P9-CLE-564

MANITOBA: A HISTORY

1975

Manitoba

A HISTORY

W. L. MORTON

UNIVERSITY OF TORONTO PRESS

Copyright, Canada, 1957
University of Toronto Press
Reprinted August, 1957, with corrections
Reprinted 1961, with corrections

Second Edition
©University of Toronto Press 1967
Reprinted 1970, with additions
Printed in the United States of America
for University of Toronto Press, Toronto
and Buffalo

ISBN 0-8020-1711-8 (cloth edition)
ISBN 0-8020-6070-6 (paper edition)

TO

My Mother and Father

Manitobans

And My Children

Manitobans

Preface

MANITOBA HAS NOT WANTED FOR HISTORIANS.
Alexander Ross, Joseph James Hargrave, Donald Gunn and
C. R. Tuttle, Alexander Begg, George Bryce, R. B. Hill, F. H.
Schofield, and Margaret McWilliams, all left histories of the Red
River Settlement, or of Manitoba. To attempt to add one's name
to the list and to rehearse again a story so often told may seem to
call for explanation. But the last history, Margaret McWilliam's
Manitoba Milestones, appeared nearly a generation ago in 1927.
What follows is perhaps a somewhat different history. Nearly all
the above were written under some immediate excitement; the
writer was a newcomer, or had a cause to promote. All, I think,
were written in the main for an audience outside Manitoba. What
follows is a general history of Manitoba for Manitobans.

This history is also different in that it has agricultural settlement as its central theme. All else, the fur trade, social development, and the play of politics, has been subordinated to that
theme. The emphasis throughout is on the narrative; I have attempted to recount and explain rather than to record. The book
may not be without its uses as a reference; I have tried to include
everything of importance and to state all accurately, but my aim
has been to tell the story rather than relate its details. In the same
spirit, while I have tried to be scholarly, I have subordinated the
apparatus of scholarship; footnotes and bibliography are highly
selective.

It is hoped, of course, that the story may be of interest to others
as well as to Manitobans. My native province has always seemed
to me an unusual and fascinating place, possessed both of a
history of great interest and of a deep sense of history. Manitoba
may have begun only in 1870, but no Manitoban thinks it of such
recent date. We have been brought up to believe, in home and

school, that our local history goes back to the Elizabethans and to Henry Hudson. Hudson and his son adrift on the icy Bay are part of the mental imagery, the historical furnishing, of every Manitoban school child. And the story of Selkirk's colony and the Red River Settlement is also part of the texture of our history. Thus we have felt that our history is as long as that of most parts of North America, and it is a history which informs and shapes our minds.

There is another element, drawn from the fact that for half a century Fort Garry was the effective centre of government of the fur trade from Hudson Straits to the Pacific; that is a sense of an imperial past. It was not easy for Manitoba to become a mere province, and something of that habit of independence and command survives, particularly in the outlook of Winnipeg, never a merely provincial city.

In sharp contrast with this ranging, imperious spirit of the metropolis is the solid rural conservatism of the province itself. With the great Ontario immigration of the 1870's and 1880's Manitoba became a land of steady ways. The countryside has been one of relatively small farms and definitely small towns. In it the simple, sturdy virtues of hard work, thrift, and neighbourliness have been cherished and transmitted. Though a western province, Manitoba has been on the whole conservative, and rural Manitoba has often been impatient with the improvidence and recklessness, by rural standards, of the great, self-centred city in its midst.

Finally, if it is too much to assert that a Manitoban can be recognized abroad, it is still true that life in Manitoba forces a common manner, not to say character on all its people. It is the manner, or mannerism, of instant understanding and agreeableness at meeting, and rises from the need for harmony in a society of many and diverse elements. This superficial friendliness is common to all North Americans, of course, but in Manitoba, a truly plural society, it is a definite and highly conscious art. Few Manitobans can pass a day without meeting at least one person of different background. It is not an easy way for ordinary folk to live, dependent as we are on our prejudices to sustain and comfort us; it is lived in Manitoba in the deliberate belief and profession that a sound, satisfactory, and enduring society can be based on no more than the possession of a common country, a common political allegiance, and the maintenance of personal freedom and equality under the law. In short, it is perhaps in Manitoba that the Canadian experiment in political bi-nationalism and cultural plurality is at its most intense.

For these reasons, together with its own inherent colour and drive, the story has seemed of interest. For help in the preparation of the text I have to thank the Social Science Research Council of Canada, the University of Manitoba, and the Manitoba Brewers' and Hotelmen's Association. The staffs of the Public Archives of Canada, the Public Archives of Manitoba, and the Library of the University of Manitoba have helped me many times with apparently inexhaustible courtesy and patience. Dr. Norman Zacour, now of the University of Pennsylvania, I remember gratefully as research assistant in two fruitful summers. My one-time teacher and colleague, Dr. R. O. Macfarlane, will, I hope, find the work of interest, for no one was better qualified to have done it than he, and he would have done it differently and better. And I would particularly record the help and inspiration given by the late J. L. Johnston, Provincial Librarian of Manitoba. Many others, whom I recall with gratitude, have aided with generous suggestions and with notes from their own researches. And finally, I acknowledge my debt to the Director and editorial staff of the University of Toronto Press, who first suggested the work, who have made its publication possible, and have lavished on it their usual exacting care both in printing and illustration.

W. L. MORTON

University of Manitoba, 1955

Preface to the Second Edition

HISTORIES END; HISTORY DOES NOT. THE HISTORY of Manitoba to 1955 possessed a certain form. That was the growth of a modern urban and agricultural community on the basis furnished by a primitive fur trade economy and society. By 1955, or even before, new lines of growth were already appearing. To live in the Canada and the world of the later twentieth century Manitoba had to develop a far more refined economy and far more sophisticated values than formerly had been thought sufficient. Yet the course of growth in a community becomes clear to view only with some lapse of time for study and reflection. The section added for this edition at page 474, therefore, has been written as an epilogue for revision, not as a further chapter to a book which has its own form and proper conclusion.

I must express my gratitude to Mr. H. W. Bowsfield for his great kindness in reading the manuscript and saving me from much error.

W.L.M.

Contents

Illustrations

PLATES

MAPS

MANITOBA: A HISTORY

1

The Fur Trade of the Bay
1612-1713

IN MID-AUGUST, 1612, THE WESTERN SHORES OF Hudson Bay lay as they had lain for unnumbered years, level and low, unmarked by headland and unrelieved by rearward hills. The rocky beaches from their ragged crests shelved slowly out beneath the shoal waters, running in their brief season's sunlight or surging sullenly beneath the quick fogs of summer. No high land was to be seen, and no deep water found.[1] Save for the cry of gulls along the breaker's wash or dash of caribou across the landward plains, the shores were still with the stillness of the sub-Arctic, and silent as their prehistory is silent. But in mid-August of 1612 that prehistory was ending. To seaward stood up the white sails of two ships, bearing down on the blue line of shore.[2]

The two ships were English and came from a world astir with doings new and old. In England itself, learned King James was betrothing his daughter Elizabeth to the Elector Palatine and busily seeking a bride for Henry, Prince of Wales. One was being sought in the Louvre, where the fair, fat widow of Henri IV, Marie de Medici, ruled unhappily as Regent in a swirl of intrigue, with neither the finesse nor the success of her house. One of her subjects, Samuel de Champlain, sickened for the woods and waters of the broad St. Lawrence as he struggled at court to save the four-year-old colony of New France. Down the coast of North America from the St. Lawrence, at Jamestown, the haggard survivors of the "Starving Time" groaned under the harsh rule of Governor Dale. Farther still, beneath the tropics and southern

latitudes, the life of century-old colonies of Spain flowed in
established and languorous patterns, fed by the streams of silver
from Potosi and Zacatecas. Across the long roll of the Pacific, in
the Further Indies, Portuguese factors in indolent unease watched
Englishmen and Hollanders press in jealous rivalry into the
spiceries which had drawn Da Gama around the Cape of Good
Hope and Columbus to the Antilles. And in the Celestial Empire
the streets of Canton and Nanking were loud with the rustle of
silk and aflare with yellow and scarlet as in the days of Marco
Polo, and its thronging millions still enjoyed under the dull Ming
emperors the spell, now threatened, of its immemorial peace. For
a new age had opened and it would leave at rest neither venerable
civilizations nor the primitive wilderness. The men of Europe in
1612 had for over a century been rifling the New World for its
precious metals and the ancient East for its silks and spices, and
were yet unsatisfied.

The white sails in Hudson Bay drove their ships on the same
quest. The vessels were the *Resolution* and the *Discovery,* Henry
Hudson's old ship, now for a second time sailing the Bay her lost
captain had scanned from her deck in 1610. Their commander
was Captain Thomas Button, later to be Admiral Sir Thomas
Button.[3] Behind the voyage stood the chivalry and wealth, and
indeed the royalty, of England, committed to the discovery of a
North West Passage to the Orient by Hudson's new-found strait
and the rumoured strait of Anian.[4] The enterprise had been
launched in full confidence that the way lay open, and now the
low shoreline ahead, stretching north and south out of sight, was
a bitter disappointment. Button named his landfall "Hopes
Checkt"[5] and stood southward down the coast to seek a westward
opening.

On August 27 he put into the estuary of a great river flowing
from the southwest, to rest and refit, and consider his future
course.[6] Before he was ready to sail, the sudden closing in of
cold weather made it necessary to prepare to winter on that forbidding shore. Dikes against the ice were built around the ships
in a little "creeke"[7] on the north shore of the estuary.

There Europeans first wintered on Manitoban soil.

There also died Francis Nelson, sailing master of the *Resolution,* and Button gave his name to the strange river coming down out of the unknown land. With him died also many of his shipmates, presumably from scurvy, and in the spring of 1613 Button sailed with the survivors in the *Discovery,* leaving the *Resolution* to perish by the Nelson. The region of his discovery and costly wintering he called New Wales in honour of his homeland.[8] After exploring the coast northward from Hopes Checkt to "Ne Ultra" in sixty-five degrees north, he sailed home to England.

Button made his way back in the confident hope, based on observation of the tides, that a passage to the west might yet be found. In 1614, 1615, and 1616 his successors, Gibbons, Bylot, and Baffin, probed deep into the ice-encumbered waters of both Hudson and Baffin Bay, until at length the painstaking Baffin concluded that there was no passage by either way. Others believed, however, that to the north or south of Button's New Wales a passage might yet be found.

In this belief Jens Munk, a Danish navigator, sailed into the Bay in 1619, and followed Button's course westward. Turning southwest with one ship while the other cast to the north, he discovered and on September 7 entered the rock-bound mouth of a large river in latitude fifty-nine degrees, long to be known as Munk's Harbour and today as Port Churchill.[9] There the onset of cold weather compelled him to pass the winter. The first months sped happily, with his men busied with cribbing the ships against the ice and cutting firewood. His Norwegian seamen hunted and trapped as in their own northern woods. Munk noted that the abundant and rich peltries were at least insurance against the financial loss of a voyage which failed to find a passage.[10] There was no trade with natives, for though traces of their wanderings were clear, none appeared during Munk's stay. These interests and activities, however, languished after Christmas, as the dreaded scurvy set in. When June cleared the harbour of ice, only two of Munk's sixty-four men survived with their commander. These three sailed one of the ships to Norway.

The brave effort of the Danes, founded on their recent Greenland voyages and the enterprise of King Christian IV, was not

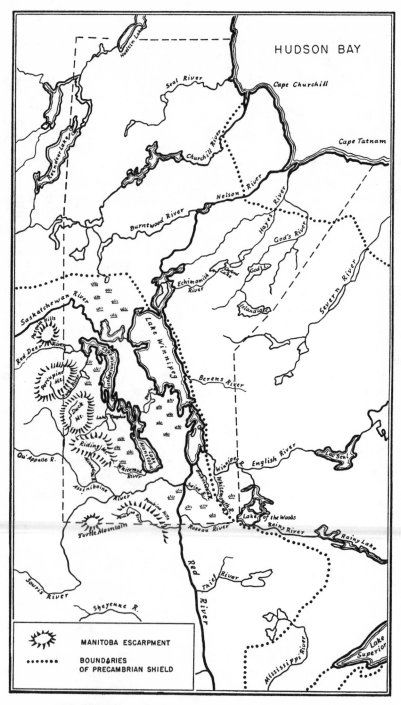

HUDSON BAY

Cape Churchill

Cape Tatnam

MANITOBA ESCARPMENT

BOUNDARIES
OF PRECAMBRIAN SHIELD

THE PHYSICAL FEATURES OF THE MANITOBA BASIN

renewed, as Denmark was drawn into the wasting Thirty Years' War. But in England interest in the North West Passage revived a decade after Munk's return. Two separate expeditions sailed in 1631 under Captains Luke Foxe and Thomas James. The bold Foxe searched the west coast from near Button's Ne Ultra at sixty-five degrees north down past Munk's and Button's winter harbours to Cape Henrietta Maria. James, a less resolute mariner, whose vivid descriptions of the perils of Arctic navigation were to influence Coleridge's *Rime of the Ancient Mariner,* skirted the perilous coast from north of Hopes Checkt down to the Bay which bears his name. There he wintered. Both, on their return, Foxe in 1631 and James in 1632, thrust northward into Foxe Channel and Basin.

These voyages made it clear that any sea passage lay to the north. Of the mainland, the continuity of which they had established, Foxe and James naturally learned little. Like Munk, they encountered no natives, though they reported many evidences of their presence along the coast.[11] Foxe noted the profusion of berries the northern summer yielded, as Munk had gratefully done,[12] and James the abundance of game.[13] These things were not enough to draw traders and settlers to remote and ice-bound coasts. With James's return to England there came to an end the great series of voyages, begun by Martin Frobisher in 1576 for the discovery of a North West Passage. Europe was sinking deeper in the Thirty Years' War, and England itself was to be rent by civil war. Not for over a generation were men to be interested in the navigation of the Bay, or the baffling and inhospitable shores of Button's New Wales.

Yet Button and Munk, Foxe and James, had made possible the rude maps of the seventeenth century on which the west coast of "Button's Bay" took rough and uncertain shape.[14] They had seen the main features of the maritime slope of Manitoba. The existence and main features of the great inland basin of the northern mid-continent were to be divined slowly by *coureurs de bois* of New France studying the sweeping gestures and sand-traced maps of Indian narrators. But the dogged Stuart mariners had seen much, and revealed more than they knew.

The keen-eyed Foxe noted that the coast north of Munk's River differed from that south and east of it. It was rocky and fringed with reefs and stony islands. "The petty islands and broken ground of the Maine"[15] which Foxe reported to the northward continued down to the estuary. Munk's Harbour itself was a cleft in a rock-bound coast: "some low rocks which form a narrow promontory,"[16] Munk recorded, and Foxe, that there was "at the south entrance of this river . . . a cliffe like unto Balsea cliffe, near Harwich."[17] To the southeastward around the present Cape Churchill ran a shelving shore of sand and stones, where low tide drew the waters far out and high tide with wind hurled the waves among the dunes and tussocks of the coastal plain. The flat shoreline and shoal waters continued around the Nelson estuary and down the coast towards James Bay: "A most shoal and perilous coast," wrote Captain James of the section below the Nelson, "in which there is not one harbour to be found."[18]

The change in the character of the coast at Munk's river was caused by the difference in the geological formations behind the two sections. Back from the indefinite shore to the southward and eastward lay the Hudson Lowlands, plains of deep sedimentary clay, trenched, as Foxe observed, by the Nelson and its tributaries.[19] Back from the northward rocky shoreline lay the vast Precambrian Shield, which enfolded Hudson's inland sea in miles of rock, water, and forest. Though the discoverers noted the differences of the two coastal areas, they could not know that they reflected the two main features of the maritime slope of the west coast of the Bay.

Neither could they know why in latitudes of temperate climate in their home waters they should have been caught by the early closing in of winter, nor why the waters they navigated should have been made dangerous by ice for seven months of the twelve. Had they considered the matter, the barren character of the country to the north of Munk's river and the coarse grasses[20] and stunted forests[21] to the south might have seemed to them unaccountable by comparison with the climate of Europe. The reason was the drift of cold Arctic air across the northern projection of the continent they fondly imagined to be sea. As a result, the maritime slope and the Bay had, not a maritime and temperate climate, but a continental and sub-Arctic one, hot in its brief summer and very cold in the prolonged, indefinite winter.[22]

The passage of the cold Arctic weather was traced on the ground by the southeastward slope of tundra vegetation down to Munk's Harbour. Southward the hot summer air of the mid-continent was more potent and the forests of the Shield thrust out across the Lowlands and down along the river courses. These features too were reported more or less clearly by Foxe and Munk and James, but none of them hazarded an estimate of the extent of the land mass before them. They clung to the hope that it might prove to be a large island and circumnavigable.

Not for the explorers from the sea, then, was the task of revealing the face of the Shield, with its stiff, archaic pattern of lake and forest, laced with dashing rivers and ribbed with grey rock ridges. Others were to toil up its three hundred mile slope to seven hundred feet of altitude at the head of the Nelson, and dazzle their eyes before the silver shield of Lake Winnipeg, or probe wearily the waterways which drained the northern mid-continent into the great swampy tract of which Lake Winnipeg was the sea, or to encounter the wandering tribes of Indian hunters who followed the waterways and the great ridgeways season after season.

It was these sea-farers who had begun the history of Manitoba, and who imbrued it with some fragrance of eastern spices and touched it with the gloss of northern furs. From ships bound to Cathay the blare of Elizabethan trumpets had broken through the mists off Hudson Straits, and the thud of Jacobean cannon had boomed dully across the mouth of the Nelson. But the ancient silence fell after that misleading fanfare. The migrating geese plied the western shore in spring and fall unseen, the slap of wave and "rut of the ice" went many years unheard in the Bay. When history advanced again, it was from the St. Lawrence, the River of Canada, and it moved in the run of the birch canoe and the soft footfall of the *coureur de bois* whose quest was furs. And in 1670, when once more a ship put into Nelson, the two themes of North West Passage and fur trade were at last united, and their union was to lead to the penetration of the basin of Winnipeg.

The solving of the puzzle of the mid-continental waterways was the work, not of Englishmen, but of Frenchmen of Canada. The first rumours of Winnipeg, the Stinking or Turbid Waters, were gathered by French traders and missionaries advancing along the Great Lakes after 1650 and interpreted, by the latter at least, in terms of the still prevailing interest in a route to the western sea.[23] In 1656 two traders, one of whom was Médard Chouart, Sieur des Groseilliers, brought down to Quebec a report of a "Nation of the sea which some have called 'Stinkards' because its people formerly lived on the shores of the sea which they call Ouinipeg, that is 'stinking water'."[24] And they had learned of the Christinos, the Crees who lived in the forests of the Shield around Hudson Bay.[25]

In 1659–60 a voyage by Groseilliers and his brother-in-law, Pierre-Esprit Radisson, to Lake Superior added greatly to this information. Moreover, these two men by a flash of insight which has led many historians to extend their wanderings much beyond the substantial evidence, grasped the geographical significance of what the Indians told them. As refined by their own minds and those of the Jesuit fathers to whom they told what they had learned, the information was that to the southwest and north of Lake Superior were three interconnected seas. These three might well be one, that which led to China.[26] To Groseilliers and Radisson, however, fur traders as they were, this possibility was less significant than the fact that from the sea to the north, which was Hudson Bay, a water route ran to the inland sea of Winnipeg, the lake of the Assiniboins, with which tribe they had traded at Lake Superior. Here was a route, cheaper and safer than the St. Lawrence and the Lakes, to the rich fur region of the mid-continent.[27]

Like Munk, Groseilliers and Radisson knew that in the north the fur trade and exploration were inseparable. Interest in the route to the East would raise money to outfit expeditions. The fur trade would yield returns to reimburse the adventurers. Exploration would open the way to new tracts of beaver lands.

It was this flash of geographic and economic insight on the part of Groseilliers and Radisson which revealed the strategic conjunction of the Bay with the great swampy tract of Winnipeg through the Nelson River, with its abounding furs and waters leading southward and westward. And it was their experienced success in wedding the fur trade and exploration which made it possible for them, after failure in New France, to reawaken interest in England in the quest for the North West Passage and the neglected voyages of the Jacobean and Carolinian seamen. The search could be fed by the fur trade, and if it failed, the fur trade was itself an enterprise of no despicable profit. In 1668 the English supporters of Groseilliers and Radisson sent the *Nonsuch* to trade in James Bay. The little ketch returned in 1669 with a rich cargo of furs. The reawakened interest and the success of the *Nonsuch* resulted in the founding of the Company of Adventurers Trading into Hudson's Bay in 1670 with a charter which granted them a monopoly of trade through Hudson Straits and exclusive possession of lands they might discover within the Straits, the lands to be the colony of Rupert's Land. The establishment of the first permanent settlements on the coast of Manitoba was to follow in due course.

Both the search for a passage to Asia and the pursuit of the fur trade were part and parcel of the exploration of North America. In the eighth decade of the seventeenth century the course of exploration flowed in two channels, one to the southwest and the Mississippi River, the other to the northwest and the interior of the northern mid-continent. Jolliet led the former, Groseilliers and Radisson the latter. As the fur trade was to furnish the means for the search for the passage, and profits besides, the immediate need was the establishment of posts and acquaintance with the lands and Indian tribes tributary to the posts. The next phase in the early history of Manitoba was the beginnings of the fur trade at the mouth of Nelson's and Munk's rivers, and the acquisition of a knowledge of the lands and waters, and of their denizens, beyond the maritime slope.

The new-founded Company of Adventurers in 1670 despatched two ships to establish fur posts on the shores of Hudson Bay.

One of these, the *Prince Rupert,* proceeded to the bottom of the Bay to resume the fur trade begun there in 1668. In the other, the *Wivenhoe,* were Radisson and Governor Charles Bayley, bound for Port Nelson, as the estuary of Nelson's river was to be called. After a mishap at Mansel Island, they reached the river on August 31, thirty-nine years after Foxe had viewed the relics of Button's winter refuge of 1612. They had not come, like their predecessors, to probe an unknown coast. The purpose of the Company, inspired by Radisson's grasp of the strategic place of the mouth of the Nelson in the fur trade, was to found a settlement there which should be its chief factory. Such an establishment would realize the master idea of the French traders, that from the water outlet of the northern mid-continent the fur trade could be carried on with greatest profit. It was a rival of Montreal and Albany, the fur marts of the St. Lawrence and the Hudson, that was planned. On September 1, 1670, Governor Bayley formally took possession for the Company of Port Nelson and the circumjacent lands.[28] From that date the Company, under the British Crown, claimed the sovereignty of Button's New Wales, henceforth to be known as Rupert's Land.

The adventurers found the region of Port Nelson much as Foxe had described it.

There is very fine Marsh land, & great plenty of wood about a mile beyond the Marshes yet not very large. There were ye remains of some of ye Natives Wigwams & Sweating houses & some pieces of dressed Beaver skins, & they supposed the Indians had not long been gone from that place further southward or higher up into the country. There is no want of food being great store of wildfowle Rabbits & Deeres. There was then upon the ground Strawberries, Gooseberries, large red currans, huckleberries & Cramberries.[29]

Port Nelson, before the flare of its bright, hot summer waned, was a not unattractive place to men just come ashore from the sullen waters of the Bay and the fierce currents around the sombre capes of Labrador. But, as Button and Munk had learned, the descent of winter may be early and is sudden on that continental coast. The delay at Mansel Island, storms in the estuary, and the weariness of the men combined with the threat of cold weather to produce a decision to postpone the attempt to build a factory. The *Wivenhoe* and its passengers and crew went down to the bottom of the Bay to winter at the new Rupert's House the other party had built. The first attempt at settlement on Manitoban soil had failed.

The open waters of Port Nelson and the uncertain autumn weather of the "West Main" were to delay settlement another dozen years, while the posts in the bottom of the Bay and on the East Main throve. Attempts were made to begin a summer trade without building a wintering post. In 1673 Governor Bayley sent a ship with Groseilliers as trader and interpreter to begin trade at Port Nelson, but no settlement was attempted.[30] Similar later attempts to trade without a post failed. The Company, doubtful of success in setting up a permanent establishment on the Nelson, was for the time content to drive a profitable trade at the bottom of the Bay. There they could compete most effectively with their French rivals on the St. Lawrence. Only from Albany, founded in 1675—as later from Severn, founded in 1685—did they begin to tap a hinterland which extended back from James Bay to the Winnipeg basin.

The pace was forced, however, both by the French competitors and other interlopers threatening to come into the Bay. Among them were the restless promoters of the Company itself, Groseilliers and Radisson. The pair had returned to France in 1675. After many disappointments, in 1682 they organized in Canada an expedition to Hudson Bay and Port Nelson under Radisson's command. The same year saw Benjamin Gillam, son of the captain of the *Nonsuch* in 1668, sail for the Nelson from New England. The New Englanders arrived first, the French shortly after, each unknown to the other. Gillam had taken up his station in the Nelson. Radisson, in the first recorded recognition of the Nelson's twin, the Hayes, or Ste-Therese as the French were to name it, made his way along the other side of the peninsula between the two streams. He ascended the river for eight days to a distance of about a hundred miles, where he met Indians and used all his arts to persuade them to bring furs down to the coast.[31] The Canadian *coureur de bois* was probably the first European to ascend the maritime slope of Manitoba. On his return about two weeks later, the presence of the New Englanders in the Nelson was discovered. While the two parties were working out an agreement, a third expedition put into Port Nelson, a ship of the Hudson's Bay Company under Captain John Bridgar. The Company had been worried by interlopers in recent years and had been preparing to occupy the mouths of the Severn and the Nelson.[32] A winter of sharp rivalry followed Bridgar's arrival, which ended in the capture of both the New Englanders and the Company men by the resourceful Radisson. French wit, as so often, overcame English numbers in a comedy of errors played out on the frozen shores of the Nelson. Yet it is from the sudden concentration of effort on the settlement of the Hayes-Nelson estuary that the permanent occupation of Manitoban soil is to be dated,[33] and also the rival claims of France and England to that soil.

When Radisson sailed for Canada in 1683 he took the New Englanders with him, and sent the Company men to posts at the bottom of the Bay. His nephew, Jean-Baptiste Chouart, Groseilliers' son, was left with seven men in the French post on the Hayes to strengthen the ties of trade with the Indians. As the explorers had noted, the Indians did not inhabit the coast, but frequented it only in summer. It was necessary to reach the inland bands and induce the tribes of the farther interior to come down with furs for trade. Tales of the white man's coming to the Nelson and Munk's river must have passed inland long before 1682; the latter then bore an Indian name meaning "strangers' river." The attempts to trade at Port Nelson between 1670 and 1682 would also have attracted the attention of the natives. Radisson's journey up the Hayes in 1682 is the first recorded attempt to reach the inland bands and persuade them to come down to a post prepared to trade. A further effort was necessary. It must have been made by young Chouart in 1683. How successful he was and how rapidly news spread by the Indian grape vine was shown by the arrival at the post on the Hayes in 1684 not only of Crees from the forest belt of the Shield, but also of Assiniboins from beyond the great swampy tract.[34] The birch canoe and the habits of a wandering life of the Indians made it possible in less than two years to bring the interior of the northern mid-continent within the fur watershed of posts on the Hayes-Nelson estuary.

This intercourse between the interior and the coast grew rapidly. Radisson, who had once more changed masters, came back to the Hayes in 1684 in the service of the Company and carried off the rich returns of 1683. The French expedition from Canada sent to collect them from young Chouart.found the furs gone, but also found the Crees and Assiniboins coming down from "a distance of fifteen to twenty days inland." Their homes were beyond "the great lake of the Assiniboines," of which, it is noted for the first time, the Nelson River was the outlet.[35] When Radisson returned for the Company in 1685, he busied himself at the new York Factory on the Hayes in improving the standard of trade, ordering up birch bark from the bottom of the Bay, and despatching young Chouart "up into the Countries."[36] He was, that is, obtaining the materials for canoe-building which were not available in the spruce woods of the lower Hayes. Only by canoe could the tortuous Indian routes be followed. He was seeking, by a favourable standard of trade, to increase the pull of his post upon the remoter tribes who would otherwise trade through middlemen with the French on Lake Superior. He was using the woodcraft and diplomacy of his nephew to induce "the Captains of the Nations to further our trade & oblige them to bring their Families Downe."[37] In these ways the slender network of commerce flung across the forest belt and the swampy tract was being widened and strengthened. And it may be, though no explicit evidence exists, that it was the young Chouart who was the first European to reach the swampy tract and see what his uncle had divined, the waters of Winnipeg straining into the Nelson on their way to the Bay.[38]

In the following year, 1686, the growing rivalry of French and English traders for the possession of the Bay passed from peaceful competition to open violence. The French under the Chevalier de Troyes captured all the English posts in James Bay, and James II, still friendly with France, forbade reprisals. The Company, thus deprived of its southern posts, began to develop new posts along the West Main. A reconnaissance of Munk's harbour in 1686, for example, led to an attempt to establish a post there in 1689. It was burned down before completion, and the setback, with other troubles, prevented for many years the occupation of the mouth of Munk's river, now renamed the Churchill after Governor Sir John Churchill.[39]

It was this enterprise, however, which was the occasion of the first of the famous inland journeys of Henry Kelsey. Kelsey, a young apprentice who had come out with Radisson in 1684 and may have caught from him the excitement of life and travel with the Indians, had displayed both a fondness and an aptitude for Indian life, just as the young Radisson had done in his early years in Canada. He was ordered northward from Churchill to find the "Northern" (the Athapascan Chipewyan) Indians. With an Indian boy he travelled two hundred miles out into the tundra from Churchill, until his companion insisted on returning for fear of the Eskimoes.

In the coastal trade, instant touch with the Indians was as necessary as the building of a post, as Radisson and Chouart had demonstrated in 1682. And it was a task that had to be repeated. There was always the pull of the French traders at Lake Superior to be counteracted. Indian "Captains" were to be kept sweet with presents and new ones found when the old grew weary or died. Above all, the desire of the nearer Indians to keep the trade to themselves and act as middlemen between the posts and the farther tribes was to be overcome. This was a fruitful source of intertribal wars as well as a restraint on trade. It was in the interest of the white traders that there should be peace among the tribes and that the farther tribes should be free to pass down to the posts. This work Radisson and Chouart had begun and it was now taken up by Kelsey, at once a pupil and a rival of the Canadian wood-runners.

In 1690 he was sent inland from York "for to understand the native language & to see their land," as he was to write in his rhymed account of the journey. Whereas there is no evidence that his French predecessors had pierced the forest belt, perhaps because the Indian canoe routes were not yet established, Kelsey travelling with the returning Indians did so. They ascended the Hayes and Foxe rivers, portaged to Cross Lake on the Nelson and passed by the Mingao River to Moose Lake. There Kelsey entered the great swampy tract at its northwestern end. He made his way by dull curving streams and stagnant flats of pea-green marsh from Moose Lake to the channel of the Saskatchewan River somewhere near its passage of a great ridge and ancient lake shore at the locality to be named The Pas. West and east of the great ridge, the Saskatchewan lost the bright speed of its swift current in wide miles of mere and marsh. In these drowned lands Kelsey's landmark was a bend on the river he named Deering's Point after Sir Edward Deering, Deputy Governor of the Company. That point was either the great bend of the Saskatchewan twelve miles below The Pas, or The Pas itself.[40]

The region was the place of concourse for the Indians going down to the Bay. There in early summer came the Crees of the forest and the Assiniboins of the park belt, the lands of mixed woods and meadows between the forest belt and the grassland plains. Canoe birch was plentiful in the region and in early summer the bark lifted readily from the trunk. There the waters of the interior plains converged for their plunge down the Grand Rapids of the Saskatchewan to Lake Winnipeg lying to the eastward. The marshlands of The Pas, divided by the great south-north ridge, were the nodal point between the Winnipeg basin and the western plains and northern forests.

Kelsey, both in 1690 and in his second journey of 1691, passed southwestward from Deering's Point through the woods and meadows of the park belt out to the open plains, "to ye outtermost edge of ye woods." There he saw the buffalo herds, moving in myriads like cloud shadows over the rolling prairies. He travelled among the Assiniboins and Crees, now pushing with their guns out onto the plains, and tried to make peace between them and an unidentifiable tribe which he called "Naywaytame Poets." In this he failed, as the middlemen Crees refused to yield their position of advantage. The traders at the coast remained imprisoned in the wide circle of their clients.

His journeys made Kelsey not only the first white man to see the park belt and the grasslands. He was also the first to pass beyond the forest belt of the maritime slope and reveal the inner zones of the swampy tract, the park belt, and the plains. He had traversed all the zones and unravelled the waterways tributary to the Bay. He had not, however, seen Lake Winnipeg or traced the outlines of the Winnipeg basin.

Yet those outlines were becoming known, presumably from the accounts of Indians trading at York, or Bourbon as it was sometimes to be called. For the local war of 1686 had been followed by a general war in 1689, in which France and England were enemies. The opportunity had come to settle the rival claims to the Bay and its hinterlands. In 1693 the English recaptured the posts in the bottom of the Bay and held them thereafter. The French, led by the brilliant Pierre le Moyne, Sieur d'Iberville, struck back with swift precision at the more valuable north. In 1694 he captured York and broke out the lilies of France again over the dark waters of the Hayes. When the Company recaptured it in 1696, he returned in the following year and in sea-fight off the shoals of the Nelson sank H.M.S. *Hampshire* with all hands and scattered her consorts. To his guns had passed the mastery of the Bay, and York was Bourbon until the red-coated infantry of that John Churchill who had given his name to Munk's river had at Ramillies, Oudenarde, and Malplaquet redressed the fortunes of war.

Thus it was the French masters of Bourbon who reaped the harvest of Chouart's and Kelsey's labours inland, and for sixteen years, from 1697 to 1713, the fur trade of the Winnipeg basin was wholly French. While enduring the cold of the long winters and the heat of the fleeting summer, and rejoicing by way of recompense in the dry purity of the air, the French traders noted the spreading marshes and stunted forests of the region, described the ptarmigan, the vast flocks of migrating geese, and the seasonal movement of the caribou.[41] One of the narrators, Nicolas Jérémie, had even learned, presumably from Kelsey whom the French had captured, of the musk-ox of the tundra to the north of Churchill.

MUNK'S WINTER HARBOUR

Woodcut in C. C. A. Gosch, *Danish Arctic Expeditions, 1605 to 1620*
(Hakluyt Society; London, 1897), II, p. 23

CREE INDIANS CELEBRATING A DOG FEAST

From the Sketch Book of Major George Seaton in the Public Archives of Canada

They lived well on the abundant game, supplemented by the white fish which Jérémie truly called "the best fish in all the world,"[42] and by bread and wine from France. Jérémie even had a garden, the first recorded on Manitoban soil, "which never failed to produce very good lettuce, green cabbage, and other small herbs which we used for making soup in the winter."[43] As they learned to live comfortably by the Bay, they learned also of the tribes of the interior and of the main features of the inland country from Kelsey and their Indian visitors.

In 1695 seven or eight different nations were in the habit of coming to Bourbon. The nearest were the Crees, or Kristinaux, of the seaward forest belt, the later "Home Indians" of Company parlance. The Maskegons, or Swampies, denizens of the great swampy tract, were also known. But the principal traders were the merry-hearted Crees of the inland forest and the stolid Assiniboins of the park belt and plains' borders, ancient allies, one of Algonkin, one of Siouan, stock. Even the Saulteaux, or Ojibways, are mentioned as already intermingled with the Crees and Assiniboins. This was not surprising, in view of the known range of Indian travel. Of the Crees Father Marest wrote from Fort Bourbon: "They reach nearly to Lake Superior, where some go to trade. I have seen some who have been at Sault Ste Marie and Michilimackinac. I have even met some who have been as far as Montreal."[44] The other "nations" were bands of these three principal tribes of Manitoban history, the Crees, the Assiniboins, and the Saulteaux intruding from the east. In addition, the Athapascan Chipewyans of the northwest were known under strange and uncouth names.[45]

The main features of the country also were taking shape with a fair degree of accuracy, as traders questioned and Indians replied. In his *Account* Jérémie first describes the lower course of the Seal River north of the Churchill; little more is known of that stream even today. The Churchill itself, with its rapids and lakes, he sketched for a hundred and fifty leagues up to the high inner edge of the Shield.[46] And he confirmed Father Silvy's report that the Nelson drained seaward the waters of "Michinipi" or "Big Water," the inland sea of Winnipeg. Beyond, he had learned, was Winnipegosis, "the little sea," and he was told of "the fine prairies" and more moderate climate of the interior.[47] No map could be made from his *Account*, but the chief characteristics of the inland Winnipeg basin are to be found in it. Even the canoe route by Dog Lake to Lake Superior was faintly known to him.[48] And the tale Radisson had heard of bearded men and a sea to the southwest was told to Jérémie.[49]

By 1713, then, the coastal fur trade had drawn the inland regions of Manitoba into its orbit, and the Indians had described to the traders its lands and waterways. But no white man had yet seen Lake Winnipeg or its sister lakes and affluents, except the yet unnamed Saskatchewan. As the Indians travelled from The Pas to the Bay by a western route along the Mingao and Grassy rivers, avoiding the stormy waters of the great lake, it was not likely that any of the coastal traders would seek the Winnipeg basin. That was to be the work of the traders of Lake Superior, endeavouring to obtain the furs of the northern mid-continent, which by Radisson's enterprise had been diverted to Hudson Bay. Like the Company of Adventurers, they would use the tales of a western sea to advance the quest for new fur regions. And in doing so they would stir the Hudson's Bay Company to attempt something more than the coastal trade.

2

The Fur Trade of the Winnipeg Basin
1714-1763

THE STRUGGLE BETWEEN FRENCH AND ENGLISH
for control of the coastal trade of Hudson Bay was ended by the
Treaty of Utrecht, 1713. The defeat of old France in Europe
spelled the defeat of New France in America. By the Treaty, Fort
Bourbon and all other posts held by the French were returned to
the Hudson's Bay Company. English sovereignty over the coasts
of Hudson Bay was acknowledged, and a boundary commission
was to settle the inland limits of French and English territory.
But the commission was never to report and the boundaries of
New France and of Rupert's Land remained in dispute, to the
ultimate loss of the future province of Manitoba.

On September 5, 1714, James Knight, Governor of the Hudson's Bay posts in the Bay, arrived at Hayes River and accepted
the surrender of Fort Bourbon, now again to be York Factory,
from Nicolas Jérémie. With York, and with Albany, which they
had held since 1693, the English were again well situated for
drawing the "upland Indians" down to the Bay. Those fickle
clients, however, might again be lured to take the canoe routes
across the height of land to Lake Superior and the French traders
who, cut off from the fur trade of the Bay, were once more thrusting into the West. It was good sense, therefore, which led
Governor Knight to plan the reoccupation of the mouth of the
Churchill River in order to trade with the "Northern Indians"
far beyond the reach of traders from Montreal.

It was not, however, hard sense alone which inspired the project of the veteran Knight. The tales of the Northern Indians of a copper mine on a great bay to the northwest, and the native copper they displayed, had aroused in Knight a passionate desire to seek the mine and the "yellow metal" of the "Mountain Indians" beyond, by the vainly sought and still possible North West Passage.[1] He was delayed two years by mischance and the failures of subordinates, but in 1717, in the heat and flies of the sub-Arctic summer, he began the construction of a factory at Churchill, on or near the site of Munk's wintering house and amid the relics of the Danish tragedy. The grim old man succeeded against all obstacles. The Northern Indians, once sought by Kelsey and now by William Stewart and Richard Norton, were persuaded henceforth to make annual journeys to Churchill along the edge of timber and tundra and over the brief summer waters of the Arctic lakes and rivers. The Cree of the Saskatchewan came also by way of Frog Portage and the long reaches of the turbulent Churchill, soon to be known inland as "English river." Knight himself, his duty done at Churchill, succeeded in inducing the Company to authorize an expedition of two vessels to seek the Passage and the copper mine. When the party sailed to the north in 1719, however, still unexplained disaster struck and the stout old trader and all his companions perished miserably on the naked rock of Marble Island.

In the factory at Churchill, the residue and base of Knight's heroic project, the Company had a preserve against the competition of the French traders, which was to pay important dividends, and which was to be made the strategic key to the Bay by the construction of the great Prince of Wales's Fort, begun in 1733. There was to be need of such a trading preserve, for the French had not only returned to the "postes du nord" on Lake Superior, but, under competition from the English to the south and north, were preparing to cross the height of land and enter the Winnipeg basin.

The French explorers and traders after 1660 had been pulled south by the Mississippi and north by Hudson Bay. La Salle had found the Gulf of Mexico; Groseilliers and Radisson had inspired the founding of the Hudson's Bay Company and the occupation of Port Nelson. The one had advanced the fur trade of the southwest, the others of the northwest; neither Louis Jolliet nor the renegade *coureurs de bois* had found the western sea. That quest remained to be pursued in the course of which the fur trade of the northern mid-continent might be drawn to Lake Superior as well as to the Mississippi and the Ohio, or to Hudson Bay.

Before the capture of the English forts in the Bay, Daniel Greyselon Du Lhut had taken up in 1678-9 the task, begun by Groseilliers and Radisson, of exploration west of Fond du Lac on Lake Superior, and with it the necessary accompaniment of attempting to appease the fierce intertribal wars of that troubled region. It was his hope that posts among the Sioux of the mid-continental lakes and plains might draw the trade of the tribes of the Winnipeg basin from their commerce with the English on the Bay.[2] The posts would also furnish a base for the advance to the western sea. His views were accepted by the government of New France, despite anxieties over the mounting costs and hazards of the lengthening St. Lawrence route.[3] The development of trade with the Sioux west of Superior was resumed from time to time thereafter, in the face of many discouragements, and posts were built in the Sioux country in 1700, 1722, and 1728.[4]

The thrust westward from Fond du Lac, however, was one of the factors which involved the French in war with the middlemen Fox Indians south of Superior and also in the old hostilities between the Sioux and the Saulteaux of the north shore of Lake Superior for possession of the wild rice lakes to the west.[5] As the French were not powerful enough to break the Foxes, or to quell the wars between the Saulteaux and the Sioux, they found it expedient to remain on good terms with the Saulteaux and to risk the hostility of the Sioux. They were thus committed to advancing westward along the southern edge of the Shield and the forest belt of the north in company with the expanding Saulteaux. They were the more disposed to do so, as that line of advance kept them in direct competition with their English rivals on the Bay and would carry them into the Winnipeg basin, the next great source of beaver. Du Lhut had accordingly founded posts at Kaministiquia, or

Thunder Bay, and at Lake Nipigon in 1684.[6] One of his associates, Jacques de Noyon, had in 1688 crossed the height of land by the Kaministiquia River to Rainy Lake and in 1689 had gone on to the Lake of the Woods.[7] The course of the canoe route into the Winnipeg basin was thus explored as the contest for the Bay was opening and in the very years the English made their first attempt to occupy the mouth of the Churchill. De Noyon had entered the Winnipeg basin by the southeast and reached the edge of the great swampy tract two years before Kelsey traversed the northwestern end. The coastal trade of the Bay and the inland trade of the St. Lawrence were converging simultaneously on the yet unexploited beaver streams of the northern mid-continent.

The impetus of the French penetration, however, had been checked by the need to exploit their advances among the Sioux, and perhaps by the capture of the English posts in the Bay. The French commanded the coastal trade for sixteen years, and the profits of that trade made it less imperative to surmount the hazards of the St. Lawrence route and follow the enterprise of de Noyon. The efforts to enter the country of the Sioux were indeed kept up, but until after 1714 the Saulteaux trading parties had either to go by the Albany or the Hayes to the Bay, or come down by the frowning capes of Superior to Sault Ste Marie and Michilimackinac.

When the English trade from the Bay was resumed after 1714, the French had to reopen the "postes du nord." In 1717 Zacharie Robutel, Sieur de la Nouë, re-established the posts at Kaministiquia, and the trade at Lake Nipigon was also resumed.[8] At Kaministiquia the French traders stood at the foot of one of the main canoe routes to the Winnipeg basin, a route known to the government of New France since de Noyon's venture of 1688–9, as a despatch of 1716 reveals;[9] the other main one by the Grand Portage of the Pigeon River was first mentioned in 1722.[10] The despatch of 1716 describes the route in detail in order to demonstrate that by it lay a feasible line of advance to the western sea. The search for the sea would lead the traders into the area tapped by the English from the Bay and enrich New France while injuring the English trade. The project to establish a line of posts

across the western slope from the height of land to the Lake of the
Assiniboins, or Winnipeg, took shape slowly after 1716, partly at
the insistence of the Saulteaux and the Crees. In 1720 La Nouë
followed in de Noyon's tracks and attempted to establish a post
at Rainy Lake.[11] He reported that the country beyond was one
of extreme cold, in which no grain could be brought to maturity
and which was inhabited by a nomadic hunting people.[12] This
report of difficulties experienced or foreseen on the northern route
westward was followed by the recommendation of Père Charlevoix, sent out by the French government to investigate and report
on the route to the western sea, that the central way through, or
preferably south of, the country of the Sioux was the most hopeful
approach to the sea of the west. The French government decided
to attempt an advance through Sioux territory, and it was this
decision which led to the founding of the post, already noted,
in 1728. In consequence the tale of the uncertain and unhappy
relations with the Sioux was resumed.

It is probable that the decade of fumbling between 1717 and
1727 for the right line of advance was not wholly caused by the
concepts of savants like Charlevoix and the directives of the
French government, reluctant to risk involvement in financing
the expansion of the fur trade of New France. In the region of
lakes and forests northwest of Superior the traders, as La Nouë's
report hints, were passing the limits at that time of the cultivation
of corn. Corn was the staple food of the *voyageur*, the fuel of
canoe transport. With parched and hulled corn for diet, and pork
grease to make it palatable, the *voyageurs* could drive the great
master canoes of the lakes from flush of dawn to fall of dusk
without pause for meals or delays to hunt and fish. The staple
food was available on the central route through the Sioux country,
but there the hostility of the tribes was never completely soothed.
Corn was brought from Michilimackinac to Kaministiquia, and
even carried over the height of land.[13] The cost in labour was
great, however, and no local supplies were to be had. Another
source of a food supply was offered in the Indian staple of the
region, wild rice. In this rich crop of the warm shallows of the
multitudinous lakes of the southern Shield, the traders were to

find a partial substitute for the corn of the canoe routes of the Great Lakes. It was to be some years, however, before the Indians were induced to bring in regularly for sale a surplus over their own wants. Fuller records, it is possible, would reveal that the French traders between 1717 and 1727 were organizing the food supply for the extension of the canoe route over the height of land and, as well, cutting portage trails and seeking the best trading sites.

In this pioneer work was probably engaged the man who in 1731 assumed charge of the expansion of the French inland trade into the Winnipeg basin, and, with what zeal or reluctance it is impossible to say, accepted also the commission to pursue the threadbare and inevitable quest for the western sea. Pierre Gaultier de Varennes, Sieur de la Vérendrye, a Canadian veteran of the War of the Spanish Succession, had been trading in the Lake Superior country for some years, possibly since 1717. In 1728, the year of the last establishment of a post and mission among the Sioux, La Vérendrye met Père Gonor, one of the missionaries to the Sioux. Père Gonor was convinced that it was impossible to advance through Sioux territory, and wrote a memoir of La Vérendrye's account of his Indian informants' description of a tidal river to the westward. Aided perhaps by this and his own past services, La Vérendrye in 1730 was granted a monopoly of the fur trade of the "postes du nord," and in the following year began to build a line of posts westward towards Lake Winnipeg, from which he hoped a westward flowing river might lead to the western sea.

The advance began by the Pigeon River route. But La Vérendrye's men rebelled at the toil of the nine-mile portage. That difficulty and fear of a shortage of provisions made it advisable to send forward only an advance party under his nephew, Christophe Dufrost, Sieur de la Jemeraye, to winter at Rainy Lake. In 1732 La Vérendrye was able to consolidate the forward movement by building Fort St. Pierre at the lake.[14] In the next year the broad flowing Rainy River carried his canoes down to the Lake of the Woods. By the west shore of the Lake of the Woods, on the north shore of Boundary Bay, he built Fort St.

Charles. At that point La Vérendrye stood on the verge of the westward slope of the Shield, stepping down in muskeg and ridge to the marshes and prairies of the Red River valley. There, however, the swift progress of 1732 and 1733 was stayed, "owing to the difficulty the savages made about the road and also owing to the impossibility of getting men on account of their fear of dying of starvation in those parts."[15] For five years these and other difficulties were to delay the French advance at Fort St. Charles.

The resistance of the Indians to their going on was to be expected. The tribes had always wanted the traders to come among them, but strove to prevent their going on to trade with remoter tribes. La Vérendrye was moving along the border of the northern forest of the Shield, the ancient march of the warring Algonkins of the northern forest and the Sioux of the southern forests and plains. He moved also with the westward infiltration of the Saulteaux among their kindred, the Crees, with whom at that time they were at war as well as with the Sioux. He sought to assuage the animosities of the tribes and to make peace among them. But in the end he was forced to ally himself with the northern tribes, dancing the war dance at Fort St. Charles and astonishing the braves with sight of the nine wounds he had received at Malplaquet.[16] One of his sons, Jean-Baptiste, took the warpath with the Crees against the Sioux. So La Vérendrye incurred the enmity of the Sioux, an enmity which was to cost him his eldest son, his missionary, Père Aulneau, and twenty-two men, all slain by a Sioux war party in 1736 at "Massacre" Island in the Lake of the Woods. The French post among the Sioux made the situation more difficult, as both Sioux and Cree were armed by the French. La Vérendrye's choice, however, was an inevitable one; the French of New France were committed by the pursuit of high quality furs to the exploitation of the Shield and its bordering forests and prairies, and to alliance with the tribes which lived in them.

No less difficult was the task of providing a staple food for supply of the canoe route and the posts. Corn was brought in from Michilimackinac for food and seed, and was sown at Fort St. Charles.[17] The Indians of the region, the Monsonis, the Crees, and the Assiniboins, were encouraged to begin its cultivation.[18] Thus did the fur trade bring agriculture, its indispensable enemy, to the Winnipeg basin. The local bands along the route and around the posts were encouraged to harvest wild rice for sale, as well as to bring in meat, canoe bark, gum, and roots for sewing.[19] Much of La Vérendrye's interest in the agricultural tribe he called Mandan undoubtedly arose from the reports that they cultivated corn and traded it with the Assiniboins for English trade goods.[20] Despite his efforts, the food supply remained precarious: high water damaged the rice crop in 1735,[21] and in 1736 needed trade goods had to be cached en route for want of food.[22] In the valley of the Red the same want of a staple was even more menacing. Not until Cree and Assiniboin hunters were persuaded to bring in meat and fats for sale was it possible to advance in force out of the forests of the Shield, and out of reach of corn and rice, into the park belt and the plains in 1738.[23] The meat, probably dried, and the fats, foreshadow the pemmican that was to be the staple of the western canoe route as corn was the staple of the eastern. Pemmican itself is not mentioned by La Vérendrye. The scanty record, however, suggests that in the future wheatlands of Manitoba the supply of food was so precarious as to constitute a check to the advance of any considerable body of men.

Yet the years from 1733 to 1738 had not been wholly spent in frustration at Fort St. Charles. The long delay cost La Vérendrye much in money and in support from the French government, but he was in fact laying the groundwork for the next stage of the French advance, the occupation of the Red River valley. Indeed he was not only stabilizing the new route behind him; he had thrust forward advance parties into the valley itself. Again his nephew, La Jemeraye, in woodcraft and the management of Indians another Radisson or Kelsey, had led the way, aided now by La Vérendrye's sons. They had explored the two waterways from the Lake of the Woods to Red River. The northern route was by the mighty Winnipeg River, which drained the Lake of the Woods in thirty thundering falls down the western slope of the Shield to Lake Winnipeg. In 1734 Pierre, second son of the explorer, descended the Winnipeg and, first of recorded Euro-

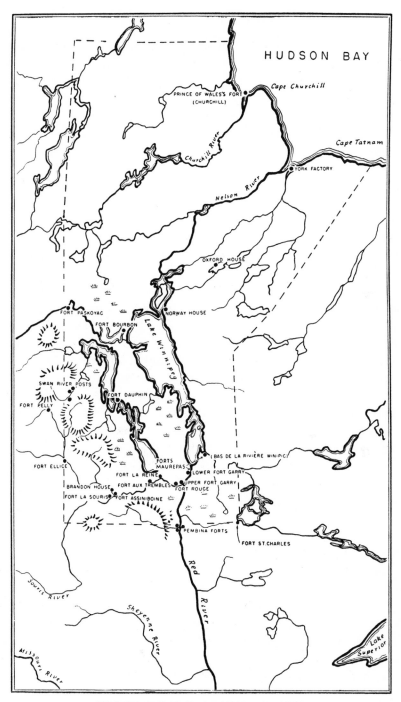

FRENCH AND ENGLISH TRADING POSTS

peans, saw the turbid waters of the southern basin of Lake Winnipeg. He made his way to the delta of the Red and just above the marshes built the first Fort Maurepas.[24] The southern route was by way of the reedy wastes of the Savanne portage to the Roseau River, tributary of the Red. At its mouth in 1736 La Jemeraye was to die, to the grief of his uncle whose chief lieutenant he had been. In December of 1736 La Vérendrye himself reached the Red by the Roseau route,[25] and in the spring of 1737 was at Maurepas.[26]

There, by the broad, unruffled Red, so unlike the rivers of the Shield, La Vérendrye took account of the new region he had entered, in the first reference to the strategic position of the site of Winnipeg.[27] He planned to shift the post to "the great fork of the Red River" in order to facilitate trade and navigation. From the Indians he learned of another great lake to the west, called the "Brother of Lake Winnipeg," and connected with it by a broad channel. The French from the east, like the English and French traders in Hudson Bay, were learning of the sister lakes of Winnipeg, Lakes Manitoba and Winnipegosis. These together La Vérendrye was to call "Lake of the Prairies." He heard, too, of "wooded mountains extending from the north to the south-west, and abounding in martens and lynxes; it is the hunting ground of the Cree and the Assiniboin."[28] The long low hills of the Manitoba escarpment, rising west of the vast cicatrix of swamps and lakes where the plains join with the Shield, were beginning to loom in the ken of the advancing traders. From the Indians also La Vérendrye gained a hazy concept of the "rivière blanche," the White River, or Saskatchewan, so called from the foaming chute of the Grand Rapids by which that great river plunged down to Lake Winnipeg; beyond that, they indicated, lay an intricate canoe route to the English traders at the Bay. They gave him more definite information of the Missouri; it did not, they said, flow westward but south; perhaps, he surmised, to the Pacific Ocean. He was resolved, he reported, to make the comparatively short journey to it, but was prevented by the fears of his men; this was perhaps an excuse trumped up by La Vérendrye, but more likely a real concern by his men for their food supply.

As La Vérendrye was not able to go himself, he gave the Assiniboin Indians who were going from Maurepas to the Mandan villages a message, saying that the French wished to trade with the Mandans also, and inviting them to come to Maurepas with horses and bring corn, beans, and minerals to trade.[29] He himself returned to New France and it was not until September 22, 1738, that he was at Maurepas again and prepared to set out for the villages of the Mandans. On September 24 he found ten cabins of Crees waiting for him at the fork of the Red River with a large quantity of dried meat as provision for the journey. The summer had been dry and the Assiniboine River was low; the canoes were likely to be delayed by the lower water and to suffer damage on the bars. Because of the lowness of the water and the many windings of the river, La Vérendrye soon decided to proceed by land, and left the canoes with their freight to thread the great oxbows of the Assiniboine. The river, he wrote, "was bordered by a fine stand of trees and by prairies of which the limits were lost to view and in which was an abundance of buffalo and deer."[30] The explorer in that fall of 1738 was crossing the great prairie of the Red River valley, the sea of grass which had succeeded to the glacial sea to be named after Louis Agassiz; a sea of grass, but dyked at intervals by the dark lines of trees along the water courses and islanded by the *îlets de bois*, the "bluffs," of oak and wild plum.[31] At the portage to the Lake of the Prairies his progress was stopped by low water and the damaged condition of the canoes. In that country, where there was no spruce, birch, or pine, it proved impossible to find gum or resin to repair them. The place where the check occurred, obviously the rendezvous for the overland and the canoe parties, was near the present Poplar Point. There La Vérendrye began the construction of the first Fort la Reine.[32] The post was on the trail by which the Assiniboins from the south moved to Lake Manitoba on the way to Hudson Bay, and would forward the work of Forts St. Charles and Maurepas in cutting off the trade to Albany on the Bay. When the building was finished, La Vérendrye sent a party back to build a depot at the fork of the Red, to be known to history as Fort Rouge.

Having thus consolidated his advance across the trade routes to the Bay, La Vérendrye on October 18 set out southward along the trail to the Mandan country. The party was in light marching order, prepared to live off the country. The route at first lay directly south, across prairie and wood-lined streams to the "first mountain," that bold and rugged part of the Manitoba escarpment known now as the Pembina hills. At that point La Vérendrye left behind the Red River valley and the lowlands of the Winnipeg basin and entered the second prairie steppe, the highlands of the escarpment. From its ascent of the Pembinas, the trail turned westward to the east end of the "second mountain," later to be named Turtle Mountain. The country between the two mountains La Vérendrye described as "a succession of hills and valleys," which made travel fatiguing, together with "some magnificent plains of three or four leagues in extent." The explorer had in fact crossed the great valley of the Pembina River, with its chain of glittering lakes, and the rolling parkland of southern Manitoba, on the far horizons of which the buttes and morainic hills loom dark and blue, claiming the name of mountain from the traveller dwarfed in the sweep of the plains. From Turtle Mountain the trail ran southwest to the Missouri and the Mandan villages. After learning much of those interesting communities, which fascinated and disappointed him, as they did all subsequent travellers, La Vérendrye in December returned over the snow-bound plains to Fort la Reine. Neither this journey, nor the longer expedition of his son, the Chevalier, in 1741–2, opened a way to the western sea, nor had it found a source of staple food supply for the canoe route. The plains La Vérendrye had crossed were later to furnish pemmican as the staple of the northwest canoe route, but until a trade in pemmican was organized for the supply of the canoes west of the wild rice country, the trade from the St. Lawrence was to be costly and halting.

Since extension of the trade southwestward was exposed to attack by the Sioux and not promising either as fur country or as a way to the western sea, the French traders now turned northwest, up the great lakes of the Winnipeg basin to the Saskatchewan River. It was a better orientation, on all counts. On that line of advance they would move among the friendly Crees, and their canoes would be in constant reach of the birch and spruce of the northern forest.[33] They would sever one by one the routes by which the bands went down to trade at York Factory. This extension of the canoe route of the inland trade to the northwest necessitated the completion of the exploration and occupation of the central lowlands of the Winnipeg basin. Even as the Chevalier was wandering over the plains of the Missouri, French posts were rising along the Manitoba lakes. In 1741 Fort Dauphin was built to serve the "mountain Crees," the Indians of the beaver-terraced escarpment west of Lakes Manitoba and Winnipegosis, on a site which cannot now be determined with certainty, but which was probably near the mouth of the Waterhen River.[34] The next year saw Fort Bourbon built on Cedar Lake above the mouth of the Saskatchewan,[35] in order to cut the route to York Factory, and to which Fort Paskoyac, at The Pas, was to be added in 1750. When Fort Maurepas was shifted to the mouth of the Winnipeg River, the French were installed along the strategic points of the fur trade of the Winnipeg basin and at the threshold of the Saskatchewan valley.

Little is known of the life and business of the French posts in what was to be Manitoba. Both Forts Maurepas seem to have been way stations; Fort Rouge, built on the north bank of the Assiniboine, only a depot. Nothing is known of Dauphin and Bourbon. Only Fort la Reine, soon moved to the neighbourhood of the great oxbow on the Assiniboine where the portage over the prairie to creeks running to Lake Manitoba was short, achieved something of the permanence of Fort St. Charles on the Lake of the Woods. And here we have one vivid picture, that of Jacques Repentigny Legardeur de Saint Pierre, La Vérendrye's successor, driving Assiniboin pillagers from the stockade by waving a flaming torch before the powder magazine. The fur trade could be dangerous, though the exploits of the traders, their long years among the Indians, cause the fact to be forgotten. But, though so little is known of their life in the forts, it is apparent that the

French traders had picked out with sure instinct the commercial sites of Manitoba, Winnipeg, Portage la Prairie, Dauphin, and The Pas.

The traders of the inland trade, both La Vérendrye and his successors, were to push up the Saskatchewan to its forks by 1750. That was to be the limit of their achievement, but it was great, the extension of the trunk canoe route of the inland trade to the Saskatchewan valley and the exploration and occupation of the great swampy tract of the Winnipeg basin. They had entered one of the richest fur regions of the continent, the peltries from which had hitherto gone to the coastal trade of York and Churchill. From La Vérendrye's establishment of Fort St. Pierre in 1732 to the fall of New France, some of the furs of the northern mid-continent, the lightest and the best, were to go down to Montreal. The inland trade and the coastal trade had come to grips in the Winnipeg basin. The competition was not absolute, for the French were less interested in beaver than the English, and sought light furs rather than heavy for the long journey and many portages to Montreal.[36] And it was competition in which the French had no advantage in price or quality of trade goods. The Montreal traders had some times to re-trade English goods from Albany to carry on in the northwest. Only their genuine friendship and matchless tact in trade with the Indians gave them an advantage over the English. But it was a competition which diminished the flow of furs to the Bay and in 1754 the Hudson's Bay Company began again to send inland men of Kelsey's kind to keep their Indian "Captains" firm and see that they brought their bands past the French traders down to the Bay.

The Company had not continued to send men inland to the tribes after the opening of trade with the Northern Indians in 1717–18, nor, after Knight's disastrous failure in 1719, had it ventured to push the search for the North West Passage or the copper mines. It had pursued the coastal trade peacefully and profitably, nor did the first intrusions of the French traders into its inland network of trading ties with the Upland Indians disturb it seriously. The War of the Austrian Succession caused a practical cessation of French competition inland, the Seven Years' War was to end it. But the failure of the Company to continue the search for the North West Passage and to colonize the lands it held had brought it under fierce attack between 1733 and 1749. An excitable and persistent Irish gentleman, Arthur Dobbs, who had made the expansion of British commerce and the discovery of the North West Passage his peculiar avocation, succeeded in having two expeditions despatched to the Bay in search of a passage. The first, under Captain Christopher Middleton in 1741, and the second under Captains William Moore and Francis Smith in 1746, both failed to find a seaway. But Dobbs and his supporters put down the failures to the opposition of the Hudson's Bay Company. As a result of their criticisms the possibility of agricultural settlement in the interior and the extension of trade beyond the fur trade was for the first time discussed at length. Among the evidence submitted by Dobbs was the narrative of Joseph la France, a *voyageur* who had deserted the French to come down to the Bay, and whose account of his travels is among the most revealing of the early descriptions of the land that was to become Manitoba. Much of the interest, however, in the attack on the Company arose from the hope of the trade of the Bay being thrown open. The upshot was a parliamentary enquiry in 1749.[37] The competition of the French traders inland, and the threatened competition of English interlopers in the Bay, had the effect of strengthening the hand of those servants of the Company who wished to resume active operations inland.[38] The new inlanders, led by Anthony Henday, won for the English that knowledge of the swampy tract and the Saskatchewan valley which the French had already gained. They went, however, not to trade but to keep the Indians coming to the coastal posts. They sought to maintain the old integration of coast and inland by means of the coastal trade.

The thrust of the French traders of the St. Lawrence into the northern mid-continent, however, created no such integration in the inland trade. It was but the trial of an idea, a rehearsal of a drama to be played by actors more favoured of fortune. The widespread American empire of France, its branches brushing the sun-bright waters of the Gulf of Mexico on the south and the grey mountain stream of the Saskatchewan on the north, was like a tree rooted in a rock cleft. The constricted root and the unconfined boughs went ill together. The sons of New France had been first in concept, in daring, and in execution. They had made their own the woodcraft and watercraft of the Indian, and so equipped had traced the main features of the great interior valleys of the continent. At the last they had added to the maps the valley of the Red and the great lakes of Manitoba. In 1760 the tree of empire was lopped at the root and fell; French dominion in America was ended, but not French achievement, French speech, French blood. From La Vérendrye's day there were to be men of French race on the waterways and the prairies of Manitoba.

3

The Union of Coast and Plain
1764-1821

BY 1760 ALL THE FRENCH POSTS IN THE NORTH-west were deserted; the traders had been called to the defence of New France. Only two or three—it may have been more—old *voyageurs* continued to live with the Indians the life of Indians. In that year the armies of Amherst closed in on Montreal; the golden lilies of the Bourbons fluttered down in the soft Laurentian light, and henceforth British bugles rang from the ramparts of Quebec across the dark strait of the river of Canada. The seat of the Northwest fur trade had become British, and was to remain British by the Treaty of Paris, 1763. The claims of the French Crown, which had extended from the Gulf of St. Lawrence to the Saskatchewan, from the Lakes to the Frozen Sea, were extinguished forever, and only the *habitants* by the great river and the straggling *voyageurs* of the vast interior of the continent remained to keep alive the memory of French empire in America.

The change of sovereignty wrought no fundamental change in the economic life of the former New France, the new province of Quebec. British merchants and capital moved to Montreal; British traders flocked to Michilimackinac, as, for example, did the first Alexander Henry.[1] But French traders went with them, and the trade was resumed with all the techniques and resources of the old French trade, the master canoe, the *voyageur*, the French posts, the French knowledge of the Indians and the waterways. The British conquest of Canada invigorated the Montreal fur trade by bringing about the union of British capital and supplies with the French inland trade. When Pontiac's warriors had given their sullen submission in 1764, the great canoes once more swung out from the sprawling fort and low shore of Michili-mackinac, some to Green Bay in the southwest; some to Sault Ste Marie and Grand Portage in the far northwest.

The drama of La Vérendrye's great advance into the northern mid-continent was now to be re-enacted, but by actors who knew their parts and carried the play with a swing the laborious re-hearsal of 1731–60 made possible. The rush to the Northwest began in 1765, despite pillaging by the Monsoni Indians on Rainy River;[2] by 1768 there were four posts on the lower Red River and the Assiniboine, Forrest Oakes' on the Red, and La Reine, Middle, and Pine forts on the Assiniboine.[3] The traders, like La Vérendrye, were occupying the line of the Assiniboine between woods and plains in order to obtain provisions from the latter and furs from the forests of Riding Mountain and the Dauphin country to the north.

When in the same year, 1768, the official prohibition of winter-ing among the Indians was withdrawn by the government of Quebec, the rush of traders swelled. Again like La Vérendrye, the traders turned northwest from the Assiniboine to the Saskatche-wan, repeating on a larger scale the same conjunction of plains provisions with forest furs.[4] In 1768 James Finlay was on the Saskatchewan, and in 1771 Thomas Corry.[5] The new Northwest traders had all but reoccupied the former fur domain of the French.

The new *élan* of the inland trade, however, did not pause at the limits of French expansion. The inland servants of the Hudson's Bay Company had reported the return of the "pedlars." In 1773 they were pained to discover Joseph Frobisher trading on the Churchill, a Montreal trader who had passed from the Saskatchewan by Portage du Traité to that hitherto intact pre-serve of the coastal trade of the Bay.[6] In 1778 Peter Pond, furnished with a common stock by traders on the Saskatchewan, passed over the Methy Portage into the Athabaska country in the basin of the Mackenzie River, and added a vast new province to the fur kingdom.[7] The inland trade of Montreal had cut clear across Rupert's Land, and was reaching out to the Pacific coast and the ultimate Northwest of the Mackenzie and the Yukon. Out of the stresses of this titanic effort arose the pooling of goods, the informal common stocks of hard-pressed traders in the interior. These were to grow to include the supply merchants of Montreal, and from these combinations sprang the successive North West partnerships and their rival concerns, until in 1804 all were to amalgamate in a great monopoly of the Northwest trade which spanned the continent from Montreal to the mouth of the Columbia.

Out of the same pressure of danger, distance, and cost was to arise the organization of the great trunk canoe route from Montreal to Grand Portage, and from Grand Portage to the Saskatchewan, the Athabaska, and the Columbia. The operation of the canoe brigades over these immense distances through the brief northern summers required a rigid discipline en route and a sure supply of provisions in depots along the way. Corn, flour, and pork grease from Detroit and Michilimackinac fed the brigades across Superior and over Grand Portage to Lake Winnipeg. At Rainy Lake supplies of wild rice were held to supplement the corn. There also was a great canoe-building establishment,[8] and there, after the beginning of the Athabaska trade, the Athabaska brigades were met by picked crews from Grand Portage, sent to hurry the cargoes over the height of land in time to reach Montreal before the St. Lawrence froze over.

From Bas de la Rivière, the post which replaced Maurepas at the mouth of the Winnipeg River, the plains south of the Assiniboine and the Saskatchewan furnished the supplies of the northbound canoemen. Buffalo pemmican was the staple food of the central portion of the trunk route, and carried the brigades to the northern posts on the Churchill and in the Athabaska, where dried white fish and caribou venison kept the lonely traders from starvation. Thus the inland trade had wedded the plains rich in meat to the forests rich in furs, and the increase in the scale and range of the trade in the last years of the eighteenth century made a sure supply of provisions from the plains only less important than the taking of furs in the forests.

Especially was this true in the Winnipeg basin, the central span of the canoe route and of the whole transcontinental trade. The posts of the Northwest traders on the Red and Assiniboine changed and shifted from year to year, but increased in number until the end of the eighteenth century.[9] They were at once fur posts and provisions posts, the trade in one or other commodity varying from time to time, but with the importance of the provisions trade steadily increasing as the scale of the whole trade grew. Only the posts on the upper reaches of the Assiniboine and on its tributaries in the forest and beaver country of Riding and Duck mountains remained primarily fur posts. The pemmican of "Upper Red River," as the Nor'Westers called the Assiniboine, became the staple supply of the central section of the canoe route. In June of each year boats and canoes moved down with cargoes of pemmican by the forks of Red River to Bas de la Rivière on the Winnipeg. There the boats were burned for their nails, which were collected from the ashes, to be returned to the upper rivers. The bags of pemmican fed the east-bound brigades on the long lift to Rainy Lake, and the west-bound canoes up the stormy stretches of Lake Winnipeg to the mouth of the Saskatchewan.[10] A supply system had come into operation, though a rude one which relied on the use of local supplies as well and much extemporization. But increasingly the movement of the brigades depended on its functioning, and any failure of the supply might have left men to starve on the northern waters, or have checked the dash of the brigades for the junction with the Montreal canoes or the passage of Methy Portage before the northern rivers froze.

To furnish adequate and reliable supplies of pemmican required the growing organization of hunting and transport. The source of supply was the buffalo of the plains. The great herds pressed down into the Red River valley at the beginning of the nineteenth century. Roving bands of them were found in the park belt, and even north of the Assiniboine. Alexander Henry the younger in 1802 recorded that they had trampled the banks of the Pembina River near its junction with the Red "like a barnyard," and that he saw them grazing from its edge.[11] In summer, the wandering herds were usually to be found along the fringes of the mixed wood and meadow lands—the park lands—of the lower Saskatchewan and the Assiniboine. Hunting buffalo for trade became the prime occupation of the Assiniboin Indians on the plains of the Souris and Qu'Appelle rivers, and of the Plains Crees who had joined them. In time Canadian "freemen," *voyageurs* who chose to remain in the Northwest after the expiration of their contracts of service, joined the Indian bands and learned from them the discipline of the hunt, which they transmitted to their progeny of mixed blood. This was the beginning of the organized buffalo hunt, which became the principal occupation of the freemen and their offspring the *métis*. They grew uncannily skilful in the art of "buffalo-running," of pursuing the stampeding animals on horseback and shooting down chosen beasts from the saddle. When the hunters turned from the chase, the women came up to dress the slaughtered animals and remove the tongue, the *depouillé* or back meat, and other choice portions. The meat not immediately consumed was cut into strips to dry in the prairie sun or over fires in dull weather. When dried hard, it was either traded in that form or pounded to powder and mixed with melted fat and tallow in bags of green buffalo hide to make pemmican. The standard bag of about ninety pounds was, in meat, fat, and hide, the yield of one buffalo. A nutritious, if not particularly palatable food was the result, which could be kept in dry storage for some years. The pemmican, together with dried meat, tongues, fat, robes, and sinews, was traded at the Assiniboine posts, and constituted the first commercial return of the western plains.

Pemmican became the staple food of the posts as well as of the canoe brigades. It was, however, a last resource rather than the preferred item of the traders' simple menu. They supplemented their diet by hunting, fishing, and gardening. These pursuits were often, indeed, the only means of subsistence. The solitary trader who had to buy fish and game for his table found in gardening a considerable aid to survival and a welcome addition to his diet. The great companies also, seeking to check costs mounting with the extension of the trade, encouraged their efforts at horticulture and even more ambitious attempts at agriculture. The Hudson's

Bay Company posts on the Bay early had gardens, even as far north as Churchill.[12] Inland traders who remained at a post for any time cultivated a garden and a potato patch. Alexander Henry the younger, while at Pembina on the Red River from 1800 to 1806, enjoyed prodigious success as a gardener.[13]

The same need to stabilize and cheapen the supply of food led to attempts to cultivate cereals. The French traders had farmed at Fort à la Corne on the Saskatchewan before 1760;[14] they surely did so at La Reine and Dauphin also. Henry grew some Indian corn at Pembina. Its cultivation by the Saulteaux at Netley Creek near the mouth of the Red began by 1806 at the latest.[15] Gabriel Franchère in 1814 spoke of Bas de la Rivière as having "more the air of a large and well cultivated farm than a fur traders' factory; a neat and elegant mansion surrounded with barns, stables, storehouses, etc., and by fields of barley, peas, oats and potatoes."[16] This bespeaks an agriculture practised for some little time, and it is probable that the fields still cultivated on the gentle slope of the south shore of the Winnipeg at Fort Alexander are the oldest continuously cultivated land in Manitoba. Some of the Canadian freemen had turned to farming in their retirement, at the forks of the Red and no doubt at other favourable spots.[17] Even more striking than these beginnings of agriculture was the presence of cattle at some of the posts; they had presumably been brought in as calves in the canoes.[18] There can be little doubt that the Committee of the Hudson's Bay Company had sufficient grounds for its belief in 1811 that the climate of the interior of Rupert's Land was good and well fitted for the cultivation of grain, though it was only prudent to believe that "the practicability of agricultural improvements" was still to be demonstrated.[19]

While the Nor'Westers had been organizing the great trunk canoe route which tapped the fur forest from Superior to Athabaska, and the growth of the trade was stimulating the beginnings of agriculture, the Hudson's Bay Company had not remained passive. The return of "pedlars" put an end to the coastal trade and to the sleep by the frozen sea of which Joseph Robson had accused the Company; those servants of the Company who had been urging a penetration of the interior in force were to have their way. The work of the inland guides like Matthew Cocking and Joseph Batt made it possible to meet the Nor'Westers in the only effective way, by changing from the coastal to the inland trade. In 1774 Cumberland House was founded on Pine Island Lake by Samuel Hearne, to command the Saskatchewan route and the country eastward to The Pas and northward to the Churchill.[20] The difficulties to be overcome in establishing posts in the interior were many: the lack of canoes and canoemen; the lack of long service men who knew the country and the Indians; after 1793, the difficulty of recruiting men in the British Isles during the Revolutionary and Napoleonic wars.[21] Slowly, however, these obstacles were surmounted or worn down, and the old English company began to match the Canadian traders, post for post, throughout western Rupert's Land. From 1774 to 1810 the Nor'Westers were subjected to patient and persistent competition.

From York Factory and Churchill a system of posts along the Saskatchewan was built up, and also in the Swan River country south of The Pas. The southern Winnipeg basin, however, was in the hinterland of Severn and Albany, not of York and Churchill. It was largely left to the Nor'Westers until 1793, when Donald Mackay and John Sutherland of the Hudson's Bay Company came in by boat along the Albany and the significantly named English River to the junction of the latter with the Winnipeg. Thereafter the Albany men and their boats spread eastward to the Lake of the Woods and Rainy Lake, and westward along the Red and Assiniboine. An extraordinary multiplication of posts, both North West and Hudson's Bay, followed their advent on the upper Assiniboine. By 1800 the Albany posts had pushed on until they were competing with those of which York was the headquarters in the Swan River and Duck Mountain country.[22] This push along the edge of the plains was for provisions at least as much as for furs; the Company's lines of communication were lengthening and the costs of their posts mounting. As the Saskatchewan posts drew on the plains of the Saskatchewan for dried meat and pemmican, so the posts of the Assiniboine and the Winnipeg drew on the plains of the Souris and Qu'Appelle. The

Hudson's Bay Company's inland trade, like that of the Nor'-
Westers, had brought about a junction of forest and plain in the
provisioning of the fur trade. The Company's posts also had
turned to gardening and a rudimentary agriculture to supply their
needs and reduce costs. So much was this so at the Assiniboine
posts that it was known in 1811 that horses, seed potatoes, and
perhaps seed grain could be obtained from Brandon House, as
well as Indian corn from the Indians at Netley Creek.[23]

The needs of the fur trade of both the Bay and the St. Lawrence, then, were calling into being the buffalo hunt and agriculture in the Winnipeg basin. As costs continued to mount
during the great war in Europe, the Hudson's Bay Company more
and more felt the need of "country provisions" and of native
labour. In 1810 these needs were crystallized into a positive and
aggressive policy by the philanthropic projects and commercial
ambition of Thomas, fifth Earl of Selkirk and his hard-headed
brother-in-law, Andrew Wedderburn-Colvile. The high-minded
and patriotic Selkirk sought to relieve the distress of the Highland
crofters and Irish cotters suffering from the agricultural revolution
which was driving them from their homes. As early as 1802, fired
by a reading of Alexander Mackenzie's *Voyages,* Selkirk had
planned the establishment of an agricultural colony on the banks
of Red River. In 1810, after experience in settling emigrants in
Prince Edward Island and Upper Canada, he returned to the
project of a colony in the Winnipeg basin. He and Colvile bought
into the Hudson's Bay Company,[24] and used their influence to
secure the adoption of a policy of aggressive competition with the
North West Company. The foundations of this policy were twofold, the invasion of the rich Athabaska country, hitherto a
preserve of the Nor'Westers, and the establishment of an agricultural colony at Red River. The two were closely related: the
penetration of the Athabaska would restore dividends and give
the North West Company effective opposition; the colony would
furnish provisions for the posts and boat brigades; it would supply
country-bred men for the service and offer a sanctuary to retired
servants and their dependents, relieving the posts of the cost of
supporting them; finally, it would confirm the Company's title

to the soil, flouted by the Montreal traders, through actual occupation.

Moved by these considerations, the Company in 1811 granted Selkirk the upper Winnipeg basin, to be known as Assiniboia, in absolute proprietorship. The northern boundary of the grant began at the height of land west of Superior, followed the canoe route by Rainy River and the Winnipeg River to Lake Winnipeg, swung up the lake to latitude fifty-two degrees and thirty minutes, ran west to the middle of Lake Winnipegosis and down to latitude fifty-two degrees and then west again to the head of the Assiniboine River. From that point, the western boundary followed longitude one hundred and two degrees and thirty minutes south to the height of land between the Souris and Missouri rivers. The southern boundary followed the height of land around the headwaters of Red River and so back to the height of land west of Superior. The bounds drawn with such magnificent freehand enclosed a great natural province, the central basin of the northern mid-continent. It was knit together by its own internal waterways and level reaches of grassland and park belt, and linked by easy passages east, west, and south over the same waterways and low divides, while to the north the tangled course of the Nelson and Hayes furnished passage to and from the Bay. The grant was the old fur region La Vérendrye had first opened, a region now much depleted of furs, but in 1811 the principal source of provisions for the Northwest fur trade.

At that time both companies were peaceably trading in the region and drawing supplies from it. It was Selkirk's intention that both should continue to do so, but the Hudson's Bay Company was to be helped by the colony, while at the same time it challenged the Nor'Westers in the Athabaska. Such twofold pressure, added to the old Company's great advantage in its cheaper sea route by the Bay, would give it competitive superiority over the North West Company. The outcome of the competition no one could foretell. Clearly, however, it was ominous for the future of the projected colony that its origins were involved in the increase in the scale and organization of the fur trade, and that its foundation should be the gambit in the mounting conflict of the two giant corporations, struggling for a monopoly of the fur trade of the great Northwest and of the Pacific coast.

Challenging these issues, Selkirk in 1811 despatched from Stornoway a party of 36 Scottish and Irish labourers[25] under his newly chosen Governor of Assiniboia, Miles Macdonell, to make preparation at Red River for the colonists who were to follow in 1812. Seldom have the foundations of a colony been better planned, and seldom has planning been more frustrated by mischance, the shortcomings of agents, and the opposition of rivals. After suffering many desertions, including that of the blacksmiths, brought about by the intrigues of agents of the North West Company, the party sailed for Hudson Bay. It reached York Factory too late to go up to Red River, and was forced to winter on the Nelson. Not until August 30, 1812, did Macdonell and his party, reduced to 18, reach the Red River. They had acquired a bull and a cow at Oxford House on the way, but lacked implements and were without provisions. The fish of Red River met their immediate needs, until the fur posts, both Nor'Wester and Hudson's Bay Company, gave them relief. It was by then too late to make much preparation for the colonists of 1812, Irish and Hebridean, 120 in number, with an unknown number of women and children not listed, who reached Red River on October 27, still less for those expected in 1813. The first necessity proved to be to make arrangements to hunt buffalo at Pembina for sustenance during the coming winter.

That year of 1812, nevertheless, saw the systematic beginning of agricultural settlement in the Red River valley. Like so many beginnings, it was insignificant, and was rendered particularly so by the magnitude and fury of contemporary events. As Miles Macdonell rode along the open prairie of Red River, selecting a site for the colony, Napoleon's lancers were pricking across the Russian plains, scouting before the Grand Army of the Empire on its march to Moscow. The great war of the Revolution and Empire was rising to its tremendous climax in Europe, and in North America Canadians and Americans were thrusting and counter-thrusting at Michilimackinac, Detroit and Queenston. Once more the base of the Northwest fur trade was threatened by conquest from the south. Yet the riders by the Red, dwarfed by the plain they crossed and forgotten by a world in agony, chose the site of their colony in just confidence, for both the Empire of Bonaparte and the Republic to the south lay gripped in the toils of British sea-power, and the mother island was secure and the seaways open. By the Bay and the St. Lawrence, the interior of the northern mid-continent could be linked with those British waters by which its first settlers were to come.

Macdonell had received from Selkirk instructions written with the precision of a man who had pored over every description of his new domain until he had fixed every feature in his mind's eye. The site of the colony was to be dry and airy; such a site as could probably be found where the Red River passed the high or outer bank of Lake Winnipeg.[26] Selkirk suggested the choice of Pelican Ripple (St. Andrew's Rapids) as described on Peter Fidler's survey. Fidler had said that by the Ripple was the first plain or opening on the way up the river, "with nearly dead water from the lake." This last feature, Selkirk thought, might make it possible for a sailing vessel to reach the colony, and help make it a place of consequence. The situation seemed to him, however, too low for a permanent settlement. If Macdonell thought it advisable to go up to the "great plains," he was to examine both branches of the river.

The site, in any event, should be on "a plain of tolerable extent," and each settler was to have "the advantage of wood, water and open lands fit for immediate cultivation."[27] Selkirk had discerned the peculiar advantages the Red River lands offered the settler, in that river-front lots gave wood, water, and cleared land in combination. And he had the rude words of Archibald Mason, a Scottish farmer who had taken to the fur trade, to assure him that from "Nattli creek" to the Sioux country west and south there was "a remarkable Rich Soil of Marl and black Mold." "These famous lands," wrote Mason, had not their equal else-where.[28]

Macdonell made a rapid inspection of the country between Netley Creek and the Forks, rejected the site at Pelican Ripple, and despite his knowledge of the flood of 1811,[29] decided that the tract of prairie along the west bank of the Red just below the mouth of the Assiniboine was the best location for the colony. He chose the large point, thereafter known as Point Douglas, a mile below the North West post of Fort Gibraltar, built in 1810 at the Forks, as the centre of the colony. It was also the place for his first sowing of grain, because some land had been cleared of brush and grass by fire. He took formal possession of the colony on September 4, set his men to work, and went on to Pembina to arrange with free Canadians and Indians to hunt meat for the winter. He took back two horses and a harrow to the Forks, where he found that little land had been prepared. On October 7, however, he himself planted some winter wheat, covering it with a hoe. As there was no blacksmith, it had been impossible to make a plough. So inauspiciously did systematic agriculture begin in the Red River valley. The arrival of a small flock of sheep with the colonists of 1812 added to the cares as well as the resources of the tiny agricultural colony.

The winter was passed at Pembina in dependence on the hunt. At the beginning of May, 1813, Macdonell returned to Point Douglas to sow spring wheat and other grains and potatoes, and to push on the clearing of land and the erection of buildings. Peter Fidler brought down provisions and buffalo robes from Brandon House, together with a bull, cow, and yearling heifer he had purchased from the Nor'Westers for the colony. He divided Point Douglas into seven lots and laid out a stretch of the west bank of the Red in one hundred acre lots. The river frontage was ten chains, as the frontage used in Quebec, which had furnished the model for the survey, was thought by Macdonnell to be too narrow.[30] So Quebec contributed the striped pattern of its *côtes* to Red River colony, a pattern which chanced to lend itself easily to the reproduction in the New World of the ancient Celtic in-field and outfield system of Scotland.

These constructive measures depended on the success of the crops and the hunt. The former had failed, both the winter and the spring wheat, the pease, rye, hemp, and English barley. Indian corn was almost a total failure, and the oats were late and were frozen. Only the potatoes yielded well. The causes of the failure,

Macdonell wrote, were bad seed, a drought after sowing, grubs, and faulty cultivation. Only one badly made plough had been in use, late in the season, as no one had the skill to make a good one. There was little from the harvest with which to feed the colonists of 1812, and the expected arrivals of 1813. That fall all but the family of John MacLean, a farmer of some means and an outstanding man, once more went south to Pembina to live by the hunt.[31] No detailed account survives, and the imagination fails to tell how these hardy people lived, men, women and children, in log huts through a Red River winter.

The colony, however, was growing despite all reverses, and by internal settlement as well as by immigration. To the freemen living at the Forks in 1812 six families were added in 1813. Other freemen were settling at Pembina, and still others were coming to begin a colony at White Horse Plain up the Assiniboine in 1814. Macdonell reckoned in that year that there were two hundred Canadians with their Indian wives and mixed progeny in the whole colony. Some had taken up land, and he had offered all of them land and free seed for three years, "but they [had] followed so long the Indian manner of living that it [was] not easy to win them from it." Even two Nor'Westers, John Pritchard and Alexander Macdonell, were talking of settling in the colony, and Pritchard was already the warm eulogist of the climatic and agricultural merits of his adopted land, as he was for many years to remain. The immigrants of 1812 were true settlers, determined to work their lands, unlike the labourers of 1811. They were settled lower down on the river on lots of three chains frontage, as a greater width was found to spread settlement too much. In 1813, moreover, had come millwright Lamont and blacksmith Macdonald.[32] The latter, with Michael Heyden who had come in 1812, helped repair the shortage of tools and of ploughs from which the planting of the first harvest had suffered.

While prospects were improving, and while it was apparent that the colony would develop by internal settlement alone, the Governor was disappointed when he went to York to meet the party of immigrants expected in 1813. These were Scottish settlers, victims of the great Sutherland clearances of 1811 and

1812, in the main from the parish of Kildonan. But they had been landed at Churchill, stricken with fever, and the ship's captain refused to take them on to York. The party was forced to winter on the Arctic banks of the Churchill and in the spring trudge overland to York. Thus not until June 21, 1814, did the third party, 83 in all, reach Red River.

The prospects for that year seemed on the whole to be propitious. Wheat—spring, not fall wheat—barley, oats, Indian corn, and buckwheat were sown, not to mention three hundred kegs of potatoes. All began to grow well. The livestock had come through the winter, except for some killing of sheep by the dogs, and the drowning of the bull from Oxford House in the water-hole. Serious as these minor losses were in the circumstances, they were forgotten as the golden summer of 1814 rounded to its close, and scythe and sickle swept through the abundant harvest. The yet small plots, however, yielded only seed for 1815, apart from the ever prolific potatoes. The arrival of the Kildonan settlers, driven from the valleys which had hitherto reared men and were now to raise sheep,[33] still further strengthened the agricultural character and the morale of the colony.[34] For these Sutherland Scots were farmers and herdsmen, and were to cling with equal tenacity to their new lands and their old ways.

Their coming, however, with that of a small party of 15 in the fall, for the moment only increased the difficulty of providing enough food for the colony. The assiduous but pedestrian Governor Macdonell, despite a warning from Selkirk of the necessity of not arousing the hostility of the fur traders, had already endeavoured to forestall a shortage of provisions by issuing on January 8, 1814, a proclamation which prohibited the export of pemmican or other provisions from Assiniboia.[35] The enforcement of this embargo of doubtful legality would have been a serious impediment to the trade of both the North West and the Hudson's Bay companies. It would have been particularly embarrassing to the former, as the recapture of Detroit by the American army in 1813 had reduced the supply of corn and flour for the canoe brigades moving west from Fort William. The Company required the pemmican of Assiniboia to provision the

DEPARTURE OF THE SECOND COLONIST TRANSPORT FROM YORK FORT TO ROCK FORT
SEPT. 6, 1821

Painting by Peter Rindisbacher in the Public Archives of Canada

SUMMER VIEW IN THE ENVIRONS OF THE COMPANY FORT DOUGLAS ON THE RED RIVER
DRAWN FROM NATURE IN JULY, 1822

Painting by Peter Rindisbacher in the Public Archives of Canada

brigades eastward as well as westward from Bas de la Rivière.[36] Though the immediate difficulties were overcome by their partners in Assiniboia in negotiation with Macdonell, the Pemmican Proclamation served to confirm the suspicion of the Nor'Westers that the Red River colony was deliberately planted athwart their supply route for the purpose of crippling their trade. So also did formal notices—not meant to be enforced but to protect Selkirk's title—to quit their posts, which were served in August, 1813, and proclaimed in October, 1814. With the ruthlessness of the vaunted "North West spirit" they determined in the council of 1815 to make the continued existence of the colony impossible.

In the attempt they could count on the support of the *métis*, or *bois-brûlés*, the free Canadians and their descendants of mixed blood, especially the wilder elements who had remained on the plains of the upper Assiniboine. Their loyalty to their old "bourgeois," or masters, had been kept alive by gifts and cajolery. Many of them had been granted their discharges on condition that they come back into service at call. Many were still attached to the Company as provisions hunters and had developed a marked *esprit de corps* in the rude discipline of the buffalo hunt. The *métis* still felt the old hostility to the Hudson's Bay Company of the *"anglais,"* with which they identified the colony. The Nor'Westers, preparing a backfire against the Hudson's Bay Company's confirmation of its title to the soil of Rupert's Land, assured the *métis* that they were a "new nation," intermediate between the whites and the Indians, and that they possessed through their Indian mothers an unextinguished title to the lands of the Northwest. They had also instilled in them some vague military notions, much in vogue in those years of war, which were speedily assimilated into the custom of the buffalo hunt. These wild, proud men constituted something of a military force in a vast territory where there was no organized police power. And Governor Macdonell incurred their suspicious hostility when he forbade the running of buffalo near the settlement, because it drove the herds away. His order seemed to the *métis* an unwarrantable interference with their accustomed mode of life.

From these causes and by these men came the first destruction of the colony, that of 1815. The North West bourgeois, Duncan Cameron, first lured many of the settlers to desert the hard life of the colony by promises of transport to Canada and aid in settlement there. These, 133 in number, were later taken east in the canoe brigades. Governor Macdonell was arrested on a Canadian warrant, and taken east for trial, as was possible under an Imperial Act of 1803, which gave the Canadian courts jurisdiction over Rupert's Land and the Indian Territories. Then the *bois-brûlés*, gathered from the upper Assiniboine, harassed the colonists who were determined to remain, and their stock, by firing from ambush and making threatening sallies. Finally they drove the remaining colonists from their lots, to flee by boat to Jack River at the north end of Lake Winnipeg. Behind them the *métis* trotted their shaggy ponies through the plots green with grain, and the smoke rolling up from the log cabins on the bank of the Red signalled the destruction of Selkirk's colony. The North West Company, the fur trade and its half-caste progeny, had struck down the farmer and trampled his fields.

The year 1815, however, was not to witness the end of the Red River colony. All that summer the grain shot blade and ear in the fierce heat of the Red River valley. When in early August Colin Robertson, a former Nor'Wester in the service of the Hudson's Bay Company, brought back the colonists from Jack River, he found a sole survivor, one MacLeod, tending an abundant and ripening harvest.[37] The settlers set themselves to cutting hay for the surviving livestock and harvesting a crop which yielded four hundred bushels of wheat, two hundred of barley, and five hundred of oats. This crop assured the colonists of seed for another year, and some food as well. When the new Governor Selkirk had sent out to relieve Macdonell came up the Red that fall he saw standing along the bank twelve or fourteen stacks of grain, brown against the blue September sky, "a sight perfectly novel in this country."[38] Fortunate as the harvest was, fish from the river and the buffalo hunt at Pembina were once more the staple support of the colony during the winter of 1815–16, as well as for the last band of immigrants to arrive, the band of 84 which came in 1815. With them had come the new Governor, Robert Semple, a sincere and earnest, but impulsive and indecisive gentleman.

The restoration of the colony by Colin Robertson at a time when the Hudson's Bay Company was about to launch the first of its expeditions in force into the Athabaska country invited a strong riposte from the North West Company. The colony, it was apparent, might be a decisive factor in the contest for the fur trade of the Northwest, and must therefore be destroyed. News of the rousing of the *métis* by the bourgeois of the North West Company and rumours of threats to exterminate the colony came down the Assiniboine during the winter.[39] On March 17, Robertson arrested the Nor'Westers at the Forks; later Semple released them on parole. Attack and counter-attack began on the upper Assiniboine that troubled spring, while the colonists laboured to sow their plots. In May Robertson seized Fort Gibraltar, which dominated the water passage at the Forks.[40] Thereafter the provisions brigades of the North West Company could pass only under the guns of Gibraltar.

The season was now at hand when pemmican was to be moved down to Bas de la Rivière to supply the Nor'Wester brigades. On June 1 the *métis* under Cuthbert Grant, half-breed son of a North West partner and boldest of the bold hunters of the plains, captured and plundered Brandon House, the Hudson's Bay post on the Assiniboine two miles above the mouth of the Souris. They then rode with the provisions boats down to Portage la Prairie, and from there proceeded down the river by land with three carts of pemmican. Robertson, when news of the descent reached him, advised Semple to pull down Fort Gibraltar, and this was done. But Robertson abruptly left Red River to go to England, and the colony was deprived of his resolute and canny leadership. The effect of the removal of Fort Gibraltar was to leave Fort Douglas dominating the Red below the Forks and capable of denying passage to the North West boats with provisions for the brigades. It is not clear whether the intention was to deny the passage, but the act implied that intention and was so interpreted by the Nor'Westers. They, for their part, were concerned not only to open the way for their own provisions, but to stop those for the Athabaska expedition of the Hudson's Bay Company.

When the *métis* reached the ford on the Assiniboine in what was to become St. James, they struck across the plains for the Red below the settlement. There were two bands, the first escorting the carts of pemmican, the second following at some distance. Whatever their intentions with respect to the colony, it is evident that their immediate purpose was to establish contact with the North West partners who were coming fresh from council at Fort William. This they hoped to do below the settlement without interference from Fort Douglas, but the swampy ground out on the plain forced them to pass closer to the fort than they desired.

Their leading party reached Frog Plain below the settlers' lots unperceived, but the second band was sighted from the watch tower of Fort Douglas. Semple, with some rashness, went out to intercept them with a straggling band of armed followers, twenty-five in number as it proved, a group too large for parley and too weak for fight. At Seven Oaks, a point where the woods along the Red jutted out into the plain, about three-quarters of a mile from Fort Douglas, the rear party of the *métis* wheeled back on seeing it was being followed. They advanced on Semple and his followers on horseback and in crescent formation. Semple, who had sent back for a field piece but had not waited for the slow-moving oxen to bring it up, had his men extend their line to three paces interval to avoid encirclement. One Boucher rode out from the silent *métis*, sitting with their guns across their horses' necks, and Semple, who had also advanced, asked what they wanted. An altercation followed, and Semple tried to seize Boucher's bridle or gun. A shot rang out and firing began, by the colony men from their extended line, by the *métis* from horseback or from behind their horses. At this moment the other party of *métis* rode out from behind the wood and, firing from horseback, swept round behind the colonists to cut off their retreat. The colonists huddled together, and a massacre followed, for Semple himself and nineteen of his officers and men were killed, only six escaping to the woods of the river bank, or being spared. The dead were stripped and mutilated, their corpses left on the plain; the victors washed the blood-stained cloaks of the slain in the Red. One *métis* at the most was killed. Infantry on the open plain were helpless before the mounted marksmen of the buffalo hunt.[41]

This sudden and deadly burst of passion at Seven Oaks—it was premeditated by neither side—gave the Nor'Westers control of the colony once more. Prisoners were again taken to Fort William in the canoes; again the boatloads of refugees pulled wearily up the long reaches of Winnipeg to Jack River, to pass a bitter winter in redoubled exile, driven from their new home and far from the old. The Nor'Westers "had cleared the two rivers,"[42] and that fall there was no harvest in Red River.

These, however, were the dregs of the cup of bitterness. The harrying of 1815 was one thing; the massacre of 1816 quite another. Lord Selkirk at once prepared to retaliate with more than North West spirit. In Canada he engaged a band of discharged soldiers from the de Wattville and de Meuron regiments; they had been mercenaries, mostly Swiss by nationality, but including Poles, Germans and other Europeans. With these men and a commission as justice of the peace, Selkirk seized Fort William in August and in January, 1817, an advance party of his veterans under Captain P. D. D'Orsonnens trudged over the snowbound Savanne portage of the Roseau to descend on and seize Fort Douglas before the Nor'Westers were aware of their approach.

In the following summer Selkirk himself reached the colony and the colonists were once more brought back from Jack River. The colony was restored, and on surer foundations. The discerning eye, the enthusiasm, and the presence of the lord proprietor gave firm direction to the details of restoration and assurance to the colonists themselves. Selkirk, so far as was possible, since the resident Saulteaux were immigrants of fairly recent date and few Crees and Assiniboins were left, extinguished the Indian title to the lands along the Red as far south as the Red Leaf River and along the Assiniboine as far west as Rat Creek beyond Portage la Prairie by treaty with the friendly chief Peguis and three other chiefs. The lots of Fidler's survey were reassigned to the surviving colonists and the de Meurons were settled along the banks of the Seine which flowed into the Red from the southeast just opposite Fort Douglas. Their presence, and that of a commission of enquiry headed by Colonel W. B. Coltman, kept an unwonted peace that summer. The ravaged seed plots were restored and crops sown; where the seed was obtained is not recorded. The crops promised well all summer, but, as the sowing had been late, were damaged by the fall frosts. What was harvested had to be kept for seed.[43]

Such tribulations, severe as they were, were all that were to afflict Red River henceforth. The Prince Regent's Proclamation of 1817 awed the contestants, and the fierce and prolonged lawsuits in the Canadian courts exhausted their funds and their pugnacity. The *métis* were no longer excited against the colony and more and more came to see it, as many had done from the first, as a place of settlement for themselves and as a market for the produce of the hunt. Orkneymen also, from the service of the Hudson's Bay Company, began to settle with their native families along the Assiniboine a little above the Forks in "Orkneytown."[44] The colony was now to be furnished with churches and schools, the work of devoted missionaries. In 1818, as a result of some years of negotiation by both the North West Company and Selkirk, came Rev. J. N. Provencher and Rev. S. Dumoulin of the Church of Rome, to resume the work of the Catholic missionaries in the Northwest and begin the work of Christianizing and pacifying the turbulent *bois-brûlés*. With them came some French Canadian families from Lower Canada to give a firm core of civilized folk to the farming settlement of the half-wild *métis*.

The Scottish Presbyterian colonists had been promised a minister of their faith, but at the last moment the one bespoken, Rev. Donald Sage, drew back and his place was not to be supplied for many years, to the bitter disappointment of the Kildonan settlers. In 1819 the Church Missionary Society, at the request of the Committee of the Hudson's Bay Company, sent Rev. John West to the colony, and in 1820 he began his ministrations to the Indians and to such colonists as found them acceptable. From these years on the missionaries in church and school were to labour to create an oasis of civilization in Red River amid the surrounding barbarism of forest and plain.

When, therefore, the crop of 1818 began to head, it seemed that the colony might be past its early trials at last. But the colonists were attempting agriculture in the midst of a vast wilderness, unbroken, undrained, uncontrolled; their tiny plots on the banks of the Red were at the mercy of tempest, flood, or pest. On August 2, locusts descended in swarms on the crops. In places they were three inches deep on the ground. The lots of the de Meurons suffered the worst losses, the potatoes most among the crops. The wheat, fortunately, was so far advanced as largely to escape.[45]

The locusts deposited their eggs in the colony, and the following spring the young were at work early in May. This time they stripped the plots, and even the prairie, so that there was little grass for hay. Not only was no grain left for food, but little or none for seed. Seed had from time to time been obtained from the posts of the upper Assiniboine,[46] and from Bas de la Rivière on the Winnipeg River; these had escaped the locusts.[47] In 1820, however, it was necessary to send a party down to Prairie du Chien in Wisconsin Territory to buy seed wheat.[48] It returned with two hundred and fifty bushels in early June, and much of the late-sown wheat matured sufficiently to escape the fall frosts.[49] From this wheat came most of the seed of the colony thereafter, and the strain was known as the Prairie du Chien. After 1820 the crops slowly improved, despite the lingering remnants of the locusts, frosts, mice, grubs, and other afflictions. The plots length- ened their black strips up the river bank, the number of ploughs was increased, and agriculture was established in Red River. Lady Selkirk's proud words to Bishop Plessis with samples of wheat grown at Red River and Rainy Lake were to be borne out: "This goes to show that these regions can supply something besides furs."[50]

Not for some years, however, was the colony to be independent of the buffalo hunt for its main supply of food. Even while the crops became more abundant, "plains provisions" remained a large part of the Red River diet. For the larger part of the popula- tion of the colony, the *métis* who had come down from the plains to settle, the buffalo hunt remained the principal occupation, by which they won their food and produce to trade for ammunition and clothing. The long years of trial had ended in a compromise between the hunt and the plough,[51] between dependence on the summer drift of the buffalo herds and the rhythm of seedtime and harvest.

Meantime, the contest for control of the fur trade had continued in the law courts of Canada and along the rivers of the Athabaska. The courts could make little of the violence and counter-violence in a wilderness fifteen hundred miles distant. In the Athabaska the Nor'Westers bore things with a high hand still, but could ill afford the strain the dogged opposition of the older company put upon their over-extended resources. Then in 1819 Governor William Williams of the Hudson's Bay Company, a hard old soldier, struck with the North West spirit the Bay men had learned only too well, and broke the back of the North West organization. With an armed schooner on Lake Winnipeg and a company of de Meurons from Red River, he seized the North West brigades at the portage of the Grand Rapids of the Saskatchewan. The furs were seized and the bourgeois taken to York for passage to England for trial.[52] This stunning blow, so much in the North West manner, was struck by a confident power. The great North West Company had yet the strength to retaliate by arresting Williams himself, but it was in fact collapsing. The finances of the merchant partners were in disorder; the winter partners were discontented as the term of the last partnership approached; the old bullying Nor'Wester spirit could no longer carry all before it; the Bay men had learned all the techniques of the inland trade and had bettered some of them; the conservative, permanent chartered corporation was wearing down the loose, short partnership; above all, the beaver lands were stripped far back into the northern Rockies. Union of the companies was imperative to restore peace in the trade and conserve the fur-bearing animals on which it depended. In 1821 a union was brought about, a union of the solid organization of the old chartered company with the Nor'-Wester techniques, of the stability of the coastal trade with the enterprise of the inland.

The union of 1821 opened the greatest of the chapters in the history of the Hudson's Bay Company as it ended the strife which was destroying the fur trade of the Northwest. It reconciled the coastal and inland trade in a great monopoly and bound interior and Bay in a great transport system centring on York Factory. The union slackened the ties between Canada and the Northwest; the

great trunk route by Fort William was abandoned, except for the
movement of local brigades and the silent passage of express
canoes. Never more would the long flotillas of the north canoes,
with their middlemen chanting to the thrust of the paddle, file
down the waters of du Bonnet, or dash to the landing at Bas de la
Rivière and check the canoes with the paddles rolled on the gun-
wales in a flash of spray. The York boats of the victor, with long
rake of stem and stern pitching down the rapids of the Hayes,
were to carry to the Bay the furs of the Northwest. But that
triumph of the Bay over the St. Lawrence was also an integration
of the maritime slope, the fur forest of the Shield, the great
swampy tract, and the southern plains, an integration of the fur
trade of the north and the provisions trade of the south. In that
union the agricultural colony of Red River, with its annual
buffalo hunts, had a secure role to play safe from the strife of
contending traders, a small and a subordinate province in the vast
empire of the fur trade.

4

The River Lot and Buffalo Hunt
1821-1856

WHEN THE UNION OF THE NORTH WEST WITH THE Hudson's Bay Company had ended the strife in the fur trade, the new Company sent a member of its Committee, Nicholas Garry, to visit the Northwest and oversee the measures necessary to the organization of the posts and operations of the new monopoly. In August, 1821, he reached the Red River by the old canoe route from Fort William. As he began the ascent of Red River, Garry found the Saulteaux Indians under Chief Peguis encamped at Netley Creek in the midst of their cornfields.[1] He noted that, like their relatives in Canada, they made sugar from the sap of the maple.[2] There also was a ranch belonging to the Company where horses were kept to transport goods overland to Brandon House. On the way up the river Garry found the water of the river muddy and ill-tasting, but thought the woods along the banks beautiful. At the rapids (Pelican or Grand Rapids) was a station where sleigh-dogs were kept during the summer. About six miles below Point Douglas the log houses of the settlers began to line the high edges of the river bank on either side. There lived the Scottish colonists, firmly settled after two dispersions. On Point Douglas, Fort Douglas still sat looking south up the broad channel of the Red and forming the centre of the colony, and in or around it lived the chief men of the settlement, Thomas Thomas, Robert Logan, James Bird, John Pritchard, Thomas Laidlaw, Rev. John West, Rev. Picard Destroismaisons. At the Forks the stubs and new sheds of dismantled Fort Gibraltar stared across the river to where the new mission church of St. Boniface, founded by Rev. J. N.

Provencher in 1818, reared the first church steeple into the diamond blue of the western sky. Around it lived the Canadian colonists who had come in from Lower Canada in 1818,[3] and behind it, along the little River Seine, were the de Meuron veterans, slovenly and restless pioneers.[4] Garry noted that there were at Red River 221 Scottish settlers, 65 de Meurons, 133 Canadians, a total of 419 people, of whom 154 were female. At Pembina were about five hundred *métis*.[5]

Such was the Red River Settlement in 1821 and there could be no stronger comment on the effect of the ill-success of agriculture and the pull of the nomad life than the disparity in numbers between the colonists at the Forks and the *métis* at Pembina. The truth was that the rude community on Red River was much more a casual settlement than it was a planned colony. Garry concluded that there was serious likelihood of the colony becoming "the Receptacle of lawless Banditti and a most dangerous thorn in the side of the Hudson's Bay Company."[6] John Halkett, executor of the Selkirk estate, shared Garry's fears when he visited the colony in 1822 and set himself to avoid this result by urging the Roman Catholic fathers to persuade their flock at Pembina to move northward to Lake Manitoba or a site less exposed to the Sioux and the temptations of the plains and the American "petty traders,"[7] free to come to the new boundary of 1818.

It was a drab and forlorn community Garry visited, and he noted that even its leading men had neither energy nor foresight.[8] Only concentrated settlement would allow the work of civilization to proceed. The practice of agriculture, the ministrations of the church, and the education of the young required that the roving life of the hunt, native to the *métis* and forced on the immigrant by the harsh circumstances of the first years of the colony, should give way to close settlement by church and school along the rivers and to the steady routine of the ploughman and the herdsman. Until the new way of life could provide a sufficiency of food, however, dispersion was necessary to survival, and even then the pull of the plains would be strong on *métis* and immigrant alike. For fifty years the Red River Settlement was to live in uneasy balance between civilization and barbarism, the river lot and the buffalo hunt.

The people of the settlement, however, remained much as Garry had found them for a whole generation. The *métis*, settled along the river banks of the Red River valley even before Selkirk founded his colony, remained the largest and most distinctive element in Red River. The sons of French and Scottish fathers[9] and Saulteaux, Cree, and Assiniboin mothers, they had adopted the hunting life, the wild freedom, and the ancient feud with the Sioux of the tribes of the park belt and its bordering plains. But their paternal tie with the white race led them to live apart as a group from the Indians and to supplement the spoils of the hunt with the potato patch of the river lot and to make the winter camp of the Indian a permanent habitation in the Red River valley. Remembering the language and the simple devotions of their fathers, they responded readily to the missionaries, and came to regard the mission churches and chapels among them as fixed centres in their still semi-nomadic life. Some of them, indeed, settled permanently and became farmers; others remained wanderers, the *hivernants* or winterers, who lived always on the plains, and came to the settlements only to trade or carouse. The *métis* as a group combined an attachment to a fixed residence in the colony with occupations which took them out into the western plains or along the northern waters as huntsmen, tripmen, and guides.

In 1823 most of those who had settled at Pembina were persuaded to leave that settlement, superior base though it was for the buffalo hunt, and to settle, some at St. Boniface, but the larger part at the old camping ground up the Assiniboine at the White Horse Plain, soon to be known as Grantown after Cuthbert Grant, leader of the *métis* at Seven Oaks, and later as St. François-Xavier. Their numbers in the colony were swelled as the rival fur posts were consolidated and relieved of their numerous dependents in the reorganization that followed the union. The colony became the refuge of the unemployed of the fur trade, and the years of the amalgamation saw bands of *métis* moving down through the park belt and in from the plains to settle along the

Red and Assiniboine and their tributaries to the south and west. From these settlements the trails struck out southwest to the valley of the Pembina, by very much the same route as La Vérendrye had followed, and on to the buffalo plains. The river settlements of the *métis* were eventually to run in a great triangle from Pembina to St. Boniface and west up the Assiniboine, a band of settlement which constituted a buffer between the colony and the Sioux and was regarded by the *métis* as the corporate possession of their race.

Their devotion to the buffalo hunt and their role as shield of the settlement served to perpetuate in the *métis* their strong sense of identity, their belief that they were a "new nation."[10] It was this sense which had led the wilder spirits among them to serve the purposes of the Nor'Westers in breaking up the colony in 1815 and 1816. When they had come to accept the restored colony and had made it the base of their semi-nomadic life, they still preserved their claim to a share in the Indian title to the lands of the Northwest and their sense of being a "nation." As their training in the discipline of the hunt and their brushes with the Sioux made them formidable warriors, their corporate sentiment made them, in the absence of regular troops at least, the only military force in Red River and as such a potentially dominant power. The careless and amiable *métis*, once aroused, could dominate Red River, as the ballad of Seven Oaks composed by their poet, Pierre Falcon, reminded them they had done in 1816.

Besides these native settlers, there were the immigrant colonists. Close to the *métis* in language and religion, and sometimes mingled with them in the hunt and their settlements, were the few free Canadians who had married white women and the more numerous families which had come from Lower Canada in 1818.[11] These French Canadian colonists lived chiefly at St. Boniface, where they furnished a steadying element among the fickle *métis*. They brought the sober industry and steady morals of old Quebec to the Northwest and maintained in Red River the civilized manners and social gaiety of their ancestral way of life. From this group most of the leaders of the French community of Red River were to trace their origin.

Seated near them were the de Meurons, largely German Swiss by race, but with a few Poles and other nationalities swept into the ranks of their old regiments in the great European upheaval of the Napoleonic Wars. These men, who had seen service on both sides in Europe, Ceylon, and America, were now trying their fortunes in the struggling colony. As they were Catholic by religion, the church of St. Boniface, patron saint of the Germans, had been set by Provencher hard by their lots on the Seine, which the English called "Germantown." The de Meuron veterans, however, were slovenly and dispirited farmers, and many were the grumblings in German, great the restlessness and too frequent the outbreaks of violence among them. The grasshoppers, the disappointing crops, the drudgery of pioneer farming, the lack of women with whom to make a decent home, all served to keep them discontented.[12]

The Scottish settlers on the river lots down the Red from Fort Douglas, in what Selkirk had named Kildonan after the parish of Kildonan in Sutherland, were very different colonists.[13] Many of the Scots and most of the Irish had left for Canada; the majority of those who remained were the Sutherland Scots, who dominated the Scottish community and gave it their character. The cruelty of the evictions from their ancestral homes, and all the hardships of pioneering in a harsh and lawless land had not shaken their constancy or altered their purpose. By their rebuilt houses they were adding rigg to rigg, while the little stock they owned ran on the plains to the rear, as on the hills at home. Already they were resuming in the river lots a pattern of cultivation curiously like the immemorial "infield" and "outfield" pattern of Scotland, in which the infield was cropped intensively year after year, the outfield from time to time, and all behind was common.

Inside the log houses as well as out there was, of course, something of Scotland brought to the new land. While the wood fire roared in the clay fireplace, the spinning wheel whirred amid the lilt and murmur of the Gaelic, language of the hills, brought now to be the language of new children of the plains. For the Scots, like the Canadians of 1818, had come as families; not for them the mingling of blood and the conflict of custom that followed. They had come as a community, lacking only the promised minister of their own tongue and faith, and a community they remained, a firm core of sober, Christian, and Scottish life in all the slovenliness and wildness of the Red River Settlement.

These were the colonists Garry saw in 1821 at Red River. At York he met an incoming party of Swiss immigrants, who had been recruited by Lord Selkirk's agents on the upper Rhine. When they arrived at Red River, they joined their fellow countrymen, the de Meurons, some of whom were able to find among the girls the wives they had wanted to share the rigours of farming. The new colonists had been badly recruited, for they were townsmen and artisans, not peasants accustomed to at least the privations of rural life in Europe. They simply lacked the primitive skills necessary to survival in Red River.[14] The few years they were to spend in the colony were miserable, and the Swiss remained discontented with their lot, as they tried unhappily to make the best of a situation they had neither anticipated nor were equipped to meet. It is a pregnant comment on their character that their one contribution to the history of Red River is the crude water colours of one of their number, Peter Rindisbacher, which are among the most valuable documents of that history.

These were the various elements of the colony, partly the result of Selkirk's mistaken zeal, largely the product of the unions of the men of the fur trade with Indian women; the Scottish and the few Irish settlers; the French Canadians; the *métis* and the Scottish half-breeds; the de Meurons—Swiss, Pole, Piedmontese, Italian; the Swiss; and odd individuals of other races. Few more immigrants were to come. In 1836 thirteen families, some Lincolnshire farmers, of whom the master farmer, Oliver Gowler, is to be noted, were brought out to work an experimental farm begun by the Hudson's Bay Company. In 1848 and 1850 Chelsea pensioners, old or disabled soldiers retired from the service, were brought out with their families, some two hundred in all, most of whom remained in the Settlement. Year by year, of course, the population was recruited by the addition of retired officers and servants of the Company. But with these exceptions the colonization of Red River was complete by 1826.

The Settlement had indeed by that year extended over much of the area and assumed much of the character it was thereafter to maintain. The buffalo hunts had become organized seasonal expeditions by 1821. The cultivation of the little riverside fields, if not very successful, was annually renewed. The sturdy log houses marched with the river banks in steadily growing numbers, marked by the stubby steeples of Provencher's church opposite the Forks and John West's two miles below. Cattle had been brought in from the United States in 1822 by Governor Bulger, and were now dispersed in tiny herds along the settlements. John Pritchard, a former Nor'Wester who had joined the colony and shared its tribulations because of his faith in the future of agriculture in Red River, could write with his wonted enthusiasm to Bulger from Red River in August, 1825: "The Settlement is wonderfully improved. [It] extends from the White Horse Plain almost to Netley Creek [in] a line of well built houses. We have an abundance of domestic cattle, and the fields at this moment present a prospect of wheat exceeding anything heretofore produced in this Country. The Wind-mill is expected to be in operation the approaching Autumn."

In the following year, however, the numbers and variety of the population were to be diminished by the first of the great Red River floods since the Settlement began. The fall of 1825 was very wet, the snowfall deep on both the Red and Assiniboine watersheds, the spring break-up late and sudden. The crests of both flooding rivers reached the Forks together, and the turbid waters spread over the great flood plain above the Grand Rapids. The colonists had to flee with their families and stock to the ridges to east and west, to Bird's Hill, Stony Mountain, and Silver Heights, and watch their houses and possessions disappear beneath or float upon the broad brown waters. When the flood drained away they came back to the river lots; the persistent Scots and the insouciant *métis* took up again the toil of the farm and the chase of the buffalo. But the unsettled de Meurons and the Swiss had borne all they would of the hazardous life of Red River. Almost all emigrated to the upper Mississippi valley, where their descendants live to this day.[15]

This loss of the Germanic element from the polyglot, variegated colony which was forming in the Red River valley was offset over the years by a steady accession of retired fur traders with their Indian wives and half-breed children. These men, too affectionate or too honourable to abandon their mates and off-spring on the completion of their service in the north, found in the colony a haven where they could invest their savings in land, spend their declining years in peace, and provide for the education of their children in circumstances not too dissimilar from that in which they had been reared. Yet another element was thus being added to the varied pattern of Red River society. The retired traders were mainly Scots or Orcadians, proud, shy, and simple men with an immense sensitivity in all matters of personal dignity. Those who were retired officers of the Company possessed both prestige and means, and shared neither the Ishmaelite wildness of the *métis* nor the careful poverty of the Kildonan Scots. They were the natural aristocracy of the primitive community of Red River. Their principal settlement was at the Grand Rapids, which was to become St. Andrew's parish. But they settled also in St. John's, around the site of Fort Douglas, and a couple of miles up the Assiniboine in what was to become St. James. Some of them became veritable squires and farmed well and seriously; others with a lazy fecklessness a *métis* could not have exceeded.[16] The great houses of these Company men, built with logs in the manner known as "Red River frame," or of the local limestone in the Norman French style the Company had brought in from Lower Canada, with their Georgian doors and fanlights gave character and a touch of grace to Red River architecture.[17] Their Indian ladies, though they might pad softly about the house in moccasins and sit on the steps smoking a pipe, were long accustomed to rule a fur post and kept house with competence and dignity. Their dark-eyed children filled the schools of the settlement. Not all their children chose the ways of civilization; even these fortunate families were not free from the half-breed's inevitable choice of the life of one parent or the other. But in their own eyes and in the esteem of the colony, they were the first families of Red River, a fact they remembered with dogged northern pride.[18]

The addition of the families of the retired officers and servants of the Company, however, had the effect of increasing the mixed blood of the Settlement, and from 1826 to 1836 the development of a predominantly half-breed society went steadily forward in Red River.

All the sections of the Red River colony were composed of independent people, accustomed to following a known pattern of life. They had little need of direction by social superiors or by government. It was well that this was so. Despite Selkirk's painstaking and imaginative planning, Red River colony had simply grown. It had begun to take shape even before 1812; thereafter the conflict of the companies and natural disasters had made orderly development impossible. The inclusion of an agricultural colony in the domain of the fur trade caused many frictions, and at best the natural antagonism of fur trade and agriculture was held in suspense.[19] The Hudson's Bay Company, both the Committee at home and the officers in the Northwest, had never been fully convinced of the feasibility of combining colonization with the fur trade, whatever the necessity of lowering the costs of provisions. The doubt was never wholly removed. Moreover, a well-organized colonial government, with governor, police, and courts, would be an inducement to an increase of settlement and a challenge to the authority of the Company over the fur trade. A weak government, on the other hand, would allow the colony to become "a den of thieves," as Governor Bulger wrote,[20] that is, of free traders who would compete with the Company and of outlaws who would plunder its defenceless posts. The colony itself was too poor to support the charges of efficient government, and the fur trade was naturally reluctant to assume them. These different dilemmas were not to be wholly resolved during the fifty years of the colony's history, and such government as there was depended upon the acquiescence of the governed. The orderliness of Red River was owing to the good sense and good nature of its people.

The government of Assiniboia was a proprietary government of the House of Douglas down to 1834, when Assiniboia was returned to the Hudson's Bay Company. Neither the Douglas family before 1834 nor the Company after that date made much provision for the government of the colony. The first Governors of Assiniboia had only limited authority, and were agents of the Selkirk estate rather than colonial governors. They were also always overshadowed by the local officers of the Hudson's Bay Company and by Governor of Rupert's Land George Simpson. The government was always conducted in, or from nearby, the Company's establishments. Usually it was Upper Fort Garry, near which the courthouse was built in 1843. But it was sometimes from the Lower Fort, which was in effect the country seat of the Governor of Rupert's Land when he was in residence in Red River. The Governors of Assiniboia, Miles Macdonell, Robert Semple, and even Alexander Macdonell,[21] were assisted by councillors, but probably the Council of Assiniboia is to be dated from the appointment of Governor Andrew Bulger in 1822.[22] There was a continuous body from that date, which while remaining appointive became representative and usually reflected the sense of the community.

The provision of a police force and courts of law was not successfully attempted before 1834.[23] While everyone realized that a garrison of regular troops was necessary to ensure order, it was also realized that neither the Imperial government nor the Company was likely to supply them. Suggestions that a local militia should be raised were many[24] but came to nothing.[25] The first Sheriff of Assiniboia was appointed in 1816 in the person of John Spencer.[26] Two constables were employed in 1823,[27] and remained in their posts down to 1834, but their duties were slight. Justice was administered by a single justice of the peace. It was understood that the law in force was the English common law and statutes applying to Assiniboia, but there was no one in the colony possessed of any professional knowledge of the law.

When the Company resumed jurisdiction over Assiniboia in 1834, it continued the office of governor and the Council of Assiniboia. But the reorganized Council increased the number of the justices to four, and in 1837 established a General Court.[28] The Company sought to supply the lack of legal science in the colony by appointing a Recorder in 1839, one Adam Thom, a Scots lawyer from Lower Canada.[29] Thom proved himself a competent law officer, but the French and *métis* were suspicious of him because he refused to use French in court, and was notorious for his savage attacks on the French party and French nationality in Lower Canada. Nothing came of this suspicion of Thom for a number of years, and from his appointment on, Assiniboia possessed a simple but effective system of courts which, with certain notorious exceptions to be noted hereafter, dispensed justice to the satisfaction of the community. At no time, however, except when regular troops were in the colony from 1846 to 1848 and from 1857 to 1861, were the courts able to pronounce, or the government to enforce, a really unpopular sentence. Government remained government by acquiescence.

That it could do so was owing not only to the growth of customs which regulated the buffalo hunts and the pastoral life of the colony, but also to the influence of the missionaries. While the medicine men still rattled their rickety lodges on the stormy shores of Lake Winnipeg and on the wooded points of the lower Red, the Cross had been brought to the Forks and the church bells called along the river to the calm of Sabbath worship.[30] The coming of Fathers Provencher and Dumoulin in 1818 had done much to persuade the turbulent *bois-brûlés* to accept the colony as part of the order of things in the Northwest and to make it a base for their roving life. Thereafter the fathers strove to make the lives of their wild charges sufficiently sedentary to render the ministrations of the church possible, if not regular.[31] The church at St. Boniface was made the centre of the mission, and in 1822 became the seat of the Bishop of Juliopolis *in partibus infidelium,* the good Provencher reluctantly assuming the duties of bishop coadjutor. A chapel at Pembina, moved to White Horse Plain in 1824, was the first outlying mission, but the number of missions grew as the *métis* were induced to settle. The attempt to immobilize the shifting nomads was a long and doubtful struggle, however, and some of the priests, notably Dumoulin and Belcourt, thought it better to follow their flocks in their wanderings than to persuade them to settle, a belief which led to some friction in the mission and which may have delayed the work of settlement.[32]

With the work of conversion, the baptism of the children, and the sanctioning of marriage unions made after the fashion of the Indians, went the beginning of education.[33] The first mission school was founded with the mission itself at St. Boniface in 1818, and by 1827 it was well established and on its way to becoming the College of St. Boniface. Scholars were not many nor success great at first, and the Catholic schools failed to produce a priest for the ministry.[34] They did, however, create a literate group among the *métis*, capable of defending the interests of their fellows. The education of the women in household arts was also attempted, and with the arrival of the Grey Sisters of Charity at St. Boniface in 1844 was thenceforth in competent hands.

The Catholic missionaries had a difficult and baffling task to perform with their responsive but wayward charges. Yet they built mightily on the foundations of the most primitive and poorest element in Red River; the steeple of Provencher's little cathedral fronting the Forks was the symbol of their achievement; its fruit the simple devotion of the buffalo hunters on the naked plains of the Souris, the endlessly patient work of the fathers, not only with the *métis*, but with the Crees and the Chipewyans of the far Northwest.

No Protestant missionary had come to the Northwest before the founding of the Red River colony. In 1820 the Hudson's Bay Company, on the motion of certain directors influenced by the Evangelical movement which was then stirring the Church of England to send missionaries to all parts of the world, co-operated with the Church Missionary Society to despatch Rev. John West to Rupert's Land as a missionary to the Indians. West arrived in the same year and at once began to plan a sedentary mission among the Indians.[35] To do so involved persuading them to turn from hunting to agriculture for subsistence; and in the corn-growing Indians at Netley he found material upon which to begin. He also hoped to train some Indian boys for the ministry, a project in which the Anglican missionaries, unlike the Roman Catholic fathers, were to have a measure of success.[36]

With the mission to the Indians, West, of course, combined ministration to the Protestant colonists and the officers and servants of the fur posts he visited on his journeys. Many were the first services, from York to Fort Garry, from Fort Alexander to the Qu'Appelle. Many, too, were the marriage services which sanctified unions made according to the "custom of the country," weddings by the witnessed consent of both parties, or unions after the simpler mode of the Indians.[37]

With West's mission, too, was associated the founding of the first non-Roman church in the Northwest, the mission church of St. John's, later like its Catholic twin to become a cathedral church. On the lot Selkirk had assigned for the purpose, a church yard and burying ground were laid out, and in 1823 the first church edifice west of the Red, a rude log building but with a steeple, was erected.[38] It served both the Anglicans and the Presbyterians of Kildonan, the service being modified, especially by Rev. David Jones, West's successor, to accord as far as was possible with the Presbyterian view of decorum in worship. Jones in 1824 began a second church, St. Paul's, six miles below St. John's, which was called Middle church when a third was founded in 1827. This was St. Andrew's, begun at Grand Rapids by Rev. Wm. Cockran to serve the growing community there. In 1836 the mission church of St. Peter's was built on the east bank of the Red to serve the Saulteaux converts of Peguis' band settled at Netley Creek. Thereafter Anglican missions spread with the growth of population along the river banks.

With the church came the school. West had taught his boys, both Indian and white, at St. John's mission. Jones and Mrs. Jones conducted schools there for both boys and girls, as did Cockran and Mrs. Cockran at St. Andrew's. Mr. John McCallum made the St. John's school into the Red River Academy in 1833, and a school run by the versatile John Pritchard in Kildonan merged with it. McCallum's school was converted by Bishop David Anderson into St. John's College in 1849. From the schools came a good number of literate and even well-educated men, a few of whom, Indian as well as white, were ordained to the Anglican ministry. These schools were really private ventures, not church schools proper, as were those of the Catholic fathers, and the various schools which followed them were also private. Thus the Protestant churches, while carrying on the work of education, did not develop that corporate interest in it which the Catholic Church did.

It is in the work of the missionaries, both in their own exclusive work as ministers of the Gospel, and also as educators and as legislators on the Council of Assiniboia, that the principal reason is to be found for the successful maintenance of civilization in Red River in its fifty years of isolation. The ever active influence of the fur trade and the plains towards barbarism was checked. As the proportion of mixed blood increased, its complications were overcome by the influence of religion and education. Red River had always a solid core of well-mannered, well-educated men and women, who lacked only a proper field for their talents and accomplishments.

Red River colony, however, could not furnish employment for its more gifted children. The economic pulse beat was always slow. The migration of the de Meurons and the Swiss to the Mississippi was but a signal instance of a slow and steady seepage of population out of the colony down to the growing settlement on the upper Mississippi.[39] This lack of economic opportunity was a major indication of the failure of the colony to grow. The causes of the failure were many, but all arose from the isolation of the colony from the settled regions of the continent. After 1821 the one commercial outlet was by York, and York and the Bay could handle only the limited commerce of the fur trade, which was carried in one or two ships annually.

The fur trade, then, was the prime mover of the colony's economy, and it afforded but a limited market for the farm produce of the river lots and the plains provisions of the hunt. There was therefore little hope of expansion in either farming, or stock-raising, or buffalo-hunting. And within the colony's economy, the farm and the hunt, to a degree, operated as a check upon one another, the produce of each competing to lower the price of the other.[40] The chief hope of economic gain, therefore, lay in trading, and the private trader at once encountered the commercial monopoly of the Hudson's Bay Company.

The introduction of the free settlers into Rupert's Land had, of course, raised serious problems for the united Company with its effective monopoly of the commerce of the Northwest. Was the Company, and the Company only, to sell goods to the colonists and trade with the Indians? The first clash occurred in 1823, when Governor Bulger attempted to buy provisions for the colonists from the freemen.[41] The Committee of the Hudson's Bay Company informed Governor George Simpson that the Company had no intention of preventing the colonists from trading with the Indians or others for furs, robes, and provisions, provided the commodities were for their own use.[42] They might not, however, exchange them. And from the same time private traders were allowed to import goods, by the Company's ships, into the settlement for sale there. One Andrew McDermot, a clerk of the Hudson's Bay Company until 1824, was among the first, if not the first, of these private traders.

So much the Company tolerated. It was engaged, however, in a long campaign of raids and skirmishes against American "petty traders," from Rainy Lake on the east to the Souris valley on the west. This competition the Company could deal with effectively, but it was anxious not to have its rivals aided by free traders from within its own territory. The Company indeed licensed selected men like Andrew McDermot, James Sinclair, and Cuthbert Grant to oppose the American traders, the first two as traders in their own interest, the last in the specially created and salaried office of "Warden of the Plains." These tolerated traders disposed of their furs and other commodities to the Company, not to American traders. Yet a little traffic in furs with the American traders over the line, or even with the American settlements at St. Peter's, later to become St. Paul, was often the only way an active young man had of earning a few pounds quickly. And it was very easy to get together a few packs of furs and robes from the Indians and métis and to carry them down to the Mississippi posts over the open plains. Nor was the Company disposed to make importation of goods from the United States too difficult, for when in 1835 the Council of Assiniboia imposed a duty of 7½ per cent on such goods,[43] the London Committee ordered it to be reduced first to 5 per cent and then to 4, at which rate it remained.

There was, in short, besides the legitimate "petty trade" in imported goods in the colony, always some "free trading" by colonists, but it reached intolerable proportions only in 1844, when Norman W. Kittson opened a post for the American Fur Company at Pembina,[44] and when a native-born generation was beginning to find the monopoly of the Company oppressive and life in Red River dull and unrewarding. The movement of immigrants to the Mississippi, the ventures of a few traders, the travels of the occasional young man in search of education, had kept open the routes to the south, the trails of North West days. Adventurous young men like Peter Garrioch began to trade with American traders on the Souris, or brought furs from the *métis*,[45] with goods imported by the Bay. The free traders themselves now carried the catch to Pembina or to St. Paul. It was a party of which Garrioch was a member that in 1844 first opened the Crow Wing Trail for bringing American goods to Red River, a trail to the east of the Red which was less exposed to stoppage by the Sioux than the older trails down the open plains of the west bank.[46]

The almost open trade for furs with goods imported into the colony by the Company's ships, and the scarcely clandestine traffic with Pembina and St. Paul, were more than the Company could tolerate.[47] In 1844 Alexander Christie, Governor of Assiniboia, tried to put a stop to it by controlling the mails and instituting the licensing of traders, the licence requiring the licensee to abstain from the trade in furs. The free traders, led by James Sinclair, opposed him and challenged the Company's monopoly on the ground that it infringed both native rights and those of British subjects.[48] When the Governor informed them that all, both half-breeds and native whites, had equal rights to trade, but that the Company had a monopoly of the fur trade, the free traders retorted with a demand for representative government in Assiniboia, their counter to the Company's use of the authority of the civil government of Assiniboia to enforce its monopoly.[49] In their opposition they were joined by Father G. A. Belcourt of the Saulteaux mission at Baie St. Paul on the Assiniboine, who was at odds with the Hudson's Bay Company; he used his influence to persuade the *métis* to join the free traders and English half-breeds in a petition to the Imperial government for free trade and representative government.[50] The *métis* were the more ready to listen to him, since their distrust of Recorder Thom's administration of justice and their dislike of his person were increasing. Moreover, they had come into contact with American cavalry patrols in the Sioux country, and had been warned they must either stop crossing the boundary or settle at Pembina. There, of course, they would prove an even greater threat to the Company's trade.

The prospect of trouble in Red River was alarming to the Company. In Oregon, American settlement was ending the régime of the fur trade; in 1844 the settlers had created a provisional government which marked the end of the Company's dominance of that country. In Red River only a military force, it was evident, could now maintain order, and this neither the colony nor the Company was able to provide.[51] Fortunately for the Company, the threat of war with the United States during the Oregon crisis made it possible to obtain the despatch of a detachment of regular troops to Red River in 1846. That summer, under the command of Major J. F. Crofton, three companies of the 6th Royal Regiment of Foot (the Warwickshires) with artillerymen and sappers to the number of 347 came in by way of York, and the plains of Red River first saw the scarlet coats of British infantry. Until the troops were withdrawn in 1848, the turbulence in the colony quietened, partly because of the presence of the troops and partly because the troops furnished the free traders with a market.[52]

The constitutional agitation that the free traders, both English and French, had begun was, however, continued by a petition to the Imperial government for relief from the monopoly and rule of the Company.[53] The petition was carried forward by Alexander Kennedy Isbister, a Scots native of the Northwest, who had won for himself a fine academic reputation in Scotland, had studied in London, and was to become a schoolmaster. The petition was seriously entertained by the Colonial Office and enquiries made, but when further action was made conditional on the petitioners taking legal action to test the validity of the Company's charter, Isbister declined to proceed.

But in Red River the discontent continued among both the English and French half-breeds, and the indictment in 1849, at the wish of Chief Factor John Ballenden, of Guillaume Sayer, a *métis*, and three others for trading furs with Indians brought the issue of free trade to a head. The powerful and volatile *métis* were to a man in sympathy with the accused. The only military force was a small body of Chelsea pensioners sent to replace the regulars in 1848, and the Governor, Major W. B. Caldwell, their commanding officer, dared not set them against the formidable warriors of the buffalo hunt.[54] No constable dared make an arrest.[55] When the trial was held, the *métis* were assembled in arms, summoned by a committee of ten of whom Louis Riel, an influential French Canadian, a miller and a man of enterprise, was probably the chief. This show of force was a protest against the use of the civil power, not resting on any representation of the people, to uphold an unpopular monopoly. The Court, however, sat; it tried three cases, and then called on Sayer to appear. In his place came James Sinclair and others who claimed to be "delegates of the people." It was agreed, after argument, that Sinclair might act as counsel for Sayer. Sayer was produced by his friends and, with Sinclair challenging, a jury of both English and French was empanelled. The evidence was heard, and the jury through its foreman, Donald Gunn, returned a verdict of guilty with a recommendation to mercy. Ballenden, having obtained a verdict of guilty, withdrew his other charges, and Sayer was not sentenced. This "pardoning" led to the assumption by the armed crowd that the accused had been acquitted and they swarmed away shouting that "trade was free."[56] After this "mock trial," trade was indeed free, as the Company did not again attempt to enforce its monopoly, but relied on its own great competitive strength and the richer resources of the fur country of the far north. From 1849 an open trade with St. Paul developed steadily, and the free traders spread over the Northwest as in the earlier days of competition.[57]

The coming of "free trade," that is, private trade in furs despite the monopoly of the Hudson's Bay Company, marked the beginning of the end of the old order in the Northwest. With free trade in Great Britain, the last of the great monopolies could not long hope for support against the free traders of its own domain. Nor could it use its own political authority to enforce its own monopoly without provoking an explosion of popular resentment it lacked the means to suppress. If representative government was not given to Red River at the same time that responsible government was granted to Canada and the Maritime Provinces, the crumbling of the commercial monopoly none the less made the advent of self-government inevitable. The fur trade could not have supported a renewal of the competition which had marked the rivalry of the great companies at the beginning of the century. Free trade could mean only the development of general commerce and the coming of the agricultural frontier and civilization.

Yet for another decade the old order in Red River was to continue unchallenged from without and with no further challenge from within. Representatives of the *métis* were taken into the Council of Assiniboia, Adam Thom was induced to withdraw to his native Scotland, and the Company reached a tacit understanding with the *métis* and the free traders. With that understanding the unique and picturesque life of the Red River colony reached and passed its prime; the old order of buffalo hunt, river lot, and fur trade continued, and the origins of the new were yet embryonic.

The power behind the defiance to the monopoly and the government of Assiniboia was the power, essentially military, of the *métis* of the buffalo hunt. The occupation of the hunt had not only kept alive the corporate sense of the *métis*, their belief in themselves as a "new nation"; it had also, as it developed, given them character as a people, a kind of government, and a very definite discipline. Hunts by individuals or small bands for the supply of a post or of the colony had come in Red River to be organized as seasonal migrations of the *métis* people, men, women, and children, to the plains of the Souris and the Coteau of the Missouri, far out on the borders of the Sioux. The movement of so many, into territory beset by hereditary enemies, for the purpose of hunting the easily stampeded buffalo, necessitated the evolution of a discipline on the march, in camp, and during the hunt. Founded on the forms and usages of the plains Indians, the organization of the hunt became the framework of *métis* society, the mode of their corporate life.

It can best be described by a description of the hunt itself. There were two annual expeditions, the "spring hunt" and the "fall hunt." The former was the more important. In June the hunters prepared their outfit, guns, ammunition, a hunting horse, a pony, and a Red River cart. This last, a copy of the wooden cart of Scotland,[58] was by mid-century a native vehicle with two high, deeply dished wheels, of wholly wood construction, which could move across plain and marsh, needing nothing for repair that the plains could not furnish, affording a raft when streams had to be crossed and grinding from its dry wooden axles a shriek more piercing than howl of coyote or cry of loon. Each hunter, so furnished, moved off with his family to the hunt, leaving only the old or disabled to tend the potato patch, the plot of oats or barley, and the rude log cabin, till once more the carts creaked back to the colony.[59] The "main river party" assembled in the parishes near Fort Garry, the White Horse Plain party at St. François-Xavier. Both made their way by the Pembina trail south of the Assiniboine to the Rivière aux Ilets de Bois, rich in sugar maple groves,[60] and so to the Pembina Hills. They passed over these to the Pembina valley, where they camped for some days until all parties had arrived and all stragglers had come up.

At this encampment the hunt was organized. A president or "chief" of the hunt was elected and with him twelve councillors, a public crier, and guides; then "captains" of tens were elected by ten hunters, as "soldiers" attaching themselves to the leader of their choice.[61] Thereafter the direction of the marches, the choice of camp site, the conduct of the hunt, the regulations which governed all movements and life in the camp, were decided by the president and his council and enforced by the soldiers. The priest who accompanied the hunt gave his sanction to all these arrangements, and celebrated mass on the scrupulously observed Sabbath. When camp was broken, the long cavalcade of hunters, carts, and plodding women moved behind two guides bearing flags; the flag of the buffalo hunt probably varied, but is said to have been white with three crosses.[62] So the people moved out into the plains, usually by the east end of Turtle Mountain (La Vérendrye's Second Mountain), but perhaps by the north flank towards the Souris valley, according to reports of the movements of the herds.

Sometimes the march was interrupted by alarms of Sioux war parties; if the alarms were followed by sight of the fierce warriors on their war ponies, the *métis* went into *laager* in a hollow, the carts forming an obstacle sufficient to check a rush of horse, while the marksmen from behind them could tumble a Sioux brave from his pony or catch a creeping warrior against the bright sky-line of the prairie night. Many such battles were fought, as in the fight at the Grand Coteau in 1857 when eighty *métis* for two days fought off the swarming Sioux, and the *métis* never hesitated to venture out onto the plains in formation. Yet they preferred and sought peace, for their object was to hunt, not fight.

If it were the dark herds which were sighted and not the flitting Sioux, camp was made at once. Then the hunters, each mounted on his best horse, rode out under the captain and approached the herd up-wind behind any convenient fold in the rolling plain. When in position they charged in line at a signal from the captain. Every man carried his gun across the neck of his trained runner, and had a handful of powder loose in his pocket, his mouth full of balls. As the buffalo turned to run, each picked his animal, usually a young cow, and rode alongside. The gun was fired across the horse's neck, aim being taken by the angle. Up to fifty or even a hundred yards, the Red River hunter could bring down his prey, though usually the shot was fired from close range. Then a palmful of powder was poured down the barrel of the gun, a ball spat into the muzzle, and the whole shaken home by knocking the butt on the thigh or the saddle. The runner had meantime carried on at a gallop to overtake a new beast. When the gun muzzle came down for the aim, the moist ball held up in the barrel for the moment necessary for accuracy, and another cow went down.[63] And so it went in the thunder of the hooves, the snorting and roaring of the herd, in the dust and glare of the summer plains, until each hunter had left behind him a string of kicking beasts, and wheeled his foam-flecked hunter back to camp. A cap, a glove, or other personal article had been dropped to identify a beast, but usually each knew his own.[64]

As the hunters trotted back to camp, the women, most of them wives and daughters but some hired for the work, came out with the carts to strip the carcasses of their robes, the fat humps, tongues, and other choice bits. The rest was left for the coyotes and the crows. On the morrow the meat was cut into long strips to dry over poles put up for the purpose; in dull weather a fire of buffalo chips aided the sun. When the meat was dry, some was bundled for sale or use in that form, some was pounded on buffalo robes into fine powder. This was placed in sacks of green buffalo hide and over it melted fat and marrow was poured, and the two mixed together and the sack sewn up. Such was the manufacture of pemmican, the concentrated produce of prairie grass and sun, the skill of the hunter, and the toil of his wife. Fat was also preserved separately in skins or bladders, and tongues, one of the delicacies of the Northwest, were pickled in brine.

When the carts were loaded, the hunt moved back by convenient routes to the colony, where the "plains provisions" were traded to the Company and the farmers. The smaller fall hunt was similar in character but its purpose was to get robes and fresh meat rather than pemmican. The numbers engaged were fewer, the organization less rigid, and many of the hunters remained to winter on the plains. Those who came back to winter in the colony quickly took in what the birds, the neighbours, and their own negligence had left of the crops sown in the spring, and set themselves to a round of masses, horse races, dances, and festivities, as well might men who had defied the Sioux and ridden their runners down the avalanche of the buffalo hunt. But if the Sioux had been troublesome, or the buffalo distant and the hunt short, then before spring there was hunger in the cabins and sometimes the charity of the wealthier and the more prudent people of Red River had to come to the relief of the brave *métis* in his distress.[65]

The buffalo hunt, colourful and unique institution as it was, was not the only occupation of the *métis* and others of Red River who did not love the drudgery of the farm. The business of the great Company, carried on in posts scattered from Superior to the Pacific, from Red River to the Yukon, called for an extensive system of transport for the movement of trade goods and furs. The York boat had replaced the canoe as cargo craft, and the *voyageur* was replaced by the tripman. The tripman was usually a *métis* of Red River, but sometimes an English mixed blood. He was under contract to act as bowman, middleman, or steersman on one of the boat brigades from the Red to York, from the Red to Norway House at the north end of Lake Winnipeg, and from Norway House by the Saskatchewan River to Portage la Loche, or Methy portage, to the Athabaska country. In June the brigades of four to eight boats put out from Lower Fort Garry to make their long journeys by perilous waters,[66] and returned as the ice was freezing the backwaters in October.

The tripmen became as addicted to their strenuous calling as the buffalo hunters to theirs. Each engaged for his familiar trip, and all were known by their districts; the Methy portage men as *poissons blancs* (white fish), the Saskatchewan men as *blaireaux* (badgers), the Red River men as *taureaux* (bulls). These nicknames, which alluded to the alleged diet of their bearers, perpetuated an old custom of the North West *voyageurs*, whose name for the eastern men, *mangeurs du lard* (pork-eaters), was still the ultimate in contempt. Brave and skilful in the navigation, tracking, and portaging of their durable but awkward craft, and in the fights which marked their carousals, the tripmen were an even more turbulent and lawless element than the hunters of the plains, to whom they were blood relations, and with whom they passed the Red River winters of festivity and famine.[67]

The opening of the free trade with St. Paul gave rise to a new occupation and a new kind of tripman, the occupation of cart-freighting and the men who contracted to carry freight by cart to St. Paul, or the Saskatchewan. It was an occupation much like that of boat tripping, seasonal, casual, and varied. After 1850 the carts were organized in brigades of indefinite and growing numbers, and wound, lurching and shrieking, by the Crow Wing and other trails over the height of land to St. Paul. When in 1858 even the Hudson's Bay Company began to bring in goods by St.

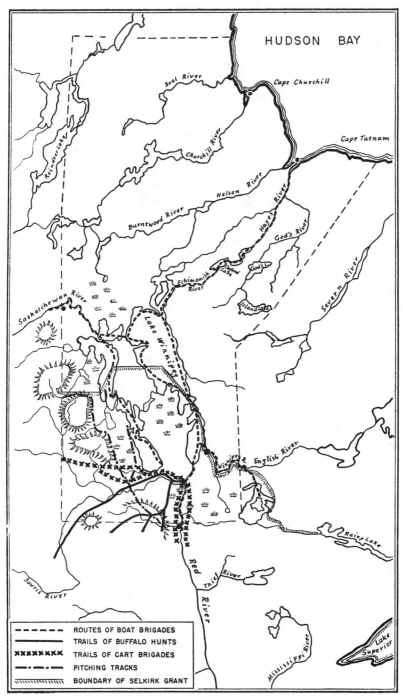

- - - - - - ROUTES OF BOAT BRIGADES
———————— TRAILS OF BUFFALO HUNTS
xxxxxxxxx TRAILS OF CART BRIGADES
-·-·-·-·- PITCHING TRACKS
⁄⁄⁄⁄⁄⁄⁄⁄⁄⁄ BOUNDARY OF SELKIRK GRANT

TRAILS AND ROUTES, 1811–1869

Paul as well as by York, it opened a new supply route to the West overland by Fort Carlton on the Saskatchewan to Edmonton. The trail to Portage la Prairie was extended to Fort Ellice and on to Carlton, and goods moved by cart all the way from the upper Mississippi to the upper Saskatchewan. But Red River remained the hub of the new transport system as it had been of the old, and only the steam boat was to end the use of the York boats on the great trunk route of Winnipeg, Hayes, and Saskatchewan and only the railroad the winding cart brigades. The web of transport held coast and inland, the fur forest and the provisions plains, firmly integrated.

Why Red River and Fort Garry should have been the centre of the trade is not evident at first sight. York and Norway House were the seats of the Council of Rupert's Land and the distributing centres for trade goods. But the pemmican of the plains, the tripmen, and the flour from the river lots made Red River the force which set the great transport shuttles weaving in the spring. When the York boats filed down the Red in June, following the ice in its northward retreat, like the wild geese flying on their way to the Arctic, they began the northern summer, the season of furious activity in the fur trade.

The farmers ploughing on the high banks of the Red watched them go, and turned their ploughs westward up the riggs[68] towards the brief golden summer of western agriculture, for many of the colonists below Fort Garry were steady farmers, whose fields and stock were their main occupation. They held their lands by the best title available, conditional long-term grants or entries in the books of the Company, unlike most of the *métis,* who were squatters merely.[69] Some Canadians in St. Boniface, some *métis* at St. François-Xavier, were solid farmers. These and the Scottish farmers of Kildonan and St. Andrew's worked their fields methodically, if not very intelligently, and the rich soil of Red River enabled them in good years to reap abundant harvests; and even in bad years there was rarely a total crop failure in the colony between 1819 and 1868. Most of the farmers were Scottish peasants evicted from their ancestral holdings by the agricultural revolution of the eighteenth century in Great Britain, or else retired hunters and traders. Naturally neither had brought the methods of the new agriculture with them, and Red River farming was simple and backward until the middle of the century. Yet such as it was, it was the anchor of the colony, which kept it civilized against the pull of the plains and the fur trade, and made Red River the metropolis of the Northwest.

The farmers' year began with the sugar-making in March, in the groves of ash-leaved maple (*acer negundo*) in the river loops of the Red and Assiniboine.[70] The crop year began in late April or early May. When the land was dry enough the riggs were ploughed with the iron and oaken ploughs in the home "parks," and, where they existed, as in the Lower Settlement, outer "parks," or fenced fields. When the soil was ready, the wheat was sowed broadcast by hand[71] and harrowed into the earth. Barley, oats, and potatoes followed, with perhaps some dwarf Indian corn,[72] especially where Indian blood ran in the veins of the farmer. The better farmers had gardens also, and grew a great range of vegetables, including melons and pumpkins. And many a doorway was bright with flowers as June gave way to July. Farming was bound to the river's edge; not a single farmstead was built away from the water side, not a lot was laid out without its river frontage. Water, shelter, ease of travel, drainage, the desire for neighbourhood, the fixed belief that it was impossible to cultivate the plains, all these kept agriculture joined to the rivers. As a result, the lots in time were narrowly subdivided, and settlement was scattered along the rivers as far south as Pembina and as far west as Portage la Prairie before it extended a mile from the rivers.

When seeding was done, farm work was largely over until the haying. The green crops had to run the gauntlet of spring frost, drought, grasshoppers, a wet fall, and early frosts. Spring frosts did little harm to the hardy wheat, and the sowing of the other cereals and crops could be held back until the danger of frost was past in early June. Drought was a serious handicap in scattered years, in the decade of 1836–46,[73] and in the years from 1862 to 1868.[74] Wet falls delayed ripening and made the danger from the fall frost serious, as in 1859,[75] but the danger was diminished by cutting the grain "on the green side." While the crops took their natural chances, the farmers repaired the fences to prevent the wandering stock from invading the fields. The fences around the buildings were often post and slab, but the standard fence was post and rail. Fencing—oak, ash, spruce, cedar, and tamarack—was obtained along the rivers, and in later years from the hills to the east, First Pines, Second Pines, and Far Pines, and the "weedy hills."[76] Post and rails were cut and hauled in winter, and put up in summer.

The cows and sheep were meanwhile pasturing on the rear of the lots under supervision, or wandering at large on the plains. The stock was inferior, as bulls and rams, despite the laws passed by the Council of Assiniboia, were little controlled. The strain was mixed, with some black Highland stock present,[77] as was to be expected. The sheep seem to have been particularly neglected, and, like the calves, suffered much from the wolves and the dogs.[78] Attempts at cattle herding "at the pine hills" had failed,[79] owing to losses from wolves and the cold, and not for many years were they to be resumed. Wintering the stock was a problem; both cattle and sheep had to be sheltered, and the better horses were stabled. Oats and barley were used for feed, but the staple winter fodder was wild hay from the prairie, and it was surprisingly difficult to obtain enough. Behind each lot was a "hay privilege" two miles in length, on which only the owner of the river front could mow. On the plains the first comer cut the heavy grass of the ponds and low spots. To prevent unfair advantages being taken, haying on the plains was forbidden before a fixed date, in late July or early August. On that date, especially in dry years, there was a rush to the plains to appropriate good fodder carefully spied out beforehand. This late haying conflicted with harvest, and the stock often suffered severely for want of hay in late winter and early spring.[80]

Though the chief wheat in Red River down to the middle of the century was the Prairie du Chien, which ripened in something over one hundred days, the time of harvest varied much from year to year.[81] As the wheat and barley ripened, the reapers moved into the parks with their sickles and scythes,[82] and struck down with smooth, repeated stroke the stiff ranks of tawny wheat and golden barley. The women and children followed, raking, binding, and stooking, "each pile of sheaves," a traveller approaching Fort Garry late in the evening tells us, "sending its long eastward shadow over the closely shaven plain. . . ."[83] The oats followed, and the sheaves were carted in from the stooks to be stacked in the barnyards. Threshing was done by flail on the barn floor; where one was lacking, on an ice floor; the grain was winnowed and sifted in the open air, and stored for grinding or for seed.

When the potatoes had been lifted, and the stock driven home for stabling, the farmer's year was over, except for the "mudding" of the house and barn, the cutting and hauling of wood and fencing, and perhaps a trip to Lake Manitoba or "Granmaree" (Grand Marais) on Lake Winnipeg for white fish.[84] Some cattle were butchered for home use or for sale, but most of the meat eaten in the Settlement, particularly among the poorer people, was "plains provisions," dried meat or pemmican.

The wheat when threshed had still to be ground. In the early days hand mills had been used, and had to be kept as standbys, for times when roads were blocked, or wind or water failed. The first mill, a windmill, had been built in 1825,[85] and thereafter windmills along the Red and Assiniboine gave another distinctive touch to the river-lot landscape. They were unreliable, even in the windy plains of the Red River valley, and attempts were made to replace them with water-mills. Cuthbert Grant spent much energy and money in trying to dam Sturgeon Creek, but failed to develop a steady head of water. The creeks below the Forks drove a number of water-wheels, particularly after the great flood of 1852 had turned the back country into a swamp. But the dry years after 1862 stilled the splash of the water-wheel, and steam-mills were begun in the village of Winnipeg and at the Lower Fort.[86]

Red River flour, ground from a soft spring wheat, gave a dark, hard loaf which seems to have rejoiced only the very hungry; bannocks, *galletes,* and scones were more popular. Oats gave oat cakes to the Scots, and barley furnished barley broth, one of the great staples of Red River diet without distinction of race or condition. Distilling offered a further outlet for surplus grain; the stills were private, and the product went into the private fur trade; the Council in 1845 urged the Hudson's Bay Company to open a public distillery to put the private, or illicit, stills out of business,[87] but though the project was taken up, it was not completed.

The truth was that the primitive and often slovenly agriculture of Red River had succeeded after 1827 in furnishing, together with the buffalo hunt, food enough for the colony and the fur trade. It had difficulty in meeting any extra demand, such as that created by the garrison in 1846, for which flour had to be brought from Canada by canoe,[88] or the exploring parties of 1857. Besides its backward methods and the natural hazards of agriculture on that far frontier, its development was checked by the lack of an export market, by the competition of the buffalo hunt, and by a shortage of labour caused by emigration to the Mississipi, the comparatively high wages to be earned by tripping, or the profits to be earned as a free trader.[89] Nobody, to be explicit, except the Kildonan settlers and a few enthusiasts in the Lower Settlement, was very much drawn to agriculture in Red River; the fur trade, the plains hunt, the long summer trips, were the attractive and profitable occupations, and dull indeed was the young man who stayed at the plough's tail in the ever narrowing river lots, "farming lanes" as scornful newcomers were soon to say.

Indeed, despite the drift of the young men into the free trade and to the United States, the river lots at St. Andrew's and St. Paul's (Middlechurch) had become congested by 1852. In that year came the second of the great floods, which, like that of 1826, turned the valley from Silver Heights to Bird's Hill into a lake. In the next year Rev. William Cockran, founder of St. Andrew's and St. Peter's parishes, led a migration of settlers from St. Andrew's and Middlechurch westward up the Assiniboine to higher land at Portage la Prairie. As early as 1851 he had begun a new settlement there despite the opposition of the Hudson's Bay Company, which feared it would become a nest of free traders. There the parish of St. Mary's was founded, and also St. Margaret's and St. Anne's a few miles east on the trail of High Bluff and Poplar Point. In these settlements the familiar pattern of Red River life was reproduced along the Assiniboine, but as

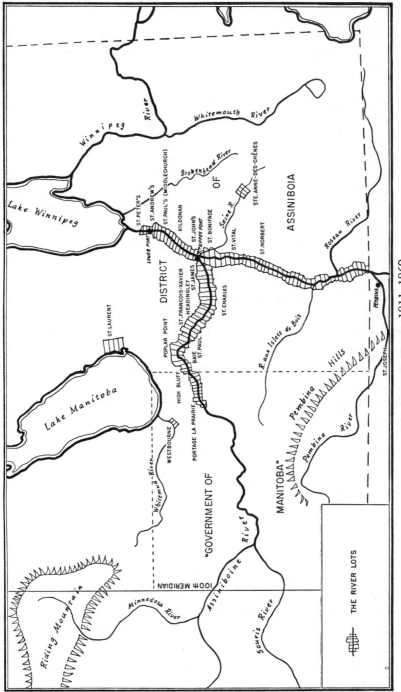

THE SETTLEMENTS, 1811–1869

THE RIVER LOTS

the settlements were outside the District of Assiniboia the missionary and his people had to organize their own simple government, a council over which Cockran presided.

Nor was this the only example of hiving off—a sure sign that the Red River Settlement had reached the limits fixed by its mode of life. In 1841 James Sinclair, Andrew McDermot's partner in the free trade, had led a party of emigrants from Red River to the Oregon country in an attempt to counter American settlement there. The effort was beyond the resources of Red River to accomplish, but in 1854 Sinclair repeated his great trek, by way of the Saskatchewan valley and the Bow River passes, with another party of settlers for the Oregon, American territory since 1846. The river lot and the buffalo hunt, the service of the great Company itself, could not employ all the energies or hold the loyalty of the children of the little colony.

Only in the great houses of St. Andrew's and the prim cottages of Kildonan, around the cathedrals and in the offices of Fort Garry, was it possible to escape the slovenly barbarism of the encamped cart brigade, the drunken revels of the tripmen back from York, the *tipis* of the visiting Indian encampments, the pungent presence of "some old smoke-eyed Bungay" wrapped in his blanket and sucking his pipe. The churches, the schools, the society of clergy and Company officers, the considerable resources of the Red River Library founded by Colonel Crofton in 1847 and enriched by Peter Fidler's bequest of his books, the influence of the historian, Alexander Ross, and of the scientist, Donald Gunn, correspondent of the Smithsonian Institution, were strong foundations of civilization. But around them washed the dull waves of an essentially primitive life, an economy founded on the hunt and the trap line, a society based on the union of the nomad and the trader.

To those who remained in the Red River parishes, it often seemed that the rhythmic, picturesque, peaceful life of the Settlement was stifling. The same quick round of summer tripping and hunting, the same long-drawn winter of dancing, racing, and gossiping, the same full exploitation of the fur trade and the buffalo, the same cropping of the half-mile strip along the river banks, the same few posts in the Company, the government, and the church, seemed to offer little future to the young men being educated in the schools or kicking their heels around the stoves at home. For the new generation, the generation of mixed blood, was facing the future in 1850. They had proved themselves in the horse-racing on the river, in the duck-shooting at Shoal Lake and Lake Manitoba. They had proved themselves in the schools and colleges of Red River. Some had gone on to win distinction in the old country, in Canada and the United States, always "thinking long" of Red River in their letters. The wealth of Red River was passing to them through their Indian mothers; they were the native aristocracy, and Red River Settlement, French and English, except in Kildonan and St. Boniface, had become a community of mixed blood. In 1861 A. K. Isbister, who himself had Indian blood in his veins, was to write in England:

. . . it is an interesting fact that the half castes or mixed race, not only far outnumber all the other races in the colony put together, but engross nearly all the more important and intellectual offices—furnishing from their number the sheriff, medical officer, the post-master, all the teachers but one, a fair proportion of the magistrates and one of the electors and proprietors of the only newspaper in the Hudson's Bay territories. The mixed race, from the inter-marriage during many generations of the Company's officers and servants with the native Indians, have, in fact, increased to such a degree that they are at the moment the dominant class in the country. The single fact that every married woman and mother of a family throughout the whole extent of the Hudson's Bay territories, from the ladies of the governors of British Columbia and of the Red River Settlement downwards, is (with the exception of the small Scotch community at Red River, and a few missionaries' wives) of this class, and, with her children, the heir to all the wealth of the country—the fortunes made in the fur trade, and the valuable property accumulated in the Red River Settlement—is alone sufficient to invest the race with a high degree of interest and importance.[90]

"What if mama were an Indian?" a half-breed son could write in defensive pride.[91] They found employment in the Company, the Council, and the church. Yet there were not enough positions, and the old order seemed to require that this would always be so: "Whatever profession I follow there will be no room for me in Red River."[92] A new order was needed, but how would the half-

breed sons of Red River share in a new order which would fuse
Red River with the larger world? William Ross in Red River
wrote to his brother James, writer of the quotations above, at the
University of Toronto:

You know the fact that Red River is half a century behind the age—no
stirring events to give life and vigour to our debilitated political life. The
incubus of the Company's monopoly—the peculiar government under
which we *vegetate* or are fostered; all hang like a nightmare on our
political and social existence—it cools our ardour—destroys our energies,
and finally annihilates our very *desires* for improvement. Such being the
state of our political atmosphere you will not be surprised that our lives
should be a dull monotonous sameness—careless of every tie that binds this
country to the mother [sic] or sister colonies—and why is this? Just for
the reasons above given and because we in R[ed] R[iver] live for our-
selves and care for no one else—nothing but the little tattle of scandal in
every one's mouth—of this we have plenty. Such a state of things cannot
last forever, sooner or later the whole fabric must be swept away, and
then and not till then will Red River move onward, slowly it may be, but
surely—it is marvellous with what apathy people look at everything here,
and yet we need not be surprised when we know that public opinion
is moulded by the circumstances of the times. We ought to have a flood
of immigration to infuse new life, new ideas, and destroy all our old
associations with the past, i.e. in so far as it hinders our progress for the
future—a regular transformation will sharpen our intellects, fill our minds
with new projects and give life and vigour to all our thoughts, words,
and actions. . . .[93]

This impatient letter was written in 1856 by a son of Alexander
Ross, historian of Red River and once Sheriff of Assiniboia, and
of "Grannie" Ross, daughter of an Okanagan chief. The next year
was to see the beginnings of that flood of immigration which was
to sweep the old order away. And much of the stimulus of the
letter no doubt came from improvements and changes already in
train. Alexander Ross himself was an energetic critic of agriculture
in Red River, and had done something for its improvement,
notably by founding an Agricultural Improvement Society in
1850. Other men were experimenting, particularly in the Lower
Settlement, with new methods of tillage and new strains of wheat,
notably Donald Gunn and Rev. Abraham Cowley.[94] The short
crop of 1846 had led to the importation of new seed from Britain,

the "Black Sea wheat" brought from the Black Sea when the repeal of the Corn Laws opened British ports.[95] This strain was probably a forerunner of Red Fife, and it was joined by others. New agricultural implements were being carted in from St. Paul, making possible a lengthening of the fields and an increase in acreage. A mail service had been opened by way of Pembina in 1853.[96] The founding of the Bishopric of Rupert's Land in 1849 and the establishment by the See of St. Boniface in 1854,[97] the increase in the number of Anglican and Roman Catholic missionaries, indicated a growing interest by those churches in the Northwest. In 1840 four Methodist missionaries had entered the Northwest from Canada. One of them was Rev. James Evans, who began near Norway House his mission of Rossville and there invented the Cree syllabics, in which with home-made press and type he printed the Psalms and the Gospels. In 1851, partly through the efforts of Alexander Ross, the Presbyterian faithful of Kildonan obtained a minister of their faith in Rev. John Black, for whose ministry Kildonan church was built. The coming of the Methodist missionaries and of John Black signified that Canada was gathering the resources which would enable it to take an interest in the Northwest, cut off from the colonies on the St. Lawrence since the union of the companies in 1821. And every year the free traders multiplied and the length of the cart brigades bound for St. Paul increased. The growing commerce with the United States had already suggested in St. Paul that the commercial connection might lead to political union.

Many signs there were which indicated that Red River was beginning to drift out of its long isolation and to move into the great stream of North American development. The compromise of river lot and buffalo hunt, of the sedentary life and the nomadic, which was Red River, was beginning to crumble. The agricultural frontier from the east was about to send out its forerunners— traders, land speculators, adventurous farmers—to disturb the balance of the half-breed society of Red River.

5

The Old Order and the Transfer
1857-1869

THE CHANGES IN THE RED RIVER SETTLEMENT up to 1849 had come largely from within; between 1849 and 1857 external events had begun to work the major changes in the Settlement. The advance of the American agricultural frontier up the Mississippi valley had been marked by the formation of the Territory of Minnesota in 1849, and by the rapid growth of St. Paul as the centre of commerce for the upper Mississippi and Red River valleys. The trade of the Red River cart brigades with St. Paul had grown yearly since 1844, and that rude hamlet began to dream of itself as the metropolis of a region extending to the Saskatchewan valley and the Rocky Mountains. In Upper Canada also there were those who called for a resumption of the old trade with the Northwest and the annexation of the lands of the Red River valley. The *Globe* of Toronto eloquently voiced at once the commercial aspirations of that rapidly growing city and the cry of the farmers of "western Canada" for a new frontier under the British flag.

These ambitions, both Canadian and American, made it evident that the commercial monopoly and political rule of the Hudson's Bay Company over Rupert's Land and the far Northwest could not endure much longer. Both had rested on isolation from the agricultural frontier of North America. Both were suited only to the fur trade. Agriculture for export would doom both. The Company and the British government perceived clearly enough that it was only a matter of time before the monopoly must be ended and a new form of government set up in the Northwest. The issues were, when and on what terms should the surrender be made, and what should the new form of government be?

An opportunity to consider these issues was afforded in 1857 by the approaching expiration in 1859 of the Company's exclusive licence to trade in the North-West Territory and on the Pacific coast of British North America. A Select Committee of the House of Commons of Great Britain was set up to hear evidence and report. The Committee sought to determine the character of the Company's rule and trade and the fitness of the Red and Saskatchewan valleys, and of the Pacific coast, for agricultural settlement. They tried, in short, to discover whether the plains of the Northwest could be used for any other purpose than the fur trade, and whether the Company's licence should be renewed, or some commercial and political changes recommended. The Company's official testimony, given by Governor Sir George Simpson himself, was that the country was unfit for settlement and that the monopoly and Company rule should be continued for another term. Among the other witnesses the evidence as to the agricultural potentialities of the Northwest was conflicting; the weight of the evidence as to the nature of the Company's conduct of its trade and of the government of its vast territories was on balance favourable to the Company.

The Committee in a majority report recommended that the Company's licence for a monopoly of trade should be continued in the northern regions, where there was no likelihood of settlement, but that a Crown colony be created in Vancouver Island and on the Pacific slope, and that the way be left open for the acquisition of the valleys of the Red and Saskatchewan by Canada.[1] It was in effect a recommendation to open to agricultural settlement the areas in which it was possible, but to leave the northern fur forest of the Shield and the Mackenzie basin under the monopoly of the Company. It was a wise decision, so far as it went, but lacked a just appreciation of the speed with which the opening of the Northwest was approaching.

The Select Committee may be excused for failing to anticipate, and to recommend immediate provision for, the imminent changes in the Northwest. There was a great lack of the climatic and geographical knowledge necessary to form an estimate of the agricultural potentialities of the Red and Saskatchewan valleys. The Northwest had been explored and occupied for the purposes of the fur trade. The need of objective information on its general character and particularly on the climate and soil was felt by both the Canadian and British governments. The result was the despatch of two exploring expeditions, each instructed and equipped to give scientific reports. The Canadian Exploring Expedition was despatched in 1857 under the leadership of the engineer, S. J. Dawson, and of Henry Youle Hind, Professor of Chemistry and Geology of Trinity College, Toronto. The British expedition was despatched in the same year under Captain John Palliser who had hunted on the American plains in the 1840's and was known for his geographical interests. Both parties first investigated the character of the rugged country between Lake Superior and the Red River valley. Then in the summers of 1857 and 1858 Red River was stirred by the visits of the Canadian party by the old canoe route of the Winnipeg River and of the British party by the cart route from St. Paul. Both parties organized in the Settlement for journeys of exploration over the plains.

Hind's own party—others were sent on other missions—first followed the cart track south to Pembina, by the open plains from tree-lined river to tree-lined river, and then back by the similar country east of the Red. They next followed the cart track westward up the Assiniboine. It was the freighting route to Forts Carlton and Edmonton on the Saskatchewan. It was also the new track of the hunters from St. François-Xavier to the buffalo herds now far out on the western plains. The party saw the new settlements at St. Anne's (Poplar Point), St. Margaret's (High Bluff) and St. Mary's (Portage la Prairie). From the last settlement they followed the buffalo hunters' track through the "Bad Woods" of the Assiniboine's prehistoric delta up into the Sand Hills of the central escarpment. They wound through clumps of spruce and by the dunes of the Dry Dance Hills to the junction of the Souris with the Assiniboine, the course of the trail later to be named after the local Indian chief, Yellow Quill. They crossed the Assiniboine into the southern borderland of the park belt, and passed along the wooded valley of the Souris to the edge of the Souris plains. This was the country of the buffalo, the plains tribes, and the locust swarms. Even then a swarm was moving into the park belt out of the limitless plains,

the sky continually changing colour from blue to silver white, ash grey and lead colour, according to the numbers in the passing clouds of insects. Opposite to the sun the prevailing hue was a silver white, perceptibly flashing. On one occasion, the whole heavens towards the south east and west appeared to radiate a soft grey tinted light with a quivering motion, and the day being calm, the hum produced by so many million of wings was quite indescribable, and more resembled the noise popularly termed "a ringing in our ears" than any other sound. The aspect of the heavens . . . produced a feeling of uneasiness, amazement, and awe in our minds, as if some terrible, unforeseen calamity were about to happen.[2]

Greeted thus by one manifestation of the teeming power of the great plains, the party pushed down the Souris to the international boundary and then struck northwest across the plains for the deep valley of the Qu'Appelle. On the return the party divided, one section following the water route by the Saskatchewan down to the mission at The Pas, through the marshlands to Grand Rapids, and back by way of Lake Winnipeg to the Settlement. The other returned by way of Fort Ellice to the aspen bluffs and tree-traced rivers of the park belt. They followed the Saskatchewan trail across the central slope and the northern affluents of the Assiniboine to the Whitemud River and the Red River lowlands.

In the following summer Hind led a party by way of Lake Winnipeg and the Dauphin or Little Saskatchewan River, Lakes Manitoba and Winnipegosis, to reach Lake Dauphin and the bold eastern front of the escarpment at Riding Mountain. In the early snow of October, the party crossed the marshes and ancient gravel beaches at the foot of the escarpment and scaled the massive, wooded slope.

The view from the summit was superb, enabling the eye to take in the whole of Dauphin Lake and the intervening country, together with part of Winnipegosis Lake. The outline of Duck Mountain rose clear and blue in the northeast [*sic; sc.* northwest], and . . . Riding and Duck Mountains appeared continuous, and preserved a uniform, bold, precipitous outline, rising abruptly from a level country lying from 800 to 1,000 feet below them. The swamps . . . were mapped in narrow strips far below; they showed by their connection with the ridges, and their parallelism to Lake Dauphin, that they had been formed by its retreating waters.[3]

Hind was gazing out over the ancient basin of Lake Agassiz, its vanished waters transformed into an Agassiz of blue distance stretching out of sight over the Manitoba lowlands. The lofty shoulder from which he surveyed the lowlands was exceeded in height only by Mount Baldy on Duck Mountain to the northwest. Hind's penetration of the northwest highlands by the old fur trade route, produced the first recorded description of that one-time fur region and future rich farming district, the Dauphin country.

The Canadian expeditions had traversed the basin of the great lakes and the tall grass plains of the lowlands. Hind had wound among the bluffs and hills of the central uplands and had viewed the forests of the northwest highlands. He had left unexamined only the southern borderlands along the Pembina valley between Pembina and Turtle Mountains.

That region of the southern parklands, however, was crossed by Palliser's party in August of 1857. Palliser, too, went south by the cart track to Pembina, then westward up the Pembina Mountain to the highlands, and west along the ancient route by the Calf's Head Mountain to the Pembina valley. The party threaded their way between the aspen poplar bluffs and across the wide prairies which La Vérendrye had crossed on his way to the Mandans, until they reached Turtle Mountain. That blue tableland they found no longer the hunting ground it had been even when Palliser shot grizzly bears there in 1847.[4] And it was passed no longer by the buffalo herds, long wont to pour around its eastern slopes to the valleys of the Red and Sheyenne. Leaving the Turtle Head on their left, the party struck northwestward like Hind across the treeless plains of the Souris to pursue the exploration of the great plains of the South Saskatchewan and the passes of the Rockies.[5]

After these scientific expeditions came parties of travellers, hunters, and gold seekers; Milton and Cheadle, the Earl of Southesk, the Nobles party from St. Paul, the Canadian over-landers of 1862, to note only the best known. The surviving accounts of their travels from Red River through the park belt and across the plains confirm the impression made by Hind's and Palliser's reports. The Winnipeg basin that La Vérendrye had explored before the horse came had been a region of water-ways linked by ancient pathways and extended portages such as the Mandan trail and the *portage des prairies*. The horse and the Red River cart had made it a region of cart tracks and Indian "pitching" trails, which sprawled across the country in a loose and slovenly network. Yet all led to Red River Settlement. There the long lines of the riverbound farmsteads formed a narrow base, not only of waterways reaching to the Bay, the Arctic, and the Pacific, but of a system of overland transport radiating to St. Paul in the south and to Edmonton in the far northwest. Over these tracks in summer men and goods, guided by the plainscraft of the *métis*, travelled freely and surely. The day stages, the camp sites, the water crossings, were familiarly known. The settler, like the traveller, might now move surely over the land by known ways.

The Indians, moreover, who drifted listlessly down the pitching tracks of the ancient ridgeways were the remnants of tribes deci-mated by smallpox; the buffalo herds, which had cut deep paths on the banks of the Souris and flowed in black masses around the slopes of Turtle Mountain, were now far out on the plains of the Souris and in the Coteau de Missouri. The land lay open to the settler from Red River to the upper Assiniboine, from the southern borderlands of the Pembina to the slopes of Riding Mountain, mile upon mile of lowland prairie, mile upon mile of poplar bluff and open meadow in the park belt of the highlands.

That the land was open to settlement was evident, but could people reach the land and would land and climate support extensive farming, not only on the river bank but back on the prairie? The Canadian expedition reported that land and water communication could be opened between Canada and Red River, but Palliser held it scarcely practicable to build a railway from

Lake Superior, possible though one was by the southern passes of the British Rockies.[6] On the agricultural possibilities of the Winnipeg basin, Hind was confident, but too confident; Palliser doubtful, but too doubtful. Hind thought the possibility of extensive agriculture proven, Palliser thought even wheat-growing precarious. There was plenty of room for difference of opinion, and each had evidence to support his views. The future with all its trial and error was to prove Hind right, and with all its failures to underline Palliser's doubts.

The agricultural settlement of the West, then, would still be a matter for experiment, in which the fortunes of many men and women would be involved. On one fact, however, Palliser and Hind were in agreement, and in agreement also with American scientists, such as the climatologist, Lorin Blodget, and advocates of northwestward expansion, such as J. W. Taylor of St. Paul. That fact was that in the valleys of the Red and the Saskatchewan, and in the park belt zone which stretched across them, lay a great corridor of potential settlement and a practicable railway route to the northern passes of the Rockies. This "fertile belt," as Palliser termed it, lay between the northern fur forest and "Palliser's triangle" to the southwest, the northward projection of the "Great American Desert" of contemporary geographers. The "Desert," a semi-arid region of the high grassland plains between the Mississippi and the Rockies, was, with its horsed Indian tribes, a barrier to settlement and an obstacle to the Pacific railway then being projected in the United States. But to the northward lay a well-watered crescent stretching from the upper Mississippi to the upper Columbia. In it, it was now being affirmed, agriculture was possible, for the northward sweep of the summer isothermal lines made the cultivation of wheat theoretically possible up to latitude 56° north in the Peace River valley. As Blodget, a leading American geographer and climatologist, wrote in a much quoted passage: "The buffalo winter on the Upper Athabaska at least as safely as in the latitude of St. Paul's, Minnesota, and the spring opens at nearly the same time along the immense line of plains from St. Paul's to Mackenzie's River."[7]

This message of both theorists and explorers was hailed at once in St. Paul and in Toronto, for it gave assurance that the Northwest could be settled by the farmer, whose wheat and cattle would furnish traffic for a Pacific railway sweeping up from St. Paul and Fort Garry to the North Saskatchewan and the low gradients of the Yellowhead (Tête Jaune) Pass.

Nor were men lacking to act on this assurance and gamble on its fulfilment. The ever growing trade with St. Paul, by which even the Hudson's Bay Company was bringing in its trade goods, called for means of transport to supplement the creaking cart brigades. The aggressive merchants of St. Paul offered a bounty for the construction of a steamboat on Red River, and in 1859 the *Anson Northup* was launched at Georgetown in Minnesota. The purpose of the proprietors was not so much commercial as to prove the navigability of the Red and the Saskatchewan. On May 19 the smoke from her double stacks rolled over the trees enfolding the new settlement of St. Norbert, south of Fort Garry, and the boom of her whistle mingled with the clash of the rejoicing bells of St. Boniface. Her life was to be brief, her navigation of the northern summer waters erratic, but she was the first of a succession of steamboats which plied the Red until the railway came.

By cart, and thereafter by steamer, American goods were trickling into Red River: cast-iron stoves, reaping machines, four-wheeled democrats to replace the lumbering carts. In 1859 came the printing press. Two young Canadian newspapermen, William Buckingham and William Coldwell, fresh from service with the Toronto *Globe* and with the wind of Northwest destiny in their nostrils, came up from St. Paul with a press and were soon set up in the little village between Fort Garry and Point Douglas. The *Nor'Wester* was the apt title of their paper, and proclaimed its character clearly: ". . . a newspaper . . . devoted to the varied and rapidly growing interests of that region."

Such a country [it affirmed] cannot now remain unpeopled. It offers temptation to the emigrant nowhere excelled. It invites alike the mechanic and the farmer. Its rivers and rolling prairies and accessible mountain passes, secure to it advantages which must belong to a highway to the Pacific. . . . What can impede its development? What can prevent the settlement around Fort Garry from becoming the political and commercial centre of a great and prosperous people?

The printing press will hasten the change. . . .[8]

And the new weekly began to urge that the rule of the Hudson's Bay Company be ended and the Northwest annexed to Canada.

The hustle of these years, breaking the stagnation at which William Ross had sickened, was increased by the discovery of gold on the Fraser in 1856 and on the North Saskatchewan in 1861. Small parties of gold seekers tried the northwest route, and for a while there was an overland trail by the Red and Saskatchewan. In the 1860's gold dust from the North Saskatchewan washings was one item swelling the commerce of Red River. Young men turned from hunting and carting to wash gold in the bars of the great western river.

There was still, however, more money to be made in fur than in gold. More and more buffalo robes came into Red River to go south in the carts to St. Paul; the Crimean and American Civil Wars swelled the demand. The great Company's licence to trade in the North-West Territory was not to be renewed and though the monopoly of trade in Rupert's Land conferred by the Charter remained, it was not likely to be respected in an age contemptuous of privilege. A rush of free traders was feared by Sir George Simpson, partly because of the agitation beginning in Canada against the Company and partly because of the establishment of an American military post at the new *métis* settlement of St. Joseph's on the Pembina just across the lines. Once more, as in 1845, the approach of American troops to the frontier gave rise to the danger that the restless *métis* might transfer their allegiance to the Republic, either by moving across the line or by inviting American intervention in Assiniboia. Simpson obtained the despatch of a detachment of the Royal Canadian Rifles to Fort Garry in 1857, under the command of Major George Seaton. The presence of the green-coated Canadian Rifles at Fort Garry quieted the turbulent spirits in the colony, but when the time for relief came in 1861, the Company declined to assume the cost of paying replacements, and the War Office to maintain troops in a location so isolated.[9] Thus it was that Samuel Taylor noted in his journal how the Rifles dropped down the Red on their way to York in August, 1861,[10] leaving the Red River without a garrison in the changeful years which had begun.

More and more free traders overran the Winnipeg basin, the Saskatchewan valley, and the plains, until their combined trade amounted to nearly half that of the Company itself. The incoming traders built storehouses for their goods, first on the east bank of the Red River, and then, after the flood of 1861, on the west side of the Red. Between the edge of the Hudson's Bay land around Upper Fort Garry and Point Douglas to the northward where Andrew McDermot and his son-in-law A. G. B. Bannatyne, long independent traders, had their storehouses, sprang up the stores of the free traders after 1862. The rude little village, the product of free and international trade in the locality La Vérendrye had once forecast would be a seat of commerce, was at first jokingly called McDermotstown and then more formally named Winnipeg to distinguish it from Fort Garry. It was the creation of Red River merchants such as McDermot and Bannatyne, and American traders such as Norman W. Kittson. In the 1860's the number of American traders increased; they were rivalled as yet by only a few Canadians.

A trickle of immigration had indeed begun to run from Canada as well as from the United States, a counter current to the slow flow of people out of the Settlement to the United States. The American immigrants were exclusively traders; the Canadians were almost wholly settlers. Canadian families were migrating by the score from Canada into Michigan, Wisconsin, and Minnesota, moved by "prairie fever" to seek prairie lands. A few individuals and even some families came on to the Winnipeg basin in the wake of the Exploring Expedition of 1857–8, or around by St. Paul. Some were drawn to Kildonan, but nearly all passed on from the cramped riverside settlements of the Red and lower Assiniboine to the growing settlement at Portage la Prairie.[11] This slight movement was significant. The Canadians were land seekers, and would remain in the country, as the American traders would not. And the Portage, isolated and without government, would favour annexation to Canada, whatever doubts the older parishes might have.

The stir caused by the exploring parties, the gold seekers, and the immigrants, though it was welcomed by many in Red River, also led to considerable unrest among Indians and *métis*. They were far too much a part of the old order not to fear its passing, and the coming changes.

Of the many changes of these years, the decline of the fur trade was the most significant. The swarming free traders, whose activities had brought Winnipeg into being and who kept the commerce of the colony thriving, where in fact the scavengers of the trade. They were sweeping up the last remnants of the once great trade of the Winnipeg basin, the westward plains, and the Saskatchewan valley. They were clearing the way for the farmer, at the same time that they ended the traffic begun by La Vérendrye and so brilliantly developed by the Nor'Westers. The trade of the great Company suffered from this competition, but its great resources of capital and skill, still fed by the vast preserves of the North and of the Mackenzie basin, little touched by the free traders, were not lightly to be overcome, and sustained it.

In the free traders' packs, the buffalo robe took steadily larger space. The Red River hunts ranged out summer and fall in ever growing brigades. But each successive year the bands had to swing farther out on the plains; by 1859 the hunts were extended as far west as the Cypress Hills, and there were years when the hunt failed. The price of pemmican, traditionally three pence a pound, began to rise. The *métis'* occupation, the buffalo hunt, was not gone, but its end was in sight, and with the fur trade and the buffalo herds would go the boat and cart freighting by which many of them lived. How could this peculiar people, so immediately a product of the fur trade, protect themselves against the crumbling of the old order, how provide for themselves in the new?

It was apparent that in the new order of agricultural settlement, land would assume an importance it had not possessed in the fur trade. Hitherto it had been of value only as the site of fishing ground, or portage road, or river-front farm. Such lands had been the prize of the first comer and retired fur traders and casual half-breed farmers had in fact squatted. Their title to their river lots was "the ancient custom of the country." While the Hudson's Bay Company were lords of the soil in Rupert's Land, they had never taken steps to extinguish Indian title to the land. Only in Lord Selkirk's grant had this been done, in a narrow strip along the Red from Lake Winnipeg to the border, and along the Assiniboine from the Red to Rat Creek a few miles west of Portage la Prairie. Here were the only land titles of record which a court would sustain, and even the validity and the meaning of Selkirk's treaty were to be disputed. Everywhere else the Indian title remained, and the *métis* claimed a share in it in right of their mothers' blood. Indians and *métis*, then, had important rights to maintain in the lands of the Northwest, and transgression of these rights by eager land seekers would meet resistance.

These things were made evident when old Peguis, chief of the Ojibway and Swampy band in St. Peter's parish, and one of the signers of the treaty which ceded the river fronts to Selkirk in 1817, protested in 1860 to the Aborigines Protection Society that the Indian title had not been properly extinguished even for these lands.[12] The resultant controversy in Red River served to awaken keen interest in the land question. It was hotly debated at a public meeting in 1861, and thereafter settler, Indian, and *métis* were aware that few, if any, land titles were secure in the Northwest. Even in Assiniboia the majority of the lots were held only by squatter's right, and on transfer the custom was to pay for improvements and no more. A land rush, or the threat of a land rush, into the Northwest when men feared dispossession from their lots and loss of rights would provoke resistance by the *métis*, if not by the Indians.

There were few thinking people in Red River by 1860 who were not aware that the near future would bring change in the Northwest. "There is a general expectation," said Bishop David Anderson, "that the present year may usher it in, and that during its course the southern portion of the land, or at least our own settlement, may become a direct Colony of the Crown."[13] It was generally accepted that economic change would require a new form of government to replace the mild, but increasingly ineffective, rule of the Governor and Council of Assiniboia. At the same time, it was realized that a new local government would mean, with the end of Company sovereignty, a new political connection with the outside world.

The possibilities were three. A Crown colony might be set up over the "fertile belt" and the plains, as the Select Committee of 1857 had recommended for Vancouver Island and as had been done for that colony in 1858. The Northwest might be united with Canada, as the Canadian government and the Toronto *Globe* had urged, and the Select Committee had advised. Finally, since 1860 was the very hey-day of Victorian anti-imperialism and *laissez-faire*, the pull of natural forces might be allowed to work itself out, and the Northwest come under American sovereignty as a new territory of Saskatchewan. The legislature of Minnesota was strongly to hint in 1862 that the United States should acquire the territories to the northwest of that rapidly developing state.[14]

If British sentiment and Imperial prestige were set aside, the last possibility offered an attractive future for the Northwest. The trade with St. Paul was fully established and rapidly growing. Annexation would lead to speedy organization as a territory and an early beginning of railway construction. It would end the monopoly, such as it now was, of the Company, and it would abolish the 4 per cent customs duties at Pembina. Such were the material advantages urged by the St. Paul merchants and their representatives, the American traders in Winnipeg. With them would come self-government and protection by the federal troops of the Republic. That was one possible future before Red River; its realization was to be dimmed by the Civil War, but it became more likely when the defeat of the South ended opposition to the addition of free soil to the North. No one, of white blood or mixed, could be unaware that, whatever befell, the Northwest would be welcome in the great Republic.

Annexation by Canada, if not indicated by contemporary commercial ties comparable with those of St. Paul, was strongly suggested by long historical connection and common political allegiance. Canadians had first explored and traded in the Northwest, and many of its people in 1860 were of Canadian descent. At the same time that the agitation began in Canada for a renewal of the Northwest trade in 1856, a demand that the Northwest be annexed to Canada was raised. Indeed, Canada revived and asserted, as against the Charter of the Hudson's Bay Company, the old French title to the Northwest.

Yet just as there had been an external check on American expansion over the Northwest, so there was one in Canada. The demand for annexation was an Upper Canadian agitation, supported chiefly by the Grit, or Reform, party. The Grits were frontier farmers who, aware that the good lands of Upper Canada were nearly all taken up, were looking for a new frontier in the Red River valley. The demand, if granted, would have extended the boundaries of Upper Canada from Superior to the Rockies, and made it the dominant, as it was already the larger, partner in the Canadian Union of 1840. Lower Canada therefore could not but be doubtful of the results of this proposed extension of its English and Protestant partner. "M. Cartier, the Canadian Prime Minister, was over here last autumn," wrote A. K. Isbister from England to Donald Gunn at Red River in 1859, detailing an interview with Sir Edward Bulwer Lytton, Colonial Secretary, "and seems to have satisfied Sir Edward of the hopelessness of annexation. He told him quite frankly that, as the head of the Lower Canadian party, any proposal of this kind would meet with his determined opposition—as it would be putting a political extinguisher upon the party and the Province he represented, and, if carried out, would lead to a dissolution of the Union."[15] In the face of this natural resistance by French Canadians to the aggrandizement of Upper Canada, only the admission of the Northwest to a new Canadian union as a separate territory could be contemplated. But until a new union was attempted, the annexation of the Northwest to Canada was delayed, and the danger of its permanent loss incurred.

There remained the possibility of the Northwest being made a Crown colony, as Vancouver Island and British Columbia had been in 1858 and 1859. A Crown colony government under

Canada was indeed suggested by Governor-General Sir Edmund Head as early as 1857. In 1863, Head, as Governor of the Hudson's Bay Company, was to repeat his proposal, and to have the support of the Duke of Newcastle, Colonial Secretary. But the Imperial government was unwilling to assume the responsibility involved. It seems reasonable to suppose, however, that that was the form of government best suited to the needs of the Northwest and the general circumstances of the time. A Governor and a Council, to be made representative in due course, would have served all political needs well enough for some years. The moribund rule and shattered monopoly of the Hudson's Bay Company could have been decently ended and removed. The Northwest might have developed its own legislature and courts and laid the foundations of its own laws. The Indian and half-breed title to the land might have been extinguished and those suspicious, but essentially docile, people reconciled to government and the coming of settlement. Finally, the Northwest so organized, might have been represented at the Quebec Conference of 1864, as some in the Northwest wished, and have taken part in planning the federation of British North America. It might have made terms, as British Columbia was to do, with the confederated provinces, and come into the Canadian Union with provincial status and with a territorial area comparable with that of the great Laurentian provinces of Ontario and Quebec.

None of these possibilities was to be realized before 1869. Before Red River could obtain self-government and unite with Canada, the rule of the Hudson's Bay Company in Rupert's Land had to be ended with proper safeguards for the commercial and financial interests of the Company. The provinces of British North America had to find a basis of union which would enable the federation they created to annex the Northwest without disturbing the equilibrium in which they came together. From 1859 to 1868 the Colonial Office declined to undertake responsibility for ending the Company's régime and setting up a Crown colony. The successive colonial secretaries wished Canada to assume the burden of government between Superior and the Rockies, and contented themselves with acting as mediators between the Company and the ambitious colony. Canadian action, however, waited on the federation of the British North American colonies, which was not to be completed until 1867. Even the grandiose project of the Grand Trunk Railway of Canada and of Sir Edward Watkin to extend that line by the United States and the Saskatchewan valley to the Pacific, and the buying out of the Hudson's Bay Company by the International Financial Society in 1864 to further the enterprise, failed to effect any change in the status or external relations of the Northwest. Red River and the Northwest therefore derived no benefit from the enquiries and expeditions of 1857–9 and remained static and isolated under the nerveless rule of the Council of Assiniboia and the Hudson's Bay Company in a continent in which the Civil War was transforming the American Union and hastening the federation of the British colonies.

The long delay, after it had been made clear in 1857 that Red River could not much longer pursue the fur trade and river-lot farming in isolation, created a political vacuum in the Settlement. That vacuum was filled by some slight mooting of the desirability of Crown colony government; some consideration, fed by the trade with St. Paul, of annexation to the United States; and the agitation by the "Canadian party" for union with Canada.

The Canadians who had come to Red River in the wake of the exploring expeditions in 1858 and 1859 had come to share in the development of a new frontier. They hoped thereby to enrich themselves, but they also had stout patriotic hopes of adding the new frontier to Canada. The proprietors of the Nor'Wester, William Buckingham and William Coldwell, were of this mind, and their paper became and remained the organ of Canadian sentiment. James Ross, son of the historian and newly returned from a brilliant academic career in Canada, bought out Buckingham in 1860, and brought his local knowledge, education, and some journalistic experience in Canada to the cause; for criticism of the Governor and Council of Assiniboia in the Nor'Wester he was dismissed from the offices of sheriff and postmaster of Assiniboia in 1862. Ross then began to use the paper to agitate for "responsible government," the Canadian term for full democratic self-government, in Assiniboia. Thus the "Canadian party," as it came to be called, had as its core the *Nor'Wester*, as its cause self-government in Assiniboia and union with Canada.

During the hazardous years of the decade after 1860, the party was led by the bold and aggressive Dr. John Christian Schultz, a Canadian immigrant of 1860. A red-blonde giant, powerful of body and crafty of eye and mind, Schultz supplemented the meagre earnings of his profession by dealing as a free trader in fur, Saskatchewan gold, and land. He proposed to grow rich with the development of the broad lands opening before the settler, and he was prepared to risk much and strike hard to promote that opening. The potentialities of the Northwest were to have few advocates more diligent or devoted. In 1864 he bought out Ross and in 1865 Coldwell, and the *Nor'Wester* passed into his hands until 1868. Schultz used it not only to continue the agitation for union with Canada, but also to recount Red River history in terms antagonistic to the Hudson's Bay Company and to advertise the agricultural prospects of the country. In 1868 his friend Walter Bown, dentist turned free trader and of the same outlook as Schultz, took over the paper and carried on the tradition of opposition to the old régime. The "Canadian party" was in fact John Schultz and such Canadians as were under his influence at any given time. This was unfortunate, for in Schultz, as one who knew him observed, "Fate had manufactured a scoundrel out of material meant by Nature for a gentleman."[16]

There were, indeed, but few Canadians in the settlement. Schultz, Bown, and Schultz's half-brother, Henry McKinney, were the only Canadian traders. The commerce of Winnipeg was in the hands of the old free traders of Red River, notably Andrew McDermot and A. G. B. Bannatyne, and of American traders from St. Paul. Alexander Begg, the later historian of the Northwest, arrived in 1867 as a Canadian salesman, but in the following year went into partnership with Bannatyne. In the Presbyterian Church in Kildonan was a tie with Canada; Rev. John Black was a Canadian by education, and the church tie had

had such results as the sending of young James Ross to pursue his studies at the University of Toronto. But, as already noted, the few Canadian settlers for the most part went westward to the Portage, to form a second centre of Canadian sentiment. In general, the Canadian party at Winnipeg was more noisy than numerous, and the quiet folk of Red River, both English and French, found it irritating when it ceased to be amusing.

In this they were not unduly intolerant, for Schultz and his followers took their tone from the Toronto *Globe* and assailed the Hudson's Bay Company with bitter indignation as an intolerable obstacle to the settlement of the Northwest and annexation by Canada. They took up the attack of the free traders of 1845 on the legality of the Government of Assiniboia. They raised, with the aid of Peguis and Donald Gunn, the question of the extinction of the Indian title, even by Selkirk's purchase of the river fronts in Assiniboia. They denied the validity of the Company's charter. In short, they so challenged all the fundamentals of the old order in Red River as to give the impression that they were trying to bring about anarchy. That indeed was to be the result, though it was not the intent, of their agitation.

Such an agitation, in so primitive a society, could not be confined to principle. It became involved in personalities, and threatened to raise the passions of race and creed. In 1863 the trial of Rev. G. O. Corbett of Headingley on a charge of attempted abortion resulted in his conviction and imprisonment. This singularly unpleasant *cause célèbre* deeply divided opinion. Corbett had been an outspoken critic of the Hudson's Bay Company; his friends and the Canadian party sprang to the quite unwarranted conclusion that he was now being made to suffer for his opinions. A group led by James Stewart, schoolmaster of St. James and a member of the party, broke open the gaol and freed Corbett. For this act Stewart was arrested, but he was immediately liberated by an armed party led by William Hallett and John Bourke, prominent half-breed leaders. The opposition of long-suffering Governor Dallas and a large force of special constables was unavailing.[17] Neither prisoner was recommitted, and the justices of the peace advised the Governor that in the absence of a military force suits having a public interest could no longer be adjudicated.[18]

The government, that is, could use force only by pitting one element of the population against another, which in effect meant that public order in Red River depended in the last resort on the will of the armed *métis*. Yet at this time they were the only defence against such a danger as the refugee Sioux, who had been driven from Minnesota after the massacre of 1862. These miserable but dangerous people had first begged menacingly around the settlement, harassed by their enemies, the local Saulteaux, and then had reluctantly settled at Portage la Prairie. In 1865 Lord Wharncliffe, who had visited the Northwest, declared in the House of Lords that there was "an absolute want of government at the Red River Settlement."[19] That fact was to be underlined by the forcible liberation of Schultz himself from imprisonment for debt in 1868. It is not surprising, therefore, that the gaol-breaking of April, 1863, should have been followed by a public meeting in St. James on June 11, at which James Stewart called for the formation of a provisional government and an elective council, "a temporary government formed by the people themselves for the time being until the British Government shall see fit to take the place into their own hands."[20] It was resolved to agitate for such a government and to pay no taxes until one had been formed.

Practically speaking, the Canadian party was right in its contention that the government and external relations of the Red River Settlement had ceased to meet the needs of the country and the times. Effective government of Red River and the Northwest by the Hudson's Bay Company had ended, as the officials of the government and Company knew. Commercial monopoly and paternal government could not survive in an age of free enterprise and political democracy. Government in the Northwest hung on a legal thread, the sovereignty of the British Crown and the charter of 1670. While it was to prove to be of strength sufficient to drag into exile a man bold enough to set up a provisional government, it did not give assurance that the people of Red River would be protected in their persons and rights. More and more men went armed in Red River. More and more it became apparent that, if the Imperial government or Canada did not furnish effective government, men must make good the deficiency by improvised governments of their own.

That the people of the Northwest might form governments of their own was revealed by both the *métis* and by Red River and Canadian settlers outside the limits of the District of Assiniboia. In 1864 the missionary, Père Albert Lacombe, and his flock organized a local government at Big Lake in the far Northwest.[21] In 1867 attention was drawn to the local government established at Portage la Prairie. This body, under the guidance of Cockran, in his last years Archdeacon, served the community well, and continued to give satisfaction as Canadian settlers came in to swell the settlement after 1860. One of these was a young Montrealer, Thomas Spence, a man of some education, intelligent but romantic and conceited. On his coming to the Portage in 1867, Spence was elected to the Council. He wished to reorganize and elevate the Council so as to make it worthy of its role as the first representative and popular government in the Northwest and worthy also, it was somewhat maliciously suggested, of Thomas Spence himself. He persuaded the Council to create the office of President, to which he was elected; to set up an Executive Council; to organize districts with representatives; to define its boundaries to include all the territory between Assiniboia to the east, the hundredth meridian to the west, and Lake Manitoba and the American boundary to the north and south; to impose taxes; to adopt the name, first, of Caledonia, then of Manitobah.[22] Finally, the Colonial Office was notified by letter dated February 19, 1868, of these important developments, in the hope, apparently, that this new colonial government—it was not called a republic by its sponsors, who were loyalists of the loyal—might be recognized by the Imperial government. The Colonial Office replied on May 30, 1868, that while Her Majesty's subjects might submit themselves to laws of their own making for municipal purposes, no government exercising authority over British subjects might be formed in British territory without express commission from the Crown.[23] The answer disposed of any claim to legal authority by a provisional government, and shook Spence's infant state. There were local objections also to the expense of this new form of government, and Spence's ambitions collapsed in a flurry of revolver shots before the resistance of the outraged shoemaker Macpherson, a western Hampden who refused to be taxed. The old Council of Portage went on functioning, however, and the episode seems to underline the fact that in 1868 there were two governments existing side by side in the Red River valley: one, the moribund government of Assiniboia, the other the native, popular government of Manitobah, both simple, both elementary, but one of the past and dying, the other of the future and growing. James Ross's demand for responsible government; James Stewart's cry for a provisional government; Father Lacombe's little venture; Thomas Spence's pretensions; all emphasized the need for new government, and furnished precedent for a larger and sterner experiment in government-making.

In these years also Red River suffered not only a want of government but, from 1862 to 1868, a want of rain. After wet seasons in the late 1850's a dry spell began in 1862. The harvest that year was fair, despite a dry spring and damage from hail and mildew. Drought set in in earnest the next year. "Dry, Dry," wrote Samuel Taylor at the Lower Fort, "the Weather was never seen, people Say, so long without rain, it Thunders often and yet no rain, sometimes it is very hot, it gets very rain like sometimes but it clears off and there is no rain."[24] Wheat was seven shillings a bushel that fall, and seed wheat ten shillings in the spring of 1864. The water-mills stood idle by the parched creeks; hay was in short supply; the steamer *International* made only one trip in the third dry summer. Grubs and grasshoppers damaged the crops, and in the fall prairie fires swept the plains and burned the swamps to the clay. In 1865 the grasshoppers were a plague, and the season again dry.

The next two years gave some relief from drought and grasshoppers, but in 1868 the two combined to cause an all but complete crop failure. And with the crop failed the other two sources

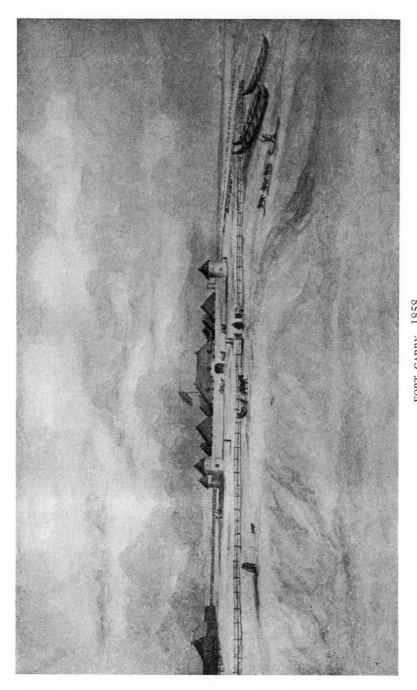

FORT GARRY, 1858

From the Sketch Book of Major George Seaton in the Public Archives of Canada

BUFFALO HUNTERS' CAMP, 1858

From the Sketch Book of Major George Seaton in the Public Archives of Canada

of food, the plains hunt and the lake fisheries. Even the rabbits, wrote both Bishop Robert Machray of Rupert's Land and Governor Mactavish, failed in that year of destitution.[25] For the poor and improvident, the winter threatened to bring hunger such as Red River had not known since the foundation of the colony. Public subscriptions for relief were opened in the Settlement, in St. Paul, and in Ontario. A Relief Committee was set up, with local committees in each parish, and during the winter food, and in the spring seed wheat, were distributed among the needy. The Canadian government combined its plans for annexing the Northwest with relief of distress in Red River. It arranged to send in a party to cut a road from St. Boniface to the North West Angle of the Lake of the Woods, as engineer S. J. Dawson had recommended in 1858. Work began in the late fall of 1868, with John Snow in charge and Charles Mair, a young poet and a protégé of Hon. William McDougall, as paymaster; he was soon a crony of Schultz and the Canadian party. Snow and Mair bought supplies and engaged workers, and these expenditures, it was hoped, would aid the relief of distress. To this pass had Red River come in the grim fall of 1868. Once more it seemed that the Northwest was a fur and Indian country only, where life was hard and food precarious.

Yet despite the bad years, the Settlement continued to flourish; the free traders of Winnipeg, stripping the country of the furs the Hudson's Bay Company had conserved, were making money; despite the drought and the grasshoppers, Canadian settlers continued to trickle in. In the worst year, 1868, Kenneth McKenzie, a master farmer from Ontario, came to spy out the land and decided that it promised well. As settler after settler staked his claim, the question of land titles became more urgent. The *Nor'Wester* bluntly informed newcomers that every man had as good a title as the Hudson's Bay Company, namely, a squatter's title. "The tenure of land is precisely the same with the new comer as it is with the Hudson's Bay Company—you hold as much as you occupy and no more." It was, it rightly wrote, the custom of the country for each man to take what he could use; that in transfers payment was made only for improvements, not

for the land itself.[26] Year after year more and more people had
been acting on those premises. The Portage settlements had been
squatters' settlements from the first. When John McLean came
from Canada in 1862, he had bought his land from previous
settlers, paying them for their improvements. When Kenneth
McKenzie passed through the Settlement, he went beyond the
farthest claim at "The Portage," and ploughed a challenging
furrow around fourteen hundred acres of grass and timber land
on Rat Creek.[27] The Canadians of the work party sent in to build
the Dawson Road were staking out claims east of the Red at Ste.
Anne des Chênes, or Oak Point, in the spring of 1869.[28] That
summer the ever pugnacious James Stewart and others began
staking claims on the very block of land the Hudson's Bay Company had reserved for itself around Upper Fort Garry.[29]

The claims of Indians, *métis,* and the Company to the lands of
the Northwest were all challenged, directly or implicitly, by
Canadians in the fall of 1868 and the spring of 1869. All the
debates of the 1860's on the land question were coming to a
climax. McKenzie's claim on Rat Creek necessitated the negotiation of a treaty by James McKay with Yellow Quill's band
of Indians, by which the lands east of Rat Creek from the Assiniboine to Lake Manitoba were ceded[30] for the time being. The
claim-staking at Oak Point and on the Hudson's Bay reserve was
repudiated by Colonel J. S. Dennis, chief of the Canadian survey
party of 1869.[31] Nevertheless, the fears of the natives had been
kindled. They could see a land rush developing in which they
would be swept aside by these aggressive newcomers who ap-
propriated the land, took the camp sites, ploughed up the trails,
drove off the game. If there were to be peace, it was imperative
that the suspicious Indians, the sensitive and formidable *métis,*
be given assurance that their rights in the land of their birth
would be recognized. The Hudson's Bay Company Governor
and the Governor and Council of Assiniboia could give them
none. It was rumoured that the newcomers had boasted that "the
half-breeds would soon be driven from the country, or kept as
cart-drivers to bring in the vehicles of the new immigrants,"[32]
and the feeling grew that the coming of strangers, as Charles

Mair, paymaster of the Dawson Road party, had told the Indians at Rat Creek, "was like the march of the sun, it could not be stopped."[33] It was not a reassuring message. They would, it seemed, have to act for themselves, and demand terms from Canada, which was now preparing confidently to annex Rupert's Land and the North-West Territory.

It was now a fact that the confederation of British North America in 1867, by ending the deadlock between French and English in Canada, made it possible to consider the admission of the Northwest into the union. Whether it came in as a federal territory or as a province, it would not lead to the aggrandizement of the old Upper Canada, now Ontario, at the expense of Quebec, but would furnish a free field for the development of the people and institutions of both the provinces of the St. Lawrence.

To the Canadian government, the annexation of the Northwest presented itself as a matter of ending the title of the Hudson's Bay Company in Rupert's Land and of assuming the government of an area extending from Labrador to the Rockies. At no time from 1857 to 1869, despite some warnings by their own servants, did the Canadian ministers ever consider the matter as one requiring consultation with or assurances addressed to the people of the Northwest. That no harm was intended those people goes without saying; that to approach them directly was impossible while the government of the country remained vested in the Hudson's Bay Company, is true. Yet no effort was made, through the government of Assiniboia, or the clergy, or the press, or by special commissioner, to give assurances to the people of the Northwest, that land titles would be guaranteed, the Indian title extinguished by treaty, and self-government in due course freely granted. These things might have been done, but they were not attempted, and the consequences were to be serious. The responsibility for the failure is perhaps to be ascribed to the Imperial rather than to the Canadian government.[34] One of the greatest transfers of territory and sovereignty in history was conducted as a mere transaction in real estate.

There could not have been much misunderstanding in Red

River of what was being prepared for the Northwest: organization as a territory after the American model, to be followed by the speedy grant of local self-government. John Schultz, who returned from a trip to Canada in May of 1869, probably told the *Nor'Wester* such was to be the likely political future of the area.[35] Territorial status with self-government would have satisfied everyone, it is reasonable to suppose, had its introduction only been made a matter of official assurance, and impartial treatment of all elements in the Northwest put beyond doubt. Unfortunately, the agitation of the Canadian party, the activities of the Canadian squatters, the boisterous assurance of some Canadians who saw themselves as the creators of a new and superior order in the Northwest, irritated and aroused misgivings among the *métis* and the Roman Catholic clergy.

When Canadian workmen on the Dawson Road began to stake claims in the spring of 1869, after buying out the Indian title with a few bottles of whiskey, the belief spread that the Canadian government itself would not prevent, or might be too tardy to repair, an invasion of Indian and *métis* rights in the land. The watchful *métis* decided that it was necessary to insure that any new régime before it established itself should recognize the Indian title and should be willing and able to safeguard existing claims. In August, 1869, amid rumours and reports in the *Nor'Wester*, but without one authoritative statement of the impending transfer of the Northwest from the Hudson's Bay Company to Canada, Canadian surveyors came in to make preliminary surveys in anticipation of the transfer and land rush. They were received with distrust by the *métis*, while the American Consul, Oscar Malmros, newly appointed from St. Paul, won golden opinions of clergy and *métis* by his bland manners and seeming disinterestedness. The surveyors had been carefully instructed that their party was in the colony by permission of the Hudson's Bay Company. They were to avoid giving offence to any and to assure the inhabitants of Red River that their rights would be respected. These instructions were faithfully observed; J. S. Dennis, chief of the survey party, even gave a long interview to Louis Riel, son of the leader of the Sayer affair, who was making himself prominent in the discussion of the coming transfer. Dennis explained at length that the *métis'* interests were to be safeguarded, and he afterwards testified that he had thought that Riel had been satisfied with his assurances. Such was not the case; the *métis* were not to be satisfied with words, and Riel was soon urging resistance to Canada from the steps of St. Boniface Cathedral after mass. In the face of this opposition Dennis stopped the local surveys and went to Pembina to run the principal meridian due north, with a base line to Ste. Anne and one to Portage la Prairie, on which townships might be surveyed for the immigrants of 1870. But Dennis too had made the error of accepting Schultz's advice and hospitality and the *métis'* distrust was confirmed.

The reports that the transfer had been arranged had already led to some discussion as to how the people of Red River should respond to this disposition of their future without any reference to them. On July 29 William Dease, a respected and prominent *métis*, had called a meeting in the Court House to discuss the transfer. As Dease's purpose was to challenge the right of the Hudson's Bay Company to dispose of the Northwest, and as he was thought to be acting for Schultz, the *métis* declined to support him.[36] A meeting early in October at the home of Thomas Sinclair, at which *métis* representatives, John Bruce and Louis Riel, were present, also failed to reach a decision,[37] as did all Riel's approaches to the English half-breeds with a view to a united protest against the reported policy of the Canadian government.[38] The English portion of the Settlement, if somewhat irritated at not having been consulted, was not prepared to protest. Neither were the more stable elements of the *métis*, the farmers and traders of St. Boniface and St. François-Xavier.[39] The tripmen and the hunters, however, particularly the turbulent Saskatchewan boatmen of St. Vital, were restless, and resentful of the attitude of the Canadian newcomers, the "Canadas," as they called them. They listened to Riel,[40] and some of the clergy, Rev. Georges Dugas, Rev. L. R. Giroux, and Rev. N. J. Ritchot, shared Riel's views and urged him to resist the pretentions of Canada. Bishop Taché, who would have restrained these hotheads, was absent in Canada on his way to Rome. One visitor from Canada who might have reassured all doubters of Canada's good intentions was singularly unsuccessful. That was Hon. Joseph Howe, Secretary of State for the Provinces, who had come to see for himself this new territory which was to come under his jurisdiction. Howe avoided contact with Schultz and the Canadian party. He talked freely, sympathetically and reassuringly to those old settlers who visited him. He even sent a message, presumably one of reassurance, through Rev. J. M. Lestanc, administrator of the diocese of St. Boniface, to Louis Riel. But he made no public statement, and left the settlement on October 16, aware that there might be some trouble but not aware of how serious it might be.

The fundamental question, however, was not so much that of land title as who would control the new government at the transfer—the native people of the Northwest, or the Canadian party and the in-swarming immigrants to follow. It seemed only too likely that the Canadian party would; Schultz and his colleagues were confident of it, and boasted of their connections with the new government. How then would the *métis* fare when the self-government they had once claimed made them a minority in the land of their fathers? The English half-breeds and the white settlers had few such fears, but among the French *métis* this fear of domination by English-speaking newcomers was strong. It would be best, the talk ran, to make a stand and exact terms while resistance was still possible. Suddenly on October 11 a party of *métis* led by Riel stopped surveyors who were running the base line to Ste. Anne towards the river lots of St. Vital; it was a symbolic act, duly considered, not a sudden local skirmish. They challenged the right of a Canadian survey party to make surveys in the Northwest before the Indian and half-breed title had been extinguished. In particular, they challenged the right of Canada to make surveys, not so much across particular lots, as in an area which the *métis* had traditionally regarded as being reserved for them. There was no title to land there, they implied, save that conferred by the custom of the country. It was a challenge which could not be taken up; the surveyors, as their instructions required, quietly withdrew in face of this resistance and went on with their work in the English parishes to the north and west. The little-known, the disregarded *métis* had defied Canada to make good, by treaty or by force, its title to the Northwest.

6

The Resistance of the Red River Métis
1869-1871

THE SYMBOLIC DEFIANCE OF THE MÉTIS RESTED on the superior strength their unity gave them. To oppose a régime they distrusted, they turned to the ancestral organization of their people, the council of the buffalo hunt. Language and faith gave them a sense of unity; they cherished the old belief that they were a "new nation" and a peculiar people; the traditional institution of the council of the plains hunt gave them a means of action.[1] When it was announced in the *Nor'Wester* that the federal Minister of Public Works, Hon. William Mc-Dougall, a Grit politician and a noted Upper Canadian annexationist, had been made Lieutenant-Governor of the North-West Territory, with a commission to take effect on the transfer of authority from the Company to Canada, it was felt that the danger was clear and immediate. Rev. N. J. Ritchot, priest of St. Norbert, later wrote to Sir George Cartier: "The council of the nation was assembled, and it was resolved to organize a military force after the custom of the country in time of danger, and to put it on foot in order to repel the invasion of the country by men in whom could be recognized no authority positively and legally constituted."[2] This force was organized among the turbulent boatmen of the Portage la Loche brigades and the hunters in from the summer hunt in the parishes of St. Vital and St. Norbert, home of the boatmen and the "main river" band of the hunt. Direction of the military force was vested in a "National Committee," elected on October 19, an adaptation of the council of the buffalo hunt and also, perhaps, of the relief committees of the previous year. The president of the Committee was John Bruce, the secretary, Louis Riel.

As the *métis* had in the council of the hunt a traditional institution, so they had in Louis Riel a leader—for Bruce was largely a figurehead—who was the son of the leader of the revolt of 1849 against the Company's monopoly. A bright boy, born in Red River in 1844, Riel had been picked out by Taché as a possible candidate for priesthood in 1858. He had been educated in the Collège de Montréal until 1865. Riel was by talent and training no common youngster, but a handsome, eloquent, and impetuous personage. But he had failed to complete his course, or had not been permitted to continue, perhaps because some instability of character had been detected by his mentors. He then spent a year in Montreal and Terrebonne, and had become familiar with the great world of the east. He had returned by way of Chicago to St. Paul in 1866 and 1867, and when he finally reached the Red River in 1868 he was educated, poor, and a failure, another young man for whom there was no place in Red River. Now at twenty-five years of age he would make himself, like his father before him, the tribune of his people, and defend for them the rights the transfer threatened.

The first step was to prevent McDougall from entering the country and quietly waiting, in conjunction with the Canadian party and the surveyors, to assume power when news of the completion of the transfer came through. At St. Norbert, where the Rivière Sale draws down its train of trees in heavy loops along the Red, a barricade was erected which closed the Pembina Trail. A messenger was sent to the border to command McDougall to stop outside the territory he was coming to govern. McDougall ignored the message and the messenger, but on October 31 was compelled by a mounted and armed party sent by the National Committee to retire across the line to Pembina, where he took up quarters to wait for the transfer to take place. The act was as definite, and as symbolic, as the stopping of the surveys.

By stopping McDougall the *métis* intended to do two things: to prevent the Canadian party, acting under McDougall's aegis, from seizing power in Red River; and to delay the transfer until the people of the Northwest might make terms with Canada. The second point was one in which success was foregone; there was in fact little they might claim that the Canadian government had not intended in due course to give. It was the struggle to gain the first point which led to the troubles of 1869–70. The Canadian party, startled and angered by the bold—and illegal—action of Riel and his Committee, jumped to the conclusion that the *métis* and their clerical friends, in resisting annexation to Canada, were preparing for annexation to the United States. They believed also that the object of their ten years of suspicions and polemics—the local officials of the Hudson's Bay Company—had connived at the organization of resistance to the transfer. The Canadians put themselves in communication with McDougall, and began to organize a force to overthrow Riel. In the developing contest between the *métis* and the Canadian party, Upper Fort Garry, by its position and because of its stores, which alone could keep any considerable force of men together in a Northwest winter, was the key to the situation. If the *métis* seized it, they could carry out their programme; if the Canadian party, they could thwart that programme and hold out until relief came from Canada in the spring.

The *métis*, already organized and accustomed to act quickly under orders, moved first and seized Fort Garry on November 2, in order, as they said, "to protect it" from a danger they declined to specify.[3] Governor William Mactavish and his officials, though warned of the danger of a seizure, had decided they could not prevent one, as most of those well affected to the Company, the tripmen and the hunters, were in fact the insurgents. By this act Riel obtained the upper hand in events. The gates of the Fort were guarded by armed men, but the business of the Company went on, and the courts of Assiniboia continued to sit. All that had been done so far was to prevent, by force of arms, the entry of one who, though governor-designate, was a private citizen until the transfer of the North-West Territory to Canada was proclaimed.

The Canadian party was quick, and not unreasonably quick in view of their reading of events, to call the action of the *métis* a rebellion and Riel and his men rebels. The movement, however, was directed, not against any constituted authority, but, as the Canadian government at once grasped, against the assumption of sovereignty in the Northwest by Canada.[4] The keen mind of Sir John Macdonald had at once seized on this essential point, and in 1874 he was to define trenchantly the legal consequences of the stopping of McDougall and the occupation of Fort Garry:

The armed resistance was a very aggravated breach of the peace, but we were anxious to hold, and did hold, that under the circumstances of the case it did not amount to treason. We were informed that the insurgents did not desire to throw off allegiance to the Queen, or sever their country from the Empire, but that their action was in the nature of an armed resistance to the entry into the country of an officer, or officers, sent by the Dominion Government. We desired, therefore, that it should be considered in the light of an unlawful assembly, although it might technically be held to come under the statute of treason. . . .[5]

If to deny the public highways to private individuals and to occupy the strong place of the Settlement at the head of armed men was only to skirt rebellion, once the proclamation was issued that would announce the transfer of the Northwest to Canada, to continue to resist McDougall would be to resist constituted authority. It was necessary for the National Committee, therefore, since no rebellion against the Hudson's Bay Company or the Queen was intended, to insist at once on being consulted by the Canadian authorities and to obtain acceptable terms of entry into Confederation. If this were to be done effectively, it must be done by a united Red River Settlement, English as well as French. The military organization of the French *métis*, which had acted so quickly and decisively in the emergency, had to be transformed into a provisional government, civilian in character, which might negotiate with Canada. Such was Riel's programme, the programme of James Stewart in 1863 and of Thomas Spence in 1868, but it was backed by four hundred to six hundred armed *métis*.

Many obstacles, the remainder of November was to disclose, lay in the way of its implementation. The French were not united themselves, a factor of prime importance throughout the insurrection. The wealthy plains traders and the well-to-do-farmers, such as Pascal Brèland, William Dease, Joseph Hamelin, and Charles Nolin, were not convinced of the emergency nor ready to place themselves under the command of the upstart Riel. The English too were divided in their sympathies. The men of Kildonan and many in St. Andrew's and the upper Assiniboine settlements, along with Henry Prince's Indians at St. Peter's, were on the whole in sympathy with the Canadian party. The remainder, though resentful at not being consulted with respect to the transfer and at the prospect of becoming "a colony of a colony," were not convinced that the strong action of the French insurgents was necessary or defensible. The Canadian party, distrusting the Company and fearful that there was American inspiration and the prospect of American aid behind the rising, were for immediate action to put down the *métis*. The "American party" in Winnipeg, the presence of American annexationists such as Enos Stutzman of Pembina and Major Henry M. Robinson around Riel, lent colour to their distrust. It would seem in fact that at first Riel could not control the Americans, and perforce accepted their sympathy and support. But it would also seem that he never considered annexation except as an implied threat and a last resort. Over all these doubts and fears hung the cloud of Indian unrest: of the local bands agitated by concern for their rights in the land; of the refugee Sioux at the Portage, landless, hungry, and menacing. Both sides began to fear that the other would invoke Indian aid; both were sure that a clash between the insurgents and the Canadians would bring the Indians down on the Settlement to plunder and kill.

Amid these menaces the resolute Riel pursued a plain and undeviating course. On November 6 he published a notice to the inhabitants of Rupert's Land, inviting ten of the English parishes to send one representative each, and the town of Winnipeg two representatives (apparently on the model of the Relief Committee of 1868)[6] to meet with the president and representatives of the French-speaking population on November 16 to consider the political state of the country and adopt measures for the future. The parishes of St. Mary's, St. Margaret's, and St.

Anne's, though outside Assiniboia, were included, as they were to be henceforth. After much discussion, the English parishes decided to send delegates, and on the day appointed twelve French and twelve English delegates met in convention at Fort Garry.

Meantime, McDougall at Pembina had been endeavouring by correspondence to push Governor Mactavish into assuming responsibility for bringing the movement to an end. Mactavish, though he little relished the role of Canute, prepared a proclamation warning the Convention that the acts of the military organization had been illegal, and of the consequences, material and legal, of the continuance of such lawlessness.[7] The Convention heard the proclamation but none the less deliberated for two days, and adjourned until November 22. When the delegates reconvened on that date, it soon became apparent that, while the English thought terms of union should be negotiated with Canada, they were not prepared to disregard the Governor and Council of Assiniboia. Riel, however, held to the position which the military organization of the *métis* and control of Fort Garry gave him and refused either to let McDougall come in or to negotiate with anyone but the Canadian government. On November 23 he proposed the formation of a provisional government, on the ground that the government of the Company was weak and incompetent, in order to treat as representatives of the Northwest with the government of Canada. The English delegates, who correctly held that the government of the Company was still in existence, then said they must consult their constituents on the new and far-reaching proposal.[8] Riel's contention that the rule of the Company had decayed to extinction, if it had not ended when the terms of transfer were settled in March, 1869, had failed to convince the English members of the First Convention. But both sides clearly realized, as a result of their debates and Mactavish's proclamation, that the crux of the affair was the existence, or absence, of a legally constituted government in Rupert's Land.

Attempts were now made by the small group of English led by A. G. B. Bannatyne, who favoured the French stand, to arrange a compromise by which the government of the Company would be retained, but remodelled into a legislative and an executive council. Aided by W. B. O'Donoghue, an Irish theological student at St. Boniface who had joined Riel, they arranged a meeting of the electors of Winnipeg at the Engine House on November 26. Bannatyne was in the chair and both Riel and Schultz were there; all present were armed as had become customary in Red River. Riel spoke in favour of a provisional government to be formed by a united settlement. No one, he said, would be coerced, not even the followers of Dr. Schultz. He was heard out and applauded at times. When a pensioner, Michael Power, made a bombastic, loyalist speech, he was squelched by Schultz himself. This fair progress came to nothing, however, because it could not be decided who had the right to be present. Indeed, the absence of a law establishing a franchise and a law of naturalization made it extremely difficult to proceed democratically, and this fact increased Riel's readiness to fall back on the military force of the *métis*. But next day he agreed, after Oscar Malmros, the American consul, and others had urged it would be the best course, to unite with the English in an executive council under the Hudson's Bay Company.

This news was sent out to the parishes down the river, where sentiment had been forming in favour of resisting the French and of bringing McDougall by force. The immediate object of the Canadian party and their friends, however, was to keep from Riel the pork the Canadian government had in store for the Dawson Road party. These provisions, stored in Dr. Schultz's house, might well prove the decisive factor in a contest of strength in a Red River winter. There was little enough food in the Settlement. The *métis* in Fort Garry had at first been fed by their wealthier friends, and then on Hudson's Bay Company provisions, for which they promised to pay. They would have enough, but the Canadians and their friends would be greatly aided if they could use the provisions to keep a force under arms. Thus when Alexander Begg the diarist carried the news of the compromise to the lower parishes he found two hundred and fifty men assembling to put the government pork beyond the reach of Riel.[9] The St.

Andrew's delegates agreed to accept the Bannatyne compromise, but on November 30 Riel, probably having been informed of the armed gathering down the river, reverted to his original position.

On the next day all was changed. Some, but not all, of the English delegates came to Fort Garry on December 1 to resume the discussions in the Convention on the basis of the Company's government continuing. While they were debating whether they should attend in view of Riel's change of mind, the news spread that the "Queen's Proclamation" had come.[10]

This new turn of affairs had been caused by William McDougall at Pembina. In cramped quarters at the desolate frontier town, dependent on slow mails for information from Ottawa, the governor-designate had been deliberating how he might discharge the duties of his office when the transfer occurred. His understanding was, as had been finally agreed by the Imperial and Canadian governments, that it would take place on December 1. When the instruments were exchanged in London, the government of the Hudson's Bay Company would end at Fort Garry— or would be held to end, he assumed, since Riel knew that December 1 had been fixed as the date of the transfer—while he remained in enforced absence on American soil at Pembina. A hiatus in government would be claimed, which the insurgents would turn to advantage by forming, as they would have a right to do under the law of nations, a provisional government which might be made a pretext for intervention by the United States. To prevent such a check to the establishment of Canadian authority, McDougall had decided to issue on his own responsibility, when December 1 came, a proclamation announcing in the Queen's name the completion of the transfer and his own assumption of the government of Rupert's Land and the Northwest. McDougall, in short, had decided to gamble on the transfer being completed on the date arranged, despite his instructions not to assume the government until informed of the completion of the transfer. He had crossed the border on the night of November 30–December 1 and read a proclamation to the dark and empty plain, by which he declared the transfer to Canadian sovereignty complete and himself the Governor of the North-West Territory of Canada. It was an act at once rash and completely illegal.

It was an advance copy of this proclamation which Colonel J. S. Dennis brought to Fort Garry on December 1. It was accepted as authentic, and the conclusion at once drawn that the government of the Hudson's Bay Company had come to an end. The English delegates then met with the French, and asked them to state what they wanted. The French withdrew and prepared a "list of rights." This they proposed should be submitted to McDougall for ratification by the Canadian Parliament. To the substance of this list, the first "Bill of Rights," the English delegates were prepared, despite its manifest American inspiration, to agree. But disagreement arose when the English delegates proposed to send a delegation to McDougall with the list and to bring him in on receiving his assent to it. Riel emphatically insisted that McDougall would in no circumstances be admitted until the list was ratified by Parliament. He dismissed the English with contempt, and at that the First Convention dissolved.

Riel's distrust was at once justified by the actions of the Canadian party. McDougall had made Dennis deputy-governor and conservator of the peace, and with this authority Dennis began after December 1 to raise and drill men, both half-breed and Indians, at Lower Fort Garry. Enlistment of the Swampies of St. Peter's by Dennis, and rumours that "Shaman," or George Racette, a notorious scoundrel and agent of Schultz, was raising the Portage Sioux, led to an Indian scare among the French and Americans. The situation had been reached in which an armed body of French at Upper Fort Garry were opposed by an armed body of English at the Lower Fort. News of the English arming at once brought to Riel's aid those French who had hitherto refused to follow him.[11]

Between the gathering forces huddled the little village of Winnipeg, and on its southern edge toward the Upper Fort stood Dr. Schultz's house with the government pork and a garrison of Canadians. This outlying post of the Canadian forces seemed to the French a menace to Fort Garry. Attempts at mediation by the influential plains guide and freighter, James McKay, and by

Bishop Machray were fruitless. Dennis, indeed, was already doubtful of success. On December 4 he had written to Schultz: "You speak of enthusiasm, I have not seen it yet with anybody but Prince's men."[12] Schultz and his Canadians, however, determined to make a stand, thus adding to their responsibility for the troubles engulfing Red River. An order from Dennis to Schultz to withdraw was ignored. And a plea by a delegation from Winnipeg that his stand was endangering the already precarious peace was cut short by the French, who marched out on December 7, surrounded Schultz's house, and made its garrison prisoner. The favourable impression made by the Bill of Rights in St. Andrew's had been the decisive blow to Dennis' efforts to raise a force to rescue Schultz.[13] The St. Peter's Indians continued resolute, but they would undoubtedly have been overwhelmed by the larger, better armed, and better organized corps of the *métis*.

Riel was now master of the situation. He held Fort Garry, and he immediately suppressed the *Nor'Wester* and the first issue of its rival, the *Red River Pioneer*. On December 8 he issued the Declaration of the People of Rupert's Land, in which a provisional government was proclaimed from November 24, on the ground that the Hudson's Bay Company had "abandoned" the people of Rupert's Land by transferring to a "strange power" its authority and had thereby exempted the people of Rupert's Land from allegiance to it. They were therefore free to set up a government to deal with the circumstances in which they found themselves. The Declaration went on to decry the right of Canada to impose "a despotic form of government" on British subjects, to assert that the denial of entry to Rupert's Land to McDougall had been justified, and to declare that the establishment of Canadian authority would be opposed until negotiations with Canada had given assurance of good government in Rupert's Land and the Northwest. Riel was now bringing his programme to its climax, but he had been forced, by McDougall's success in causing division, to proceed not on the basis of a united settlement as he had desired, but by means of the military organization of the *métis*. So evidently did that force dominate the Settlement that on December 9 Dennis listened to the pleadings of Bishop Machray and others, ordered his followers to cease their preparations, and made his way over the border by way of Headingley and Pembina Mountain. For the unfortunate McDougall there was no recourse but retreat across the snows to St. Paul. He was followed by the mocking air of a *métis chanson*, composed by old Pierre Falcon to be sung to the air of "The Wandering Jew." It sang of a man who had come seeking a throne and had enjoyed nothing better than the domestic convenience he had brought with him. The Canadian party was now imprisoned or scattered, and Riel was in control of Red River.

The course of the insurrection had hitherto been governed by local events and personalities. The real controls, however, were external, for on the date of actual transfer of the government of Rupert's Land and the Northwest depended—or was thought to depend by all participants in the Northwest and Canada—the legality of all acts, both Riel's and McDougall's. Here the action of the Canadian government was decisive. On learning that McDougall had been stopped at the border, Prime Minister Macdonald cabled to London on November 22 to ask whether the £300,000 Canada was to pay the Hudson's Bay Company in settlement of its rights in Rupert's Land had been handed over to the Company. When assured it had not been, he at once took the stand that Canada was entitled to peaceable possession, and requested the Colonial Office to postpone the transfer.[14] This was done, and the government of Rupert's Land beyond a doubt remained vested in the Hudson's Bay Company and its officials, headed by Governor William Mactavish at Fort Garry. Legally, both Riel and McDougall had had the ground cut from underneath their feet.

At the same time, despite faulty and contradictory communications, the Canadian Prime Minister and his cabinet had grasped the true import of the rising. Though they could not ignore the evidence and many rumours of American interest in the rising and the possibility of American intervention, they held firmly to the line that the purpose of the insurgents was not annexation to the United States, but negotiation with Canada.

Having grasped this true premise, the Canadian government recalled the unhappy McDougall and set out to find means of conciliation. On December 6 the Governor-General, Sir John

Young, issued a proclamation promising an amnesty to all who would lay down their arms and desist from their lawless proceedings. It was then decided to send commissioners to discover what terms would satisfy the insurgents. Colonel de Salaberry, a French Canadian who had been with Hind's party in 1857-8, and the Grand Vicar Thibault, long known and beloved as pastor of St. François-Xavier, were first despatched, primarily on a mission of pacification to the French. They reached Red River, Father Thibault on December 24, de Salaberry, who was stopped at Pembina, not until January 6. Riel, who had become president of the provisional government on December 27, was shown their commissions and, on grasping the fact that theirs was a mission of reassurance only, treated them with scant respect. A third and special commissioner, Donald A. Smith of the Hudson's Bay Company service, was empowered not only to seek to calm suspicion, but "also to take such steps, in concert with Mr. Mc-Dougall and Governor Mactavish, as may seem most proper for effecting the peaceable transfer of the country and the government from the Hudson Bay authorities to the Government of the Dominion."[15] With the despatch of the commissioners, Macdonald also began preparation for a military expedition in the spring as a demonstration to all concerned that Canada and the United Kingdom meant to complete the transfer and hold the Northwest.

Smith reached Fort Garry on December 27, having cautiously left his commission at Pembina. He did not announce his mission and was received simply as an officer of the Company, but was detained within Fort Garry on the orders of the suspicious Riel. Smith arrived in the midst of continued efforts by the moderates to bring the French and English together, and a drive by the American annexationists to swing the movement in favour of union with the United States. When on January 7, 1870, a newspaper once more appeared in Red River, it was called the *New Nation*, in deference to the traditional boast of the *métis*, but it was edited by Major Robinson and its tone was strongly annexationist. It was edited for circulation in the United States, not in Red River, but that Riel should have tolerated its tone reveals how fluid the situation was at this time. In circumstances so uncertain, it was no difficult matter for Smith to undertake, as he had been instructed and furnished with means to do,[16] to create a "Canadian party" among the French. In this he succeeded with the aid of Richard Hardisty, his brother-in-law, and two *métis* who now opposed Riel, Pierre Léveillé and Charles Nolin. When he had made his preparations, Smith revealed his mission and (in defiance of Riel) had his papers brought in by Hardisty and an armed party of *métis* under Léveillé on January 18. The ensuing conflict between the two men turned on Riel's insistence that Canada treat with his provisional government, while Smith was determined to deal only with the people of Red River. Since Riel could not on this occasion play his trump card of the military organization of the *métis* without provoking a conflict among his own people, Smith won the first round of the contest.

But the Dominion commissioners were working at cross purposes.[17] On the night of January 18 Rev. J. M. Lestanc, administrator of St. Boniface, and the other commissioners, Thibault and de Salaberry, reunited the French under Riel, and Riel was once more able to dispute the leadership of Red River with Smith. A mass meeting convoked from the whole Settlement was held on January 19 in the court yard of Fort Garry to hear Smith's commission read. The meeting in the bitter cold of that day heard the Canadian government's assurances of liberal treatment expounded by Smith, and it was resolved the next day, on the motion of Riel and Bannatyne, that on January 25 a convention of twenty French and twenty English delegates should meet to discuss Smith's message and decide on a course of action. The meeting broke up in a spirit of mutual good feeling. French and English had been united by Smith, who, having divided Riel's people, had used the policy Riel had tried to follow in November; Riel could therefore go along with Smith. From this point on the influence of the Americans Stutzman and Robinson, whose aid Riel had accepted and may have needed, and whose support he seems to have wished to keep as a last resort, steadily diminished and soon ceased to count.

In a hotly contested election of delegates to the Second Convention, Riel's followers were returned in a majority over the supporters of Nolin and Léveillé.[18] Among the English the only excitement was caused by the disputed election of the American candidate in Winnipeg, Alfred H. Scott, who defeated A. G. B. Bannatyne. A second election was ordered, but Bannatyne declined to contest it. When the Convention met, therefore, Riel was still in the ascendant among the French, a fact perhaps aided by the escape of Schultz from Fort Garry on January 23. As a result of Riel's victory, the outcome of the Convention was twofold. On the one hand, as Smith wished, the Convention drew up a second list of rights, which he approved in general terms. He also invited the Convention to choose delegates to go to Ottawa to discuss the list with the Canadian government. Riel was defeated in the Convention by the votes of the English and the anti-Riel French on motions to have the Northwest enter Confederation as a province, and to have the terms of the transfer annulled. Yet, on the other hand, he was strong enough in his military position, his retention of the prisoners, and his use of arbitrary arrest and detention, to nominate the delegates and to force the Convention to agree to the formation of a new provisional government representative of both English and French. Delegates from the Convention were assured by Governor Mactavish that they should form a temporary government. They therefore agreed, for the sake of peace and in the hope of the prisoners being released, to join with Riel in a provisional government. A council of twenty-four members was proposed, to be elected from the French and English parishes equally, and an executive to consist of President, Secretary, Treasurer, and Adjutant-General. A list of magistrates was approved and James Ross was made Chief Justice. Riel was elected President after much opposition. It was then that the delegates were nominated and elected, Father Ritchot, Judge Black, and Alfred H. Scott to represent respectively the French, English, and American elements in Red River. Riel thereupon announced that the prisoners, both those of December and later, would be released, and on February 11 the Convention came to an end.[19]

With the agreement to negotiate the terms of entrance into Confederation and the formation of a representative provisional government, Riel's programme as taken over in its first part by Smith was nearing fulfilment. The English parishes, however reluctantly, were prepared to fall in with his plans for the sake of peace. Peace and the completion of union with Canada on acceptable terms now seemed assured, and the release of the prisoners was begun.

The prospect of peace, however, was destroyed by the action of the friends of the Canadian party in the lower parishes, where the escaped Schultz was at large, and at Portage la Prairie. Though Portage, with High Bluff and Poplar Point, had sent delegates to the Convention, the western settlement remained a centre of Canadian feeling. There members of the Canadian survey parties had congregated, together with prisoners escaped from Fort Garry, such as Thomas Scott of the Dawson Road work party. Worried and angered by the continued detention of their friends by Riel, they decided early in February to make their way to Red River, join their sympathizers in Kildonan and St. Andrew's, and demand, if necessary enforce, the release of the prisoners. On February 10 they were reported to have reached Headingley, where they were held four days by a blizzard. Their presence there, and the refusal of some of the prisoners in Fort Garry to promise not to oppose the Provisional Government, on the misunderstanding that to do so meant to undertake to support it, delayed the promised release of the prisoners. Another complication was the capture by Riel's men of one of the Portage scouts, William Gaddy, a half-breed from Portage la Prairie. Gaddy bore a message for William Dease, who lived south of St. Norbert and was opposed to Riel, urging him to attack the homes of the *métis* soldiers and draw them from Fort Garry. At this news, the French sank their differences, as in December, and rallied behind Riel.

On the night of February 14 the Portage party moved through Winnipeg to Kildonan where they met Schultz bringing up a force from St. Andrew's and St. Peter's. The men of the lower parishes were dragging a cannon as they marched up to Kildonan to the tune of "Hey, Johnny Cope":

Riel sits in his chamber of state
With his stolen silver forks and his stolen silver plate,
An' a' his braw things spread out in style so great,
He'll not breakfast alone this morning.

Hey, Riel, are ye waking yet,
Or are ye're drums a-beating yet,
If ye're nae waking we'll nae wait,
For we'll take the fort this morning.

Riel, however, continued the release of the prisoners, and in spite
of the unhappy killing, during the mustering in Kildonan, of
young John Hugh Sutherland and of his slayer, Norbert Parisien
—the first violent deaths in the insurrection—moderate counsels
prevailed and the Portage men decided to go home. But as they
floundered through the snow past Winnipeg the next day, they
were surrounded by mounted men from the Fort and taken
prisoner. This sudden return to violence by Riel is probably to
be explained by the exasperation of his headstrong men. Akin to
that, however, was his own conviction, strengthened by the
capture of Gaddy with his incriminating message, that the Canadian party was determined to destroy the union of the settlement
behind his newly formed government.[20]

In face of this seeming refusal of the revived Canadian party
to accept the government which the delegates of the parishes in
Convention assembled had approved, Riel fell back once more on
the military organization by which he had risen and from which
it seemed he could not divorce his power. Captain Charles Arkell
Boulton, who had led the Portage party largely to keep them in
hand, was singled out as an example, tried by "court martial" of
the *métis* military organization on February 17, found guilty of
defying the Council, and condemned to be shot. The intercession
of Smith and others induced Riel to spare him, but only on condition that they use their influence to have the Provisional Government accepted and the election of representatives to its Council completed. Smith undertook to reconcile the people of the
Lower Settlement and Bishop Machray wrote to the Portage
people to ask them to accept the Government. Riel instituted a
feverish search for Schultz, already embarked on his great wilder-

ness march to Duluth, and sent a party to White Horse Plain to guard against a descent of the Portage Sioux. The strain he was under is revealed by the attack of "brain fever" which prostrated him on February 24. By the end of the month, after a visit by Smith and Archdeacon John McLean to the western settlements, Alexander Begg could record that the whole settlement had accepted the Provisional Government. The election of representatives was finished on February 26. It seemed that the crisis caused by the well-meant but nearly fatal march of the Portage men had been surmounted.[21] "Captain Bolton and Riel," Begg noted, "had many arguments together on the state of the country and Bolton, it is said, is beginning to see things in a different light from what he did."[22] Riel himself was recovering completely from his illness.

Upon this growing peace the execution of Thomas Scott broke in with tragic and seemingly inexplicable violence. Scott, an Ontario man from Perth, had been a workman on the Dawson Road. The last act of a court of Assiniboia had been to fine him and three companions £4 for an assault on the foreman, Snow, in a dispute over wages,[23] and Scott was reported to have remarked on hearing sentence that it was a pity they had not ducked Snow when they were at it, as they had not got their money's worth.[24] He had been captured in Schultz's house on December 7, had escaped to the Portage, and had been captured again with the Portage party. Apparently a man of excitable temper and rough ways, learned perhaps in the lumber shanties of the Ottawa valley, he proved, by the accounts of his enemies, to be an impatient and contemptuous prisoner. On Scott's part, there was cause for resentment of an imprisonment which rested on nothing but superior force, for the prison rooms were crowded and cold, the food was scanty and rough, and the guards were neither trained wardens nor disciplined troops. Scott was also, it seems, at times made frantic by dysentery. His offence seems, however, in want of any acceptable or revealing evidence by either friend or foe, to have been twofold. For one thing, he refused stoutly to recognize the Provisional Government and urged his companions to refuse also. For another, he seems to have displayed that sense of superiority, that contempt for the half-breed, which lay at the root of the trouble the Ontario men raised for themselves and which the sensitive *métis* particularly resented. From that contempt sprang, in part, the refusal to accept the Provisional Government, which to the Canadian seemed a silly and disloyal mockery, but which Riel took so very seriously. So much did Scott's rough defiance irritate the *métis* guards, that they at length seized him and in exasperation were about to shoot him out of hand. Besides these difficulties with Scott inside the walls, it is to be remembered that Schultz, the instigator of the February rising, was still thought to be at large in the Settlement, stirring up the Indians. Moreover, the Provisional Government of the Convention was not yet constituted and what Scott had offended was not a civil government, however provisional, but the military organization of the *métis*. This was founded on a rough and swift military organization among the *métis* which had used the forms of a court martial as early as 1817,[25] and which in 1870 "was determined to make itself respected."[26] On March 3, at a court-martial presided over by the easy-going giant, Ambroise Lépine, Scott was tried on the charge of "insubordination and striking the guards," found guilty after debate, and condemned to be shot on March 4. The initiative in bringing on the trial seems to have come, not from Riel or Lépine, but from the exasperated guards. Once sentence was passed Riel, sensing the danger to his government in Scott's defiance and knowing he could not break with his men, was obdurate to all pleas for mercy. "We must make Canada respect us," he told Smith when the Commissioner pleaded for Scott,[27] and after a brief delay for spiritual preparation Scott was led out on March 4 and shot before the walls of Fort Garry.

Why the resistance, hitherto so restrained, rose so suddenly to this pitch of brutal violence, is an obscure and complex question. If Riel was forced to accept the decision of his angered men, he was destroyed by the very force which had raised him to power, the military organization of the *métis*. His frantic, often admirable, efforts amid the menace of the Canadian risings, the intrigues of the Americans, the divisions and instability of his own people, to shift the basis of power from the military organization to the civil authority of a provisional government had ended in unmitigated tragedy. The shooting of Scott was a blunder, so much a blunder that it is difficult to believe a man of Riel's quality could have committed it except under the compulsion of the guards' exasperation and the threat of an Indian rising fomented by Schultz. It was, unhappily, worse than a blunder—it was un-necessary.[28] The Provisional Government had been accepted and peace was returning to Red River. Schultz was actually in flight and the Indians were quiet. After the shooting of Scott the peace of Red River, it is true, remained unbroken, but it was the peace which shock induces. For Riel thereafter there was to be no peace in the Northwest he loved, no peace anywhere but the forlorn peace of exile and the final peace of the gibbet at Regina.

Tragic also was the fact that the unhappy Scott was shot just four days before Bishop Taché reached the Settlement. The good bishop, devoted to his children yet but half won from barbarism, had feared the results of annexation and had warned Cartier in October, 1869, when on his way to the Oecumenical Council in Rome, that there would be trouble in Red River. But that too confident politician had waved his fears aside. When the troubles began, the Canadian government had requested him to return, and leaving the Council, he had come back to Ottawa. There he was asked to use his influence to quiet the *métis* and to assure them that none of their rights would suffer by the transfer. He raised the question of an amnesty for illegal acts committed. For answer he was shown Sir John Young's Proclamation of December 6, and was assured verbally by Cartier and Macdonald that amnesty was a matter for the Imperial government, but that he need have no fear that amnesty would be granted. The assurance was given, Taché was to testify later, despite his warning that there might be bloodshed.[29] Taché then made his way to Red River. At first he was kept under guard in his palace by Riel, who had come to distrust any emissary from Canada. Riel had already arrested M. Nolin, Joseph Hamelin, Angus McKay, and John F. Grant, prominent *métis* who had been influenced by Smith, and it is probable that he feared a similar undermining of his power by Taché.[30] By March 14, however, Taché and Riel were reconciled, and the beneficent influence of the Bishop became evident during the ensuing month in the release of prisoners, the changed tone and editorship of the *New Nation*, the final elimination of American influence, and the raising of the Union Jack over Fort Garry beside the "party flag" of the insurrection. There was a fair prospect from the last days of April that union with Canada would be accomplished with the support of all Red River.

To this end, the delegates to Ottawa set out on March 23 and 24, with a third list of rights, this one drawn up by the Provisional Government, requiring admission of the Northwest as a province rather than as a territory of Confederation, a governor who could speak both French and English, and a general amnesty. Thus Riel, busy as President in organizing the executive of the Provisional Government, undid the victory Smith had won over him in the Convention and most unethically repudiated a major decision of the Convention. But even this did not end the evolution of the list of rights, the outcome of compromise by the English and of the settled determination of the French to safeguard the existence of their group in the Northwest. There was in fact a fourth list, inspired, it would seem, by Bishop Taché, which added a request for a Senate and for denominational schools.[31]

While the delegates were absent on their journey to Ottawa the legislative assembly of the Provisional Government met twice, on March 23 to organize the government of "Assiniboia," a name now extended to the whole Northwest, and on April 26 to enact a code of laws. The institution of the new government ended the "martial law" which Riel had used so arbitrarily; from this point on the Provisional Government was civilian as it had not been before. The debates in the assembly reveal that the chief concerns of the people of Red River were the administration of justice, the liquor laws, prairie fires, and lands held only by custom of the country, in particular the two-mile "hay privilege" behind the river lots.[32] The President issued two proclamations to the people of the Northwest, informing them of the establishment of the Provisional Government and assuring them that their rights would be respected. The Portage Sioux were quieted with presents; the Hudson's Bay Company was permitted, indeed urged, to resume trading; and an American railway party of exploration from St.

Paul representing the Northern Pacific was given no political encouragement. As the hunters went out to the plains, and the winterers came in with their furs, life at Red River resumed its wonted rhythm.

In Ottawa the anger caused by the execution of Thomas Scott led to the arrest of Ritchot and Alfred Scott. When they were released, the three delegates were received, though not recognized, by Macdonald, Howe, and Cartier. After discussions which were brief but intense, as the Canadian ministers knew what they could give and what withhold, the "rights" of Assiniboia were embodied in a bill which was enacted on May 12, to come into force on proclamation. There was to be a new province with a Legislative Council and Assembly, a constitution similar to that of the old provinces, and representation in the Parliament of Canada. But it was to be a minute province, the old district of Assiniboia, which was only enlarged to include the Portage settlement on petition of Dr. J. S. Lynch, a Canadian from Red River, on behalf of settlers there, and at the insistence of the opposition. The vast remainder of the Northwest was to be a territory governed by Ottawa, and by Fort Garry. Thus was Riel's demand for provincehood at once granted and made almost a mockery. The public lands of the new province, contrary to Canadian precedent, were to be controlled by the federal government "for the purposes of the Dominion," namely, railway building and land settlement. And the name of the province, at Riel's suggestion, was to be, not the historic Assiniboia, but that of Thomas Spence's upstart government of 1868, Manitoba, the "Spirit Strait" of the Crees, the "Lake of the Prairies" of the Assiniboins. Manitoba, however, stood for self-government and a new beginning, and self-government had been one of the main demands of the people of Red River since 1846. A guarantee of land titles and a land grant of 1,400,000 acres to be allotted in reserves to the unmarried children of half-breed families dealt with the vexed land question. Provisions for the official use of the French language and a guarantee of the existence of the educational rights held by the various denominations "by law or practice at the union" perpetuated in the constitution of the new province the old duality of Red River and the balance of English and French nationality on which Confederation rested. The new province, the first of Canadian creation, embodied the old rivalry and the long co-existence of French and English in the Northwest. It embodied also the Red River Settlement, its mixed blood, its old-fashioned ways, and the rivalry of "old settler" and "Canadian." On July 15, the Act was proclaimed, and the legal existence of Manitoba began.

Though the Manitoba of the Manitoba Act was very different from the Assiniboia which the Provisional Government claimed to govern, the fact did not prevent the legislative assembly of the Provisional Government formally and indeed gladly accepting the Act when its terms were laid before it by Ritchot on his return to Red River.[33] Not even Riel dissented in any particular. The rights of the people of Red River, it was felt, had been vindicated and soundly established. It remained only to turn over the government of the country to the new governor from Canada.

Two great anxieties yet remained. One was the grant of an amnesty, the other the object of the military expedition already making its way to Red River over the old canoe route from Fort William. An amnesty was needed to conciliate French Canada, the expedition was necessary both to allay the anger of Ontario and to impress Americans and Indians. A general amnesty had previously been promised, on the condition that the insurgents would lay down their arms, by the Proclamation of the Governor-General, Sir John Young, on December 6, 1869. It had not been published by the Commissioners in Red River, however, as there was then no prospect of the insurrection stopping, and publication before the *métis* could lay down their arms would simply have forced them to be contumacious. Taché had received assurances in Ottawa that the Proclamation held good and would cover all cases, but that had been before the news of the shooting of Scott had reached Ontario. Schultz and his friends had quite deliberately whipped up an agitation in Ontario against "the murderers of Scott,"[34] and it was vital for Riel to know whether the amnesty would in fact cover responsibility for Scott's death.

Riel's anxiety was shown by the retention of a considerable force in Fort Garry, and the drilling of his men.[35] Ritchot, however, brought new assurances, and in June Bishop Taché took his fate in his hands and pledged his word to Riel that a complete and general amnesty had been promised.[36] Both Ritchot and Taché exceeded the assurances given them; both, it may be surmised, were misled by Cartier's jaunty assurance that he would get his way by hook or by crook. The storm of anger in Ontario, indeed, was making it impossible for the Canadian government to consign the shooting of Scott to legal oblivion. Taché's assurances nevertheless satisfied Riel; the garrison at Fort Garry was dismissed and the President of Assiniboia lived on in Fort Garry, comfortably ensconced in the gubernatorial furniture William McDougall had forwarded, surrounded by the members of his government and a few guards, waiting to yield peaceable possession of the Northwest to Canada's representative, the new governor, Adams G. Archibald.

This disposition was quite unknown to the men of the First Red River Expedition who were toiling over the portages west of Fort William. To the men of the 60th Rifles, Imperial troops who symbolized the United Kingdom's interest in the transfer, the great march was but another of those routine operations in far parts of the world which fell to the Imperial Army, another Abyssinian expedition. To the men of the Ontario Rifles, volunteers from the Ontario militia, it was an expedition to avenge the murder of Scott, and to the men of the Quebec Rifles, for the most part Ontario volunteers also, it was the same. The commander of the expedition, Colonel Garnet Wolseley, despite his proclamation that this was a mission of peace, took much the same view as the volunteers. Something of their temper was learned by Bishop Taché, and he therefore endeavoured to have Governor Archibald reach Red River, accept the transfer, and have civil government installed before the troops arrived. Archibald was to be met at the North West Angle of the Lake of the Woods by a party from Red River and taken overland by the road Snow had been building. But when the Lieutenant-Governor arrived there, no party was found, an omission by Taché and Riel which has never been explained, and he had perforce to follow the troops around by the Winnipeg River.

It was the troops, then, who reached Red River first; the Imperial regulars, moving up through the Lower Settlement, landed in drenching rain at Point Douglas on August 24. They advanced around the village of Winnipeg in skirmishing order, then dashed forward and occupied Fort Garry which they found sitting empty and silent. Riel, warned at the last minute of the temper of the expedition, had fled to St. Boniface and was soon on his way to the border. The Provisional Government he had reared on the military organization of the buffalo hunt was swept away by the military forces of the Crown. It had no legal basis in the eyes of the Canadian government, and Wolseley at once recognized the Hudson's Bay Company as the only existing government. For a few days before Archibald arrived Donald Smith was head of a reconstituted Company government. Thus all Riel's pretensions were overthrown as though they had never been.

It was perhaps a pity that the affair ended in this way. The Provisional Government had played some part in reconciling the differences of opinion which the transfer had created among the people of Red River and it had brought the *métis* to accept a union on terms with Canada. Some informal exchanges between Riel and Archibald would have ended the matter harmlessly and started the new régime on a basis of reconciliation. Bishop Machray and leading Red River people such as John Sutherland of Kildonan and A. G. B. Bannatyne had already done much to mollify the exasperation of both sides. They might have persuaded the English-speaking "old settlers," buffeted and neutral between the contending French and Canadians and angered by the shooting of Scott, to have tolerated such a show for the sake of peace. Riel, however, like Schultz before him, was not allowed to capture a governor, and Archibald came in on the bayonets which had sprung from the blood of Scott.

When the new Governor did arrive on September 2, he found the regular troops, their mission completed, preparing to return to Canada. He was to be left to govern the colony with the embers of the insurrection still warm beneath his feet; on the one hand, the Ontario volunteers in possession of Winnipeg and Fort Garry, on the other the still unbroken military organization of the buffalo hunt. He must listen to the insistent advice of Taché and employ the young men the Bishop had brought out from Quebec—Royal, Dubuc, Girard. He must hearken to the clamours of Schultz and the Canadian party for indemnity and revenge. Against the urgings of the French for amnesty rose the cry of the Ontario extremists for vengeance. Order had to be maintained while the volunteers fought with half-breeds in the saloons of Winnipeg, brawling which on at least one occasion ended in the unpunished killing of the *métis* Elzèar Goulet, and while Riel flitted through the French parishes and the buffalo hunters brooded in resentment. And beyond the limits of Manitoba and its welter of passions lay the vast Northwest, his to govern too, as Lieutenant-Governor of the North-West Territories, with its empty spaces, its wandering tribes, and its reckless traders.

Seldom had a Canadian statesman a more difficult task to perform. The tall, quiet Nova Scotian brought to his duties the qualities the circumstances required, dignity, courage, tolerance, and the slow temper of his native province. To keep the peace, to create the institution of executive and representative government, to treat with the Indians, to avoid falling into the hands of any party, these things required force and tact combined. How well Archibald was to succeed in this exacting task is perhaps declared by the fact that neither English nor French have adequately honoured his memory in the province he saved from the dangers which beset its foundation.

The Lieutenant-Governor at once began the work of organization. He appointed to his executive council Alfred Boyd of Redwood in St. John's parish, a merchant of English birth, and M. A. Girard, a young French Canadian sent out by Cartier. Commissions were issued to the magistrates and a small mounted police force recruited. A census was taken; the population of Manitoba was found to be 11,963, of whom 558 were Indians, 5,757 *métis*, 4,083 English half-breeds, and 1,565 whites. Catholics numbered 6,247 and Protestants 5,716.[37] Twenty-four electoral districts were formed from the parishes along the rivers and outlying settlements, twelve of which were French and twelve English. In December, 1870, the elections for the Legislative Assembly were held, and the members of the Legislative Council were appointed in March. In January the executive council had been enlarged to include Thomas Howard, a moderate Protestant from Quebec, H. J. Clarke, a Roman Catholic lawyer from Montreal, and James McKay, the famous plains guide from St. James parish and a Roman Catholic. Though it was to be known as the Clarke ministry, it was not a cabinet responsible to the legislature. The troubled conditions of the province and the lack of experience of parliamentary institutions among its people made it necessary for Archibald and his immediate successor to be their own prime ministers, to be, indeed, the "paternal despots" Sir John A. Macdonald had advised.[38] On March 15 the first legislature of Manitoba met in the house of A. G. B. Bannatyne, no public building being available, with a ceremonial guard drawn from the Ontario Rifles and with such other pomp as could be mustered. When the legislature was prorogued, the province was left in possession of a system of courts, a system of education, and a body of statute law sufficient for the needs of a yet small and simple community. The courts, moreover, were to be carefully modelled on those of Great Britain by the first chief justice, Alexander Morris,[39] and the statute law, after some use of Nova Scotian models by Archibald, on that of Ontario. The common law, of course, continued in force as before the transfer, and it was thus assured that the law of Manitoba would be English, not French.

Two things characterized Archibald's council and the legislature: the balance of French and English, Catholic and Protestant; and the exclusion, by both the Governor and the electors, of the two extremes in the late troubles, Schultz and the Canadian party, and Riel and the leaders of the Provisional Government. The Governor surrounded himself with moderate men, insisted that Riel keep in the background, and resisted both the public agitation and the private blandishments of Schultz. The great moderate majority of the "old settlers" exercised through the fran-

THE RED RIVER CART, 1862–3

Painting by W. G. R. Hind in the John Ross Robertson Collection

BREAKING PRAIRIE

Painting by E. Roper in the Public Archives of Canada

chise the power they could not exert in the days of armed insurrection. The Canadians were generally unpopular, and the men
of the Provisional Government were for the most part repudiated.
The policy of balance and moderation was defended in the *Manitoban*, a newspaper which succeeded the *New Nation* and was
the Lieutenant-Governor's official organ. That policy was justified
in the fall of 1871 when the Fenians threatened to invade the
province after the disbanding of the volunteer battalions of the
First Expedition. Both English and French volunteered to defend
the province, the former at once and as a whole, the French after
delay, but with few exceptions and under Riel's leadership.

When, however, Archibald welcomed their services and shook
hands with their leader—who was carefully not named—in a
famous scene at an inspection of the *métis* troops at St. Boniface, the
outcry from the Canadian party revealed that intense suspicion
between the two elements of the population remained. It would
so remain until the amnesty question was settled. Ontario sentiment demanded the arrest and trial of Riel and others responsible
for the shooting of Scott. Bishop Taché and Riel, holding that the
Provisional Government and its acts had been legal and had been
recognized as such, and holding also that an unqualified amnesty
had been promised, were angered that Riel and his associates had
to remain concealed in their parishes or in exile at St. Joseph's
across the boundary on the Pembina River. The harassed federal
government, torn between its Quebec and Ontario supporters,
insisted the matter was an Imperial responsibility, as technically
it was. There could be no peace in Manitoba if the amnesty were
granted, none if it were denied. Macdonald tried to avoid trouble
by paying Riel to stay out of the country. Archibald had to retire
because he had accepted Riel's services, and his successor, Alexander Morris, played for time.

In 1874, however, a number of events brought the issue to a
head. Riel, after having repeatedly stood aside for other candidates, insisted on running for election in the federal district
of Provencher and was returned, but was not allowed to take his
seat. Warrants had been obtained in 1873 from a sympathetic
local magistrate for the arrest of Riel and Ambroise Lépine, and

Lépine had been taken into custody. In 1874 the trial and conviction of Lépine for the murder of Scott brought to an end the long attempt to smother the implications of the rising of 1869. The Manitoba court and the Imperial authorities could not but hold that the Provisional Government had, and could have had, no legal basis, since under the British constitution all executive authority emanates from the Crown.[40] The acts of the insurgents in stopping McDougall and setting up a provisional government had not been directed against the authority of the Crown, and might be held not to be rebellious or treasonable; but in the light of all the circumstances, deliberate trial and execution of a fellow subject by such a government, and still more, by the military organization of the *métis*, was not to be covered by a similar plea. The custom of the buffalo hunt was neither the custom of an indigenous tribe, nor the law of the land. For the death of Scott, therefore, those responsible had to be punished, but in view of the political nature of their offence, justice might be tempered with mercy. Lépine's death-sentence was commuted by the Governor-General to two years' imprisonment and forfeiture of civil rights.

The government of Alexander Mackenzie perforce appointed a Select Committee of Enquiry in the House of Commons into the events of 1869–70 in the Northwest. By resolution of the House of Commons following the Report of the Select Committee, a full amnesty was granted to all participants in the troubles, except Riel, Lépine, and W. B. O'Donoghue. To Riel and Lépine amnesty was to be granted, conditional on five years' banishment; and later the banishment of O'Donoghue was also limited.

With this, the amnesty question and Riel pass out of the history of Manitoba. But the fundamental issue of the troubles, the relation of French and English in Canada and in Manitoba, was assuming a new form. The establishment of civil government in September, 1870, had seen a renewal of claim-staking, and in 1871 an influx of settlers from Ontario began. Not until 1874 was it to be rivalled, and then by a much smaller flow of French Canadians from Massachusetts. Steadily the balance of population turned against the French. Steadily the old settlers, both

French and English, were outnumbered by the new, almost wholly until 1874 from Ontario.

The principle of duality was imperilled politically also. In 1874 trouble arose over a bill to alter the electoral districts so as to give some representation to the new settlers. The Canadian settlers were also critical of the dual school system, Catholic and Protestant, established in 1871. They protested against the official use of the French language and the maintenance of a Legislative Council in the tiny province when Ontario did without one. This agitation resulted in the fall, first, of the administration of H. J. Clarke, and then of the brief M. A. Girard ministry, both in 1874. The resultant administration of R. A. Davis reflected the shifting balance of population, although Davis and his colleague, John Norquay, were careful to compromise:[41] the division of school funds was made proportionate to the numbers of Roman Catholic and Protestant children, but the "old settlers" electoral districts were spared. It was well that this moderate temper prevailed, for Lieutenant-Governor Morris was now treating his ministers as his responsible advisers. Hard times and the need of economy in government enforced the Canadian protests, and when in 1875 Prime Minister Mackenzie granted increased federal aid to the struggling province, it was on condition that the Legislative Council be abolished. In 1876 this was accomplished, and the modification of the constitution of 1870 and of the principle of duality embodied by the growing weight of Ontario settlers in the electorate had begun. The French of Manitoba, said Hon. Joseph Royal, did not oppose the abolition of the Council, as they relied on the guarantees of the British North America Act;[42] that is, they were henceforth dependent for the special position of their group in Manitoba on the courts and the political weight of Quebec in Confederation.

Meantime, the weight of numbers passed steadily from the French to the English, from the old settlers to the new, as the newcomers in search of homesteads followed the surveyors out along the trails the buffalo hunters and the freighters had traced. Even the English "old settlers" began that withdrawal into themselves before the aggressive newcomers which was to keep many of them, for years to come, a race apart. The old order was remembered with some wistfulness:

> O, for the times that some despise,
> At least I liked them, me whatever,
> Before the Transfer made us wise
> Or politics had made us clever.

And the tilt of the balance was quickened as the half-breeds, French and some English, in growing numbers abandoned their lots or sold the scrip titles to land issued under the Manitoba Act, and followed the dwindling buffalo herds to the still empty plains and the unoccupied river fronts of the Saskatchewan. The many who remained withdrew into themselves on the old riverside farms. The *métis*, as the militant element of the native population of the old Northwest, had won a victory for their land rights, language, and faith. This victory had been consolidated in the Manitoba Act. They had not, however, won a victory for their mode of life. The old order by which they had lived was disintegrating before the inflow of Ontario settlers and the rise of a new society founded on agriculture, the railway, and the complex commerce of the nineteenth century.

7

The New Pattern of Settlement
1871-1875

IN 1871 THE RED RIVER SETTLEMENT, NOW THE
Province of Manitoba, was about to be inundated in a new kind
of settlement. Sprung from the infield and outfield of old Scotland, from the river "ranges" of Quebec, mediaeval in its far
origins, and sanctioned by the slow life of fifty years of Red River
history, the old framework of the Red River community of farmer
and hunter was to be submerged and dissolved in a flood of eager
land seekers, each desirous of a separate homestead. Yet the old
Red River survey was to survive the passing of village agriculture
and the plains hunt, to form the basis of the new settlements which
grew up beyond the river lots.

By 1871 the various settlements of old Red River had occupied
the bank of the lower Red from Netley Creek to the Assiniboine.
From the Indian settlement at St. Peter's to the village of Winnipeg, the river front was solidly occupied, and the farmsteads of
the half-breeds and the Orkney and Kildonan Scottish settlers
presented an almost unbroken line along the west bank. In the
rear of the houses and riverside fields ran the highway across the
lots, passing over the creeks by rude timber bridges and "cordu-
roy" grades. The houses were fewer on the east bank, but at Cook's
Creek and Bird's Hill settlement had begun. The parish of St.
John's abutted on Winnipeg and the Hudson's Bay reserve at
Fort Garry, which extended from the Red to Colony Creek and
from the Assiniboine to the Saskatchewan, or Portage, Trail.
Opposite the mouth of the Assiniboine was St. Boniface, centring

on the cathedral; to the south up the Red the dwellings of the *métis* clustered in the deep woods of the river loops of St. Vital. South again St. Norbert spread out on either side of the crossing of the Rivière Sale, and beyond, along the riverside trail to Pembina, Ste. Agathe was taking shape.

Up the Assiniboine from Fort Garry, the quiet English settlements of St. James and Holy Trinity (Headingley) had slowly established themselves in the hardwood fringe of the river. Between them the small French parish of St. Charles with its chapel had arisen in the sixties, and perpetuated the name La Vérendrye had bestowed on the Assiniboine. Beyond, on the edge of the White Horse Plain, stretched the larger St. François-Xavier, home of Cuthbert Grant and centre of the White Horse Plain hunt. Lane's Post at Pigeon Lake, a Hudson's Bay establishment, and Baie St. Paul, a French and Indian settlement, prolonged the Assiniboine settlements westward towards the Portage settlements. These were English half-breed settlements, with a handful of Canadians come in since 1860. All were threaded together by the Saskatchewan Trail which followed the north bank of the Assiniboine. Beyond Portage the Trail forked, the South Trail running to Rat Creek and the edge of the Manitoba Escarpment at the "Bad Woods," the North Trail to the crossings of the Whitemud River. At Rat Creek a few Canadians along with Kenneth McKenzie had taken up claims and begun to farm in 1868 and 1869.

These, except the last, were the river-front settlements in what the surveyors were to call the Settlement Belt, and in which the river-lot survey was to survive, embedding the old pattern of Red River life among the square survey sections of the new order. Beyond the Belt were a few scattered settlements—fishing stations and cattle-grazing camps for the most part. At the southeast curve of Lake Manitoba was St. Laurent, a fishing station and also the point where travellers Saskatchewan-bound took to the water or the ice of Lakes Manitoba and Winnipegosis. At the mouth of the Whitemud River, just off the North Saskatchewan Trail, a fishing station had been established in 1858 by the Portage people and named Westbourne. At Grand Marais on the southeast shore of Lake Winnipeg was another fishing station, which, however, was not yet a permanent settlement. Southeast from St. Boniface, where the Seine emerged from the ridges and forests of the eastern highlands into a land of meadows and oak groves, *métis* had settled in the late fifties at Oak Point, and the mission of Ste. Anne-des-Chênes had been founded. The settlers here were hunters, turning farmers and graziers under the leadership of the church and in response to the rich, broad grasslands. A similar settlement had begun to develop where the Pembina trail from Headingley crossed the Rivière aux Ilets de Bois. In 1871 its lands were the occasion of a conflict between the *métis* and immigrants.

This episode was typical of settlement at that time and of the basic issues of the land question. Up to 1870, no settlement had been made away from the river fronts, with the partial exception of that at Portage la Prairie. The Red River farmsteads lined the water front, for there water and wood were available. No one had settled out on the prairies. It was believed in Red River that water could not be reached by sinking wells on the plains. There was no wood for fuel, building, or fencing. In consequence, the old settlers and the new sought to establish claims to the river fronts of the tree-lined streams, and passed over the "main prairie" indifferently.

The Rivière aux Ilets de Bois was such a stream. It rose in the heavily wooded Assiniboine Delta lands south of Portage la Prairie, wound through the meadows, marshes, and bluffs (*îlets de bois*) north of the Pembina Mountain, and lost itself in a great marsh in the flat lands west of the Red. In the hardwood groves along its banks, long used for sugaring by the people of St. François-Xavier, were shelter, fuel, and timber. The river lay on the route to the plains of the main river party of the buffalo hunt. The soil was fertile and would yield heavily of potatoes and barley. It had long been noted as a camping ground, and here in 1868 a number of *métis* from Montana staked claims, according to the custom of the country that natives might take and use land no one else had claimed.[1] In July, 1871, a body of Ontario land seekers, attracted by the fertility and advantages of the site, ignored the signs of *métis* occupation and staked their own claims. The *métis* on their return from the plains protested indignantly and organized to eject the newcomers. Only the intervention of Governor Archibald prevented an open struggle for possession. In the end the *métis* gave way and the newcomers remained undisturbed on their farms by the stream they had defiantly renamed the Boyne.

The land question, as this episode suggests, was the fundamental issue of the times. Whoever possessed the soil would give the new province their language, faith, and laws. Within the District of Assiniboia land had been held by one of two means: a lease from the Hudson's Bay Company as lords of the soil, and squatters' right, validated by long possession and acknowledged by the custom of the country. Possession of land acquired by squatting was acknowledged by the government and courts of Assiniboia. On transfer by sale, compensation was for improvements only. When a new claim was taken, it was sufficient to indicate intention by staking, a practice of which Canadian settlers had taken advantage in the absence of surveys and a land law.

Such possession did not make for certainty for two reasons: the Charter of the Hudson's Bay Company had been assailed, and the Indian title had not been extinguished, except in the Settlement Belt by Selkirk's purchase of 1817, and even there doubtfully. The Manitoba Act had confirmed Hudson's Bay titles and prescriptive titles; it had granted 1,400,000 acres, yet to be located, to the children, unmarried, of half-breed families. It did not, however, deal with recent squatters' claims or staked claims, and, of course, it did not extinguish the Indian title. That must await a treaty. Thus there was plenty of room for disputes over land even after the Manitoba Act was passed.

There was yet another uncertain claim in the "hay privilege," the exclusive right to cut hay on a two-mile extension of the river lots. It was a valuable right in the Red River economy and the settlers now sought to ensure it in perpetuity by converting their customary right into full ownership. The Legislative Council of Assiniboia had so decreed, but the Manitoba Act did not deal with the hay privilege, and it remained a source of anxiety to the old settlers until it was conceded in 1877.

The new administration, however, was moving with all possible speed to quiet fears and to ensure that the land rush would be peaceful and orderly. In 1871 by Treaty No. 1, negotiated by Commissioner Wemyss Simpson and Governor Archibald at the Lower Fort with the Ojibways and the Crees, all the lands of Manitoba and a band to the north and west were ceded by the Indians to the Queen in right of Canada in return for reserves, annual presents, and money payments. Though it gave rise to disputes over the meaning of the "outside promises," the Treaty did at last extinguish the Indian title to the lands of the original Province. The land surveys, so brusquely interrupted in 1869, were resumed in the summer of 1871, and were pushed with such speed that by 1873 all Manitoba was divided into the square survey of townships six miles square and sections one mile square with ninety-nine foot "road allowances" between all sections. The river lots of all the old settlements were resurveyed and fitted into the new survey, and titles issued.

With this simple system imposed on the Red River valley and the western highlands, it was possible to begin the work of locating the half-breed reserves, and great blocks of individual and combined townships were reserved from settlement and held for occupation or sale by the children of half-breed families; after 1877 this privilege was extended to the heads of families, and to old settlers of white blood also. In all, 2,448,160 acres of Manitoba land was granted to the old settlers of all kinds. Thus the grievances and uncertainties respecting land were diminished or settled. Special cases, such as the conflicting claims to the Winnipeg Common on Point Douglas, were settled by the courts. Land unaffected by pre–1870 claims and not designated as reserves, the great remainder of the province, was available for grants as homesteads under the Dominion Lands Act of 1872, or as grants to railways. Some, of course, had to be set aside for the Hudson's Bay Company and some was reserved as school lands; in practice, a section and three-quarters in every four townships and two sections in every fifth for the Company, and two sections in every township for schools.

The old settlements, the new claims, the various uncertainties, the half-breed reserves, all influenced the direction and progress

of settlement, holding one district empty and causing another to
be filled. The selection of a route for the Pacific railway, the great
undertaking which was to complete the transcontinental federation of British North America, also affected the direction and
increased the speculative element in settlement. Lands on or near
the route would obviously be of greater value than those more
distant. Only one thing was certain, that the railway must cross
the new province. The question was, where? At first the surveyors
recommended a route south of Lake Manitoba and the prospect
pulled settlers westward from Winnipeg to the Portage and the
Whitemud River. Then came delay and uncertainty with the
Pacific Scandal of 1873 and the fall of the Macdonald government, and not until 1874 was it announced that the railway would
cross the Red River below the Lower Fort and run northwestward
between Lakes Winnipeg and Manitoba to cross the Narrows of
the latter. That meant that railways in the Red River valley and
the highlands would be branch lines and that settlement could be
scattered.

The settlement of the old land claims and the taking up of new
land were carried on during the resumption of the Ontario migration in 1871. In that province Manitoba had been well advertised
by the troubles of 1869. Many of the volunteers came to see the
country; many remained when the militia battalions were disbanded in the spring of 1871. Everyone in Ontario had heard of
the new frontier, with its prairie land which held neither stone
nor stump to check the plough. Farmers on the thin soil of the
Precambrian Shield in Lanark County, farmers hemmed in by
the waters of Huron in Bruce and Huron counties, men with large
families for whom to find farms, the hard pressed, the adventurous, all listened to the reports of deep soil to be had cheaply, of
a climate where wheat throve free of midge and smut. Already
thousands of Ontario farmers had moved to the prairies of the
mid-western United States; now hundreds decided to seek the
prairies of Manitoba. In 1871, by the newly opened Dawson route
and by Lake Superior and the railway to Red River, the first
"parties" came to Fort Garry, a name only slowly yielding to that
of Winnipeg. The parties had been organized in the home town-

ship in Ontario, or made up on the way: the *Manitoba Weekly Free Press*, for example, reported on May 22, 1875: "A short time ago a meeting was held in Southampton, Ontario, to consider the proposal to form an organization for planting a colony in Manitoba."[2] The men left the womenfolk and household goods in Winnipeg and drove through the country near by or far out on the trails to make their location. When they had found a site to their liking, they returned to Winnipeg for families and outfits, and with horse team or oxen and waggon box covered with canvas, set out for the homestead.

Some chose to settle on the prairie lands northeast and northwest from Winnipeg. First and largest of these peripheral settlements in the rear of the river lots was Springfield, soon to be followed by Sunnyside to the east.[3] The two townships lay to the south of Bird's Hill and Pine Ridge, divided on the north by the wooded protuberance of the Moose Head. The broad sweep of the prairie southward invited the plough and the mower, while the oak bluffs of the ridges and the poplar and spruce of the hills gave assurance of shelter and wood for all purposes. Other settlers struck northwest across the prairies to Stony Mountain and its surrounding limestone ridges and oak bluffs, succinctly described in the new name of Rockwood. It was a region as inviting as Springfield but open to the north and less sharply defined by hill and ridge. Still others went eastwards from Winnipeg to found settlements at Prairie Grove and Clear Springs, some simply turning off from the Dawson Road.[4]

To many the Canadian settlements at Portage and Rat Creek proved an attraction, and they took the Saskatchewan Trail to join their compatriots in those settlements, or pushed beyond to choose sites on the wooded banks of the Whitemud River. In 1871 the party led by Walter Lynch settled at the three crossings of the North Trail on the Whitemud. Others struck south from Headingley along the trail to St. Joseph's and found on the Rivière aux Ilets de Bois the sites of their choice, not, as has been seen, without trouble. But the St. Paul Trail along the Red, crossed as it was by French settlements, did not at first attract Ontario immigrants.

In the next three years the new settlements grew steadily, as long as claims with sufficient timber on them lasted. No one yet was prepared to settle on the open prairie, not even on the Portage plains, without access to wood and running water. The settlements were additions to and extensions of the old pattern of Red River Settlement, and were controlled by the same element, the desirability, verging on necessity, of having wood lot and water front. All could also hope to be on or near the route of the Pacific railway.

Not everyone, however, could find a suitable site in these few settlements on the fringes of the old pattern, and in 1874 the dispersion of settlement over the lands untouched by Red River colonization began. In that year a colonization party from Michigan and Wisconsin was organized to take up the two townships east of the Red on the border. The Emerson settlement was thus begun,[5] throve immediately, and became a point of dispersion for settlers pushing east, or more often west, along the trails the International Boundary Commission had marked out in 1873.[6] In the same year Ontario settlement began at Scratching River on the St. Paul Trail south of the last French settlement at Ste. Agathe, and the town of Morris was founded.[7]

Thus two lines of approach to the region of the Pembina Mountain had been opened: the old one from the north by Headingley and the new Boyne Settlement, the new one across the prairies of the west Red River valley from Emerson or Morris to the foot of the Pembina Escarpment. On the wooded creeks that cut across the two ranges of townships extending along the lower slopes of the Escarpment small settlements began, which in their first years were collectively called Pembina Mountain. These dispersed and isolated colonies were united with the older settlements only by the Pembina Trail to Headingley, a trail much subject to floods. It was difficult in the early years of settlement to obtain either supplies or news, as many letters of complaint in the Winnipeg press still testify. The first homesteaders, however, had found the most favoured lands of Manitoba in climate, fertility, and beauty, and were forming below the long, blue front of the Escarpment a base from which the rolling uplands would be occupied.

The Ontario immigration had been almost the only movement into the province from 1871 to 1874, though there had, of course, been some settlers from the Eastern Townships of Quebec, from the Maritimes, and the British Isles. It had the effect, therefore, of continuing the duality of language and faith with which Manitoba began, but it weighed down the balance in favour of the English tongue and the Protestant faith. The years 1874 and 1875, however, saw the beginning of "group" colonization and the introduction of settlers who were neither French nor English. The Ontario immigrants were a distinct group in that they were readily identifiable by speech and manner as "Canadians." They had come, however, as individuals, or in parties organized by themselves. Moreover, they had come to obtain, without aid or direction, the best individual farm each could find for himself; no townships were reserved for Canadian or British settlers. For the other groups, who would be minorities among the English-speaking majority, ethnic islands in a Canadian sea, blocks of land were reserved by the federal government, as they had been for the half-breeds. The racial compromise which lay at the foundation of the new federal state, the right of a defined minority to preserve its identity, had been extended to Manitoba by the Manitoba Act. The logic of that compromise was now being carried into land settlement, consciously or unconsciously— in part, at least, merely to attract prospective settlers away from the United States—and with significant consequences for the future of the new province.

The first to begin group settlement were, of course, the French. The necessity of safeguarding the land rights of the *métis*, the need of close settlement for parish life, the certainty of the French becoming a minority before the influx from Ontario, had inspired the safeguards for language and church schools and the half-breed reserves in the Manitoba Act. The next necessity was to strengthen the French element in Manitoba by bringing in educated men to lead the group and French Canadian farmers to take up land with the *métis* in the reserves. The hope of immigration to Manitoba from Quebec was soon disappointed. The Church in Quebec was not certain that it was not best to hold fast by Quebec and continue to take over the Eastern Townships and press back the forest frontier to the north. A French Colonization Aid Society was therefore organized in St. Boniface, and at a later date another in Montreal,[8] partly to encourage migration from Quebec, but more especially to bring back to Canadian soil the French attracted since the 1850's to the factories of Massachusetts. New reserves were obtained on the Red at what was to become Letellier and in 1875 the first settlers from Massachusetts arrived.[9] Others from the same place and some from Quebec joined the *métis* who were opening the new settlements at what were to become the parishes of St. Pierre-Jolys and St. Malo to the eastward on Rat River. Still others went to the old settlements at Ste. Anne-des-Chênes and Ile-des-Chênes. The area east of the Red and south of the Seine, the federal electoral district of Provencher, would not, it was hoped, lose its French character but would remain a French territorial bloc. But around these French settlements Ontario settlers pressed, sometimes with trouble as the result, as over the reserves at Letellier,[10] sometimes with a developing good neighbourliness, as at Caledonia east of Winnipeg. There Rev. George Bryce of Manitoba College was to speak on "What we need to make a strong Canadian nationality" to an audience consisting of forty-eight from Ontario, thirty-one Manitoban born, ten from Scotland, ten from Quebec, three from England, four from Ireland, three from the United States, and one each from France and Nova Scotia.[11]

Any hope that the southeast of the province might be wholly French, indeed, was ended when in 1874 the first Mennonite reserve was formed in the townships north and east of Rat River. The Russian colonies of the Mennonite sect, of a simple, quietist, and pacificist faith, had been deeply disturbed by the revocation by the Russian Imperial Government of their exemption from compulsory military service. Some decided to emigrate, and sent emissaries to the United States and Canada to seek new lands like their own on the south Russian steppes and guarantees of the quiet enjoyment of their religious tenets. The Canadian government welcomed the approaches of this sturdy farmer folk, and by order-in-council issued in 1873 promised religious freedom, exemption from military service, and their church schools "so far as the law allowed." Guided by their co-religionist from Ontario, Jacob Shantz, the Mennonite emissaries visited Manitoba in 1873 and were moved by the prospect of countryside and soil so like that of the steppes to ask that a reserve be set aside for a colony of their people. This was done and in August, 1874, the first party of Mennonites arrived in Winnipeg, and outfitted themselves to go to the reserve.[12] Their Low German speech, strange dress, and sharp haggling caused some comment, but the gold in which they paid for their many purchases silenced all doubts in Winnipeg, where business had been slow. After a hard winter spent in primitive shelters, the new settlers began to show their mettle as pioneers on prairie land. The cellar dwelling, the Russian stove fired with twisted grass and cakes of cow dung, the agricultural village, the practice of summer fallow, the culture of flax, were immediate contributions of the Mennonites to life in the parkland.

Fresh parties in successive years helped to people the reserve and in 1876 a new one was established west of Red River, along the border toward the Pembina Mountain settlements. The country was tall grass prairie and here the Mennonites first completely demonstrated their capacity for living and thriving on the open plain. To this "west reserve" the later parties largely came, and some groups moved from the less favoured "east reserve." They imposed on the square survey, designed for individual homesteads, the pattern of the agricultural village they had carried from the early modern Netherlands to Prussia and Russia. They set trees around the close-grouped dwellings, house in front and barn behind, and soon the prairie horizon was broken by clustered *dörfer* and springing cottonwoods. Old Europe had sent forth one more organic community to take root in the New World, one founded fast not only on an immemorial peasant way of life but also on a much-enduring religious faith. These simple and sturdy folk, not without suffering and heavy labour, were soon masters of their new-old environment and prosperous in self-sufficient plenty. Like the bulk of the Ontario settlers, they had been well-to-do farmers in their homeland, and had a modest amount of capital. This was augmented by loans from the federal government and their co-religionists in Ontario, which enabled them to begin farming at once on a considerable scale.[13]

Not so fortunate was the next group to vary and extend the ethnic composition of Manitoba. In the Icelanders the new province was to receive a group as deeply marked by their singular and isolated history as the Mennonites were by their faith. To their stark homeland and stormy seas the Icelanders had remained faithful through nine centuries of hard living and natural disaster. Now a few venturesome spirits were writing home of the land and waters of that America their ancestors, first of Europeans, had discovered. In 1873 Mount Hecla erupted and buried miles of pasture beneath a flood of lava and a drift of ash. The people were now too many for the remaining land, and some must break the bond which held them to a home the dearer for its harshness. They sought a country as like the old as possible, in which the pastoralist could graze his herds over broad acres and the fisherman cast his nets in wide waters. By the chance of Governor-General Lord Dufferin's affection for Iceland, their attention was directed to Canada. The first comers were not satisfied in the Muskoka district of Ontario, and in 1875, guided by Rev. John Taylor of Muskoka, their prospectors came to Manitoba. The party directed its search to the west shore of Lake Winnipeg beyond the northern boundary of Manitoba, and at Willow Point in a broad bay with white sand beaches, they chose a site for their colony.

In the fall of the year the first party came, to the number of two hundred and eighty-five.[14] They came with the stark pride of their race, the fierce shyness of the northerner, their tools, their books and their love of letters, and little else. These were people who must wrest by native wit and stubborn will every material thing, food, field, house, and furniture, from the raw bushland and turbid waters of their new home. The first winter was to be bitter, with short rations and long snowbound nights in damp log shanties, before spring loosened the ice on Winnipeg. Yet as the flatboats which had brought them down the Red and across Upper Winnipeg turned slowly into the bay, they had responded, as all settlers did, to the exciting promise of new land and named the colony "Gimli," which in the decadent language of the English means "Paradise."[15]

Icelander and Mennonite ended the duality of the ethnic composition of Manitoba. Both were Protestant, the Icelanders being Lutheran by faith, yet each group was distinct and exclusive, the Icelander by tradition, the Mennonite by faith. The former had come to create a New Iceland, the latter to find a new haven from the world. Both would have to meet the challenges of an individualistic and commercial society in a region which was a continental crossroads and was soon to prove itself one of the great farmlands of the world. Yet even if Icelanders and Mennonites blended with English or French, or both, the result would be, as the population grew with immigration, an amalgam not English, French, Icelandic, or Mennonite. Nor were these the only elements of the amalgam; the population of Red River had from the first been very mixed and immigrants of other nationalities were coming to Manitoba. In 1871, for example, a German Society had been organized in Winnipeg by local Germans. Uniformity of language and culture could at best be only an ideal, while duality had become even more unlikely, and plurality the working rule for an indefinite time. But plurality indefinitely multiplied would imperil duality and lead, by an inevitable paradox, to uniformity. The new province was committed to an experiment in the making of a community which its founders had scarcely foreseen.

The separate colonies in a yet scantily peopled land suggested little as yet of these consequences for the future. All settlers of whatever origin were laboriously engaged in "getting started" in their new homes. The procedure was much the same everywhere, the Ontario settler, individualist though he was, matching the community work of the Mennonites by the "bees" of his native province, gatherings of neighbours to raise a house, break a field, or thresh a crop. The first weeks on the homestead might be spent under the waggon or under canvas according to season. The first work was to plough a field in the prairie sod—potatoes might even be planted if the settler were on the land early enough—or to get out logs to build a house. It was soon found that Ontario ploughs did poor work in the heavy clay and tough sod of the Red River valley. American ploughs designed for the work, especially the "John Deere" with its chilled steel mouldboard, were indispensable. The sod was turned in shallow furrows to rot, and usually was "backset" at a deeper level before sowing the following spring to turn up a loose soil for a seed bed. The house was built of poplar logs, with oak for a foundation. Ontario men were skilled in the use of the broad axe and hewed the sides to a smoothness marked only by the bite of the axe cutting the chips. As long logs could be obtained in the new settlements, the old Red River frame method of building was discarded for the speedier "notch and saddle." Rafters and cross pieces of poles reared the roof over the gables built up of logs, and thatch of straw or "thatch grass" furnished a roof both warm and dry. Lumber was usually available for the flooring of ground floor and attic, but a hasty and hardy bachelor might make do on the virgin sod. These tasks were the necessities if winter were to be weathered and the new year started on time. Winter itself gave time for wood-cutting, hauling supplies, buying stock, and the "socials" and dances which gave relief to the labour and loneliness of the pioneer.

When the fields cleared of snow and the soil softened in the spring, the first season's sowing was usually done by broadcasting. Mechanical seed drills were already in use in Kildonan and at Portage, but in the out-settlements the seeder strode his first rough acres scattering seed to right and left in the immemorial way. The breaking of more land followed in late June and early July. Oxen were usually employed in the first years, because they could work better than horses with no fodder to supplement their grazing. Not until oats were in good supply was it advisable to abandon dogged Buck and Bright for the quicker, more tractable horse. Haying was sometimes done by scything and hand raking, but mechanical mowers and rakers were the earliest and most numerous machines brought into Red River. Their use was widespread because of the great dependence of both old and new settlers on the natural meadows for hay to carry the livestock through the long winter. When August had ripened the wheat, scythe and cradle were in almost universal use; mechanical reapers there were, but not many. The hand-bound sheaves were "shocked" or "stooked," and then hauled in cart or waggon to the barnyard or some dry knoll to be stacked. The flail was used on many a makeshift threshing floor in the new settlements, and the grain winnowed when the wind was right, but threshing machines driven with horses by means of a capstan roundabout were in use in most settlements. The owners did custom-threshing from farm to farm into the late fall, and in early spring.

The crops were fenced by post and rail in those early days as they had been in Red River. The supply of these was another demand on the sparse timber of the bluffs and riverside. Cattle ran at large and the soft clang of the cow bell and the call of "co-boss" were familiar sounds along the lines of settlement. Some few farmers experimented with ditch-fencing and hedges, but most could only view with concern the day when rails would be too few and fields too large.

The truth was that in the years from 1871 to 1875 the new settlers had not overcome the limitations of Red River farming. Like the old settlers they were bound to the river fronts by the need for wood and water. They lacked the equipment with which to farm the prairies. In the machines which were being brought into the country in increasing numbers, and in the railways which were so eagerly anticipated, were the means by which commercial farming on the tall grass prairies and the meadows of the park belt would be possible. The pioneers of the early seventies were holding advanced positions, secure in their choice of site, but dependent on the progress of the railways to reward their boldness.

The new settlements of 1871–5, except those along Pembina Mountain, were merely extensions of the river-front settlements. They belonged still to the old order, though nourishing the seed of the new. The same observation applied to the still unrivalled focus of the expanding settlements, the village of Winnipeg. Its growth, it is true, was more rapid; a village of 100 in the spring of 1871, by the fall of 1875 it had been for almost two years an incorporated city, and its population had risen to the number of some five thousand persons. This rapid growth is to be explained by the fact that Winnipeg and Fort Garry—the two were rapidly merging—remained as in Red River days the seat of government and centre of commerce for the whole Northwest. Ottawa had not yet taken from Fort Garry sway over the traders and tribes of the plains and northern forest; Archibald was Lieutenant-Governor of the North-West Territories as well as of Manitoba, two offices in one person, and his successor, Morris, held both offices until 1876. In that year the North-West Territories were given a separate government but the District of Keewatin was created to afford some government to the unbounded wilderness north and east of Manitoba, and placed under the Lieutenant-Governor of that province. The government of a growing province. small though it was, greatly exceeded in volume and importance the petty business of the District of Assiniboia. In Winnipeg, too, was the first Dominion Lands Office in the West, which handled the large and vexatious business of adjusting the titles of old inhabitants, administering the half-breed reserves, and registering the claims of new settlers. There the Canadian garrison was stationed, at Upper and Lower Fort Garry until the Fort Osborne barracks were completed in 1872. When the Quebec and Ontario volunteers were disbanded in 1871, they were replaced late in that year by the Provisional Battalion of Ontario militia, and Ontario militia remained in garrison until 1877. The troops were a prominent element in the social life of the little frontier town until their duties were assumed by North West Mounted Police and local militia companies.

It was not, however, so much as the seat of government and a garrison town that Winnipeg continued to play and expand the old role of Fort Garry in the Northwest. As the village of Winnipeg, foundation of the free traders, was absorbing Fort Garry, seat of government and commercial monopoly, so the growth of Winnipeg as commercial centre exceeded and quite overshadowed its growth as political capital of Manitoba. It was to Winnipeg that the traders and land speculators flocked, it was there that the settlers bought their outfits, and it was Winnipeg that continued to be the one place in the Red River valley known in the outside world. The plains traders still brought the long lines of their cart brigades there in mid-summer, and the freight brigades creaked forth from it to Fort Ellice, Carlton, and distant Edmonton. This was no provincial city, but an emporium, a metropolis, driving a prosperous trade still, not only in furs and robes but also in the equipping of the new farms which in a few years would pour a stream of grain and stock eastward through the Winnipeg market.

Until 1875, in the blending of old and new by the growing commerce of Winnipeg, the old continued to dominate. The fur trade remained the chief business of the city. The Hudson's Bay Company continued its great annual outfits as in the past. Its cart brigades were prominent among those on the Saskatchewan Trail. The York boats still swung down stream from the Lower Fort in June and in the fall put in from York Factory. The Company, however, was beginning to replace them with steamboats on Lake Winnipeg, first with the S.S. *Chief Commissioner*, and then with the S.S. *Colvile*. Plans were afoot for steamboats on the Saskatchewan, which would reduce the cost of west-bound freight. The old private traders, especially A. G. B. Bannatyne, maintained a vigorous trade with the plains. Many newcomers entered the field, notably the firm of Kew, Eden and Company, which as Stobart, Eden and Company was to become, next to the great Company, the largest dealer in furs and robes in the West.[16]

Yet none of these firms or their competitors confined themselves to the fur trade. They all had retail stores in Winnipeg and some were beginning to supply the merchants of the new settlements. Even the Hudson's Bay Company prepared to enter the retail and wholesale business and compete for the growing trade of Winnipeg and the rising settlements with merchant firms such as that of Higgins and Young, which, having begun in a small way as retailers, were becoming wholesalers also. This versatility was appropriate to a period of rapid transition from a fur to an agricultural economy, and reached its climax when some of these firms became the first grain buyers of Winnipeg.

The commerce of Winnipeg, then, rested still on the fur trade but anticipated the development of agriculture. Accordingly, much of the business of Winnipeg was in real estate. There was a lively business in advertising the qualities of Manitoban land, in informing and directing land seekers, in arranging sales of land and scrip, and in buying on speculation both town lots and farm lands. There was from 1871 to 1873 a mild boom in Winnipeg lots and in well-situated agricultural lands. This declined with the general depression in 1874 and 1875, but by 1876 the great boom of 1880–1 was beginning to gather way. Conditions were not ripe before 1875 for a major boom and early real estate men like A. W. Burrows of Ottawa and E. Brokovski of Toronto spent much time and effort to little avail in extolling the future of the great Northwest. In the depression years people were not disposed to move in sufficient numbers to drive up land values rapidly.

It was in real estate, however, that the great fortunes would be made, and even before 1875 much money was being sunk in Manitoba lands. Much also was being invested in homesteads and farm outfits, much in building, some in government services, roads, bridges, and buildings, more still in goods, machinery, livestock, and all the necessities of a new community, even the basic foodstuffs the new farms could not yet supply in sufficient quantity. Some indication of the inflow of capital is gained from noting the steady excess of the value of imports over exports at the Port of Winnipeg in these years, $1,037,185 in 1872, $671,353 in 1873, $634,351 in 1874.[17] Some of the capital import is glimpsed in the Mennonite gold, in the statements that such and such a settler brought in so much capital in money or livestock. Nearly all this capital passed through the hands of Winnipeg business men, and financial facilities were soon needed. The first to supply them were the Dominion Savings Bank and the Merchants Bank of Ontario in 1872. Private bankers also flourished, of whom W. F. Alloway, founder of the banking firm of Alloway and Champion, was first to emerge.

The opening of the agricultural era, however, demanded physical goods in a way the fur trade did not, and to the services of commerce and finance Winnipeg added the supply of lumber, flour and other manufactured goods. Lumber was in chief demand and, surprising though it may seem in retrospect, the lumber industry was the first and for some years the largest of Winnipeg industries. Logs were floated down the eastern tributaries of the Red from the Minnesota pineries and rafted down to Winnipeg. By 1872 the sawmills of Dick and Banning, of Macaulay, Sprague and Company and others were loud with the shriek of saws as they turned out the boards and scantlings for the multiplying business firms which were building the new stores on Main Street and the citizens who proudly reared the new houses on Point Douglas. The firm of Brown and Rutherford opened as a cabinet factory and carpentry establishment in 1872. Brick-making was begun in 1871, at first only for use in chimneys, but as the quality improved the use of brick was extended and the buildings of Winnipeg began to assume a more permanent character. By 1875 flour-milling was overtaking the lumber industry and Andrew McDermot's old mill was overshadowed by the great warehouse and towering smokestacks of MacMillan's. The millers were soon to introduce the new "patent process" which with chilled steel rollers and silken bolts could grind a superfine white flour from the hard spring wheat of the Red River valley. The flour went to local bakers, to the cart brigades going west, to the outfits of new settlers, to the survey and construction gangs on the railway lines. Some of it went to the Chambers biscuit factory opened on May 1, 1876.[18]

Lumber and flour dominated the early industry of Winnipeg. But smithing was important and with it harness-making and carriage-making. George MacVicar started the St. Boniface woollen mills in 1873 and other minor industries required by an outfitting centre sprang up from time to time.

The provision of so many goods and services was made possible by a rapid growth of population. In the Winnipeg of December, 1870, there were about 100 people; in 1871, 215; in 1872, 1,467; by 1874, 3,700; in 1875, some 5,000.[19] The town was a turbulent aggressive democracy, in which mob violence was easy and not infrequent. On one occasion in 1871 a jeering mob reduced the Attorney-General of the province to drawing his revolver in self-defence. But this rough civic democracy preferred to function through the mass meeting of citizens and in these the leadership of the steadier elements usually prevailed. The core of the city's democracy, its leading element, was a fusion of the old private traders with newcomers after 1870, many of them volunteers of the First Expedition. They were, with few exceptions, Old Countrymen and Ontario men by origin, but they became by interest and connection passionate Winnipeggers and stalwart champions of the city's future. Their first foe was the old commercial rival of the free traders, the Hudson's Bay Company, an antagonism now perpetuated by the great land-holding of the Company on the southern half of the projected site of Winnipeg. Their next enemy was any town which challenged the metropolitan role envisaged for Winnipeg as the commercial emporium of the Northwest and as the Pacific railway crossing of the Red. To the traders—the Bannatynes, Ashdowns, Stobarts, Higgins— there were rapidly added the lawyers, real estate men, bankers, and journalists—the Cornishes, Blanchards, Burrows, Luxtons, Duncans, Alloways, and McArthurs. They were not so much Manitobans as Winnipeggers; their interests were not provincial but as wide as the Northwest; and from that distinct origin sprang the peculiar character of the Winnipegger, self-centred and aggressive, it may be, but always broad-viewed and never provincial.

The tone and purposes of the central group were caught early by the Winnipeg press, whether in the *Manitoba Free Press*, founded in 1872, which W. F. Luxton soon made not merely a sharp-tongued organ of Liberal party views but the most representative voice of the Northwest, or in the line of newspapers which began with the *Manitoban* and passed down through the *Winnipeg Times* and the *Standard*. The interests of the Northwest in Confederation, the interest of Winnipeg in the Pacific railway, and the expansion of Manitoba and the West were their congenial themes which consistently overshadowed local and provincial interests. The press, too, was metropolitan rather than provincial.

To the business and professional core which directed the city's growth were added other elements more variegated and more picturesque. The hotel keepers and saloon proprietors were a large and prosperous group, frequently of Irish or German descent, to judge by their names. The Winnipeg saloons were notorious for their rowdiness, and the police court was crowded with drunks and prostitutes. The influx of immigrants, many of them single men of the roughest kind, the visits of the cartmen and the boatmen, made Winnipeg in these years a "Wild West" frontier town. In 1876 it was noted that "Winnipeg and Barrie are the two most evil places in Canada," and both were prayed for at the Y.M.C.A. Convention of that year. This character, as a place for outfitting and returning, the city was never wholly to lose. The stage and livery men were a prominent group in an age of horse transport. Smiths and bakers, printers and photographers, may be discerned, but otherwise the records reveal only a large mass of clerical and manual workers; the carpenters and bricklayers who built early Winnipeg may be assumed, but the great body of workers must have been unskilled and transient. Again, while the British-Ontario element made up the great majority, there is evidence that from the first the population of Winnipeg was varied and polyglot; seventeen languages were spoken on its streets, it was said, though on no statistical authority. The workers were not organized, as was to be expected in so new and so rapidly changing a community. A Typographical Union was formed in 1872, and an attempt made to form a workmen's union in 1874, but it seems to have had no immediate sequel.

With the vision of metropolitan growth before them, and a rapid increase in population in three years to justify them, the dominant group in 1873 set out to have Winnipeg incorporated as a city. A bill of incorporation was prepared in a "mass meeting," that great organ of early Winnipeg democracy, and was introduced in the Legislature. There it was so amended as to be unacceptable. Its supporters charged that the changes were made through the influence of Donald A. Smith, then a member of the Legislature and a growing power in the Hudson's Bay Company. The point at issue was civic taxation, from which the Hudson's

Bay Company, like other large property holders, might well fear to suffer, given its large holdings and the old antagonism between Winnipeg and the Company. Feeling ran high and found violent expression in the tarring of Speaker C. J. Bird, a crime whose perpetrators were never detected.

In December, 1873, however, a satisfactory act of incorporation was passed and on January 1, 1874, the new council was organized under Mayor F. E. Cornish. With civic taxes, money could be raised for civic improvements. The streets were surveyed along the lines of the river lots and the Hudson's Bay reserve, and Main and Portage, the old Red River trails, confirmed in their magnificent width of 132 feet bestowed on them by the Council of Assiniboia in 1835. The roadways were graded, and plank sidewalks were built to afford the pedestrian some footing in the terrible Winnipeg mud, as slippery as grease and as tenacious as glue. A sewer was dug to drain the stagnant waters of a level site. A city hall and market were begun, and mayor and aldermen were soon engaged in enduring controversies of civic government. In the civic coat of arms and heraldic symbols, three wheat sheaves d'or and a locomotive were representative of the city's hopes; the motto, "Commerce, prudence, industry," were certainly not inspiring and scarcely just. Commerce, yes, but "daring, imagination" would better have represented the qualities of this commercial metropolis which was also a provincial capital, a city which to be significant at all had to be large in grasp and broad in vision.

The incorporation of the city was only the major example of a rapidly forming organized society. In 1872 the Winnipeg General Hospital was also begun by private action and set up in restricted quarters on the bank of the Red. In 1875 it was incorporated and later was moved to its present site, the gift of Andrew McDermot and A. G. B. Bannatyne. There was a particular need for a hospital in Winnipeg for the care of the ill and injured among the immigrants and the transient population. Much the same corporate spirit as founded the General Hospital found expression in the beginning of the Manitoba Club in 1874, a club which was not partisan or professional, but select in that membership in it was practically a certificate of leadership in the commercial community of Winnipeg. Similarly the professional associations were taking shape; the Manitoba Law Society was incorporated in 1877, the Manitoba College of Physicians and Surgeons in the same year. Thus one by one the institutions, public, semi-public, and private, sprang up in the early formative years of Winnipeg, the tentative and hopeful years of the mid-seventies. Nor is it irrelevant to note the formation in these years of the national societies, St. Andrew's, St. George's, and St. Patrick's in Winnipeg and the smaller towns, and certainly the beginning of the Caledonian Curling Club in 1876 is to be recorded, for curling was to become the most general and most typical of sports in Manitoba.

The settlement of the Red River valley and the interest in the Pacific railway was slowly changing the orientation of the Northwest economy from north-south to east-west. Yet the Red River steamboats, pouring goods and immigrants into Winnipeg from June to October, though their competition had ended the trips of the cart brigades, kept alive the old north-south connection, indeed brought it to its most active years. And the projected Pembina Branch, planned as a branch of the Canadian Pacific railway to connect with an American line at Pembina, would perpetuate the north-south axis into the day of the railway. So also did a developing traffic on Lake Winnipeg. Not only the yet surviving brigades of York boats and the new Hudson's Bay Company steamers, but lumber schooners and tugs, the *Venture*, the *Lady Ellen*, the *Maggie*, and the *Swallow*, plied the waters of upper Winnipeg. They carried cargoes and towed flatboats of lumber from mills at Fort Alexander on the Winnipeg River and from Big Island. By 1875 they were bringing in cargoes of white fish and pickerel and carrying supplies to the Icelandic colony at Gimli. The Red River prairies and the uplands beyond the Manitoba Escarpment, the farm lands, were to occupy the immediate future of Manitoba, but the forests and waters of the Shield and the great swampy tract were to play some part in the growth of the province until their day should come again.

By 1875, then, Manitoba had not quite taken leave of the old order, or quite entered on the new. But immigration had brought about two fundamental changes in Manitoba: the equality of English and French, Protestant and Catholic, had been upset in favour of the English and Protestant, and the principle of duality in language and education brought into jeopardy. The establishment of the Mennonite and Icelandic colonies had transformed the ethnic pattern from a bilingual to a multilingual one, with consequences not to be felt for another generation. The political shift recorded in the redistribution of 1874 and the formation of the Davis ministry was slight, having been checked by the refusal of the Premier and John Norquay to countenance racial politics,[20] but it was significant. If the trends of population growth established between 1871 and 1875 were to continue, the pressure for further change in the constitution of 1870 would grow. And imposed on this small provincial community, tense with conflicts of national import, was the polyglot, dynamic commercial capital of the Northwest.

The year 1874 was marked not only by a political crisis, but also by the deepening of the commercial depression which began in 1873 and by the announcement of the policy of the Mackenzie government with respect to the Pacific railway. The Liberal government of Alexander Mackenzie had failed to find parties willing to undertake, in a time of depression, so gigantic an undertaking. It had therefore decided to build the railway piecemeal, as revenues permitted, meantime developing the use of the natural lines of communication. Manitoba would thus have to wait longer than had been anticipated for railway communication with eastern Canada. The new policy also involved three other decisions of importance to Manitoba. The first was the adoption of a route for the Pacific line which would cross the Red at the head of navigation at a point soon to be named first The Crossing and then Selkirk. From there it was to run northwestward to the Narrows of Lake Manitoba and proceed by way of the Swan River valley to the Saskatchewan. This meant that Winnipeg would be denied the advantage of being at the crossing of the Red by the Pacific railway and that the settlers westward along the Saskatchewan Trail would not be on the first and main line of railway, as they had confidently anticipated. The second decision was to begin construction of the line from the crossing of the Red eastward and from Fort William westward to connect the Red River valley with Lake Superior. The third was to build a line southward from the crossing to the boundary, there to connect with an American line. This, the Pembina Branch, was authorized in 1874 and grading begun in 1875, while work on the first section eastward of the Canadian Pacific was begun in 1876. The old canoe route from Fort William, and the cart trail to St. Paul, were to be duplicated in the iron track of the railway. The purpose was to give railway communication quickly by the southern, American route, and to build the more difficult Canadian route as rapidly as funds permitted. The effect was to create two rivals for Winnipeg in the towns of Selkirk and Emerson, and to cause the western settlers to begin a clamour for branch lines.

The commercial depressions and the delay in building the railways was not the only setback of the years from 1873 to 1875. The old plague of Red River valley agriculture, the grasshopper or Rocky Mountain locust, the devastating visitor from the high plains of 1818–20 and 1865–8, now struck once more. In the westernmost settlements and the Mennonite reserves the damage was heavy; in 1875 the settlements at the crossings of the Whitemud lost everything, even their potatoes. Other settlements escaped with less loss, the import of food was well organized, and there was little of the actual want experienced in 1868. Work on government building, the Saskatchewan cart brigades, and the Pembina Branch helped those who had lost their crops. The great want was for seed grain. In 1875 and 1876 loans for supplies and seed grain were advanced by the federal government and the Provincial Agricultural Society.[21] Thus the immediate danger of crop failure through lack of seed was averted, and though the government mortgages were long a source of difficulty, the crop of 1876 was abundant enough to make the grasshopper years but one among many of the memories of pioneer hardship. By 1875 the new way of life, the new pattern of settlement, was firmly emplanted in the Red River valley.

8

The Growing Pattern of Settlement
1876-1881

THE RESILIENT STRENGTH OF THE NEW AGRICUL-
tural settlements is apparent when all the difficulties of the mid-
seventies are reviewed. Only a self-sustaining society could have
survived them, and that the economy of the new province did so
is a testimony to its primitive strength. The wonder is rather that
the depression and its accompanying evils did not check the course
of settlement more than they did. The number of immigrants in
1875 was 11,970 and in 1876 it was 3,000 to 4,000, together an
increase over the total figures for 1873 and 1874.[1] The truth was
that neither depression nor grasshoppers were ills peculiar to
Manitoba. The former was universal, the latter plagued the competitive areas of settlement south of the border. The established
and the thrifty settler in Manitoba was able to ride out more than
two bad years. The pioneer society was simple, hard working,
and capable of living at a very modest level. Like all pioneer communities, it lived and worked for the morrow which was sure to
compensate for present hardship. The very lushness of the crops
the grasshoppers had devoured was the guarantee of future success. Hence it was that while the middle seventies saw a slowing
down in the settlement of new lands and the growth of towns,
there was no crippling break in the life of the new community.

The group colonies, Mennonite, Icelandic, and French, indeed
grew steadily during these years. New Mennonite parties continued to arrive each year down to 1879, to a total of some 6,000
souls in both reserves,[2] and the laying out of the villages and the

renewing of the old community ways went forward year by year. The Icelandic immigration in 1876 numbered 1,226; in 1878, the last year, with one later exception, of mass immigration by the group, 220.[3] The colony was sorely smitten in the winter of 1876–7 by smallpox, which flared and smouldered periodically along the Indian frontier during these years of rapid immigration by whites. The official quarantine imposed at the northern boundary of Manitoba seemed to the suffering people an act of unnecessary cruelty, only scantily made good by such help as was extended. Yet from 1877 on the colony slowly struggled to its feet; the fields widened in the bush, nets and boats were adapted to the Winnipeg fisheries. In 1877 a council for the local self-government of New Iceland was formed which in 1878 was given a constitution as the Republic of New Iceland, a venture in local self-government made necessary by the almost complete absence of administration in the Territory of Keewatin created in 1876. The French Colonization Society strengthened the *métis* settlements at Ste. Anne-des-Chênes, at Ile-des-Chênes, and along the Rat River, and founded the new settlements of Letellier and St. Jean Baptiste on reserved townships between Emerson and Morris. The imperfect statistics suggest that well over 2,000 French Canadians came to Manitoba from the United States between 1874 and 1887.[4] And the flow of settlers from Ontario and the British Isles mounted steadily after the low year of 1876, contributing the largest part of an estimated total of 11,500 immigrants in 1879, 18,000 in 1880, and 28,600 in 1881.[5] The significant changes in the immigration of the late seventies were the falling off of non-British immigrants and the rising proportion of people from the British Isles, an immigration spurred by the great agricultural depression which began in 1877. In Manitoba its beginning was marked by the visit of the delegates of the British tenant farmers in 1879.[6] Noteworthy also was the rising number of immigrants from the mid-western states, many of them repatriated Canadians. The census of 1881 was to report a population of 65,954 for the province within its new boundaries of that year.[7]

The immigration of these years had two points of dispersal

over the province, Winnipeg as in the past and the rising town of Emerson, together with the customs and immigration station of Dufferin across the Red. Emerson town had grown rapidly since its foundation in 1874 and the prairie townships north to the Roseau and east to the forested ridges had been filling up rapidly. The town saw itself developing as the port of entry to Manitoba, an ambition hampered only by the long start of Winnipeg and by the persistence of the federal government in maintaining the customs house at Fort Dufferin, and of the Hudson's Bay Company in trying to develop the lands around its Pembina post as the town of West Lynne, both on the west bank of the Red across from Emerson. Not only the Canadian and American settlers east of the Red used Emerson as a base. The survey of the international boundary in 1873–4 and the westward march of the Mounted Police from Fort Dufferin in 1874 had opened a trail to Pembina Mountain. The settlers along the base of the Escarpment and the Mennonites of the west reserve also made Emerson their base for outfitting. The approach of the St. Paul, Minnesota, and Manitoba railway promised to make the hopeful village, with the aid of a bridge across the Red, the point from which railways would radiate northwestward across the province.

The course of settlement from 1876 to 1881 did much to encourage these great expectations of the "Gateway City." The late seventies were years of excessive rainfall and the lowlands of Manitoba were waterlogged. The reserves for half-breed and group settlements together with the holding of land by speculators created a "landlock" which was vigorously denounced. The two factors of flooding and the reserves combined to encourage prospective settlers to push up into the highlands beyond Pembina Mountain and the Assiniboine delta. Emerson benefited greatly when in 1876 there broke out among Ontario immigrants the "Pembina fever," a rush to occupy the remainder of the lands in the townships in ranges 5 and 6 along the broad terraces at the foot of the Mountain. In 1877 the towns of Mountain City and Nelsonville were formed. In 1878 the occupation of the uplands began, and settlements sprang up in the bluff-studded rolling countryside between the Escarpment and the deep wooded valley of the Pembina River. In 1878 Thomas Greenway, soon to be a leading man in his adopted province, brought in a party of Ontario settlers and began the settlement along Crystal Creek from which Crystal City sprang, and to the north the Paisley Colony was begun in the same year. At Rock Lake and Swan Lake settlement also began in 1878.[8] In 1879 settlement pushed north to Cypress Creek and the Assiniboine watershed and westward to Badger Creek and Turtle Mountain. Much of the best land in southern upland Manitoba had been claimed by 1880 and the rush of settlement had crossed the western boundary of the province.

The settlers were almost wholly from Ontario, with a sprinkling of British immigrants, and almost wholly Protestant, except for the French Catholic settlement of St. Léon. Nearly all were practical farmers with means, a few were graduates of the Ontario Agricultural College at Guelph, and they brought to the parklands of the southern highlands a high degree of agricultural experience and skill.

The same westward rush beyond the boundary of the province characterized the stream of immigration through Winnipeg to the west along the Saskatchewan Trail. While new settlements were formed back of the old ones along the Trail, as at Ossawa north of Poplar Point and at Richmond north of Gladstone, most continued westward to the highlands of the south central slope. On the North Trail newcomers for the most part passed through Palestine to enter the beautiful upper valley of the Whitemud. Settlements began at the Beautiful Plain in 1877, westward at Boggy Creek, at Stoney Creek, and at Tanner's Crossing of the Little Saskatchewan.[9] In 1878 the establishment of a Mounted Police barracks at the junction of the trails at Shoal Lake led to the beginning of settlement there. By the South Trail settlers passed through the Bad Woods and over the Big Plain, fertile but bare of wood, to the crossing of the Little Saskatchewan. Here the Ralston party of 312 miners from Michigan had attempted to settle in 1874, but, soon wearying of pioneer agriculture, many had abandoned the colony.[10] The settlement of the valley of the Little Saskatchewan did not start in earnest until 1878 when the energetic colonizing agent, R. W. Prittie, began to bring in his organized parties from the eastern provinces and the United States.[11] Some of these went to Pembina Mountain but most continued on to Winnipeg and the Little Saskatchewan. The centre of the settlement was at the crossing of the South Trail, where soon a flour mill and saw mill rose on the site of Rapid City. Settlement spread north and south along the valley, and the "dry and rolling" parklands were claimed by just such Ontario farmers and repatriating Canadians as were moving in west of Pembina Mountain. Many British immigrants were attracted to the Little Saskatchewan country, and the Whellams party of two hundred British settlers marked the beginning of British—chiefly English—settlement of the valley and the country west.[12] In 1879 settlers had reached Shoal Lake by the South Trail and the Hamilton and North-West Colonization Society had begun the settlement of the Birdtail valley with Ontario farmers.[13] By 1881 these settlements, at first in the North-West Territories and in that year incorporated in Manitoba, had reached the Assessippi, or Shell River, valley and the Assiniboine valley in its southward course to Fort Ellice. The Saskatchewan Trail had carried settlers to the western limits of the extended province.

The years from 1876 to 1881, years of much rain and high water in the rivers, had also seen the steam navigation of the Assiniboine begun. From 1876 the *Prince Rupert, Marquette,* and *Alpha* plied regularly between Winnipeg and Portage. In 1879 the steamer *Marquette* made the voyage through the Sand Hills, passed the Grand Rapids above the Sourismouth, and triumphantly steamed on to Fort Ellice.[14] The voyage, to be repeated during the same season of high water, called attention to the great central valley, and in 1879 settlements at Grand Rapids on the Assiniboine, at the Sourismouth, and around the Blue Hills of Brandon began to fill the front between the Little Saskatchewan settlements and those to the south at Turtle Mountain. The majority of the settlers came in by Portage and over the Yellow Quill Trail, named after the local Cree chief, which wound southwest through the Sand Hills to the mouth of the Souris.[15] All of highland Manitoba south of Riding

Mountain had been occupied, the Canadian base of the park-belt crescent had been settled, and the extension of Manitoba's boundaries in 1881 added the newly settled highlands to the lowlands which had constituted the greater part of the province from 1870.

This great influx of some forty thousand immigrants between 1876 and 1881, the years of the "Manitoba [land] fever," was in response to the fact that the possibilities of the Red River valley as a wheat-growing country both north and south of the border had been demonstrated. The hard spring wheat belt of the Northwest was coming into being. The new milling process for making a white, high-gluten flour from hard spring wheat had founded the milling industry of Minneapolis and started the great rush for the rich black wheatlands of the Red River valley in Minnesota, Dakota Territory, and Manitoba. The mechanical drill, the sulky and gang ploughs with chilled steel mouldboards, the self-binding reaper, the steam thresher, and barbed wire, combined in the late seventies to make prairie farming possible and profitable. Its supreme achievement, the bonanza farms of Minnesota and Dakota, did not occur in Manitoba; only the James and the Lowe farms west of Morris approached the size and suggested the character of the bonanzas to the south. But the same machinery which made the bonanza a wheat factory was equally useful on the quarter-section or half-section farm which were the standard sizes in Manitoba. By 1878–9 all the new machinery and the new cheap fencing material had appeared on Manitoban farms.[16]

The equipment of farm with machines and of field with barbed wire was justified, for Manitoba wheat by the late seventies had made its name in the great wheat markets. That the old Red River strains continued to be grown is certain; that many varieties were tried out is plain from the scattered records. Two varieties, however, predominated in the commercial notices and the prize lists of the provincial and county agricultural societies. One was Golden Drop, a soft white spring wheat, popular with farmers because it was a heavy yielder. The other was the famous Red Fife, sometimes called Glasgow, a hard, amber-coloured spring wheat, which yielded well, usually matured before the fall frosts struck in the Manitoba lowlands, and gave a white smooth flour of exceptional baking strength.[17] In Fife wheat, Manitoba found an agricultural staple to replace the prime beaver which had drawn the fur traders westward and begun its history. The virtues of northern-grown seed had long been advertised and the expectation among seedsmen was that the soil and climate of the Red River valley would yield wheat to replace the failing strains of the southern farmlands. In the fall of 1876 the Winnipeg firm of Higgins and Young gathered in, from Kildonan, Springfield, Rockwood, and the settlements near to Winnipeg, 857⅙ bushels of "hard" wheat, and consigned it, the first commercial export of wheat from Manitoba, to Steele Bros. of Toronto.[18] The firm, because of a shortage of seed in Ontario, had ordered 5,000 bushels but no more could be collected so late in the season. The samples shown to millers and farmers in Ontario convinced them that on the cheap lands of Manitoba the failing wheat farming of Ontario might be revived, and the reports of the "glorious harvest of 1876," the first to yield the new province a surplus of grain, made it plain that the export was no flash in the pan.[19] The "Manitoba fever" burned high, and the settlement of the western highlands was the result. The crops of the next few years were of similar quality, and under pressure from the buyers farmers turned more and more to the growing of Fife and the culture of wheat. The mounting surpluses were milled in the mills which sprang up in every settlement, but especially in Winnipeg and Portage, for local consumption and export to the North-West Territories. Only railway communication with the east, however, could handle the increasing harvests. The steamboats did their best, carrying surprising cargoes on their decks and on flatboats from Portage to Winnipeg, and from Winnipeg to railhead in the United States. Wheat from the east, from the Mennonite reserves, and from Pembina Mountain and Morris, went out by Emerson. But the steamers, with their limited capacity and in the short season, could not hope, even in years of high water, to deal with the mounting surpluses.

With such limited transport facilities, however, the grain trade had begun. From 1876 the leading business houses of Winnipeg, A. G. B. Bannatyne, Gerrie and Company, Higgins and Young, Kew, Stobart and Eden, and others, many of which were still dealing in furs, advertised that they would pay cash for wheat.[20] J. H. Ashdown and Co. was buying and exporting wheat from Emerson in 1877 and 1878.[21] Flat warehouses for storing and trans-shipping grain were built at Portage, Winnipeg, and Emerson. At the last point, W. J. S. Traill of Georgetown, Minnesota, a Canadian son of a distinguished literary family, who had served in the Hudson's Bay Company on the upper Assiniboine and left its service at Georgetown, began buying wheat in 1878. The following year he extended his grain-buying from Minnesota down the Red River valley to Winnipeg along the recently completed Pembina Branch and was apparently the first exclusive grain buyer in Manitoba.[22] His venture at this time neatly illustrates the way in which Manitoba settlement after 1876 was part of the northwestward extension of the hard spring wheat belt of the continent and of the techniques of its exploitation. Yet Canadian millers, no less than Canadian farmers, were quick to grasp the significance of the new wheatlands for Canada. In 1877 R. Gerrie and Co. shipped a consignment of Manitoba wheat by Duluth to the Goderich, Ontario, mills of the well-known Montreal firm of A. W. Ogilvie and Co.[23] Others followed, and buyers for Ogilvie were soon themselves in Manitoba, confirming a connection which was to grow and strengthen. The milling industry of the St. Lawrence, like the Canadian fur trade, was to find new sources of supply in the Red River valley and the Northwest, and the commercial system of the St. Lawrence would struggle to preserve this new agricultural hinterland from becoming subject to St. Paul and Minneapolis.

Methods of grain buying and handling were improvised at first, but became more systematic after 1879 with the construction of the flat warehouses for storing and shipping grain. By 1880 the construction of an elevator in St. Boniface was undertaken, and thereafter elevators began slowly to replace the warehouses, their red towers by the railway tracks becoming the most eye-catching of prairie landmarks. The great task of providing the grain trade with physical equipment had begun, and was in fact an extension into Manitoba of the methods and equipment already under development in the wheatlands south of the border.

Both the success of wheat farmer and grain trader, however, hung on the coming of the railway. The Mackenzie programme had been pushed on steadily, but slowly. The grading of the Pembina Branch was begun in 1876, but not until December, 1878, was the laying of the iron over the sixty miles of grade completed, and the first train welcomed demonstratively at "Paddington" on the St. Boniface side of the Red.[24] The building of the main line eastward went on slowly across the forest and muskeg of the eastern highlands. The crossing of the Red remained fixed at Selkirk, despite efforts by Winnipeg to have it changed. In consequence Selkirk enjoyed a considerable boom and like Emerson began to think of itself as a rival of Winnipeg. Winnipeg and the western settlements had therefore to bestir themselves. Mass meetings were held in Winnipeg during 1877 to seek federal aid in building a railway bridge across the Red, and the support of the western settlements was enlisted for an attempt to obtain federal aid to build a railway from Winnipeg to Portage and the Whitemud.[25] The bridge would have enabled the new railway to connect with the Pembina Branch and also with the main line. Municipalities were promptly established, Westbourne and Portage, in order to bonus this "westward extension" of the Pembina Branch. Federal aid for a bridge was offered only on unacceptable conditions, however, and before new measures could be tried, the defeat of the Mackenzie government in the election of 1878 and the return of the Conservatives to power offered the possibility of a new policy being adopted. But some time was to elapse before the character of that policy became evident.

If Manitoba was being peopled, if it had found the export staple which would carry the costs of its settlement, it had not yet found a voice to awaken it to a sense of community. Spokesmen for groups there were: Archbishop Taché and Joseph Royal for the French, John Schultz and W. F. Luxton for the Ontario-bred; E. H. G. G. Hay for the English old settlers. There was

even solid John Norquay, rising in all men's esteem, to speak
out boldly for understanding between groups. But there was no
one yet to see the whole in the perspective of a future of continued
growth. In 1877 Lord Dufferin, Governor-General of Canada,
with Lady Dufferin spent some weeks in the province; he visited
the settlements in the Red River valley, the Mennonites of the
east reserve, the Icelanders at Gimli. In the speeches which
marked his progress he emphasized to the new province its
national destiny, its place in the sisterhood of Canadian provinces,
its role as the "keystone of that mighty arch of sister provinces."
To the French he spoke in flowing French, to Mennonites and
Icelanders he spoke in terms both understanding and sympathetic,
terms which could only hearten them at once to preserve their
peculiar qualities in the new land while committing themselves
wholly to it. Then in Winnipeg he brought his visit to its climax
with the great oration which Manitobans long treasured and
fondly quoted. The classic oratory of Dufferin, of Tennysonian
richness and vividness, however forced the orator himself may
have felt it to be, left the peoples of Manitoba with a first consciousness of their place in Canadian life and their particular
task of achieving, as peoples of diverse origins, a strong Canadian
community based on unity in diversity. He had remarked, he
said, the degree to which "a community of interests, the sense
of being engaged in a common undertaking—has amalgamated
the various sections of the population of this Province originally
so diverse in race, origin and religions, into a patriotic, closely
welded and united whole."[26] These were wise and timely words.

That the new province should have had its larger destiny
delineated by a man of broad mind and a master of memorable
phrase was fitting, for its local institutions, the intimate and
inner modes of community life, were taking shape in the late
seventies. Chief of these was the Red River parish, both Catholic
and Protestant. In Red River society, in which the missionary
was the only educated man whose efforts were not devoted to the
fur trade, it had been natural that local communities should be
organized in parishes around church and school. It was inevitable,
given the local circumstances in which government was at a

minimum, and the belief of both Anglican and Catholic that the education of the young was an office of religion, that church and school should be inseparable. In practice, there was some difference between the Anglican and the Catholic schools; in the former, the teacher was much more likely to be a layman and the school was likely to be considered his concern, rather than the parson's; in the latter, the school was unmistakably clerical, and, except in the larger school at St. Boniface, lay teachers exceptional. Both churches, however, as in England and in Quebec, took it for granted that education came under their jurisdiction.

The denominational school system guaranteed by the Manitoba Act and established by the provincial School Act of 1871 perpetuated the educational scheme of Red River. Local schools, classified as Protestant or Roman Catholic, might be established under the Act on local initiative and be administered by local trustees under the superintendence of the Protestant or Catholic section of a provincial Board of Education. The Board was independent of the provincial government but received grants from it, which the sections divided among their schools. Until 1875 the two sections received grants equal in amount; in that year the disparity of population and the Protestant attack on dualism made it necessary to divide the grants on the basis of the number of pupils enrolled in the schools of each section.

With the Act of 1871, the Anglican schools became part of the "Protestant" system and, except for St. John's College, lost their particular connection with the Church of England. In the Catholic parishes, however, the intimate union of faith and tongue, reinforced by clerical policy, ensured the perpetuation of the union of church and school, and of the parish as the organ of local community life. The colonies founded by the group settlements of the mid-seventies established not dissimilar organic communities. In the Mennonite villages, governed in local matters by elected *schultz* and *oberschultz*, and in church matters by elected elders and bishops, church and school were united in that both were agents of the organic village community. As long as the village community retained its vitality, the absence of a distinct clergy was not a material difference between Mennonite village and the Catholic parish. Among the Icelanders the Lutheran Church professed the same principles with respect to education as did the Anglican, but in practice was as indefinite. In the form of government, or republic, instituted for New Iceland in 1878, education was made the responsibility of the local divisions. Anglicans, Catholics, Mennonites, and Lutherans, all, to a greater or less degree, brought to Manitoba the European union of church and school born of the fierce religious struggles of the Reformation when control of the education of the young was necessary for denominational survival.

The Ontario settlers brought with them a quite different tradition. The greater number of them were Presbyterians, and held the conviction of that denomination that education was a matter to be dealt with by the laity as well as the ministry. The next largest group, the Methodist churches, were by religious tradition on the whole disposed to favour the union of church and school, but the long struggle in Upper Canada against the efforts of Bishop Strachan and the Church of England to retain a privileged position in education had made the Methodists champions of the separation of church and state. That had been accomplished in Upper Canada by 1854, though modified in fact by the Separate Schools Act of 1863, and the Ontario Protestants were firm supporters of the principle of free, secular public schools.

In Upper Canada also Lord Durham and his followers had introduced the municipal institutions which under the leadership of Jeremy Bentham and his Utilitarian disciples were in England replacing the old government of parson and squire by that of elected representatives. The township and county, not the parish, were the units of Ontario local society; the atmosphere of secular and utilitarian democracy, not that of traditional, religious custom, was the air in which it flourished. In the first settlements, therefore, the Ontario immigrants, like the French or the Mennonites, endeavoured to settle a township with their own kind, for the township, with its secular school and its voluntary churches, required a fair density of like-minded people just as much as the parish or the agricultural village. Like them, too, it needed a name, and the first names of settlements in Manitoba were actually names of townships after the old Ontario usage, names such as Springfield, Palestine, Rosebank. The expectation was that settlement would be dense and uniform enough to make most townships local units for the support of school and church. The school, however, would be non-denominational, and the church, or churches, voluntary.

In these various local communities were the roots of the new society, and also of causes of conflict. Not infrequent were struggles over the possession of land or woodlots by one group or another, as in the French reserve at Letellier in 1877 and the woodlands beyond the Mennonite western reserve in 1877 and 1878. Possession of adjoining land by its members in sufficient density was the basis for survival of the group as a group. "We feel aggrieved to know that for years at least we must be surrounded by a people who refuse to affiliate with us in school, church, municipal or other institutions," wrote an Ontario settler from Scratching River, adding, "we welcome all, but we wish all to have equal privileges. . . ."[27] These disputes could be and were adjusted. Fundamental, however, was the difference between the groups which were essentially religious groups, such as the French and the Mennonite, and those essentially secular, such as the English and the Icelandic. The former were devoted to the perpetuation of the faith; the latter to the full realization of the individual. It was a deep-seated conflict, symbolized not inaptly by the ecclesiastical parish on the one hand, the political municipality on the other.

While the French maintained their parishes, then, the Ontario settlers proceeded to introduce municipal institutions. The first municipal act, that of 1871, recognized the parishes as units of local administration and, indeed, having been drawn by Archibald from Nova Scotian legislation, reflected the older institutions of that province. The next act, that of 1873, was an attempt to approximate to Ontario institutions, and permitted one or more townships to incorporate as municipalities. Springfield and Sunnyside did so in that year, to constitute the first municipality of the province. Kildonan and St. John's, a Red River parish and the Scottish Presbyterian settlement, followed in 1875. The act was not considered satisfactory, however, and a demand by Ontario settlers for efficient municipal institutions was one of the issues of the election of 1874. The outcome was the County Municipality Act of 1877, which introduced the Ontario municipal system as far as local circumstances permitted.[28] The desire for municipal institutions in the new settlements sprang largely from the desire to raise local revenues for local improvements, chiefly roads, bridges and drains; but by 1878, when the first county municipality, that of Westbourne, was formed, a new factor was at work, the desire to use local credit to offer bonuses for railway construction. The same device was employed later to promote the building of grist mills. The municipalities also helped to repair the inability of the provincial government to furnish adequate funds for local improvements. From these beginnings the municipal system of Manitoba sprang; and although much legislation was yet to be passed the municipal organization of the province henceforth went forward steadily. The French parishes, the old Red River parishes, and even the Mennonite villages were incorporated smoothly into the general system and assumed the new functions of local government, without ceasing, in the instance of the French parish and the Mennonite village, to carry on their religious and educational functions. None the less, the spirit of the new system was alien to that of the old, and the new municipal system was certain to attempt to assimilate to itself the distinct educational system of denominational schools and to raise religious and racial controversy in so doing.

The rural municipalities were soon to be joined by urban ones other than Winnipeg, already incorporated in 1873. The rival town of Emerson, confident in its future as gateway to the province and in its population of over 2,000, followed in 1879. Selkirk, Portage la Prairie, Gladstone, and a small host of others, fired by the advent of the railway and the need for incipient local improvements to draw capital and population, were to plunge in 1880–1. The more cautious, like Portage, were to benefit from the assumption of municipal dignity; other communities, left with vacant lots, abandoned buildings, and heavy debts, were bitterly to regret the hopeful rashness of too eager promoters.

While municipal institutions were developing, the schools, both Catholic and Protestant, continued under the control of the independent Board of Education. The schools were financed by local taxes, levied by local boards of trustees, and by provincial grants to the Board for allocation among the schools. Under this system the Catholic schools, both those of the French and those of the English-speaking Irish Catholics, remained truly denominational. The Protestant schools, being multi-denominational, became in effect secular, though not, of course, anti-religious institutions. Many factors contributed to this trend: the mixture of denominations; the lack of positive doctrine in a general Protestantism; the principle of the undenominational public school; the strong sense of a need for uniformity in a forming community; the lack of a sufficient density of population to support more than one school. The trend towards secularism combined with the growth of municipal institutions to foster the concept of a general municipal system of which the public schools should be a co-ordinate part.

The same community effort which established the schools also built the first churches for the missionary clergy, who served the new settlements with great devotion spent in long travel and much hardship. The old established parish churches of the Roman Catholic and Anglican communions continued to serve the bulk of the membership of those churches. These denominations expanded with relative slowness. It was necessary for the Catholic Church to be sure a parish could be maintained before it felt justified in erecting a mission into a parish, and similar considerations delayed the extension of the ministrations of the Anglican Church. Presbyterian, Methodist, and Baptist ministers served the new settlements with something of the energy and ubiquity of the circuit riders of old Ontario; and the first churches of the new settlements were therefore usually of one of those denominations. Often they were available to more than one denomination; in practice they were open to all, and in the very early stages one building served as school and church of the whole settlement.[29] Frontier conditions and scanty population made for union and uniformity, or denominational existence at a very simple level. "One's denominational prejudices are wonderfully overcome by moving out west," wrote a settler at Emerson.[30]

The founding of the local institutions of church and state were accompanied by the introduction of the fraternal and semi-public societies of the mother communities. There were active St. Andrew's, St. George's, and St. Patrick's societies in Winnipeg, and in some other towns, as the "Old Country" settlers strove to cherish the memory of their origins. The French brought the Society of St. Jean Baptiste, the Ontario settlers the Loyal Orange Order. On June 24 and July 12 the dusty trails of the new settlements were lined by spectators to watch the Society march past with sword and banner, or to see the Orangemen "walk" and "King Billy" ride again to thud of drum and squeal of fife.

All loyally joined, however, in the two national holidays of the Twenty-fourth of May, Queen Victoria's birthday, and Dominion Day. The celebrations consisted of "pic-nics" and games in local groves or available meadows. The sports were foot races, jumping, throwing the hammer, tugs-of-war and an enthusiastic version of baseball. The British settlers were devoted to athletics; small and new was the community which did not have its baseball and football (soccer) clubs. Where there were English there was cricket, where Canadians, a lacrosse or baseball club. In fall boys and men sought the marshes for duck shooting or flushed the prairie chicken on the uplands. Horse-racing remained the pastime it had been in Red River days, as did driving on the river ice. In winter curling soon became the game of the middle-aged, while the young skated on the frozen rivers and in rinks; ice hockey had not yet emerged as an organized sport. Snow-shoeing was popular with many, but the indoor dance, the Red River jig in the old parishes, the barn-dance or the house-warming in the new settlements, the "social" evening of the churches, and the Literary or "Mutual Improvement" societies were the chief diversions of the cold season.

It was a society which could amuse itself by sport or other diversions. Among the British and Ontario settlers nothing like folk art or folk music existed, nor did the Mennonites and Icelanders bring anything of the kind. But a certain conscious cultivation of the arts continued among the people, and local poets like William Gerrond of High Bluff or Holmes R. Mair of Westbourne could find an appreciative audience for their occasional verse, however rough or however pretentious. The *chansons* of Pierre Falcon, who survived at St. François-Xavier until 1876, were treasured and sung among the *métis*. Even an occasional ballad, popular in the sense that no author was known and that it was widely sung, could spring up, such as that of "John Taylor and his Daughters Three," which commemorated a tragedy of the great blizzard of 1883; and in "Remember the Red River Valley" the Manitoban settlers had a song which, if not indigenous, was local in theme and a true folk song.[31] Assuredly, at any rate, it was a time and a community in which everyone could sing, at church or social; not a settlement lacked its fiddler, not a chance gathering but could divert itself with song and dance. In Winnipeg the church choirs were beginning to cultivate that love of music which was to flower in later years.

Not all the creative urge was expended in play, however, and beside the founding of the local institutions of church and municipality with their attendant societies and diversions went the establishment of specialized and semi-public organizations devoted to science and the arts. Higher education, for example, had been left to the denominational colleges sprung from the Red River missions. In 1871 St. Boniface, St. John's, and Manitoba colleges were incorporated by the provincial legislature, and in 1877, at the initiative of Lieutenant-Governor Morris, the three were united to form the University of Manitoba. The Methodist churches, Wesleyan and Episcopalian, were not yet strong enough to maintain colleges of university standing and the Baptists were to support the Prairie College founded at Rapid City in 1880. The new university was an examining body only, but even so was a remarkable attempt, possible only in the existing conditions in Manitoba, to reconcile denominational differences in one university and diverse teaching traditions in a common system of examination.[32] An effort had been made in 1874 to found an historical society, but not until 1878 was this accomplished,[33] to be followed by the incorporation of the Historical and Scientific Society of Manitoba in 1879. This body, formed by such men as the local historians Alexander Begg and Rev. George Bryce, and by businessmen like Alderman Mc-Micken, was devoted not only to the advancement of science but also to the promotion of the interests of Manitoba. In both objects it was to win a creditable measure of success, not least in the provision of the only public library, other than the Legislative Library, that Winnipeg or Manitoba was to have until 1905. The devotees of the fine arts were not able to establish permanent organizations. The active E. Brokovski and his gifted wife inspired the formation of both the Dramatic and Literary Association and the Philharmonic Society in 1876, but neither survived the return of the Brokovskis to the East. Winnipeg and the province had not yet, and were not to have for many years, a society confident enough in taste and wealth to maintain the cultivation of the drama or of concert music at even a low level of amateur performance. But the interest and desire were present, and were never to fail.

The new society taking form in Manitoba had settled the best lands of the province and in pursuit of favoured sites on river front or railway line had spread out to the limits of the southern Canadian park belt. The spread of settlement from 1876 to 1881 had been in response not only to the lure of rich wheatlands but also to the quickening of railway construction. The completion of the Pembina Branch in December, 1878, had furnished an effective outlet for the wheat crops, and the breaking of land, the sowing of Red Fife, and the development of the grain trade boomed. The construction of the Canadian Pacific between Selkirk and Fort William had gone steadily ahead. The Macdonald government, formed after the Conservative victory in the election of 1878, applied its National Policy of a protective tariff and returned to the policy of building the Pacific railway by means of a contract with a private company. In 1880 the Cana-

dian Pacific Railway Syndicate was formed and undertook to
complete the line. To aid it, a large land grant and a money
subsidy were voted by Parliament, and the contract forbade the
construction of any competing line to the American boundary,
the famous "monopoly clause" of later controversy. Construction
now quickened and the choice of route was reviewed. In 1879,
as a result of W. A. Macoun's survey of the southern plains and
of engineers' surveys of the Manitoba highlands, it was determined to carry the main line westward across the plains to a
southern pass in the Rockies. The decision meant a southern
route in Manitoba also, but crossing of the Red was still to be at
Selkirk. The historic route by the Saskatchewan to the northwest
passes was abandoned and the forests and lakes of the north fell
even more into the background of Manitoban history.

Selkirk had remained a speculator's town, despite its natural
advantages, a brick yard opened and pottery works begun, together with its paper of the proud title of the *Inter-Ocean*.
Winnipeg, on the contrary, was driving ahead as an aggressive
commercial and industrial city. From 1875 to 1881 its population
increased from 5,000 to 8,000. But to hold its lead it must command the railway to the West. Once more its leading men rallied.
A new and last attempt to have a bridge built at Winnipeg and
the main line brought south was complicated by the chartering in
1879 of the Manitoba and South Western Railway, which proposed to build from the main line to Winnipeg and the southwest
of the province and was empowered by its charter to build a
bridge at Winnipeg.[34] This difficulty was surmounted, and negotiations were opened in 1880 with Ottawa and the new
Canadian Pacific Railway. This time Winnipeg was to gain the
prize, but at a price. The city undertook to build the bridge
itself, at first for a branch line from Selkirk. Then, by contract
with the Company, the city in 1881 granted the railway, on condition that its main line came through Winnipeg and that its
shops be located there, exemption from municipal taxation in
perpetuity, together with right of way and land for station and
yards.[35] Winnipeg had triumphed at last, and had drawn the
main line of the transcontinental railway to itself. Selkirk

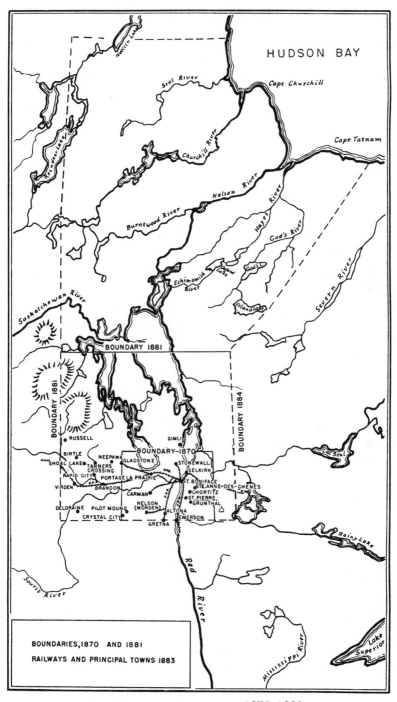

BOUNDARIES AND RAILWAYS, 1870–1883

remained only as the river port of Lake Winnipeg. Hopeful
Emerson to the south went bankrupt in an attempt to construct
a bridge across the Red and in any event was largely cut off from
the territory to the south by the tariff of the new National Policy.
Winnipeg's "metropolitan character," as Alderman McMicken
has justly termed it in 1877,[36] had been confirmed, and the outfitting centre of the fur trade was made by rail and tariff the
distribution centre and wheat market of the whole Northwest.
The day of the railway had come and with it the beginning of an
east-west flow of trade. Winnipeg was the gateway between east
and west through which that trade would pass.

For the province as a whole, however, the rapid growth of 1876
created pressing problems. The ever inadequate finances of the
provincial government were severely strained and there was a
general belief that only by an increased federal subsidy and extension of the provincial boundaries could the growth of Manitoba
be sustained. The situation was complicated, moreover, by dis-
sension within the government. In 1878 Premier Davis had retired from politics and had been succeeded by John Norquay.
Norquay, son of an old Red River family, had won a deserved
reputation as a conciliator of new and old settlers, and of French
and English. His first year of office, however, was signalized by
an attempt on the part of Joseph Royal, leader of the French
group, to institute party politics in the province in place of the
old dual system of equal representation of the two racial groups
in the legislature and the cabinet. Since responsible government
had at last been realized, he maintained, party government should
follow.

In reality Royal was attempting to maintain the principle of
duality in the cabinet.[37] The provincial cabinet was by that time
indeed responsible to the legislature, and parliamentary government had matured in Manitoba. But the dual system of representation had broken down; the French had become a minority
in the province and the legislature. Yet as a united minority in a
two-party system they might still hold a balance of power. Party
government, moreover, as Norquay feared, would mean the subordination of provincial political life to the needs of the federal

political parties—a situation which would augment the power of the French minority in the legislature—and Norquay declined to follow Royal's lead. The English members vigorously supported him, and undertook to mark the end of dualism by ending the official use of French. Norquay's cabinet became for a year a wholly English one, until the quarrel was adjusted and the French were once more represented in the provincial government. The Act abolishing the official use of French was disallowed by the Macdonald government. Nor was Norquay ready to part wholly with the system of communal representation and the recognition of racial groups in the composition of the government. The redistribution measure of 1878 rested still on the communal principle. Norquay believed that the government should represent not a party but the province, both to conciliate groups within it, and also to strengthen the province in negotiation with Ottawa.[38]

The request for better financial terms met with little success in 1879 and the years following. But the negotiations for extension of the boundaries were successful and in 1881 the western boundary of Manitoba was set at the twenty-ninth range of townships, where it has remained, the northern at 53° of latitude. The eastern boundary was to be the western boundary of Ontario, but the whole area from the North West Angle of the Lake of the Woods to the height of land west of Fort William was in dispute between Ontario and the federal government, and (arbitration having failed) could not be settled until the courts had handed down a decision. Whatever the outcome to the east might be, the province received in 1881 the territory into which some 16,000 settlers had gone since 1876, the new settlements from Riding Mountain and the Assessippi valley on the north to Turtle Mountain and the Souris plains on the south. To the northward all of the great lakes of the Winnipeg basin were brought into the province and the forest lands to east and west of the lakes. If the eastern boundary were found to be far to the east, Manitoba would be a large province indeed, and one lying along the east-west axis of the new Canada.

The territorial gains, however, were of little immediate use to a hard-pressed government, as the public lands remained under federal control and the subsidies did not meet the pressing needs of a pioneer community. Perhaps the one immediate effect was political, the further reduction of the strength of the French in Manitoba. An Ontario majority was rooted in the lands of the province, and pattern of settlement would determine the pattern of the community.

9

The Triumph of Ontario Democracy
1881-1888

THE OLD MANITOBA OF 1870 HAD BEEN ENGULFED in the new Manitoba of 1881. In one decade of swift change the province had seen the fur trade give way to the grain trade, the cart brigade to the railway train. The *métis* had withdrawn to the wooded river lots, or trekked to the plains of the Saskatchewan to shoot down the last bands of buffalo. The loose beauty of the park belt, the landscape of shimmering meadows flowing around the clumped poplar bluffs and down ragged willow runs, was giving way to a new pattern, the rectangular pattern of ploughed field and quarter-section farm. The wandering trail of Indian and trader was cut by fence and furrow and the rigid road allowance of the surveyor was beginning to grid the face of lowland and upland. At the river crossings towns were rising and bridges springing. The last cart brigade had creaked along the Portage Trail, and no more, as in 1879, would the plains traders come in to Winnipeg, camping at Silver Heights and "marking the sky line with their pointed and picturesque lodges."[1] The new Manitoba was confident of its future, sure that field could be added to field, that wheat could be poured to the lakehead in ever growing volume, that town could sprout beside town and abundance remain for the newcomer. In this confidence it plunged into the land boom of 1881–2, and from 1881 to 1887 the steady spread of settlement is lost to sight in the furious endeavour of the young community to equip itself with the capital goods of an agricultural economy, to protect its local interests in the national frame-

work of Confederation, and to define the character of the new
order.

The first symptom of the crisis that the advent of the railway
had caused was the boom itself. The coming of the railway brought
to a sudden climax the slow growth of the preceding decade.
Settlement from 1871 to 1881 had been a speculative venture in
anticipation of the railway following settlement. The old trails
and river crossings, the river fronts, and the bluff and meadow
areas of the park belt had been occupied. Farming, however, had
been carried on for the local market, and the rise in land values,
though relatively great, absolutely had been small. But when the
Pembina Branch began to operate in 1879 and the main line of
the C.P.R. was located westward and construction began in 1880
and 1881, the Manitoba boom began.

It was a speculative boom in land values. In Winnipeg, for
example, population, industry, and capital had grown steadily from 1871. All quickened their rate of growth during the
boom years of 1881 and 1882, until the city seemed to be a city
of tents,[2] but not proportionately to the rate of increase of land
values. City lots had commanded a good price in 1872 and 1873,
and prices were rising again in the late seventies. In the spring
of 1881, however, they began to soar, and for twelve hectic
months Winnipeg lived in a frenzy of speculation. Lots on Main
Street were exchanged for higher prices than those then commanded on Michigan Avenue in Chicago. Auctioneers chanted
day in, day out, and far into the dusk on every street corner. The
advertisements screamed out the fleeting opportunities to invest
in the limitless future of the boundless West. All were drawn
into the whirl—tradesmen, workmen, lawyers, ministers—buying
lots on margin, on options, and on agreements of sale, in mush-
room subdivisions and bubble town sites. Syndicates, the latest
financial device of the day, were formed to provide the easy credit
which buoyed up the boom. Canada had never seen anything
like it before, nor was it ever to see quite such a delirium again.
By the spring of 1882, even though the first train came through
from Fort William in March, the boom was slackening. An
attempt to promote the far distant site of Edmonton failed, the

boom began to subside, and not even the professional assurance of an imported auctioneer, one Coolican, could swell the glittering bubble again. Rapid building maintained prosperity for a time, but the crash came in 1883, insolvencies multiplied, and many of the new rich became the old poor once more.

Even more fantastically daring was the Emerson boom. That enterprising and hopeful city had been incorporated in 1879, five years after its foundation on a virgin site. Though annoyed by the attempt of the Hudson's Bay Company to develop the rival town of West Lynne on the west bank of the Red River, Emerson had aspired, by means of a projected railway, the Emerson and North-Western, to become at least one of the gateways to the Northwest. These hopes had inspired an extensive subdivision of the town site and in 1880 speculation in the lots of the new city became feverish. It reached its peak in 1881 and collapsed calamitously in 1882 when the charter of its railway was disallowed and it became apparent that Winnipeg was to be the railway and wholesale centre for the West. The stillborn city was left a small town, struggling to keep open the bridge across the Red on which it had staked its future, and burdened with a debt which was its only urban characteristic. Only by reversion to the status of a town and through the assumption of its obligations by the provincial government was Emerson to be relieved of the dead weight of the too rash and sadly frustrated ambitions of 1881.

If one city died aborning in 1881, another sprang to life in 1882. Just above Grand Valley, where the Canadian Pacific crossed the Assiniboine on its westward route, Brandon started up at the touch of the rail on the southern slope of the valley. A town site was laid out by the railway on a higher site than that of Grand Valley, and soon stores and houses were rising along the staked-out streets. The speculators poured in, and soon lots on which the startled gophers still whistled were changing hands at very high prices.[3] The future of Brandon, however, was one worth speculating upon: unlike Emerson, it had rich farmlands to south as well as north; unlike unhappy Selkirk, it was on the main line of the Pacific railway; and unlike Portage la Prairie, it was far enough from giant Winnipeg to have a chance of independent growth as a lesser industrial and distributive centre. By 1883 Brandon was to be a respectable small city, by prairie standards, with a population of over two thousand.

As the urban land values were pushed towards their limits, the speculators began to take an interest in the outlying towns. Portage had had its boom in 1880-1 as the main line went through. It was not until late in 1881 that the small towns caught the specu- lator's eye. They were eager enough to attract attention, as the proud names of some in these years suggest: Rapid City, Crystal City, Dominion City, Mountain City. Town after town was in- corporated at the instigation of hopeful citizens and professional promoters; large town sites were subdivided—that of Gladstone was four miles square—and the merry business of buying and selling at inflated values began. Some of the booms were founded on the approach, actual or prospective, of a railway; some were decidedly forced. They all collapsed like pricked bubbles in 1882 and citizens were left in a time of low prices to pay taxes on debts incurred to pay for local improvements commensurate with the hopes blown up by the boom.

The Manitoba boom was essentially a boom in urban real estate. Agricultural land values rose, of course, with the coming of the railroads, but speculation in farmlands did not reach the fantastic proportions of that in town lots. There was speculation, however, particularly in the lands of the Canadian Pacific Rail- way and in the half-breed land in the immediate vicinity of Win- nipeg. Perhaps the chief effect of the boom on agriculture was to create, by driving up the price of land, a sense of wealth among farmers and to encourage them to buy more land at advanced prices, to extend their purchases of equipment, and also, as the land regulations then permitted, to acquire a second homestead. Scarcely less significant was the tendency of increased prices in settled districts to drive the newcomers out to the cheaper lands and so to scatter settlement with grave resultant problems for municipalities and the school system.[4]

The boom in farmlands ended with that in town sites, and land values settled to the comparatively low levels at which they were to remain for the remainder of the century. The decline was a blow both to the speculator and the actual settler. In fact, however, cheap land was Manitoba's principal asset as an area of settlement, and the chief means of discounting the high freight rates and the high costs of agricultural implements of which loud complaint was made even as the boom broke. This factor it is which explains why the years subsequent to the boom did not witness a cessation of settlement but, on the contrary, its steady spread, accompanied by the constant if slow growth of the older settlements. Manitoba's agricultural economy was well founded, and for the rest of the century was to grow surely, nourished by the same hopes as the earlier settlement: cheap land, railway communications, and the export staple of a hard spring wheat commanding a premium of ten to fifteen cents a bushel on the world market. Not until the public lands of the American trans-Mississippi West were filled could there be a general land rush to Manitoba and the Northwest. Meantime, the first generation of settlers were given twenty years in which to consolidate themselves and adapt their ways and institutions to the new land.

The great boom, however, affected not only the pockets of Manitobans. In the hurry and whirl of those years the pattern of settlement in southern Manitoba was set. Winnipeg had triumphed over Selkirk and Emerson, and went on to grow ever greater in metropolitan stature as the distributive centre for Manitoba and the Northwest, prolonging into the days of wheat the supremacy of Fort Garry in the days of fur.[5] Brandon sprang into being and ousted Rapid City as the commercial centre of western Manitoba. The other towns fell into place as local markets along the great central spine of the Canadian Pacific, or the slowly spreading network of the branch line railways. The surrounding farms along the railway lines saw field added to field, frame house succeed to log, frame barn to hay-roofed shed, and quickly lost the marks of pioneer settlement.[6] The western frontier passed on into the Territories. Little internal frontiers formed around the central sandhills and moraines and along the bases of the hills of the Escarpment. Only to the east along the Shield and to the north along the lakes and forests of the great swampy tract and the Riding and Duck mountains did the unbroken frontier re-

main in Manitoba. The boom ended the pioneer days in southern
agricultural Manitoba, and confirmed the work of the first decade.
It left a community established with all its essential characteristics
delineated: an agricultural province; in the majority populated
with a British-Ontario stock; and with a political capital in a
commercial metropolis, too large in population and ambition for
its provincial setting.

While the boom lasted it also gave an added impetus to the
spread of settlement. The settlement of the southern uplands and
of the country along the Saskatchewan Trail in the late seventies
had left the central region of the Assiniboine valley uninhabited.
The wooded and rugged country of the Assiniboine Delta, the
Sand Hills, and the Tiger Hills had been avoided. But when the
main line of the Canadian Pacific Railway was built westward
from Portage to Brandon, settlers flocked to the good lands along
the route. De Winton, soon to become Carberry, was founded
at the south end of the Great Plain, and Melbourne and Edrans
established on the clay terraces among the Sand Hills. Westward
from Brandon, Virden, Pipestone, and Oak Lake sprang up as
the railway passed on in 1882, and the rolling prairie, where
plain and parkland merge south of the great eastward curve of
the Assiniboine, was dotted with settlers' shacks and the black
squares of ploughed fields.

Southward from Brandon, settlement joined up with settlers
who had come to the Blue Hills in 1879 and then, by way of the
Souris valley, with the settlements in the Turtle Mountain region.
Here were forming the towns of Killarney on the uppermost of
the Pembina lakes, Boissevain on the plain at the northern foot
of Turtle Mountain, and Deloraine on the eastern verge of the
Souris plains. In this district and at this time Manitoban pioneers
were first venturing out on the open plains, to share the trials and
hardships of farming on the grasslands with their fellows in
Dakota Territory to the south and along the line of the Canadian
Pacific through the North-West Territories. They were able,
however, to make the transition more easily because the railway,
agricultural machinery, and barbed wire moved with them, and
because the woods of Turtle Mountain and the lignite beds of the

Souris valley yielded fuel. Yet they added a new region to agricultural Manitoba and the prairie dwellers of the Souris Plains were in many respects to have a history of their own within the province.[7]

The advance into the southwestern corner of the province was matched by an advance to the northwest. The flow of settlers along the Saskatchewan Trail to Fort Ellice had reached the Birdtail River by 1879 and Shell River by 1881. The flow increased in 1880 when the Portage, Westbourne, and North Western Railway, later the Manitoba and North Western, began to follow the old North Trail. It ran through country already partly settled, but its coming increased the settlement and called new towns into being: Neepawa on the upper Whitemud, Minnedosa at Tanner's Crossing, Strathclair and Newdale beyond. Settlement ran ahead of it. More people moved into the Assessippi country and there in 1883 the town of Russell was laid out under the direction of that Major C. A. Boulton who had led the Portage party to free the prisoners of Riel.

The limits of easy settlement in the parklands, however, were being reached. To the north, heavy forests barred the way of the settlers and the broad plateau of Riding Mountain remained a few years longer the great game country it had always been. Even so, a few hardy spirits had crossed Riding Mountain from the south to enter the Dauphin country as early as 1881. But much filling in of settlement remained to be done in districts already occupied. The southward sloping valleys of Riding Mountain above Minnedosa, Shoal Lake, and Birtle drew many settlers and some speculators, among them Lord Elphinstone, a large investor in Manitoban land. A small Swedish colony was formed on the Rolling River, well up in the forests of the Mountain. South of the railway around Rapid City the farms spread out towards the Assiniboine over the new municipalities of Odanah, Miniota, and Oak River, to complete the occupation of the south-central slope. And to the east behind the older settlements, the new farmsteads multiplied until checked by forest or rock. On the Portage Plains the fertile clays were taken up until the marshy lands of Lake Manitoba and the limestone rubble of the Long Ridge north of Poplar Point were encountered. The Plains had become one solid wheatfield by 1881.[8] Northwest of Winnipeg, the same limestone uplands and the wooded country of the interlake region checked the advance of settlement. East of the Red also settlement stopped along the wooded ridges, for Manitoba was the "Prairie Province" where the pioneer had only to sink his share in the sod and run his furrow as he pleased. For future settlers of the north and east a heavier task was in store.

In the upper Red River valley the occupation of the prairie lands by Canadian and Mennonite settlers went steadily forward as the difficulties of farming and living on the open, long-grass plains were overcome. The great marshes, particularly that of the Boyne, checked the occupation of the valley lands, but in 1881 the provincial government, spurred on by the wet seasons and the grant of swamp lands by the federal government, began a series of drainage schemes, the greatest of which was the Norquay Dike to empty the Boyne marsh.

On the southern uplands, while the good vacant lands of the older districts were being taken up by purchase or homestead, the general movement of settlement was across the Pembina valley and northward towards the Tiger Hills. Beaconsfield, Somerset, Belmont, and Swan Lake date from these years, as do the French settlements of Notre Dame de Lourdes, Bruxelles, and St. Alphonse, the last like some south Italian town with church and houses huddled on its hill. At the same time Holland and Treherne were founded on the northern slope of the Tiger Hills and the occupation of the Cypress River country was completed. The lowlands stretching north to the Assiniboine were too heavily wooded on the Delta lands and too wet on the valley clays to be occupied in the early 1880's.

While the farms spread over the province, the methods and aims of farming were changing. The subsistence and mixed agriculture of the first years of settlement began to give way to wheat as the railways furnished a means of export. From among the varieties of grain grown before 1881 Red Fife, the hard red spring wheat, was emerging in definite supremacy. In 1881 the Canadian Pacific Railway and the Provincial Agricultural Society both furnished pure Fife seed to farmers, and every effort was made to encourage its cultivation.[9] As settlement thickened on the Escarpment, with its 800-foot increase in altitude and the late wet springs, fall frosts began to be reported in 1880 for the first time since 1871.[10] The average period of growth from seeding to harvest for Red Fife was 110 days, and August and September frosts, on the clear nights of the full moon, became a worry of the Manitoban farmer. Early harvesting, smoke smudges, fall ploughing to permit early seeding, were all tried as remedies, and the search for an earlier maturing variety of equal quality began. For a quarter of a century, however, Fife was to know no effective challenger.

At the same time the use of machinery continued to spread. The self-binder was steadily ousting the reaper, and the widening fields demanded the use of the seed drill. As the sulky and the gang plough came in, the horse—usually a "Montana cross" of Ontario stock with bronchos from Montana Territory—was replacing the ox. The walking plough came more and more to be used only for breaking, and the ancient art of the ploughman was transmitted by fewer and fewer fathers to ever fewer sons. Barbed wire lined the new fields, or, with local "herd laws," kept the cattle in their pastures while the grain grew unfenced. The locomotive steam engine reached Manitoba in the early eighties, and during threshing the quaver of its whistle for straw or grain bags echoed the deeper note of the railway locomotive throughout the days and late in the clear October nights. The threshing separators were reaching the form and size of their later development. Threshing was done almost wholly "from the stack," for outfits were still few and labour scarce. The separator was pulled between a double row of stacks and from dawn to dusk pitcher and spike pitchers toiled to keep the sheaves moving steadily to band-cutter who fed the roaring cylinder. The grain was bagged as it came from the machine, the straw swept away with pole or sweep. And when the stacks were gone, the outfit moved out and the tumbled piles of straw, gleaming and golden in the sun, were fired and touched the night with their yellow and crimson flares.

Yet, though straight grain farming on large farms with machinery developed in the Red River valley, the Portage Plains, and across the southern uplands and central slope, the Ontario tradition of mixed farming with stock remained unshaken in most of the province. The pure-bred herds and flocks of such leading farmers and ranchmen as Walter Lynch and Donald Stewart at Totogan, of George Morton at Turtle Mountain, of Alex. Boyd in the Sand Hills south of Carberry, were not characteristic of Manitoba, any more than were the wheat farms of the Red River valley and the Portage Plains. The old tradition that every farm should furnish its own milk, meat, and eggs maintained itself, and most farmers preferred to guard against crop failure by keeping up at least a small herd of grade cattle where pasture and water permitted. The tradition was to be reinforced when drought and depression decreased the returns from grain farming after 1882. Old ways of farming and new were to be tested by economic and climatic difficulties in the new land.

Among these difficulties were troubles over railways. The coming of the railway had brought the inflated prosperity of the boom. With the collapse of the boom came the realization that the establishment of railway communication with eastern Canada and the United States was only the beginning of the construction of a transport system. The new lines had to be equipped with water tanks, stations, loading platforms, warehouses, elevators. Branch lines had to be constructed. Towns had to be built on, or moved to, the railway line. Roads were needed to move grain to the railways. Railway cars were needed in mounting numbers to move the wheat crop which year by year was larger, in bad years as well as good.

All these things could not be done at once over the whole settled area of the province, and they could only be done at a price, much of which had to be paid in freight rates. The early rates were therefore high in comparison with those charged by American railways. The Canadian Pacific Railway Company, moreover, naturally put its main effort into the construction of the main line to the Pacific, and gave second place to the construction of local facilities and branch lines in the settled area of Manitoba.

In fact, the Company was prepared to leave branch line construction to local companies.

Of these many were incorporated and a few actually began construction. The Portage, Westbourne, and North Western indeed did fairly well as a feeder of the Canadian Pacific. Begun in 1880, it reached Gladstone by 1881 and Minnedosa by 1882, and by 1885 had crossed the boundary into the Territories. It received much local support from municipal bonuses and gained the backing of the Allan interests and a land grant from the federal government. It opened a rich territory in which for many years it had no rival. But it gave an inferior service and failed to earn reasonable returns. In 1894 it was to be taken over by the Canadian Pacific. The Manitoba and South Western, despite the excitement its incorporation had produced and the voting of bonuses by municipalities along its proposed right of way, barely succeeded in reaching the Boyne by 1881. There it stopped. The Canadian Pacific bought it out in 1882 and pushed on to the southwest by way of Morden and Manitou in the middle eighties. The construction of a branch from Brandon to the Souris valley the Canadian Pacific undertook itself, and by 1886 the line was to reach the site of the new town of Souris. Other projects, such as the Pembina and Turtle Mountain out of Emerson, failed to obtain a charter, or if chartered failed to begin construction. Such slow and sketchy railway building, of course, quite failed to overtake the spread of settlement since 1875, and many settlers, hopeful and expectant of finding themselves somewhere near the economic limits of the grain haul with waggon or sleigh, were left enraged far from the end of construction.

Even when the lines came through, trouble followed. The mounting surplus of grain could not be handled until the equipment of the grain trade, platforms, warehouses or elevators, had been built. The Winnipeg and local grain buyers hastened to furnish them, but it took time and capital to do so. Nor could the new railway companies, including even the Canadian Pacific, supply grain cars enough to move the harvest from all points. In 1883 the management of the Canadian Pacific, in an effort to prevent large-scale monopolies in elevators and warehouses growing up, placed a minimum of 25,000 bushels of capacity on elevators and warehouses on its lines.[11] The result was to create local monopolies which buyers exploited and to produce an outburst of anger from the farmers and the demand that the restriction be removed. These early inadequacies of the transport system and of the grain trade, which included the terminal facilities at Fort William, were frequently emphasized locally by the growing surplus of wheat produced on the expanding farmlands, until the bumper crop of 1887 made the "grain blockade" general, and the grain was piled in long dykes of bags along the tracks at every shipping point.

These troubles, inevitable and irritating in themselves, occurred as the depression set in and frost and drought injured the crops. All prices fell, but farm prices fell farthest. Wheat prices fell to levels not touched for a century; in 1886 No. 1 Hard Wheat sold in Brandon for 53 cents a bushel. In 1883 the duties on agricultural implements were raised from 25 per cent *ad valorem* to 35 per cent. For men struggling with the heavy costs of building, breaking land, and buying farm machinery, this blow was severe. The seasons of 1883, 1884, and 1885 were dry marked by severe fall frosts and that of 1886 was a year of drought. In Manitoba the drought did not sear the land as it did farther west and south, but it reduced the hay and grain crops severely and in the fall the prairie fires raged as in the days before settlement.

Similar conditions obtained in eastern Canada and the United States and one of the great waves of agricultural discontent which mark North American history began to form. All across the farmlands of the continent the farmers were organizing in their anger. In the early 1870's agricultural depression had helped the spread of the Grange, a farmers' fraternal and educational organization. One lodge had been set up in Winnipeg in 1874 as a political caucus, and one each had been organized at Headingley and High Bluff in 1878 in protest against prices charged by Winnipeg merchants. But Manitoba had not really known a farmers' organization. Now, however, that the cotton growers of the southern states were organizing in the Southern Alliance and the corn and wheat growers of the west central states in the Northern Alliance, Manitoba, with its developing and depressed agriculture, was to produce a farmers' organization, at once its own and yet inspired by the great associations of the United States.

The Farmers' Protective Union of Manitoba originated late in 1883 in the settlements across the southern highlands, and especially in the area centring on Langvale south of Brandon. The farmers organized local unions, and delegates from the locals met in convention at Brandon in early December, 1883. There the leadership of the movement was taken from men like James Lang of Langvale, a rugged Ontario farmer, by excitable men like Charles Stewart of Rounthwaite and budding politicians like Clifford Sifton, to whose names were to be added later those of Joseph Martin and R. P. Roblin. A provincial convention then met in Winnipeg on December 19. The deep frustration and anger of the delegates, who represented not so much the Union as the province, was strikingly expressed by the dramatic and drastic act of drafting a "Bill of Rights," just as Louis Riel and his embattled *métis* had done, as an expression of protest and as a farmers' platform. The Bill of Rights demanded that Manitoba be granted its "provincial rights," including control of its public lands; that withholding of land from actual settlers by speculation and federal government reserves be ended; that the national tariff be made once more a revenue tariff; that the Canadian Pacific Railway monopoly be ended; that the elevator "monopoly" be broken; that the government of Manitoba be allowed to charter railways; and that the construction of branch lines be hastened.[12]

The resolutions of the convention were pressed on the sympathetic provincial government and a skeptical federal cabinet, which interpreted the agitation as being largely an outburst of disappointed speculators. To consider the reception of its delegates, a second convention was called to meet in Winnipeg in March, 1884. The membership in the Farmers' Union by that date had grown in striking fashion as the movement spread to other parts of the province. Local unions had been organized in most of the principal settlements. Not content with organization, some unions had formed farmers' companies to build elevators. Moreover, the farmers' cause was supported by the businessmen of Winnipeg, themselves engaged in a dispute with the Canadian Pacific Railway over freight rates on incoming goods and critical of the "monopoly clause." Even the local attempts to build elevators to compete with the Winnipeg-owned "line" elevators did not break the union of rural Manitoba and Winnipeg, and further cement was found in the Manitoba Rights League, which was headed by prominent Winnipeggers and absorbed in the Union in 1884.

Under moderate leadership the Union might have become the voice of a united province. But there were extreme elements in the movement, including those prepared to urge secession from Confederation and even annexation to the United States. Many an impoverished speculator supported an agitation which might lead to measures to restore land values. Moreover, the Union had become involved in party politics. Under Thomas Greenway the opposition in the Legislative Assembly was becoming increasingly partisan and definitely Liberal. It had taken up the cry of "provincial rights," first raised by Premier Oliver Mowat of Ontario, and had seized on the Farmers' Union and its demonstrations of discontent as evidence of dissatisfaction with the Norquay government and the Conservative federal administration of Sir John A. Macdonald. Some prominent men in the Union were well-known Liberals, and this sympathy and connection were enough to enable the opponents of the Union, with sufficient truth to be damning, to declare it to be "just a Grit organization." In an age when politics were fiercely partisan, and party lines were forming swiftly, such a charge was enough to prevent many a Conservative farmer from supporting the Union.

The failure of the Winnipeg convention, however, was assured, and the Union ruined, by a resolution passed by the convention and by a threat uttered by Stewart. The resolution asserted that, until the grievances alleged by the Union had been remedied, further immigration into Manitoba and the Northwest should be discouraged. In a new community, to which a steady inflow of capital and population were the prime conditions of prosperity, this was local treason of the worst sort. The Winnipeg businessmen, hitherto by no means unsympathetic with the plight of the farmers and the campaign of the Union, at once turned solidly against it and set themselves to destroy it. Even more disastrous was Stewart's threat that, if redress of grievances were not speedy, Manitoba would secede from Confederation. In a province which was largely colonized out of loyalist Ontario, which had known the threat of annexation during the Red River troubles, which had seen with bitterness many of its settlers leave for Dakota Territory in the preceding two years, the threat of secession was deeply angering. Not only did the press denounce Stewart's speech as being at once disloyal and unrepresentative; many a quiet farmer drew back from the Union which was led by such a man. Stewart shortly after left for the United States, sped on his way by the execrations of the Winnipeg papers, and the Union he had led to ignominious failure collapsed and disappeared.[13]

The rise of the Farmers' Union was Manitoba's counterpart to the rising of Indians and the *métis*, once more under Louis Riel, on the Saskatchewan in 1885. The collapse of the farmers' protest against railway monopoly and federal tariff policies did not mean that Manitoba's troubles had been ended. The agitation begun by the Union had in fact merged with another, the growing opposition in the province to the use of the federal power to disallow provincial charters of railways which infringed the charter of the Canadian Pacific Railway Company.

The agitation in Manitoba against the federal disallowance of provincial railway charters was a complex movement. It contained three elements, Manitoba's perennial attempt to obtain "better terms" of union in Confederation, the question of the union or separation of provincial and federal political parties, and that of "provincial rights," in particular the right of the provincial Legislative Assembly to charter railways to run anywhere in the province. "Provincial rights," of course, was a slogan brought into Manitoba by the Grit democracy, the Liberal party of Ontario.

The struggle for better terms has been touched on already; indeed, viewed in this light, the Red River troubles of 1869 were

only an attempt to win better terms than those laid down by the
Canadian Parliament in the Rupert's Land Act of 1868. The
Davis government had won a revision of the financial terms in
1875. Norquay took up the struggle in 1879, and the boundary
extension of 1881 was given in the belief that the larger territory
would enable the government of Manitoba to meet the financial
demands upon it more successfully. Despite the greater taxable
area, however, and despite the general municipal organization of
1880, the provincial government was in continual financial difficulties. It was caught between the clamant needs of a rapidly
growing new community and the financial scheme of Confederation, devised for provinces which, relatively speaking, were old
and settled areas. The perpetual financial stringency was made
more galling to Manitobans by the fact that Manitoba, alone
among the provinces of Canada, did not have control of its public
lands. The government and people of the province were persuaded, perhaps erroneously, that Manitoba would enjoy a larger
revenue if, like the other provinces, it could administer its public
lands. The federal government, which paid a subsidy to the province in lieu of its lands, was determined to retain control of them
in order to ensure rapid colonization and railway construction.

Closely allied to the struggle to obtain better terms of union
was the question of the relation of provincial to federal politics.
During the 1870's while responsible government was being slowly
developed, and the passions aroused by the troubles of 1869 were
slowly subsiding, Manitoban politics had been governed by communal loyalties. With the end of the decade the question of
organizing political parties arose, and with it the allied question
of the relations between provincial parties and the federal. Norquay's stand in 1879, that partisanship should be avoided in
provincial politics and that the administration of the province
should be kept free from the passions and manœuvres of federal
party politics, won general assent at that time.

There was also general assent at the beginning of the 1880's to
Norquay's further proposition that the best way to win better
terms from Ottawa was through the agency of a government
supported by a united legislature. Such a government could nego-

tiate firmly, yet in a conciliatory manner, with more hope of success than a provincial administration compelled by party ties to oppose and attack the federal government of the day if of opposite political complexion, or, if of the same, to accept and defend whatever treatment the federal administration might choose to accord to the province. And even after party lines had been formed, there were many who agreed with the *Commercial*, a Winnipeg trade review, that, even within the parties, Manitoban politics should be "distinctly western and progressive," loyal to the British connection but not trammelled by the "fogeyism" of Ottawa.

These questions of the relationships between federal and provincial politics came to focus in the dispute over the disallowance of provincial railway charters. The coming of the railway, with the completion of the Pembina Branch and the westward extension of the Canadian Pacific Railway, was the signal for the chartering of a number of railways which were designed to serve as branch lines for the Canadian Pacific. A few sought federal charters, as the Manitoba and South Western had done; most, however, turned to the provincial legislature. The latter, secure in its power to incorporate commercial companies, granted no less than six charters in the session of 1880. One of these, the Manitoba and South Eastern Railway, violated clause 16, soon to be famous as the "monopoly clause," of the charter of the Canadian Pacific Railway, which prohibited the construction of any line running in a southerly direction from the main line of that railway. The object of this clause was, of course, to prevent competition from branch lines of American railways, particularly of the Northern Pacific. Its effect, however, was to make the construction of branch lines in the southern uplands dependent on the grace and means of the Canadian Pacific Railway, and to deny, since the Pembina Branch was part of the Canadian Pacific system, any alternative route to shippers of wheat from Manitoba. The freight rates of the Canadian Pacific were therefore not competitive rates, and those charged on the Pembina Branch were in fact prohibitive.[14]

There was thus a direct conflict between the need of the grain grower for branch line construction and competitive freight rates and the policy of the federal government, which was by means of the tariff and the Canadian Pacific Railway to make Manitoba and the Northwest an economic hinterland of eastern Canada and to prevent it being drawn into the hinterland of St. Paul and Chicago. The conflict between local interest and national policy became a political struggle in which the Manitoban farmers turned increasingly to the provincial government as a means of fighting their battle, and the federal government was compelled to use at once its powers of disallowance and the bait of better terms to maintain its policy of nation building and to try to conciliate the angry western province.

This struggle raged until 1887. It was to raise anew the question of Manitoba's place in Confederation and to transform the character of provincial politics. Its ramifications are exemplified by the involvement in the controversy of the question of a railway to Hudson Bay and of the boundary between Manitoba and Ontario.

The historic route to York Factory, sole outlet for western furs from 1821, had begun to decline in importance from mid-century, as the cart brigades to St. Paul carried more and more of the freight of the Northwest. It continued to be used by the Hudson's Bay Company until the 1880's, but the new province of Manitoba had had little interest in it, looking rather to railway communication with the outside world by way of St. Paul and Fort William. Both history and geography, indeed, suggested the use of the route by the Bay, and in the late seventies the budding town of Emerson, inspired perhaps by its neighbours across the border, had its exponents of a railway to the Bay. When the St. Paul and Fort William routes came into operation in 1879 and 1882, however, it was found that the Canadian tariff of 1879 and the control of the Pembina Branch by the Canadian Pacific greatly reduced the usefulness of the St. Paul line and that Fort William in effect had a monopoly of the traffic of the province. A search for alternative outlets began, either by way of a competitive railway to the border or by way of a railway to York Factory. Even the threat of such a route might serve to bring down the rates charged by the Canadian Pacific. Professor Bell's surveys of the Nelson and Hayes rivers in 1880 for the Geological Survey of Canada had revived interest in the route, and when the railway troubles began the search for alternative outlets it was possible to quote scientific evidence in support of the feasibility of a railroad to the Bay. The exponents of the scheme received much support, both in Manitoba and in Minnesota and Dakota, as the struggle over disallowance grew heated, and the federal government, seeking to win time and relieve the pressure, despatched an expedition by sea to Hudson Bay in 1884, 1885, and 1886. The object was to determine the length of the season of navigation in the Bay, and the expedition, under the command of Captain A. R. Gordon, and with Professor Bell in charge of the scientific investigation, reported that it was of at least four months' duration.[15] In 1885 a federal charter was granted to the Hudson's Bay Railway Company under the presidency of Mr. Hugh Sutherland, M.P., and in 1886 it began to build northwestward from Winnipeg. The work was soon to be halted in a scandal, but a strand from the history of the old Northwest was woven into that of the new province, and was to reappear in the future.

The project of a railway to the Bay had also raised the question of boundary extension to the north, at a time when the settlement of the Manitoba-Ontario boundary was causing dispute. The controversy over the boundary with Ontario, like the movement to resume export by the Bay, went far back into the history of the Northwest. The Hudson's Bay Company and Great Britain under the charter of 1670 had claimed all the land drained by the rivers flowing into Hudson's Bay. The claim had not been made good by settlement inland, and the French government of New France had always contested it. A commission to settle the dispute had been provided in the Treaty of Utrecht, 1713, as already noted, but it had never come to any conclusion, no doubt because the treaty was followed by an Anglo-French entente. With the cession of Canada in 1763, the French claims passed to the Crown of Great Britain, first in right of the province of Quebec from 1774 to 1791, and, after 1791, of the colony of Upper Canada. The western boundary of Quebec and of Upper Canada was not definitely established, and in consequence, when the Hudson's Bay Company yielded its title to Rupert's Land in 1869, the federal government inherited from the Company a potential boundary dispute with the province of Ontario. The Upper Canadian attempt before the Confederation to revive the old French claims to a boundary at the Rocky Mountains had been ended finally by the creation of Manitoba, but under the terms of the Quebec Act Ontario had strong claims to a western boundary at the North West Angle of the Lake of the Woods.

The first eastern boundary of Manitoba at 97° west longitude was to the west of that famous landmark. In 1878 a commission sat on the question of the western boundary of Ontario and fixed it at a line passing through the North West Angle from the 49th parallel of north latitude to the Winnipeg River. The award was not accepted by the federal government but no dispute arose until the extension of the boundaries of Manitoba in 1881. By the federal act the eastern boundary of Manitoba was made the western boundary of Ontario. Ottawa claimed for Manitoba a line due north of the junction of the Ohio and the Mississippi rivers which ran just west of Fort William; Ontario the line of the North West Angle. The question was made a practical one by the entry of Ontario lumbermen into the area with the Canadian Pacific Railway. If the district was in Manitoba, it was for the federal government to grant the leases; if in Ontario, for the government of that province. As the federal government was Conservative and the Ontario government Liberal, and the granting of timber leases a partisan matter, the controversy was one of some political urgency. Moreover, the building of the railway, the Rat Portage gold strike of 1882, and the beginning of settlement at Rat Portage raised questions of law and order, and also of political representation, since the Territory of Keewatin no longer included the area under dispute. Was the government of Ontario or of Manitoba to police the district, and to which assembly, that of Manitoba or that of Ontario, should the representative of the settlers be elected? Both provinces claimed jurisdiction, and in 1883 their respective police forces came into conflict over the arrest of some disturbers of the peace. A member for Rat Portage actually sat in the Manitoba legislature in the session of 1883. But the boundary "war," really one between Ontario and the federal government, was not allowed to widen, and was referred to the Judicial Committee of the Privy Council. In 1884 the Committee found in favour of Ontario and the boundary was fixed at the North West Angle.[16]

The decision was no doubt good law and it ended an intolerable uncertainty. It did, however, fly in the face of both history and geography and deprived Manitoba of an area which by historical and physical ties had always been part of the Red River basin. It ended, moreover, the possibility of Manitoba's becoming a great central province in Confederation with an east to west orientation and was to force it back on northward expansion to achieve a balance of resources. Manitoba had had little interest in the matter at the first, as the area had little agricultural land and the federal government would have administered its forests and minerals. In the fierceness of the controversy over railway disallowance, however, it seemed but another instance of the refusal of equality of rights or territory to the "Cinderella of the provinces." The tradition of grievance which was forming was reinforced. And there was an object lesson in the fact that the province which had challenged Ottawa had been successful, while that which had relied on the federal government had gone empty away.

The boundary award was made in the same year that the Farmers' Union was at its height and the depression in its first, most painful stage. The Manitoba and South Eastern Railway had been rechartered and its charter had again been disallowed. The issue was clearly joined: public sentiment in Manitoba had hardened in favour of a strong assertion of provincial rights, and the Macdonald government was resolved to maintain its railway policy. The Norquay government had been sustained in the election of 1882, but was increasingly constrained, while negotiating for better financial terms with the federal government, to yield to the pressure of the Assembly and to support the chartering of railways south of the main line and protest the resultant disallowance. It was a difficult role and one that could be effectively maintained only by an administration which was in fact what that of Premier Norquay had been, a representative provincial administration, and not a party government.

Norquay's essential purpose, and his main contribution to the political life of the province, was to bridge the gap between old and new settlers and to preserve harmony between French and English. In this task he was strikingly successful during the first years of his premiership. But only by sustained success in dealing with the political issues of the day could he hope to keep most of the Assembly behind him. There had always been a few opposition members, and after 1882, as Manitoban grievances grew, a definite and partisan opposition to the Norquay government began to form under the leadership of Thomas Greenway. Greenway had been a Liberal member of Parliament for South Huron before he moved to Manitoba, and some of his followers were Ontario Grits. It was natural for the opposition to take up the cry against the unpopular federal policies and set themselves up as the champions of "provincial rights." Something of the party organization of the eastern provinces had appeared locally in Manitoba in the late seventies; by the mid-eighties an organized provincial Liberal party was taking shape.

The rise of a partisan organization not only destroyed the character Norquay had striven to impart to provincial politics; it had also had the effect of forcing his administration into the position of being defenders, not infrequently reluctant defenders, of the Macdonald government and finally of forcing it to assume the role of provincial Conservative administration. Norquay and his followers were such in seeming rather than reality. The relations between Norquay and Macdonald were not those of party chief and sub-chief. Nevertheless the desire to co-operate where co-operation was possible, the essentially conservative cast of the Premier's own mind and of his concept of politics, added to the appearance of being allied with the federal Conservatives, brought him the support of Manitoban Conservatives. The day of provincial political parties had begun in Manitoba.

Norquay never acquiesced in this change of political method, but persisted in his own policy of attempting to put a fair case well with general provincial support. The federal government was glad to find some means of offsetting the violent unpopularity of disallowance in Manitoba, and in 1886 Norquay's persistence was rewarded by the grant of better terms to Manitoba. The main provisions were an increase in the "debt allowance" of the province and in the subsidy in lieu of public lands. A total addition of some $300,000 was made to the annual revenue of the province. With this success in hand, Norquay was able to go to the polls. The election of 1886 was the first really partisan provincial election in Manitoba, and the Liberals showed remarkable strength, particularly in western Manitoba. Had the distribution of seats not still favoured the old settlements of the province, it is doubtful whether Norquay could have carried the day.

This set-back, for such it was, was followed by a renewal of the controversy over disallowance. The Red River Valley Railway had been chartered to run from Winnipeg west of the Red to the border, where it would make connection with the Northern Pacific. Such a line would, it was hoped, offer an alternative outlet and effective competition in rates to the Canadian Pacific. The charter was disallowed, and the long-suffering Norquay, buffeted between the anger of his own people and the adamantine stand of Ottawa, was at last roused to fight. He proposed to build the line in defiance of the disallowance, as a provincial public work. He set resolutely to work, only to become entangled in a web of legal injunctions sued out by the Canadian Pacific Railway and to find himself begging fruitlessly in the money markets of New York and London for funds wherewith to proceed.

At this juncture, the hard-pressed administration was charged by one of its erstwhile supporters with an irregularity in the financial transactions between the government and the Hudson's Bay Railway. Further investigation revealed that a serious irregularity had in fact occurred. Norquay and his Provincial Treasurer, Hon. A. A. C. Larivière, were forced to resign. In a powerful and moving speech, the heart-broken man, first and last of native premiers in two generations, defended his political career and established his personal honour beyond reproach. But two years more and this most distinguished of the sons of old Red River was dead of a sudden illness and at peace among his people in St. John's Cathedral cemetery.

The year 1887, which saw Norquay's government fall, saw also a bumper crop result in a great grain blockade, and political agitation over disallowance swell to a pitch of bitterness scarcely to be kept within constitutional bounds. There was indeed cause to wonder whether Manitoba, heir of Red River and the Northwest fur trade, could make a place for itself in the Canadian federation, and whether the new agricultural economy could call into being and maintain a stable and cohesive society. But there was to be a swift resolution of the controversy and a *dénouement* which was to reveal that the character of the pioneer society of Manitoba had formed.

The years of political agitation from 1882 to 1887 were the years of depression also. Those years, which tried the new agricultural economy so severely, were years of slackening immigration. The annual influx fell from an estimated 60,000 in 1882 to an estimated total of 21,000 for Manitoba and the Northwest in 1887.[17] Indeed, they were years which saw emigration from the province; settlers, thwarted by the holding of the reserves and railway lands from the market, went to Dakota Territory across the line; many Icelanders, weary of the floods and bush of Gimli, went there also; other settlers were lured farther west to the lands along the new line of the Canadian Pacific. The greatest change in the formation of the provincial population, however, was that the agricultural exodus from Ontario was ending. The solid British-Ontario core of rural Manitoba had been formed. In the first half of the 1880's it had been largely reinforced by English, Scottish, and Irish settlers. At the same time the French Canadian immigration from New England ended, and the colonization of Manitoba by Canadian farming stock ceased to be the dominant feature of its growth.

People were still needed to take up the great areas of agricultural land yet vacant, but the vast flow of European emigration poured into the cities and over the plains of the western

United States. Efforts to attract them to the Canadian West were vain as yet, and appeals had to be resumed to special groups, such as had been made to the Mennonites and Icelanders in the seventies. Even these had little effect and it was private philanthropy which brought in the most noteworthy groups. In 1883 Lady Cathcart was moved to assist a group migration of Highland crofters to western Manitoba and the Territory of Assiniboia. The trials and successes of these people, reminiscent of those of the Selkirk settlers, were followed with keen interest in the press. In 1885 Count Esterhazy assisted the migration of a group of Hungarian colonists to the valley of Stony Creek northwest of Neepawa. A successful settlement was established there which came to be known, rather unhappily, as Huns' Valley. In 1887 another large contingent of Icelanders arrived and scattered to Gimli, Argyle, and other Icelandic settlements. Swedes, Danes, and Norwegians were also coming in small numbers. But these isolated groups witnessed to the difficulty of obtaining immigrants rather than marked the beginning of the great influx of British and European people which was to begin after 1896. For another decade Manitoba was to be predominantly a new, western Ontario.

It was, it is true, to be an Ontario with a difference, for the rainfall was less and the summer shorter. The frosts of the eighties led to an emphasis on the need for early sowing and hence for fall ploughing. It became the mark of the good farmer to have the stooks in stack by early October and the fields black by November. With a few years of cultivation and the onset of dry summers, the new technique of dry farming by summer-fallowing began. Fallowing, to clean the lands of weeds, had been advocated by the historian Alexander Ross as early as 1850. By 1884 it was being advocated and by a few practised, to clean the land of Canada thistle, wild oats, mustard, and pigweed, the most troublesome weeds;[18] that it was a useful practice to conserve moisture became evident in the dry years of the future. Manitoba was a zone of transition from the moist forest lands to the semi-arid plains, and its farmers had to work out a flexible compromise between the tillage of forested Ontario and the new "dry-farming" of the plains. Mennonite example had something to do with the introduction of summer-fallow; still more perhaps, American example on the great plains of Dakota and Nebraska. The practice became firmly embedded in Manitoban farming, until it was standard to have up to one-third or even one-half of the tillage in fallow. The hardy wheat plant, for which the fallow land was reserved, would reach maturity on good fallow, it was found, in an almost rainless summer.

Despite the limitations of the climate, aggravated as they were to be by dry years, the face of rural Manitoba was assuming a new aspect, in many ways like, in others unlike, rural Ontario. The straggling bluffs were being trimmed square by the plough; on the prairie of the Mennonite reserves, on the Portage Plains, and on the bare skylines of the uplands, the bluffs were being matched by the sapling platoons of the shelter belts to north of house and barn. The soaring cottonwood and bushy Manitoba maple were the chief recruits in a campaign against the north wind. The campaign was inspired by the love of trees brought from wooded Ontario and by the Forestry and Horticultural Association founded at the instigation of Rev. W. A. Burman of Griswold in 1883.[19] In 1886 Arbor Day, the day of annual tree-planting, was introduced in Manitoba and the Territories. Ploughed field and travelled road checked the prairie fires and on woodlot and on road allowance the native trees and shrubs were soon growing more abundantly than in the days before settlement. The bluffs of the park belt were fitting themselves into the checkerboard landscape, as the heavy roll of standing wheat had replaced the flow of prairie grass.

The shaping of the new landscape was accompanied by the shaping of a new provincial consciousness. The small colony of Red River had succeeded to a surprising degree in transmitting to the immigrant its sense of being a people apart. The greatness of the break made by the newcomers had created a strong sense of identity with the old-new community of the Red River basin, and the strange new land became familiar quickly because of its distance from the old homes. The struggle for better terms and provincial rights, moreover, hardened the consciousness of identity. With a speed which was often amusing the new settler of yesterday became the Manitoban of the morrow. But under these more brilliant stars and amid these wider horizons the farm-steads continued the rural life of Ontario, to which the British settlers were assimilated. The difference of habitat was not great enough to force any fundamental change. The major modification of social and political life was caused by the less density of population and the larger size of the farm. It was a struggle, for example, to maintain the local school districts; the Ontario county system, introduced in 1880, had to be altered in 1884 by the creation of a rural municipality which was a compromise between the county and the township. The Ontario township never became a unit of local government, and the county was too costly for a thin population to support. The small towns also, in spirit replicas of those of Ontario, failed to develop the small industries and the population of their originals. They remained the agents of the railways and the local grain trade.

While rural Manitoba was establishing and adjusting the wonted ways of Old Ontario in the new land, bustling Winnipeg was driving on its imperious way. Westward from Point Douglas the railway yards of the Canadian Pacific sent out fork and parallel, track by track. On the site of the old village where Mc-Dermot's store had stood alone forty years before, the great ware-houses were rising from which goods went out to the whole Northwest. The Board of Trade worked energetically to let no occasion slip to add to the business of the metropolis. After four years of struggle, it won from the Canadian Pacific Railway the differential freight rates which ensured its role as distributing agent for the Canadian West.[20] It fought fiercely to have the grading of the wheat crop according to the newly established grain grades, ranging down from the famous "Manitoba No. 1 Hard," done in Winnipeg and not at the terminal elevators of Fort William. It fastened on the grain trade as the great enter-prise which should make the city greater, and in 1887, the year of a bumper crop, the Winnipeg Grain Exchange was organ-ized.[21] The buying and selling, the grading of the swelling wheat crops of the West were to be centred in the city which stood on the edge of the wheatlands, half way to the great lakehead terminal at Fort William.

The consciousness that Winnipeg was the metropolis of the West, and not just the principal city and capital of Manitoba, grew during this formative period. The press spoke more and more for the Northwest. Among the leading men, the grain men, the lawyers, the journalists, those who had foregathered in the Manitoba Club since its founding in 1874, there developed that strong sense of sectional interest, to be advanced only by national policies, which was to form the mind of the Winni-pegger and establish the character of the city. The sense of sectional and national destiny found exemplary expression when in 1885 Riel's ill-starred rising on the Saskatchewan threatened to plunge the West into the chaos of an Indian war. Winnipeg despatched a field battery and two new battalions of militia, the Winnipeg Rifles and the Winnipeg Light Infantry, units one day to be famous. Volunteers came in from the country and Major Boulton raised his Scouts in the northwest of the Province, but it was Winnipeg, as was fitting, which organized the rally of men to put down the insurrection and ensure the peaceful develop-ment of the West in Confederation.

The achievement of this formative period was, of course, largely material. The school system was extended, the University of Manitoba continued its sober growth; the Historical and Scientific Society of Manitoba was in its most active and fruitful phase. But there was no equal to Ross's or Hargrave's historical writing; not even George Bryce's first work, *Manitoba, Its Infancy and Growth*, possesses the literary charm or factual content of their work. Alexander Begg, an industrious notetaker and com-piler, usually accurate when working from documents or direct observation, had published his *The Creation of Manitoba* in 1871, the best contemporary account of the troubles of 1869–70, and his rather haphazard *Ten Years in Winnipeg* with Walter Nursey in 1879. Begg had also published *Dot-it-Down*, a tale of the Red River troubles, in 1871 and at least one story in the *Winnipeg Times*. R. B. Hill's *History of Manitoba* provided a sober and useful account of the history of Portage la Prairie and the settlement of Manitoba down to 1888. But the literature of travel, so striking in the thirty years before 1870, had practically ended. Its place was taken by the journal of the tourist and the narrative of the settler. Lady Dufferin's chapters on Manitoba in her *Journal*, Mary Fitzgibbon's *A Trip to Manitoba*, are the most charming examples. No imaginative work in verse or prose was produced. Among the Sand Hills and by Chaska-water, it is true, a young naturalist was training the eye, and exercising the pen from which were to come *The Trail of a Sand Hill Stag* and some of the essays of *Wild Animals I Have Known*, but the time of Ernest Thompson Seton was not yet come.

The provincial society which had taken form in Manitoba by 1887 had in fact little time for arts and letters; it was preoccupied with its own growth and its own urgent future. It was self-centred, if not self-satisfied. Yet it was not isolated, either in sentiment or in fact. On the contrary, Manitoba was part of a developing nation and an outer margin of the great industrial system which, spreading from England, was setting up new centres of power in the United States and in Germany, and was bringing the Far East and the Far West within the commercial and industrial web of western Europe and America. The wheat from the new fields of Manitoba went to feed the workers of Lancashire and the Midlands; the railways and the steamships which carried it were the agents and carriers of that industrial order which was calling a new agricultural society into being on the prairies where the buffalo bones were yet white and the occasional Indian band still wandered, not yet broken to the reserve. The provincial society of Manitoba was itself a province of an industrial and cultural empire that was ocean wide and in some ways world wide.

Not only was Manitoba an outer part of that great society; the very rhythm of its growth was a reflex of the cyclical rise and fall of enterprise in the great world of international commerce. In the late eighties that world was suffering from a deepening of the prolonged depression which had set in during 1873 and which save for the upturn of 1879–81, marked in Canada by the Manitoba boom, was not to end until 1896. It was this long-drawn depression which had disappointed the high hopes of Confederation and left Canada in 1887, despite the building of the Canadian Pacific Railway, the development of the National Policy, and the creation of a transcontinental union, burdened with stagnant industry, alarmed by the loss of population to the United States, and shaken by the heavy commitments of the annexation and opening of the Northwest. In 1887 even England, still supreme in finance and industry and still mistress of the seas and of an unchallenged empire, was disturbed by the decline of its agriculture before the cheap wheat of the prairie lands and the threat to its exports of the rising industrial power of the United States and Imperial Germany. These changes were as yet only premonitions of a harsher age, but they signified that it was into an age of world commerce, big business, and power politics that the new province had entered.

It was also an age of nationalism, democracy, and public education. The new industrialism required national markets, the new industrial society hastened the spread of democracy, and the machine age demanded general literacy. All these factors made for elimination of differences between peoples and classes, and for assimilation to a common standard. Nowhere was this more true than in the United States, which had become a melting pot of peoples. Canadian eyes turned frequently to the American scene and as English Canadians aspired to emulate the great material achievements of the Republic, they assumed they must imitate the immigration and social policies also. But the same factors were at work in Europe as well, often resulting in class conflict, and the clash of creeds and of church and state, as in the *Kulturkampf* in Germany or in the struggle to control the schools in France.

Under the influence of these factors, as well as of its own circumstances as they had developed since 1870, Manitoba was to complete its integration with old Canada and to become part of the commercial system of the world. Its growth, so precipitous since 1878, was to be slowed by the general depression, but in that slowness lay an opportunity to consolidate the developments of its first seventeen years, and to confirm the provincial character already formed by 1887. That character was the character of the British-Ontario majority, and it was responsive to all the influences of nationalism and democracy.

The work of consolidation was to be entrusted to new hands. The fall of Norquay's government in December, 1887, ended completely the Red River era in Manitoban politics, the period of government on the basis of joint participation of the French and English and of a communal representative system. It also ended the attempt to better Manitoba's position in Confederation and to gain competing railway outlets by co-operation with the federal government. For communal representation, representation by population was to be substituted, and for political dependence, an aggressive assertion of "provincial rights."

Norquay was first succeeded as premier by one of his own ministers, Hon. D. H. Harrison of Minnedosa, but the new government failed in its first test, the re-election of the new ministers on their acceptance of office, as constitutional law then required. One of these by-elections, that in the district of St. François-Xavier, was later to become famous. The minister seeking election was Hon. Joseph Burke, despite his name the French representative in the new government. He was opposed by the Liberal nominee, F. H. Francis of Headingley. As the French vote was decisive in the old French settlement from which the district took its name, it was necessary to conciliate French sentiment. When the Liberal candidate and his friends were questioned as to the attitude of the Liberals towards French representation in the government, a significant question as the resignation of the Harrison government was generally anticipated, assurances were given that they would be treated as in the past.[22] The assurances were accepted and Francis was elected. This victory for the Liberals in one of the old Red River districts, with the defeat of two other ministers, brought the weak administration to a swift and timely end. When the legislature met on January 18, 1888, the government resigned and the Liberal leader, Thomas Greenway, was called to form an administration. He did so, and true to the pledges given at St. François-Xavier and to Manitoban tradition, he took James E. Prendergast into the Executive Council as Provincial Secretary, after consultation with Archbishop Taché. There seems to be no reason to doubt the sincerity of the pledges or the action of bringing in a representative of the French. The Liberals at that time were not committed to the elimination of the French from the government of the province or to any measure a French representative could not accept. The decisive factor was the narrow division of the legislature, in which the Liberals had been in a minority until the events of December and January. Even with the victories in the by-elections, they could be sure of controlling the House only with the support of the French members.

The new Premier requested adjournment of the Assembly until he had completed the formation of his Council, which consisted of Hon. Lyman Jones, Provincial Treasurer, Hon. Joseph Martin, Attorney-General, Hon. James Smart, Minister of Public Works, and Prendergast and Greenway, the latter as Minister of Agriculture. When the Assembly reconvened it immediately adjourned once more, for the Premier had been invited to Ottawa to discuss the burning question of disallowance. The Premier and the Attorney-General journeyed east, leaving an excited and speculating province behind. Was the Goliath who had rebuffed Norquay so often to yield before the Davids of provincial rights?

The negotiations were protracted and difficult, and were brought to a conclusion only when Greenway and Martin at last left Ottawa for Winnipeg, and were requested to return by Prime Minister Macdonald. The obstacle lay not in anything between the two governments, for the federal government had already made up its mind to end the disallowance of railway charters in Manitoba. The completion of the Canadian Pacific, the mounting agitation in Manitoba, and, the decisive factor, the grain blockade of 1887,[23] had convinced the Macdonald government that the time had come when the monopoly clause was no longer enforceable. The difficulty lay in reaching terms with the management of the Canadian Pacific Railway. As the monopoly clause was to run for twenty years from 1880, the Railway had a strong claim to compensation for an earlier termination. Terms were at length agreed upon, and the federal government pledged itself to disallow no more railway charters of lines in the "old province" of Manitoba, that is within the boundaries of 1870. It was a proud Greenway who assured an excited crowd of Winnipeggers at the railway station on his return that monopoly was at an end, that there would be no more disallowance of provincial railway charters, and that the construction of the Red River Valley Railway would be completed. The power of disallowance had indeed been practically ended and the functioning of the national constitution gravely modified by Manitoban resistance. The "rights" of Manitoba had been vindicated and the new government as their uncompromised champions was most popular and practically without an opposition.

Seldom indeed has a government begun its term of office under happier circumstances, in that the great object both of its rival and predecessor and of itself was granted to it almost without effort on its own part. Yet the provision of railways to compete with the Canadian Pacific Railway was only one of the main lines of policy of the Greenway administration. There were three other objects the new government had in view: the enforcement of economy in the government service and expenditures; the increase of immigration into the province by all practicable means; a redistribution of the electoral districts on the old Grit principle of Ontario, the principle of representation by population coupled with introduction of manhood suffrage.

Economy was at once enforced by administrative order, and included the dismissal of a number of civil servants. Expenditures were restricted, and the provincial finances, in a slovenly state after the lax supervision of the Norquay administration, were overhauled. The only major increase of expenditure was one in the provincial grant to the struggling school districts of the province, the greater part of which was a frontier less than ten years occupied.

These strokes of the new broom were reported to the session of the legislature called in March, 1888. The principal measure laid before the Assembly was that providing for a sweeping redistribution of the province into thirty-eight electoral districts.

The measure was drastic and reasonably effective in applying the principle of representation by population. The population of the majority of the new districts was fairly close to the standard unit of 2,600 people. The three Winnipeg seats, it is true, contained a population of between 6,000 and 7,000 each, and the northern districts, such as Russell, as few as 1,600. The size of urban constituencies, however, was defended on the ground of the advantages of proximity to the seat of government and their representatives, while the population of the northern districts was expected to increase. The significant feature of the bill, however, was that it completely ignored the old concept of communal representation. It was considered at the time that only one of the old districts, that of Kildonan, had survived. The old Red River districts of the "old settlers" and of the French survived, in so far as they survived at all, only in virtue of density of settlement, as in Kildonan or to a lesser degree in Provencher. With them went the "colony" electoral districts such as Gimli, which was absorbed in St. Andrew's.[24] The newly settled areas of "new Manitoba," on the other hand, were for the first time effectively enfranchised. When an amended Elections Act introduced manhood suffrage into the provincial franchise, the triumph of Grit democracy in Manitoba was complete. The old order, whether the dual system in language and schools with all it meant to the French, or the influence the old settlers had exercised through their communal constituencies and their own representatives led by John Norquay, now existed only at the discretion of the new majority, largely Ontario-bred and Protestant by creed.

Redistribution was followed by the dissolution of the legislature and a general election in June, 1888. It was an election, but scarcely a contested one. Ten of Greenway's supporters, including the Premier himself, were returned by acclamation. Norquay's followers, and even professed Conservatives, voted for Greenway candidates. When the new Assembly met in August, the government backed with thirty-five supporters faced an opposition of five, strong only in dauntless John Norquay, returned by the old settlers of Kildonan. Of the whole house only six were French.

This election of mid–1888 marked the triumph of Ontario

over Quebec in Manitoba. The decision of 1870, the work of Riel's daring and Taché's diplomacy, was tacitly undone. The Grit democracy of rural Ontario, thwarted in 1870 by more involved considerations than its simple principles took account of, was triumphant in 1888 in the possession of the major part of the soil of the province, in the flush of a sweeping political majority, and in the easy achievement of "provincial rights."

10

A British and Canadian Province

1889-1890

THE POLITICAL STRUGGLE WHICH FOLLOWED THE collapse of the Manitoba boom of 1881 was a struggle to win for the province a tolerable position in Confederation and to knit its new agriculture into the commercial system of the nineteenth century. The key to success in the latter endeavour was low freight rates. Low freight rates, it was thought, could be obtained if only railways competitive with the Canadian Pacific Railway were built. The victory of the Greenway Liberals and the ending of disallowance opened the way to the provision of such competition.

Even before the election of June, 1888, Greenway and Martin, who was Railway Commissioner as well as Attorney-General, had been working out the railway policy of the administration. In the spring the decision had been made not to complete and operate the Red River Valley Railway as a public work, but to lease it to a private company to complete and operate. To this decision there was little opposition then or later. But the choice of a company to lease it involved the administration in a controversy which split the cabinet and badly shook a government which had begun so brilliantly and which seemed so strong after the victory of June.

Of the private companies available, the Canadian Pacific was impossible, since the purpose was to provide competition for that line. The Canadian Pacific, none the less, made strenuous efforts to persuade the government to buy or lease the old Pembina line east of the Red to Emerson, but Greenway was suspicious of its affiliations with its American outlet, the St. Paul, Minnesota and Manitoba Railway, J. J. Hill's line, and declined to make an offer the Canadian Pacific could accept.[1] Three other railway companies presented themselves. One was the Hudson's Bay Railway, as yet only begun but already notorious from its connection with the fall of the Norquay government, a notoriety it was never to lose. The second was the Manitoba Central, a line only chartered, but which proposed to build from some point west of Portage parallel with the Manitoba and North Western. The third was the great Northern Pacific of St. Paul, recovering from the disasters the reckless financing of Jay Cooke had involved, and ready, now its connections with Duluth to the east and Puget Sound to the west were completed, to do battle with its contemporary in origin and completion, the Canadian Pacific. Both because the Manitoba Central would have had to seek an outlet over either Northern Pacific or St. Paul, Minnesota and Manitoba lines, and because the Hudson's Bay Railway would be costly to complete, the Greenway government was beyond doubt prudent on the ground of economy in deciding to entrust the Red River Valley Railway to a Manitoban subsidiary of the Northern Pacific, to be known as the Northern Pacific and Manitoba.

The decision resulted in the notorious "Northern Pacific contract," by which the Northern Pacific and Manitoba undertook to complete and operate the Red River Valley Railway from Winnipeg to a connection with Northern Pacific lines at the border, to build branch lines westward from the Red River line, and to operate the system under maximum rates fixed by the Lieutenant-Governor-in-Council. Though there were difficulties in arriving at a satisfactory method of fixing maximum rates— the attempt was indeed abandoned in 1889—and though the hope of obtaining lower rates through competition was to be realized only to a minor degree, the contract in retrospect seems to have been an honest, if ineffectual, attempt to find a means of regulating railway rates.

The announcement that the Red River Valley Railway was to

be leased to the Northern Pacific, however, produced one of the most furious outbursts in Manitoban political history. The *Manitoba Free Press* and its fiery editor, W. F. Luxton, a fierce opponent of railway monopoly and Liberal member for Rockwood, were in close contact with the supporters of both the Hudson's Bay Railway and the Manitoba Central. So also was Lyman F. Jones, the Provincial Treasurer. The *Free Press* furiously charged Greenway and Martin with having agreed to lease the Red River Valley Railway to the Manitoba Central for a contribution to their party's campaign fund and then, in betrayal both of this alleged corrupt bargain and of the interests of Manitoba in ending railway monopoly, leasing it to the Northern Pacific, also, it was alleged, for a consideration but this time for personal bribes. As the *Free Press* was then the most powerful of western papers and a recent and fervent supporter of the Greenway government, these charges of another "Pacific Scandal" greatly injured the government. The consequences were the dismissal of Jones and his replacement by D. H. MacMillan, and a libel suit brought by Martin against the *Free Press*. A disagreement of the grand jury prevented the case being brought before the courts, else the political records of Manitoba might have been much enriched. A Royal Commission of Enquiry was appointed and reported on November 15, 1888, that no evidence had been advanced to support the charges against the ministers.

It would seem that Greenway and Martin, comparatively inexperienced men dealing with powerful and avid interests in an age in which men were as ready to cry corruption as they were to practise it, may have been precipitate and inconsiderate of local interests and party commitments. It yet remains to be proved that they had been corrupt, or that they had sacrificed the interests of Manitoba. The fact that Martin became a director of the Northern Pacific and Manitoba did nothing to allay suspicion, but was not incompatible with the easy public morality of the day. The impetuosity of Luxton and the bitter disappointment of those interested in the Hudson's Bay and Manitoba Central railways was the fire that caused the smoke which hung over the government of the province in the summer of 1888.

When the legislature had debated the contract in late August and early September, the conclusion of the majority, despite much public concern caused by the *Free Press*, was that the contract, if not flawless, was the best procurable, and it was duly ratified. This result was largely the work of the new member for Brandon, Clifford Sifton. Only one dissentient note marred the comfort the ministry drew from the support of their followers. That was the powerful opposition of Rodmond Palen Roblin, member for North Dufferin. He was the most outstanding of the new members brought into the Assembly in by-elections which preceded the June election; his maiden speech had made an instant and deep impression on the House, and deservedly.[2] The grounds of his opposition were that the ministers had gone back on an agreement with the Manitoba Central Railway and that they had made a bad bargain for Manitoba.[3] As Roblin was himself a director of the Manitoba Central, he was an interested party and presumably an informed one. His bitter attack, however, neither proved his points nor detached support from the government. The result of this breach was that Roblin, a firm Ontario Liberal, a rising man of business in Carman and Winnipeg, and one of the most effective political speakers in the province, became an independent and began to tread the path which was to lead him to the leadership of the Conservative party and the premiership.

While the political battle raged, the contractors of the Northern Pacific and Manitoba were completing the Red River Valley Railway and beginning a branch south of the Assiniboine River to Portage la Prairie; if grain were to move south to the border in volume over the Red River Valley line, it would have to be brought by feeders from the west. South of Headingley, however, it was necessary for the branch line to cross the tracks of the old Manitoba and South Western, now part of the Canadian Pacific system. The crossing was reached in October, 1888. The management of that line, being desirous, despite the decision of the federal government to end disallowance, to test the constitutional right of the Legislature of Manitoba to charter railways in the province, sought and obtained an injunction to restrain the Northern Pacific and Manitoba from crossing its line. When the

Northern Pacific contractors, spurred on by the hot-headed Commissioner of Railways, Joseph Martin, sought to make a crossing by trickery and even by threat of force, the management of the Canadian Pacific decided to resist. Locomotives and flat cars, manned by extra crews, stood on the line at the point of crossing. Even when the injunction was withdrawn, the Canadian Pacific men maintained their guard. Meantime, the forces of the Northern Pacific were swollen by bands of special constables sworn in by the irate Martin, Attorney-General as well as Commissioner of Railways. The likelihood of a breach of the peace precipitated by the Commissioner of Railways, for the suppression of which the Attorney-General was responsible, was a matter for concern to Lieutenant-Governor Schultz but it in no wise restrained the pugnacious Joseph,[4] who never more than on this occasion deserved his sobriquet of "Fighting Joe." The "battle of Fort Whyte," so called after the western manager of the Canadian Pacific, Mr. William (later Sir William) Whyte, fortunately proved to be one of threats and manœuvres only. No breach of the peace occurred and the dispute was referred to the Supreme Court of Canada, which in February, 1889, ruled that the legislature of Manitoba had the power to charter railways within the bounds of "Old Manitoba." In the result the completion of the Portage branch was delayed a few months, the reputation of the Canadian Pacific Railway as a selfish grasper at monopoly was increased in Manitoba, and the Greenway government had another victory to its credit. The loss of public confidence it had incurred from the attacks on the Northern Pacific contract was to some degree made good.

The breach with the *Free Press* and that with R. P. Roblin were never to be healed, but though they continued their criticism of the railway policy of the Greenway government, the alternative outlet for Manitoba grain came to be regarded by the public of Manitoba as the great achievement of the Greenway government in railway affairs and was so accepted despite the fact that Northern Pacific and Canadian Pacific rates soon ceased to be competitive.[5] The failure to arrive at a method of controlling rates was to leave freight rates as an issue in provincial politics for many a year, but at the time the public was not to be aroused against the government on that issue. Neither did its refusal to give the Hudson's Bay Railway the support it required to continue, and so provide a northern alternative outlet, tell against it, despite a steady public demand in Manitoba for the building of the line to the Bay. In 1891 a cash subsidy of $1,500,000 was offered on condition that the federal grant was earned and the line completed in five years. The offer proved insufficient to revive the line, but enough to turn the edge of criticism from the government.

The summer of 1889, then, saw the completion of the Portage branch of the Northern Pacific and Manitoba. It also saw the beginning of a new westward branch from Morris, a line designed to cross the Red River valley to the northern shoulder of the Pembina Escarpment, pass south of the Tiger Hills, and make its way north of the Pembina Valley to Brandon. As it thrust forward from Morris in 1889, new towns sprang up along its course, Miami on the lower terraces of the Escarpment, Somerset among the rolling prairies of the Cypress River headwaters, Wawanesa in the great loop of the Souris River gorge betwen the Tiger Hills and the Blue Hills of Brandon. Thus one of the fairest and most fertile tracts of the province was crossed by the life-giving railway. In 1890 the line was pushed forward into Brandon, from which the Manitoba Central had begun a short and inglorious course to the northwestward. That controversial and ill-fated line gave Rapid City a second railway—for it had been reached in 1885 by a spur from the Manitoba and North Western—and then came to an end at Hamiota for want of funds.

The fate of the Manitoba Central, indeed, was only indicative of the fate which befell most western railway building from 1890 to 1895. Railway construction in the West during those years came to an end for want of funds, and for want of prospective traffic to warrant the raising of funds. The settlement of the West and of Manitoba had slowed almost to a halt by 1890. Before it had become apparent, however, that the government of Premier Greenway was not to preside over a new era of railway construction, rapid immigration, and booming land values, there had arisen between May, 1889, and February, 1890, an issue which was to make Manitoba more widely known than ever the Manitoba boom had done, and which was, to the eyes of outsiders and of history, to dominate Manitoba politics for the next eight years. That was the Manitoba School Question.

The time was ripe for the raising of the School Question in Manitoba in 1889; yet the impulse to do so came not so much from within the province as from without. Since the attack on the dual school system and the abolition of the Legislative Council in 1876, and the attempt to limit the official use of French in 1879, there had been peace between English and French, Protestant and Catholic. For thirteen years the dual system of Manitoba had continued as modified in 1876, without public criticism from the English-speaking and without public complaint from the French. The former cannot be said to have accepted dualism finally or from conviction as to its merits; they were simply preoccupied with the tasks of settlement and of transplanting in Manitoba their own familiar institutions in church, state, and school. The French, for their part, proceeded with the slow work of filling their parishes and of developing the parish church and school, as the framework within which they might live their own life without disturbance from the busy and aggressive society their neighbours were creating in the rest of the province. The territorial separation of English and French which obtained in all but a few districts made this peaceful development of two distinct and incompatible sets of institutions possible.

As the tide of numbers turned against them, and as they became a permanent minority in Manitoba, the French of Manitoba assumed an attitude at once defensive and resigned. Their preoccupation was to preserve the results of the insurrection of 1869, "the movement which had saved the French race from destruction," as Taché's biographer was to describe it.[6] They were aware that their rights in the province were always subject to attack by the growing majority of the English Protestants; they feared, despite the constitutional guarantees, that such an attack might be successful.[7] If the attack came, they would defend their rights with all the sturdy courage of their Canadian ancestry. Meanwhile they would live quietly, in good neighbourliness with their English, Mennonite, and other fellow settlers. For it is to be recorded that neither before 1889 nor after did the controversies over schools and language in Manitoba terminate the friendly, if not intimate, relations between English and French which the days of settlement had established. Had those questions been dealt with in Manitoba, they would have been settled quietly, though not without pain. They were not to be so dealt with, because the Roman Catholic clergy, resisting throughout Europe the growing pretensions of the secular state, were bound to resist any attack on the dual system in Manitoba and in resisting, to invoke the aid of the powerful Catholic hierarchy of Quebec. Thus the School Question in Manitoba was certain to be, once raised, a national issue.

It was perhaps appropriate, therefore, that it should have first been reopened, not by events in Manitoba, but by events in Quebec and Ontario. In Manitoba the political ascendancy of the Protestant Ontario settlers had been established. Their greater numbers, the creation of a general municipal system, and, finally, the redistribution of 1888, had made their institutions and numbers dominant in the province. That ascendancy, however, had not led to any attack on the dual system; the opposition in principle to dualism was quiescent and might long have remained so. The prairies were dry, the grasses dun and grey after summer's heat; a spark would set the fires running, a rain would lay the sodden grass along the ground.

A spark was to fall, a spark generated by the Jesuits Estates Act passed in 1888 by the Mercier government of Quebec. This Act settled the long vexed question of the Canadian lands of the Jesuit Order, which had passed to the British Crown at the Conquest and to the province of Quebec at Confederation. The Act wisely directed the greater part of the monetary compensation voted to the Jesuit Order to the uses of education, but requested the Pope as head of the Church of Rome to arbitrate certain disputed claims. This reference to His Holiness, natural to a Catholic community, provoked an outcry among strong Protestants, and particularly among Orangemen in Ontario, that papal intervention was being invited in Canadian politics. A rising young member of the Conservative party, Dalton McCarthy, made himself leader of the protest, and became the champion of a crusade by the Equal Rights Association, against the allegedly growing political power of the Catholic clergy in Canada The disallowance of the Act was demanded.

The campaign aroused strong feeling in the Orange lodges, both in Ontario and in central and southwestern Manitoba. The English press also gave much space to McCarthy's attack, for religious controversy was favoured reading matter in hundreds of English Canadian homes. The excitement caused by the Jesuits Estates Act and McCarthy's campaign thus spread to Manitoba in the early summer of 1889. Only too obviously, if the Roman Catholic clergy and their French laity were seeking to extend the political power of Catholicism and the French in Canada, the special position of the Catholic denominational schools and the official status of the French language in Manitoba invited the attention of all loyal British Protestants.

In May the then inevitable outcry for the abolition of the dual school system was raised in the Liberal *Brandon Sun*.[8] Brandon was the political centre of the southwest, so largely settled by Ontario Protestants. The Orange Order was active there, as it was also in Portage la Prairie. In all the province from the Assiniboine River south, and from the foot of the Pembina Escarpment westward, in that south-central and south-western Manitoba which was a new Ontario, the anti-Catholic cry was certain to start the echoes ringing. The purpose of McCarthy's campaign, it is true, was to have the Jesuits Estates Act disallowed. In this cry Manitoba, fresh from successful opposition to disallowance, could scarcely join. But if religious feeling was checked by the recent memories of federal disallowance, the difficulties encountered in building up the school system in districts yet thinly settled, and the remoteness from the French settlements and the lack of any knowledge of or sympathy with the French, were bound to inspire a feeling that the rights of the French Catholic were costly privileges beyond the means of a pioneer society and not in accord with the spirit of a young democracy engaged in the work of creating a new nation out of diverse elements.[9] The

Sun therefore kept up the cry during June and July and was quoted with approving comments in a number of papers of the south and southwest.

The campaign, if such it may be called, for it did not arouse any immediate or general fervour, provoked a surprisingly quick response from the government. Late in July, it would seem, though the evidence is not explicit, three members of the Executive Council, the Premier, Martin, and Smart, the ministers from the region in which the agitation had sprung up, determined to abolish the dual school system. What moved them, as what moved the *Brandon Sun* to begin its campaign, is not a matter of record. That the *Sun* responded to the McCarthy campaign seems likely on the surface. The ministers, at the prompting of J. B. Somerset, Superintendent of Protestant Schools, were genuinely concerned both with economy in administration of the schools and with an increase in the school grants. But the possibility that they sought a popular issue with which to recover the strength lost in the controversy over the Northern Pacific contract is not to be overlooked.[10] They made their decision without consulting their two other colleagues, D. H. MacMillan and Prendergast. Their decision was announced, as a decision of the government, by Hon. James Smart in a speech at Souris on August 1 and another at Clearwater on August 2. The government, said Smart, had already come to the aid of the struggling school districts, and was anxious to do more. It had discovered, however, that the Catholic schools were receiving more than their due share of the provincial school grant. It was only just, therefore, to remove this inequality, and aid the Protestant schools by abolishing the dual system, creating one uniform, non-denominational system of public schools. To ensure efficiency of administration, the School Board also would be abolished and a Department of Education set up under a minister responsible to the legislature.[11] Economy and the abolition of privilege, that is, were the grounds on which Smart based the government's decision. He expressed no anti-Catholic sentiment and spoke with no heat. On such grounds and in such a temper, the School Question might well have been debated on its merits, though the dual system would have undoubtedly been abolished. The great majority of English-speaking Protestants were quietly and resolutely opposed to it and sooner or later would enforce major modifications in it.

The Question was not to be debated quietly, however, for on August 5 Dalton McCarthy made a fiery anti-Catholic speech at Portage la Prairie. Hon. Joseph Martin was on the platform and, responding to the excitement of the meeting, pledged himself, and by implication the government, to the abolition not only of the dual system of schools but of the official use of the French language in Manitoba.[12] The abolition of French had not been mentioned by Smart, though it had been predicted in the *Winnipeg Sun* on August 1, and the journalist, J. W. Dafoe, in two articles for that paper, wrote later in 1889 that the government had decided to abolish it in 1888.[13] Martin in an abject letter of apology to Greenway after the Portage speech made it clear, however, that no decision had been taken on the abolition of the official use of French.[14] The subject, of course, was in the air as it had been for years and was certain to have been raised by Martin or another. However that might be, the abolition of French could also be defended on grounds of economy. But the temper of the meeting and the manifest intention to destroy dualism in its entirety at once placed the government's decision to amend the School Act on a new footing and revealed the anti-French and anti-Catholic animus which lay behind the decision. Martin, whether by calculation or carried away by excitement, had exceeded his powers, and was privately rebuked and publicly repudiated by the Premier for proposing the abolition of the official use of French.[15] He and McCarthy, however, had let the genie out of the bottle and neither Greenway nor any other man was to persuade it to return. The Premier now had to go forward with the betrayal of his French colleague and supporters and the abolition of the dual system in school and language. "The country was ablaze with a prairie fire and a strong wind was blowing."[16]

Once the movement had begun, there was to be no checking the sweep towards the abolition of the dual system. The Ontario Protestant ascendancy with its sense of unchallengeable strength, the difficulties and the need for rigid economy in creating a school

system in the thin and scattered elements, the belief that no injustice was being done the French in taking from them a "special
privilege," all sprang to the surface following the pronouncements
of Smart and Martin. Added to them and underlying them was a
deep-set conviction among the British settlers of all kinds that
Manitoba must be made British and that a "national" school system should be the agent to accomplish the task.[17] Already the
presence of the Mennonites and the Icelanders, together with the
smaller ethnic groups, had raised the question of how these diverse
elements were to be assimilated to one common Canadian nationality. The attempts at group settlement, the formation of colonies,
the old communal principle which had affected the distribution
of electoral representation in the province from 1871 to 1888,
had all worked to make the issue more urgent. Anything which
made for division, such as the dual system in language and
schools, seemed to invite a perpetuation of differences, and was
condemned in the general opinion of the British and Protestant
majority. They were determined that Manitoba should be a
British and Canadian province, and were convinced that they
were right and justified in that determination. The old drive
of Ontario to possess the West was prevailing over the counter-
claim of Quebec that the West should be the dual heritage of
French and English. The limited union of two nationalities each
secure in the possession of its cultural institutions, in which Quebec and Ontario joined at Confederation, was, it was thought,
neither desirable nor workable within the limits of a single province. Neither should the future of Manitoba and the Northwest
be prejudiced by an extension of the racial and religious differences, indefinitely multiplied by the immigration of new groups,
which periodically disturbed the public life of Ontario and
Quebec.

This general support for the abolition of the dual system was
speedily modified by a further consideration. Were the schools
under the new system to be secular? The Protestant schools had
not been denominational in any exact sense or any particular way.
The schools under the new system would be definitely non-
denominational. So far there was general agreement among Pro-

testants. The Protestant clergy, however, were not prepared to accept schools which should be merely secular, or, as it was conventional to put it, "godless." Some further pronouncements of Attorney-General Martin, on these occasions in favour of the principle of secular education, aroused the fears of the Protestant clergy. A ringing declaration against secular schools by Rev. Dr. J. M. King, Principal of Manitoba College, made the position of the Presbyterian ministry clear, and an outspoken protest by Bishop Robert Machray of the Church of England added the weight of the Anglican communion and of a leading educationalist to the opposition to purely secular schools. If the government ever had any intention of being bound by the declarations of the Attorney-General, it did not proceed with it. Religious exercises, it was announced, would be permitted in the schools, and so the stigma of godlessness was avoided and a possible source of opposition to the changing of the school system removed.

Sustained and impassioned opposition came, of course, from the Roman Catholic clergy and the French minority. In August Prendergast, who had detected and feared the coming storm, had protested and resigned. He did so in the conviction that he had been tricked and betrayed, from the time of the St. François-Xavier by-election, into joining and supporting a government which now proposed to destroy the constitutional rights of his co-religionists and French compatriots. It must be said that Premier Greenway and his colleagues never succeeded in refuting this charge of deception and disloyalty. At the same time it must also be said that an examination of the whole sequence of events from January, 1888, to the introduction of the school and language legislation in February, 1890, suggests that Greenway was led from one position to another, from dependence on the French vote to independence of it, from the determination to amend the school laws to the abolition of the dual system in both language and schools, by the pressure of events and the fretful irascibility of Martin, until in the end he had betrayed colleagues whom he had not planned to betray and abolished constitutional rights he had not proposed to abolish. It was an obtuse disloyalty, it would seem, not a Machiavellian treachery, of which he was guilty. But he was guilty, and the plea that the French had to submit to the will of the majority does not involve as corollary that Premier Greenway should have led that majority.

To the injured and indignant protests of Prendergast were added the spirited pamphlets and the restrained but accusing letters of Archbishop Taché. The fate he had always feared for his people had come upon them with appalling suddenness. With despair in his heart, Taché fought with every weapon at his command, the letter and the spirit of the constitution, appeals to honour and fair play, and refutations of the financial and legal arguments of the supporters of the abolition of the dual system. The secret history of the preparation of the third and fourth Bills of Rights and of the negotiations between the delegates of the Provisional Government and the federal authorities was laid bare in the controversy, and the fundamentals of Manitoban history were revealed in the press in December, 1889. It was all to no avail. The majority, convinced that the French and Catholic case was specious and that no injustice was being done to French or Catholics in treating them in common with all their compatriots in a general democracy, pushed on to its goal. There were to be those who thought that injustice was being done, notably James Fisher, Q.C., and J. S. Ewart of the legal firm of Fisher and Ewart. These men thought, and were to argue while the School Question remained in dispute, that the proper reform of the system would have been to introduce the Ontario system of separate schools, by which Catholic parents in defined circumstances and as a matter of personal relief might require that their taxes be applied to the support of Catholic schools. Such a compromise was to suggest itself again and again in the course of the controversy, but in 1889 and 1890 the majority of the electorate and the legislature of Manitoba were determined to abolish the Quebec dual system of denominational schools and replace it with a system of "national" schools on the American model.

In the session of the legislature which began in January, 1890, a bill was introduced to abolish the official use of the French language in the Legislative Assembly, the civil service, government publications, and the provincial courts. With the last went also the

right of a French Manitoban to trial by a French jury in a provincial court. The change in government publications had already
been put in train in September, 1889, when the printing of the
Manitoba Gazette in both languages had been discontinued. The
French members, led by A. F. Martin and Prendergast, made a
spirited defence of the rights of the French language, but they
received no support and no overt sympathy. It is plain from the
reports of the debates that they expected none, and had no hope
of altering the determination of the majority, but were speaking
for the record and for posterity.

The bill to alter the school system followed. It was a copy of
the contemporary School Act of Ontario, with the provision for
separate schools omitted and also the clauses providing for compulsory school attendance. These last were struck out in committee, for the legal position of the government, assumed at a
last-minute meeting of the cabinet, was that the Catholics of
Manitoba had no constitutional right to schools supported by
public taxation, but did have a right to schools such as they had
before the entry of Manitoba into Confederation, private schools
supported by fees and gifts.[18] Because of this right, children of
Catholic parents could not be compelled under the constitution
to attend state-supported schools. The bill provided for a system
of non-denominational schools, to be administered by local boards
of trustees and a Department of Education with a minister responsible to the legislature. Religious exercises in the schools were
permitted, though not required, under defined conditions. The
minister was to be advised on scholastic matters by an Advisory
Board, a pale vestige of the former School Board.

Once again the French members, aided now by three English-
speaking Catholics, courageously but despairingly rang the
changes on the violation of long-cherished constitutional rights,
and presented the petitions against the bill which had poured in
from the French parishes. Again it was to no avail. Joseph Martin
asserted the need for a national school system if a Canadian nation
were to be created within the British Empire. He argued and was
supported by the member for Brandon, Clifford Sifton, that the
bill would deprive Catholics of nothing which they had enjoyed

at the time of the union with Canada. Sifton also stressed the fundamental issue, the separation of church and state. Smart reproduced his arguments for economy and a fair distribution of the provincial grant. The Premier defended the course of the government, but with neither clarity nor distinction. The back benchers had little to say, assured as they were of the support of their constituents if they remained silent and voted for the bill. Not much was made in the debate of the charge, popular among the anti-Catholic speakers and pamphleteers, that the Catholic schools were inefficient. Only one Protestant member, R. P. Roblin, already in opposition to the government because of its railway policy, spoke against the bill, and then on the ground that he was opposed to the introduction of a Department of Education to replace the School Board. Education, he insisted, must be kept out of politics. On the second reading the bill passed, twenty-seven to eight.[19]

The mere passage of the bill, of course, did not end the School Question. On the contrary, it opened six years of controversy. On the face of it, the Act seemed to be a violation of established and admitted constitutional right. Section 22 of the Manitoba Act said explicitly that the Catholics of Manitoba had a right to such schools as they had "by law or practice" at the time of the union. Such schools they had enjoyed for nineteen years, supported by local taxes and provincial grants. They might therefore hope that the federal government or the courts would right the wrong, as they saw it, done by the legislature and the democracy of Manitoba. Justice might be obtained in a variety of ways. The Lieutenant-Governor might veto the bill, or reserve it for consideration by the federal government. The Lieutenant-Governor of Manitoba since 1889 had been that John Christian Schultz whom Riel had imprisoned and whom the French had feared and hated as leader of the Canadian party before the union. Much had happened since, however, and Schultz was the agent of the federal government, which was controlled by the Conservative party. In that party the influence of Quebec and the Catholic hierarchy was strong. For one moment, as the Lieutenant-Governor stood before the legislature giving the royal assent one by one to the

bills passed during the session, a wild hope rose in the breasts of
the French as the titles of language and school bills were not read
out in the order in which they had been passed. Were they to be
reserved? But they had only been placed inadvertently at the
bottom of the pile by the clerk. The harsh voice of Schultz in-
toned the formula of assent, the work of Taché and Riel was swept
away, and the bills became the law of the province.[20]

There remained the possibility of disallowance by the federal
government. But the exercise of that power had already involved
the Conservative administration in too much trouble with Manitoba, and Taché was persuaded to withdraw his appeal for the
disallowance of the School Act. Then he was persuaded to withhold an appeal to the courts until after the election of 1891. Thus
it was not until late in that year that, by way of the case of *Barrett*
vs. *Winnipeg*, the Manitoba School Question began its tortuous
progress through the courts. There for the moment it may be
left.

By the School Act of 1890 the School Question was concluded
to the satisfaction of the British and Protestant majority in Manitoba. The Ontario immigrants had made the old dual community
over in the image of their natal province, and by refusing even
separate schools on the Ontario model, had made the copy what
they would have had the original be. Manitoba was to be a melting pot, a crucible of Canadian nationalism. The only question
still in doubt was whether the courts might upset the Act, or the
federal government be moved to intervene. Either event would
have been regarded, and hotly resented, as an attack on the "provincial rights" and domestic institutions of the province. Unless
such intervention occurred, however, Manitoba would go on its
way, holding that the School Question was closed.

11

The Quiet Times of the Nineties
1891-1896

AFTER 1890, DESPITE THE INTEREST AND EXCITE-
ment the Manitoba School Question had caused in eastern
Canada, in the United States, and even in Europe, it was of
secondary concern to Manitobans. The interest of the majority
of Manitobans and the activities of the government were turned
to other subjects. The government, indeed, had had its day of
notoriety. In 1891 Hon. Joseph Martin resigned after renewed
differences with Premier Greenway. He was succeeded as Attorney-General by Hon. Clifford Sifton, a rising young man who
had already proved his mettle in the railway controversy and in
the management of the school legislation. But the government
became a humdrum administration which brought few issues to
a conclusion. A temperance movement, for example, had been
developing in Manitoba with the Ontario immigration, and in
1892 was strong enough to have a plebiscite held on the question
of provincial prohibition of the sale of liquor. Despite a majority
for prohibition, the government found itself unable to act because
of uncertainties as to its constitutional powers. Nor was it to push
vigorously the establishment of an agricultural college and a
teaching university, both of which had been under discussion
since the late eighties. The government, like the province, was
caught in a deadwater, and seemed incapable of progressing until
swept on once more by a new wave of immigration and railway
expansion. The extension of the railway system and the increase

of immigration were, therefore, the principal interests of the province and of the government.

By 1890, the rapid railway construction of the preceding decade had come to a pause. The basic pattern of the Manitoban railway network had been set; Winnipeg had emerged clearly and definitely as the railway centre, the great nodal point of the railway web radiating out over the province and the Northwest. All railroads led to Winnipeg. Even the opening of the new line to the south made little difference to Winnipeg or to the Canadian Pacific Railway. The tariff prevented any great inflow of manufactured imports from the United States, and Winnipeg remained the distributing and wholesale emporium of the Canadian Northwest. As a shrewd American observer was to write: "Nature on the one side and the tariff on the other have isolated the Canadian Northwest and made Winnipeg the unrivalled mistress of its trade."[1] The Canadian Pacific moved grain to Fort William as cheaply as, or more cheaply than, it could be moved to Duluth, and in consequence remained the main outlet and main railway system of the Northwest. After 1890 the agitation for the building of the Hudson Bay railway continued sporadically, and there was much talk of the completion of a line from Duluth to Winnipeg through southeastern Manitoba. The line, an attempt to realize the project of the once notorious Manitoba South Eastern Railway, was pushed forward from Duluth, but nothing was accomplished in Manitoba before 1897.

The pause in railway construction was accompanied by a continued slackening of the inflow of immigrants. The falling off had continued despite the active and intelligent immigration policy of the Greenway government. The Premier, as Minister of Agriculture, made immigration his personal responsibility and it was indeed a role for which he was well fitted as the leading colonizer of the Pembina Mountain district. He at once set himself to the task of stimulating a renewal of the movement of Ontario farmers to Manitoba. An immigration office was opened in Toronto in 1889, where literature on Manitoba was distributed, questions answered, and everything possible done to attract the intending settler to choose Manitoba rather than the western

United States. In 1890 a similar office was opened in Liverpool, England, in the hope of reviving the movement of English and Scottish emigrants to Manitoba. Lecturers were engaged to explain the advantages of settlement in a province of cheap and fertile lands, returning settlers come to visit their old homes were employed to do the same work, and press stories unfavourable to Manitoba were answered. In Canada and the United States agents were employed on commission to attract settlers to Manitoba, excursions of parties of "delegates" were organized from Ontario and the mid-western States, and the famous harvester expeditions were begun, with a view not only to supplying labour for the harvest but also of inducing young men to settle and try their fortunes in the province. Here indeed, except for an attempt to attract European settlers, was in embryo the immigration policy which Clifford Sifton was later to apply with such brilliant success after 1896 in the federal field.[2]

It cannot be said that these projects, though persisted in from 1889 to 1896, produced results equal to the effort. The immigration from Ontario had practically ceased. The parties of enthusiastic colonists in the years of the "Manitoba fever" had given way to the immigration of individuals. The sons and daughters of Ontario farmers were going into the factories, either in Ontario or across the border, in ever increasing numbers. Of those few who still followed the frontier westward, the greater number were attracted as always to the American trans-Mississippi West rather than to Manitoba or the Territories. British immigration had also declined to a trickle. The exodus of tenant farmers in the eighties had relieved the pressure on British agriculture; the farm labourer tended to prefer the low annual wages of his home to the relatively higher seasonal wages of Canada. British urban labourers also, influenced perhaps by the spread of trade union organization to the unskilled workers and a rise in real wages, preferred to remain at home. The various individuals and societies which aided emigration of the distressed from the Highlands and the slums of London continued their efforts, but were a comparatively small source of immigrants.[3]

The first half of the nineties, however, did see the beginnings of two streams of immigration which were to swell to floodtide before 1900. One was the movement of American farmers, often former Canadians, to the comparatively cheap lands of the Canadian West. By 1892 this movement was attracting excited comment,[4] though it was a swallow which did not make a spring before 1896. The other was the beginning of the immigration of eastern European people to the Canadian West. The first Ukrainian pioneers came in 1891, the harbingers of the great movement after 1896, but again it took some time for the movement to gather way. Little note was taken of this significant beginning at the time, which was to add so many people to the province and to change so greatly the composition of its population. But one by one the factors were coming into play which would produce a new land rush, and keen-eyed watchers noted them. In 1896 an Immigration Convention was held in Winnipeg which, though it seemed to fail to achieve its immediate objects, was in fact the herald of another wave of immigration and another boom.[5]

The reasons for the falling off of immigration are numerous and obvious. The first was the prevailing low price of wheat, and indeed of all farm produce. From 1888 to 1896 the price of wheat in Manitoba seldom rose above seventy-five cents a bushel, and other produce commanded similar or even lower prices. Added to this was the long period of years of low rainfall, which of course kept down the yield of wheat and other grains. From the very dry year of 1886 to that of 1897, the rainfall in all years but 1887 was below average. In Manitoba also most of the good lands from the lakes of the Winnipeg basin and Riding Mountain south to the border had already been taken up by actual settlers or were held by speculators. The new settler had to buy land at prices which were comparatively high for a time of low produce prices and short crops, or go into the bush and forest lands of the north. For these reasons, the various attempts to start a new boom failed, and so the province failed to obtain the hectic and perhaps deleterious advertising of a boom. In consequence of these factors, capital was tight and development was still further slowed down. And finally there were the external factors touched on above, which operated at the source and diminished the number of prospective settlers.

Thus it was that the first half of the nineties was a period of very slow growth of population and settlement in Manitoba. But it was still a period of growth and, above all, of consolidation. In farming the trends begun in the eighties were continued. The use of machinery had become universal and was extended. Even the new settler began with a minimum of machinery; the established farmer added new machines and improved models of old ones to his equipment. The seed drill, whether furnished with covering teeth or shoe drills, did all the sowing. The gang plough with its two furrows had become the standard plough for fields now mellow with five to ten or more years of tillage; the sulky was used for sod-breaking, while the walking-plough, the symbol of immemorial generations of agriculture, was relegated to the hard tasks of brush breaking or the simple job of ploughing the garden and the potato patch. The binder had replaced the reaper as the reaper the cradle; it cut a swath of seven feet, required four horses for its draught, and had become standard equipment. The locomotive steam engine was approaching its climax of lumbering but stately power, while the self-feeding separator was displacing the old hand-fed machine. Another change in threshing practice, one considered reprehensible by old-timers and which was certainly indicative of the haste and temper of farming in Manitoba, was that of threshing grain from the stook instead of from the stack.

The growth of mixed farming, notably from 1885 on, became more pronounced in most districts. The increase in the number of cattle marketed, and therefore of those carried on the farms, was large and indeed surprising in a province which had been importing meat a decade before. A growing interest in improving the strain of cattle was also evident, particularly among breeders of Shorthorn and Aberdeen Angus. New men were making names for themselves as stockmen, such as J. D. McGregor of Brandon, proprietor of the Glencarnock Farms, and John Barron of Carberry. The completion of the Canadian Pacific and favourable rail and ocean rates prompted the beginning of cattle exports to eastern Canada and Great Britain by 1889. Shipments from the Manitou and Crystal City district were especially noted, and there it was that the firm of Gordon and Ironside took its rise. Pat Burns of Minnedosa was already buying and selling cattle, in preparation for the railway supply contracts which would start him on the way to wealth. Dairying and cheese making also developed, not without the difficulties incidental to the development of those skilled enterprises, but with fairly encouraging results. Writers on Manitoba agriculture and the Winnipeg Board of Trade continued to deplore the slowness with which Manitoban farmers took up the culture of barley, but that sturdy, heavy-yielding but bearded cereal could not easily replace wheat as the cash crop dear to the heart of the farmers who had come west to grow wheat. In hog raising and poultry breeding for sale the Manitoban farmers were also backward, perhaps because of their addiction to wheat growing, but mostly because they felt these occupations did not pay, and because of the perennial shortage of reliable labour. Gardening in Manitoba was highly successful, for the soil and hot summer were suitable for most vegetables, but there was little market gardening, for want of market and labour. Only the hardier fruits could be grown, but already Alexander Stevenson of Morden was demonstrating that a skilled man in a favourable spot could grow most temperate-zone fruits, and especially the apple.

The efforts to diversify and make Manitoban agriculture more efficient led to the foundation in 1890 of the Farmers' Institutes, with governmental encouragement and support.[6] The older Agricultural Societies had done useful work by means of fairs and the competitive display of stock and other produce, and this work continued. But the Institutes were designed to bring agricultural science directly to the individual farmer and to apply it on the individual farm. They were to do useful, unspectacular work among the more progressive farmers.[7] The same movement gave rise to demands for the foundation of an agricultural college and the placing of agricultural studies on the curriculum of the schools. The latter was done in 1893, but, though the Greenway government approved a grant for the purchase of a site for an agricultural college in 1892,[8] no action was taken to establish one at that time, it would seem because of difficulties over finance and choice of site. To these aids to improved agriculture must be added the work of the Brandon Experimental Farm, opened by the federal Department of Agriculture in 1886. Its first work was chiefly experiment with shorter-season wheats, but it also aided the attempts at diversification. And agricultural scientist and practising farmer were to find a co-ordinator in a young, hard-driving woman journalist, E. Cora Hind, whose stocky figure and direct manner were becoming known across the province and whose articles were appearing in the *Free Press*.

Manitoba remained on the whole a grain-growing province, however, and pre-eminently a wheat-growing one. The growing and the shipping of wheat were its two main occupations. When the grain was threshed, it was either hauled direct to the railway, if the supply of waggons and the condition of the roads permitted, or it was stored in the farmyard granary, or the small field granary, or even in the open field until freeze-up and snowfall made it possible to haul it in bobsleighs to the elevators or flat warehouses. Increasingly the hauling was done at threshing time, and the long lines of teams waiting to pull up the ramps to the elevator scales or to the unloading platforms of the warehouses became a familiar scene in fall in all the small towns of the province, as the rumble of the empty waggons hurrying to the frantic call of the steam whistle for bags was a familiar sound of the countryside. The pressure on the railways for cars for shipping became urgent, as more and more farmers had enough wheat—one thousand bushels —to make up a carload. The allotment of cars by the railways became a delicate problem, as the railways preferred to allot cars to the elevator companies which loaded them quickly, rather than to farmers who had to fill a car waggonload by waggonload.

In this difficulty, and in the vexed questions which arose in the grading of grain, lay the germ of the grain growers' associations of the next century. In the first half of the nineties, the farmers' concern with grain shipments and the costs of production led to the formation first of farmers' elevator companies at a number of points in the province,[9] such as had been attempted by the Farmers' Union, and then of the farmers' organization known as the Patrons of Industry. The Patrons had arisen in the mid-western United States and in Ontario in succession to the Grange. In 1891 the first lodges were organized around Portage la Prairie and others soon followed in south-central and western Manitoba.[10] They were primarily a fraternal and educational organization, but soon ventured into consumers' co-operation, notably in the buying of binder twine, coal, and coal oil. When the Patrons of the Portage district attempted the production of binder twine by a producers' co-operative, they unhappily failed, and this discouraged the co-operative movement. The Patrons' organ, the *Patron's Advocate*, voiced the discontent of the Manitoban farmers under a régime of low prices for farm produce and of high costs of production, increased by protective duties on binder twine, farm implements, and other necessities of machine agriculture in the grain-growing regions. In 1895 demands for political action by the Patrons arose and there was a threat of a considerable number of Patrons' candidates in the provincial election of 1896. But many of these candidatures failed to materialize, and of the seven Patrons who finally ran, only two were elected.[11]

The comparatively slight effect of the Patrons' movement and its collapse after 1896 signify that the state of Manitoban agriculture, if not prosperous, was also not desperate. Low prices and short crops were being offset by the breaking of new land, by hard work and skill; and Manitoban agriculture grew slowly but steadily in strength and productiveness. The growth of the small towns which served the farms as shipping points and market towns was of the same kind, as it was a function of the growth of agriculture. One by one the older towns had recovered from the after-effects of the boom of 1881. Two emerged as small cities, Brandon and Portage la Prairie. Brandon, indeed, had escaped the mismanagement which the boom had inspired in many towns, and forged ahead steadily as the capital city of western Manitoba. By 1896 it had a population of some four thousand. Portage had first to suffer the shame of repudiating its debts before a settlement was reached with its creditors. A long-drawn-out rivalry between the widely separated east end and west end had to be laid aside as the result of a devastating fire, and what was practically a new town came into being midway between the rival ends, along broad Saskatchewan Avenue. As centre of the rich farmlands of the plains and a railway divisional point, the growth of Portage was assured, if within limits.

The fate of Emerson, the once proud Gateway City, was less happy. It too bogged down in indebtedness from which a government commission rescued it in 1889. When it had shaken off the burdens imposed by its thwarted and extravagant ambitions, it could settle down, not without some proud regrets, to the role of country town. Selkirk too, though not overwhelmed by indebtedness, had to give up its one-time rivalry with Winnipeg. Its position as the port of Lake Winnipeg, its export trade in white fish to the United States market, its lumbering and shipping, however, gave it a distinctive character and a solid prosperity.

Smaller towns which had yielded to the temptations of the boom, like Gladstone and Crystal City, after tribulations arising from debt and over-expansion, freed themselves of debt or were freed by assumption of their indebtedness by the provincial government. When they had consolidated themselves within limits proportionate to their prospects, they too settled down as quiet market towns, their sleepy quiet emphasized only by the rumble of a farmer's waggon and the clang of the blacksmith's hammer. Few Manitoban towns increased in size, but the log buildings and hastily built false-front stores gave way one by one to more substantial frame, brick, or even stone structures. One by one the new churches went up with modest tower or spire a landmark on the skyline, soon to be borne on the swelling tops of Manitoba maples planted in churchyard or street. And slowly the new schools, town halls, court houses, and post offices, often built of the buff brick coming from the local brickyard, lent solidity to town after town.

Most of the towns were not content to be merely shipping points and market centres, but strove to develop local industries. Brickyards were opened where there was suitable clay and some local capital, as at Morden and Sydney. Most towns had flour mills, some the new roller mills, as at Crystal City. A few had sawmills, as Birtle and Shellmouth, where logs were brought down from Riding Mountain on the spring freshets of the Birdtail and the Shell. Portage la Prairie had an unusual industry in its paper mill, which for many years turned out building paper. At Rapid City the enterprise of the citizens of that hopeful but thwarted town was especially prominent; there a brickyard, a pottery, a flour mill, and a woollen mill were begun and carried on with varying degrees of success. Creameries were numerous, and some very successful, as that at Shoal Lake; others had uncertain fortunes. Cheese factories were not so numerous, or so successful, but some succeeded in turning out a fair brand of cheddar. It cannot be said that many of these local industries really prospered. The flour mills were most useful and longest lived, but had increasingly to compete with the standard brands of the large companies such as Ogilvie's or the Lake of the Woods Milling Company. The sawmills and brickyards served a need in the years when towns and farmsteads were being built, but the growing use of British Columbian lumber and the cessation of the growth of the towns closed them one after another. The pottery at Rapid City had a brief life, as did the woollen mill, for such manufacture had to meet the competition of pottery and woollens imported from eastern Canada and Great Britain. The creameries and cheese factories were attempts to meet the depression by diversifying farming, but had to contend with low prices and the shortage of skilled labour.

Businesses other than manufacturing tended to remain small and personal. But two were to achieve provincial stature in this epoch and a national scope later, the Portage la Prairie Mutual Insurance Company, and the Wawanesa Mutual Insurance Company. The rise of these companies witnessed at once to the extent of the small capital funds of the new communities and the prudence of their businessmen.

If the number of local industries was few and their success uncertain, every town had a basic pattern of trades and professions. The blacksmith was a necessity in the days of the horse and the plough, and his forge flamed and his anvil rang from morning till evening of the busy summer months. The harnessmaker plied his quieter trade behind windows filled with glossy black harness bright with brass studs and hanging trace chains. Every town required the services of a carpenter and a tinsmith, a shoemaker, and perhaps a tailor; other trades such as bricklaying or plastering were likely to fall to some handyman, more or less skilful. Every town also required a doctor, a lawyer, a town clerk, and a bank manager; these, with the ministers of the gospel and the school principal, constituted the professional corps of the town and district. A number of general stores, one or more hardware stores, a butcher shop or two, a lumber yard, a restaurant, Greek, Italian, or Chinese, with one or more commonplace Canadian ones, and a Chinese laundry, constituted the basic services a town had to offer. The sale of farm implements and of insurance, also of special lines of goods, such as cream separators or sewing machines, were handled by agencies; farm implement agencies were usually handled by hardware merchants, insurance agencies by clerical handymen such as school teachers in summer vacations. The railway men, the shop clerks and girls, the draymen, the elevator men, the casual workers, completed the working force of the town. The whole was a fairly rigid pattern of professional, commercial, and trades occupations which varied little, though individuals might and frequently did move from a position or business in one town to a corresponding one in another.

In these years of quiet consolidation the simple pleasures of rural and small-town life assumed a familiar and conventional form. The surprise party—the descent of neighbours in force on the family chosen for the "surprise," to stay all day or over the weekend—remained a favourite diversion in the country, where distances were still great, roads bad, and transport confined to buggy, buckboard, or waggon and in winter to cutter or bobsleigh. June, July, and August were the months for picnics— school picnics, church picnics, Orange picnics—and the groves and riverside meadows which were good picnic grounds were in the nineties already familiar and remembered places. Foot races, tugs-of-war, and baseball were the conventional sports. In winter,

skating and ice hockey for the young, and curling for the middle-
aged and the oldsters, were the chief games, and the long, low
skating and curling rink became a characteristic feature of every
town. In the winter the "social" (evening) took the place of the
picnic, and the school and church socials were occasions for much
visiting among winterbound neighbours and for much good eat-
ing, especially at the "box socials" for which the ladies filled a box
for auctioning to the gentlemen, and then shared its contents with
the lucky bidder. The box social was undoubtedly the most fun-
provoking way of raising money ever devised, especially when
signals were misunderstood and the box of the local belle was
"bid" by the homeliest or least desirable of bachelors.

Organized and strictly amateur sport was keenly followed and
highly developed. It was the age of football, baseball, and rifle
shooting. It was a poor town which could not field a football or
a baseball team, or put up a good shot, as could also many a rural
district. Horse-racing also was keenly followed by its devotees, and
the summer fairs, which were grain and livestock exhibits accompanied by sports, were the scene of tournaments and races keenly
contested for prizes of trophies or cash. The influence of the English immigrants was shown not only in the popularity of association football, but also in a number of cricket clubs and annual
matches, and even in the organization of a few hunt clubs, as at
Minnedosa and Winnipeg, to chase, not the red fox of tradition,
but the startled and indignant coyote. It was a hardy and athletic
race which had peopled the Red River valley and the Manitoba
park belt, and they prized highly physical prowess in man and
horse. The man who was a good sport, good shot, and good horse-
man was sure of esteem from young and old, and the ideal within
its limits was a proud and manly one.

This rural society, stable yet mobile, had its natural acquisitive-
ness and dynamism checked and quietened by the long depression. The experience of Winnipeg, still metropolitan rather than
provincial, but in the nineties more provincial than before or
after, was the same. By 1887 the liquidation of the bad effects of
the great boom was pretty well completed, and growth of a more
normal kind renewed. But it was a slow growth. The population

of the city in 1881 had been at least twenty-five thousand; in 1896 it was only thirty-five thousand. Though many of the residents of 1881 were transient, and most of those of 1896 permanent, the increase in population was very slight and less than that of the province outside Winnipeg. The excited hopes of the boom, the dreams of metropolitan greatness, were damped by these years of relative stagnation, and Winnipeg, from being a roaring frontier town, the town of the plains traders, the lumber men, and the railway workers, had become for the time being a quiet provincial capital, slow-going, sedate and, conservative. An American visitor in 1894 remarked on these characteristics, on the leisurely habits of the businessmen who got down to their offices at ten in the morning and left at four for the tennis courts or the canoe club. He remarked also, as other American visitors had done, on the solidity of the town, for a western town, and a certain character and charm given by the prevalence of the buff Manitoba brick in business buildings and private houses.[12] It was a Winnipeg which stretched from Point Douglas to the Assiniboine and Armstrong's Point, with suburban villages in St. John's, St. James, and Fort Rouge. Between Portage Avenue and the Assiniboine, the best residential area in succession to that of Point Douglas, was a district of large lawns, large Victorian houses of brick, with wide verandas, sharp gables, or mansard roofs, with a leisurely spaciousness and quaint homeliness of its own. Tree planting had been started soon after the incorporation of the prairie city, and in 1893 the work was systematized and a beginning made at regular provision for the beauty and amenity of the city by the foundation of the Public Parks Board.

This quiet town was, however, the offspring of the fur trader's continental base, and in the wide sweep of Main Street, in the westward thrust of Portage Avenue, in the massive warehouses and the spreading railyards was a latent and gathering strength, an earnest of the metropolitan ambition to control the grain and wholesale trade of the West. The leisurely businessmen had not let any grass grow in Main Street. They had made Winnipeg the railway centre of Manitoba and the focus of the westward-fanning lines. The Board of Trade had wrested a freight rate structure favourable to the wholesale trade of Winnipeg from the Canadian Pacific Railway. The Winnipeg Grain Exchange was steadily increasing in strength and efficiency as it marketed crop after crop. Nor were new ventures lacking. In 1891 the Winnipeg Industrial Exhibition was begun in the hope of its becoming an annual event to draw attention, capital, and population to the city. The founding in 1892 by a group of leading Winnipeggers of the Great-West Life Assurance Company, which over the years was to become a national and international company, was an indication of the soundness and vigour of the business community. And the Immigration Convention of 1896 was inspired and organized largely by Winnipeggers. It needed but a new rush of settlers to the West, an increased demand for prairie wheat, to start Winnipeg booming and growing again.

In the professions the city had seen little change. In industry, changes had occurred. Lumbering had declined, until in the nineties only one mill remained. Flour milling, on the other hand, had increased, both in the number and size of the plants. The first small beginnings of the meat packing industry were appearing. Pork packing was well established and the company of J. Y. Griffin had a plant of considerable size. The separate Winnipeg stockyards were already capable of handling hundreds of cattle, but there was neither an abattoir nor a cold storage plant in the city. In the other trades and industries there was little change. In 1892, street transport was improved, and a new service industry made much more important, by the change from the old horse cars to the electric street cars of the Winnipeg Electric Company organized in that year. Winnipeg labour organization had been stimulated by the coming of the railways: in the mid-eighties the Knights of Labour had a branch in the city, and the Winnipeg Trades and Labour Council had first been organized in 1884 on the basis of the industrial unionism of the Knights; in 1894 it was reorganized on the principle of craft unionism. Strikes were infrequent, however, and organized labour during these years sought shorter hours and improvements in working conditions rather than higher money wages.

The pleasures of Winnipeggers in the nineties were much the same as those of rural Manitoba. Picnics, socials, and concerts were the staple. The only distinctive sports were canoeing and rowing, which flourished under the care of the Winnipeg Canoe Club, organized in 1883. The old Red River sport of horse racing was more highly organized, of course, and the races were a social event of the summer season. The annual curling bonspiel had become a leading event of the Winnipeg winter season. In February, 1894, the legislature was unable on one occasion to obtain a quorum because honourable members were at the bonspiel. An other ice sport, hockey, came into its own in the nineties, and at once rose to a primacy it was thereafter to maintain. When the famous team, the Victorias, went east in 1896, it won the Stanley Cup and much attention for its fierce attack and the high shot on goal known then as "the Winnipeg scoop." The bicycling craze which developed in the mid-nineties was largely, but by no means wholly, confined to Winnipeg and gave an interest to those seeking exercise and a new "line" to Winnipeg shops.

In the arts and sciences little was done or appreciated. The theatre and music, though not neglected, were at their lowest ebb of interest in Winnipeg. The city had no public library save that furnished by the Historical and Scientific Society. Even that active organization was beginning to leave behind the first vigour of its youth and verge on a decay which followed from a failure to recruit new members with new interests. The University of Manitoba had been empowered to teach as well as examine in 1889, but a long deadlock followed over the provision of funds and buildings for the establishment of a faculty. In literature and music there was a hiatus in these years also. Travellers now passed through Manitoba, and few settlers' reminiscences were of the quality of William Pennefather's *Thirteen Years on the Prairie* published in 1892. Of the older historians Alexander Begg published in 1894 his valuable *History of the North-West* in three volumes, but Begg had ceased to be a Manitoban and the history of the province is only a part of his narrative. The indefatigable Dr. Bryce, however, was doing the research which was soon to yield a flood of publications, and the nature stories of Ernest Thompson Seton were soon to appear.[13] The nineties, if largely barren, were also fallow years.

The one great and permanent change in Winnipeg's social life was the rise of the Lake of the Woods region as a summer resort. As early as 1881 a Winnipeg Sanitary Association had been formed to develop a resort at the Lake of the Woods.[14] At Keewatin and Rat Portage, at Coney Island, at Devil's Gap, and in Clearwater Bay, well-to-do families were building summer cottages and collecting all the camp gear—boats, fishing tackle, beds, and stoves —which go with holidays "at the lake." As Toronto was to populate Muskoka in the summer months, so Winnipeg began to make the Lake of the Woods a summer suburb. The Manitoban lakes, Winnipeg, Manitoba, Rock Lake, and Killarney, were sought as yet only for picnics, fishing, or shooting.

Between 1887 and 1897 Manitoba grew little and slowly in population, but not inconsiderably in strength and character. The work of widening the fields, of adapting institutions, of making the new land and the new peoples British and Canadian, went steadily forward. The work of pioneering was not, however, ended. On almost every farm, in every district, the prairie sod or native bush called for the breaking plough, rougher and less fertile or less accessible lands called for farmers' sons or new immigrants. And one new district was opened, one new frontier begun, in the Lake Dauphin country to the northwest between Riding and Duck Mountains. Some scouting settlers, a few ranchers, and many deer hunters had pushed their way over Riding Mountain to this famous old beaver country from the settlements along the line of the Manitoba and North Western Railway. The first settlers had gone into the district in the early eighties, and a few individuals followed over the years. In 1886 settlement may be said to have begun, stimulated in part by the drilling for oil which was started in that year.[15] These later settlers came in from west of Riding Mountain down the great valley between the Riding and Duck mountains and over the terraced levels to the great prairie west of Lake Dauphin. It was a region of deep soil and tall grass, with heavy timber on the heights, ridges, and river courses. To the south the blue terraces of Riding Mountain ran out massive and bold; to the northwest the blue shoulders of the Duck Mountain lay flat against the sky. It was a frontier such as old Manitoba had been before 1880, a frontier which outran the railway, one on which men, for the sake of a free choice of cheap lands of the first quality, were prepared to risk and endure long years before they could market a crop. By 1888 settlers were pushing up the old pitching track of the Arden Ridge from Neepawa and Gladstone. Some continued to pass over Riding Mountain by way of the valley of the Rolling River, where the small Swedish colony of New Sweden still continued. None who pushed into this fertile district regretted having done so, but the need of communication with the outside world made itself felt with increasing urgency as settlement spread and crop surpluses began to mount.

In 1889 a railway to the northwest, known as the Lake Manitoba Railway and Canal Company, had been chartered with a land grant of 6,000 acres a mile, but no money was found for the project in the years that followed. Not until early in 1896 did two energetic railway projectors, William Mackenzie and Donald Mann, aided by the contractor, Herbert Holt, all names of later fame, take up the charter and persuade the Manitoba legislature to grant them a guarantee of bonds up to $8,000 a mile for a railway to the Dauphin country.[16] Construction began at Gladstone, on the Manitoba and North Western line, and by the close of the season the railway had reached what was to be the town of Dauphin, the centre of the great bay of land which lay between the mountains. Settlers began to pour in, among them Polish immigrants. In the summer, a town, formed of the two pre-railway villages of Lake Dauphin and Gartmore, sprang up in the midst of a field of golden wheat; and at the end of the quiet years Manitoba had gained a new, booming frontier to the northwest. It had also gained another railway line, which was to become the Canadian Northern, a makeshift, daring, ever economical pioneering line of the northern fringe of settlement, and for the next twenty years was to be at the centre of Manitoban politics as the Canadian Pacific had been for the twenty past. And Messrs. Mackenzie and Mann had begun a venture which was to grow into the Canadian Northern Railway Company, the realization, long delayed but now swiftly carried out, of Sanford Fleming's vision of a great northern line to pass through the Saskatchewan valley and pierce the Rockies by the easy grades of the Yellowhead Pass. The east-west axis of Manitoban life was not yet to be reorientated, but only broadened. Yet at the same time this northern agricultural frontier was to be the base from which a new frontier of lumbering and mining was to spring. Beyond the Dauphin region lay the fertile valley of Swan River, which pioneers were already exploring; beyond Swan River rose the forests of Porcupine Mountain and across the barren lands beyond the Red Deer river stood the old fur fort and mission of The Pas on the mighty Saskatchewan; beyond that river lay the Shield, the country of the fur trade still.

There to the north and east in the Territory of Keewatin, indeed, the fur trade had continued its way undisturbed by the creation of the farming society on the southern plains. It had ceased, however, to be the land of chief interest to the new traders on Red River or to the men charged with government there. The wandering bands of Crees and Chipewyans still came to the Hudson's Bay Company posts to trade, to the lowly missions to pray and beg; from time to time the boatmen would still trim a "lobstick," a tree made a landmark by having all its branches but the top lopped off, to honour their employer and to earn a "regale"; the York boats still ran the rapids of the Hayes. But the whole vast country had been left a backwater by the westward drive of Confederation, the railways, and the farming frontier. When Lieutenant-Governor Patterson of both Manitoba and Keewatin, like his predecessors, went in 1897 to visit the Nelson valley of the vast territory under his dual commission, it was as though he had entered a *terra incognita*, this country in which the history of Manitoba began.[17]

Even as the new frontier and a new era of growth were beginning, the years of controversy over the School Act of 1890 were drawing to a close. In 1891, as already noted, Dr. J. K. Barrett, a Catholic ratepayer of Winnipeg, had challenged in the courts the right of the School District of Winnipeg to compel him to pay taxes for the support of the new, non-denominational schools. The Manitoba courts gave judgment against him; on appeal to the Supreme Court of Canada, the judgment was reversed; on further appeal to the Judicial Committee of the Privy Council, their lordships reversed the judgment of the Supreme Court.[18] The Greenway government had been justified, for their decision that Catholics possessed at the union only the right to maintain private schools by gifts and fees, and that the legislature of Manitoba under the constitution could create a tax-supported public school system, had been sustained in the highest court of the Empire. A similar fate attended the suit of Anglican taxpayers in the case of *Alexander Logan* vs. *Winnipeg*. No denominational school in Manitoba could claim a share of the school taxes.

The British North America Act provided, however, one further remedy for the wrong the Catholics of Manitoba claimed to have suffered. Under section 93 of that Act a minority deprived by a provincial legislature of educational rights enjoyed at the time of union might seek remedial legislation by the Parliament of Canada. To this remedy the Manitoban Catholics now had recourse. Their petition naturally embarrassed the Conservative government of the day, for the School Question threatened to create a breach between its Protestant and its Catholic supporters. The latter would demand remedial legislation for the Manitoba Catholics, the former would resist it. If the government introduced remedial legislation, it would enable the Liberal opposition to raise the cry of "provincial rights," and education, except as provided in section 93, clearly was a subject of provincial jurisdiction; if it did not, it would suffer the loss of political support in the province of Quebec.

Feverishly the Conservative government, weakened by the death by Sir John A. Macdonald in 1891 and of Sir John Thompson in 1894, sought to avoid the menacing dilemma. They referred to the Supreme Court the question whether the federal Parliament was empowered to take action on a petition submitted under section 93 and the Manitoba Act. The Supreme Court returned a negative decision, but on reference to the Judicial

Committee in 1895 the decision was reversed. Twice the Judicial Committee had formally returned to the government the poisoned chalice of the dreaded obligation to deal with the Manitoba School Question.

Some evasion was still possible, and a commission was sent out to Manitoba to try to reach agreement on remedial legislation. The federal commissioners proposed a system of separate schools for Catholic children on the Ontario model, the basis of which was the right of a parent to require in definite circumstances that his taxes be used to maintain a separate school, something different in principle from the dual system of Quebec and of Manitoba before 1890.[19] The Manitoba government refused to yield, and at this point the federal cabinet and the Conservative party began to break up. Seven ministers resigned in protest against the leadership of the Prime Minister, Sir Mackenzie Bowell. The quarrel was patched up, but only on condition that Sir Charles Tupper be recalled from the High Commissionership in London to become Prime Minister. A private attempt by Donald A. Smith to have Greenway compromise on the School Question also failed.[20] Tupper assumed office in 1896 and undertook to drive a remedial bill through Parliament in the face of Liberal opposition and of the dissident Conservatives led by Dalton McCarthy.

The federal Liberals, however, astutely led by Wilfrid Laurier, had stood fast on "provincial rights" and claimed that they could by "sunny ways" reach a compromise with the Manitoba government which would satisfy the Catholic claims. Firm on this ground, they blocked the passage of the Remedial Bill until the life of the Parliament elected in 1891 ran out. The Conservatives were thus forced to fight a general election on the School Question in June, 1896, and the Liberals won a great victory, especially in the province of Quebec, in which they carried forty-nine seats. In Manitoba, however, where the Greenway government had been returned to office without serious opposition both in 1892 and early in 1896, the voters, regarding the School Question as settled in Manitoba, returned five Conservatives to three Liberal candidates. This vote "for its own coercion" really reflected the settled belief of the electorate that the school system was no longer an open issue. With such indifference did Manitoba treat the question which wrought a revolution in the federal politics of Canada.

The new administration of Prime Minister Laurier at once entered on negotiations with the Greenway government for a compromise on the School Question. Laurier's agents, Hon. Israel Tarte and Henri Bourassa, opened the discussions in Winnipeg,[21] and they were then completed in Ottawa by Hon. Clifford Sifton on behalf of the Greenway government.[22] Agreement was reached in November, and in the 1897 session of the Manitoba legislature the Schools Act was amended in accord with the Laurier-Greenway compromise. By the amendment Catholic teachers were to be employed when there were forty Catholic children in an urban school or ten in a country school. When requested by ten heads of families, school trustees were to allow religious instruction to be held in the school from three thirty o'clock to four by a minister of the faith of the children whose parents had made the request. No child of another faith was to be required to attend these classes and there was to be no separation by denomination during the hours of secular instruction. (Religious exercises of a non-denominational character were already permitted under the Act.) When ten pupils in any school spoke French or any language other than English, the teaching of these was to be "in French, or such other language, and English upon the bi-lingual system."[23] Such were the simple terms of the compromise that was intended to end eight years of controversy.

It was not without difficulty that the two governments won acceptance of the compromise. Only intervention by the papacy prevailed on the Catholic hierarchy of Quebec to desist from open opposition. The Greenway government found no difficulty in having the religious clauses accepted on the ground that no privilege had been granted to a religious sect or a section of the population, but that concessions had been made only to the religious beliefs of individuals. The bilingual clause provoked opposition, however, particularly in Brandon and the southwest, and it had to be quietened by the explanation that the clause was inserted to conciliate the Liberal following from Quebec and that other languages had been included but none named in order not to offend Ontario by giving a special privilege to the French.[24]

So the School Question was formally closed as Manitoba and Canada entered upon a new era of development. Catholics were left with the conviction that they had suffered a moral wrong at the hands of the majority, and some of the majority were uneasy as to the effect of the bilingual clause on the future of a province of which the population was already diversified, and which was to become even more so as new currents of immigration flowed in. Hon. Clifford Sifton was now federal member for Brandon, where the agitation against the dual system had begun in Manitoba. His policy of vigorous stimulation of immigration, a policy which was an enlarged application in more favourable circumstances of Greenway's modest efforts, was to increase that diversity of population until the operation of the bilingual clause was to produce linguistic chaos in Manitoba schools.

That possibility could for the time being be ignored, for the quiet years were over; the period of consolidation in the life of the province was ended. In 1896 the price of wheat began once more to rise; railway and ocean steamship rates had already fallen. It was once more to pay well to grow wheat in Manitoba and the West. A flood of immigrants was setting in towards the plains of the Canadian West and Manitoba was to leave behind its first generation, the pioneer generation which had made it a British and Canadian province, to grow with the expanding West and move with the great commercial and political currents of the twentieth century.

12

The First Decade of the Great Boom
1897-1907

AFTER THE LONG YEARS OF DEPRESSION CAME THE years of prosperity, which were to run their golden course until 1912 and leave Manitoba transformed. The origins of the great boom developed outside the province. The flood of South African gold, following on the discovery of the mines of the Witwatersrand in 1888, was to be swollen by the great strike in the Yukon Territory in 1897. The gold backing of the world's currencies was increased, and money and credit were available again for railway stocks, government bonds, and farm mortgages. Railway rates and ocean steamship rates had fallen during the nineties and were to continue to fall for some years; Manitoban wheat and cattle were moving more cheaply to the eastern and British markets. Wheat prices had begun to rise in 1896 and moved steadily up as the demand of Europe's industrial population made itself effective; the prices of manufactured goods followed more slowly and for once there was a price differential in the farmer's favour. After the dry year of 1897, the seasons were to be kindly, and yields were high as acreage increased. In 1901 came a bumper crop of over 50,000,000 bushels of wheat. Manitoba and the Canadian West, last of the great agricultural frontiers, were coming into their own after twenty years of preparation and disappointment. The world, it soon became apparent after 1897, would buy all the wheat Manitoban farmers could grow, and would loan all the money Manitobans could spend on the development of the province's resources.

Good prices for wheat, cheap lands, and a high flow of investment meant that immigration also would quicken and the old
problems of land settlement and national assimilation assume new
proportions. The old streams from eastern Canada and the British
Isles began to swell again, and particularly the latter. The new
trickles from the United States and from eastern Europe rose
even more rapidly. The steamship lines and the railways strove
by cheapened passages and aggressive advertising to increase the
movement which gave them unprecedented traffic. The Department of the Interior, driven by Clifford Sifton, doubled and redoubled its efforts to attract immigrants to Canada, and with ever growing success. European peasants could be drawn to the homestead
lands of Canada now that those of the United States were taken
up; American farmers, often of Canadian origin, seeking lands
for their sons, or for investment, turned to the Canadian West
as once to the West of their own country. At last the empty spaces
were to be filled and the vacant lands taken up from the Red to
the Rockies. One of the great population movements of history
was beginning, which was to leave the farmlands of Manitoba
occupied and the province a polyglot mosaic of diverse peoples.
Many of them were to be alien in origin and of faiths and traditions unknown to the West, and with their coming was to begin
a testing of Canadian nationality such as it had not yet under-
gone. In Manitoba the testing was to be especially severe, for its
new settlers were to settle in definite zones and in the growing
metropolis of Winnipeg. And at the base of Manitoba's life lay
the School Question, closed but not ended.

The testing was to be in the future, however, and the present
held only the new prosperity and the new hopes of a development
far exceeding that of the Manitoba boom of 1881. In the last
years of the century Manitoba was astir with pioneering once
more. All through the province, to the east and north against the
forests, through the Tiger Hills and along the slopes of Riding
Mountain, on the short grass plains of the extreme southwest,
settlers were seeking out new lands and bringing the rough lands
under the plough. In the extreme northwest one wholly new
frontier district was opened and settled with an eager rush. The

MAIN STREET, WINNIPEG, 1880

Painting by F. B. Schell in the John Ross Robertson Collection

A VIEW OF WINNIPEG IN 1912

Painting by Harold Copping in the John Ross Robertson Collection

famous fur country of the Swan River valley had dropped out of notice after 1879 when the route of the Pacific railway had been swung southward. The trails had grown up with brush, the old fur posts had decayed, and the Indian and the elk had taken possession once more. But the settlement of the Dauphin district and the coming of the railway to Dauphin in 1896 had formed a base for a new advance. There were soon seekers after unclaimed land and the forerunners of a new rush of settlement were probing the forests and marshes around the eastern terraces of Duck Mountain.

Settlement and the railway first turned westward up the valley of the Valley River between Riding and Duck mountains. On the plains named after the half breed Gilbert Ross, the village of Gilbert Plains sprang up in 1898 after G. P. Campbell, an enterprising young lawyer of Dauphin, bought Ross's nearby land. In 1899 the town of Grandview began in the pass between the mountains. Settlement spread quickly over the prairies to the wooded slopes to north and south, and westward towards the rolling uplands which connected with the Shell River district to the southwest and the upper valley of the Assiniboine.[1]

The main line of the railway, now reorganized and renamed the Canadian Northern, crept northward along the foot of Duck Mountain, aiming for the valley of the Saskatchewan and the realization of Sanford Fleming's vision of a Pacific railway by the Yellowhead Pass. In 1899 it had reached Cowan, and from railhead here the first settlers of the Swan River jumped off, to make their difficult way across the northern spurs of the Duck Mountain plateau down into the valleys of the Roaring and Favel rivers. By fall over four hundred settlers were in the valley of the Swan, and the Canadian Northern had swung round Duck Mountain and was across the valley heading for the blue shoulder of Porcupine Mountain.[2]

The rush of 1899 and the rushes of the years immediately following were long to remain a memory in the valley and the province. It was a concerted thrust of experienced landseekers, pushing into the prairie lands of the valley, family by family, with their stock and equipment, picking their lands and occupy-

ing them with the practised skill of Boer *voortrekkers*. The railway and the builders of towns moved in their immediate wake
and by the end of 1899 Minitonas, Swan River, and Bowsman
villages had sprung up. It was a goodly land they had possessed,
another Dauphin district in structure, a terraced plain between
plateaux, but more wooded and more northern in aspect with the
dark hues of the spruce and the more frequent willow meadows
and tamarack swamps. And to the westward the abrupt tableland of Thunder Hill stood sentinel in lonely eminence in the
gap between the mountains. From all the slopes poured down
the many tributaries of the Swan, and in the rich loam the water
table lay close beneath the surface. Wood, water, and fertile
land in abundance made the last of Manitoba's westward frontiers
the best, and in the comparative isolation of the valley was to
grow up a community proud of its district and sure, as crop succeeded crop in unbroken succession, that they had lighted on a
land specially favoured by Providence.

The settlers on this new frontier were almost wholly Canadian
or British; later, American settlers followed. Many of the first
comers were Manitobans moving out to their second frontier to
pit the skills and capital of the first against the familiar hazards.
One of these, A. J. Cotton of Treherne, was an established
farmer in the south. In 1899 he took up twenty-four hundred
acres in the valley, which was to become his home and where he
was to leave a respected name as master farmer and public servant.
Year by year the labour and skill of such men was to make the
Swan River a garden land, heaviest in yield of all Manitoba for
many unchallenged years, and most beautiful as it lay checkered
with the green and gold of its fields, laced by its wooded rivers
in the blue arc of the hills.

It was in the rush of its opening, however, that Swan River
was typical of the first years of the boom. A similar but greater,
more straggling and scattered rush was setting in over the wide
plains of the Territories. Nor was land settlement the only stir of
these quickened years. Men by the hundreds were leaving in the
Yukon gold rush, to join the thousands trudging on the trail of
'98. In the following year the tension between the British and the

Boers of the Transvaal in far South Africa broke in war, and Canadian contingents were despatched. Scores of volunteers, the restless and the adventurous lads, the hard riders and the good shots, were drawn to take part in a struggle about which they knew little, against men with whom they soon formed a ready sympathy born of not dissimilar ways of life. Many Manitobans enlisted in the Strathcona Horse raised by Donald A. Smith, who thought that the prairies might furnish a match for the mounted marksmen of the Transvaal. Soon they were back, the veterans, men always a little different, who never quite forgot the high veldt and the strong South African sun. The ties which were binding the little province to the great world were stretching farther and becoming more numerous.

The times were stirring and there was need for government to bestir itself with the times. The record of the Greenway government had not been impressive. If it had struggled against adverse circumstances, it still was true that its railway policy had proved a disappointment. The Northern Pacific had built an alternative system in Manitoba, which was popular with its patrons, but it had not attempted to offer serious competition with the Canadian Pacific. There was no need to, as there was enough traffic for both. Now, however, that immigrants and capital were beginning to flow into Manitoba again, and the wheat crop to increase rapidly, there was need for more railways, and there remained the pressing need for ever lower rates if Manitoban grain and cattle were to compete on the world market.

The Greenway government, it is true, in guaranteeing the construction of the Dauphin railway in 1896, had stumbled on a new railway policy. It was put before them by the astute and aggressive Mackenzie and Mann, who were already beginning to think of a second transcontinental line. The plan was to revive the once much agitated project of a southeastern railway from Winnipeg to the international border and Duluth; now it was proposed to continue it by Rainy River to Port Arthur. The result would be a second and increasingly needed outlet for western grain by a Canadian route. The line could later be linked up with the Dauphin railway to make the trans-Manitoban link of a major system. The charter was granted in 1898, with a government guarantee of bonds up to $8,000 a mile and tax exemption during the period of construction, and encountered little criticism from the opposition. Only James Fisher, independent Liberal, censured the government for failing to make effective provision for the control of rates charged for transport on the line, a criticism to which Greenway could only reply that guarantees had been sought on cordwood hauled to Winnipeg.[3] Thus faintly were struck two dominant notes of the new era, railway construction with government aid, and government control of freight rates.

The Greenway government was not to survive into the new era. It had been long in office and its original force was abated. The loss of the boisterous Martin and the hard-driving Sifton had not been made good by the appointment of the assiduous J. D. Cameron as Attorney-General. The Premier himself had never risen above a shrewd mediocrity. The failure of the government's railway policy, masked by the depression, was to become more and more significant as the demand for railway services increased with the rise of the boom. The Compromise of 1897 had taken the School Question out of federal politics, but it had started the return of former Conservatives to their party, and the Orange Order, which had been critical of the Compromise as a return to separate schools, was becoming hostile. Even the immigration policy of Sifton, which was so greatly to aid the establishment of federal Liberal power in the West, had effects adverse to the provincial Liberals of Manitoba. The eastern Europeans, the peasants in their sheepskin coats, and especially the strange sect of Doukhobors, produced a hostile reaction among the British-born which the local Conservatives were to turn to advantage with the cry of "Canada First." In addition, there were the charges, common in that age of fierce partisanship, of governmental extravagance and of manipulating the voters' lists for party advantage. So constant and so reciprocal were such charges that they must, on most occasions, have simply cancelled out. To the former, however, the deficit of 1899 in the provincial revenues, to the amount of $250,000, lent some substance.

These growing weaknesses meant that the Greenway ministry was entering on a decline. At the same time, it was faced by a reinvigorated provincial Conservative party. Since 1888 that party had been weakened and divided by the circumstances of the breakup of the Norquay government and by the School Question. The representation of the party in the legislature had been small. Even in 1896 it had not been greatly increased. In that year, however, it found a leader in R. P. Roblin. Roblin had been defeated in 1892 and had turned to the building up of his personal fortune and especially of his interests in the grain trade. In 1896 this vigorous and able independent was elected for Woodlands and accepted the leadership of the opposition in the House. As the term of the legislature ran out and it became apparent that the Conservatives would have a good chance of winning, he decided that the party required a leader with an established Conservative pedigree,[4] and in 1898 he retired to make way for Hugh John Macdonald, son and heir of the great Sir John Alexander Macdonald. Hugh John, as he was known in Manitoba, had first come to the province, like so many of its leading men, with the Red River Expedition. In later years he had returned to the West and entered the practice of law in Winnipeg. A modest man who knew his limitations, he was none the less a winning personality, loved for his sunny disposition and gentle courtesy among a wide circle of friends, and the bearer of a great name. His elevation to the leadership was a call to battle to all Conservatives in the province and a sign that the party was seeking victory after years of practical acquiescence in the policies of the Liberal party.

Macdonald began a series of addresses throughout Manitoba early in 1899. He was welcomed by large meetings and won adherents by the warmth of his personality and his skilful appeal to British sentiment and Orange feeling. Organization meetings were held, and the party spirit and organization revived. There were many signs of "McCarthy-ite" Conservatives returning to the fold and even reports of Liberals abandoning their party for the Conservative.[5] The party platform, the first issued by the Conservatives of Manitoba, was simple and forthright. It pledged the party to economy and efficiency in government finance. It grappled resolutely with the prohibition question, and promised to enact a measure to end the public sale of liquor in the province. On the School Question it was silent, except to call for a restoration of the Board of Education, on the ground that education should be kept out of politics. Macdonald in his speeches had declared himself unequivocally in favour of national schools, but made it clear that the School Question should not be revived by an attack on the Compromise. The remainder of the platform was of less significance but of similar character.[6]

The revival of the Manitoba Conservative party was a challenge not only to the provincial Liberals but also to the federal government. A Conservative victory in Manitoba would be hailed across Canada as marking the recovery of the federal Conservatives from the great defeat of 1896. Coming, as it would, on the eve of a federal election, such a victory might affect the Liberal chances of success. Accordingly, Sifton and other federal ministers spoke in the province in July and October in support of the Greenway government and federal policies. Sifton was at particular pains to defend his immigration policy, but his success was doubtful. The same calculation appealed to the federal Conservatives also, and in November Sir Charles Tupper and other Conservative leaders stumped the province. The denunciation of this "brigade of strangers" by the *Free Press*, now restored to support of the Liberal party after some years of control by interests connected with the Canadian Pacific Railway, perhaps indicates its effectiveness.

When the elections were held in December, the Conservatives were in a position to contest every seat, whereas in 1896 nine Greenway candidates had been elected by acclamation. Such was the *élan* they had developed in a year of campaigning that they elected twenty-three of their candidates over fifteen Liberals returned. The party carried all south-central and southwestern Manitoba, except Mountain where Greenway held fast, and two of Winnipeg's three seats. The Liberals won the constituencies of the Red River valley and the northwest, among them three of the seats in which the French vote was decisive.[7] The pattern of 1888, when the south and southwest, the area of predominantly Ontario settlement, had returned the Liberals, was being reversed. The Greenway government had been defeated by the charges of financial extravagance and "machine" politics, and by the weakness of its railway policy. To this result the Compromise of 1897 had also contributed, though to what extent it is, of course, impossible to say. The personal popularity of Hugh John Macdonald and the vigorous intervention of Tupper were also effective in what was to a great extent a trial of strength between Sifton and Tupper. For it cannot be said that the election marked either any profound dissatisfaction with the Greenway government or any significant change in the history of the province; it was a change of government merely. It was to be significant in the long run, however, for it once more put the government of Manitoba in opposition to the federal government, and so confirmed what was becoming almost a provincial tradition.

But it would be unjust to the new government to suggest that the change of administration produced no change in the spirit or direction of Manitoban politics. The government of Premier Macdonald was fresh and vigorous. The strongest man in the party, R. P. Roblin, it is true, was not for private reasons in the ministry. None the less Roblin was a pillar of strength to the government he was soon to lead. A man of great energy, simplicity, and directness of mind, and possessed of a trenchant grasp of principle, Roblin brought to his party a range of ability none of his predecessors in Manitoban politics had possessed with the sole exception of Clifford Sifton. These qualities were modified by a broad tolerance of differing views, a vigilant realism in reading public opinion, and a keen sense of human foibles and weaknesses. A certain pomposity of speech and manner, a self-confidence which verged on arrogance, a personal loyalty which approached blind trust of colleagues, were to mar the strong characteristics of Roblin as they hardened into fixed habits.

Most of his colleagues had something of the same hard confidence and the new administration as it ran its long course was never to want either assurance or capacity. To ability was added the fiery partisanship of the day, which the new ministers shared above the common measure. It was a fighting government from the beginning, and in the fierce feud with the federal Liberal party this partisan spirit was to be kept keen. There is little doubt that much of the strength of the new government was to be drawn from this pugnacious spirit and the fervour with which it exploited the feud with Liberal Ottawa.

Macdonald's premiership was marked by the attempt to deal effectively with the difficult question of prohibition. The Greenway government had declined to implement, because of doubts of its constitutional powers, the plebiscite of 1892, but the Judicial Committee of the Privy Council of 1896 had transferred control of the liquor traffic in the provinces to the provinces. A federal plebiscite in 1898 in favour of federal control of the interprovincial trade had not been acted on by the federal government because of the large majority against control in the province of Quebec. The Manitoban Conservatives, however, had pledged themselves to bring in a provincial Act, and Macdonald now insisted that this be done. A bill prohibiting the sale of liquor in the province by hotels or merchants was passed in the session of 1900. Doubts at once arose, however, as to its constitutionality, and as to the rights of the Hudson's Bay Company under its charter. When Macdonald resigned to contest a seat in the federal election of 1900, he was succeeded by Roblin, and the new Premier insisted that the doubts be referred to the courts. When these were resolved in 1901, still further doubts had arisen as to the practicality of enforcing the Act in view of the legal right of private individuals to import liquor, and as to whether public sentiment was sufficiently against the consumption of liquor to make enforcement practicable. Roblin therefore insisted on the question being submitted once more to the people. Leaders of the temperance movement, angered by what they regarded as evasion, urged that the plebiscite be ignored. Their efforts were not without effect, and contributed to the defeat of prohibition in a small vote. Thereafter the Roblin government held that there was nothing to be done but to enforce the existing provincial Liquor Act as well as possible, to support local prohibition, and to tighten the terms of the Act as experience revealed its weaknesses. To this policy it was stoutly to adhere despite growing pressure from the temperance associations, the Dominion Alliance and the Royal Templars of Temperance, and many of the Protestant clergy.

The Roblin government was to be harassed by the "liquor question" to the end of its days. It was to be no less troubled, and in large part undone, by the question of compulsory school attendance. Legal provision for compelling attendance of children at the public schools had been held in 1890 to be impossible in face of the rights of Catholic parents under the Manitoba Act. Now, however, the flood of newcomers from eastern Europe, suspicious of attempts at assimilation in the schools of their homelands, raised the question of how their children were to be educated as Canadians. The education of the "Galician" children became an urgent question. Allied with this question was that of "juvenile delinquency" among idle children on the streets of fast-growing Winnipeg. What was the government to do? It took the stand that the School Question must not be reopened, that therefore legislation to enforce attendance was impossible, and that such other means as were available must be used to the utmost. But an insistent demand for compulsory attendance began to spread and was eventually and rather inconsistently to be taken up by the Liberal opposition. No escape from the constitutional dilemma of 1890 was to be found for some years, however, and meantime the work of education and nation-building fell into serious arrears in Manitoba.

In its financial policy the new government was more fortunate. It had inherited a deficit from its predecessor, of which it was to make much political capital for years. It undertook a thorough revision of financial procedures, as Greenway had done in 1888, and there is little reason to doubt that on both occasions the overhaul was necessary and beneficial. Thereafter careful administration of the provincial finances by Hon. J. A. Davidson and his successors retired the Greenway deficit and gave the government a series of mounting annual surpluses which ran unbroken to 1912. These surpluses undoubtedly were caused by the growing prosperity of the province, and the accompanying sale of the provincial swamp lands. Yet careful administration was necessary, for demands for expenditure increased with the growth of population and the spread of settlement, and the revision of the federal subsidies was to be delayed by the controversy with the federal government. Accordingly, the financial resources of the province were limited for many years, and provincial services, notably education, were impoverished. The direct taxation of corporations, including railways, was begun under Premier Macdonald and also contributed to the success of the Conservative financial policy. A novelty in its day, it was much debated, but, though it was extolled by the government and proved remunerative, it could not, despite careful administration, repair the want of adequate subsidies.

The government's financial policy was a year-by-year accomplishment, cumulative in its effect. Its railway policy, initiated in 1901, was its most spectacular achievement and quickest success. In that year the government took over the lines of the Northern Pacific in the province on a 999-year lease. It at once transferred them to the Canadian Northern on a similar lease, the company to operate the lines under a provincial guarantee. By the contract, however, the government took power to fix rates on the Canadian Northern lines within the province, and fixed as its object rates of ten cents on a hundred pounds of wheat outgoing and fifteen per cent on the value of freight incoming. At the same time it guaranteed the bonds of the Canadian Northern up to $8,000 a mile in Manitoba and $20,000 a mile on construction in the rocky country along the Rainy River.[8] Thus it proposed to bring freight rates down in Manitoba and to afford a second Canadian outlet for Manitoban grain. It was the Greenway policy in its aims, but in method it substituted the fixing of rates by government for competitive rates and extended the use of guarantees of bonds adopted by Greenway in 1898. The contract was fiercely criticized in the House and press, as pledging the credit of the province to the fortunes of a railway company, and for a time the attack seemed likely to shake the government. Roblin's stout defence, however, carried the measure and it was fully implemented. When in 1902 the line to Port Arthur was opened, the second outlet was obtained and the competition of the fixed Canadian Northern rates brought down those of the Canadian Pacific.[9] Thereafter the Roblin government year by year guaranteed the bonds of the Canadian Northern for the construction of branch lines in the province, and the Manitoba railway network assumed its final shape, except for the transcontinental line of the Grand Trunk Pacific built across the province between 1905 and 1909.

The expansion of the railway system of Manitoba was, of course, in response to the settlement of the North-West Territories as well as to the growth of the province itself. The rapid development of the prairie lands of the Territories and the new sense of confidence engendered by the boom raised again the old question of boundary extension. It was clear that the Territories would soon have to be granted provincial status; indeed, the question of "autonomy" had already been raised. The old Manitoban belief that the province had been denied its proper boundaries by a jealous federal government had not died out, and in 1901 the legislature, on the motion of the Liberal opposition, unanimously passed a resolution asking that, as Manitoba had been denied expansion eastward, it be enlarged to reach Hudson Bay and also, if the federal Parliament should so decide, to the west.[10]

An enlargement to the west would have greatly increased the agricultural lands of the province, given it most of the Assiniboine watershed, and carried it out along the east-west axis of Canada. In 1902 Premier Roblin went into Assiniboia to advocate union with Manitoba and met Premier F. W. G. Haultain of the North-West Territories in friendly debate at Indian Head. But the people of Assiniboia did not welcome the proposal, either when first made by the legislature of Manitoba or when urged by Roblin. They had no wish to assume a share of the debt of Manitoba, or of the possible burden of the guarantees to the Canadian

Northern Railway. They were also sure that they could make better terms with the federal government than Manitoba had succeeded in doing. So definite was their opposition that the proposal of boundary extension westward had to be dropped, and replaced by one to extend the boundaries northward. Thus Manitoba's early development as a province and the costs of its provincial development stood in the way of its acquiring the agricultural lands which would have made it one of the major provinces of Confederation and furnished an adequate base for the development of the north. The question of extending the boundaries, so raised, was to remain a central issue in Manitoban politics for the next decade.

By making itself the champion of boundary extension, the Roblin government adopted what was to prove a popular and rewarding cause. It allied itself with another when in 1901 Premier Roblin announced the appointment of a Commission to investigate the desirability of founding an agricultural college in Manitoba.[11] As early as 1884 Lieutenant-Governor J. C. Aikins had urged that one be founded; in 1893 the Greenway government had taken steps to do so; now the measure was to be taken up in earnest. In 1903 the Commission reported in favour of the establishment of a college, the necessary legislation was passed and funds were voted. A site of 170 acres was selected on the south bank of the Assiniboine near Winnipeg, and construction of the necessary buildings began.

This vigorous identification of itself with progressive measures served to consolidate the hold of the government on the electorate. The Liberal opposition had stoutly criticized the acts of government and defended the record of the Greenway government. Under the leadership of the aging Greenway it failed, however, to evolve an alternative programme on which to appeal to the electorate. When a general election was held in 1903, the Conservatives won thirty-one seats and were able to carry on with a larger majority and against a weakened opposition. In 1904 the Liberal opposition was still further weakened by Greenway's resignation to contest a seat in the federal election of that year, and by their inability to decide on a successor. In the interim C. J. Mickle of Birtle acted as leader in the House.

The efforts of the Roblin government to identify itself with the urgent needs and aspirations of the growing province were one reflection of the primary endeavour of a society which was still largely a pioneering agricultural society, to equip itself with railways, elevators, stockyards, and all the necessary facilities for moving produce rapidly and in volume. Most of the task was performed by the railway and elevator companies. But now, as in the earlier phases of development, it proved impossible for them to expand their equipment rapidly enough to carry the swelling output of the grain fields of Manitoba and the Territories. In 1901 there had been a great grain blockade, and in 1902 another. The hardships of the blockade, inability to ship grain hauled in for weary miles or to sell crops to meet bills, were aggravated by the railways' old practice of assigning freight cars to elevators in preference to assigning them to individual farmers. While the purpose was to speed the movement of grain by confining handling to the elevators, one effect was to give the elevators a monopoly of the local market and to force down the local price. Farmers wished to have the alternative of selling or of shipping their grain for sale direct to the exporters. In the great blockades of 1901 and 1902 resentment at the discrimination practised by the railways rose high, and a number of farmers in Assiniboia decided that the remedy was for farmers to organize in defence of their interests. In 1902, under the leadership of E. A. Partridge and W. R. Motherwell, the Territorial Grain Growers' Association was formed, the latest in the line of farmers' organizations, from the Grange through the Farmers' Union to the Patrons of Industry.

In January of 1903 the movement spread eastward along the Canadian Pacific main line to Manitoba and the first local organization of the grain growers of Manitoba was brought into being at a meeting at Virden at which W. R. Motherwell was principal speaker. J. W. Scallion, a farmer of the Virden district, was elected president. Among the purposes defined in the con-

stitution of the local organization was "to watch legislation
relating to the grain growers' interests, particularly that affecting
the marketing, grading and transportation of grain."[12] The movement rapidly spread across the southwest, down to the Portage
Plains and into the Red River valley. In March of 1903 the
Manitoba Grain Growers' Association was organized at Brandon,
already established as the agricultural capital of Manitoba.
Scallion was elected president of the provincial association and
Roderick McKenzie, a farmer of the Brandon district, was elected
secretary.[13]

Scallion retired after a year in office and was replaced by D. W.
McCuaig of Portage la Prairie. But McKenzie, a hard-headed
Ontario Scot of iron resolution, was to be re-elected year after
year as secretary, and principal organizer, of the Association. The
Association prospered and spread, and few were the farming districts which did not have a local more or less active, and more
or less filled with the burning zeal of the Grain Growers to defend
the farmer's interests and claim his proper position in the country.
So widespread and active did the Association become in its rapid
growth that almost from the first it was regarded as representing
and speaking for the farmers of Manitoba as a body. To this
representative role it had in these years a remarkable claim, and
in the activities of the locals and in the great annual conventions
of the Association guided by an executive of growing experience
and skill, there was a genuine focus of the interests and desires
of Manitoban farmers. To the will of the farming community,
thus expressed by an organization no political party could match,
the Roblin government and both political parties gave instant and
respectful heed.

How powerful the Association had become was revealed when
in 1906 the Grain Growers' Associations of Manitoba and the
Territories supported the formation of the Grain Growers' Grain
Company. The Company was to handle members' grain, compete with the private companies, and pay a dividend, after the
fashion of co-operative societies, to shareholders on shareholder's
grain handled. In 1907 the Company attempted to obtain a seat
in the Winnipeg Grain Exchange, only to be debarred on the

ground that the co-operative principle was incompatible with the by-laws of the Exchange. The Grain Growers interpreted the action as the expression of an intention to destroy the Company by denying it the indispensable facilities of the Exchange, and sought the aid of the Roblin government. The government at once took up the cause of the Grain Growers and attempted to settle the dispute by a conference of the representatives of the two parties. When this failed the government, defying a threat of the Exchange to remove to Fort William, put through in 1908 legislation which compelled the Exchange to admit the Grain Growers' Grain Company. The victory was qualified by the Company dropping the co-operative clause from its by-laws, but the struggle was an early and clear indication of the power of the organized farmers and of their influence on government.

Equally significant, if less direct, was the influence of the Grain Growers' Association on the government's policy with respect to telephone services. There was growing dissatisfaction in Winnipeg, during the early years of the century, with the high rates charged by the Bell Telephone Company under its franchise, and in the province with the inefficiency and costliness of the various municipal telephone systems. When other private companies sought franchises in Winnipeg a public demand, strongly supported by the Grain Growers, arose for the creation of a publicly owned system. The Roblin government acceded to the demand and in 1906 the necessary legislation was enacted for the expropriation of the Bell Telephone Company and the establishment of a government owned and operated system in the cities, together with long distance lines to link rural municipal systems. The development of the Manitoba Government Telephones, the first such system on the continent, was begun in response to a demand in large part rural and to a growing support for the principle of public ownership of utilities. The Roblin government had assumed in the Government Telephones one of its most onerous and troublesome responsibilities and had carried one of its most enlightened measures: "a stroke of inspired statesmanship," wrote an English observer of the business and social effects of the telephone in the country.[14]

The ready adoption by a Conservative government of the principle of public ownership of community services monopolistic in character was not surprising, as the principle was one widely advocated at the time without regard to party. It was indeed regarded in Manitoba, when combined with the use of independent public commissions to operate the publicly owned utilities, as a means of reducing political corruption. Public ownership was therefore often combined with another proposal which had the same end in view. This was direct legislation, or the use of the initiative, the referendum, and the recall by the electorate, to introduce and pass laws directly and to recall members of the legislature. Direct legislation in turn was allied with the ever growing demand for the enfranchisement of women and the prohibition of the liquor trade. All these movements found a ready response from the Grain Growers' Association and by it were pressed on the government. The Roblin government, however, while responsive to public opinion, was determined not to depart from the principles of responsible government, or to mistake pressure groups for public opinion. It refused to appoint a commission to operate the Government Telephones, and kept them under the control of a Department of Telephones. It was flatly opposed to direct legislation, and sceptical of the merits of women's suffrage and prohibition. In consequence, its early response to the Grain Growers' Association was not followed by an equal response to the power of a growing movement for economic and political reform. In particular it was incapable, as a party and a partisan government, of responding to the growing dislike of partisanship among the progressive elements of Manitoban society.

The province was stirring with new ideas, the novelties of the times, as it was stirring with the influx of settlers. And there was a connection between the new ideas and the newcomers, as many of the ideas were brought in or advocated by newcomers. For the moment, however, it was the mere growth of population which was the moving force in the political life of the West. The autonomy question in the North-West Territories, a demand for provincial status and increased federal subsidies, was ripe for settlement because of the rapid settlement of the Territories. In

1905 the Laurier government proceeded to develop its policy. It had rejected the claim of Manitoba to eastern Assiniboia and in so doing practically decided the question whether the Territories should be made into one province, as the Territorial Premier, F. W. G. Haultain, urged, or two. By the Autonomy Bills there were to be two provinces of Saskatchewan and Alberta, each running north to 60° north latitude, each over 250,000 square miles in area, and each with generous subsidies.

The legislature of Manitoba met this new situation by advancing its claims to the territory to north and east.[15] It was prompted to do so because in that direction only lay any hope of extension and because the project of a Hudson Bay railway had been revived and a branch line of the Canadian Northern was building to The Pas. The legislature, in reverting to the northern claims, however, was turning from the east-west axis which the Canadian annexation of the Northwest had created, to the historic north-south axis of fur trade days. The reunion of the Bay and the Shield with the southern plains would recreate a historic pattern of commerce, if wheat from the western plains should move outward from the Bay as the furs of the northern forest had once done. The claims of Manitoba to the north had also some shadow of right, as nearly all the territory claimed was in the District of Keewatin. The District had been governed by the Lieutenant-Governor of Manitoba and the provincial courts had exercised jurisdiction over it since its creation in 1876. The debates on the Keewatin Bill in that year made it clear that the anticipation of the legislators was that the Territory would some day be incorporated in Manitoba.

Northward extension, however, was to fare no better in 1905 than westward extension. The claims of Manitoba were at once countered by a demand from the government of Ontario that its claims should be considered, and the federal government had at once to defer to this new and powerful party to the discussions. The immediate effect of Ontario's intervention was to retard the possibility of extension, but its claim when formulated was to be the extension of its then western boundary straight northward. The result would have been to cut Manitoba off completely from Hudson Bay and to give to Ontario the ports of Nelson and

Churchill. Manitoba replied that an Imperial Act of 1889 had permanently fixed the northern boundary of Ontario on the Albany River. More subtle and perhaps more effective than Ontario's objections was the opposition of Quebec and the Catholic hierarchy to the extension of boundaries that carried with it the public school system of Manitoba. The Archbishop of St. Boniface, Mgr Langevin, had never hesitated to make known his continuing opposition to the Compromise of 1897, and the Autonomy Bills of 1905 had precipitated a bitter struggle over separate schools in the new provinces. During the by-election in Mountain in 1905, Hon. Robert Rogers, Minister of Public Works for Manitoba, revealed that Cardinal Sbaretti, Papal Delegate in Canada, had suggested to Attorney-General Campbell a modification of the Manitoba School Act which would have permitted separate instruction of Catholic pupils by Catholic teachers. Such a concession, the Cardinal implied, would ease the extension of Manitoba's boundaries.[16] The Roman Catholic Church was, of course, anxious to preserve its existing separate schools in Keewatin and at The Pas. While too much weight ought not to be given to this episode, it did reveal the difficulties with which the federal government had to contend, and also the readiness of the Roblin government to use boundary extension for partisan advantage.

An even more serious obstacle to the extension of the boundaries was the matter of a revision of the federal subsidies. From 1905 on the Roblin government's demand on the federal government was for "equality"; equality of subsidies with Saskatchewan to the west, or of control of public lands with Ontario to the east. One or other, with boundary extension, it was claimed, would at last give Manitoba that full stature in Confederation which it had always been denied. But the Laurier government resolutely declined to reopen the question of subsidies for old Manitoba, and offered only an additional subsidy for the new territory. Despite all the difficulties, however, all of which were greatly increased by the partisan feud between the two governments, Parliament did in 1908 pass a resolution which proposed the extension of the boundaries of Manitoba to their present limits, but with no concessions as to financial terms. Whether this act was seriously meant, or was an election manœuvre in an election year, it is impossible to say. The negotiations were deadlocked on the issue of the financial terms and were so to remain during the term of the Laurier government in Ottawa.

The failure of the Roblin government to obtain an extension of the boundaries of the province in no wise diminished its hold on the electorate of Manitoba. On the contrary, it was able to stand forth as the champion of a province wilfully mistreated— "cabined, cribbed, confined," declared Roblin—by a Liberal government dominated from Quebec. The issue even masked the growing problems of educational administration and of the assimilation of the alien immigrants and their children into the society of the province and nation. For the government was revealing a tendency to treat these problems in a brusque and superficial way, as exemplified by the flag legislation of 1906. By the Act the school trustees were required to have the Union Jack flown over the schools in school hours. Such legislation, necessary and desirable as it was in a society which threatened to dissolve from extreme dilution, ignored the fact that appalling numbers of Manitoban children were simply not attending the schools over which the flag of the Empire was to fly. And the issue of boundary extension, while significant in terms of provincial pride, was also illusory. The hope of Manitoba's being one of the major provinces of Confederation had been destroyed by the boundary decisions of 1884 and 1905.

Yet the next provincial election, that of 1907, was to bring the Roblin government to the peak of its power. Its administrative record, its championship of popular causes, its fighting partisanship, made an irresistible combination. Meanwhile, the provincial Liberal party had failed to find either a popular platform or a popular leader. In convention in March, 1906, the Liberals had drawn up a platform that was either merely critical of, or in accord with, government policies. The convention elected as leader Edward Brown, Mayor of Portage la Prairie, a man of established integrity and ability but of little popular appeal and no experience of provincial politics—"a kindergarten politician," jibed Roblin in the ensuing campaign. In the House itself T. C. Norris, who had been returned for Landsdowne in 1899, was coming to the front as a competent speaker and amiable personality. In the ranks of the party the names of some able young men, A. B. Hudson and T. H. Johnson, were beginning to carry weight. But the opposition lacked the vigour, the craft, and the genuine popularity of the governing party,

The election was fought on the government's record, on the burning question of boundary extension, on the perennial issue of the voters' lists and the "thin red line" charges that federal Liberal returning officers had stricken Conservative names from the voters' lists and that on appeal the action had been condoned by Liberal appointees on the Bench. The turbulent flood of partisanship, the outstanding characteristic of these years, had risen until it washed at the portals of the courts. If such judicial decisions continued, Hon. Robert Rogers, himself the fiercest of partisans, had asserted in the Legislative Assembly, "the judiciary . . . will be despised by the dogs and the crows of this country."[17] The truth was that both parties practised flagrant electoral corruption, that all appointments to the Bench and civil service were political, and that Manitoban politics were the scene of an unresting struggle between the provincial political machine and its federal rival. And the fires of partisanship were fiercely fanned by the press. The *Free Press*, edited by J. W. Dafoe and owned by Clifford Sifton, was the hard-hitting party organ of the Liberals; it was matched in ferocity by the *Winnipeg Telegram*, the Conservative paper; while the independent *Tribune* of R. L. Richardson found ample occasion for trenchant comment in the activities of the political parties and press.

The underground struggle for power between the parties did not, of course, prevent major public issues from being raised. When Brown in his manifesto and speeches attempted to introduce the subject of compulsory school attendance, Roblin turned it aside by declaring that he would never allow the School Question to be reopened. But even such an issue, relevant as it was to the fundamental problem of creating a viable community out of the ever multiplying elements of provincial life, soon led back to the political underworld. It was in this campaign that the charges were first made that the government had an understanding with the Catholic Church with respect to the lenient administration of the School Act, and that it was in league with the liquor interests. This counter-attack was of little avail, however, for the Liberals gained only three seats and failed to elect their leader. With twenty-eight seats in a House of forty-one, the Roblin régime was more firmly entrenched than before. It was in fact to justify its retention of power by the intermittent passage of progressive legislation. So much did it do so, as the following two chapters will reveal, that when replaced by an opposition committed to reform, that government, except with respect to school attendance, prohibition, direct legislation, and women's franchise, found little to do except amend what the Roblin government had done. It had in fact enacted much of what the Progressive movement of the day desired. But by its adherence to party politics, the Roblin régime forfeited the political support of former Patrons, radicals of all kinds, and reformers fired by the new ills of growing Winnipeg. As a party it lived, as a party it was overthrown, and the Liberals swept to office on a tide of progressive reform.[18]

13

The New Manitoba of the Great Boom
1908-1912

THE ROBLIN GOVERNMENT WAS CONFIRMED IN power in 1907, both because it was fortunate in having come to power on the upswing of the greatest boom the province had yet known, and because it had served the material interests of a rapidly growing community well. From this time on, however, it was to decline because it failed to align itself with new concepts of democratic government and to respond to new needs in the rapidly growing and changing population of Manitoba. And as the power of the government waned, the great boom also faltered and subsided.

The provincial population had reached a figure of 150,000 in 1891. The great bulk was British born and English speaking. The three considerable minority groups were the French, the Mennonites, and the Icelanders. In 1901 the population stood at 255,000; the majority was still British born and English speaking, the three old minorities were relatively little changed, but new minority groups, numbering 16,000 all told, had been added. By 1906 the population numbered 365,000 and the new minority groups numbered 73,000.

The great immigration which began in 1897 had been greeted with mingled hope and apprehension, hope that the West was at last coming into its own, apprehension that it would not be possible to assimilate the newcomers to the British-Canadian way of life which had been established in the first generation of settlement. It was taken for granted that they would and should be assimilated, and it was to this end that the flag legislation of 1906 had been directed and that the agitation for compulsory school attendance was now being raised.

Though the question of the future character and composition of the population of the province was thrusting itself forward, it was still only a question, and Manitobans were still on the whole content to busy themselves with the development of the province. This had been proceeding lustily. Between 1901 and 1903, the provincial Department of Agriculture reported, land values had doubled in Manitoba. As measured in terms of wheat acreage and yield, 999,598 acres in 1896 had yielded 14,371,806 bushels of wheat; 2,011,835 acres in 1901 yielded 50,502,085 bushels; 2,720,424 acres in 1906 yielded 54,460,124 bushels; and in 1911 Manitoba reached the record production of 60,275,000 bushels from 2,979,734 acres. The story could be repeated in terms of livestock, in both numbers and quality of horses and cattle. It was in these years that John Barron, J. D. McGregor, and Alex. Galbraith made the purebred livestock of Manitoba famous. And the line of master farmers and plant breeders which had begun with Alexander Stevenson of Morden and A. J. Cotton of Treherne and Swan River lengthened as new men added their patient work—Samuel Larcombe, Devon's gift to Birtle, for one. Even the production of hogs, sheep, dairy produce, and poultry was greatly increased and improved, for the predominance of grain farming did not, over the whole province, prevent the development of stock farming and mixed farming. Good prices for wheat, the short summers and severe winters, and the perennial shortage of farm labour prevented the development of a high, mixed farming economy such as prevailed in Ontario, but even in the years of the great wheat boom Manitoba, except in the southwest or regions like the Portage Plains or the upper Red River valley, did not specialize in grain farming as did Saskatchewan.

The wealth drawn from this vigorously productive agriculture went into the breaking of new land, the purchase of livestock and machinery, the great new hip-roofed barns, and the sturdy new houses. The country fairs and the great fair at Brandon saw horses and cattle shown of the best strains of the British Isles. The

Clydesdale and the Percheron were in their glory, and the Short-
horns and Aberdeen Angus displayed in bovine complacency the
last refinements of the showman's art. In the fields the quick-
stepping teams were more and more often challenged by the
lumbering steam tractor or even the first thundering combustion
engine tractors. Machine power, as well as machine implements,
was coming to the farm, and farm management and farm costs
were becoming ever more difficult matters.

In the old settled districts the landscape was changing anew.
The prosperous farmstead nestled in its windbreak showed first
its windmill tower, and perhaps its silo. Then the hip-roof of the
great red barn and peaked hay hoist rose above the trees. To one
side, with lawn and garden, rose the new farm house, square and
grave, or ell-shaped with faintly anxious gables peering across
the wide, surrounding fields. The old log stable and the first
shanty had vanished, or were tucked away in the background as
rough outhouses. In the new districts, or on the poor lands, the
log house was still common, and certainly more picturesque than
the tar paper shanty which now rivalled it. But even there the
farm machinery and the broad fields broken by the steam plough
or eight-horse team revealed that this pioneering was in a new
era, and would last a much shorter time than in the earlier years.

The later pioneers of Swan River, of the bush lands of Dauphin
and Riding Mountain, of the Brokenhead valley east of Winnipeg, had not thrust ahead of the railways but had come with
them. The railways carried off their produce and supplied their
needs as rapidly as their labour could produce and earn. And the
railways continued to multiply, cutting across every untraversed
space in the province, thrusting into the unoccupied interlake
district, poking out northeastward from Winnipeg. The Canadian
Northern, backed by guarantees of its bonds by the provincial
legislature, was particularly active, but the Canadian Pacific also
filled out its network of branch lines. From 1905 to 1909 the
third transcontinental system of Canada, represented in the West
by the Grand Trunk Pacific, drove its main line across the province and in 1908 called the new town of Rivers into being. It
found little space for development of branch lines in Manitoba,

however, and was in fact the through line its name signified. The railways, however, were in effect supplying the place of roads in the grain growing districts and were attempting to bring the haulage by road down to something like ten miles.

With the proliferation of railways went the multiplication of elevators. The elevator was almost as necessary as the railway in the rush of harvest, for few farmers could store their grain on the farm. The flat warehouse still survived and was popular among farmers as a check on the local elevator, but in itself was a laborious and tardy way of loading grain. It was because of their dependence on the railway and the elevator, a dependence which might give the local grain buyer a monopoly of the market, that the farmers were so sensitive to all that affected the shipment of grain and which explained the rapid rise of the Grain Growers' Association. Closely allied to facilities for shipping grain was the matter of grain grading. The farmer often questioned the grade given his grain by the local buyer. He fought for and won the right to appeal to an impartial board for a fresh grade, and the federal Board of Grain Commissioners was established in 1908. He was anxious to maintain the reputation of Manitoba wheat, and conducted a long agitation against "mixing" of grades by the grain exporters, demanding instead terminal elevators owned and operated by the government to ensure adequate storage and to check "mixing." In short, the whole complex and hurried process of shipping wheat for export to a distant market gave rise to many occasions for abuse of the farmer's interests by the elevator and railway companies and the grain buyers, and the farmer persistently sought redress.

The idea sprang up that public ownership of both line and terminal elevators would check local monopoly and other abuses, and from 1906 to 1909 the Grain Growers took over the idea and pressed it on the provincial government. The Roblin government had already shown itself disposed to respond to pressure from the Grain Growers; but it hesitated to undertake this highly doubtful venture. When in 1909, however, a by-election in Birtle was lost to a Liberal candidate who was also a Grain Grower, G. H. J. Malcolm, after a campaign in which government ownership of

elevators had been an issue, the government was prompt to announce in December, 1909, that it had accepted the principle of
government ownership. A committee of the government met with
a committee of the executive of the Grain Growers' Association,
and worked out a plan for the purchase and building of elevators
with public funds, the resulting system to be operated by an independent commission. The government accepted the plan, including the commission, and the Manitoba Government Elevators
began operation in 1910 under a commission of which the president was D. W. McCuaig, who had been president of the Manitoba Grain Growers' Association since 1904.

The attempt to supply the essential equipment of the expanding
agricultural economy by government action, if necessary, to protect the producers' interest, was made for the livestock industry
as well as the grain growers. Their demand was for union stockyards, where livestock could be held and cared for until sold,
without pressure from a single railway or buyer. The livestock
men were also anxious that central abattoirs and cold storage
plants should be established, so that Manitoba cattle, instead of
going east or west as "feeders," might be fattened on Manitoba
farms and dressed in Manitoba to be exported as beef. To this
demand also the Roblin government turned a sympathetic ear,
and promised help in 1912. As yet, however, existing facilities
served and the growth of the meat packing industry in Manitoba
proceeded slowly.

The demand for increased equipment was, of course, a reflection of the growth of population and production. But the great
immigration which followed 1897 went largely to Saskatchewan
and Alberta, or to Winnipeg. The total population of Manitoba,
by natural increase and immigration, rose between 1901 and 1911
from 250,000 to 450,000 in round numbers, an increase of
200,000. Of this increase, 100,000 was in the population of the
city of Winnipeg, exclusive of its rising suburbs. The population
of the city in 1901 was 42,000; in 1911 it was 142,000. Winnipeg, that is to say, was continuing to develop as a metropolitan
rather than a provincial city, and its increase of population was
proportionate to the increase in the whole West and not to the

increase in the province of Manitoba. The years of the great western boom saw Winnipeg rise to metropolitan stature, and realize in large part the aspirations of its founders.

The mere physical growth of the city was impressive in itself. The building boom reached heights of expenditure never reached before, and not to be reached again for almost half a century. In 1907 the building contracts totalled $12,000,000. Whole streets of houses sprang up, row on row; the hollow pounding of the hammers rose and fell from dawn to dusk. On Main Street and the increasingly important Portage Avenue, tall office buildings, with column and cornice and plate glass, were rising from the City Hall around by the corner of Portage and Main down past the brick bulk of T. Eaton's departmental store. That building had been completed in 1905; the Union Bank Building rose high above the City Hall in 1904; the McArthur "skyscraper" of fourteen stories in 1910 marked the peak of the boom and remained the highest of Winnipeg buildings. Out from the piled-up mass of the business centre, the new streets were spreading westward across the plain to the city limits. North beyond the Canadian Pacific Railway, and between the tracks and St. John's, the "North End" was rising, a new community of alien immigrants. South of the Assiniboine, Fort Rouge had become the residential district of the well-to-do, and the decline of the old district south of Portage Avenue had begun. The great mansions of the Nantons, the Ashdowns, the Macdonalds, and other wealthy business families were pushing along the south bank of the Assiniboine to form Wellington Crescent, where the brisk clip-clop of the carriage horses was already being challenged by the roar of the automobile. Beyond the Crescent, Crescentwood was beginning to rise among the oak trees which spread out towards the willows and sloughs westward.

The growth of Winnipeg by the end of the first decade of the century had reached such proportions that it was beginning to stimulate the growth of suburbs. The cathedral city of St. Boniface, a separate municipality in law and population, was beginning to be made an industrial suburb of its great neighbour. The convergence of railway lines on its northern and eastern

limits drew to the city the processing plants of an agricultural
economy, and the old missionary city of Provencher and Taché
was slowly being engulfed in an arc of flour mills and abattoirs.
Similarly the old cathedral village of St. John's within the city
limits of Winnipeg was being surrounded by the featureless
rows of houses of the North End. St. James was ceasing to be a
river-front village along the Assiniboine, and was turning to face
the empty width of Portage Avenue as that thoroughfare swung
westward to the still rural and wooded heights of Deer Lodge, as
Silver Heights was now called.

Even as the physical limits of the city spread to accommodate
its growing population, so the physical equipment by which it
served the West grew. The marshalling yards of the Canadian
Pacific grew wider and longer year by year, as more and longer
freight trains drew in from the plains fall after fall. A new station
and a new hotel, the Royal Alexandra, dominated Main and
Higgins, and a subway was built to carry the traffic of Main Street
under the endless traffic of the main line. At the other end of
Main Street the Canadian Northern, in this heir to the Northern
Pacific and Manitoba, and the Grand Trunk Pacific united to
build marshalling yards along the Red on the old river flats, and
in 1911 to build a Union Station on Main Street facing westward
down Broadway. On that tree-lined avenue the Fort Garry Hotel
reared in 1913 its tall height and chateau-like roof. The smoke
of the yards and shops by day and the thud of coupling cars by
night never allowed Winnipeg to forget that it lived by the
coming and going of the trains as a seaport lives by its shipping.
How completely Winnipeg had become a railway city is illustrated also by the all but complete extinction of its river traffic.
Only an occasional steamboat whistled its way through the great
iron bridges which carried the railways. Even the building, at
long last, of the control dam at Lockport in 1910 to flood St.
Andrew's Rapids produced no revival of commercial traffic on the
Red. The once bustling waterfront became a neglected back yard
of a too busy city which had sprung from the traffic of its rivers,
and now left in slattern neglect the streams which were its sole
natural adornment.

As the railways expanded, so did the warehouses, the Grain Exchange, the real estate firms, through which Winnipeg served the West and grew rich in serving. The development of local firms such as J. H. Ashdown's and the Great-West Life Assurance Company, both in the expansion of their Winnipeg headquarters and in the establishment of branches in the rising cities of the West, was characteristic of Winnipeg's business growth. The rise of Winnipeg branch offices and stores, such as the real estate and loan office of Osler, Hammond and Nanton, or T. Eaton's store, to stature comparable with their main offices and stores in eastern Canada was an even more striking example of this growth. The Grain Exchange occupied its great new building on Lombard Street in 1908, and was reorganized in 1910. In the tense clamour of its Pit, in the flickering change of the quotations on the blackboard, was focussed the essence of the western economy in this age of wheat. The Winnipeg Stock Exchange, incorporated in 1907, did a brisk business in these years of boom, although it never acquired the vigour or the fame of the Grain Exchange.

The governing commercial group was enlarged during these years, but remained essentially unchanged. Old names, Ashdown, Alloway, Macdonald, remained; young men had made themselves names, A. M. Nanton, R. T. Riley, N. Bawlf; new men were coming up. The grain trade and the wholesale trade were still the dominant occupations. Membership in the Manitoba Club remained the symbol of success and the club itself the centre of that informal exchange of opinion and information, access to which marks the "insider." The legal profession had increased in number and weight, and wealthy firms and powerful counsel served the grain trade, the railways, and the real estate business with great profit in money and prestige. More and more of these men in business and law acquired national reputations and were called to directorships in national firms or to the service of the federal government. The most striking example of the reputation of the Winnipeg business community, perhaps, was the formation in 1913 of the Canadian Committee of the Hudson's Bay Company, composed of Sir William Whyte, A. M. Nanton, and G. W. Allan. It was a deserved reputation, for in the boom days the Winnipeg business community had proved itself at once progressive and conservative and had maintained a high standard of commercial morality and a high sense of public duty.[1] The prudent conservatism of the business community is well exemplified by its support of the introduction of a Board of Control in the civic government of Winnipeg to restrain any financial rashness of the City Council in guiding the growth of the booming city. It was in its relations with labour and with farmers that it was to reveal its limitations and the weaknesses of its business code.

There was to be occasion for this revelation, for Winnipeg was ceasing to be merely a commercial city; industry was beginning to become important. The service industries, the railway shops, the iron works, the carriage and saddlery shops, had been significant from the first. Secondary processing industries such as flour milling, important from the late seventies, were now expanding, and to it was added the growing meat packing industry. Food industries, such as Paulin Chambers' biscuit factory, or Dyson's pickling plant, were increasing. The industrial output of the province, in large part that of Winnipeg, was valued at $13,000,000 in 1900 and $54,000,000 in 1910 and the labour force grew from 5,000 in the former year to an estimated 17,000 in the latter.

The growth of industry of course brought with it the growth of industrial labour, and Winnipeg labour took part in the great development of the labour movement in Canada between 1900 and 1912. By the end of the century the principal Winnipeg trades had unions, organized since 1897 in the flourishing Winnipeg Trades and Labour Congress. In the Labour Day parade of 1899 twenty-seven unions took part.[2] Other events of that year illustrated the vigour of the labour movement of Winnipeg. The railway machinists struck in October, and were joined by the boilermakers and blacksmiths in what became an outstanding strike in Winnipeg labour history.[3] In the same month Eugene V. Debs, the American Socialist leader, spoke on "Labor and Liberty," to members of the Independent Labour party.[4] The party, first organized in 1895, had been busy since February with preparations to enter the provincial election on a farmer-labour platform.[5] These glimpses of an intense and vigorous life are typical of succeeding years. They were years punctuated by the growth of the Labour party, the coming of European Social Democrats and British Labour party men, the establishment in 1904 of both the Social Democratic party and the Socialist party of Canada, growth in the numbers of union men, the faint beginning of labour legislation, and one fierce strike in 1906, ending in violence and the use of troops, the strike of the Winnipeg Street Railway men for higher wages and recognition of the union. They were years of growth, but of growth diverse and unco-ordinated and still on the margins of the law and public esteem, for public opinion in Winnipeg and the province was not prepared as yet to accept organized labour or to grant direct recognition to trades unions.

Labour, however, was growing in social importance, as may be illustrated by the agitation for Sunday street cars. Hitherto Protestant sabbatarianism and middle class *mores* had prohibited the cars from running on Sundays, and the sabbath calm of the streets was broken only by the cries of children playing and the passing carriages or cars of the well-to-do. Working men and enlightened citizens now began to demand that the cars be available to take people out of the cities and to the parks, and indeed to church, on Sundays. It was a very lively issue, fought with some heat for years, until in 1906 Sunday street cars were authorized. The opening of Winnipeg beach in 1903 on the west shore of Lake Winnipeg was to furnish cause for a similar struggle for Sunday trains to the beach in later years. What was involved was a change of manners—the matter was scarcely one of morals—to create a more humane society and allow the families of workers and the lower middle class some chance to share amenities the well-to-do took for granted.

These various indications of the significant growth of Winnipeg industry raised the question of how power was to be supplied for future growth. Alberta and Pennsylvania coal were made costly by the long haul from the mines. The one cheap and local source of power was the hydro-electricity to which eastern Canada was turning during the early years of the century. The multitudinous waters of the Canadian Shield, spilling down the granite ridges of that wilderness just to the north of the larger Canadian cities, furnished abundant water power which the engineers were making cheap. Sixty-odd miles to the northeast of Winnipeg the Winnipeg River, long-abandoned route of the fur trade, still plunged down its many falls from the Lake of the Woods, a great stabilizing reservoir fed by the seepings of millions of muskegs and the quick run-off of the granite ridges. Here, the engineers estimated, a half million horse power of electrical energy might be developed.

Electricity had first been developed in Winnipeg in 1881 by steam generation for lighting. By 1888–9 the growth of the city and the desire to replace the horse-drawn street cars with an electrified system gave rise to a project to develop the water power of the Assiniboine at the St. James rapids, but nothing came of the proposal. In 1892 the Winnipeg Electric Street Railway Company was formed, with a franchise to operate an electric street railway system; later, by the absorption of other companies, it acquired rights to generate and distribute power. The electric railway began operation in that year, and the drone of the wheels became one of the characteristic sounds of Winnipeg streets. The Assiniboine power project was once more taken up, but was abandoned because the company was required to build a navigation canal as part of the enterprise. As a result, the generation of power and the manufacture of gas remained scattered among a number of small firms, and when the rapid growth of the city began at the century's end the supply of power became quite inadequate.

In 1901 the organization of the Manitoba Water Power Electric Company was undertaken by the Winnipeg Electric Railway Company to develop hydro-electric power on the Pinawa channel of the Winnipeg River. Construction began in 1903. In that year the City Council, alarmed by the prospect of a shortage of power and of a private monopoly, took up the question of providing cheap and adequate power. A long and bitterly contested struggle followed, both as to how power should be provided, and

PRAIRIE LAND IN WESTERN CANADA, 1912

Painting by Harold Copping in the John Ross Robertson Collection

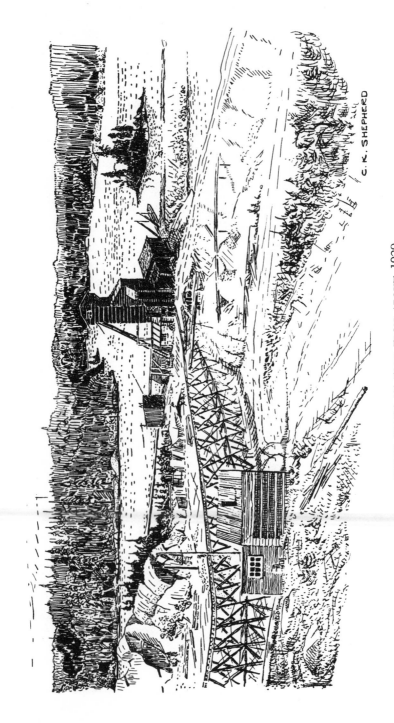

EARLY SHAFT AT FLIN FLON ABOUT 1929
Drawing by C. K. Shepherd, from a photograph

as to whether the City Charter should be amended to allow the city to generate power itself. Those who favoured the ownership and management of the power plants by the city were led by Mayor Thomas Sharpe and Alderman J. W. Cockburn, two of Winnipeg's greatest public servants. While the struggle was still undecided in 1903, Cockburn, to safeguard what he believed to be the city's interests, secured the power site at Pointe du Bois falls in his own name for ultimate transfer to the city. In the course of the struggle the old Assiniboine project was re-examined and vigorously supported, but was dropped on what now seem the obvious grounds that it could not supply the needs of the growing city. The relative merits of electrical and gas power were disputed, while the city grew and industry's need for power multiplied.

Meantime, the Winnipeg Electric Street Railway Company, backed by the powerful interests of William Mackenzie of the Canadian Northern and the Nesbitt Thomson bond company of Toronto, had continued to gather together the street railway, power plant, and gas utilities. In 1906 the first hydro-electric power from the Pinawa Channel plant on the Winnipeg River flowed to Winnipeg over the company's transmission lines, but the rates for light and power remained high. Now at last the City Council responded to the pressure of public opinion, organized by a Citizens' Committee and mass meetings called by the Board of Trade. The civic democracy of Winnipeg was at its strongest and best at this time, and had its way. The Charter was amended to allow the development of a civic power utility. Offers by various private firms to compete with the Winnipeg Electric were rejected, and by a by-law approved by the electors on June 28, 1906, the Winnipeg City Hydro was formed. In 1907 the Council voted to develop Cockburn's site at Pointe du Bois, but the financial crisis of that year delayed action. In 1908 the project went forward under Mayor J. H. Ashdown, elected on a platform of public ownership, and his successor, W. Sanford Evans. In 1911 the first power came from Pointe du Bois. The rates were set at 3½ cents a kilowatt hour less a 10 per cent discount for prompt payment, and these rates the Winnipeg Electric met. Winnipeg now had cheap power in abundance and under the management of J. G. Glassco the City Hydro became an efficient utility. Winnipeg from 1911 was to have two hydro-electric systems, one private, one public, in competition, a dual system which, with the natural advantages of the Winnipeg River, gave the city power rates which for long were the lowest on the continent.[6]

The rejection of the Assiniboine power project and the bold determination to develop the falls of the Winnipeg were a measure of the new concept the city had formed of its growth and destiny. The planning of the city's development was being done by 1906 in terms of a population of 300,000 by 1911 and 450,000 by 1921. The impetus carried on even when the great boom slackened, as the formation of the Greater Winnipeg Water District in 1913 to build an aqueduct from Shoal Lake, a branch of the Lake of the Woods, was to demonstrate, both in the magnitude of the project and in the enthusiasm with which it was undertaken. But even as paved roads were run out to Headingley and St. Norbert and city lots were subdivided across the prairie, even as the last blasts rang out from the rocks of Pointe du Bois, the great land boom was passing its crest and the charges were blasting out the Panama Canal which, far down in tropic waters, was to turn the gateway of Winnipeg and sap the traffic that fed its growth.

Nor were the results of the decade of development to be wholly pleasant for the province as a whole. As the great boom built up to its climax and material prosperity became a frame of mind, as the increase of railway and steamship rates, the rise in real wages, and the fear of war were undercutting the boom, so within the province the boom was setting up ever sharper strains in the structure of the community. None was severer, or more feared, than the strain of incorporating the thousands of European immigrants. The American settlers caused little concern in the West, though the "Americanization" of the West aroused fears in eastern Canada. Nor were doubts entertained as to the power of the old community to absorb the north European immigrants.

the Scandinavians, Germans, and other people of related stock and Protestant faith. It was the Slavs, "the Galicians," in fact principally the Ukrainians who were feared as "strangers within the gates." These sturdy peasants, with their strange costumes and the inevitable sheepskin coat, were more alien than a mere difference of language and background made inevitable. They brought the peasant's fierce attachment to the soil and a sense of ethnic nationalism, born at once of oppression and the teachings of their leaders, which were new in Manitoba. The Anglo-Saxon farmer was attached to the land as a way of life, but his farming was as commercial in its management as banking or store-keeping; he would never have joined the Ukrainian peasant in the sudden, impulsive act of kissing the sacred earth. Most groups in Manitoba, English, Scottish, Icelandic, were conscious of their ethnic backgrounds, but all assumed the possibility of easy good fellowship and community life. Only the French and the Mennonites may have understood the desire of the Ukrainians to maintain their nationality in the new land; to the others it was a menace to a basic assumption taking shape in the new province, that in the new land all things were new and what each group possessed was to be put into the common stock.

The two main Slavic groups to settle in Manitoba were the Ukrainians, then for the most part called Galicians from the district of origin of the majority of them, and the Poles. Of these the Ukrainians were much the more numerous, and also the more assertive. They were, in fact, soon to begin to assimilate the Poles to a considerable degree to themselves. Their separateness was intensified by the fact that the remaining homestead and cheap lands of Manitoba lay along the bushland frontier extending from the southeastern corner of the province to Lake Winnipeg, up through Interlake district, and northwestward around Lake Manitoba to the slopes of Riding and Duck Mountain. Into these rugged bushlands the new settlers went of necessity, but also, it is recorded, not unwillingly, since the bushlands in some ways resembled the wooded foothills of the Carpathians from which most of them had come. There they re-enacted, with variants drawn from their peasant background, the toilful drama of the pioneer. The potato patch, the first narrow fields, the log house plastered with clay and thatched deep with straw, all were multiplied along the new eastern and northern woodland frontier these hardy people brought into being. One eye-catching thing they brought to Manitoba, their love of colour, and the blank white of the Anglo-Saxon's log house was replaced by robin's egg blue and other soft tints which recalled far Galicia and the Bukovina.

Not all these peasant folk went on the land. They had come with little money, and became labourers on the railways and on construction in the city to earn wages to bring out their people, buy their land, and feed their families. Many never succeeded in acquiring land, but became wedded to the wage-earner's life. They formed new communities in Winnipeg and in the railway divisional towns of Portage la Prairie, Brandon, and Dauphin. In Winnipeg they joined in the peopling of the North End between the Canadian Pacific tracks and old St. John's. There long rows of cheap houses were run up, but never fast enough to house the inflow decently or to furnish cheap enough lodgings. In squalor and poverty, in a mixture of races living under strange laws and in a strange land, began the life of one of the city's most vigorous and vivid districts, the North End.[7]

It was in the North End also that the Manitoba Jewish community rooted itself. Few Jews had come to Manitoba in the first generation of settlement. Those who did were traders and peddlers along the main line of the Canadian Pacific, or merchants in the Mennonite towns of the south. When the east European immigration began in the nineties, most Jewish immigrants settled in the North End, as merchants and traders serving the immigrant community. As the Jewish community formed and the synagogues were founded, the Jews of the rural towns tended to remove thither with their families to ensure that their children should receive a Jewish education. Soon Jewish children were displaying their characteristic precocity in the schools and some Jewish names were known among the most respected in Winnipeg. Winnipeg was not to escape the curse of anti-semitism, but it was possible there for a gifted and persecuted people to win for their children a new life of freedom and opportunity, and Winnipeg was soon to be repaid in over-measure for such toleration as it showed and such good fellowship as it practised.[8]

When the tale of the immigrants was counted, it was apparent that all the diversity of Europe, in race and creed, had been imposed on the already diversified population of the Manitoba of the first generation. The leading question of the day was whether this conglomeration of peoples could be fused with the British Canadian majority to make a real community which would preserve the salient features of the old British allegiance, English speech, the rule of law, the democratic process, and the creed of common friendliness and good neighbourhood. The great agency of assimilation in North America was the public school, and Manitoba, at the cost of a severe struggle, had established a common, or national, school system partly in anticipation of the need of unifying a diverse population. That system, as an instrument of assimilation, however, had been weakened by the bilingual clause of the Compromise of 1897. The clause imposed no limitation on the mother tongue which might be taught with English, whenever there were ten children of a language other than English in a school. The clause in its first years operated as it was intended, to allow French and Mennonite parents to have their children taught in the speech of their homes as well as in English, the language of the community. The privilege of bilingual instruction appealed to the nationalist aspirations of the Ukrainians, some of whose leaders dreamed of the creation of a new Ukraine in western Canada, and to the natural dispositions of parents in all groups not to have their children alienated from them by education in a strange tongue, even if it was the language of the law and the community. Soon bilingual instruction was being demanded in many school districts where the number of children warranted, and the Department of Education had to endeavour to meet these lawful requests. There is little doubt that the demands were sometimes stimulated by the Roman Catholic clergy, hopeful of obtaining among their Polish and Ukrainian co-religionists allies for the overthrow of the school system,[9] and by political organizers of both parties seeking to curry favour with newly enfranchised voters. The Department of Education was hard pressed to supply teachers, let alone bilingual teachers, to the school districts rapidly rising in the new settlements. It was indeed difficult to find teachers willing to endure the hardships of life among these pioneer peasant communities. To meet the need for Ukrainian bilingual teachers, special training schools were founded at Brandon and Winnipeg in 1907, as had been done in St. Boniface for French teachers in 1899. In the same way, the Department made every effort to comply with the law and to meet the desires, sometimes exacting, of the parents and trustees in the new districts.

Sympathetic administration, however, could only help develop the chaos latent in the loose phrasing of the bilingual clause. The standard of English suffered, with the teachers themselves barely bilingual; children of minority groups of less than ten in a school were taught English and another language other than their own; the languages to be taught altered abruptly as the numbers of children from different groups changed in a school from term to term; there were bitter struggles for control of school boards, struggles ultimately to be settled by possession of the soil. Finally, because of the lack of a school attendance law, many children were receiving little or no education; and if the bilingual clause were removed from the School Act, or any other change made which was obnoxious to any group, it could resist it, at the expense of its children, by refusing to allow them to attend school. These were some of the considerations which lay behind the growing agitation for a compulsory school attendance act. The Roblin government, determined as it was to avoid reopening the School Question, held to the ground that such an act would violate the constitutional rights of Roman Catholic parents. On a reference to a distinguished counsel in 1907, this opinion had been confirmed.[10] The government therefore confined its efforts to dealing with truancy in Winnipeg and the province by tightening the enforcement of the Children's Act and by urging the consolidation of schools in the country and the provision of transport to take the children to them. It was in fact able to point to a steady rise in the average school attendance, but the averages were still shamefully low.

The great immigration had brought this difficult and delicate question with it. The mere growth of population and the advance from the pioneer stage of society brought demands for new extended services by the municipal and provincial governments. The creation of the Manitoba Government Telephones had been a response to one such demand. The provision of telephones in Winnipeg and the province proved to be a difficult and costly undertaking, increased, it was charged, by inefficiency consequent on political interference. In 1911–12, it was found necessary to raise the rates to cover mounting deficits, which provoked a strong outcry, and further charges of mismanagement. Another government project, the Grain Elevators, however, proved to be a complete failure. An ambitious programme of purchase and building undertaken by the commission resulted in annual deficits, which the government had to meet. It seemed that while farmers desired the check which the Government Elevators imposed on the private companies, they were not prepared to patronize them exclusively. This disposition may have been increased by criticism of the government system by the Liberals and the Grain Growers. So heavy did the deficits become that in 1912 the government ended the experiment and leased the elevators to the Grain Growers' Grain Company.

With the coming of agricultural prosperity, and also of the motor car, it became possible to think of continuous highways of superior quality in addition to the local roads which served the farms and market towns. These were the responsibility of the municipalities; the province had hitherto confined its public works largely to the drainage of the provincial swamp lands, the building of bridges over the larger rivers, and similar undertakings. Now a demand arose for a "good roads" programme to consist of provincial highways and provincial assistance for municipal market roads. It was a demand to which the Roblin government did not yield until 1914 when the Good Roads Act was passed. This need for better roads was to do much to transform relations between the province and its municipalities, and to lead eventually to the creation of a system of provincial highways similar to the network of railways which was then nearing completion.

Manitoba had made do for the most part with the public buildings which had been built with federal grants in the eighties, but these were now becoming too small for their purposes, or unworthy of the new prosperity of the province. There were also new services to be provided in health and education. The buildings of the Agricultural College at Tuxedo had been the first large undertaking of the Roblin government. By 1911 the Tuxedo site had become too small, both in lands and buildings, and a new site was purchased in St. Vital, six miles south of Winnipeg. Here in 1912 began the erection of buildings for lectures and laboratories and a students' residence of large size and expensive construction. At the same time the Agricultural College was separated from the University of Manitoba and made a degree-granting institution. The growing demand that the University of Manitoba be made a state university with an adequate grant and a site and buildings furnished by the provincial government was not met by the Roblin government, because of obstacles within the University council to a reorganization acceptable to the government. Normal schools were built in Winnipeg, St. Boniface, Manitou, Portage la Prairie, and Brandon, and an industrial school at Portage la Prairie. In 1910 a sanatorium for tubercular patients was opened at Ninette in the sun-filled Pembina valley, and the mental hospitals at Selkirk and Brandon were rebuilt on a generous scale. In Winnipeg a new Law Courts was planned and, by action of a bipartisan committee of the Legislature in 1911, a new Legislative Building. The design of F. W. Simon of Liverpool, England, was selected by a similar committee from sixty-five submitted in competition. The building was to cost just over $2,000,000 and in 1912 the first estimates for its construction were voted. It would be, said the Premier with a rare revelation of feeling, "a thing of beauty"; in it, indeed, and in the other great buildings of the period, the prosperity and the aspirations of the long boom were to be incorporated.

The cost of this heavy programme of public building would, it was thought, be easily borne by a province whose future seemed to promise an unlimited growth. But the province and Winnipeg, inspired by the long succession of years each more prosperous than its predecessor, were on the point of over-reaching themselves. One ominous sign was the collapse of the grandiose plans for the Selkirk Centennial in 1911. The celebration was to mark a century of settlement in the valley of the Red and to advertise to the world the still unexplored potentialities of the West, and it was intended to outdo the Chicago Columbian Exposition of 1893. But the federal government refused to grant the $2,500,000 asked of it, and efforts to raise that amount and its equivalent locally failed. In the end the Centennial was a rather commonplace display of Red River relics and a local industrial and agricultural exhibition. Winnipeg had acquired the grand manner but not the deep purse of Chicago. The failure of the Centennial was a forecast of the outcome of the expenditures on public works. These were indeed carried out on a scale not incommensurate with the future envisioned for the province. But the cost was to prove to be one of the heaviest strains on a community which was still borrowing against the future, and the splendid new buildings were to prove so many ornate millstones round the neck of the future taxpayer. The material strain of equipping the province with public buildings, moreover, was to be matched by the psychological strain of adopting ideas fitted to the new age with its new conditions.

One of these ideas was an old one intensified, the idea of prohibiting the use of alcoholic liquor. The prohibition movement had been in progress for over half a century, in the Red River Settlement and Manitoba as elsewhere. It was intensified at the turn of the century by two factors of increasing importance, the growth of industrialism and the emancipation of women. Intemperance, an evil under any conditions, was increasingly dangerous in an industrial age and increasingly intolerable to the women who were emancipating their sex from the legal and social discrimination which had confined them to private life under the rule of husband or father. It was the Women's Christian Temperance Union which in 1893 first petitioned for the extension of the suffrage to women in Manitoba. The agitation was carried on from 1898 by Margret Benedictson of Selkirk in her publication *Freyja*, and was to be organized in the Political Equality League by Lillian Beynon Thomas in 1912.[11] Meanwhile, the advocates of prohibition had increased their efforts, following the defeat of the plebiscite of 1902 on the Macdonald Prohibition Act, and were putting steady pressure on government and the parties "to banish the bar." The temperance societies were joined by the churches one by one, and the political parties had to weigh the loss of votes to be caused by supporting prohibition against that to be suffered by refusing to do so. The Roblin government declined to adopt a policy of prohibition, and continued its policy of enforcing the Liquor Act and making licences to retail liquor more expensive and more difficult to obtain. The operation of the local option clause made more and more municipalities in the province "dry," but Winnipeg and especially the "foreign" districts remained obstinately "wet." As a result, the demands for prohibition and for the extension of the franchise to women were now combining with the determination to assimilate the foreign immigrant to native ways, to become a confused but explosive movement. The Liberal party began in 1910 to incorporate these elements in its programme. In this crusade, in which temperance was quite lost sight of, it is possible to detect a certain exasperation under the stresses of the times and an attempt to deal with them decisively by a sweeping, idealistic gesture.

The growing ferment of a new society under strain was apparent on every side. The agitation of the Direct Legislation League revealed a profound distrust of the political parties and conventional governmental procedures, and a desire to find a short cut to clean and popular government.[12] It also expressed the strong democratic feeling of the times that the people as a whole ought to control government, instead of the politicians and the "vested" and "special" interests which, it was alleged, were so powerful. The League expressed at once the growing revulsion against partisan politics and the hope that in a direct appeal to the people lay a remedy for political and social evils. The growth of the

Labour party in Winnipeg and the spread of socialist ideas, particularly by British and European immigrants, the beginnings of social work in Winnipeg by Margaret Scott, the Jane Addams of Winnipeg, and the All People's Mission of the Methodist Church, were a further indication of new forces at work, and forces which the Conservative and Liberal parties could not completely satisfy. The ferment of the times was evident also in the Grain Growers' conventions. It began to spread to the Liberal party, as was made apparent by the adoption of direct legislation in the party's platform in 1910.

Many of the new elements in political thought of the day derived from the steady growth of the Labour movement in Winnipeg. The movement was basically one for the recognition of the rights of labour in an industrial age, but it was also a lively and intimate part of the general reform movement. Many labour leaders, though not necessarily the rank and file, were keenly interested in temperance, women's rights, and direct legislation, as was exemplified in the early career of F. J. Dixon, the organizer of the Direct Legislation League, and S. J. Farmer, an advocate of that reform. Both men were leaders of the Independent Labour party of Manitoba. That party was gradually making a place for itself in Winnipeg, but elected no candidate before 1914, and its chief effect was to force the old parties to turn their attention to the new problems of industrial society, and to make a beginning in industrial legislation, such as the Workmen's Compensation Act of 1910. A new element, industrial labour, inspired by the ideas of the Labour movement in Europe and the United States, was making a place for itself in Manitoban life, but the adjustment would be easy on neither side.

The Roblin government and the general character of Manitoban society, however, were not yet to be greatly affected by these developing changes. In the election of 1910 the government was sustained by its record, its political craft and sturdy political machine, and the cry for boundary extension and equality of treatment in Confederation. The Workmen's Compensation Act was cited as evidence that the government was alert to the needs of the times. The Liberal opposition had a new leader in T. C.

Norris, who had led the party in the House since 1907, and his candid and genial personality accorded well with the growing desire for simple and straightforward government. The Liberal platform of 1910, moreover, had a positive quality which that of 1907 had lacked, though it still failed to take a decisive stand on two of the most important questions of the day, compulsory school attendance and prohibition. The multiplicity of issues, and their social nature, was accompanied by the appearance of new parties and independent candidates, almost wholly in Winnipeg. In 1910 three Socialists and two Independents stood for election, although all but one drew too few votes to be listed. Once more the Roblin government was returned with twenty-eight supporters; the Liberals, however, with T. H. Johnson and Dr. R. S. Thornton in the House, for the first time since 1899 constituted an alternative government.

If the politicians were reluctant to come to grips with issues other than the strictly practical and material, they were no more so than the writers who might have been expected to be more reflective. Of these the most famous in his day, and the most ephemeral in his fame, was "Ralph Connor," Rev. C. W. Gordon, minister of St. Stephen's Broadway Presbyterian church. Gordon had achieved reputation as a novelist with the publication of *Black Rock* and *The Man from Glengarry*, novels of some feeling and characterization. Thereafter there flowed from his pen a series of novels descriptive of western Canadian life, which were widely read and translated into many languages. They served the need for some description of the land to which thousands were flocking; they discussed Canadian life in that tone of manly Christian endeavour which Canadians then found satisfying because it did fill the gap between the roughness of the frontier and the pieties of the home. But the novels afford no authentic note of the times, not a single penetrating comment on the inwardness of Canadian life. *The Foreigner*, for example, is a novel of the North End of Winnipeg; it might have captured imaginatively the spiritual stress of that human crucible, but it is, in fact, a melodrama of Russian intrigue. Gordon's novels were part of the great boom, themselves inflated, brittle, and hollow.

Nearer to the heart of Manitoba, more authentic, touched with genuine sentiment and lilting with Irish laughter, were the stories of Nellie McClung. Helen Mooney, to give her maiden name, had come in as a child with her family from Ontario to settle at the Sourismouth. Her first stories were of farm life in south-central Manitoba, of which the best were published in *The Black Creek Stopping House*. Her vein of sentiment and intimacy made her writings popular among western Canadians, and *Sowing Seeds in Danny* is typical of rural Manitoban life of that time in its observance of the convention of bright superficiality and reso-lute refusal to admit in public the existence of the sordid and sinful. When Nellie McClung turned to sterner things, it was not to treat of them in literature but to campaign on the platform for prohibition and women's suffrage, at once a more courageous and an easier thing to do. More literary than the work of either Ralph Connor or Mrs. McClung was E. A. Wharton Gill's *Love in Manitoba*, a simply told and well-constructed novel of life in the Swedish Settlement on Riding Mountain, but thoroughly conventional and imitative of the standard English novel to the point of exquisiteness. More robust, and a genuine document, was the same author's *Letters of a Manitoba Choreboy*.

Another literature, the continuation of a long tradition, was springing up in Manitoba during these years, that of the Ice-landic Manitobans. At Riverton, for example, the farmer poet, Guttormur J. Guttormsson, was preparing his first volume for publication. A rich poetry and a promising prose were being added to the cultural wealth of the new land, but were denied to the majority of Manitobans by the barrier of language, a phenomenon the years were to multiply.

In historical literature the years of the great boom were more productive than the previous period had been. R. G. McBeth began the publication of his numerous books; the best, *The Making of the Canadian West*, appeared in 1898. The author was too little disposed to report from first-hand evidence and too much disposed to moralize and romanticize. The same year saw the publication of Archer Martin's *Hudson's Bay Company Land Tenures*, a work of severe legal scholarship on one of the fundamental issues of early Manitoban history. The volumes of reminiscences continued to appear from time to time, as the participants in the events of the creation of the province were moved to put their recollections on record. J. H. O'Donnell's *Manitoba as I saw it* was the best of the kind in this period. In 1910 Father Morice's monumental *History of the Catholic Church in Western Canada* appeared in English, and in 1912 in French. A fine venture in the same field of church history and also in biography was Rev. C. W. Gordon's (Ralph Connor) *Life of James Robertson*, organizer of the Presbyterian Church in the West, published in 1908. F. H. Schofield was actively compiling his three-volume history of Manitoba during these years and it appeared in 1912, a sober and useful work. The appointment of Chester Martin to the Chair of History in the University of Manitoba in 1909 brought to the province the future student of Lord Selkirk's work in Canada, but his flowing narrative history of Manitoba was not to appear in *Canada and Its Provinces* until 1914. None of the historians of the period, except Archer Martin, can be said to have attempted any very penetrative analysis of Manitoban history or society.

Indeed, no one did in the hurry and preoccupation of the surging growth in the great boom. Rev. J. S. Woodsworth's *Strangers within the Gates* is concerned with the multitudinous problems of the immigrants' life in the North End, as the author was bound to be as the leader of the Methodist All People's Mission. The book, however, is the hurried work of a busy man, a man in need of a philosophy adequate to the circumstances in which he found himself. It is a compilation of writings on immigration problems by writers who themselves lacked the equipment for interpreting, or even faithfully reporting, what they saw. Little is to be learned from it, and Woodsworth was himself to go on in search of a "social gospel" which would throw some light into the dark places in which he had chosen to work.

It was to be a lonely search, for Manitoba was yet preoccupied with the great work of physical development. In the country the old ways still served. The churches taught the old doctrines, ever a little more hollowly, as the gap between the old formulations of creed and the demands of the new age widened. There were still revivals and still backslidings, but indifference quietly grew. Many became dissatisfied with the organized churches and turned to the farmers' organizations or the Labour movement for a cause to serve. No outward change occurred, however, although the union of the Protestant denominations was already under discussion. For the rest, the old recreations still served in sport and social gathering. But the zest they had once aroused was wanting; pioneer days and pioneer ways were nearly done in Manitoba.

Of Winnipeg the same was broadly true, but with a difference. Winnipeg was still the great outfitting and supply centre, the place where the immigrant set out for his land and the workman took his job, the place to which all returned from construction, harvesting, or "the bush" to "blow a pile" and release the tension of a summer's or a winter's work. To the West "The Peg" was a raucous, lesser Chicago, the outfitter, the exploiter, and the city of the fleshpots. And the city catered to the wants of the transient and exploited the inexperienced. The great bars of this frenzied decade, with the brass rail for the uplifted foot and the glittering array of bottles to tempt the eye, were at once the goal of the thirsty and the target of the prohibitionist. They were western bars, in which men drank, and were encouraged to drink, to intoxication, not places of social relaxation. Allied with them were the card sharpers and shell game men.[13] As notorious as the bars were the Winnipeg houses of prostitution. How to deal with this problem was a major irritant in civic administration. A resolute attempt at suppression in 1904, following on a period of attempted regulation, caused the dispersion of the houses all over the city. The chief of police and the Mayor were driven to think segregation and licensing preferable, and in 1910 the matter was an issue in the mayoralty election.[14] The growth of Winnipeg had carried with it the organization of vice and the beginning of an underworld with which the liquor trade and both civic and provincial politics had intimate if reluctant ties, and which gave the social reformers their most urgent task.

That was the seamy side—the muddied hem—of the new metropolis. Another, more pleasing aspect but no less a part of the new life of the city, was the growth of the commercial theatre.

This was not a matter of amateur theatricals, such as the seventies had known, but of travelling companies, which had begun to reach the city in the eighties when the Winnipeg Theatre was built. Now the revival of theatre in London and New York, the new easy money of the boom, the combined demand of old Winnipeggers and of British and American newcomers, both transient and permanent, created a hunger for drama, opera, and vaudeville which seemed insatiable. During the season the city knew the excitement of good theatre, of the company of actors and singers, of dressing for the circle or of huddling in "the gods," and of coffee after the show in Mariaggi's famed café.

To the Winnipeg were added the Orpheum, the Pantages, and then in 1908 the great Walker Theatre, a stage and auditorium for which any city might have been grateful. There two princes of their profession, Mr. and Mrs. C. P. Walker, offered to delighted Winnipeggers and Manitobans, their guests and the passing traveller, year after year the best that London and New York could be persuaded to send travelling.[15] They gave the public lasting and memorable pleasure, and for many years they were rewarded financially and to the end were held in affectionate honour by their adopted city. But Winnipeg had few amateurs of the stage and produced no artist in these years.

What could be the outcome of the strong contrasts of commercial vice and puritanical reform, of a booming commercial theatre and the swamping of the local cultivation of the arts? No one could say, and the period itself was not to reveal. It did not do to discuss Winnipeg as a Canadian Chicago, for in these years Chicago was contesting the leadership of letters in the United States. In any event, Winnipeg did not impress sensitive observers as being just another Chicago, or even another Toronto. There was, it seemed to them, some elusive difference. Perhaps it was its uniqueness. Bernard McEvoy, fresh from Ontario, wrote in 1901:

Winnipeg reveals itself, if you stay in it for a few days, as a city of very considerable actualities, and very great possibilities. As a commercial, educational, governmental, and social centre it is a capital city that holds a distinct and unique place. Its wide streets are typical of the breadth of its notions. Winnipeggers have not the slightest doubt about their city. They have heard of New York and London, and they have some dim remembrance that there is a city called Toronto, and one called Montreal—also that on the west coast there are a couple of thriving communities that some people call cities. But, O pshaw! People will do these things. But look around you. Ask some old fellow what this was twenty years ago. Very well, then—There you are.[16]

Winnipeg, in defiance of all the prophets, had grown as no city before had grown; it had a certain Pallas Athena quality of having sprung full grown from the prairie.

Perhaps also the precocious prairie child had some promise, born of its unique growth and fresh beginning, of future grace of mind and manner. The poet, Rupert Brooke, who visited the city in 1913, was disposed to think so:

A new city: a little more American than the other Canadian cities, but not unpleasantly so. The streets are wider, and full of a bustle which keeps clear of hustle. The people have something of the free swing of Americans, without the bumptiousness; a tempered democracy, a mitigated independence of bearing. The manners of the Winnipeg, of the West, impress the stranger as better than those of the East, more friendly, more hearty, more certain to achieve graciousness, if not grace. . . . one can't help finding a tiny hope that Winnipeg, the city of buildings and the city of human beings, may yet come to something. . . . *That* hope [of material growth] is sure to be fulfilled. But the other timid prayer, that something different, something more worth having, may come out of Winnipeg, exists, and not quite unreasonably.[17]

These were comments that the future would test; how, perhaps the foundation of the Men's Musical Club in 1912 was to show. But that they could be made indicates that over the rough growth of the city and the province still hung some auroral hint that the settlement of prairie and parkland, the building of a great commercial emporium on the Forks of the Red and the Assiniboine, was not merely utilitarian and material, but might also open new trails for mind and spirit.

The surface of events in the last years of the great boom, however, gave little indication of such possibilities. The fierce pace of building and land breaking was unslackened, the bitter contests of politics waxed more hotly. In 1911 the negotiation of the Reciprocity Agreement with the United States suddenly gave a new turn to federal politics and this in turn broke the deadlock on boundary extension and better terms which had lasted since 1905. The federal Conservative party, after initial hesitation, came out in opposition to reciprocity in trade with the United States. Reciprocity was attacked as a deadly threat to the whole work of nation building in Canada and to the east-west flow of trade which made Canadian nationalism viable. In this it was supported—indeed, had been anticipated—by Premier Roblin and the Manitoban Conservative party. As the provincial party had fought for the federal in the elections of 1900, 1904, and 1908, so would it fight in 1911. In return R. L. Borden, the Conservative leader, pledged his party to extend the boundaries of Manitoba, to revise the financial terms, to push the Hudson's Bay Railway with vigour, and to build government terminal elevators at Fort William.

The Reciprocity Agreement promised Manitoban farmers relief from the tariff burdens against which they had often protested and were protesting anew, and a Liberal victory might have been expected. Such was the force of the Conservative campaign and the appeal of its promises, however; such were the deep, underlying interests of Manitoba, and particularly of Winnipeg and the railway towns in the east-west flow of trade; such was the strength of old Ontario loyalties and British Canadian nationalism in a province the first child of Confederation, that eight of the ten Manitoban seats returned Conservative candidates though the Liberals carried most of the seats in Saskatchewan and Alberta. This was the most noteworthy expression of the strength of national purpose and sentiment which underlay and could override Manitoba's often vocal sense of provincial and sectional interest.

The victory was a triumph for the Roblin government, and richly was it rewarded. The long-standing feud between Manitoba and Ottawa was ended, and the "Cinderella of Confederation" became for the time being the favourite child. In 1912 the boundaries of Manitoba were extended northward to the line of 60° north latitude—the line of Button's landfall in 1612—and northeastward to the Bay, to the point due north of the junction of the Ohio and the Mississippi. The prairie province became a maritime province also with a seacoast of 500 miles and the two ports of Nelson and Churchill. One hundred and eighty thousand square miles of territory across the Shield and the Hudson Bay lowlands raised the total area of the province to 250,000 square miles. Once more Hudson's great and desolate bay, the voyages of the seamen, and the toil of the fur posts and the fur brigades came back into the history of Manitoba. Once more the Bay, the Shield, and the southern plains were integrated, as in the days of the fur trade, and the Hudson's Bay Railway was to realize the integration. The north-south axis of the basin of Winnipeg was re-established, and the long dominance of Manitoban life by the east-west thrust of eastern Canada might at last be eased.

At the same time, the federal subsidies were generously enlarged. In return for the surrender of the remaining swamp lands, Manitoba was granted a total subsidy of $1,349,345.39 per annum. The federal government retained control of the Crown lands. But the Roblin government could claim that it had achieved equality for Manitoba with Saskatchewan and Alberta.

Such were the fruits of victory. There was to be criticism, however, and there was a price to be paid. The Liberal opposition criticized the failure to obtain control of the Crown lands, without which the royalties it was hoped the minerals of New Manitoba would yield would go into the federal treasury. Ontario, on the strength of its claim to the west coast of the Bay, exacted the concession of a railway corridor five miles wide to Nelson and Churchill. Both Ontario and Quebec had been brought to support the extension of Manitoba's boundaries by the extension of their own northward to the Bay and Hudson Straits. And the Manitoban Minister of Education, Hon. G. R. Coldwell, rather mysteriously and ambiguously amended the School Act in 1912 in a way which might have permitted the segregation of Catholic pupils in the cities, as Mgr Sbaretti had suggested in 1905. Thus, it would seem, was Catholic opposition to the extension of the jurisdiction of the Manitoba School Act conciliated, to the growing consternation of Manitoba Orangemen.[18] The amendments were in fact

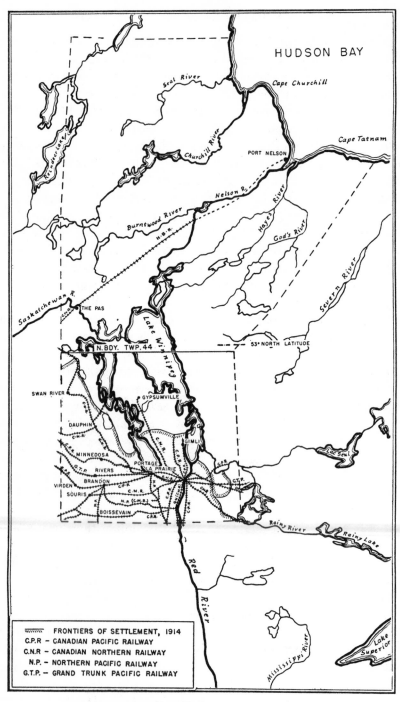

HUDSON BAY

Cape Churchill

Cape Tatnam

Seal River

Churchill River

PORT NELSON

Nelson R.

Hayes River

God's River

Burntwood River

H.B.R.

Severn River

Reindeer Lake

Saskatchewan R.

THE PAS

53° NORTH LATITUDE

N.BDY. TWP. 44

Lake Winnipeg

SWAN RIVER

GYPSUMVILLE

DAUPHIN

C.N.R.

C.N.R.

C.P.R.

GIMLI

Lac Seul

MINNEDOSA

G.T.P.

RIVERS

PORTAGE
LA PRAIRIE

G.T.P.

G.T.P.

VIRDEN

BRANDON

C.P.R.

C.N.R.

SOURIS

N.P. (C.N.R.)

BOISSEVAIN

C.P.R.

Rainy River

Rainy Lake

Red River

Mississippi River

Lake Superior

FRONTIERS OF SETTLEMENT, 1914
C.P.R – CANADIAN PACIFIC RAILWAY
C.N.R – CANADIAN NORTHERN RAILWAY
N.P. – NORTHERN PACIFIC RAILWAY
G.T.P. – GRAND TRUNK PACIFIC RAILWAY

RAILWAYS AND SETTLEMENT BY 1914

only an attempt to provide some relief for Catholic parents supporting private schools in Winnipeg and Brandon; in the French rural districts lenient inspection by the Department of Education had in effect made the public schools parochial ones. But the "Coldwell amendments" failed to give a similar relief in the cities and were to help destroy the political fruits of boundary extension.

New Manitoba, which in a sense was the oldest Manitoba, was incorporated into the province on May 15, 1912, forty-two years after that May 12 which had seen the Manitoba Act become law. It was a lonely wilderness of forest, rock, and water, in the main unchanged from the days when Henry Kelsey had threaded his way across it to the Saskatchewan and the plains. But at The Pas, Kelsey's base and old fur post and mission, a lusty new town had sprung up with the coming of the Canadian Northern Railway in 1910. Since that date the old agitation for a railway to the Bay had been renewed. The first steps towards a Hudson Bay railway were taken by the Oliver Land Act of 1908 and by the beginning of the bridging of the Saskatchewan in 1910. And in the campaign of 1911 the Conservative leader, Sir Robert Borden, had promised it would be built by his government if elected. Now, with the bridge thrown across the Saskatchewan to carry the railway, with the fur trade and a flourishing new lumber industry, The Pas was setting out to be the capital of Manitoba "north of 53°," the base for the exploitation of a new frontier of forest and mine. The Borden government quickly redeemed its pledge, and in 1913 the sledges were clanging in rhythm on the spikes of the railway to the Bay; lumbermen were cruising the northern woods, and prospectors following the waterways in search of mineral showings. The laws and magistrates of Manitoba went into the north, and a new electoral district of The Pas was created. A member was elected and went south to Winnipeg to tell the legislators from the farms and rural towns of the south of the vast extent and illimitable resources of the new Manitoba.

The boundary extension of 1912 was the climax of the great boom in Manitoba. Already land values were falling, and the basic conditions of world commerce were altering to the disadvantage of the West. The census of 1911 revealed that in population Manitoba was falling behind Saskatchewan and Alberta. A Million for Manitoba League was promptly organized to ensure that settlers did not pass the province by, but the cause of the League's concern was a clear indication that the boundary extension of 1912 could not undo the results of the boundary decisions of 1884 and 1905. The addition of New Manitoba was also the climax of the career of Premier Roblin, a climax marked by the bestowal on him of the K.C.M.G. But for Sir Rodmond's régime also the basic conditions of its continuation in office were altering to its disadvantage. Manitoba was to enter a new era, to face the major consequence of the boom, the unresolved questions of race and class relationships and, in over-measure, the agony of a great war.

14

The War and Political Crisis
1913-1917

AS THE EXTENSION OF THE BOUNDARIES IN 1912 had brought a new Manitoba into being "north of 53," so the events of the succeeding decade were to create a new Manitoba in the old settled areas of the south. These events sprang in part from changes within the province itself. But in Europe, still the centre of world power, there was a mounting tension among nations, and a sharpening of class conflicts within states. In Manitoba, also, racial and class tensions were to intensify, as first depression and then war brought to an end the golden years of hopeful and prosperous growth.

The end of the great western boom had been prepared by rising freight rates and falling farm and land prices. It was precipitated when in 1912 and 1913 the Balkan Wars, by the demand for money and the fear of war they created, dried up the flow of British loans to Canada. The stream of pounds sterling which had made possible the building of the railways and elevators, the purchase and equipment of farms, the building of the towns and cities, diminished quickly and soon was to be cut off entirely.

The collapse of real estate values followed; while prices of farm lands fell, those of urban lots tumbled. The real estate agents and the land speculators found it difficult to dispose of farm lands and impossible to interest buyers in suburban developments. The continuance of immigration and the falling prices kept the market for farm lands alive, but holders of urban lands were left holding them. Scores of subdivisions, dozens of attractively named suburbs, died on the agents' prospectuses and on the drafting boards. Winnipeg once more found itself surrounded with a belt of lands held for speculation, this time a belt of suburban lands.

More fundamental and more serious was the end of the wheat boom. The falling returns from what was the main and the "cash" crop of even the old settled districts of Manitoba imposed a severe strain on Manitoban agriculture. Despite the growing importance of other crops, especially of oats and barley, despite the great development of livestock farming, the great majority of Manitoban farmers relied on the wheat crop to pay the costs of operation. Manitoban farming was dependent on the wheat crop and, while the farmer could meet depression by the sale of livestock and by increasing the production of milk, hogs, and poultry, he could not prosper by doing so. He could not clear land, build buildings, and buy machinery without good wheat crops and profitable prices for the great staple grain. The Grain Growers' Association, based on wheat farming, remained not only the greatest of the agricultural associations of the province, but one which represented the agricultural community in its entirety.

The shock of the depression was even severer in the cities. Building permits in Winnipeg fell to a mere $6,000,000 in 1913, and the pounding of the carpenters' hammers died away. In a city which had not commanded labour enough for over a decade, unemployment appeared. Thousands of men who had been sure of a job of some kind, at what were accounted good wages, now became acquainted with the wearing uncertainty which depression spells for the working man. The period in which unemployment was severe was comparatively brief, the ever demanding harvest fields gave seasonal employment, and the completion of private and public buildings kept many hands at work. The memory of the uncertainty of these hard times was, however, to sink into the minds of Winnipeg labour.

Even as farming was dependent on the export of wheat and the labour market on the furnishing of the facilities necessary for the movement of grain, so was public and private investment. But a slackening of the flow of investment could not bring the whole economy of the province to a halt. In particular the govern-

ment of Manitoba was committed to a great and unfinished programme of public works, some of which had to be finished. The
Manitoba Agricultural College was nearing completion at St.
Vital; work was begun in 1913 on the new Legislative Buildings
on Broadway. These costly projects had to be completed if they
were to be of use, and the government pushed on with them. In
doing so, it was responding to the spirit of the times, for the spirit
of the boom was still at work. Men looked eagerly to the ending
of the financial stringency which obtained all over Canada, and
of the depression of real estate values which was exceptionally
severe in the West.

These hopes were not foolish. The maintenance of peace in
Europe would presumably have led to a resumption of the development of Manitoba's resources by British capital, aided, no
doubt, by an increased flow of American capital into the developments to which it was attracted, the grain trade and the minerals
and wood pulp of the Shield. The exploitation of the province's
resources, so greatly advanced between 1897 and 1912, had only
been begun. Especially was this true of New Manitoba and the
new northern frontier on the Shield. During these years of depression there occurred the first mining flurry Manitoba had
known since the discovery of gold at Rat Portage in 1883. Following the great Cobalt strike of 1903, prospectors had been working
along the edge of the Shield northwestward, seeking the famous
"Cobalt bloom," the ore which had characterized that rich mineral
complex, and for the quartz lodes which bore gold. In 1911 gold
had been found at Rice Lake east of Lake Winnipeg, and a rush
of prospectors followed over the next year. By 1914 some gold
was being taken out, and the intensive exploration of the southeastern mineral belt of Manitoba, with its numerous low grade
ores, was begun.

With the beginning of the Hudson's Bay Railway prospectors
fanned out northward and eastward from The Pas, and in 1914
the gold of Herb Lake or Wekusko, in 1915 the sulphide ores
of the Flin Flon area, the copper deposit of the Mandy claims,
were discovered. A considerable rush began, thousands of claims
were staked, and American capital became interested. It seemed

that Northern Manitoba was about to prove itself another Northern Ontario and that a mining boom would be added to the agricultural boom which everyone hoped to see resumed in the south.

That such promising finds should have been made on the outermost edge of the Shield gave grounds for hope that the vast interior might be no less rich. If Winnipeg and the towns of the
south were stagnant, The Pas was booming in virtue of these
hopes, and because of the construction of the Hudson's Bay Railway. Since 1908 The Pas had regarded itself as the advance base
for the building of the railway to the Bay and the development of
the Shield. Now its time had come, as the railway thrust out
towards the Nelson, and as the prospectors came in from north
of the Saskatchewan to file their claims and forgather in the bars.
The town grew rapidly, and the fine site on the great ridge between the Pasquia River and the wide marshlands to the east was
laid out in town lots far to the south. There was good reason for
its hopes, for not only had The Pas become a divisional point on
the Hudson's Bay Railway and the base for prospectors probing
the Shield, but it continued to enjoy its old trade in furs, and the
trappers brought in their catches as in times past. The lumber
industry, which had followed the railway up from the Dauphin
country under the leadership of T. A. Burrows, was also growing,
and by means of the rivers and the development of horse and
tractor "trains" was drawing the timber from north of the river
down to the mills on the waterfront. In 1916 The Pas was to
become the administrative as well as the economic capital of
Northern Manitoba when the administration of the great territory
north of 53° was placed under a Commissioner for Northern
Manitoba, Mr. G. P. Campbell of Dauphin.*

The Pas was not only a boom town in a time of depression;
it also was a frontier town of a kind new to Manitoba. It was not
a market town flung up to serve the agricultural frontier, and
after early hopes of greatness to lapse into quiet subservience to
the countryside. The Pas was northern, a mining, lumbering, and
fur trade town, committed to the service of the rough and turbulent men who unravelled the tangled waterways of the Shield
and endured the rigours of northern winters. Its business was

seasonal, its bars and stores alternating between stagnation and boisterous demand. Its life was rough, colourful, and optimistic, and The Pas was conscious of its difference and prided itself on its northern isolation and lusty character. New Manitoba was new indeed, and doubtful whether the distant and conservative south would realize the promise of the "land of the lobstick" and support its claims. Even so, the main hope of The Pas was that the Hudson's Bay Railway would pull much of the western wheat crop through its yards to the Bay, and in these years the railway drove steadily towards the Nelson and added new, strange names to the map, Rawebb, Wekusko, Wabowden.[1]

While the north was exuberant with its incipient boom, old Manitoba lived in hope of the great boom resuming. The newspapers and commercial periodicals were filled with anticipation of a new surge of prosperity; the plans of business and government were laid in anticipation of an upward swing of the business cycle. Meantime, the depression years, in part because they were years of depression, witnessed an intensification of the drive for reform. The beginning of unemployment in Winnipeg aggravated all the social evils, poverty, bad housing, juvenile delinquency, and the strains on family ties, with which the new profession of social workers had begun to struggle; in 1916 Winnipeg was for the first time the place of meeting for a Social Welfare Congress.[2] The increase of industry had brought with it sweat shops, long hours, and insanitary factory conditions. With these evils not only the growing Labour movement contended, but also many public-spirited citizens who resented the extinction of the promise of the new land by the century-old ills of the Industrial Revolution. The backwardness of Manitoban schools was becoming notorious in Canada and the English-speaking world, as the comment of Mr. Herbert Samuel revealed in 1913 when he remarked that in the matter of education Manitoba was a generation behind the civilized world. The comment stung, and public opinion was at last being aroused to face the shortcomings of the rural schools. A series of sixty-four articles exposing the defects of the bilingual schools in the *Manitoba Free Press* during 1913 made it quite impossible thereafter to avoid the issue. By resolving its internal differences and agreeing on a common programme, the temperance movement had acquired a force and public backing it had not enjoyed before. And the vigorous Political Equality League not only pushed the cause of women's suffrage and legal emancipation hard in these years, but gave further impetus to the whole reform movement, in the various aspects of which women were deeply interested, and especially in temperance. A generation of able women, led by Lillian Beynon Thomas and inspired by the gay, fighting spirit of Nellie McClung, was thrusting to the front. Their action ensured the triumph of the reform movement and a change in the character of Manitoban public life.

For the moment, however, it seemed that the old political ways were becoming more deeply ingrained. Party politics were more furious, bitter, and corrupt than ever. In 1912 and 1913 three notorious by-elections were held in the province, a federal by-election in Macdonald in 1912, and provincial by-elections in Kildonan–St. Andrew's and Gimli in 1913. The Macdonald by-election was a refighting of the issue of reciprocity; and the federal Liberal party, aided by the Saskatchewan Liberal machine, made a strenuous attempt to win the seat from the Conservatives who had captured it in 1911. They were opposed by the provincial Conservative party, and the result was a trial of strength between two political machines versed in all the arts of electoral corruption. The Conservative candidate won, and the election left behind it a cloud of charges and countercharges which darkened the political atmosphere. Even more vicious were the provincial by-elections of 1913. In Kildonan–St. Andrew's the new Minister of Public Works, Dr. W. H. Montague, appointed to succeed Hon. Colin Campbell, was seeking election. The Liberal opposition used his membership in the federal cabinet in 1896 and his support of remedial legislation against him, and even made accusations of personal dishonesty. Both sides charged the other with the staple offences of false voting, free treating, and bribery. Montague was victorious, but the ferocity of the campaign seemed to have brought Manitoban politics to the mudsills of public life. The saturnalia of political corruption, of which the parties mutually indicted one another in Gimli, however, revealed that there were yet lower levels to be churned up. Again the Conservative candidate won, and the exasperation of the thrice defeated Liberals undoubtedly goes far to explain the fierce resentment with which the memory of these elections was kept alive. At the same time the average voter was beginning to ask whether politics need be conducted in this fashion, what was the morality of public men who could use such charges, even if they did not employ the methods of which they accused their opponents, what was the character of a government sustained by such victories, and whether this furious partisanship had indeed anything to do with the straightforward issues of provincial administration.

The contrast between the need for reform, if the laws and customs of a predominantly rural society were to be reshaped to meet the needs of industrial society and of an industrialized agriculture, and the crescendo of partisanship which marked the years 1912 and 1913, was a challenge to the political parties of Manitoba. It was an especial challenge to the Conservative party, which was completing its fourth term of highly successful administration. That party had governed the province well; it had moved with the times; it could point to a long record of concrete achievement. It had in fact been progressive in its practical measures, and, while it had been conservative in that it stood by what was established, as in the School Question, and demanded that the need of reform be thoroughly proved before adoption, it responded to the new demands in given instances, such as the Workmen's Compensation Act of 1910 and the creation of a Public Utilities Commission in 1913 and a Bureau of Labour in 1915. Yet it can well be asked whether the extreme partisanship of Manitoban politics at this time was not owing in the main to the attitude of the leaders of the Conservative party and the Roblin administration. They were all hard-headed, practical men who took life as they found it, were sceptical of reform and, with the possible exception of the Premier, indifferent to idealism. They could not fully respond to the new spirit of the times. Success had made them arrogant. They were bound by their record. Above all,

Macdonald, Kildonan–St. Andrew's, and Gimli raised the question whether the party and the government had not become the prisoners and dupes of the party machine.

Much happier was the lot of the Liberal party. As an opposition of fifteen years standing, it had no record to embarrass or to bind. It had found an amiable and candid leader in T. C. Norris, a man who stood above the rancorous partisanship of the party struggle and who could appeal to the independent voter. The party leadership was greatly enriched in talent by the rise of T. H. Johnson, an Icelandic Canadian and Winnipeg lawyer, of C. D. McPherson of Portage la Prairie, and of A. B. Hudson, a Winnipeg lawyer of great gifts. With such freedom and such new leadership, the party was able to respond to the reform movement. It had done so, though not entirely, in 1910. In the convention of 1914 the work was completed. The platform adopted then was a detailed endorsement of the reform programme. Direct legislation, a pledge to introduce effective temperance legislation if a referendum should authorize it, women's suffrage, compulsory education with allowance for the constitutional rights of Catholic parents, were the chief planks of an elaborate document. Another was a demand for the transfer of its natural resources from federal control to the province, a demand which was at once a criticism of the Roblin government's success in the boundary extension of 1912, and a return to that tradition of grievance against Ottawa which had always been so effective in Manitoba.[3] It was a reinvigorated and rearmed Liberal party which went into the provincial election of 1914.

A Redistribution Act of 1914 had increased the number of seats in the legislature to forty-nine, three of these being for electoral districts in Northern Manitoba. In the contest the Liberals were openly supported by, or assured of the sympathy of, the Grain Growers' Association, the temperance organizations, the Orange Order, now formally demanding the abolition of the Compromise of 1897, and the Political Equality League. Dr. C. W. Gordon—Ralph Connor—a leader of the temperance movement, openly called for the election of Liberal candidates. Nellie McClung stumped the province for temperance and the

Liberal party. In a great meeting in the Walker Theatre, a feminine David, she won a personal triumph by wit and courage over the arrogance of the Premier, a frank and uncompromising opponent of women's entry into "the mess of politics." Norris himself was an effective leader, not least in his reassurance of the French leaders as to the effect of the educational policy of the Liberal party.

As a result, the Conservative party did not receive the undivided support of those organizations which were not allied with the Liberals. Despite the public approval by Archbishop Langevin of the school policy of the Roblin government, despite the presence in the cabinet of Hon. Joseph Bernier, the first French minister since 1889, the French were divided politically on the School Question and the Coldwell amendments.[4] In consequence the party had to rely on its record, its organization, and the powerful campaigning of Premier Roblin. All were strained to the uttermost and the election of 1914 was the hardest fought and most evenly contested in the history of Manitoba. No political trick was left unused, no ruse untried by either side. It was a contest between the past and the future, and the past was strong and deeply entrenched. When the votes were counted, the Conservatives had won twenty-five seats, the Liberals twenty-one. The seven independent members, two Labour, four Socialist, and one Ukrainian Nationalist, were defeated. The elections in the three northern seats had been deferred and the outcome there might yet reduce the government to a minority in the legislature.

The result was unsatisfactory to everyone. The Roblin government had lost much of its usual following, notably, as the Premier said, the Orange vote. It is possible that only the "immigrant vote" prevented its defeat. The south and west had for the most gone Liberal; the Conservative members were returned from the old districts of the Red River valley and from the frontier constituencies. The Liberals had been confident of victory, and were bitterly disappointed. The popular vote, 62,798 for the Liberals and 15,654 for the independents, against 71,616 for the Conservatives, lent substance to their claims that the Roblin government had been virtually defeated, and the fact that of five French seats the Liberals had carried one showed that their appeal was neither narrow nor racial. They therefore made a determined effort to win the three northern seats. They were set back, however, by the resignation of their candidate in The Pas in the face of threatened prosecution for violations of the Election Act, and the three seats, as was the way of frontier districts, returned government candidates. The Conservative majority was therefore a reasonably secure one of seven, and Manitoba seemed destined to be governed for four or five years more by the Roblin government. The bitterness of the elections, however, following on the three by-elections of 1912 and 1913, resulted in a long list of petitions contesting the returns, and Manitoban political life was certain to be neither dull nor serene during the life of the new legislature. There was a general belief that the Roblin régime was drawing to a close, and a stubborn refusal by its opponents to accept the results of the election as either honest or final.

The fierce preoccupation with provincial politics in the summer of 1914 was abruptly interrupted by the outbreak of the World War in August, 1914. Manitoba was a provincial society, engaged in the work of building a new community on a frontier far distant from Sarajevo and the line of the Vosges or the plains of Flanders. Yet it was a frontier of that great European society which had dominated the world for a century and which had now plunged into the first of the great wars that were to shake the supremacy of Europe in the world. Trade, immigration, and Canada's membership in the British Empire had kept Manitoba closely bound by interest and sentiment to the fortunes of that larger world. Now the declaration of war by the government of the United Kingdom committed the Empire to war with Germany and its allies. The European balance of power was at stake, on the preservation of which depended the freedom of Manitoba to continue to develop in its wonted ways. Isolation from the conflict was impossible and was not considered.

The response of the province was, in fact, much simpler. To those of British descent the fact of Britain's participation was enough to determine their sympathies and their action. Anger at the invasion of Belgium and the ruthlessness of German "militarism" clinched the matter for those of radical sympathies who had watched with fear and distaste the growing tension in Europe. Among no element of the population was there actual or immediate opposition to Canadian participation in the war. The fact of commitment was accepted and an early victory hoped for; the question was, what had to be done?

Manitoba lay in Military District No. 10, which also included the province of Saskatchewan and northwestern Ontario. There were no units of the Permanent Force of Canada in Manitoba, but there were a number of militia units. Four infantry regiments had headquarters in Winnipeg: the 90th Regiment, or Royal Winnipeg Rifles, formed in 1883, the "Little Black Devils" of Fish Creek; the 106th Regiment, or the Winnipeg Light Infantry, raised during the Saskatchewan Rebellion; the 100th Winnipeg Grenadiers, raised in 1908; and the 79th Cameron Highlanders of Canada, organized in 1910. There were besides cavalry units, the 12th Manitoba Dragoons and the 99th Manitoba Rangers, both of Brandon; the 18th Mounted Rifles of Portage la Prairie; the 20th Border Horse of Pipestone; the 32nd Manitoba Horse of Roblin; and the 34th Fort Garry Horse of Winnipeg. These units were in peacetime little more than the military clubs of a martial race, but in war they proved extraordinarily effective rallying centres. On August 6 the Minister of Militia sent out the first call for volunteers for an overseas contingent, the volunteers to come from the existing militia units or those who, though unconnected with the militia, had had previous military experience. By August 18, M.D. 10 reported that over 5,500 officers and men had been recruited for the Canadian Expeditionary Force. Although the quota for the first contingent was quickly filled, more volunteers were immediately requested of the western military districts "in order that the force might benefit by the enthusiasm of the West." Infantry units, as a rule, were called upon to provide a quota, but some, like the Winnipeg Light Infantry, recruited over strength, and won exemption from the restrictions of the quota by direct appeal to the Minister. On August 23, the first units to move from Manitoba, the 106th

Winnipeg Light Infantry and the 79th Cameron Highlanders, entrained for Valcartier en route to England. The 90th and 100th followed the next day, and it was by these militia units of Manitoba, so far as their identities could be retained under the new system of numbering of battalions, that the province was represented in the First Canadian Contingent.[5]

Soon the recruiting of further battalions of volunteers began, individual commanding officers raising their units in Winnipeg and the province in the traditional way. A training camp, named Camp Hughes after the Canadian Minister of Militia, was established on the main line of the Canadian Pacific Railway in the western sand hills, where soil and terrain furnished a dry and ample training ground. A city of tents soon gleamed on the plain in the centre of the Camp, and great trenches, zigzagging and revetted, cut yellow gashes through the soft soil. There, in the fierce heat and dust of western summers, thousands of Manitoban lads from the desk and the plough were to learn the rudiments of soldiering before they left those wide horizons which had never known war for England and Flanders.

In addition to this response of the volunteers, the Manitoba legislature in special session voted a gift of 50,000 bags of flour to the Imperial government and one of $5,000 to the Belgian Relief Fund. Private citizens at the same time began the organization of the Manitoba Patriotic Fund to raise by private subscription money for the many needs of war not covered by governmental expenditures.

By the spring of 1915 the first Canadian formations were in the trenches, and in April of 1915 the headlines carried the agonizing news of Second Ypres. In the stand of the outflanked Canadian brigades at St. Julien against the yellow fog of chlorine gas and the grey waves of the German infantry, the 8th (90th) and the 10th (106th) battalions held firm with their fellow Canadians, a militia which displayed the steadiness of veteran troops. The reeking mud of Gravenstafel ridge was a far cry from the firm sod and clear air of the Saskatchewan, where the Rifles and the Light Infantry had received their baptism of fire. But the ordeal was endured and the Manitoban units shared the fame

Second Ypres conferred on Canadian infantry, "the Thermopylae of Canadian arms," the quiet-spoken John Buchan was to term it. The battle brought the war home to Manitoba, and from then on the political struggle, to which the election of 1914 was but a prelude, and the slowly growing racial and class tension in the province, developed in the heat and pressure of a community not yet fully formed or mature, yet committed to one of the fiercest of all wars.

Even sharper than the contrast of Second Ypres and Batoche was the contrast between the stark courage of the soldiers and the sordid corruption of Manitoba politics revealed in the spring and summer of 1915. The headlines of the battle news were to struggle for space with the headlines of the "Parliament Building Scandal." In 1913 the firm of Thomas Kelly and Sons had undertaken to construct the new Legislative Buildings on Simon's plans for the sum of $2,859,750, and work was begun. Shortly thereafter, however, on the recommendation of the Provincial Architect, V. W. Horwood, supported by other professional advice, it was determined to change from pile foundations to caisson foundations sunk to bedrock, and from reinforced concrete construction to steel and concrete construction. The former change was well advised, the latter probably so. The effect, however, was to revise the cost of construction from the contract figure of $2,859,750 to an estimated $4,500,000. Of this the legislature was informed in the session of 1914. Construction continued without question, being interrupted for a few weeks only by the outbreak of war. But rumours began to circulate of faulty construction of the caissons and of slack supervision by the government inspectors.

In the first session of the new legislature in 1915, the Liberals, invigorated by their near victory and animated by resentment at a defeat they attributed to corruption, pushed for a thorough investigation of expenditures on the Legislative Buildings in the Public Accounts Committee from March 11 to March 30. Their enquiry was ably conducted by A. B. Hudson and T. H. Johnson, but was foiled of its purpose by the Conservative chairman and majority and, as was later proved, by the perjury of V. W.

Horwood, the Provincial Architect, and other civil servants. The enquiry was also foiled by the absence of the inspector of the caisson construction, one William Salt, who was in the United States at this inconvenient time, on the advice, as it was later proved, of the Provincial Architect and a member of the cabinet who was also a member of the Public Accounts Committee, Hon. George Coldwell. The Committee's report approved the expenditures on the building, and the supervision of the construction.

From what had been revealed, however, and from what was privately known, the Liberals were now sure of their ground. On March 31, A. B. Hudson moved a resolution charging culpable negligence in the construction and the defrauding of the Provincial Treasury of the sum of $800,000, and calling for investigation by a Royal Commission of Enquiry. The accusation was harsh, the charges specific, and Hudson made it clear he acted in no spirit of mere partisan vindictiveness, but out of a deep sense of public responsibility. The government stood firm against the resolution, basing its stand on the report of the Public Accounts Committee. When the House rose at 1:20 A.M. on April 1, Premier Roblin had refused to agree to an investigation.

At the same time, however, on March 31, the Liberals had laid a petition before Lieutenant-Governor Sir Douglas Cameron, praying that a Royal Commission be appointed to enquire into the charges. When the House met on the afternoon of April 1, the Premier informed the members that a Royal Commission would be granted. It was generally understood at the time that on the morning of April 1 the Lieutenant-Governor had given Premier Roblin the choice of recommending the appointment of a Commission or of being requested to submit his resignation.[6] Such strong action by a Lieutenant-Governor was not without precedent in Canada, and electoral conditions in Manitoba in the spring of 1915 were such as to make an appeal to the people a mortal danger to the Roblin government. A Royal Commission was therefore appointed, consisting of Chief Justice T. A. Mathers of the Manitoba Court of King's Bench, Hon. D. A. Macdonald of the Court of King's Bench, and Sir Hugh John Macdonald.

Under the Chief Justice as chairman, the Commission began its enquiry on April 27, and by May 7 enough had been revealed to substantiate the Liberal charges. On May 12, Premier Roblin submitted the resignation of his government, on the ground that a new government was necessary to make the adjustments which had to be made between the province and the contractor. On May 13 an administration was formed by T. C. Norris, with A. B. Hudson as Attorney-General.

When the fact of fraud and political corruption had been established, two main purposes emerged and were accepted by both parties. One was to put an end to political corruption, the other was to recover the moneys fraudulently acquired by Thomas Kelly and Sons. The new government would do the former, the latter might best be achieved by a civil suit against the contractors. Might it not be better to discontinue the Royal Commission with its expense, and employ a departmental committee to prosecute the enquiry? This matter was discussed before the resignation of the Roblin government by its legal advisor, C. P. Fullerton, K.C., and the leaders of the Liberal party. Norris and Hudson agreed to a departmental committee, provided the Commissioners consented and provided Premier Roblin would sign a letter of resignation written by them, to include an admission of the justice of the Liberal charges. When the Premier's letter of resignation failed to contain the admission, the agreement was not carried out. But certain Conservatives, attempting to create a diversion when their party was in such embarrassing circumstances, charged through the agency of C. P. Fullerton that the agreement was part of a corrupt bargain to procure the withdrawal of election protests involving Liberal as well as Conservative members then before the House and the accession to office of the Liberal party. A second Royal Commission, consisting of Hon. W. E. Perdue of the Manitoba Court of Appeal, Hon. A. C. Galt of the Court of King's Bench, and H. A. Robson, Public Utilities Commissioner, was appointed on June 24 to deal with this accusation. Its report, signed on July 26, completely exonerated the leaders of the Liberal party from the charges of attempting a corrupt bargain. The evidence, however, did reveal how the party organizers conducted the private affairs of the parties and implicated Hon. J. H. Howden, former Attorney-General.[7]

On July 22 a civil suit was begun against Thomas Kelly and Sons, but the action was held up until Kelly could be extradited from the United States, where he had retired. The Mathers Commission had meantime continued its investigation and on August 24 completed its report. The report was largely based on the evidence of V. W. Horwood, the Provincial Architect, and William Salt, inspector of construction, whose evidence the Commission was forced to take in Minneapolis as that gentleman refused to place himself under the protection of the laws of his native land. The Commission found that all the charges had been fully proven, that there had been a conspiracy to obtain election funds from "extras" in the contract for the Legislative Buildings, that the contractors had been overpaid to the amount of $892,098.10, and that "large sums" of money had been paid by the contractor to Dr. R. M. Simpson, the president of the Provincial Conservative Association. The report also purported to show that the former Premier, Sir Rodmond Roblin, Attorney-General J. H. Howden, Hon. George R. Coldwell, Minister of Education, and Dr. W. H. Montague, Minister of Public Works, had been parties to this fraudulent conspiracy.[8]

The detailed findings of wrongdoing by Sir Rodmond Roblin, W. H. Montague, J. H. Howden, and George Coldwell, the four ex-ministers, was followed on August 28 by their arrest on charges of conspiracy to defraud the Crown. Sir Hugh John Macdonald, as Police Magistrate, refused to hear the indictment and the Master in Equity was appointed to act. On the evidence of Horwood and Salt, the ex-ministers were committed to trial on October 6. Not until July 24, 1916, were Sir Rodmond, Howden, and Coldwell brought to trial, Dr. Montague having died in the interval. On August 28 the trial ended in the disagreement of the jury, and a new trial was ordered.

Departmental investigations had meanwhile given grounds to suspect further wrongdoing. A Special Commission under Chief Justice T. A. Mathers enquired into the construction of the new Law Courts on Broadway and the Central Power House. It reported on May 5, 1916, that in the construction of these buildings there had been laxity, but no positive impropriety or attempts to obtain election funds.[9] On July 14, 1916, a Commission consisting of Hon. A. C. Galt of the Court of King's Bench began a prolonged enquiry into the construction of the buildings of the Manitoba Agricultural College. A first interim report, signed on January 26, 1917, involved Hon. Robert Rogers, federal Minister of Public Works, and Coldwell and Howden, as did a second of May 25, 1917.[10] Rogers hotly repudiated the findings, and obtained a federal Royal Commission, consisting of Hon. Sir Ezekiel McLeod, Chief Justice of New Brunswick, and Hon. Louis Tellier, a retired judge of the Superior Court of Quebec, to review the findings of the Galt Commission. The report of the commissioners on July 26, 1917, completely exonerated the Minister and his colleagues of the charge of improper dealing in real estate adjoining the site of the Agricultural College.[11] In the session of 1916, too, the Public Accounts Committee had unearthed evidence of the padding of roadwork accounts for political purposes by the Conservative representatives and party agents in Russell, Rockwood, and Gimli. A Royal Commission consisting of Hon. G. Paterson sustained the charges, based on this evidence, in a report signed February 20, 1917.[12]

The civil suit against Kelly had begun on June 18, 1916. Kelly defended himself, on withdrawal of his counsel, and was convicted on all charges but one. The conviction and sentence of two and one-half years imprisonment was sustained by the Supreme Court of Canada, together with the award of a claim for the refunding of $1,207,351.65 to the province. The judgment with interest to November, 1917, remained on the books of the province until 1941 when it was written down to a nominal valuation of $25,000. At that date some $30,000 had been recovered.

On June 25, 1917, Sir Rodmond Roblin, J. H. Howden, and George Coldwell were discharged from the criminal charges which had hung over them for two years, the grounds being the ill-health of Sir Rodmond and of Howden. No further public service, it was clear, was to be rendered by pressing charges against men known to be personally honourable, but who had been engulfed by the underworld of politics everyone now hoped was destroyed. The Galt Commission was withdrawn, and the quashing of charges of fraud by one Baribault against McDiarmid and Co., the new contractors for the Legislative Buildings, by the Public Accounts Committee in 1917,[13] ended the sickening tale of political corruption and hardened partisanship.

The effects of the scandals were deep and long lasting. They involved more than a change of administration and the discrediting of the Roblin government. The revelations of the moral obtuseness of party workers and even ministers of the Crown, of the things which were done to raise funds to fight the blindly partisan elections of the day, discredited the party system in Manitoba. It was apparent that the Roblin government had been subdued to what it worked in, coarse and completely immoral party politics, and that the Conservative party had been captured by its machine. For this the ministers and public leaders of the party, however personally incorrupt, were responsible, and their public reputations had to suffer the consequences of their being the victims of a political order which they had tolerated when it had become intolerable. The old kind of politics would no longer do, and had to go. The pity of it was that men of marked ability and fine achievements had to be swept away with it. Sir Rodmond Roblin deserved a better fate and the historic party he had led with such distinction a more loyal and honest service from its agents. When that is said, however, it remains to be added that the scandals marked the end of one era and the beginning of a new which Sir Rodmond and his party would have found uncongenial. The simple and crude political methods of the boom days had become inadequate, even had they been reasonably honest. The scandals were opening the way to non-partisan government, and the triumph of the reform movement.

The slow stain of the scandals spread across the political life of Manitoba for three years. These years of shame, however, were also years of new beginnings and lasting changes for the better. The Norris government had come to power as a Liberal government pledged to implement the platform of 1914. The party had been forged and strengthened during its fifteen years in opposition; the platform of 1914 had embodied the reform movement. The government and party, standing on such a platform, were prepared and willing to represent all those elements in Manitoba which, without respect to party, were desirous of reform. The Norris government, though formally a party government, was required by the circumstances in which it came to office to transcend its origins and become a non-partisan administration.

Its first weeks in office were devoted to the immense task of "cleaning up the mess" left by its predecessors. The various enquiries were pushed, the public accounts audited. The Premier then recommended the dissolution of the legislature elected in 1914, and went to the country on the platform of 1914, with the temperance plank changed from the banishing of the bar to the prohibition of the liquor trade in the province. The campaign, however, was necessarily a plebiscite on the record of the Roblin government and the result was foregone.

It was distinguished, however, by the courageous, if forlorn, fight of the Conservative party under a new leader, Sir James Aikins. The party had met in convention on July 14 in Winnipeg, with some 1,500 delegates present. In the convention, the party was reclaimed from the organization which had misled and corrupted it. A platform was adopted calling for political reforms, one of which was the appointment of an auditor-general responsible to the legislature alone, to prevent a repetition of the recent evils and laxities. The platform declared, among other things, for the Macdonald Temperance Act, the repeal of the Coldwell amendments, women's suffrage, improved education with adequate instruction in English, and more scope for the Bureau of Labour.[14] Thus was the Conservative party belatedly brought abreast of the times. The new leader, a distinguished lawyer, churchman, and citizen, stumped the province in a sturdy effort to vindicate the new character of the party. It was a fine and courageous act, but he fought almost single-handed. One only of the former ministers was in the field, Hon. George Lawrence, and the federal Conservative party stood almost ostentatiously aloof. Hon. Arthur Meighen, Conservative member for Portage

la Prairie since 1908 and a rising man in the federal party, alone
lent aid.

The polls gave the Norris government a landslide victory.
Forty-two of its supporters were returned to a legislature of forty-
nine. Only five Conservatives were elected, four of them from the
five seats in which the French vote was decisive. Sir James Aikins
was defeated in Brandon, George Lawrence in Killarney. It was a
leaderless rump, four-fifths French, which represented the party
of Macdonald and Roblin. Of nine independent candidates,
Labour and Socialist, two Labour members, the first of their party,
were returned from North and Centre Winnipeg, R. A. Rigg and
F. J. Dixon. The latter, an able, courageous, and attractive man,
had been elected as a Labour candidate with Liberal support in
1914. The Norris government had an enormous majority and a
sweeping mandate with which to carry out its legislative programme. No mere party victory could have been so complete.

The government was at once put under heavy pressure by the
temperance societies, the Social Welfare Council, and the League
for Political Equality to carry out its pledges to enact temperance
legislation. Such was the temper of the time, that this *ignis fatuus*
of temperance reform was given precedence over more substantial
matters. The Premier held fast to two principles, that there should
be a referendum and that the temperance organizations should
prepare the draft legislation on which the referendum was to be
held. This latter unorthodox procedure was undoubtedly wise, as
it committed the most likely critics of legislation by the government to full responsibility. A committee drawn from the organizations reported in favour of the Macdonald Act of 1900, and
this was accepted by the government. The committee also asked
that women be given the vote prior to the referendum, a request
in which they were strongly supported by the League for Political
Equality. The request was one the government could not grant
until the legislature met; but the pressure is of interest as revealing the intimate connection between the temperance movement
and that for women's suffrage. Once the Act had been agreed
upon, the campaign for the carrying of the referendum, as it was
incorrectly called, went forward vigorously, with only the liquor

interests and the extreme prohibitionists opposing, until the vote was taken on March 13, 1916. The result, with the newly enfranchised women voting, was 50,484 for and 26,052 against. Only St. Boniface and North Winnipeg gave adverse majorities. The Manitoba Temperance Act, already passed in the session of 1916, was then proclaimed. By the Act, the sale of liquor within the province, except by druggists on prescription by a medical doctor, was forbidden. Liquor, however, could still be imported into the province by private individuals for consumption or by wholesalers for re-export. Manitoba, it was confidently hoped, had ended a public controversy running back to 1892 and had taken a step towards a better social life. Whether the law which many still thought a violation of private right could stand the strain of enforcement remained to be seen.

The Temperance Act was part of the programme of the Norris government, yet a part in which it was careful to place the responsibility for the Act squarely on the organizations which demanded it and on the electorate. It was wise to have done so, for Roblin had been perfectly right in thinking that temperance legislation is no stronger than the public opinion which supports it. The rest of the government's programme was entirely its own. In the session of 1916, which opened on January 11, the Norris government implemented fully the programme to which it was committed and for which its mandate was unqualified. Indeed, the legislature divided on only one item of legislation in the session, the abolition of the bilingual teaching clause of the School Act. Thereafter, the flood of legislation was to diminish in 1917 and 1918 and with the diminution the near unanimity of 1916.

The major political reforms of the Norris government were four in number, of which two were completed in 1916. First was the Initiative and Referendum Act, by which direct legislation was introduced into Manitoba. The Act was inspired by American example, and its introduction by the Norris government suggests either an imperfect grasp of the principles of parliamentary government, or considerable political naïveté. While this Act was to be declared unconstitutional by the courts on the ground that it infringed the prerogatives of the Lieutenant-Governor as a component branch of the legislature, it was a striking manifestation of the democratic spirit of the times and of the distrust of politicians and legislatures which the long years of political corruption had engendered, a distrust which the scandals seemed to justify. The next act was that which conferred on women the right to vote and to be elected to public office, the first such act passed by a Canadian legislature. The third was a remodelled Elections Act, which, however, as such acts do, called forth so much discussion that it was stood over and not passed until 1917. Fourth, the Civil Service was reorganized and a Civil Service Commission appointed in 1918 to recruit the service by competitive examination.

More fundamental to the life of the community, however, were the two acts respecting education and the abolition of the ill-fated Coldwell amendments. The first act was a School Attendance Act, which required that all children between the ages of five and fourteen attend some school, public or private, provided the latter were satisfactory to the inspectorate of the Department of Education. The ground had been carefully explored and was well prepared, as this passage from the Speech from the Throne indicates: "A measure of compulsory education which, while respecting the personal rights and religious convictions of the individual shall make it obligatory on parents and guardians of all children that such children shall receive a proper elementary education either by attendance at the public schools or by such substitute within the choice of parents or of guardians as shall attain that end."[15] The provisions of the Act thus respected the constitutional rights of Catholic parents, as defined by the courts. School attendance officials were to be appointed by local boards, with central supervision, and exemptions were to be granted for seeding and harvest work, or other reasonable excuse. The Act steered a nice course between the needs of education and the work of rural children on the farms in the busy seasons, an imperative need in the Manitoba of that day and especially in time of war. The actual change made in attendance was to be slight for many years in rural areas, both because administration was left to the local boards, and because a two- and three-mile limit was placed by the Act on the distance within which attendance was compulsory.

The School Attendance Act provoked little controversy, but the bill to amend the School Act by striking out the clause providing for bilingual teaching under the Laurier-Greenway Compromise provoked a spirited opposition from the French members of the House, aided by the first and only Ukrainian member. The growing campaign against bilingual instruction, largely led by the *Manitoba Free Press*, had been directed against the teaching of Ukrainian and Polish in schools. The rights of the French and the Mennonites, the languages covered by the Compromise in 1897, had generally been respected. The extended enquiry made by the *Free Press* in 1914 into bilingual teaching in the new districts of the province had revealed that the schools were in effect perpetuating the immigrant tongues without adding English to them But even in 1915 the *Free Press* and Premier Norris had been careful to admit the special position of French under the School Act. The report of the Department of Education in 1915, however, and a special report prepared by Inspector C. K. Newcombe, revealed that linguistic chaos had been produced in many districts. "The situation," the Deputy Minister of Education, Robert Fletcher, was reported to have informed his Minister, Dr. R. S. Thornton, "is just about out of hand."[16] The consequence of this study of the situation by the Minister of Education was a decision that French and German were inextricably involved with the newer languages. In Dr. Thornton's opinion the only remedy for a chaotic situation was to abolish the bilingual system entirely and make English the sole language of instruction in the schools.

Indeed, there were grounds for thinking that efforts had been made, under the cover of the Roblin government's defence of the bilingual system, to unite the Ukrainians and Poles with the French to resist any change. The result was to confound French with languages the clause had not been intended to cover. A considerable body of professional opinion also held that instruction in the mother tongue was not necessary in the elementary grades and this helped open the way to abolition. Despite doubts in the

Liberal caucus, and an attempt to preserve a special position for French, Dr. Thornton had his way, and it was resolved to abolish the bilingual system in its entirety.[17]

It was to the above, as it seemed, sudden and arbitrary decision that the French members objected, including the Liberal, P. A. Talbot. The latter eloquently affirmed the principle of dual nationality in Canada. "If any single member expects the English to assimilate the French in this Dominion I might give them the friendly advice to disabuse themselves. The French are a distinctive race, and we will not be assimilated whether you like it or not. We have been given our rights as a separate nationality and we will hold them."[18] It was the cry Henri Bourassa and the Nationalists had raised in Quebec. Talbot's Conservative colleagues pleaded eloquently the rights of French as the language of the original pioneers of Manitoba and the West and the natural right to education in the mother tongue, but to no avail. The great majority of the legislature were convinced that, in a population of 500,000, residents to the number of 100,000 speaking languages other than English, together with 30,000 French, menaced the stability and cohesion of the community. Better firm action now than worse trouble in the future, was their thought. In short, they proposed to make the public school and the English language the agencies of assimilation in a community which the immigration of the boom years had made increasingly heterogeneous and polyglot. The position taken by Thornton had been moderate but firm, and he maintained it:

It is necessary to deal with this law [the bilingual clause] both in our own interests and in the interests of the strangers within our gates who have come to make their homes with us with the purpose of becoming a part of this nation. The first essential to individual progress in any land is to know the language of the country. In an English-speaking country, as this is, a knowledge of English is more necessary than a knowledge of arithmetic. No matter what a man's attainments may be, the doors of opportunity are closed to him if he has not a knowledge of English, the common tongue. . . . We are building for the Canada of tomorrow, and our common school is one of the most important factors in the work. In this Dominion we are building up, under the British flag, a new nationality. We come from many lands and cast in our lot, and from these various factors there must evolve a new nationality which shall be simply Canadian and British.[19]

The School Act was amended accordingly and the complex and delicate problem was, not solved, indeed, but turned over to the administration of the Department of Education, now given a free hand by the School Attendance Act and the abolition of bilingual teaching. The further consequences of the Acts were to remove the historic anomalies which were the consequences of the old dual system of 1871, and to give Manitoba a school system which might be brought up to the standard of the English-speaking provinces and the states of the American Union.

The major educational legislation of the Norris government was completed in 1917 with the passage of an Act to enable the Provincial Treasury to loan money to needy school districts for the erection of schoolhouses, and by the amendment of the University Act. The reorganization of the University of Manitoba had been delayed since 1907 both by the differences of opinion as to the relationship of the denominational colleges to the University, and the question of a permanent site. By the Act of 1917 the University of Manitoba was made a semi-state university, with a Board of Governors appointed by the provincial government. The colleges remained in affiliation, St. Boniface only after being assured of the integrity of its curriculum in Latin Philosophy. The provincial grant was increased with the passage of the Act, and the question of the site reopened. The previous decision to place the University with the Manitoba Agricultural College at St. Vital was rescinded and the site in the suburb of Tuxedo, chosen by the University Council in 1911, was once more adopted. The government, unfortunately, could not spare the funds necessary for building. The Agricultural College had been reorganized and brought back into affiliation with the University in the previous year.

The school legislation of 1916 was essentially an attempt to raise the standard of rural education, and especially to deal with the aggravation of the difficulties of rural education by foreign settlement on the frontiers and bilingual teaching. The University Act was meant to crown the provincial system of education,

by establishing a university of high standing at its apex. Another
group of acts passed in this busy session of 1916 constituted an
attempt to bring the laws of Manitoba into line with the needs
of industrial labour and the standards of contemporary legislation.
The Workmen's Compensation Act was amended in ways desired
by labour. Amendments were also made to the Factories Act and
the Building Trades Protection Act. An Act gave additional duties
to the Bureau of Labour and a Fair Wage Board was set up. The
Shops Regulation Act was amended, as it applied to the employment of young people, to conform with the School Attendance
Act. These acts were continuations of that response to the needs
of labour in the growing industries of Winnipeg which the Roblin
government had begun, and which the Norris government was to
carry yet further. Neither party had experienced any theoretical
difficulty in thus practising state intervention on behalf of labour;
neither, on the other hand, would, or could, accept the full labour
programme of union recognition and collective bargaining. The
Norris government indeed was perhaps more sympathetic with
the cause of labour than was prudent in an agrarian province.

In the yet little-developed field of public health and welfare,
the one outstanding act among a number of minor acts and
amendments was the Mothers' Allowance Act, by which the province was to assist widowed mothers in rearing their children in
their own homes. The extension of aid by the state to minors and
incapacitated or handicapped people was slowly going forward
in Manitoba, but it had not yet passed the line at which it was
forbidden to aid those who might theoretically be expected to
help themselves. Relief of the indigent remained a matter of
municipal responsibility and discretion.

Legislation on behalf of agriculture was surprisingly small in
1916. The establishment of a Weeds Commission to administer
a strengthened Noxious Weeds Act was a valuable piece of legislation which reflected a growing problem of Manitoba agriculture.
These were the years when the sow thistle was the despair of the
farmer. The Settlers Animal Purchase Act, a personal project of
the Minister of Agriculture, Hon. Valentine Winkler, authorized
assistance by the province to settlers in the Interlake district and

other needy areas for the purchase of up to five head of cattle. More significant was the demand, inspired by G. W. Prout, M.L.A., for a study of ways and means of providing a system of rural credits. Since the amendment of the Canada Bank Act in 1912 and the coming of the depression, western farmers had become more and more concerned with the provision of credit on terms adapted to the special circumstances of agriculture.

In 1917 the legislation to provide agricultural credit from local and provincial sources was the chief feature of the session. A Farm Loans Act was passed to provide long-term mortgages at low rates of interest on the guarantee of the Provincial Treasury. A Farm Loans Board was set up under the Act to administer the scheme. A Rural Credits Act followed, which authorized the formation of local rural credit societies for the subscription of funds to provide loans. One-quarter of the funds of each society were to be subscribed by the members, one-quarter by the municipality, and one-half by the Provincial Treasury, the whole to form a basis for bank loans to individuals. This use of local and provincial funds to lower interest rates and prime the pump of credit was one of the most interesting experiments of the Norris government, and one of the most daring.

15

The Years of Social Crisis
1917-1922

THE ENLIGHTENED AND COURAGEOUS PROGRAMME
of legislation pursued by the Norris government during its first
term of office did much to redeem the public life of the province
from the shame of the scandals. It was carried through despite
the increasing distraction and strain caused by the ever intensi-
fying war effort. The province was giving freely of its men at the
same time that it was trying to increase the production of the
farms. Winnipeg's industries and the railways were under equal
pressure. That energy should have been found for progressive
reform was a striking display of character by the people and leaders of Manitoba.

The prime contribution of Manitoba to the war was its wheat
and livestock. The war found the agriculture of the province in
good shape, established and well furnished in all respects save
labour. The demand created by war speedily ended the depression
of farm prices. The crop of 1914 was only average, but in the
following year a large acreage of summer fallow and breaking
combined with ample rainfall to produce the memorable crop of
1915. This heaviest of all crops was increased in size and value
by perhaps the greatest triumph of cereal breeding, the plump,
high-quality, and quick-ripening Marquis wheat produced by
Dr. Charles Saunders of the Ottawa Experimental Farm. The
only problem was to get the crop off, and the threshers hummed
early and late, the railway yards rumbled day and night, handling
the millions of bushels of high-grade wheat. In 1916, however,

stem rust struck with unprecedented severity, yields were light, and the sample shrivelled. Dry seasons came in 1917 and 1918 and the crops were short. And in Manitoba, for the first time, there was soil-drifting on a large scale. On the light lands of the Assiniboine delta, the scouring winds drifted the overworked top soil in grey dunes along the fences.

To these trials others were added in these bitter years. Recruiting, the demands of war industry, and the cessation of immigration caused a crippling labour shortage. Children who should have been in school, women already overworked in the kitchen, old men and lads, men on leave from Camp Hughes, toiled in the fields at seedtime and harvest. Wages rose, as did the cost of the machinery which had to be bought to offset the labour shortage. Indeed, rising costs of land and of all the needs of farm production steadily pursued the rising prices of wheat. So much did the latter rise that in 1917 the federal government appointed a Board of Grain Supervisors to handle the wheat crop of Canada and steady the soaring market. In this race of rising prices and costs lay the possibility of disaster for the farmer, urged to produce to the limit and driven to increase his outlay in order to do so.

The drain of men into the cities for war industry and into the army created difficulties for the farmers, but it filled the factories and the battalions. By the end of July, 1915, it was claimed that Manitoba had raised 18,000 volunteers, and seventeen battalions were formed, or forming, in the province.[1] The lists of local casualties lengthened in the papers, particularly after the great Somme offensive of 1916, and with them came the lengthening of the list of battle honours. More and more pressure, by recruiting officers and public opinion, had to be used to keep up the flow of volunteers. The contrast between the sacrifice of those who served overseas and those who stayed at home in the prosperity of the war boom deepened and darkened. The merits of the voluntary system, accepted without question in 1914, began to be doubted. By the end of 1916 a demand for conscription was taking shape, and by 1917, when Prime Minister Borden declared it necessary after his visit to the United Kingdom, public opinion in Manitoba was almost solid for it among those of British descent.

With the demand for conscription came a cry for a union, or coalition government, to carry conscription and prosecute the war. As early as 1915, indeed, Premier Norris and the *Free Press* had declared such a government to be necessary. The thought was natural in a province which had suffered the worst excesses of partisanship and was turning away from the old parties.

In the summer of 1917 the movement for union government and conscription came to a head. Manitoban Conservatives supported it with no difficulty. For Manitoban Liberals it was a matter of divided loyalties. The federal Liberal leader, Sir Wilfrid Laurier, conscious of the feeling of his own people in Quebec, had declined to support conscription or union government. The leaders of the Manitoban Liberals were convinced of the necessity of both, and came to the determination that a western Liberal party must be formed to support a coalition. For this purpose a convention of the Liberals of western Canada was held in Winnipeg in August, 1917. The Laurier Liberals succeeded in defeating the purposes of the unionist Liberals, however, and it was necessary for the provincial Liberal party to break away from the federal party to support the Union Government which was formed in October, 1917. These events split the federal Liberal party, severed the ties between the provincial Liberal party and the federal, and still further increased the growth of non-partisanship in the province. When the Union Government appealed to the electorate in 1917, it carried all the Manitoba seats except Provencher, an adequate measure at once of Manitoba's commitment to the war and of its turning away from the old party system.

The year 1917 saw not only the introduction of conscription and the formation of the Union Government, but also the change in the character of the war caused by the beginning of the revolution in Russia and the entry of the United States into the war. Both events seemed to be victories for the democratic ideals for which Manitobans believed the war was being fought by the Western powers, but neither immediately increased the military force of the allies. The task of holding the front until the Russian armies began to fight again, and those of the United States were trained, fell particularly on the British Army. In the fall of 1917 the prolonged and bloody fighting at Passchendaele held the German army down, yet with appalling losses many a Manitoban home had sad occasion to remember. But it was in 1917, also, that the Canadian Corps under a Canadian commander captured the ridge of Vimy, where the 43rd Camerons (the 79th) particularly distinguished themselves. The army had become the vehicle of a proud national feeling, which not only strengthened national sentiment in Canada, but overcame much of that provincial narrowness which always threatened to grow to excess in the Canadian provinces, Manitoba among them. The war had not only recalled the province to a sense of its being part of a larger world, but had also given it a new sense of being part of the Canadian nation. In the press and in the schools the name of Canadian was being used with a new pride and a deepening significance. The tale of battle honours indeed gave cause for pride. Fourteen men from the province won the Victoria Cross. Three came from one short street in Winnipeg, thereafter to be called Valour Road. In the new sphere of war, the air over the battle, one Manitoban youngster born and bred and of Red River stock, Flight Sergeant Alan MacLeod, won the cross of simple valour. Here was a common bond for all Canadians, old and new, of whatever stock or origin. One Manitoban fighting man of note, for example, was Sniper Pte. P. Riel, nephew of "the rebel."

Neither the tense days of the great German offensive of March, 1918, nor the heady weeks of victory which followed the great offensive of August 8, did anything to lower that high sense of achievement. For one proud day on November 11 the guns boomed in Winnipeg and Camp Hughes, and the anvils banged in the towns across the province. Then came the relaxation of victory, the continuing sorrow, the problems of rehabilitation, the tensions of a war-wrung society. In Manitoba the stern resolution of wartime fell away, to reveal what it had masked, agriculture harassed by short crops and high costs, long hours and low real wages in Winnipeg's industries, thousands of unassimilated immigrants and their bewildered children, and continuing resistance to the School Act.

All during the spring and summer of 1918–19 the discharged

soldiers came flooding back. The brisk drum and fife of the
Grenadiers was heard once more on Main and Portage, and the
swing and skirl of the Camerons' pipes, splendidly barbarous,
as the massed khaki columns flowed endlessly in a last victory
parade down the rejoicing width of the great streets paralleling
the Red and Assiniboine. When the khaki uniforms were laid
aside, there were jobs to be sought or farms to be taken up. The
main effort at rehabilitation was to induce the veterans to go on
the land, and the federal government's Soldier Settlers' Board was
set up to obtain land on favourable terms for veterans and to start
them in farming with stock and equipment. The provincial government assisted in such ways as it could, and the frontier districts, particularly the Interlake, and in the old settled areas the
farms given up by old men who had held on during the war years,
received hundreds of new farmers, eager to forget the war in
quiet toil of the fields. Neither jobs nor lands were always immediately available, and much of the land was poor. In Winnipeg
discharged soldiers were among the unemployed or those who
feared unemployment. In the country there was often high feeling at the sight of land being tilled by men who had not served,
but had increased their holdings when the soldiers were overseas.
Some of this resentment was directed against Mennonites, although many of them had served, usually in non-combatant services, and always at a heavy cost in terms of bitter disapproval by
their own people. There was a vehement outburst against Hut-
terite settlers who had come in from the United States in 1918
and settled at Eli and Oakville south of the Assiniboine. A pie-
tistic sect of agrarian pacifists, they were good farmers, but their
communal system of land holding clashed with the individualistic
system of the country and their pacifism was an offence to many
at that time.

The return of the veterans added to other strains in the community. The cost of living was soaring in a practically unchecked
inflation. The real wages of labour in Winnipeg were falling
rapidly, and aggravated the evils of insanitary factories and the
shortage of housing. The epidemic of influenza which swept the
country in the winter of 1918–19 added a burden of further loss

and depression. And the effort to fuse the heterogeneous elements of the population by means of the schools was still encountering much quiet but obstinate resistance. The new office of Official Trustee, an officer of the Department of Education empowered to organize schools where the residents of a district refused to act, did make it possible to extend the system into the "foreign settlements." This task was carried out with combined firmness and tact by Ira Stratton, one of the province's finest servants. In the French districts trouble was avoided by both Catholics and Protestants. But the Mennonites, especially those of the Old Colony sect, were deeply disturbed by the loss of their right to teach in German, the language of their church, and were carrying an appeal, based on the alleged privilege of having their own schools conferred on them by federal order-in-council, to the Judicial Committee of the Privy Council.

This general malaise in the province was completing the dissolution of the old political parties, which had acted, in their quest for political support, as bonds of society and agents of assimilation. Class feeling, which had played so small a part in the simple society of pioneer days and was rejected by the democratic spirit sprung from those days, was becoming prominent. Classes were organizing, and society dissolving, as the farmers' organizations became more radical and labour organized and listened to more radical voices. In the first post-war years the organized farmers and organized labour emerged as aspirants to power in Manitoba.

The farmers had continued the routine work of their organizations, of which the Manitoba Grain Growers' Association was chief, and had lent their powerful support to the war effort. Since the defeat of reciprocity in 1911, however, they had become more and more antagonistic to the protective tariff, and more distrustful of the political parties. Suggestions that the farmers enter politics as a class by means of their organizations became frequent. In 1916 the Canadian Council of Agriculture consolidated the farmers' political demands in what it termed the Farmers' Platform. The Platform consisted largely of a detailed proposal for a reduction of the tariff and the elimination of protection. It was disregarded in the election of 1917, but in 1919 it was revised and published as the New National Policy. In the same year Hon. T. A. Crerar, Minister of Agriculture, resigned from the Union Government on the ground that it had declined to reduce the tariff on agricultural implements, and then formed around him in Parliament a group of western "Progressives." The signal had been given for a western revolt against the national tariff policy. In 1920 the Manitoba Grain Growers' Association, along with the Saskatchewan Grain Growers and the United Farmers of Alberta, adopted the Platform and committed their organizations to the support of candidates pledged to implement it.

The resolution to enter federal politics, of course, raised the question of the farmers entering provincial politics also. The United Farmers of Ontario had already done so in 1919, and their representatives had captured the government of Ontario; the United Farmers of Alberta had won the Cochrane by-election in that province the same year. Only approval by many members of the personnel and policies of the Norris government prevented the Manitoba convention of 1920 from approving similar action in Manitoba. As it was, it was determined that the locals might decide on political action, and, if a majority of them did so, the executive of the Association would call a convention to draft a platform. At the same time the Association was reorganized as the United Farmers of Manitoba, a change of name which was a response to a growing membership and a more militant spirit in the rank and file of the Association. The decision, compromised as it was, revealed the growing discontent of farmers with the place accorded agriculture in the national economy, with the parties and government, and even with their own organization. Already many Manitoba Grain Growers, and particularly the many new members of these years, were coming to believe that their Association should sever its association with the increasingly conservative United Grain Growers' Grain Company and take on a more radical character. And there were some who looked to common action with labour.

Just as the organized farmers were becoming more numerous and more militant, so too was organized labour in the cities and large towns. Since 1914 the number of workers in industry in Winnipeg had increased and there had been a steady growth in the numbers and membership of the trades unions. These were craft unions, organized under the Trades and Labour Council of Winnipeg, and most of them affiliates of the Trades and Labour Congress of Canada. During the last years of the war, however, the dominance of these conservative craft unions in the leadership of Winnipeg labour had been sharply challenged by the One Big Union movement. This movement, derived from the radical International Workers of the World of the United States and the radical wing of labour in Australia, was an attempt to organize labour industrially in one comprehensive union and to convert it to the doctrines of class war and Marxian socialism. One of the main tenets of the movement was the right and capacity of labour to assert its power in the community by the general, or sympathetic, strike. A strong sectional feeling was also embodied in the O.B.U. movement, because it first entered the West and was in opposition to the craft unions controlled from eastern head offices. The Russian Revolution gave a great impetus to the radical elements in the O.B.U. movement, as it also stimulated wild hopes among the immigrant Social Democrats.

The ferment caused by deteriorating conditions of labour and by the radical movement was very evident throughout 1918. There was an increasing number of strikes in Winnipeg as there was in other western cities. A strike which began on May 2 among civic workers of Winnipeg spread until it had almost reached the proportions of a general strike. From then on the idea of a general strike was constantly in the minds and often on the lips of the extremes leaders of Winnipeg labour, and in many ways the strike of May, 1918, was a rehearsal of the events of May and June, 1919. The impairment of civic services raised the question of whether public servants were in fact in the same position as workers in private industry. A motion by Alderman Frank Fowler challenged the right of civic workers to strike, and the threat to the community brought about the organization of a citizens' committee under A. L. Crossin to protect the public interest. There the resemblance of the spring strikes of 1918 and 1919 ended.

That of 1918 was not made general, and was settled by the mediation of the citizens' committee and of the federal Minister of Labour, Hon. Gideon Robertson. But serious issues had been raised, and in July a strike in the metal trades raised that of recognition by the employers of the Metal Trades Council as bargaining agent for the workers.

The labour unrest was combined with political opposition to the anti-soviet policy of the Allies and the Canadian government. The latter opposition was expressed in public meetings called by the Socialist party in the Walker Theatre in December, 1918, and the Majestic Theatre in January, 1919. The general tenor of the speeches was, of course, socialistic, the Russian Revolution was defended, and the victory of workers over the capitalists everywhere was forecast. In this continuation of labour unrest and political discontent the O.B.U. movement and the idea of the general strike flourished, as they seemed to offer a direct path to better conditions and political power for the working class. In January, 1919, the organization of the One Big Union was approved at a meeting in Vancouver, and in March a convention of those attracted by the ideas of the O.B.U. was held in Calgary. From Winnipeg went Rev. William Ivens and Rev. Salem G. Bland, Methodist ministers sympathetic with labour, and R. B. Russell and R. J. Johns, labour radicals. There the idea of the general strike, leading to a seizure of power by labour, was approved, and the delegates departed to spread the new policy among industrial workers. There was much wild talk at Calgary and subsequently, which was serious enough, but perhaps not to be taken as seriously as the authorities were to do. The high cost of living, threatened unemployment, and the general unrest of the post-war months gave the O.B.U. and the Labour movement a tremendous stimulus. The early months of 1919 witnessed a rush of new members into the Winnipeg unions.

In this way the radicalism of the O.B.U. movement, the idea of the general strike, and a struggle between the orthodox unionists and the radicals of the O.B.U. for the leadership of the Labour movement were introduced into Winnipeg in the spring of 1919. The result was to increase the unrest of labour, an unrest to which both the influx into the unions and the passage of an Industrial Conciliation Act by the legislature bore witness. The discontent sprang from genuine and legitimate grievances, long hours, low real wages, bad housing, a depressed status in a society which had not yet admitted labour to terms of equality. One especial grievance was the refusal of some employers to admit the practice of collective bargaining and the reservations of others respecting it.

These grievances were expressed on May 1 when the metal workers struck against three companies, the Vulcan Iron Works, the Manitoba Bridge and Iron, and the Dominion Bridge and Iron, because the management refused to agree to collective bargaining by all the metal workers' unions and ratification of a settlement by the Metal Trades Council. The companies were prepared to deal only with the unions in their own works. On the same day the building trades struck for higher wages, on the ground that the current rates did not enable them to live during the winter off season. Both sets of unions referred their cases to the Trades and Labour Council of Winnipeg. The Council, despite differences between conservatives and radicals, resolved to take a ballot among the unions on the calling of a sympathetic strike. The ballot was taken hastily but fairly, and in fifty-two affiliated unions the vote was 11,112 votes for to 524 against; seventeen unions did not report. Among those voting were the unions of the city firemen and the police. The Council then set the date for the strike at 11 o'clock, May 15, and announced that "all public utilities [would] be tied up in order to enforce the principle of collective bargaining."[2]

The strike, then, began with two immediate aims and two subsidiary but increasingly important aspects. One aim was the redress of legitimate grievances with respect to wages and collective bargaining; the other was the trial of a new instrument of economic action, the general strike, the purpose of which was to put pressure on the employers involved in the dispute through the general public. The first subsidiary aspect was that the general strike, however, might be a prelude to the seizure of power in the community by Labour, and both the utterances and the policies

of the O.B.U. leaders pointed in that direction. The second subsidiary aspect was that, as a struggle for leadership in the Labour
movement was being waged as the strike began, it was not made
clear which object, the legitimate and limited one, or the revolutionary and general one, was the true purpose of the strike. It is
now apparent that the majority of both strikers and strike leaders
were concerned only to win the strike. The general public at
large, however, subjected to the sudden coercion of the general
strike, was only too likely to decide that a revolutionary seizure
of power was in view.

The organization of the strike proceeded quickly under an
interim committee of five. On May 21 a Central Strike Committee of fifteen was set up by the General Strike Committee of
about three hundred representing each affiliated union. The
Interim committee consisted of James Winning, president of the
Trades and Labour Council, H. G. Veitch, past president, Ernest
Robinson, secretary, R. B. Russell of the Metal Workers' Council,
and J. L. McBride, a conservative unionist. Ten other members
were added to it to constitute the Central Strike Committee.
Under the direction of the Committee the strike speedily became
general in fact as well as aim. In particular, the public services,
the mails, telephone, street cars, telegraphs, and milk deliveries,
were cut off at once. The police and waterworks men were technically on strike, but remained on duty, the water pressure, however, being kept low. The railway running trades did not come
out, despite a local vote to do so, because the vote was overridden
by the head offices of the Union.[3] Had they done so Winnipeg,
still wholly dependent on its railways for communication, would
have been isolated. On May 18 the pressmen were called out, and
the newspapers had to cease publication. The city was given over
to rumour, as the *Strike Bulletin* and the *Western Labour News*,
the organs of the Committee and the Trades and Labour Council,
were for a few days the only papers issued. These, of course, were
taken up by the work of the Committee and the exhorting of the
strikers to stand firm.

Problems at once arose, of the supply of food and especially
milk to children, the sick, and hospitals, of essential services, such

as fire protection and of what to do with a population in enforced idleness and in need of amusement. On May 17 the Committee authorized the resumption of bread and milk deliveries, after an attempt to deliver only to working-class homes had proved impracticable. Placards bearing the words "By permission of the Strike Committee" were posted on the milk waggons, as was done on the theatres, which were allowed to open at the same time. This was a necessary measure to prevent strikers stopping deliveries or entry, but gave the impression that the Committee had arrogated to itself general authority in the city.

These placards played a major part in alienating the sympathies of the general public, that always forgotten majority of people who are neither workers nor capitalists. (The leaders of the O.B.U., it is to be noted, emphatically denied the existence of any third party between capital and labour.) The growing animosity of the public was increased by the fears the Bolshevik seizure of power in Russia was arousing, and by distrust of the "alien" element in labour. It was easy at that time to misinterpret the purpose and spirit of the strike. There were some wild-eyed advocates of bloody revolution at work. There was a taut determination in all the leaders to maintain the strike, though suffering might be caused to participants or the public. But much of their effort went to keeping the strike quiet and orderly, to avoiding clashes with the authorities, and to preventing any alienation of public sympathy. In all this they were successful during the first weeks of the strike. And it is of the greatest importance to note that more influential than the Marxian apostles of the O.B.U. were the militant Methodist ministers, William Ivens, Salem G. Bland, and J. S. Woodsworth. These men, preaching a "social gospel" drawn from Scripture, from the muckraking literature of the day, and from their own evangelical creed, were prophesying a new age and a new order, in which labour would come into its own and social justice prevail. Their message was in the right Christian and British tradition which ran from John Ball to George Lansbury. It was a message more appealing to the great majority of workers than the class war frenzy of the Marxists. Nor is the straight labour element among the strikers to be forgotten, the men who were not socialists, or who, if socialists, were not revolutionaries. They were the great majority. In addition to evangelical fervour and solid union spirit, there was a rollicking, experimental spirit in the air, defiant, cocky, good-humoured, as the men came out in the fine spring weather to have a round with the bosses. The numbers who came out, the membership of seventy unions together with new ones organized during the strike, exceeded all expectation; 24,000 men were estimated to have struck. It was this mood of defiant hilarity which was dominant in the first weeks of the strike, and it meant that the men and their leaders were open to any conciliatory, sincere, and reasonable approach.

Such an approach, however, was made impossible for the civic and provincial authorities by the stand they took that they would not attempt conciliation or negotiation as long as the city lay under the pressure of the general strike. Both Mayor C. F. Gray and Premier Norris insisted on a quiet and unprovocative attitude towards the strike, but both were unyielding on the principle of no negotiation until the sympathetic strike had ended. The result, of course, was deadlock. The federal government was deeply involved also, both because the postal workers had gone out on strike and because of the threat to national communications in the strike of the telegraphers and the possible strike of the railway workers. When Hon. Gideon Robertson, the level-headed Minister of Labour in the federal cabinet, had visited Winnipeg, his report was neither alarmist nor unsympathetic. But the police reports to the Ministry of Justice were alarming, and quiet preparations were made to deal with any attempted seizure of power. Detachments of Royal North West Mounted Police were moved into the city, and the troops at Fort Osborne were held in readiness.

The neutral attitude of the civic and provincial governments was not adopted or approved by the Winnipeg public not participating in the strike. Spontaneous and vigorous action was taken. On May 19 a Citizens' Committee of One Thousand was formed. The purpose of this action was to raise and organize volunteers to man the public services. The Committee also issued a paper, *The*

Citizen. Thus the general strike provoked its natural reply, the spontaneous rising of the general community to repel the threat to its existence. The Committee frankly intended not only to keep the public utilities working, but to maintain order by means of special constables patrolling the streets and moving in squads by motor car to any disorderly area. The semi-provisional government of the Strike Committee was now faced—it is almost true to say challenged—by a similar government of the Citizens' Committee. The sporadic violence of strikers in attempting to police the striking by picketing and intimidation was now met by the similar roughness on the part of citizen squads keeping the streets and local stores open. And there were from time to time some merry fights with baseball bats and neck yokes sawed in two, but as yet no general violence and no deep hostility.

By the end of May the original causes of the strike were being lost to sight in the larger issue of the legitimacy of the general strike. The danger was that the constituted authorities would lose power to the committees, and the city be plunged into a struggle between the two for mastery. On the second week of the strike the Mayor and Council began to yield to pressure from the Citizens' Committee. On May 26 the Council voted nine to five on a revival of the Fowler motion of 1918 to prohibit sympathetic strikes by city firemen and to dismiss those then on strike. A second motion passed by the same majority extended the principle of the first to all civic employees, including the police. This challenge to the principle of the general strike was not taken up by the Strike Committee at once and in consequence many strikers worried by the hiring of replacements became restless. On May 31 veterans who supported the strike paraded the streets. Parades of large delegations of strikers to the Legislative Buildings and street demonstrations became numerous. The leading elements in these were veterans, whether strikers or opponents of the strike. The Strike Committee tried to renew pressure on the community on June 4 by once more suspending deliveries of bread, milk, and ice, but the substitute services of the Citizens' Committee defeated the attempt. On June 5 the Mayor by proclamation forbade further parades, an order which was promptly challenged by

marchers. No stronger measures against the strikers were possible at that time. But on June 9, the police force was dismissed and a new chief appointed. Special constables already
organized by the Citizens' Committee were sworn in in large
numbers. The immediate result was a rough test of strength
between the strikers and specials on Portage and Main which
ended indecisively. The issue was becoming the straight issue of
control of the streets, and on June 11 there was a further two-
hour demonstration by strikers against the use of special constables. That the veterans, who would probably have been the
decisive element in a show-down, were divided, illustrated the
extent of the division in the community which the strike had
revealed.

The settlement of the original dispute, however, was being
attempted by the railway running trades unions acting as mediators. After a number of hitches, an agreement was reached on
June 16, by which the three companies undertook to bargain
collectively with the representatives of the metals trades unions,
excluding, however, the powerful railway unions. On this basis
of compromise negotiation for a complete settlement could begin
and the original cause of the strike was diminished, if not removed. The first result was a weakening of the strike.

The general strike had now lasted a month; the strikers were
feeling the strain; and many workers were returning to their jobs.
The strike was failing, and as the sense of defeat spread, the
remaining strikers, many of whom knew they would not get their
jobs back, became more bitter. The federal authorities, who had
hitherto kept in the background, but held an exaggerated view of
the revolutionary potential of the strike, now decided that the
time had come to intervene, and on June 17, by order from
Ottawa, eight strike leaders, George Armstrong, R. E. Bray, Alderman A. A. Heaps, William Ivens, R. J. Johns, W. A. Pritchard,
Alderman John Queen, and R. B. Russell, were ordered arrested.
One Sam Blumenberg was also sought, but escaped to the United
States. Four foreigners, alleged Bolsheviks, were also taken into
custody. All except Pritchard and Johns, who were returning to
Winnipeg from speaking tours, were rushed to Stony Mountain

and charged with seditious conspiracy and seditious libel. The six Labour leaders were immediately released on bail, but a great demonstration before the City Hall on June 21 was the first result of the arrests. Mayor Gray called in the Mounted Police to disperse the crowd. They moved north down Main Street in line, endeavouring to clear the street, but were met by stout defiance. Clubs swung and bricks flew, and the Police fought their way back on Main. Mayor Gray now read the Riot Act from the steps of the City Hall. In a second charge the Police, in serious danger of being overwhelmed and killed, fired into the crowded street. One man was killed and an unknown number wounded, one of whom died of a gangrened wound.[4] The crowd broke up, and when the troops drove up in cars from Fort Osborne, the great wide street was empty and silent.

The general strike had failed and the last resistance had been broken. On June 25 the Trades and Labour Council declared the strike was over, the seizure of documents was completed, and J. S. Woodsworth and F. J. Dixon, who had together edited the *Western Labour News* after the arrests, were themselves arrested on charges of seditious libel, and the *News* temporarily suspended. On July 3 the fourteen men arrested, a very mixed bag of idealists, solid Labour men and radicals, were remanded for trial after preliminary hearing and released on bail. They straightway proceeded to tour Canada and stimulate the unrest prevalent in all the great cities. On the same day the provincial government set up a Royal Commission, with H. A. Robson, K.C., as Commissioner, to enquire into the causes of the strike. On November 6 the Commissioner, to his honour, submitted a moderate and sympathetic report which laid proper stress on the legitimate grievances from which the strike had originated.[5]

Only ten of the arrested men, Armstrong, Bray, Dixon, Heaps, Ivens, Johns, Pritchard, Queen, Russell, and Woodsworth, were remanded for trial, eight on the charges of seditious conspiracy, illegal combinations, and seditious libel, Dixon and Woodsworth on the separate charge of seditious libel only. The four unfortunate aliens were deported under an amended section of the Immigration Act. The trial of R. B. Russell began on November 26.

The evidence submitted by the Crown was of a general nature and much of doubtful validity, except on the unproven assumption that the strike was an attempt to seize power. Only by attributing to the accused the flamboyant statements of the extremists before as well as during the strike, and by a narrow construction of the laws relating to sedition, could seditious intent be established. As an impartial jury was not likely to be found in Winnipeg, the jurors were drawn from the rural part of the Eastern Judicial District, but it may be questioned whether they were more than technically impartial. Rural Manitoba had viewed the strike with shocked indignation; only in Brandon and the larger railway towns was there any sympathy. The jury on December 24 found the accused guilty and genial "Bob" Russell, most warm-hearted of firebrands, was sentenced to two years imprisonment. Labour spokesmen expressed indignation at the verdict, but five of the other leaders in due course were similarly convicted and imprisoned for one year. A. A. Heaps was acquitted and Bray convicted on one count only. F. J. Dixon won acquittal by a brilliant self-defence to be set beside that of Joseph Howe, and the charge against J. S. Woodsworth was never proceeded with, and never withdrawn. Thus shamefacedly closed a shameful episode; the trials and the sentences were an abuse of the processes of justice by class fear and class rancour. It is to be noted, however, that the strike had been a real challenge to public order; it had caused deep fears; the victors were comparatively lenient and the sentences in the circumstances relatively mild.

The general strike left Labour in Winnipeg weakened and divided. The Trades and Labour Congress of Canada had denounced the strike; the Trades and Labour Council of Winnipeg split in two, the Winnipeg Central Labour Council of the O.B.U., and a reorganized Trades and Labour Council. The community of Winnipeg was also weakened and divided into two camps, and Labour and the Citizens' League, successor to the Citizens' Committee, became lasting political opponents in civic politics. Winnipeg, in the province and across Canada, acquired the reputation of being a radical and unsafe community. Labour, if it was bound to suffer for the wilder utterances of its extremist leaders, was left with a sense of injustice arising from the trials.

The same spirit was to inspire the notorious section 98, passed as a result of the Strike, which until 1936 defaced the Criminal Code of Canada. But by the strike Labour none the less established itself in the community; it was not again to be neglected or ignored by employer or public. Under the leadership of the men who suffered arrest and imprisonment a new Independent Labour Party was organized in 1920 which was to achieve public respect and unquestioned standing in the city, although the I.L.P. was not able then or later to represent all elements of labour. The European Social Democratic movement was to give rise to a local Communist party, which was to represent a hard core of unassimilated aliens and unrelieved social discontent.

The turbulent year of 1919 led on to a year scarcely less turbulent in 1920. The term of the legislature elected in 1915 was to expire and a provincial election was to reduce the great majority of the Norris government in 1915 to a minority, without, however, providing another government. One cause of this political instability was the loss of popular support suffered by Premier Norris and his administration.

The end of its first term found the Norris government sadly weakened, despite its initial strength and outstanding record of reform. It had maintained its record of honest administration. It had continued to give the most enlightened leadership to which the province was capable of responding. In the administration of the School Act it had made good progress and ensured the future integrity of the community. By the work of the official trustees, Ira Stratton and from 1919, F. Greenway, school districts had been organized in the immigrant and Mennonite districts. The courts had found that the Mennonites must accept the School Law, and the result was the emigration of the Old Colony sect to Mexico in 1921. But this sad result of the abolition of the bilingual system was offset by happier results in other areas. The building of teachers' houses had made it possible to persuade teachers to accept posts in the frontier districts. The schools were actively instilling a Canadian patriotism in the children of immigrant parents, and the Minister of Education, Dr. Thornton, had given almost official currency to the then happy term "new Canadian." The Minister and his staff could justly pride themselves that "the foundations of Canada were being laid in the frontier districts of our province."[6] The flow of legislation had diminished, but the establishment of the Manitoba Hydro-Electric Commission in 1919 to transmit electric power through the province, and of the Hail Insurance Commission in 1920 were notable achievements. As the Temperance Act of 1916 had failed to give satisfaction to its supporters, and as federal law now permitted, complete prohibition was introduced in 1920. The Redistribution Act of 1920 created a multiple member constituency of Winnipeg, with ten members to be elected by proportional representation, and raised the number of members in the House to fifty-five.

The resignation of A. B. Hudson in 1918, however, of his successor T. H. Johnson, and of G. J. H. Malcolm, successor to Valentine Winkler as Minister of Agriculture, in 1920, left the administration weakened in personnel. The very extensiveness of the Norris reforms, the multiplication of government commissions, together with the rising costs of the times, left it with deficits in three years out of five, and prompted charges of extravagance from both friends and opponents. The break-up of parties and the growth of non-partisanship told against it, and approaches by the federal Liberals led to the discounting of Norris' disclaimers that his was not a party government. Finally, as the platform published in 1920 revealed, the party was exhausted of ideas.

Meanwhile the United Farmers of Manitoba had given a conditional recognition to the entry of its locals into provincial politics. The result was political chaos in the rural constituencies, with the one idea dominant that the old parties were no longer to be trusted to give honest government or to represent the farmers' interest. The farmers must therefore elect farmers to represent farmers in a frank adoption of non-partisan politics and occupational representation. "Desirous of breaking entirely away from the shackles of old time partisanship," wrote the *Killarney Guide*, "they have decided, against the advice of their leaders, to . . . enter the field of provincial politics."[7] The movement was not general, however, but confined to the more discontented and radical elements of the United Farmers. Among many of these there was considerable sympathy with the cause of labour and with labour methods of organization, enough to lead to actual electoral co-operation in some instances, as at Dauphin where G. H. Palmer was nominated in a joint farmer and labour convention.[8] Both Liberals and Conservatives attempted, with success in some districts, to prevent, or to secure for themselves, the nomination of farmers' candidates. The opponents of the school legislation of 1916, both French and Ukrainian, attempted to use the farmers' discontent in the same way. The result was confusion worse confounded in the nominating conventions, from which twenty-six farmers' candidates emerged, some with political platforms of extreme simplicity, such as that of the candidate who declared he was "prepared to go to parliament not to follow any leader but to serve what he thinks the common good," and, producing the Bible, affirmed that his platform was the word of God, which ought to be good enough for the province of Manitoba.[9] No issue clarified the campaign, no leader appeared to dominate the new movement in politics. Even the farmers' entry into politics was to a considerable degree a cloak for opposition to the school legislation of 1916. To this chaos in the rural electoral districts was added the intervention of eighteen Labour and Socialist candidates in Winnipeg, Brandon, and Dauphin, in the latter seat, as noted, in alliance with the farmers. Yet even labour was divided between the candidates of the Independent Labour Party and of the O.B.U.

The result of the voting reflected the confusion of the election. The government had twenty-one out of fifty-three candidates returned, to constitute the largest group in the House. The Conservatives elected only seven out of twenty-seven, and their new leader, R. G. Willis, was defeated. The United Farmers elected twelve out of twenty-six, Labour eleven out of eighteen, and there were four Independents. This nominal division of the legislature did not truly reflect its character, as a School Question group was discernible, and the bounds between the Farmers and the Liberals and the Farmers and Labour were indefinite and easily crossed, especially the former. The one clear result was the dissolution of the party system in provincial politics, the outcome of the excessive partisanship of the old parties and of the growth, incoherent and forced, of Manitoban society during the great boom and the Great War.

If in the world of affairs all was turbulence and change, the builders and craftsmen were progressing in orderly fashion to create one stable work of art. While the character of Manitoban politics was being transformed in the election of 1920 the new Legislative Buildings were nearing completion. "The thing of beauty" Premier Roblin had envisaged in 1912 had taken form, by some stroke of fortune, not as just another "state capitol," but as a structure of rare, if unoriginal, grace. The talent of F. W. Simon had produced a neo-classical building which, while true to its type, had a strong claim to be considered functional. North wing and south wing with portico and colonnade now stood completed in clean cut stone, the tapestry limestone from the Tyndall quarry east of Selkirk. The towered dome soared with easy thrust to bear the gilded statue of a heroic youth holding the torch of progress towards the northwest, the quarter of Manitoba's destiny, a statue come to its lofty rest after years of tossing in the ballast of a ship commandeered for war. Within the front portals a low arch gave on the marble cascade of the stairway coming down between two bronze heroic bison striding serenely under the calm eyes of the caryatids, supporting with easy poise the roof of the skylit entrance chamber three stories above. The stairway carried the visitor up beneath the central dome where a Frank Brangwyn battle mural glowed, and on to the Legislative Chamber where the House was to sit at the feet of statues of Moses and of Solon, examples, perhaps, of overwhelming weight. Somehow, out of the corruption and the muddle of its building, the "thing of beauty" had emerged, the fine result of all the plastic arts, a summation of all classical architecture and of the engineering of the day, free of the grossness and sham which made most public buildings of its age a mockery of architecture. Now it stood against the diamond blue Manitoba sky, poised in achieved simplicity and ready to enter into the history of the people whose toil was to pay for its costly rearing.

To the new Legislative Buildings came a strange and incomplete Assembly for the session of 1921. It was strange, for many of its members were new to politics and the legislature, and incomplete because three of its members were still in Stony Mountain penitentiary. Another novelty was the presence of the first woman member of the legislature, Mrs. R. A. Rogers, a leader of her sex and, fittingly, a daughter of Red River. Most novel, however, was the absence of a majority. Manitoba had all unwittingly embarked on an experiment in what was called "group government" from an idea advocated by leaders of the farmers in Alberta and Ontario. The Norris government, supported by twenty-one Liberals, the largest group in the House, continued in office. The next largest group, the U.F.M. members, refused either to join the Norris government or to become the official opposition. Their stand was that it was their function to represent their constituents and to support such legislation as met with their approval. The necessity of maintaining a stable administration was no part of their political philosophy. The Conservatives therefore continued as the official opposition, while the Labour and Independent members skirmished vigorously and noisily as they pleased.

Under these conditions little could be accomplished, and the sessions of 1921 and 1922 were barren of significant legislation. Two resolutions of the session of 1921 are to be noted. The first was moved by A. E. Smith, Labour member for Brandon, that the cabinet should be elected by the groups in the House in proportion to their numbers—this was "group government" fully developed. The motion was defeated only by the casting vote of the Speaker. The second was a resolution, which carried, to abolish the Public Utilities Commission. The government, however, failed to act on the resolution and in 1922 a motion by P. A. Talbot, the opponent of the abolition of bilingual teaching in 1916, and a critic with a personal animus against the Commission, called them to task for it. The government considered the motion as a vote of censure on the passage of which it would resign. Discussions with the Farmers' group failed to win their united support, and the Conservatives, Labour, most of the Farmers, and the anti-school-law members combined to carry the resolution. Norris promptly tendered the resignation of his government, assuming it involved a dissolution of the legislature. But on the insistence of Lieutenant-Governor Sir James Aikins, the Premier and the various groups in the Assembly agreed to complete the essential business of the session.[10] Then the "group" legislature was dissolved and an election called.

The two years of the "group" legislature had been years of uncertainty and agricultural depression. Wheat prices threatened to fall and were maintained only by the Wheat Board. When it was ended in 1921, the prices collapsed. Efforts to revive it failed, but from them was to come the idea of a co-operative wheat pool. In 1921 the American Congress, struggling with the same conditions, passed the Fordney-McCumber tariff act, which stopped the shipment of Canadian cattle into the United States. Cattle prices slumped disastrously. Drought and rust aggravated the hard times. Farmers were caught in the spread between their obligations, many of which were fixed, and falling prices. In the federal election of 1921 their discontent and their break with the old parties was expressed by the election of sixty-five Progressive, or farmer, members of Parliament. In Manitoba twelve of the fifteen federal constituencies returned Progressive candidates. The three Winnipeg seats were shared by one Labour member (J. S. Woodsworth) and two Liberals, one of whom, A. B. Hudson, was known to be sympathetic with the Progressives. The postwar industrial slump began in 1921 and unemployment reappeared. Nor did the hoped-for mining boom in Northern Manitoba begin, despite fresh discoveries and the beginning of interest by American capital in Rice Lake and Flin Flon mines.

Such circumstances it would have been difficult for any provincial government to survive. The Norris government was now, however, discredited as well as weak. To the former charges of extravagance were added charges of waste and mismanagement. The farmers through the U.F.M. began to demand economy; the Winnipeg Board of Trade joined in the criticism, and it was this combination of the two main centres of power in the province, the organized farmers and the commercial interests of Winnipeg, which doomed the Norris government. The farmers knew that power was theirs for the taking; the business interests desired them to take it, because they hoped that a farmers' government would be a conservative and economical one. In these circumstances a change of government was certain and the new government would be both novel and strictly provincial in its aims and ties. "Whatever developments there may be in provincial politics," the *Free Press* remarked editorially when the legislature was dissolved. "they will be in the direction of building up agencies and methods of government that will be purely provincial in character."[11] The provincial old parties were in disrepute and suspect because of their affiliation with the federal parties and their commitments to "politics."

The adoption of a moderate and mildly progressive platform by the U.F M., the organization of its political campaign, and the election of 1922 were in the circumstances formalities. Despite a courageous campaign by Norris, and a new attempt at recovery by the Conservative party under a new leader, F. G. Taylor of Portage, the U.F.M. candidates won the election of 1922, despite the simplicity of their local campaigns and their nomination of only forty candidates. Twenty-seven of these candidates were returned, which, with the deferred elections in the three northern constituencies, gave them a secure majority. Seven Liberals were returned, only Norris and Hon. Robert Jacob among the ministers, six Conservatives, six Labour, and, a continuation of the confusion of 1920, eight Independents. Stability of government had been restored, but party government had been ended in Manitoba.

The election of 1922 was a political divide in Manitoban history. It marked the culmination of the effort to get rid of "politics." It also marked the attempt by a province still predominantly agricultural to find relief from the stresses of rapid change, an exhausting war, and a deep depression by returning to its origins, the rural virtues of thrift, sobriety, and patient labour. Such a return was a partial solution of the troubles of the times, but there remained the great sub-metropolis of Winnipeg with its complex economy and heterogeneous population, the vast north still largely unexplored and unexploited, and a future not likely to be more stable than the past, to challenge the adequacy of those homespun virtues.

16

The End of Farm Pioneering
1923-1930

THE COMING OF THE FARMERS TO POWER IN MANI-
toba was a local response to the world-wide depression which
followed the close of the Great War of 1914. When the immediate needs of a world starved of goods during the years of
war were satisfied, prices fell, factories closed and unemployment
grew in Europe and America. Especially did the prices of farm
produce and raw materials fall, and thus Manitoba was particularly afflicted. After the great expansion of the war years and the
lavish expenditures of the Roblin and the Norris administrations,
the province was forced by its dwindling income to begin a grim
process of retrenchment.

The post-war slump showed itself most forcibly in the fall of
the price of wheat from an average price of $3.19¾ a bushel in
December, 1920, to one of $1.10¾ a bushel in August, 1922; the
purchasing power of a bushel of wheat, by the index of 100 for
1912, was 68.73 in September, 1922. The price was to continue
at unprofitable levels until 1924. Prices of livestock tumbled also,
and indeed prices of all other farm produce turned downwards
at the same time. Not until 1924 was the bottom of the depression
to be reached and passed. Fixed charges, of course, decreased
hardly at all, and the prices of manufactured goods were reduced
more slowly and not as far as the prices of farm produce. The
farmers were caught, therefore, by a severe spread between their
selling and their buying prices; only the well established could
withstand the strain, and none without loss. The new settler,

burdened with debt, was helpless; the farmers on marginal lands in the Interlake and in the southeast were driven to ever more unrewarding toil. To this distress was added the further affliction of dry years and short crops. On the Souris Plains of the southwest, indeed, the years from 1919 to 1923 were years of actual drought, and abandoned farmsteads and deserted fields were a common and a dreary sight over the broad reaches of that shortgrass region. Nature, like the market, was once more, as in the 1880's and 1890's, betraying the farmers who had been lured to the cheap and open lands of the West.

The suffering of the depression fell not only on the farmer. Industrial unemployment rose to hitherto unknown levels in 1921 and 1922. Men tramped the streets of Winnipeg looking for work where none was to be had, and lounged on the street corners in idleness. On the packed new streets of the North End, with their swarms of children and babel of tongues; in all the new suburbs, East and West Kildonan, Elmwood, Norwood, St. James, with their little cottages and luxuriant gardens, there was anxiety and want. All over Manitoba men were realizing bitterly that the new land, the new start in life, and the will to work were not enough.

The entry of the farmers into politics from 1920 to 1922 had been indicative of this realization that the fine promise of the pioneer years, the hope sprung from the new soil and the new start, had been expended and that henceforth the new land was to be burdened with the old issues of human life. The result was a new temper in politics, non-partisan, experimental, pragmatic. It was a new temper in politics only, however, and was limited to politics by the intellectual narrowness of the farmers and the doctrinal blinkers of the Labour men. It did not extend to matters of religion or morality. Manitoban provincial life had been scarcely touched by the intellectual ferment of Europe and the United States. Even the decay of the old tenets of organized religion, though noted and deplored, went on without its implications being grasped by public or pulpit. Thus when a new and native author, Martha Ostenso, published in 1922 a novel, *Wild Geese*, a graceful and promising story of the Interlake, but touched by the new realism, it caused a mild scandal and much shocked discussion in communities, a record of the life of any one of which would have revealed true stories of the same kind. When Miss Ostenso eloped with Douglas Durkin, author of *The Lobstick Trail* and *The Heart of Cherry McBain* (stories of some authenticity of the northern Manitoba frontier) but also a married man, the scandal seemed to be confirmed. But perhaps the flight was symbolic of their rejection by a community which, though driven to strike out in new ways in politics, remained fast wedded to the old ways in manners and morals.

The new government reflected at once the new temper and the continuing instability of Manitoban life. It was new and inexperienced, and rested on the support of the farmers' representatives who, until the northern seats were filled, made up only half the legislature. The United Farmers had deliberately kept political organization to a minimum, had fought the election without a leader, and had nominated candidates who were bound only to support the platform of the U.F.M. and to represent their constituents. When the Norris government submitted its resignation, the new "group" had to choose a leader who would form an administration. Before the election three men had been mentioned as possible leaders; Colin H. Burnell, president of the U.F.M., George F. Chipman, editor of the *Grain Growers' Guide*, and John Bracken, president of the Manitoba Agricultural College. Burnell, however, failed to obtain nomination as a candidate; the able and idealistic Chipman was defeated in Winnipeg; only Bracken, who had taken no part in the election, remained with prestige unimpaired. A caucus of the U.F.M. candidates unanimously decided to approach Bracken, who accepted their invitation to form the first farmers' government in Manitoba.

In choosing John Bracken as leader the farmers revealed at once their determination to be led by one of their own kind and their sense of the need of a new beginning in politics. Bracken had been reared on an Ontario farm and was a graduate of the Ontario College of Agriculture. He had spent his brief professional career in Saskatchewan and Manitoba, where he made a name for himself as an authority on dry farming and as a scientist sympathetic with the actual difficulties of farming. He had no experience of politics; indeed, he now admitted that he had never cast a vote. Young, intense, and direct, this good-looking and simple-mannered man embodied that union of moral simplicity and applied science for which rural Manitoba craved. That his intellectual range was little wider, the abrupt limits of his interests almost as narrow as those of the people he had undertaken to lead, were in themselves qualifications for his new post.

Equally new to government, if not to political life, was the government Premier Bracken formed. Only Hon. W. R. Clubb, Minister of Public Works, had sat in the legislature before, and he only from 1920 to 1922. The government was fortunate in having an able lawyer available for the office of Attorney-General, R. W. Craig, K.C, who had been elected as a Progressive in Winnipeg, and a man of financial training, F. M. Black, for the office of Provincial Treasurer. It was this fund of ability and the grinding labour of the new Premier which was to carry the first Bracken ministry over its obstacles and to enable it to avoid the pitfalls of inexperience and incompetence which were to ruin the farmers' government in Ontario and give that of Alberta a bad start.

That a new administration could have been toppled by a united and resolute opposition was plain to everyone. The opposition groups, however, were neither united nor resolute. The Liberals, though somewhat bitter at being displaced by men with whom they differed not at all on policy, were not disposed to be actively unfriendly. Labour, which at first had some hope of establishing certain bonds of co-operation with the new administration, was not otherwise hopeful of obtaining power, and was content to co-operate so long as the interests of its supporters were not in question. The Conservatives, the ablest group in the House despite the defeat of their leader, R. G. Willis, were more critical, were more disposed to keep alive the tension of the party system, and were in fact the opposition, a position the Liberals nominally occupied. Of the eight Independents five remained independent, one joining the government supporters and two the Conservatives.

In fact, political independence was an easy role for any member to maintain in the new legislature. It was made plain by the new administration at the beginning that government was not to be by party, group, or class but, so far as honest difference of opinion allowed, by co-operation and the open meeting of minds. The Speech from the Throne referred pointedly to the desirability of proceeding with the business of the House "in the spirit of united citizenship," and affirmed the government's "obligations to the whole people of Manitoba."[1] The Premier declared in his opening speech: "We are not here to play politics or to represent a single class, but to get down to the serious business of giving this province an efficient government, and in that task we will welcome all the co-operation offered to us from the opposite side of the House."[2] In this spirit the new session opened and proceeded, and it was the spirit which was to govern Manitoban politics in the years ahead. Certain at least of the old animosities dissolved; the election of P. A. Talbot as Speaker and the later admission of Albert Prefontaine to the Executive Council marked the disappearance of the School Question from the foreground of Manitoban politics. The farmers' movement offered the French representatives a haven from the party divisions and personal antagonisms of 1916 and gave them a means of joining in the government of their province without loss of their identity. The same fundamental principle of local representation by local men was later to bring Ukrainians into the main stream of Manitoban political life.

The new spirit actually produced a new method of government at once flexible and lasting. A strict adherence to the doctrines of cabinet responsibility would probably have brought the administration down before the term of the legislature expired. A strict adherence to the doctrine of cabinet solidarity was in fact impossible, because of the U.F.M. insistence on the responsibility of members, including members of the Executive Council, to their constituents. The result was necessarily a free resort, to which the outlook of the ministers disposed them before-hand, to the device of declaring issues before the House "open" ones, on which members might vote as they pleased. The practice had, of course, been common in Parliament before the rise of rigidly organized democratic parties. The outstanding instance in the new legislature was the vote on the Wheat Board in the first session of 1923. The reaction of the organized farmers of Saskatchewan and Alberta to the falling price of wheat had been to demand the re-establishment of the Wheat Board. In Manitoba, where the harvest was earlier and the grain moved soon enough to get the best of the new crop prices, the farmers were divided on the issue. Parliament in 1922 passed an Act to re-establish the Board for a year, provided the three grain-growing provinces passed enabling acts to make the constitutionality of the legislation secure. The legislatures of Saskatchewan and Alberta complied. Everything then depended on the deeply divided legislature of Manitoba. Premier Bracken, though a majority of his Council favoured the Wheat Board bill, declined to make it a government measure. It was introduced by a private member and defeated by a vote of twenty-four to twenty-one. Three members of the Executive Council voted against the bill, the rest for. Such procedure was a striking refusal to follow the conventions of party and responsible government, but it did exemplify the new spirit in Manitoban politics. The effect, of course, was to reduce the legislature to an office of record of constituency opinion, and to divide the power hitherto vested in the Crown and the legislature between the Executive Council and the electoral districts of rural Manitoba. Grass roots democracy, first articulate in the demand for direct legislation, had prevailed by making the representative a delegate of his constituency and by making the Executive Council a composite committee responding rather to the direct voice of the constituencies than to the collective opinion of the representative assembly.

Whether a government, following the new procedure, could be defeated in the legislature, was a question, perhaps a purely theoretical one. It is to be presumed that an explicit vote of want of confidence would have led to the resignation of the cabinet. But it was soon apparent that the Bracken government was as secure in the face of the inability of the other groups to combine to defeat it as it was rendered immune to defeat by its refusal to impose a party line and risk division and defeat on a major issue.

Such were the first revealed characteristics of the new government as it faced the session of 1923. The new men and the new spirit, however, had to face the old issues. The depression had deepened and the deficit had increased between the change of government and the meeting of the new legislature. The deficit for nine months of 1922 had been $1,346,182; in 1922–3 it was $901,069. The deficit had been caused by the costly reforms of the Norris government, its slowness in economizing, its inability to impose new taxation. The demand for new services, particularly roads, had been insistent and had not been resisted. Urban and rural municipalities were heavily in debt and unable in many instances to meet their obligations despite heavy taxation. Many school districts were in difficulties and some insolvent.

To the ungrateful task of economy the new administration addressed itself resolutely. Expenditures were reduced, even on Mothers' Allowances and education. Civil servants were dismissed and not replaced. As it was not possible, however, to balance the budget only by reducing expenditures, recourse to higher taxation was necessary. A provincial income tax, estimated to produce a million dollars in the next year, was included in the budget of 1923, despite frantic protests by the business community of Winnipeg, which had expected retrenchment but not a provincial income tax from the farmers' government. It was, of course, easy for a farmers' government to impose such a tax, because of the notorious difficulty of collecting income tax from farmers. At the same time the tax on gasoline was increased, with the result that reduced expenditures and increased taxes promised to bring the budget into balance in 1925, if not before. And concurrently, the first steps were taken towards the reduction of the Municipal Commissioners Levy, a tax on land, which were to lead to its eventual abolition. A farmers' government was determined, and rightly determined, to shift the onus of taxation from land to income, and the first budget of 1923 set the pattern of provincial taxation for the coming years.

These sharp and painful measures revealed the character of the new administration sharply. It was a government devoted to economy, and its concept of economy was the simple one of reduction of expenditures. But its heritage from the Norris government was not only one of debt. There was also the reform legislation on education and social welfare which was the finer achievement of the Norris government. This the Bracken administration maintained, even when enforcing economies and so perpetuated the reform movement of the years before 1923. The experimental agricultural finance legislation of the Norris administration, however, could not be dealt with so simply. The various acts authorizing loans to farmers for purchase of livestock had simply to be terminated, with a total indebtedness of the province of $360,000. There were, too, a number of agencies, set up to administer particular acts, which had got into difficulties and were adding deficit to deficit. The chief of these were the Rural Credits Societies, a direct governmental responsibility since 1920, the Farm Loans Board, the Joint Industrial Council, and the Manitoba Power Commission. The Rural Credits Societies had been slackly administered and diverted from their original purpose of giving only small loans for immediately productive purposes.[3] The depression had placed an irresistible strain on the credit of the Societies. After an enquiry by a Royal Commission, they were reorganized and their commitments reduced. The Farm Loans Board had already adopted a policy of refusing most applications for loans and of deferring collection of repayments where hardship would have resulted in enforcement. The Joint Industrial Council was abolished on the grounds of expense, an action which showed a certain disposition not to sympathize with the real needs of labour, as did the defeat of a bill introduced by John Queen to make peaceful picketing legal. The expansion of the Power Commission's lines was slowed down, and every effort made to diminish its deficits. But the Bracken administration was left

responsible for these well-intentioned but costly undertakings
of its predecessor, which bore heavily on its budgets and might,
if bad times continued or recurred, become even heavier.

Still another heritage from the Norris government was the
liquor question, which neither the abolition of the bar in 1916
nor the introduction of prohibition in 1920 had ended. The wise
doubt of Roblin and other experienced administrators as to whether
a law could be enforced against the belief and desires of any considerable minority had been justified. Prohibition had led to home
brewing of liquor and its illegal sale by bootleggers on a scale the
police and courts could not suppress. The integrity of the police
force and public respect for law were indeed seriously threatened
by the evil. As a result the Moderation League, which had resisted prohibition, had grown in strength and in 1923 its petition
for a plebiscite on the proposal to introduce government sale of
liquor and for one on the sale of beer and wine was granted by
the legislature. The plebiscite on government sale was favourable
by a vote of 107,609 to 68,879. That on the sale of beer and wine
resulted in a rejection of the proposal by a vote of 63,601 to
20,463, which revealed that public opinion in Manitoba was prepared to leave the private use of liquor to taste or conscience, but
would not yet accept a return to its public sale and use. (In 1928,
however, the public sale of beer was to be legalized.) A Government Liquor Control Act was passed in a special session of the
Legislature, and a Government Liquor Commission set up to
administer the purchase and sale of liquor in the province. The
profits were to be paid into the consolidated fund of the province,
and soon became a major item of provincial revenue. This un-
anticipated result of the attempt to regulate private conduct by
legislation, though it made everyone in Manitoba a party to the
liquor trade, did attempt to strike a compromise, however awkward, between the excesses of the old bars and the moderate use
of drink as a stimulant.

The remaining major issue of 1923 was the plight of the schools
and the cost of higher education. In the field of education the
Norris government had done much. It had put the School Question on a new and tolerable basis; it had, by firm and tactful

administration through official trustees, extended the school system into the new districts of foreign settlement. One of its failures had been the exodus of those Old Church Mennonites who refused to accept the School Act of 1916 and in 1921 and 1922 migrated to Mexico to preserve their Bible schools and teaching in Low German. Another, not wholly to be attributed to the government, was the failure to settle the question of an adequate site for the University. It was the Norris government's successes, however, which had increased the provincial grants to education fourfold. Now both the province and the weakened school districts were in financial distress. The University was painfully overcrowded on the Broadway site, despite the erection of temporary buildings, and the Agricultural College, burdened by the overhead costs of its grandiose building, was costing heavily for each student trained.

In 1923 the Premier, as Minister of Education, had a Royal Commission under President W. C. Murray of the University of Saskatchewan enquire into the plight of public and secondary education and the adaptation of the curriculum to the rural school, and study the means of co-ordinating the institutions of higher education in the province. The report of the Commission on public and secondary education revealed a startling situation. One hundred and four schools out of some twelve hundred were entirely closed. Many of the remainder were open for only part of the school year of two hundred days. The root of the trouble was the small school district and the flat provincial grant, which made it impossible to use the resources of rich districts with high assessments to aid poor districts with low assessments and high tax rates to keep their schools open, or to base the provincial grant on need. The Commission recommended special provincial grants, the use of larger school units, and an equalized assessment to bring taxation into a tolerable relation with the productivity of the soil.[4] In the face of the strong prejudice in favour of the small district and local control of the school, and the stringency of the provincial revenues little could be done to carry out the recommendations at the time, and they were to remain largely a programme for the Department of Education to carry out as opportunity offered. The further recommendations of the Commission as to agricultural education in the rural schools were so slight and inconclusive, as of necessity they had to be, that they failed to furnish the sugar which might have coated the pill of larger units and a wider tax base.

The report of the Commission on the University was separate and in part consisted of a report, which the Commission approved, by Dr. W. S. Learned of the Carnegie Foundation. The reports frankly exposed the neglect of the University by the province in the past, a neglect only in part palliated by the war and the differences of opinion within the University. They also pointed out the heavy costs and the dangerous academic isolation of the Agricultural College. Dr. Learned's frank amazement at the neglect of the University by the government and public was only saved from being scathing by his obvious admiration of the achievement of the University under the handicaps it suffered. The Commission found clearly against the continued physical separation of the University and the Agricultural College. It recommended their amalgamation on the St. Vital, or Fort Garry, site, with the College becoming the Faculty of Agriculture of the University. It looked forward to the eventual association of the affiliated colleges with the University on their own sites at the new campus. While the Commission made it clear that it was led to this conclusion by the need of spreading the enormous overhead costs of the Agricultural College over the whole University, it also argued that the academic benefits would be considerable, particularly for the Faculty of Agriculture.[5] Again, the recommendations could not be fully carried out, as a considerable body of opinion in Winnipeg still favoured the removal of the University to Tuxedo, while the provincial budget could not allow the undertaking of the necessary new buildings on the Fort Garry site. Again, however, a programme had been laid down and a first step was taken when in 1925 the Agricultural College was made the Faculty of Agriculture in the University of Manitoba.

What the report of the Murray Commission on public and secondary schools had actually revealed was that the broad limits of agricultural settlement in Manitoba had been reached and overrun by 1922. Much of the breakdown of the school system, much of the rural distress and urban unemployment, were caused by the settlement of late comers, whether immigrants or soldier settlers, on marginal and sub-marginal lands. These lands, costly to clear and of low fertility, might afford a living when farm prices were high. In the depression of 1921 to 1924, hundreds of settlers were foreclosed or starved out, farms were abandoned and schools closed. The depression had revealed that the era of agricultural settlement in southern Manitoba, except for special areas and in special circumstances, was ended. The great land rush which had begun in 1871 had closed after ebbing and flowing for half a century. By the improvement of its agriculture on lands already settled and the development of new resources and new industries was Manitoba to thrive in the future. But it would do so bearing the cost, financial and social, of having allowed settlers to push onto the water-logged slopes of the Shield, into the Interlake and the bush and marsh west of Lakes Manitoba and Winnipegosis. In 1927 R. W. Murchie and H. C. Grant's *Survey of the Unused Lands of Manitoba* was to make explicit this revelation of the Murray Commission.

By 1923 the depression had run its course and in 1924 the upswing began. Farm prices, especially those of coarse grains, rose; the number of unemployed decreased. The revival was part of a world-wide movement, which by the following year was confirmed. The Pact of Locarno created the illusion of stability in Europe; the boom the illusion of permanent prosperity in the United States. In Manitoba the strained economy was relieved, for, although the crop of 1924 was not much better than that of 1923, the rise in prices almost doubled its value. The farmers could once more take hope. The provincial budget for 1924 yielded the first of the surpluses of the Bracken administration, the fruit of the severe economies and taxation of 1923.

Not all farmers were looking only to rising prices to restore prosperity. Many Manitoban farmers, though not as great a proportion as those of Saskatchewan and Alberta, had put their faith in a new method of marketing, co-operative marketing by means of a "pool." This method had been tested successfully by tobacco growers in Kentucky and orange growers in California. The idea was taken up in Canada in 1921 and 1922. The defeat of the Wheat Board by the Legislature of Manitoba left the pool a clear field, and in 1923 the farmers' organizations approved its trial. A great campaign was launched in the three provinces to sign up enough farmers to contract to deliver their wheat to provincial pools in 1923. Aaron Sapiro, an American lawyer who had served the American pools, was brought to speak in support of the drive. His evangelistic fervour acquainted thousands of western farmers with the idea that the old law of supply and demand could be replaced by co-operative marketing, a heady doctrine for men who had come to believe that the price of wheat was determined by speculation on the Grain Exchange. What the pool offered, of course, was the possibility that the farmer might receive the average price for wheat in any crop year rather than the price at the moment he sold, and that he, not the speculator, assumed the risk of fluctuation.[6] Only Alberta formed a pool for the 1923 crop, but in 1924 pools were formed in Saskatchewan and Manitoba and a Central Selling Agency set up. Forty per cent of Manitoba's farmers signed contracts to deliver their wheat to the Pool, the Manitoba Co-operative Wheat Producers, Limited, which was organized in locals and administered by an elected directorate and executive officers. As such it was a notable experiment in economic democracy. It was co-operative in that all wheat delivered was "pooled" by grade and sold together. On delivery to the elevator the Pool farmer received an initial payment, set for each crop year in view of world market conditions, and such further payments as the returns from the sale of that year's pool permitted; these further payments were made before seeding and harvest to meet the expenses of those seasons. Such was the plan which had been adopted with such speed, a speed made possible only by the great body of experience in co-operative action that the organized farmers had developed over the past twenty years. And the Pools were mercifully aided by the continuing rise in farm prices.

Many Manitoban farmers, however, continued to believe that the free market was more in the interest of the farmer than a Wheat Board, or a Wheat Pool. Wheat also was losing its old dominant part in the Manitoban farm economy. The history of Manitoban farming in these years is not so much the history of the rise of the Wheat Pool as one of ever more diversified farming, though the change was to bring about the organization of a coarse grain Pool. The soils of Manitoba were losing their virgin fertility and commercial fertilizer was as yet little used. The now mellow fields were infested with sow thistles, couch grass, wild oats, and other noxious weeds to the point where cleaning the land became a major concern of the farmer. Crop rotation promised to do this more profitably than the sequence of fallow and wheat. The low price of wheat forced attention on other crops, which promised better returns through higher prices or cheaper cultivation. Barley, especially new varieties promoted by the skill and devoted work of T. J. Harrison of the Manitoba Agricultural College, provided the major alternative, until in 1926 the total yield of barley was almost equal to the total yield of wheat. But rye, flax, and fodder grasses became more important year by year. As always in times of depression, farmers turned to dairying and poultry raising and the output from these occupations rose. The Manitoban farmer, accustomed to deal only in lordly wheat, now learned many new skills, and came to respect the lowly egg and the ever hungry hog.[7] Even honey, the sweet yield of long northern days and lime-fed flowers, began to become a staple product of some Manitoban farms. In the drought area of the southwest, the Durum wheats replaced the bread wheats, and kept many of the sore-tried farmers of the Souris Plains on their farms.

Other changes in agriculture were stopped or delayed by the prevailing depression. The marked increase in the number of tractors and power machines, which the last years of the war boom had witnessed, stopped after 1921. The number fell during the twenties, as machines wore out and were not replaced, and the farm horse, fed by fodder grown on the farm, came into his own again. The new farm machines, the threshing combine and the new cultivators, came into use but slowly, as farmers strove to keep their costs down and repaired the old machinery; it was the day of hay wire and the handy man.

It was not only agriculture, however, that was being diversified.

The whole economy of the province was beginning to respond to the great facts of the end of agricultural settlement and the opening of the northern frontier. It was the whole economy that was to be diversified, and perhaps the most signal instance of this was the rise of the mining industry.* Actual mining at the Maundy Mine had stopped with the fall in base metal prices, but prospecting continued. By 1925 development had begun at Rice Lake in the Central Manitoba gold fields, and diamond drilling on the sulphide ores of the Flin Flon. The known deposits at Herb Lake, Schist Lake, and Cold Lake in The Pas mineral area still awaited rising prices to stimulate their development. By 1926 interest had become so great that the legislature approved a provincial guarantee for a branch of the Hudson's Bay Railway to Flin Flon. A railway would mean the beginning of large-scale development. But northern transport had already developed methods sufficient for initial development or temporary exploitation in the sleigh "swing," a train of sleighs pulled over frozen muskeg and lake by horses or caterpillar tractors, a development of the lumber industry, and in "bush flying," an outcome of the Great War. The airplane, equipped with pontoons for summer flying and skis for winter, was revealing itself as endlessly adaptable in the northern bush for prospecting, aerial photographing, and transporting of men and materials. In 1920 F. H. Ellis and H. Dougall made one of the first strictly commercial flights in northern flying in a flight from Winnipeg to The Pas. By 1926 the daring experiments of the first bush pilots had so proved the value of the airplane in the north that James A. Richardson of Winnipeg brought the wealth of the grain trade to support the new venture, and formed Western Canada Airways Incorporated.[8]

The forests and rivers of Northern Manitoba were to contribute their wealth to the province as well as the mines. The old lumber industry of Lake Winnipeg and The Pas continued to saw the spruce timber of those regions. It was, however, a minor and dwindling industry in Manitoba, whose forests of mixed stands were better adapted to exploitation by the great forest industry of central Canada, the manufacture of pulp and paper. In the early twenties the industry became interested in entering Mani-

toba. Despite the efforts of J. D. McArthur of Winnipeg to establish the first pulp mill in Manitoba, the federal government in
1925 granted timber berths on Lake Winnipeg to the Manitoba
Pulp and Paper Company, a subsidiary of the Backus interests
which then dominated the power and paper industries of northern Minnesota and northwestern Ontario. The company opened
a pulp mill at Pine Falls on the Winnipeg River in 1926 and in
1927 the first Manitoba paper was used by the provincial press.

The Pine Falls plant was driven by electrical power supplied
by the Manitoba Power Company, a subsidiary of the Winnipeg
Electric. The industrial demand for power had once raised the
question of how the waterpower of the Winnipeg River was to be
developed. The Manitoba Power Company in 1923 had added
the Great Falls power plant to its original plant at Pinawa. The
Winnipeg City Hydro, nearing the full use of power developed
at Pointe du Bois in 1911, was looking to the newly begun development of Slave Falls for its future needs. The next great
source of power on the Winnipeg was the Seven Sisters Falls,
and in 1925 both the provincial government, looking to the future
of the Manitoba Power Commission, and the Manitoba Power
Company, in view of the rising demand for industrial power in
Winnipeg, applied to the federal government for a lease of the
power site.

The development of more hydro-electric power was becoming
urgent, not only because forestry and mining industries would
require it, but also because industrial growth was beginning again
in Winnipeg. In 1925 the Manitoba Industrial Development Board
was set up to survey the possibilities of growth and to encourage
the investment of capital in manufacturing, especially of industries supplementary to agriculture. A sugar beet factory was proposed and a company was formed, though no further action followed. By 1927 the Board could report that there were in Greater
Winnipeg 437 plants engaged in 43 branches of manufacturing.
Of the 437, 38 had been opened in 1926.

The growth of industry and the consequent pressure for the
development of new power sites, particularly that of Seven Sisters, in turn brought up the old question of the transfer of the

natural resources of Manitoba to the province. Attempts by the Norris government in 1918 to bring the transfer about had failed by 1920. The obstacles encountered were twofold, the claims of the other provinces for compensation if the Prairie Provinces were given their public lands, and the claims of the three provinces for compensation for the alienation of public lands, in the instance of Manitoba, since 1870. In 1922 the new Liberal government at Ottawa made a fresh start by a resolution of the House of Commons accepting the principle that the western provinces must be given control of their natural resources if they were to have equality within Confederation, and proposing that, if the transfer could not be arranged by direct negotiation, differences should be submitted to arbitration. The Bracken government accepted the resolution, but direct negotiations failed. Manitoba declined to accept the chances of arbitration, and the question of transfer remained in suspense. The request of the province in 1924 that the administration of the School Lands Fund, the invested proceeds of the sale of the school sections in each township, should be transferred to the province was refused. The Department of the Interior, however, now followed the practice of consulting the provincial government before alienating any more natural resources. In consequence, the provincial government had the deciding voice in the decision as to whether the Seven Sisters power site should be developed by the Power Commission or the Manitoba Power Company.

Before the difficulties which encumbered the transfer of natural resources were to be resolved, however, and the provincial government brought face to face with the necessity of a final decision with respect to the development of Seven Sisters, Manitoba was to play a considerable role in federal politics and the development of Canadian nationalism. Manitoba was a mid-western province. The dominance of Ontario-bred men in its public life and the metropolitan character of Winnipeg ensured that, while it shared the strong sectional sentiment of western Canada, it was also sensitive to national feeling and interest. Many Manitobans, like most western Canadians, resented certain national policies, such as the protective tariff, which benefited central Canada directly, but not the West. Yet many perceived or sensed that Manitoba and particularly Winnipeg throve as part of a national economy. When some sentiment for secession from Confederation developed in the West at the depth of the agricultural depression, its expression was firmly suppressed by public opinion in Manitoba. In the farmers' revolt of 1921, the majority of the Manitoban Progressives had regarded themselves as advanced Liberals engaged in a protest against the domination of the Liberal party by powerful influences in central Canada. Only one or two of them shared the strong sectional and non-partisan views of the extreme Progressives, notably of the U.F.A. representatives of Alberta. It was in part by the efforts of the Manitoban Progressives and their numerous allies among the Saskatchewan Progressives that the first King government was kept in office, and it was commonly considered by outsiders that their ultimate destiny would be absorption by the Liberal party. There can be little doubt that the Manitoban leaders of the federal Progressives, Hon. T. A. Crerar and Robert Forke, shared this view, though they could have accepted absorption only on terms.

In consequence of this difference over the nature and future of the Progressive movement, the movement was divided and lost its force. Whereas sixty-five Progressives were elected in 1921, in 1925 only twenty-four were returned. In Manitoba it proved impossible, because of old loyalties and personal rivalries, to bring Progressives and Liberals together, with the result that seven Conservatives, one Liberal, and only seven Progressives in place of the eleven of 1921 were returned. It was in this Parliament, during the session of 1926, that the "constitutional crisis" occurred, the effect of which, with the outcome of the preceding election, was to prepare the way for a Liberal-Progressive alliance in a number of Manitoban constituencies. In the election of 1926 Manitoba returned one Labour member, four Liberals, four Progressives, and seven Liberal-Progressives. The Liberals and Liberal-Progressives of Saskatchewan and Manitoba in effect constituted the parliamentary majority of the Liberal party from 1926 to 1930, and practically restored the national two-party system after the great breach of 1921. It was inevitable in such circumstances that the representations of Manitoban members should be influential, and that the West should be able to have its views taken into account in the making of national policy.

The contribution of Manitoba to national politics and the growth of national sentiment was greater and more subtle than an examination of party politics would indicate. These years saw the growth of the national and international reputation of John W. Dafoe, the editor of the *Manitoba Free Press*. The hard-hitting partisan of the first decade of the century, the bitter foe of the Roblin Conservatives, had been changed by the defeat of reciprocity, the Great War, and the Union Government into a journalist-statesman of broad views and more than partisan loyalties. The old Grit would often out, but Dafoe and his paper, strongly supported by the proprietor, Sir Clifford Sifton, became the advocates, not only of progressive liberal policies, but more especially of the development of a Canadian nation, autonomous in the British Empire and an active member of the League of Nations. This Manitoban voice became one heard with respect in Ottawa and abroad, and the course the Manitoban Progressives followed in 1926 was that which Dafoe had counselled. In particular, Dafoe was influential in shaping the tactics of the Liberal party in the crisis of 1926, and he made the long-prevalent but misleading Liberal interpretation of that crisis particularly his own. He acted as a militant partisan, not as a constitutional purist, and helped to twist events, which threatened to destroy the federal Liberals, to serve the immediate ends of the Liberal party and of the Liberal version of Canadian nationalism. But partisan tactics need not determine constitutional convention. The Liberal-Progressive victory in that year, hardly won in the face of the great embarrassment of the Customs Scandal, was in great part a victory for Canadian national sentiment, and a factor contributing to the Balfour Declaration of the Imperial Conference of 1926, by which the Dominions were declared to be autonomous members of a British Commonwealth of Nations. And the victory led not only to the definition of the Commonwealth of Nations but to the healing of the divisions within Canada which conscription in 1917 and the farmers' revolt in 1921 had caused.

In the new conditions and the new atmosphere it was possible to proceed with the work of re-establishing the harmony of Confederation. A Dominion-provincial conference was held in Ottawa in 1927. To this conference Manitoba made an indirect contribution in the founding in Winnipeg in September, 1925, of the Canadian League, a group of able and liberal men from across Canada and among whom Dafoe was a major influence.[9] The League advanced a proposal for a method of amending the constitution of Canada by Canadian action, a matter of concern now that the Imperial Conference of 1926 had made the full legislative sovereignty of Canada only a matter of removing the vestigial restrictions. To the conference the government of Manitoba had two less fundamental but important proposals to submit. One, a particular theme of Premier Bracken then and thereafter, was that in view of the growing responsibilities of the provinces for services of a national character and of their narrowly limited fields of taxation, a new delimitation of federal and provincial taxing powers be undertaken, with an increase of provincial subsidies by 10 per cent of the customs and excise duties. The other was that the transfer of its public lands be carried out.

The views on constitutional amendment formulated by the Canadian League did not prevail, as a similar proposal by the federal government was rejected by Ontario and Quebec on the ground that Confederation was a compact and that any change in the constitution must receive the assent of every province. None the less, the broadly national views of the Manitoba nationalists were made known and became the continuing attitude of the province. The delimitation of federal and provincial taxing powers, unhappily, was not undertaken at that time, but the maritime and central provinces withdrew the claims they had made for compensation in 1918 if the natural resources were to be returned to the western provinces.[10] When in the next year Manitoba itself accepted arbitration of the financial settlement of its claims for Manitoban lands alienated by the federal government, the way was clear for the ending of the long controversy and the admission of Manitoba to equal status in the Confederation of a sovereign nation.

By a happy coincidence, the year 1927 was the sixtieth year of Confederation, and the celebration of the Diamond Jubilee in the province did much to confirm the new sentiment of a Canadian nationhood in which all might share. The patriotic teaching of the tattered textbooks in weather-beaten schools, the labours of many teachers, all the shy pride of a taciturn northern race, came to the surface in that year, and the sectionalism of 1921, with the exaggerated provincialism which had accompanied it, were put behind. There seemed to be some reason for pride and some relaxation of tension. The grim years of war were behind, recollected though they were year by year at the memorials in every little town on Remembrance Day. The hard times and the dry years of the early twenties were behind also, though they had left their marks on stooped shoulders, unpainted houses, and the drab streets of the Winnipeg slums. But crops were good again and prices fair, and the world boom of the late twenties was lifting the Manitoban economy also.

It was in these easing circumstances that the provincial general election of 1927 was held. The manifesto issued by Premier Bracken called for a balanced development of agriculture, the secondary industries, and natural resources, the business management of public utilities, and the reorganization of the social welfare and educational agencies of the province. On this platform twenty-nine supporters of the government were returned. The more noteworthy result of the election was the revival of the Conservative party, which, under the steady leadership of F. G. Taylor of Portage la Prairie, elected fifteen members. The Liberals won seven seats and Labour only three, with one Independent. With a secure majority, the Bracken government could now face the easier task, after a successful administration in hard times, of governing a province with an economy in boom.

The boom of the late twenties was an industrial boom which became a speculative one, and it affected agriculture less than industry. None the less, the farmers enjoyed comparative prosperity. The wheat crop of 1927 was badly rusted, but barley and livestock helped to keep farm income up. That year saw 174,762 cattle sold by Manitoban farmers, a record number up to that time. The farmer was reaping the reward of diversification. In 1928 came one of the West's great crops; in Manitoba wheat yielded 52,383,000 bushels, oats 53,376,000, and barley 52,569,000. Mortgages were lifted, houses painted, cars bought. The horse and buggy now rarely rattled by on the road, and on Saturday nights the streets of the towns were jammed with farm-ers' cars.

Rough as rural Manitoban roads still were, they afforded pas-sage to the ubiquitous and irresistible Model T Ford and even to more pretentious cars. The rural municipalities from 1918 to 1921 and again after 1924 had been busily improving their mar-ket roads and participating in the Good Roads programme. Miles of graded earth roads led into every market town, and concrete bridges replaced the old plank and pile ones. The provincial government aided in the construction of the highways brought under the Good Roads Act. In 1925 certain highways, that south from Selkirk to the border and that west from Winnipeg to Portage, Brandon, and the Saskatchewan line, were declared trunk highways and taken under provincial jurisdiction. This was the beginning of the provincial highway system, which in 1928–30 was extended eastward by Beausejour and Whitemouth to the Ontario border. Provincial road construction was thereafter to be a steady process, pushed as a public work in time of depression and to meet public insistence on better communications in time of boom.

It was elsewhere than in rural Manitoba, however, that the boom was most evident. At long last the north was to realize some of the eager hopes of 1912. In the election of 1926 the Liberal party had pledged itself to complete the Hudson's Bay Railway, unfinished since 1917. In 1927 the rehabilitation of the line laid in 1914–17 was begun. After investigation by an English engi-neer, F. Palmer, the terminus of the line was changed from Port Nelson, an open roadstead, to Churchill, a natural harbour, and in 1928 construction of the line to that port began. Manitoba was returning to the scenes of its first beginnings. The same year saw the construction of a line to the Flin Flon mine, and the building of the new town of Flin Flon. In 1929 a cyanide and a flotation plant were begun, to extract the complex ores of the mine. The Mandy copper mine was reopened and work on the Sherritt Gordon mine at Cold Lake was begun. In the Central Manitoba field, gold was being produced, and the mineral output of the province, metallic and non-metallic, was placed at $4,925,403. The output of the mines was now making a small but appreciable addition to provincial income.

The growth of manufacturing was quickening also. In 1927 fifty-six new industries began in Manitoba. The needle trades of Winnipeg, based on the cheap labour of the North End, were becoming notable, while the packing plants of St. Boniface, based on cheap labour also and the flow of cattle from the increasingly diversified agriculture, grew both in number and in size. Though there was reason to believe that the industrial growth of Manitoba was not all that might have been expected—Winnipeg, for example, was not keeping pace with Montreal, Toronto, or Vancouver—it was diversifying the economy of the province. In 1928, W. H. Carter, president of the Industrial Development Board, claimed that for the first time in the history of the province the value of industrial production exceeded that of agricultural production, a significant claim even when allowance is made for the fact that the major industries of Manitoba were still those engaged in processing farm products.

This industrial expansion increased the demand for power and made it necessary to decide the manner in which the Seven Sisters power site should be developed. The provincial government in 1928 called Dr. T. A. Hogg of the Ontario Hydro-Electric Power Commission to advise them. The Hogg Report, in March, 1928, declared it would be uneconomical to develop the site under public ownership and recommended that the site be leased to a private company. The government, thereupon, without informing or consulting the legislature, entered into a contract with the Northwestern Power Company and the Winnipeg Electric Company, whereby the power companies would develop the site and supply the Manitoba Power Commission with up to 30,000 horse power a year for thirty years at a price of $13.80 the horse power.

That the decision was a wise and proper one, in the short run at least, there seems little reason to doubt. The province was still heavily in debt, and encumbered with a number of costly provincial enterprises. The heavy borrowing which the building of the plant and transmission lines would involve would have been a major addition to the provincial debt, even if one incurred for productive purposes. The bargain driven with the Winnipeg Electric Company was a shrewd one, in view of that Company's need of more power. The needs of the Manitoba Power Commission, still largely confined to supplying light and power to rural towns because of the reluctance of farmers to incur the initial charges of electrical installations, were taken care of for many years at rates which were then most moderate.

The contract, however, provoked a loud and sustained public outcry, which in fact proclaimed that hydro-electric power had become as sensitive an element in Manitoban politics as railways and freight rates once had been. The objections to the contract were two. One was that the principle of public ownership had been repudiated. This, of course, was true, at least for the thirty-year period. The Bracken government and the organized farmers had a certain predisposition in favour of public ownership, but it was not a principle to which the government or its supporters were pledged. In its strictly pragmatic way, the government had considered public ownership first and had then set it aside because of its estimated cost. This objection came from the supporters of the Winnipeg Hydro, notably the Labour party, who were, of course, convinced advocates of the public ownership of power and prepared to pay a price to see their principle upheld. An attempt to have the Winnipeg Hydro acquire the Seven Sisters site was defeated in the City Council, however, and public interest was diverted to the second objection.

This, in its way, was more formidable and certainly more sensational. It consisted of charges made in July, 1928, by F. G. Taylor, leader of the Conservative party, that the contract had been entered into improperly, both because the legislature had not been consulted and because the Winnipeg Electric Company had been unduly favoured. The contract, Taylor declared, was "the worst political bargain that has ever been made in this province."[11] The charges were coupled with criticism of the government for abandoning the policy of public development. In November the charge was increased to the effect that a "corrupt deal" had been made in that the Winnipeg Electric Company had donated $50,000 to the campaign fund of the Bracken government in the election of 1927. For the first time since 1915 there was intense excitement in the provincial politics of Manitoba.

Probably the government should have contented itself with denials in the press and, in the legislature, with a tussle in special committee. The sensitive pride of the Premier demanded a more formal procedure, however, and in January of 1929 a Royal Commission consisting of Chief Justice D. A. Macdonald of the Court of King's Bench, Mr. Justice A. K. Dysart, and Mr. Justice J. F. Kilgour was appointed to investigate the charge of a "corrupt deal." The Commission's enquiries were hampered, to say the least, by their own refusal to order the production of the books of the Winnipeg Electric Company, and by the tight-lipped evasiveness of the company's officials. The president of the company was detained by illness in California and was particularly uncommunicative even when visited there by the Commissioners. At the same time, a sensation was caused by the admission on the stand of Hon. W. R. Clubb that he had twice purchased Winnipeg Electric stock after the Executive Council had decided to accept the Hogg Report. Clubb maintained that he had not meant to benefit by his special knowledge, but certainly his act displayed a singular disregard both of what was to be expected of Caesar's wife and of the Marconi case in England in 1912. This revelation was followed by others; the law firm of Hon. W. J. Major, the Attorney-General, the wife of Hon. R. A. Hoey, the Minister of Education, and the Speaker of the House, all had purchased Winnipeg Electric stock in more or less extenuating circumstances. The stock indeed seems to have been popular at a time when every one with a little cash was taking a "flyer" on the stock market and few thought that those involved had offended.

Clubb and Major of course resigned from the Executive Council. The Commissioners in their report exonerated them, but only "without commenting on the rules of prudence applicable to cabinet ministers, as to which it is no part of our present function to pass judgment. . . ." The Commissioners also found that there had been no "corrupt deal," but that so far as they could discover the Winnipeg Electric Company had given $3,500 to the Conservative party, $3,000 to the Bracken campaign supporters, and $500 to the Liberal party, $7,000 in all. In a minority report Mr. Justice Dysart objected that the matter of campaign contributions had in his opinion been inadequately investigated, as was indeed the truth.[12] With the report the Seven Sisters controversy, an attempt at a revival of old-style politics given flavour only by the naïve imprudence of the two ministers and others who had purchased stock, died away, leaving the government with its confidence impaired, the Conservatives with a glow of vindication. After an interval Clubb and Major returned to their former positions in the Executive Council, and the episode was closed.

So badly had the government been shaken by the strong Conservative attack that it moved perceptibly closer to the Liberals. The withdrawal of the United Farmers of Manitoba from politics in 1928—and the waning strength of that organization—had indeed left the Bracken government in mid-air. From now on its non-partisanship was to be modified by an *entente* with the Liberals. While the Liberal party was not yet ready to ally itself with Bracken's supporters, the Liberal members in the legislature gave the government steady support for the remainder of the term of the Assembly.

The political controversy on the issues of power development could not diminish the satisfaction with which Manitoba welcomed the report of the Royal Commission on the transfer of its natural resources to the province. In 1929 that Commission found in favour of transferring the resources with compensation for alienation. The "purposes of the Dominion" for which the natural resources had been taken under federal control, the Commission found, had been fulfilled; "the railways had been built, and the lands settled." The compensation owing to Manitoba for resources alienated the Commission fixed, by a rough computation, at $4,584,212.49.[13] The Report was accepted by the federal government and the government of Manitoba. The date of the transfer was to be July 15, 1930, sixty years to the day from the coming into force of the Manitoba Act in 1870. After two generations of subordination to the needs of Canadian nation-building, the once small province of 1870 had come into its own. Sprung from resistance to Canadian authority; blocked in its hopes of expansion into a great mid-western province, it had seemed doomed to play the part of the "Cinderella of the Confederation." But in 1912 it had acquired boundaries which gave it a balance of natural resources. With control of those resources, it now had achieved that equality in Confederation which Norquay and Roblin, Norris and Bracken, had demanded as its right. A cycle had been completed in the history of the province, the cycle from colony to province, and from wilderness to field. The lands of Manitoba were settled, the cities built, a new frontier opened in the north. Once more, as in the days of the fur trade, the plains of the south and the Shield of the north were bound together in one economy and one government. The echoes of history rang back across the years in Manitoba that summer of 1930.

17

The Province and the Nation
1930-1936

THE ECHOES, INDEED, HAD BEGUN TO RING IN THE fall of 1929, when the steel of the Hudson's Bay Railway, after a half century of agitation by the West, reached the grey waters of Churchill harbour. By the first train in, the firm of James Richardson and Sons sent one ton of Manitoba No. 1 Hard wheat, sewn in two-pound canvas sacks, to be transported to England by the S.S. *Nascopie*, ship of that Hudson's Bay Company which two hundred and sixty years before had dispatched the first trading vessels into the great bay Hudson had discovered and Button traversed on his way to the Indies. Now golden wheat, first of its kind in all the world's markets, was going out with the furs which had solaced Button's successors for the want of a route to the Indies, and from which the great Company had won that sober wealth which had kept it strong over the changing centuries. In 1930 a tall terminal elevator to store 2,000,000 bushels of grain reared its grey cylinders at Churchill. In 1931 the harbour works were completed and in August S.S. *Farnworth* put in between the capes of the harbour mouth, by the ruins of Prince of Wales's Fort, to take on the first commercial cargo of western wheat to go out by the Bay.

It was with a full consciousness of the range and sweep of their history, then, that the people of Manitoba in 1930 celebrated the Diamond Jubilee of the province's entrance into Confederation. The celebration, from the gathering at the Legislative Buildings to that in the smallest village, was a tribute to the pioneers who had broken the prairie lands and the bush and made it possible for 700,000 people to dwell in comfort where 15,000 had lived precariously. The instinct which carried the memory back to Red River days and the years of settlement was sound, for the province, as it stood, was the work, and the fruit of the work, of the pioneers from Selkirk's settlers to the last comer from the Ukraine.

The people who celebrated the work of the pioneers were not themselves, after two generations, a formed or definitive people. The Manitoban Canadian was yet in process of formation. Among the 700,000 who made up the population of the province in 1930 there were few whose origins might not be detected. The mark of the Scot, of the Irish, Welsh, or Englishman was still discernible even when blended; the descendant of Red River stock was almost as sure to betray his background as the Polish or German Canadian. Yet certain broad characteristics established as early as the 1880's were still in the ascendant. They were those of the British-Ontario group, dominant yet in business and in government. In manners, speech, and outlook it was this group which was the formative force in provincial society. Their direct manners, clipped, flat speech, and concern with material success overlaying an ancestral concern with moral values, gave Manitoban life its tone. The prevailing outlook and way of life were still rural, simple, and unpretentious. Even that central core of Winnipeg, the Winnipeggers who were such by settlement and descent, were only a suaver version of the rural people, with whom their ties by blood and business were intimate. Even on Wellington Crescent, Manitoban life was essentially unsophisticated.

The British-Ontario and rural Manitoban might still dominate Manitoban life, but he had not yet assimilated the other stocks to his pattern. The Icelandic Manitoban and the French had both succeeded in preserving their identity as groups, an identity sprung from a proud self-consciousness, and had both succeeded in establishing an honourable working partnership in politics, the professions, and business with the British-Ontario stock. The Icelander had done it by sheer ability, aided by a certain kinship, the

French more often by group pressure. The German folk, whether Mennonite or German, had also preserved their identity, equally proudly, but not in partnership. They had proved themselves a singularly domestic people, given to keeping themselves to themselves and their own houses in unsurpassed order. While the Germans remained out of the main stream of provincial life, however, a newer group, the Ukrainian, was thrusting aggressively in. The Ukrainians, fired by the recent birth of national sentiment among their people in Europe and in the majority opposed to the incorporation of the Ukrainian Republic in the Soviet Union, turned the zeal of their nationalism to the preservation of their group in Manitoba and to making their way in business and politics. Their drive and courage won them reluctant admiration from the British-Ontario majority and entrance to business and public life. So virile was the Ukrainian group that, while avoiding complete assimilation itself, it was tending still more than at first to absorb the Poles, a leaderless group scattered among the Ukrainian settlements.

The process of assimilation was delayed, not only by the efforts of the larger ethnic group to maintain their identity, but also by the renewed flow of immigration in the twenties. The newcomers, whether British or European, found it difficult to mingle intimately even with Manitobans of their own kind. This factor operated both to check assimilation and to blur the mosaic which had been taking form. The immigrant Ukrainian found the Canadian Ukrainian more Canadian than Ukrainian. As a result, even while Manitobans were preparing to reject the "melting pot" theory of assimilation, which had been current early in the century, in favour of the mosaic concept, that concept itself was becoming untenable. Only some more intricate synthesis, some assimilation to an evolving, but not predetermined, type promised to produce an intimate cohesion among the people of Manitoba.

Manitoba might be a congeries of distinct groups, each the bearer of a particular culture, and the result of the ultimate blending of those groups and cultures a matter of speculation. The pangs of transition to a new way of life, the gulf between the immigrant and the Canadian-born generation breaching family ties, delinquency among the younger generation, the decline of politeness, the debasement of English speech—all were increased by the general lowering of the standards of manners and morals in a commercialized and mechanized society. There could, however, by no question that the various groups were reaching a *modus vivendi*, a collective way of life which, if superficial, made for accommodation. In creating a common citizenship, embracing all groups and giving free play to all cultures, the simple democracy of the farmers' movement, the building up of the farmers' organizations, and the schools of the province played effective and distinctive parts. In Strathcona High School in Winnipeg, children of fourteen different nationalities were in attendance, yet under the sympathetic and inspired leadership of the principal, W. J. Sisler, the young people passed out every year glad and confident Canadians.[1] The work of R. S. Thornton, the patient labours of the teachers, the wise guidance of kindly, weather-beaten school inspectors, was making itself felt year by year, and through the common schools of 1890 helping the growth of a viable community founded on a common citizenship but not on cultural uniformity.

The influence of a common environment and, in the country, of a common occupation and way of life, of course, worked powerfully to bring people of different backgrounds together. The fundamental rural life of the province was the great moulder of its people, and its influence was for uniformity, a uniformity not superficial, but deep, because founded on attachment to the soil and the home. Whether a Ukrainian pioneer in the bush frontier of the Swan River or a son of Ontario stock on the well-cultivated terrace lands of the Pembinas, whether a druggist in Beausejour or a bank manager in Dauphin, the typical Manitoban was a country man, at home with country ways and at ease in the steady rhythm of country life.

The countryside in which rural Manitobans lived had only deepened and confirmed its earlier lineaments. In the old districts the small towns snuggled deeper in their maples; the slope-shouldered giant elevators had increased their numbers. The square fields were widened out to the section lines; most of the road allowances were opened and the grid pattern stamped fair and firm on the wide land. In the Red River valley and on the plains of Portage and the Souris, the shelter bluffs stood up higher to the north wind. In the Interlake and on the rugged bush frontier of the southeast and northwest, the farmsteads on the good lands were coming to conform with those of the older districts. On the poor soils the hard struggle continued, the log shacks were patched and repatched, or, where the contest had been lost, sagged in slow decay.

This countryside, ripening towards the final form of a culti-vated mid-western landscape, was the home of a rural life enter-ing on a great transformation. The old rural isolation, the reason for the little rural school districts, the scene of the local picnics and their improvised sports, was breaking up before the opening of the country roads, the extension of rural telephones and the improvement of the rural mail service. The motor car had re-placed the buck board. Friendly visits became more frequent and shorter. While Saturday night remained the time set aside for shopping, more and more the farmer or the farmer's wife could be expected to run into town during the week. The lonely house-wife, the slave of chores and children, could now find relief in gossip over the telephone, or in a hurried trip to the neighbours. In more and more homes, of an evening, the family sat silent, in earphones, before the wonder of the radio. And in the hydro-electric pylons marching across the land from horizon to horizon was a promise, though one that few farmers could yet afford, that the unrelenting weight of lonely drudgery on the farm might be yet further lightened for man and wife and child.

Much of the work of ending rural isolation had been done by the locals, both men's and women's, of the Grain Growers' As-sociation and the United Farmers of Manitoba. The greatest work of both had been, as they said, educational, the persuading of farmers and farmers' wives to take time, to make the effort which was in fact a release of the spirit, to be thoughtful and active citizens. But no organization had done or was doing more in this respect than the Women's Institutes. Begun first in On-tario, a companion to the Farmers' Institutes of that province, they had been introduced into Manitoba in 1910, where they began a vigorous and wholly feminine existence. Their chief achievement was that they took the women away from duties too long and too faithfully performed, and brought them together in one another's homes and in the towns. But their ostensible purpose was to unite women in an effort to improve their communities, and in that too they did good work, by which the life of the province was made the richer. Indeed, without such work by the women in the Institutes, the church associations, and other organizations, life in rural Manitoba might have become even more a matter of raising grain and hogs and selling farm machinery.

The new range and wider neighbourhood of rural life meant that the old ways were dropped one by one. The farmer became less a craftsman, proud of his competence with axe and plough, and more a mechanic and a manager. The picnics became fewer; the box socials old fashioned; the sports more organized; the fairs more commercialized. The moving picture theatre had been added to the prominent buildings of the town; the radio was in more and more homes. The barn dance had given way, with its local fiddler, to the dance in town with a hired band to furnish the music.

With the decline of the old ways a new restlessness had spread. Rural life had indeed always been restless, for no rule of inheritance in the family obtained. The usual practice among those of British descent was for the children, both sons and daughters, to inherit equally. The result was that no one was bound to the family farm by the hope of succession. Accordingly, unless the matter were arranged beforehand, all the children were impelled, consciously or unconsciously, to strike out on their own. Down to the decade of the twenties the sons tended to seek new land further West, the daughters to teach school. They left home but not the land. From the war on, however, the restlessness had a new quality and the migration from the farm a new direction. The restlessness was increased by the spread of urban tastes, by the movies, the radio, the press, the mail-order catalogue in the country. And it was to the city that the children were going. The agricultural depression naturally weakened the hold of the land, the increase of industry created jobs to be filled not merely by urban natural increase and immigration, but by a migration from the farm to the cities. Manitoba was conforming to a trend which had been strengthening in North America since the 1870's. This depopulation of the countryside was a bitter loss, publicly lamented by farm leaders, a loss at once sentimental and economic. The farm now had to compete with the city for both the affection and the labour of its children. It was, however, a loss which could not be checked until the farm offered its young people opportunities of a good life comparable with those, real or fancied, offered by the city; until, in short, the steady remaking of the old rural life in the ways and to the standards of the city had been accomplished. When urban ways prevailed, and not before, the farm would know peace and the drain of population be slowed.

The transformation of rural life, and the subordination of the country to the city, did not mean that Winnipeg had continued since 1921 to sweep on the imperial way its growth from 1901 to 1911 had promised. Winnipeg also had been in the grip of a profound malaise since the opening of the twenties. Conceived and built as the metropolis of the West, it had thrived while the people and goods drawn to the West by the great boom of the opening decade of the century had passed through its railway yards and warehouses. Then it had been the Gateway City, giving ingress and egress to the booming farmlands of the prairies. In 1915, however, the Panama Canal had been opened, with the result that freight for British Columbia and Alberta could move more cheaply by that long water route than by rail across the continent. The growth of Vancouver surged forward, and the economic watershed between the two rival cities moved steadily eastward, to Winnipeg's disadvantage. By 1924 Alberta wheat was moving in volume over the Rockies to Vancouver. Winnipeg suffered, therefore, not only from the long agricultural depression in the West, but from a steady diminution of the territory its

wholesale trade and grain market served. The gateway of the
West had been turned, and the third city of Canada yielded its
place to Vancouver.

The slow sapping of its old position was not easy to accept or
admit, and it was reluctantly that the city came to recognize that
its great commercial concerns had reached their limits, or could
grow only with the growth of its new restricted territory. Only
slowly did it turn to newer opportunities in the development of
manufacturing and of the northern frontier. Even here opportunities were limited, for the market for Winnipeg products
was limited to the slowly growing population of the West, and
the Manitoban north had yielded neither a Cobalt nor a Noranda.
The change was made, however, and by 1930 the tough and
strenuous city, wounded perhaps in spirit, was turning to the
task of building a new future in its own factories and the developing north.

The malaise arose not only from a constriction of the economic
roots of Winnipeg. The cleft which the general strike of 1919
had driven between labour and the remainder of the city did not
close quickly. It had, on the contrary, been transferred to civic
politics, and the Labour party disputed with candidates of the
Citizens' Election Committee for the office of Mayor, and for a
majority in the School Board and the City Council. The basic
issue was whether the better-to-do of the city should pay more
taxes to improve and increase the services given by the schools
and the civic departments, by which the less fortunate benefited
more, or whether these agencies should give a decent but frugal
service, and anything better be left to private initiative and
personal fortune. The struggle was fairly evenly contested over the
years, with Labour in the minority during the twenties. In 1922
Labour had won the mayoralty when S. J. Farmer, who had not
been a leader in the strike, was elected, but in 1924 Farmer was
defeated by Colonel Ralph Webb. A popular mayor, Webb
brought to his office a dash and personal sincerity which won him
election for the remainder of the decade. His gift of provocative
statement, however, and his intense suspicion of Communism,
then viewed much differently by Labour than now, did nothing

to heal, and something to keep raw, the old wound of 1919. And indeed the strength of the Communist party in the North End, the election of Communist candidates to the City Council and the provincial legislature, indicated at once the failure of Manitoban democracy to win the loyalty of all its people and its capacity to tolerate dissent. But it was in the rise of Labour as a strong and permanent element in civic life that there lay the only true basis of reconciliation between the sections of the city, and as the Labour leaders matured under the influence of office and their opponents learned to practise tolerance, Winnipeggers began to take a pride, assertive or wry according to class, in being citizens of a "radical" city.

In the city as in the country, customs and attitudes were changing. The old sharp division between worker and employer was closing as the unions won increased acceptance and as more informal manners became general and dress became uniform. The growth of the city and the influence of the British and European newcomers made for a sloughing off of the rural prejudices of the old Canadian stock and the "bourgeois" antipathies of the old Winnipeg middle class with its Victorian, Ontario background. The great test of strength between the new ways and the old was Labour representative John Queen's bill to permit the running of special Sunday trains to the beaches of Lake Winnipeg. There and at the Lake of the Woods well-to-do families had spent the hot summer months since the 1880's, but the families of working people, free to travel only on Sundays, had been held in the city by the clause of the Lord's Day Act, a federal law, which prohibited the operation of special trains on Sunday. The bill was stoutly opposed by the Lord's Day Alliance. The legislature passed and the courts sustained the Act in 1924, and bluff John Queen had won a pleasant victory on behalf of his constituents. The old sabbatarianism was breaking down, as formal religion lost its hold, and private pastimes, such as golf, were more and more indulged in on Sunday.

If British and European influences made for a more indulgent way of life, the commercial entertainment evolved in the United States was also at work to provide entertainment which required nothing but the cash of the spectator. The moving picture theatres flaunted their electric signs and flamboyant portals from near Portage and Main to the remotest suburbs. The younger generation, fretting against the old-fashioned limit of a Saturday movie, was becoming addicted to the screen's hypnotic flicker, and added new favourites to old in Harold Lloyd, Gloria Swanson, and Charlie Chaplin. With the movies came the imbecilities of American slang and popular music, and youthful Winnipeggers were impelled, like others of their generation, to mimic the banalities of the mechanized and commercialized entertainment purveyed by Hollywood.

The coming of the motion pictures, in Winnipeg as elsewhere outside the great metropolitan centres, forced the theatre into decline. The older generation still loyally went to the Winnipeg, the Pantages, and the Walker, where C. P. Walker struggled nobly to keep the stage alive. The younger generation, thanks to the work of the high schools and the University, would still throng "the gods" when Shakespeare was played or Gilbert and Sullivan ran. But "the road" could no longer support a steady supply of good theatre, plays and vaudeville declined in quality, and the houses grew smaller and smaller.[2]

That the great days of the theatre were over would not have been so sad, had local talent and local effort been strong enough to take the place of professional productions. A brave effort was made by the Winnipeg Little Theatre in the twenties, but the uncertainty of amateur talent and the temperamentality of amateur producers led to friction and loss of public support. Talent there was and the love of theatre, but want of firm group action or the drive of a dominant personality led to wasted effort and the loss of talent like Judith Evelyn's or Tommie Tweed's, which might have lighted the Winnipeg stage a little longer until the call came to Toronto or New York.

Music in Winnipeg fared better, resting as it did, and as theatre did not, on firm bases in the church, school, and individual study. The choir masters and music teachers had been training a wealth of native talent for years when in 1919 the Manitoba Music Festival was founded. Alberta since 1907 and

Saskatchewan since 1909 had had provincial festivals, but Manitoba had a strong foundation for choral work in the Male Voice Choir founded in 1916 and for instrumental music in a corps of gifted teachers and societies like the Men's and the Women's Music Clubs. In the years after 1919, years of such stress and uncertainty for Winnipeg and Manitoba, the Festival was built up into something rich and unique, the pride of Manitoba and the delight of the British adjudicators who gladly came to judge this folk festival in the raw, new city set on the edge of the prairies which within living memory had been an unpeopled wilderness. This was a fine and lasting achievement, but in the higher reaches of musical accomplishment Winnipeg was just not strong enough. The Men's Male Voice Choir reached a high level of performance; but efforts to found a Winnipeg Symphony Orchestra, begun in 1920, had only partial success during these years for want of a suitable auditorium and of general and united public support.[3] The foundations, however, were secure, the supply of talent, reinforced as it was by the Jewish, Ukrainian, and Polish groups in Winnipeg, was great, and music had become for many younger Manitobans at least not so much an art as one of life's natural graces.

Art had not flourished in the province as music had done; it had not found a similar popular basis, nor uncovered the talent that the stage and music had. The Winnipeg Society of Artists had since 1903 ministered to the interests of a small group; since 1913 the Winnipeg School of Art had led a struggling existence until it was so fortunate as to obtain as instructor in 1924 Manitoban-born Lemoyne Fitzgerald, often associated with the School of Seven, who became Principal in 1929. His influence as teacher and artist was in the direction of bolder and more original work, but no one man could overcome the disadvantages of the lack of an art gallery and of a public of discrimination and taste. Only one other local artist, W. J. Phillips, had won a more than local reputation. Phillips had seized on the prairie elevator as a subject and had caught its essential appeal to the eye, the vertical thrust of the massive red shaft challenging the prairie horizontal. The delicate if conventional charm of his water colours and wood blocks of the Lake of the Woods country was also winning his work a place in Manitoban homes as well as in the galleries.

The decade of the twenties had been rich in letters; writing more nearly authentic than any since Ernest Thompson Seton's and George Bryce's appeared in some volume. The appearance of imaginative as well as historical literature which attempted to deal with actual life in Manitoba was a challenge to Manitobans, their sophistication and sense of humour. Martha Ostenso's *Wild Geese*, it has been noted, had provoked a mild scandal, and Douglas Durkin's novels caused some discomfort. A similar popular rejection was the fate of the most earnest and talented of the novelists who made Manitoba life his subject, Frederick Philip Grove. An Anglo-Swedish immigrant, well educated, observant, and driven by a brooding urge to write, Grove had come to Manitoba in 1893. He became a teacher in 1912 and taught in various parts of the province. In 1922 appeared his first book, *Over Prairie Trails*, a volume of essays finely descriptive of the Manitoban landscape and seasons. A companion volume, *The Turn of the Year*, was published in 1923, and revealed the same descriptive power. His novels, however, which aroused in the local critics pride that authentic literature was at last being produced in Manitoba, in the public merely provoked resentment at what they thought a harsh and uncalled-for portrayal of the worse aspects of rural life. In *Fruits of the Earth* (1933), a novel of farming near Lowe Farm, Grove painfully worked out the slow cramping of the spirit and of the affections that the unending drudgery of farming inflicted on many. In *Settlers of the Marsh* (1925), a story of settlement in the rough country north of the Big Grass Marsh, he revealed how under the drab routine of the settler's life human passions ran their powerful and often destructive course. The offence Grove gave arose from his adherence to the literary convention of realism, which could appeal only to sophisticated readers. Life in Manitoba was still too simple and realistic in itself for realistic literature either to inform or inspire.

The public therefore continued to follow the old favourites, Nellie McClung and Ralph Connor, though Mrs. McClung had ceased to develop and Ralph Connor's meagre talent had long since been played out. The reading public, which was very limited, was not yet prepared, apart from a small group in Winnipeg, to relish the strong meat of which so much of the literature of the day consisted. On the shelves of Russell Lang's, the chief Winnipeg bookstore and a place of musty charm, were crowded the English classics; the Victorian writers were dominant, and modern prose and verse appeared only in discreet selection and modest reserve. A welcome addition to their number, in part because it was that rare thing in Manitoban literature, a work both light and humorous, was H. G. G. Herklots' *The First Winter*.

A similar fate to that of Grove's novels, but a fate richly deserved, attended the novels of Maurice Constantin-Weyer, a French writer whose *Un Homme se penche sur son passé* received the Prix Goncourt in 1928. His *Manitoba*, an autobiographical work, and *La Bourrasque*, a novel with Riel as hero, though starred with brilliant descriptive passages, were highly coloured, inaccurate, and brutal sketches of life among the Manitoban French. These libels were exposed by Donatien Frémont in *Sur le ranch de Constantin-Weyer*.

Behind the veil, to most Manitobans, of the languages of the ethnic groups, literatures of surprising richness were growing up, especially in Icelandic and Ukrainian. In 1923 Laura Goodman Salverson's *The Viking Heart* appeared in English, a romantic story of Viking days, which was widely read, and which indicated how rich and diverse Manitoban literature was in its entirety. Her *Confessions of an Immigrant's Daughter*, published in 1939, was to tell with a sharpness disturbing to the dominant stock the inner bitterness with which a proud and cultured people undergo the essential indignity of assimilation. But the tales and poetry, both traditional and new, of these other Manitobans remained unknown to the British stock until the English translations of the versatile Watson Kirkconnell of Wesley College began to draw the veils of many languages.

Historical literature also flourished and began to make the first break from the fixation with Red River and pioneer days. J. W. Dafoe's *Laurier: A Study in Canadian Politics* (1922) and his

Clifford Sifton: His Life and Times (1931) were Canadian books on national subjects. So also was Professor Chester Martin's *Empire and Commonwealth* (1929). *Women of Red River* (1923), edited by W J. Healy, was one work more in the old vein, but in itself a graceful tribute to its subject and a work of genuine historical value. One of its compilers, Mrs. R. F. Mc-Williams, published in 1927 her *Manitoba Milestones*, a history of the province which, first among its kind, achieved a fair balance between the "romantic" story of the fur trade and the more realistic and more significant story of settlement. Professor A. H. R. Buller's *Essays on Wheat* (1919) was also a valuable contribution by a distinguished natural scientist of the University of Manitoba to the history of settlement in that it made plain the extent to which the settlement of the West had depended on the work of the agricultural scientist. The chief interest of this body of historical work was that, with the legitimate exception of *Women of Red River,* it was not written in a provincial spirit or from a provincial point of view.

That this should have been so was not a matter for surprise. A "nationalist" tradition had been founded in Manitoba by John S. Ewart with his *Kingdom of Canada and Other Papers,* published in book form after his removal to Ontario in 1904, and continued by John W. Dafoe. It was nationalist in the sense both that it was non-provincial and that it was anti-imperialist. It was at the same time internationalist, as the economic interests of Manitoba and the West required. This development was perpetuated among the younger generation by, among other influences, that of the University of Manitoba, which in its faculty and outlook was anything but a "provincial" university. More significant still, however, was the effect of the history of Manitoba, however slightly that history had yet been made explicit. A province of federal creation, the necessary stepping-stone to the farther West and for sixty years subordinated to the nation-building purposes of Confederation, Manitoba, despite its full share of western sentiment and provincial resentment at that subordination, was a national province as Winnipeg was an international market. For two generations the life of the province had been the strings across which the bow of national purpose and national destiny had been drawn. In 1930 it had become in virtue of its history and of constitutional recognition, a province in full right but a province involved in the Canadian nation.

How deep, and how necessary, that involvement was, the harshest years in the history of the province were now to demonstrate. In October, 1929, the crash of the speculative boom on Wall Street began the end of the great boom of the twenties. The summer and fall of 1929 also saw the beginning of the most intense and prolonged of the dry cycles in the history of the West. The great depression of the thirties, aggravated in the West by drought, had begun and in its course was to wreck the structure, painfully shored up since the Great War, of the world-wide economy of the nineteenth century, the economy by which Manitoba had been called into being and as a part of which it had lived.

In itself the return of the dry years would have been trial enough. The Souris Plains were once more whipped by searing winds and the light lands everywhere scoured of their precious top soil. Once more the fences disappeared under grey-black dunes as the rose bushes and the wolf willow held the driving sand. Day after day in seedtime the whipping wind had obliterated the wheelmark of the drill before the "round" could be repeated across the field. Later, on the knolls, the sprouted seed was often laid bare by the ceaseless wind to the scorching sun. On the heavy lands the wheat and coarse grain parched under a brazen sun whose heat brought no rain out of the west. With the drought came the pests which throve on drought, the grasshoppers and the Russian thistle. Even rust continued its ravages, destroying the value of Marquis wheat as the staple variety and shrinking the sample of the short crops. Year by year in 1929, 1930, 1931, the drought and pests continued, until the wheat crop of Manitoba fell to 28,000,000 bushels and the barley crop to 15,000,000.

The short crops were mercilessly accompanied by low prices. The world wheat markets had been broken in 1929 by large crops in the exporting countries and by restrictions imposed by European countries which could not earn enough foreign exchange to buy wheat. The precipitate drop in the price of wheat caught the Wheat Pools with an initial payment too high for their subsequent selling prices. They were therefore unable to meet the advances the banks had made them, or to make further payments to their members. As the great world "carry-over" weighed down the price of wheat, and as European countries, plunged into the world crisis, increased their restrictions, farmers and the Pools alike faced and underwent financial disaster. By 1932 wheat had fallen to its lowest recorded price, 34 cents a bushel.

The threatened collapse of the Pools would probably have dragged western agriculture down with them, and in 1930 the provincial government guaranteed the advances the banks had made to the Manitoba Wheat Pool. A lien was taken on the assets of the Pool and a liability, as it was then reckoned, of about $3,500,000 was assumed. Charges of mismanagement and over-expansion of the Pool elevator system made by J. R. Murray, a leading grain trader, were on the whole sustained by a Royal Commission of Enquiry.[4] The Pool locals had been too keen in undertaking expansion of the elevator system and central direction too weak to control them. The government accepted the substance of the report of the Commission, and the Manitoba Co-operative Wheat Producers, Limited, was reorganized as the Manitoba Pool Elevators, Limited, still, however, as a co-operative organization controlled by its locals.

The guarantee of the Pool was only a first step in salvage of the agricultural economy. The government had also to take a series of measures to check the breakdown of the economy and alleviate the distress. An Act to Facilitate the Adjustment of Debt was passed in 1930, to terminate in 1933; it provided means of voluntary debt adjustment by debtor and creditor. A Seed Grain Act was passed to furnish seed to farmers in the dried-out areas. So severe had the crisis become by September, 1930, that Premier Bracken called a conference of bankers, municipal officials, and representatives of the agricultural association to discuss ways and means of extending credit to farmers in order that they might keep their cattle off the market and avoid a downrush of prices.

As the farm economy crumbled, industry and commerce suffered; the swing of the trains in and out of Winnipeg slackened, the factories closed. In the winter of 1929–30 unemployment on a large scale appeared again in Winnipeg as it had in 1921–2. Thousands of workers were idle, and hundreds of families on relief. Relief works were provided by the city, province, and federal governments, in the woodyards, on the roads, in the provincial forests and the new national park on Riding Mountain, in the construction of a civic auditorium, a federal office building, and a sewage disposal plant in Winnipeg. But neither the provincial nor the federal government had provided any buffer against unemployment, either by insurance or a workable system of relief. Not until 1931, indeed, did Manitoba establish its Department of Labour. The constitutional responsibility for relief lay with the municipalities but their limited resources were soon overwhelmed by the weight of mass unemployment. In Manitoba, as in the other provinces of Canada, the provincial government was compelled to come to the aid of the municipalities. Because of the magnitude and universal character of the depression, the province had then to ask aid of the federal government. The demand became an issue in the federal general election of 1930, and not until the Conservative party had defeated the Liberals did the new government under Prime Minister R. B. Bennett come to the aid of the provinces in distress. Meantime the municipalities of Manitoba, among which Winnipeg was pre-eminent in the number of unemployed and the cost of relief, with aid from the province met the mounting costs. In 1929 $70,000 was voted by the provincial legislature for unemployment relief; in 1930, $1,300,000, the amount the province was to pay under the new agreement with the federal government by which the municipalities and the federal government were each to bear a third. By 1932 the provincial government had spent $8,000,000 on relief, and no abatement was in sight. Yet these expenditures, tremendous as they were in relation to the revenues of the municipalities and the province, had done nothing to end the depression, nor could they do anything. The workers who thronged Market Square, or marched to the Legislative Building demanding work, could not be satisfied. The federal public works programme—which gave Winnipeg in its misery the auditorium it could not afford in prosperity, subways, and a new sewer system—the steady extension of the provincial highway system, the work in the camps set up for single men in the forest reserves at Riding Mountain and on the Bedford Hills at Sandilands, these and other projects did not take the place of a normally functioning economy.

In the midst of these attempts to maintain the agricultural economy of the province and to furnish relief to the unemployed, the provincial government was itself in grave difficulties. The depression fell as heavily on the enterprises of the province as on private ones. The Federal Farm Loans Board had assumed the burden of agricultural credit, but the Rural Credit Societies and the provincial Farm Loans Board, now amalgamated, had to be liquidated, and a heavy loss from debts which could not be collected was certain. The Government Telephones, which had just become fully self supporting, and the Manitoba Power Commission, still an annual charge on the provincial treasury, suffered loss of revenue. Provincial credit fell, and the resolute maintenance of the Canadian dollar by the federal government, with the result that its value rose above that of the American dollar, heavily increased the payment of interest and principal of loans which had been made in New York. There was a serious likelihood of the province being dragged down by the dead weight of the municipalities and the sagging economy. Only the greater resources of federal government could ward off provincial bankruptcy.

It was in these circumstances that in 1931 Premier Bracken suggested that a non-partisan government should be formed to deal with the crisis. Labour rejected the proposals. The Conservative party, fired by its own recovery in 1927 and the victory of the federal party in 1930, denounced the suggestion as fraudulent. The Liberals, however, who had been moving closer to the Bracken government since the Seven Sisters affair and the Conservative victory of 1930, after some hesitation accepted. Three Liberals were admitted to the cabinet, and the tentative provincial Liberal-Progressive alliance of 1928–31 became effective.

The new Bracken ministry won a smashing victory, and carried thirty-eight seats. The Conservatives were reduced from fifteen seats to ten, partly because their stand on party government was unpopular in the rural constituencies and partly, it was said, because of the appearance of Sir Rodmond Roblin in the campaign. Manitoba was not yet ready wholly to abandon the non-partisan politics introduced in 1922, and still preferred to keep provincial politics separate from federal.

The new government was just returned to govern a province in serious distress when public morale received the shock of learning that the Chairman of the Board of Governors of the University, who was also its Bursar, J. A. Machray, had embezzled $901,175, almost the whole of the University's endowments. He had also made away with $800,000 entrusted to his care by the Church of England, as well as lesser funds. A Royal Commission of Enquiry revealed that the defalcations of University funds had begun as far back as 1903. The report of the Commission rebuked the Board of Governors for appointing Machray both Bursar and Investment Counsel, the Norris government for appointing him to the Board while he continued in both offices, and the Bracken government for making him Chairman of the Board while he continued in both offices and for failing from 1925 to 1931 to obtain annual audits and reports of the investment of University funds, as the Act required.[5] Machray was convicted and sentenced to imprisonment. It was a tale of excessive personal trust and of administrative laxity and indifference in high quarters. The breaking of this long-hidden abscess, inevitable though it was, seriously shook the University of Manitoba and shocked the public perhaps even more than the Legislative Buildings scandal of 1915.

In the atmosphere of the day, however, the Machray defalcations were soon lost to sight. The government took up the main preoccupations of its new term of office, the meeting of the costs of relief and the maintenance of the credit of the province. In company with the governments of Alberta and Saskatchewan, it attempted to persuade the federal government to assume one-half of the cost of relief. It refused to do so, however, until the provincial budget of Manitoba had been balanced, or the deficit at least brought below $1,000,000 a year. If this were not done, Prime Minister Bennett wrote, a financial controller "satisfactory to the Dominion Government, would have to be appointed."[6] Premier Bracken protested that the costs of relief could not be reduced, but, as the banks would extend no more credit, the province had no choice but to accept the terms laid down. This was perhaps the lowest point of the depression, when the province of Manitoba had in effect become the financial ward of the federal government. The new Provincial Treasurer, Hon. E. A. McPherson, however, proceeded to make heroic reductions of expenditure, and imposed a flat 2 per cent tax on all wages and salaries above $480 for single persons. The result was an anticipated deficit of only $495,855. But money for relief was to be borrowed, and kept in a separate account for settlement when the crisis had passed.

By these drastic measures the financial crisis was surmounted, and for the next three years Manitobans lived grimly in a régime of harsh economy. They were bitter years, as worklessness became the accustomed mode of life of the unemployed, as every freight train had its row of transient unemployed, as the fires gleamed nightly in the "jungles" where the wandering workless lived before moving on. On the farms the equipment grew older year by year, houses and barns more weatherbeaten; the "Bennett buggy" appeared, an old car horse-drawn; the towns became more rundown as year by year the dust from the blowing fields swirled down their empty streets.

It seemed that the depression would never lift, or the seasonable rains come again. Even when in 1935 the Liberal party, after sweeping the Conservatives from office, established the Wheat Board the farmers had been demanding again since 1931, agriculture failed to respond. The further diversification which the depression forced, the increase in the production of livestock, butter, and honey, could only alleviate the depression, not restore prosperity. Nor could the timid beginnings of new industries, such as the growth of the needle and garment trades in Winnipeg, absorb the mass of unemployed labour. Only the growing output of Flin Flon, where the new mining town was spreading over the Precambrian rock and the muskeg, and of the San Antonio gold mine in the Central Manitoban field, gave indication of new life and growth.

The depression had given rise to new political movements, and in 1932 the Co-operative Commonwealth Federation, a fusion of the Labour and farmer movements of the previous decade, had been organized. In 1933 a provincial party was formed in Manitoba and the first provincial convention held at Portage la Prairie. The new party was an attempt to bring farmers and Labour together in a single party devoted to a programme largely inspired by socialist doctrine. It absorbed the Independent Labour Party of Winnipeg, but failed to persuade the United Farmers to reverse its decision of 1928 not to affiliate with any political party. It remained to be seen whether the C.C.F. could become more than the old Labour party of Manitoba, menaced as that now was by the formation of a Communist party. In 1935 a second new party was added in the Social Credit movement which had just captured power in Alberta. What the influence of this new movement would be no one could say.

The political scene was as uncertain as the economic, therefore, when in 1936 the Bracken government went to the country. It suffered a stinging defeat, caused by resentment of its heavy taxation as well as by the number and variety of its opponents. Out of a total of one hundred and thirty-one candidates, the Liberal-Progressives had twenty-two elected, the Conservatives sixteen, the C.C.F. six, Social Credit five, Independents three, and the Communists one. To attempt to bring stability out of this chaos, reminiscent as it was of 1920, Premier Bracken was authorized by his followers to undertake to form a coalition ministry. The Conservatives, under their new leader Errick F. Willis, rebuffed the approach, but the five Social Credit members agreed to co-operate with the Bracken government. On this slender basis the ministry was reconstituted, though without a Social Credit member. Manitoba under the stress of the depression had turned neither to right nor left; it had simply plunged headlong into political confusion, from which it was saved only by the endless flexibility of the non-partisan doctrine the farmers had carried into provincial politics in 1920–2.

If the economy remained depressed, however, and if the path of politics was obscure, some things were clear in Manitoba. The purely agricultural economy of the days of settlement could exist in the averaging-out of boom and depression only at a level which made all public services, including education, difficult to maintain even at low levels. The agricultural economy matured in two generations of pioneering could not maintain the way of life to which Manitobans aspired as citizens of Canada in the twentieth century. The economy must be diversified, therefore, if a Canadian standard of living was to be maintained. Even so, Manitoba could not achieve such a standard by its own material and financial resources, or by its own efforts alone. The full provincial status achieved in 1930 was far from being enough, even as the national policies pursued in the past were far from adequate to the needs of all Canada. The province could not bear the consequences of national policies and the costs of the new welfare services society demanded, unless there was available to it a larger share of the national income. Such a revision of the financial relations between the federal government and the province could come about, however, only if a new sense of national obligation were to develop in all Canada. It was to the task of creating such a sense that the Manitoba government now addressed itself.

18

The Decisions War Deferred
1937-1945

THE OLD CONCEPTS OF "EQUALITY IN CONFEDERA-
tion" and "provincial rights," vindicated though they were in the
events of 1930, had broken down by 1936. By that year it was
apparent that Manitoba could not continue to carry the mounting
weight of indebtedness which the depression had piled upon the
province and its municipalities. They had survived since 1932
only because the financial aid from the federal government had
been generous. Now it was becoming clear that the mounting
indebtedness, apart from that owed to Ottawa, would soon become
insupportable. Out of a provincial expenditure in 1935–6 of
$14,097,549, $5,934,402 was paid in interest charges. The public
had become restive under a heavy burden of municipal and provincial taxes, especially the hated "wage tax," the highest income
tax in North America on small incomes. The destruction of the
Bracken government's majority and the rise of new parties in
1936 had exposed this resentment. The victory of the Social
Credit party in Alberta in 1935 had raised hopes of new and
unorthodox ways of dealing with debt, and in 1936 Alberta had
repudiated half its debt. Unless some relief were granted, the
probability was that Manitoba would follow Alberta along the
path of repudiation.

The one hope of relief lay in a readjustment of financial responsibilities between the provinces and the federal government.
Commercial and industrial recovery from the depression would
not be enough to restore the financial mobility of the province.

Recovery was already under way in Canada, but it had little effect on the West. The Wheat Board had stabilized wheat prices, but 1937 was one of the worst of the drought years. In Winnipeg the number of unemployed remained high. And no conceivable recovery would have enabled the province to shake off its load of debt, except by a reduction of services and a weight of taxation which would have driven its people to more fortunate parts of Canada. The province and its municipalities could not meet their responsibilities under the constitution, increased as these were by the growth of social welfare services and the weight of mass unemployment. They could not raise, with the taxing powers accorded them by the constitution, sufficient revenue out of a provincial income which fluctuated as widely as that of Manitoba had done since 1900.

The danger of the situation had already been recognized in Ottawa. The federal government had suggested the formation of a Dominion-provincial loan council to supervise the refunding of provincial debt. This, however, was to be rejected both by the Senate and by the province of Alberta. In December of 1935 a Dominion-provincial conference had been held in Ottawa to seek ways and means of rescuing the western provinces. The Manitoban delegation, led by Premier Bracken, had asked for a realistic facing of the problems of relief, an extension of provincial taxing powers or a reduction of provincial responsibility for social services, and the maintenance and more sympathetic administration of the federal Farmers' Creditors Arrangement Act.[1]

The truth was that the federal government was not unsympathetic or uninformed, but that the other provinces, less affected by the depression and well on the way to recovery, had to be convinced that the western provinces were not simply endeavouring to deposit on the national treasury the results of their own past extravagance. The new Bank of Canada, established in 1935, had been asked by the National Finance Committee set up by the Dominion-Provincial Conference of 1935 to make a study of the provincial finances of Manitoba, Saskatchewan, and Alberta. It did so, and reported in February, 1937. After demonstrating the extent to which the provincial income of Manitoba had fallen during the depression, the report criticized the provincial government for its expenditures during the boom following 1926, and for its failure to create reserves and to reduce expenditures when the depression began. As a whole, however, the report found that the provincial finances had been wisely and courageously managed during the depression. The province had done about all that was humanly possible to discharge its responsibilities and remain solvent. The situation was now, however, so serious in Manitoba, and in Saskatchewan, that a Royal Commission of Enquiry into Dominion-provincial financial relations should be appointed.[2]

This recommendation was at once followed on August 18, 1937, by an announcement by Prime Minister King that a Royal Commission would be appointed, in the hope that it might recommend means by which the Dominion and the provinces would be able to function more independently within the spheres of their jurisdictions and be able financially to stand upon their own feet. The terms of reference, because of the failure of the Dominion-Provincial Conference of 1935 to agree on a method of amending the British North America Act, was restricted to an examination of Dominion-provincial financial relations.[3] The announcement was greeted with satisfaction, almost with jubilation, in Manitoba, for it seemed to be a tacit acknowledgment of the province's claim that the western provinces had been the victims rather than the beneficiaries of national policies and that the constitutional allocation of responsibilities and revenues had become intolerable. The Commission was organized under Hon. N. S. Rowell as chairman, and its members, whose task it would be to conduct an inquest into the state of the nation at a time when national unity had been reduced to the lowest point since Confederation, were carefully chosen to represent the five regions of Canada. The representative of Manitoba and the prairie West was John W. Dafoe, in whose person the defence of western and provincial interests, the assertion of Canadian nationalism, and the overriding importance of international relations combined in proportions which at once reflected and informed the outlook of his province. Because of the leadership Manitoba and Premier Bracken had given to the movement for a readjustment of

Dominion-provincial relations, the first hearing of the Commission was held in Winnipeg in the fall of 1937.

The submission made by the government of Manitoba had been prepared by its senior civil servants and a staff of distinguished economists. It was an elaborate and painstaking demonstration of costs inflicted on the province by national tariff and monetary policies, of income catastrophically diminished, and of a weight of taxation and debt aggravated at once by relief charges and low income. It was presented, however, in no sectional or merely provincial spirit. Manitoba was true to its slowly formed character as a national province, part and parcel of the nation. The Manitoba Premier, who in these years became nationally known for his firm, insistent, but moderate presentation of the claim of the West to a reconsideration of Dominion-provincial and sectional relations in Canada, left no doubt of the spirit in which Manitoba appeared before the Commission, not as a suppliant for favours, but as the advocate of a new concept of national obligation and purpose. "In what we have to say," said Premier Bracken, "we shall speak as Canadians, not as sectionalists. What we shall say we shall say as Canadians who happen to live in this part of Canada. What we shall say will be said because it needs saying in the interests of Canada as well as of Manitoba." The purpose of the inquiry appeared to Bracken to be "the strengthening of the spirit of Canadian unity and . . . binding more closely together the different economic areas within the nation." It was to establish "confidence on the part of all Canadians, wherever they may be domiciled, that this country means to assure to them in their instruments of government a means by which they may hope to achieve the greatest possible measure of political and social justice for all areas and all individuals."[4]

The submission which followed was a sustained argument for a reduction of debt charges by federal aid in refunding and for a reallocation of constitutional responsibilities between the provinces and the nation. In especial Manitoba urged that the federal government assume the whole costs of relief and old age pensions and one-half the costs of certain other services. The submission, in short, was an argument for federal assumption of responsibilities which were national and for provincial revenues which would enable all the provinces to maintain the social services public opinion demanded at a level comparable with that of the more favoured sections of the nation. The unuttered alternative was repudiation of debt by the weaker provinces and the migration of their populations into the stronger provinces, with the possible result that their social services also would be overwhelmed. If the new standards were to be provincial, not national, the results would be disastrous for western Canada and serious for the remainder. Only a new concept of the nature and purpose of Confederation could alleviate the distress in the West and restore the unity of the nation.

Such was Manitoba's submission. The Commission then departed, to continue its hearings across Canada and the studies its staff was pursuing at Ottawa. Its course was pursued with keen attention and high hopes by Manitobans, but the two years which were to elapse before its report was published were years of continuing strain.

The agricultural economy of the province had found some relief in the stabilization of the price of wheat by the Wheat Board, in debt relief under Farmers' Creditors Arrangement Act, and in continuing diversification. The new strains of early maturing wheat, Garnet, Ruby, and Reward, were beginning to avert the menace of rust. To these was added Axminster, the product of the loving labours of Samuel Larcombe, now in his latter years become Manitoba's best-known farmer citizen, jolly, green-thumbed, and tireless.[5] But agricultural prices remained low, and the rust of 1935, the drought of 1937, prevented any significant recovery. In 1938 a heavy crop was harvested, in 1939 a fair one, but the world price of wheat collapsed in the face of large world crops and the growing threat of war in Europe. In December of 1938 Premier Bracken summoned a conference of agricultural experts to seek ways of alleviating the situation by increasing the industrial uses of grain and the degree of diversification on the farms. The organized farmers themselves were seeking to escape the old predominance of grain growing. The Canadian Federation of Agriculture, organized in 1935 and joined by the U.F.M.

in 1939 as the Manitoban Federation of Agriculture, was an attempt to bring all farm organizations together. But in the immediate circumstances wheat and the price of wheat remained the key to the maintenance of the solvency of western agriculture. A serious political struggle developed between eastern and western Canada over the price at which the Wheat Board should accept delivery of grain. After much indecision, the price was set at sixty cents a bushel, Fort William, a price which meant a heavy commitment by the national treasury and a disastrous price for the wheat grower. Coupled with this was provision for payments for each acre of wheat in areas stricken with drought. The West received the news with bitter disappointment. After a visit to Ottawa by Premier Bracken and Premier W. J. Patterson of Saskatchewan, the price was increased to seventy cents a bushel. Nothing could have illustrated more vividly the continuing plight of western and Manitoban agriculture than this attempt to have the federal government underwrite the wheat economy of the West, unless it was the proposal of the Manitoba government to barter Manitoban honey for German machinery in the spring of 1939.

The plight of agriculture was matched by the plight of Winnipeg. Even though the relief rolls were shortening, the number of unemployed remained high; despite a considerable industrial growth, led by the needle trades, the volume of employment could increase little while the agricultural economy with the processing industries languished. There was little construction, since the last of the relief works, the sewage disposal system, was completed in 1937. Real estate values were low; houses were run down; the slums along both sides of the Canadian Pacific tracks from Point Douglas to the westward became even more slatternly and noisome. Assessment, however, remained high, and the mill rate high. More and more citizens were growing restive under the weight of taxation and the never-ending burden of relief. Yet the credit of the city remained high, for the annual payments into the sinking fund, first made effective in 1908, remained fixed, and with the earnings of the fund more than provided for the retirement of the civic debt. In 1938 the City Council revolted at the burden of unemployment relief and sought to obtain further aid from the province. The provincial government, whose credit was less well supported by the provincial sinking fund, refused to help on the grounds that the city might safely find additional funds for expenditure by decreasing the payments into the sinking fund. As the sinking fund had become sacrosanct in the eyes of the city treasury officials and the Citizens' Election Committee aldermen, the council refused to take the recommended action, or indeed to give information which the provincial government wished. The dispute was referred to a Royal Commission of Enquiry, consisting of Mr. Carl Goldenberg, who was appointed by the provincial government but paid by the city. The Commissioner found that the financial position of the city was basically sound, and that payments into the sinking fund need not be continued at the established rate.[6] The provincial government, thus vindicated, continued its stand. Winnipeg was left to shoulder its heavy burden, and urban real estate and urban business to carry the municipal share of relief.

The years between 1936 and the report of the Royal Commission on Dominion-Provincial Relations, however, were not spent only in demands for federal aid and in contests between the province and the municipalities. There was a constant endeavour by individuals to find new sources of income, an endeavour which showed in the further diversification of agriculture, the beginnings of small industry in the towns, and the rise of new industries in Winnipeg. These beginnings were of slight effect, but significant both of the spirit of the people and of new hope for the future. And the provincial government gave increasingly effective leadership to the attempt to broaden the base of the economic life of the province. The acquisition of the natural resources in 1930, which at the time seemed rather a transfer of responsibilities than of resources, had produced in the Department of Mines and Natural Resources and throughout the government service a spirit of stewardship, proud of its responsibility and increasingly enlightened in its administration. During the depression that spirit had fused with the pragmatic character of the government, and the need of government to lead and initiate, to change the character of governmental activity from that of a caretaker to that of a manager. It was not that the principle of private enterprise had been replaced by that of socialism; neither extreme of doctrine entered into the matter. It was rather that government and people formed a working partnership to conserve and develop the wealth of Manitoba's rugged natural heritage. That partnership was the result of the easy and intimate union of a democratic people with a government they made their own in outlook and manner, and the response of the civil service, now one of great ability and loyalty, was quick and effective.

The first and finest example of this co-operation of people and government had been the rehabilitation of the muskrat marshes of the Saskatchewan Delta. There the muskrats had been decimated by the falling water levels, and the trappers, Indians and half-breeds of The Pas and surrounding country, reduced from poverty to destitution by poor catches and low prices. In 1934 the Department of Mines and Natural Resources, following the bold lead of Tom Lamb, trapper and fur buyer of The Pas, began to restore the water levels by building dams and controlling the flood waters which maintained the marshes. Then as the muskrats multiplied in their restored environment, the Department imposed closed and open seasons, fixed the number of furs a trapper might take, paid an initial price for the catch, made additional payments as prices permitted, and formed a reserve against the return of hard times. The result was the stabilization of an area of Manitoba's oldest industry and an increase in the security and comfort of the humble descendants of those Indians Kelsey had sought out to persuade them to take their furs to York Factory. The same system was extended to other areas of marshland, at Delta, Netley Marsh, and Fisher Bay on Lakes Manitoba and Winnipeg. The same aim and spirit guided the introduction of the registered trap line system into the eastern and northern reaches of the province. By this system the trapper was given an exclusive lease to a trap line, with right of transmission to his heir. As a result, instead of stripping its furs for fear of rivals, he was encouraged to conserve its animal life, and take only a fair annual yield. In somewhat the same way, it would seem, had the Indians of Manitoba regulated their season's trapping in the days of John Tanner, the captive boy raised among the Ojibways, and who hunted over southern Manitoba early in the nineteenth century.[7] Again, the result was a stabilizing of income among the Indians and half-breeds, still the poorest and least regarded of Manitoba's people. This revival and stabilization of the province's old industry was accompanied by the rapid expansion of the Winnipeg fur market, which handled some $4,500,000 of furs in 1938.

The same spirit and similar methods informed the work of the lands, forestry, fishery, and water services. The creation of the provincial forest reserves, in the spruce woods of the Sand Hills of central Manitoba, on Duck and Porcupine mountains and at Sandilands in the southeast, the beginning of reafforestation; the increasing use of soil surveys to govern the course of settlement; the restocking of the lake fisheries and the rivers; the study of water power resources and the control of water run-off; here were great areas of beneficent government enterprise by which the conditions for successful private enterprise were created. And more and more the old agricultural region of the south was knit to the new north by the work of the Department in encouraging the advance of the mining frontier, by the coming and going of its survey parties, by the daily flights in winter and summer of its air service.

The value of this enterprise was revealed by the steadily mounting output of the Flin Flon mine during these years and the rapid growth of the town of Flin Flon. The straggling shanty town of the early thirties had become a well-organized community, complete with churches, schools, and cinemas, but rugged as the rock on which it stood and lively with the spirit of a new frontier. And the gold mines of San Antonio and Gunnar Gold had given rise to the town of Bissett in the Central Manitoba mining field. Alone of all the productive enterprises of the province, the mining industry stood up to the depression and pointed to the desirability of broadening the base of Manitoba's economy.

How to do so remained a question. In 1937, as one of the conditions made by the Social Credit members of the legislature on which they would support the Bracken government, an economic survey of the province was undertaken. From 1938 to 1940 these studies appeared. Based on careful compilation of statistics, broad historical surveys of the various aspects of provincial life and governmental work, and considerable individual training and talent, they constituted a Manitoba Domesday which revealed the resources and limitations of the province and the character and shortcoming of the achievement of its people. The survey made it plain that the province could make little further progress on the basis of a widely fluctuating income derived from primary production for an international market. A multiplication of sources of income, a conservation of resources for steady use, a quest for sources of income less directly related to the vagaries of the world market were necessary, if the life of the province was not to be wrecked by every depression and its economy wrought to frenzy by every boom.

The economic distress of the depression had, of course, been greatly aggravated by the great drought of 1929 to 1937. The climatic cycles of the West, erratic and unpredictable, were to be recognized as a factor in the life of the province henceforth. But even in the face of these recurring natural calamities there was hope that man might do much to soften the blows of drought. In 1934 the federal government had passed the Prairie Farm Rehabilitation Act, which set up a permanent agency to combat drought in the West. South-central and southwestern Manitoba were brought within the area of its operation in 1935. The P.F.R.A. endeavoured to make provision against dry years, so as to enable the farmer to survive and carry on until the rains came again. The re-seeding of abandoned land was begun, and the use of drought-resistant grasses, the employment of new methods of tillage to preserve moisture and protect the soil with a covering of trash, were encouraged. Community pastures were established to enable grain farmers to carry stock, one at McAuley in western Manitoba, one on the Long (St. Mark's) Ridge south of Lake Manitoba. Dams were put in to check the spring run-off of the prairie rivers, first on the Souris and the Long River in Manitoba. Most widespread, however, was the digging of dugouts on farms to provide water for stock and gardens. The whole concept was to diversify the grain economy so as to provide the farm with the means of survival in the cycles of low rainfall and low prices. More deeply, it was an attempt, far-reaching in its significance, to come to terms with the environment of the West. In these years of post-depression, the people of Manitoba were taking, in a slow, unconscious way, a resolution to live in their province and to work out a satisfactory way of life within the limits nature opposed to the courage and ingenuity of man.

All these things, however, were only beginnings. The outlines of the changing provincial economy were projecting from the pattern established in the late twenties. The year 1938 saw the inception, with a government guarantee, of a sugar beet factory in Fort Garry, such as had first been planned in 1926. A new industry was thus added to those of Winnipeg, and a new crop to those of the Red River valley. The Manitoba Power Commission and the Manitoba Telephone System, as reorganized in 1931 and 1934 respectively, had continued to ride out the depression on their reserves, but expansion had ceased since 1930 and was only just being resumed. Yet no great expansion could be achieved without an extension of services to the farms and a considerable increase of industry in Winnipeg. Similarly, the power developments completed in 1931 had met all demands during the thirties, and both the Winnipeg Hydro plant at Slave Falls and the Winnipeg Electric plant at Seven Sisters had great undeveloped capacity. There had been no occasion to complete these plants, and none seemed likely to arise. Until the growing prosperity of the rest of Canada spread to the West and until the base of the economic life of the province was widened, the remaining falls of the Winnipeg would run unharnessed.

There were, however, more palliatives for the depression than a quest for new economic opportunities. Life was not wholly depressed even in the Great Depression; in the leisure, even the too abundant leisure of these unprosperous years, a respite was to be found in the arts and sports. In the schools, kept open at great cost in many a rural district, teachers still trained their choirs, and the Music Festival of Winnipeg, now accompanied by local festivals across the province, went on to ever finer achievement. A Miss Gweneth Lloyd had opened a school of ballet dancing in 1937 from which a company was to emerge to offer ballet to small and doubtful audiences. And in sport as in art the old flourished and the new came in. The great Winnipeg Bonspiel yearly broke the long winter, and brought together hundreds of men from city and country in a game at once keen and relaxing. It was in these years that Abe Gowanlock of Glenboro and Ken Watson of the Strathcona Club carried the game to its highest pitch, with a skill unrivalled elsewhere. More exciting, and more popular, if only because so thoroughly commercialized, was the addition to spectator sports of rugby football. In 1930 the team of the Winnipeg Blue Bombers had been formed and was maintained with the aid of imported American players. The game and the team had become immensely popular by 1935, rivalling the native hockey. Thereafter a Bomber triumph in the annual contest with an eastern Canadian team for the Grey Cup, emblematic of the Canadian championship, or a broken field run by Fritzie Hansen, made all Winnipeggers one and oblivious of the depression.

While Manitoba awaited the findings of the Royal Commission, sought new sources of wealth, or cheered the Bombers, the rise of Nazi Germany had upset the balance of power in Europe and threatened the peace with crisis after crisis. Even if Manitobans had not remembered the Great War, and not had an ingrained sense of their involvement in the fate of Britain and of Europe, they would have been forced to be aware of the significance of events in the Pacific and Europe from 1931 to 1939 by the campaign fiercely fought by J. W. Dafoe in the editorial columns of the *Winnipeg Free Press* for firm support of the League of Nations in the Manchurian, Ethiopian, and Munich crises of those years.[8] The general outlook of Manitobans did not differ from that of other Canadians: they hoped against hope that the logic of events might be disproved. They did not accept the thesis of Dafoe that, if the League were not upheld, the peace settlement of 1919 would be destroyed and Canada involved in war; indeed, the circulation of the *Free Press* suffered from its editorial views. But Manitobans were conditioned by the campaign to expect the worst, and when war came in September,

1939, Manitoba was solid in support of Canadian participation on Canadian initiative. While one of its representatives at Ottawa, J. S. Woodsworth, voted against the declaration of war, he did so on grounds of strictly personal conviction, and his action was respected and indeed honoured. Once more the hurry and anxiety of war came to the streets of Winnipeg and to the far, lone fields of Manitoba which had never known war since the days of the Assiniboin and the Cree. The reserve battalions, each rich in tradition and battle honours now, were put on active service and the recruits flowed in. Once more the guns thudded across the Sand Hills, as the great training camp, now moved to Shilo on the Canadian National Railways, sprang to life and began a furious expansion. And all across the province the long black runways of air training stations were laid across the fields chosen for the purpose, as the great Commonwealth air-training plan of the Royal Canadian Air Force was developed, in which allied airmen learned in Canadian skies the skill to meet the German pilots who had terrorized Europe. In Winnipeg the women eager to help made Monica McQueen's Central Volunteer Bureau a brilliant success and a model for the country.

These beginnings of the war effort, however, unlike the rush of 1914, impinged but slowly on the wonted tenor of life. Manitoba, still faced with an indebtedness it could hardly hope to carry, awaited with undiminished interest the report of the Royal Commission. In February of 1940 it appeared. It recommended, in summary, a readjustment of federal-provincial finances which would enable each province to meet its obligations and maintain a level of social and educational services consistent with the Canadian way of life. The provinces were to be left free to decide how they would administer such incomes. The Report was received with unqualified enthusiasm in Manitoba, and was held to be a vindication in substance of the province's case and of the efforts made to obtain such an enquiry. The Report, however, was not received with enthusiasm in the central provinces, both for reasons which were legitimate and natural and for others which were political and personal, such as the rivalry between the then Premier of Ontario and Prime Minister King.

It was plain, therefore, that a special effort would have to be made if the Report were to be implemented; the conduct of government during the war and after would also require a united effort. These considerations led Mr. Errick Willis, the Conservative leader, and Premier Bracken, to agree on coalition, to which the other groups were invited to adhere. All consented and a non-partisan administration was formed in November, 1940, consisting of Liberal-Progressive, Conservative, C.C.F., and Social Credit ministers. It was not a true coalition, but a joint administration, based on the proportionate representation of groups used in legislative committees. It left each group autonomous, uncompromised as to principle, and committed to co-operation in administration only for the duration of the emergency. This latest coalition was, in fact, a first, full trial of the political concept of the Bracken government since 1922, that provincial government was a matter of administration only. The unwritten premise of the administration, of course, was abstention by each provincial group from participation in federal politics. The return of the coalition candidates, as they were called, in the general election of December, 1940, was opposed only by a few sturdy party men and independents.

The need of political unity, apart from the war, was demonstrated when in January, 1941, the proposals of the federal government for the adoption of the recommendations of the Royal Commission were curtly and scornfully rejected by the government of Ontario. This rejection was the more unhappy as any major implementation of the Report was unlikely during the war. When the rejection had occurred there was nothing to be done but to postpone the readjustment of Dominion-provincial financial relations until the restoration of peace. Meanwhile, temporary, or partial, adjustments must be made. In 1940 the federal government had assumed by constitutional amendment the responsibility for the relief of employable unemployed. This greatly lightened the load on the weaker provinces. In 1942 the provinces surrendered to the federal government for the duration of the war and one year beyond the levying of income and corporation taxes, in return for subsidies which compensated for the loss on the basis of the yield of those taxes in 1941. Thus the hopes of Manitoba for a permanent and helpful readjustment of federal-provincial finances had to be laid aside for the duration.

The formation of the coalition government of 1940 was inspired, as the subsequent rejection of the Report of the Royal Commission on Dominion-Provincial Relations was dwarfed, by the titanic events of 1940 and 1941; the fall of France, the Battle of Britain, the invasion of Russia, the Japanese attack on Pearl Harbor. The old familiar world in which Manitoba had come into being, and which had seemed to survive even the wars and revolutions of 1914–18, was crumbling in ruin all round the world horizon. During these two terrible years, Canada—and Manitoba—could only work and train for the day when the counter-attack could be mounted. Not until the very end of 1941 was a Manitoban unit to see action.

In 1939 the Permanent Force unit in the Manitoban Section of Military District No. 10 was the Princess Patricia's Canadian Light Infantry, the crack regiment of the First World War. The reserve units were the Winnipeg Grenadiers, the Royal Winnipeg Rifles, the Winnipeg Light Infantry, the Queen's Own Cameron Highlanders of Canada, as the 79th Battalion had been renamed, the 12th Manitoba Dragoons, the Manitoba Mounted Rifles, the Fort Garry Horse, the 2nd Armoured Car Regiment, and sixteen units of supporting arms. In 1939 the Patricias had joined the First Canadian Division and by the spring of 1940 were in Great Britain. Three of the reserve regiments, the Rifles, the Camerons, and the Grenadiers, were called out on active service, and allowed this time to preserve their own identities. Soon the first battalions of each were in training at Shilo and Fort Osborne. In the spring of 1940 the Grenadiers were despatched to Jamaica for garrison duty there; the Camerons joined the Second Division and reached England late in 1940; the Rifles joined the Third Division; the Light Infantry, now a machine gun unit, remained on garrison duty as a training battalion, later serving on the west coast. The Dragoons served as the 18th Armoured Car Regiment, the Fort Garry Horse as the 10th Armoured Regiment. These formations, bearing the proud memories of the first war, were as they had been then, keen, hard-driving units; but their battalion rolls revealed the change that had occurred in the population of the province since 1900. The names were drawn from every land in Europe, from the highlands of Scotland to the steppes of the Ukraine, but they were now all Canadian names.

In the Navy and the Air Force Manitoban recruits preserved no such identity as in the Army, but the Air Force and the Navy, actively engaged while the Army stood on the defensive, had their pick of the youngest and most eager men. The schools of the great air-training camps at Gimli, Macdonald, Portage, Rivers, Brandon, and Souris, were soon filled, and the peaceful Manitoban skies were loud with the drone of planes. Manitoban airmen in R.C.A.F. formations joined their Canadian comrades in the R.A.F. by 1940 in the Battle of Britain. And it is to be recorded that the Alan MacLeod of the Second World War was Pilot Officer Andrew Charles Mynarski, V.C. H.M.C.S. *Chippawa*, the naval depot in Winnipeg, was swamped with the prairie lads who were drawn to the seas, to those seaways by which indeed the prairies lived. And in H.M.C.S. *Assiniboine* the name of a prairie river was made famous by the hard-fighting destroyer which bore that historic name.

It was for the first two years a strange war for people who in 1914 had seen their men thrown quickly into the fiercest fighting. When at the end of 1941 Canadian forces became engaged, it was to be a stranger experience still for people whose troops had come to stand for the attack and victory. Now Canadians were to know the bitter taste of defeat. In the summer of 1941 the Grenadiers, still without battle training, were moved from garrison duty in Jamaica to garrison duty in Hong Kong. When the Japanese overran the island, the Grenadiers with the rest of the garrison were forced to surrender on that terrible Christmas, followed by the grim silence of the four years of captivity. And this blow was renewed when in the spring of 1942 the Second Canadian Division raided Dieppe to test the defences of Hitler's Europe. The Camerons suffered terribly on the fire-swept beaches, and lost many men, among them Major Norman Young, headmaster of Winnipeg's Ravenscourt School, and gentlest of men. But the Camerons, before ordered to withdraw, "had penetrated further inland than any other battalion engaged that day."[9]

It is defeat which tries the quality of men and the resolution of Manitoba to do its part in the war steadily hardened as the bad news came. By the beginning of 1942 it was apparent that the pledge not to introduce conscription with which the King government had led a united Canada into the war must be reconsidered. In April a national plebiscite was taken on the question of releasing the government from its pledge: for the whole of Canada the affirmative vote was over 60 per cent; for Manitoba, over 80 per cent.

While conscription for overseas service was not to be introduced for two years more, the plebiscite did register the degree of Manitoba's commitment to the war effort of Canada. How deeply Manitobans, sensitive to the deeper issues of the struggle against totalitarian brutality, were committed to the war is illustrated by their service in the effort to help the French Resistance, and by the death of Captain Frank Pickersgill in the grey horror of Buchenwald.[10] The commitment to battle began when R.C.A.F. bomber formations joined the air war in 1942, and in 1943 the Canadian Corps under Manitoba-born General Guy Simonds joined Montgomery's Eighth Army in the Sicilian and Italian campaigns. From then on, in Italy, in Normandy, and in Germany, Manitoban men and units were involved and lost in the wild fighting of the Canadian army among the Dutch islands and in the forests of the lower Rhine, until the surge of victory which destroyed Nazi Germany.

The war effort of Canada revealed itself in the field, but its sources were the factory and the farm. The war had brought about an industrial boom, which absorbed the great body of unemployed and drew labour from retirement and the home. The war boom led to a tremendous expansion of Canadian industry, but almost wholly in central Canada. Manitoban industry was prosperous as it had never been before, but comparatively little industrial growth occurred, and comparatively few war orders were placed in the province. This was a source of grievance, which both private industry and the provincial government set themselves to have redressed. As a result, some contracts were diverted to Manitoban firms, and this did something to aid the continuing efforts to broaden the base of the provincial economy. The effect of the war, however, was to enhance enormously the industrial supremacy of central Canada and to leave Manitoba, comparatively speaking, more than ever dependent on its agriculture and other primary production.

It was wheat and other foodstuffs that the war demanded of the province, as well as its base metals and wood pulp. Agriculture, like industry, revived and was prosperous, but entered on no new expansion and knew no boom prosperity. Labour was scanty, for recruiting and war industry swept the young people into the forces and the cities; farm machinery was in short supply and increasingly costly. Only towards the end of the war did farm equipment and power machinery begin to increase significantly. Once more, as in 1914–18, the Manitoban farmer had to work long hours with such help and equipment as he could muster. But there the resemblance ended. He increased his production, but not by breaking new land. Better tillage and crop rotation, the growing use of artificial fertilizer, the generally higher level of farming skill and management, a generation bred to the soil, drew more from the land which had been under the plough for from thirty to sixty years. Wheat, its prices stabilized by the Wheat Board and the steady demand of the besieged British Isles, though still the chief crop of the province, had ceased to be the great, general staple. Fields were familiarly known, the potentialities of districts gauged; each was required to bear what it was best fitted to bear. The long years of trial and error, the patient teachings of the field men of the Department of Agriculture and of the Faculty of Agriculture, had produced an adaptation of farming practice to soil and climate which meant that southern Manitoba was now a mature agricultural region. On the Portage Plains wheat still rolled to the horizon every golden August, and down the Red River valley and in the Swan River. But on the lighter lands of the Assiniboine Delta it was oats and barley for cattle and hogs which filled the fields. And more exotic crops were handled with greater confidence, fall rye, the very "chancy" flax, field peas, alfalfa, and other forage crops. In the Gretna and Morden districts, with their warm soils and longer frost-free season, hybrid corn was bringing the corn belt northward into Manitoba. Above all, the dry years were over, though their memory endured, and the P.F.R.A. continued to dig the ugly dugouts and to build the dams which were an insurance against their return.

If the agriculture of southern Manitoba seemed to have reached a stable adjustment to conditions of soil and climate, there were in these years, none the less, developments which suggested that a new agricultural frontier might be opening to north and east along the line of the forested verge of the Shield. Farmers were moving on to the moist forest and marsh lands of the Cat Creek district on Lake Winnipeg, of Fisher Bay on Lake Winnipeg, on Birch River north of Swan River and into the flatlands of the Carrot River near the Saskatchewan. If the era of prairie settlement was over, was a new agricultural frontier about to open on the clay soils of that half of glacial Lake Agassiz which lay east and north of the great lakes of Manitoba? Robert Bell and J. B. Tyrrell in their reports to the Geological Survey of Canada in 1879 and 1896–7 had noted the quality soil of the Burntwood River valley and the east shore of Winnipeg. It might be that time would yet reveal that half of the agricultural soils of Manitoba remained to be occupied.

However that might be, it was a restored, but spare and hard-driven agricultural economy which emerged from the war. The whole province emerged from the war restored, tested, but oppressed by the fear of the return of the hard years and the burden of debt. The return of the troops, the airmen, and the seamen from victory in Europe, the return of the survivors of the Grenadiers from Hong Kong, lifted the heart. But it was to a province marked by the ordeal of the depression and the wrench of war that they returned; a province which had lost the reckless confidence of the early years of the century, which knew itself to be one of the minor provinces of Confederation, which for fifteen years had seen its young people leave for British Columbia, for central Canada, for wartime service around the world. It was a province so long braced to endure that it did not find it easy to rejoice in victory or to expect much of the future. The concern of the provincial government and the mood of the people was to set themselves to fight the post-war depression which was assumed to be inevitable.

19

The Growth of Province in Nation
1945-1955

THIS GRIMNESS WAS NOT UNWARRANTED, FOR THE
war had only deferred, and had not decided, the resolution of the
issues with which the great depression had confronted Manitoba.
Was Manitoba to live within the revenues which its economy and
the constitutional limits of the British North America Act allowed
it? That might yet mean repudiation of debt and a reduction of
governmental services to a level which would have driven population out of the province. Or was it to be relieved of the drain
caused by discriminatory national policies and of the weight of
debt incurred by unemployment caused by national and international policies? That might mean a fair standard of life for its
present population and a modest contribution to the life of the
Canadian nation in whose growth the province had been so
intimately and curiously involved since 1870. The answer depended upon whether the central provinces and the federal government were at length prepared to recognize that since 1870 a
nation had been created, in which the provinces, large as well as
small, were interdependent. Manitoba had made its case in 1938;
the war had made Canada a nation as never before; the issues
were posed even more challengingly than in 1939.

It was the need of winning a favourable settlement of these
issues which, with the war, had led to the coalition of Manitoban
parties in 1940. The coalition had lasted throughout the war,
but with one important change in 1942 — Premier Bracken had
accepted the leadership of the national Conservative party and

the premiership had passed to Hon. S. S. Garson. A Liberal who had entered the legislature from the Interlake in 1932 and the Bracken government as Provincial Treasurer in 1936, Garson was a typical Manitoban, Ontario-born and Manitoba-bred, intense and dry-minded. He was an able politician and administrator. As Provincial Treasurer he had lived with the spectre of debt before him, and had made the subject of federal-provincial relations peculiarly his own. Indeed, it became almost an obsession and in this, too, he was typical of his province. He had bitterly deplored the rejection of the Royal Commission Report in 1941 and had set himself to obtain its implementation or a fair equivalent. Under his leadership the coalition held together until 1945 when the C.C.F., fearing the effect of continued membership on the provincial and national fortunes of the party, withdrew and went into opposition. In the provincial election of 1945, however, the coalition was easily victorious, and the C.C.F. remained an urban party confined to Winnipeg.

That dry years and hard times would sooner or later come again all the history of Manitoba proclaimed, and the union of political forces to ensure that the province would be better equipped to deal with their consequences was only prudent. Neither dry years nor hard times, however, returned in the first post-war years. The rains fell in the crop season year after year, and the fields yielded heavily harvest after harvest, until it seemed that the years of drought were something dreamed in torment and not an actual experience. New credit policies and new skills in government kept interest rates low, prices high, and the country's labour force at work. The Canadian Federation of Agriculture had won for the farmer a secure and influential place in the counsels of government, and agricultural policy was as urgent and complex a question as ever tariff policy had been. And demand from Europe and the United States for Canadian wheat, livestock, base metals, wood pulp, and manufactured goods had launched Canada on the greatest boom of its history. In this boom Manitoba shared definitely though not spectacularly.

It shared, because it was equipped and ready both to make the most of its established industries, primary and secondary, and to widen the base of its economic life. In agriculture the recovery achieved during the war was the groundwork for a steadily growing prosperity. The mood of the farmer, the hardy survivor of the fluctuations of a generation, was to go slow, to husband reserves, and to put stability of income before the quick and swollen profits of a boom. This mood found steadfast expression in the support given the Canadian Federation of Agriculture and its policy of attempting to stabilize the price of wheat by means of long-term contracts with the British government between 1946 and 1950, and by means of the International Wheat Agreement thereafter. Manitoba had its numerous and vocal advocates of the free market in grain, led by the *Winnipeg Free Press*, but the mind of the majority of farmers was expressed in the plebiscite on the compulsory marketing of coarse grains through the Wheat Board in 1950. The plebiscite was in favour of compulsory marketing by a large majority. To most Manitoban farmers the return of the free market meant the return of incalculably varying prices, on which the Winnipeg Grain Exchange alone seemed to thrive and which the majority of farmers associated with the hard times of the past. Anything which promised to stabilize farm income won his firm, if hard-headed support. The beliefs of the typical farmer with respect to the free market may have been mistaken, but there was no doubt of his mood, born at once of the harsh experience of the past and the high costs of mechanized farming in the present. That many farmers were still ready to take organized and sweeping action to defend the new-found place of agriculture in the national economy was indicated by the rise and growth of the Farmers' Union, the latest in the series of farmers' organizations.

The acceptance by the farmer of government control of the grain market was one characteristic of post-war agriculture in Manitoba. It signified that western grain farming was no longer to be left exposed to the full sweep of world price fluctuations, but had been made one with that national industrial economy which the federal government had been concerned to maintain by protective tariffs and subsidies ever since 1879. With his basic income thus secured so far as human ingenuity and a wealthy nation could secure it, the Manitoban farmer was free to develop his industry. The rapid power mechanization of agriculture was one indication of how he did so. The sale of farm implements in Manitoba rose from $9,987,683 in 1946 to $37,474,620 in 1949. The tractor finally replaced the horse; the threshing combine, the threshing separator and the threshing gang. In five short years the rhythm and tempo of the farm day was altered from the horse-set pace to the quick run of the tractor, of the farm season from the rush of seedtime and harvest to a few swift days and nights in April and August.

The quickened tempo of farming was matched by an increased ease and efficiency. The new cultivators and chemicals cleaned the fields of accumulated weeds. The hay baler eliminated the long, hot toil of the hay field, and yielded a better cured fodder. The new strains of the plant scientists, still, as since the days of the Saunders, the primary producers in western agriculture, matured more quickly and yielded more heavily. In particular, the rust-resistant wheats stood straight and golden before the combine knife, no longer black and dusty as in the bad years when rust destroyed that princely grain of former years, Saunders' Marquis.

The new stability and efficiency made it possible to push even farther the diversification which had begun in the twenties and thirties. Not only did dairying, poultry raising, and livestock continue to form an important part of Manitoba agriculture; not only was honey now an established staple of the province: still newer crops were being cultivated in favoured districts. Along the Pembina terraces from Carman south to Gretna, the new hybrid corn was more and more grown. To it was added the cultivation of the sunflower, chiefly by the Mennonite farmers whose fathers had brought it from Russia, for the extraction of oil from the seed. An oil-extracting plant at Altona was a local and co-operative industry based on this new crop. At Morden and Carman canning factories were established; at Portage a pilot plant to test the possibilities of the manufacture of hemp, which earlier experiments had shown would grow well in the district. In these districts the unit of land-holding began to grow smaller with the coming of intensive agriculture, whereas in the rest of the province, under the stress of the overhead costs of mechanized power farming, the unit tended to become larger. Thus, slowly and painfully, within the narrow limits of a northern and mid-continental climate the plant scientist and the farmer were extending the range of Manitoban agriculture and increasing its economic stability.

The post-war prosperity meant, of course, that not only the character of agriculture was modified, but that the appearance of the countryside was changed. Houses were repainted, often after many years; new houses became common, and new tractor sheds and new cattle shelters sprang up, modelled on the Nissen huts of the war, all curved roof and no wall. The day of the great barn was passing and few new ones rose. The greater revenues of the province and the municipalities, as well as a generation of work, meant that the roads were steadily, if slowly, improved. The provincial highway system was completed in the agricultural south and by 1950 had been pushed north to Flin Flon. Standards of construction were still low, but gravel was giving way to blacktop on the major highways. On the springy gumbo clays of the Red River valley, indeed, concrete highways were under construction and No. 75 to the United States border was completed in 1952. The great area and small population of the southern settled part of Manitoba and the scanty provincial revenues kept the provincial highways and the municipal roads far below the standards of central Canada or the United States. But even the municipal market roads were well graded and maintained and the side roads could be used by cars in most seasons. This was a far cry from the seasonal traffic of thirty years before, when only the railways furnished sure means of transport. Most striking of all changes was the fact that the main roads were kept open in winter. The cutter and bob-sleigh had followed the buggy and the waggon to oblivion. Their places had been taken by the car and the truck.

The increased mobility which the better roads and new vehicles conferred completed the breakdown of the one-time isolation of the farms. Saturday night had lost its old pre-eminence in the week. The towns became weekly marketing centres, dealing more in cash and less on credit than in former times. The small tank town and cross-roads village declined, but the medium towns and larger centres benefited from the wider shopping range of the farmer and the farmer's wife. Improved streets, new store fronts, new arrangements of the goods, marked the new prosperity and growing urbanization of the towns.

Nothing did more, however, to complete the changeover to urban standards and urban ways than the launching and swift progress of the programme of rural electrification undertaken by the Manitoba Power Commission in 1946. The Commission had succeeded in distributing power only to cities, towns, and villages since its establishment in 1919. The cost of installing electrical wiring and appliances in individual farms had been too great to allow many farmers to use its services. There were only 480 farmers on the Power Commission lines in 1941, despite the fact that the grid covered most of the settled part of the province. The City Hydro and the private companies served only about as many more. In 1942 a committee had been set up to study the problems of bringing electrical energy to the farms of the province. After a thorough study of the possible benefits of electrification to the economy of the province and of the success of the Rural Electrification Administration in the United States, the committee decided that it would be feasible to undertake the bringing of electrical power to at least half of Manitoba's 58,000 farms after the war and recommended that the work be undertaken.[1]

In 1946 the work was begun in the most thickly settled areas within reach of the Commission's lines. The work of enlisting subscribers was done by local committees, and the necessary 1,000 farms were soon under contract to electrify their houses and barns. Reasonable rates were promised, half the cost of wiring was assumed by the Commission, and the Commission acted as agent to supply "packets" of the most needed electrical appliances to the subscribers at cost. The programme succeeded beyond hope and expectation, despite rising costs. Great ingenuity was shown in enlisting local enterprise and help, both in obtaining the original contracts and in servicing the lines when erected and in operation. Care was taken to use provincial resources and to encourage provincial industry. Means were discovered for treating

Manitoba jack pine to supply cheap and durable poles; the manufacture of parts and appliances was undertaken by provincial firms, assured of a market for at least the ten years of the programme. The result was a great stimulus to the whole economy of the province. By 1950 there were over 20,000 farms with electrical services, and in 1954 the programme was practically completed. The use of electrical power in the cities and towns rose rapidly also, the sale of appliances and motors to the farms exceeded the estimates, and soon the "drag" on the power lines became serious. The rural habit of cooking the roast for dinner at noon created a peak load of alarming proportions.

Rural electrification was in a fair way to completing that transformation of rural life to urban ways and standards which had begun in the twenties, but which had been checked by the great depression and the war. In ease of labour and comfort of home the rural dweller had nothing to envy the city man, and he had in addition all the pleasures of country life. And the transformation was extending to outlook and manners also, as the radio brought the farm family into the national family, and the electrical motor took over the drudgery of the chores. The hope of two generations, that rural life might be as free and commodious as that of the city, but still rural, was at last on the verge of realization.

Not less significant was the effect of the province-wide distribution of cheap power on the possibility of diversifying the economic life of Manitoba. The hope of supplementing the income of the small towns by local industries was brought closer by the availability and growing use of electrical energy and by the market afforded by a prosperous agriculture. Local industries began to multiply; the Mennonite towns of Steinbach and Altona led the way, but in every town at least some new service shops were opened. So promising was the outlook that in 1947 and 1948 the newly functioning Bureau of Commerce and Industry conducted a survey of industrial resources and opportunities in the province, and came to the conclusion that only a growing market was needed to bring the industrialization of rural Manitoba to a head. As it was, the industrial growth of the province, including Greater

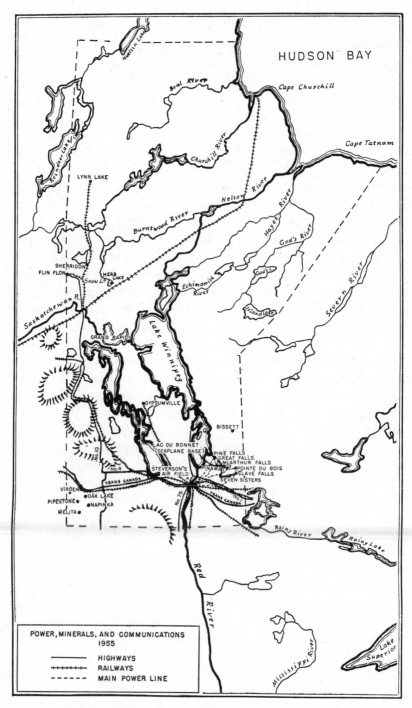

HUDSON BAY

Cape Churchill

Cape Tatnam

Nueltin Lake

Seal River

Churchill River

Reindeer Lake

LYNN LAKE

Nelson River

Hayes River

God's River

Burntwood River

SHERRIDON
FLIN FLON
HERB
Snow Lake

Saskatchewan R.

Echimamish River

God's

Island Lake

Severn River

GRAND RAPIDS

Lake Winnipeg

GYPSUMVILLE

BISSETT

LAC DU BONNET
(SEAPLANE BASE)

PINE FALLS
GREAT FALLS
MCARTHUR FALLS
PINAWA
POINTE DU BOIS
SLAVE FALLS
SEVEN SISTERS

STEVERSON'S
AIR FIELD

No.10

No.4

TRANS CANADA

VIRDEN
OAK LAKE
PIPESTONE
NAPINKA
MELITA

No.75

TRANS CANADA

Rainy River

Rainy Lake

Red River

Lake Superior

Mississippi River

POWER, MINERALS, AND COMMUNICATIONS
1955

——————— HIGHWAYS
+++++++ RAILWAYS
– – – – – MAIN POWER LINE

POWER, MINERALS, AND COMMUNICATIONS, 1955

Winnipeg, was rapid, some 200 new industries being started between 1946 and 1950. Among these was the Imperial Oil refinery in East St. Paul, built to refine oil brought by pipe line from the new oil fields of Alberta and that developed at Virden, Manitoba, in 1950. The new manufacturing plants were light industries or service industries. Most were branch plants, attracted by the growing wealth of the West and increasingly protected by rising freight rates. There was in Manitoba relatively little industry that was locally owned, and no heavy industry. The old processing industries, flour milling and meat packing, retained their pre-eminence. In short, the new industrialization depended on agricultural prosperity and national growth and was not as securely founded as could be desired. But as the dollar value of the industrial production of new industries and old rose year by year it became apparent that the economy of the province was leaving its old narrow limits and shifting to broader foundations.

To this diversification mining continued to make a growing contribution. The great Flin Flon mine still yielded heavily, although the Sherritt Gordon mine was nearing its end. But in 1946 the Sherritt Gordon Company staked rich nickel and copper claims one hundred and fifty miles to the north at Lynn Lake. A rush of prospecting in 1947 confirmed the existence of a new mineralized area beyond the Churchill. By 1950 plans were completed for the new mine, a new town of Lynn Lake, and a railway to connect the mine with the outside world. The same years saw the beginning of the production of gold at Snow Lake in the Herb Lake district, and the formation of a new mining town connected with the Hudson's Bay Railway by road. The new mining boom brought, as was inevitable, new stories year by year of new strikes in the reaches of the vast Precambrian.

The expansion of industry and mining, the rising consumption of power in rural Manitoba, brought up once more the question of new power developments. Since 1932 the established plants on the Winnipeg River had furnished an abundance of cheap electrical energy. Now it was necessary to complete the plants at Slave Falls and Seven Sisters. It soon became apparent that the production of the new installations would be insufficient to keep pace with the rising curve of power use. New plants would be needed, and the power developed at these would be more costly than that which came from existing installations. The day of cheap power in Manitoba was passing and the question was how the higher cost of new power should be distributed among the users of power in Manitoba. To find answers to this question the provincial government asked Dr. Hogg of the Ontario Hydro Commission to make a study and make recommendations in 1948. The Hogg Report presented a number of alternative plans, but recommended Plan C for adoption. This proposed the creation of a provincial power monopoly to be administered by a commission. The provincial government and legislature accepted Plan C, and, in preparation for its implementation, authorized the construction of a new plant at Pine Falls on the Winnipeg River, and set up a Manitoba Hydro-Electric Board under D. M. Stephens, Deputy Minister of Mines and Natural Resources, to administer the proposed public system. Stephens, a graduate in engineering of the University of Manitoba, had given a wide-visioned and spirited leadership to the new stewardship of that Department.

There remained only the task of preparing a general scheme into which the City Hydro and the various properties, power plants, distributing systems, and street railway system could be fitted. In 1951 the Hydro-Electric Development Act was amended by the Legislature, giving the government power to expropriate the Winnipeg Electric Company. Detailed and secret negotiations followed with the City Council, the result of which was the acceptance by Council of Plan C. Sudden and forcible opposition by the *Winnipeg Free Press* to a public power monopoly succeeded in arousing antagonism to the measure, and brought about a submission of the plan to a plebiscite of the voters of Winnipeg. Despite the pleadings of the experts and the reasoned support of the *Winnipeg Tribune*, Plan C was defeated. The situation was then that the original problem of pooling the old cheap power with the new dearer power was still unsolved. A new solution was applied when in 1952 the province purchased the plants and the distributing and street transport system of the Winnipeg Electric Company, and resold the systems to the City of Winnipeg, a complicated series of transactions completed in 1955. Two publicly owned systems then emerged, the Provincial Hydro System and the Winnipeg City Hydro, both under the supervision of the Board. The production and distribution of electrical power in Manitoba thus became a public function, though not formally a public monopoly. On the Board rested responsibility for the development of electrical power ahead of demand. In 1952 the development of McArthur Falls, the last of the Winnipeg River sites, began and was completed in 1955. The surveying of the power sites of the Nelson was also pushed forward, but in 1954 it was decided to build steam plants in the south before developing the northern sites.

The controversy over electrical power was only a symptom of a struggle for economic power. The business community of Winnipeg, like that of Canada and the United States generally, with returning and continued prosperity, was regaining confidence. The control by private interests of the new power resources of Manitoba would yield profit and prestige to the business community. On the other hand, power development was but part and parcel of the general development of all natural resources which the Department of Mines and Natural Resources had been fostering as best it could since 1930. The removal of D. M. Stephens from the deputy ministership of the Department of Mines and Natural Resources to head the Hydro-Electric Board was a symbol of the fact that the development of hydro-electric power was both basic to the industrial development of Manitoba and a part of the conservation for use of the province's resources. The keen rivalry between the advocates of private management and the leader of the new stewardship was a measure of Manitoba's economic revival, for hydro-electric development in the province was no longer a burden to assume but a prize to contest.

That such a rivalry should have arisen was at first sight surprising. The government of Manitoba had retained the undoctrinaire and wholly pragmatic character it had assumed with the coming of the farmers to power in 1922. It was committed neither to policies of public ownership nor to policies of governmental restraint. Under the non-partisan, unpolitical leadership of Premier Bracken there had developed an able and devoted civil service, commanding in such men as R. M. Pearson, deputy provincial treasurer, and R. M. Fisher, deputy municipal commissioner, a high order of talent and a driving sense of duty. The various ministries of Premier Bracken had been governed by the belief that their task was a straightforward administration of provincial business. The unintended result of this partnership of able civil servants and non-political ministers was, not a theory of government, but a habit of administration, which has been called here the new stewardship. It was this spirit, sharpened and made explicit as it was by Stephens, that the business community of Winnipeg had challenged.

In the nature of the case, the government itself, being committed to no stand on principle, was not involved in the challenge; the rivalry had developed beneath its feet. It could claim, however, to have discharged its duty as it saw it in this and on the larger issue of the financial relations between the federal and the provincial governments. Indeed, only a newly established relationship with the federal government had made possible the great financial operation involved in the taking over of the Winnipeg Electric Company. In 1946 the tax agreement of 1942 had come to an end. The federal government had called a conference in August, 1945, to make proposals for future financial relations between the provinces. Manitoba's hope that the recommendations of the Rowell-Sirois Commission might be taken up anew were dashed; the unchanging opposition of the central provinces had defeated that attempt to create the conditions of an enlightened and comprehensive nationalism. The federal government now sought to remedy only one obvious evil, the fact that the central provinces were able to tax, not only income earned within their jurisdictions, but also that earned in the other provinces by individuals and corporations situated in the central provinces. It proposed therefore that it continue to collect, as under the 1942 agreements, the income and corporation taxes, and, as well, succession duties. In return, it undertook to pay a subsidy of twelve dollars a head of population as of 1941 with adjustments as population changes were confirmed. The federal treasury would assume the cost of old age pensions for those seventy and over, and half the cost of pensions for those between sixty-five and sixty-nine, and of a health insurance scheme. The federal responsibility for the unemployed employables would be extended, and the government would contribute to a federal-provincial scheme of public works of a developmental nature in frontier and mining regions. The proposed agreement should last for three years.

The provinces sought time to study the proposals, and the conference was resumed early in 1946. The federal government now raised its subsidy to the figure of fifteen dollars a head, an amount to be increased only with a rise in national income above the level of 1942. With this and other minor modifications, seven of the provinces signified their willingness to accept; Ontario and Quebec declined. The federal budget of 1946 therefore authorized the government to enter into the agreement with the provinces individually, and in November, 1946, Premier Garson signed a tax agreement, revised upwards in January, 1947, by which Manitoba undertook not to levy income or corporation taxes, or succession duties, for a five-year period for a minimum annual payment of $13,512,000 which might be increased by both a rise in population and a rise in national income. The result was an increase of at least $5,500,000 a year in provincial revenue.

For this great gain and long-delayed fiscal justice Manitoba was properly thankful. It was a cold-blooded and impermanent financial adjustment, far removed from the national vision of the Rowell-Sirois Report. But it at last gave the government of Manitoba the means with which to govern well, and to lift some of the costs of education and the social services from the hard-pressed municipalities and school boards. When to the agreements was added the cancellation of one-half of the province's debt for relief still owed the federal government, it was clear that the Garson government had won a large measure of success in its long battle for a tolerable financial position for Manitoba in Confederation. The premature province of 1870 might at last be able to support the dignity of provincehood.

The new revenues and the debt relief were at once shared half

and half with the municipalities. The amounts would increase
with increases in provincial revenues, but be distributed as agreed.
Of the $2,750,000 apportioned to the municipalities, $1,900,000
was devoted to education. This last was distributed by bringing
in a comprehensive scheme of school taxation and grants such
as had been proposed by the Murray Commission in 1924. On
the basis of an equalized provincial assessment, municipalities
were to levy a rate of six mills, and unorganized districts one of
ten mills. The difference between the yield and $1,400 a year for
each school room in each district would be met by provincial
grant. The effect was to make the provincial grants an equalizer
of school revenues across the province; wealthy districts received
comparatively small, poor districts comparatively large grants. A
long step towards the realization of equal opportunity for education had been taken. In the same way the new revenues and
special federal grants to the provinces made possible the launching of a hospitalization scheme designed to make the latest treatment and most up-to-date medical care available to all parts of
the province. In a dry, hard-headed way, the government of Manitoba was building a welfare state in Manitoba, but only in response to proven need and only on the basis of assured means.
The long ordeal of the twenties and the thirties had imposed a
saving prudence on both the provincial administration and the
provincial electorate, while the pragmatic character of the government assured its abstention from extremes of doctrine. Nothing
revealed this attitude more clearly than the adoption of a plan
of retirement of deadweight debt at a rate and on a scale which
severely reduced the funds available for public services. (There
was, indeed, a touch of extravagance in this haste to retire a debt
dwindling in the steady inflation; the Garson and Campbell administrations were debt-depressive.)

That prudent, pragmatic character was not altered when in
1948 Premier Garson, his special task of establishing Manitoban
revenues on a sound base accomplished, resigned to become Minister of Justice at Ottawa. He was succeeded by Hon. Douglas
Campbell, who had first entered the legislature when barely of
age in 1922 as a United Farmers' representative. Premier Camp-

bell was the first native Manitoban since John Norquay to hold
the highest political office in the province. A son of the Portage
Plains, of Scottish-Ontario descent, a farmer by occupation but
deft in word and ready in sympathy, a firm believer in non-
partisan provincial administration, the new Premier embodied
and personified all the main political tendencies of the province
in his generation. His rise to the premiership and the victory of
his government in the general elections of 1949 and 1953 were
clear indications that the electorate of Manitoba, as represented
by the dominant rural constituencies, still approved the political
changes of 1922. The more the long-continuing administration
begun in 1922 changed, the more it was the same thing, an
agrarian and rural government, non-partisan, non-political, and
independent of, if not unco-operative with, the national Liberal
party. For as long as there were national parties, non-partisanship
could not be complete. The coalition of 1940 had been a near
realization of the political ideal of 1922. But the Social Credit
movement had faded out, the C.C.F. had withdrawn in 1945,
and the Conservatives, leader and party, had followed in 1950,
except for two cabinet ministers who chose to remain.

This enduring administration had given the province simple,
honest, straightforward government, uninspired but not unpro-
gressive. The negative democracy it practised accorded well with
the rural political temper. In these later years, however, the source
of its character and durability was becoming painfully apparent.
The rural representation of the province had not been substantially changed since the redistribution of 1907. Since that time
the urban population of Manitoba had increased from 138,090 to
337,331, the rural from 227,598 to 389,592 in 1951.[2] The consequence was a steadily increasing over-representation of the rural
element and a corresponding under-representation of the urban.
While it had always been conceded in practice that rural members should represent territory as well as people, the need for
the differential had been steadily diminishing with the improvement of roads, the spread of telephones, and the use of the radio,
while the actual differential was increasing. At the same time the
growing diversification of industry in the province raised the

question whether a government so preponderantly rural and agrarian could adequately represent the desires and meet the needs of the new stage in the growth of the province. By 1949 the question of representation had become one of some irritation and when the new redistribution measure of that year left the foundations of rural domination of the Legislature undiminished, the irritation became acute. The result was a renewal, in a time of high prosperity in both city and country, and when social and economic differences between urban and rural life were steadily diminishing, of the old urban-rural jealousy. This expressed itself in petty bickering over municipal plebiscites on such trivial things as daylight saving and the colouring of oleomargarine. These were indications that the distribution of political power in Manitoba was in need of being made broader and more flexible. This was in fact attempted by a new Redistribution Act in 1955, which increased the ratio of urban to rural representation and provided for an independent Commission for redistribution.

The constriction of the representative system was one indication that the pragmatic mind which had governed Manitoba for a generation, and served it well in hard and trying times, was now revealing its inherent limitations. Parliamentary and responsible government had been seriously, if not fatally, impaired by the persistent confusion of government with administration. The task of democratic government, to lead, inform, and inspire, had been deliberately neglected by ministers who bound themselves to their desks, doing the administrative work which should have been left to their departments. And the same ministers, largely trained in municipal affairs, reduced provincial government to municipal administration. This led them to look to the electorate, not to the legislature, as the source of power. The result was the creation of a plebiscitary democracy and the degradation both of the legislature and the Crown by a cabinet exercising an excessive and usurped influence. The long stifling of debate on political principle, the long insistence on administration rather than politics, had ended in a groove of routine, an incapacity to comprehend opposing points of view, or to envisage new opportunities and new lines of advance. Renewal by recruitment of new men to the government offered only slight hope that men of genuine independence and challenging capacity would be chosen. The impatient surge of a new generation of public men, to whom the past might be a springboard rather than a pedestal, and who might feel impelled to develop talent rather than demonstrate mediocrity, was much to be desired.

Whether Manitoba was capable of producing such a generation was in doubt. For twenty years of depression and war thousands of Manitoban youth had had, in a flight of all the talents, to seek opportunity elsewhere in Canada. The census of 1941 revealed that Manitoba had failed to hold its natural increase; that of 1951, that the rate of increase of its population of 776,541 was the second lowest in Canada, though the population of the sister province of Saskatchewan had actually declined. The drain of energy and talent from so young and small a community had been severe and telling. For those who found a place in their native society, the cautious mood the depression had inspired, the loss of confidence the retarded growth of Winnipeg and the province had caused, were muffling impediments to initiative and daring. The limitations of the matter-of-fact mind reinforced these barriers, for utilitarianism was the common cast of thought of the British-Ontario stock of Manitoba. Civic politics and private business in Winnipeg, Brandon, St. Boniface, Portage, were dominated by adherence to routine and precedent, and conducted in an aura of genial babbittry. Not since the lamented death of J. A. Richardson in 1939 had the Winnipeg business community known creative leadership; not since the defeat of jolly Mayor John Queen had it known anything but formal rectitude at best in civic leadership. It was the era of bureaucratic competence, of the heir succeeding to the established business. The dreams of 1911 were no longer dreamed, and the vision was lacking to see that the continuance of Communism in the North End was a challenge to civic democracy, that local industry was necessary to offset the effects of head office controls and a transient managerial class, that a new concept of the city's future was needed, and that in the cultivation of the inner resources of mind and spirit by education and the arts was a civic enterprise which could both add to the well-being of the city and transcend any limitation of material resources. Only, on the whole, among the non-Anglo-Saxon Canadians of Winnipeg and the Mennonites of Steinbach and Altona were there at once that enterprise which made two industries flourish where none was before, and the capacity to live a whole and vigorous life.

The day of material pioneering, of subduing the wilderness with axe and plough, was over, and the British-Ontario stock, which had borne the shock of that attack and founded the institutions of the province, had exhausted itself in the process and had not yet found for itself other fields of endeavour. It was the newer stocks which were the more dynamic, more content with small beginnings, more prepared to dare. They had not yet succumbed to the cult of material comfort, the ashen goal of the practical mind. Hope, for there was ground for hope, lay in the younger generation, broadened and toughened by the war years, and fired by the opportunities of the post-war boom. The election of Mayor George Sharpe, son of Mayor Thomas Sharpe, in 1954 was perhaps a sign of a new day in civic politics, as the appointment of Dr. H. H. Saunderson, a native son and an alumnus, to the presidency of the University of Manitoba was perhaps a sign that the province was shedding its intellectual colonialism.

The grey pall of pragmatism hung heavy over all areas of provincial life. The churches, whether shaken like the Protestant churches by the collapse of the old theology, or engaged in maintaining a traditional theology against the corrosion of the "scientific" mind, were, like the community they served, weary with the task of maintaining the results of their pioneering and missionary work against the effects of the great depression and the growth of materialism. The decline of the Church of England in rural Manitoba and the union of the Presbyterian, Methodist, and Congregational churches, consummated in 1925, were, among other things, indications of the weakening of the religious spirit as the pioneering years gave way to the years of material accomplishment. The Protestant laity were largely indifferent or complacent, ignorant of the theological foundations of their churches, and blinded by the false doctrine of the "social gospel" to the spiritual truths of religion. The strength of the malaise was revealed by the proliferation, on the one hand, of evangelical and fundamentalist "Bible" churches, and by the beginnings, on the other, of ritualism in the Protestant churches. The fundamentalists refused to admit that science had destroyed the literal acceptance of Scripture; the established churches were beginning to reinforce the Word with timid approaches to sacramentalism. The Catholic churches, both Roman and Greek, were still so deeply engaged in struggling to preserve their flocks and build up their parochial and diocesan organizations that they could yet claim to be the church militant. So also was the Greek Orthodox, the bulbous domes of whose churches gave a new outline on the Manitoba horizon and brought into every neighbourhood a branch of the Christian church after ten centuries of separation. But it was generally true that religion had ceased to be of major significance in the public life of the province: it was, however, still a vital spring of private life for many in a society still basically conservative, and its potential force was what it had always been.

The churches, however, were autonomous societies and in them convinced believers might resist the mass pressures of a commercialized and mechanized civilization by a resolute stand. It was not so in public education. In the schools the prevailing pragmatism led to an exaltation of the physical sciences and mathematics over the liberal disciplines, and to the adoption of the American emphasis on social adjustment rather than on intellectual training. The results were at once a remarkable success of the schools in making Canadians out of the varied stocks fed into them by immigration, and a serious threat to intellectual standards. The competence of the professions, the integrity of science, the quality of taste, were being steadily lowered by the influx of young people of fine natural endowment and inadequate intellectual training. The decadence of intellectual standards, the maintenance of which was the greatest need of a society emerging from pioneering, was increased by the contempt in which a materialistic community held the teaching profession. The really fine achievement of the University of Manitoba in its first generation was similarly threatened and the University, like the schools,

was starved of that public understanding and appreciation without which the education of the young and the pursuit of knowledge become mechanical and defeatist occupations.

In such a climate the arts and letters had little opportunity to
flourish. They were cultivated only by inspired individuals and
devoted groups. Music, as it had been for a generation, was the
great exception, with its popular roots and its snobbish appeal.
The Musical Festival had grown from strength to strength and
finally in 1947 the musical life of Winnipeg reached full stature
in the founding of the Winnipeg Symphony Orchestra, with
Walter Kaufman as conductor. And in the Trepel sisters and
Donna Grescoe, Winnipeg had produced artists, and in Barbara
Pentland and Ross Pratt composers, of promising performance.
In music Manitoba had developed something of the tough mind
and sharp sophisticated taste of a mature community.

One exotic art, by the genius of one person and the rigorous
devotion of its artists, reached a similar stature. Gweneth Lloyd's
Winnipeg Ballet Company had built itself up since 1937 into a
troupe which commanded national and international acclaim,
and gave promise of becoming as indigenous and popular as
music. The dance, like music, was capable of gaining the loyalty
of all sections of Manitoba's mosaic community, and "Visages"
and "The Shooting of Dan McGrew" gave Manitoba a common
joy and a possession forever. When in 1952 the Winnipeg Ballet
was allowed by royal permission to entitle itself the Royal Winnipeg Ballet, it was the certificate that this band of amateurs had
achieved the standing of professional artists dependent not on the
acclaim of local audiences but the approval of critics concerned
with the performance alone. And when disaster struck in the fire
of 1954 which destroyed both the properties and choreography of
the company, the Ballet was strong enough to recover and go on.

Drama and plastic arts, however, remained limited to cultivation by amateurs and the support of groups and coteries. They
had not yet succeeded either in allying themselves with the tastes
fostered by commercial art and the radio, or in finding a general
following in a yet incoherent society. For them perhaps only the
production of a local drama and art of force and point could com-

mand a popular following. The revival of the Winnipeg Little Theatre and the annual Drama Festival kept the love of the theatre alive but did little to produce actors or playwrights. The taking over of the Winnipeg School of Art by the University of Manitoba in 1949 and the invigoration of the Art Gallery by a group of interested citizens gave cause for hope of a wider love and more original cultivation of painting and sculpture.

Letters, always the product of the individual artist, were more backward still. The fact seemed to be that the British-Ontario stock had come to Manitoba divested of the folk culture of their ancestors, and comparatively untouched by the sophisticated culture of the British Isles. The dearth of libraries and the disappearance of the theatre had made it difficult to maintain a tenuous connection with the cultural development of the twentieth century. The rejection of Frederick Philip Grove had been the result of the general failure to keep abreast. Until some fair proportion of the British Canadian stock resumed that contact, their intellectual and imaginative powers would be spent in the arid pursuit of politics, the law, and the social sciences. Perhaps the most characteristic Manitoban book of the years of depression and war from 1930 to 1945 had been E. Cora Hind's *Seeing for Myself* (1937). The agricultural editor of the *Free Press*, the woman with a crop in her eye, had become famous for her ability to predict the wheat yield of the western crop. The book is an account of a tour of the world's agricultural regions, a shrewd and vivid account. But how the Manitoban mind failed to carry the same tough competence in matters of spirit is revealed in K. M. Haig's *Brave Harvest*, a loving but sentimental biography of Miss Hind. The simple, flawless prose of T. B. Roberton of the *Free Press* was a priceless possession, but scarcely a local product. The poet Thomas Saunders' *Horizontal World* showed in its theme, the Manitoban country side, at once the limitations of, and the hope of redemption for, the British Manitoban mind, that it bring to bear on actual life the resources of a neglected cultural heritage. Hopeful too was the undertaking by the revived Historical and Scientific Society of studies of ethnic groups in the province, of which Paul Yuzyk's *The Ukrainians of Manitoba*, and E. K. Francis' *In Search of Utopia*, were the first and second to appear. And Nan Shipley's *Anna and the Indians* revealed how much of tenderness and bravery there was in Manitoban history.

Manitobans of other stocks, however, had not lost their folk cultures, and in them lay a possibility of a literary development which might ultimately make English its vehicle and ensure its use once more in Manitoba as an artistic medium. The vernacular literatures in Icelandic, French, and Ukrainian continued to grow, and some of their authors published in English as well. Gabrielle Roy's *Where Nests the Waterhen* made the reedy islands and poplar bluffs of the west lake country the scene of simple and moving sketches. Mrs. Kristine Benson Kristofferson's *Tanya* followed Laura Goodman Salverson's novels in giving the Icelandic genius an English dress. And Paul Hiebert's *Sarah Binks*, rich with the soft laughter of the Mennonite, wrung laughter and tears from the bleak and arid life of the plains, not only of Saskatchewan. It is in such transmutation of the folk cultures and genius into the vernacular English that the hope of Manitoban letters seems to lie when at the end of eighty years of provincial history some evidence of more than material achievement is sought.

If indeed anything distinctive in the arts and letters were to arise in the province, it would come from the mingling and fusion of its many peoples. Otherwise, Manitoba's culture was merely part of the Canadian aspect of North American civilization. Manitoba had little claim to, and little likelihood of, a coherent and distinctive life. As a geographical area it had been reduced by the boundary settlements of 1818, 1881, and 1884 to much less than the natural limits of the Winnipeg basin. The boundary extension of 1912 had imposed on the small agricultural area of the south the heavy task of developing the vast and forbidding Precambrian north. The province was too small for political or cultural autonomy.

As a political division of Confederation, it was a subordinate community by definition, and it was neither possible nor desirable that a provincial patriotism should develop beyond the level of a decent pride in one's neighbourhood. In so far as the province as a political community operated to create a social community, it functioned as a subordinate agency, and the community it shaped was primarily and consciously Canadian. A viable political society had been formed in the province, one of a surprising coherence in view of the diversity of its constituent peoples, and one capable of common effort in peace or war. As a community, however, a social order capable of fulfilling all the needs of its members, Manitoba was, in the first place, only an area of Canadian society, and in the second place, incapable of discharging the full obligations of society. It had not produced even a definite art or literature, which are the elementary fruits of a formed community. While it is true that only a world society and a universal religion can fulfil the potential needs of human nature, and the cultivated man draws on all human culture for his needs, most men are satisfied with what is near and familiar. For Manitobans, on the whole, the arts, letters, and religious life were neither near nor familiar, whether local or universal. Manitobans lived either flatly provincial lives, or insubstantial exotic ones. Only the development of a provincial culture, a regional variant of a larger whole, from the foundation of an established material society could bring the two extremes into balance, and yield an art and literature rich with all the tang of all the province's peoples, as Manitoban as the reek of poplar smoke, as the Winnipeg goldeye, or as its summer's lucid honey.

Whether such a society would ever crystallize in Manitoba the future would reveal. Meantime the past had brought into being a community in ever closer adjustment to its harsh and confining environment. In the three and a half centuries since Button's sails hove over the horizon on the Bay, an advanced material civilization had been imposed on the stone age savagery of that day. The southern plains had been brought into cultivation and united in commerce with the northern Shield. The plains which had fed the fur trade now fed the mines, and where the fur brigades had filed down the rivers the grain cars now rolled into Churchill. With this great change much had remained un-changed; the Indian followed in essentials the wandering life of his ancestors; spring and fall the geese plied their ancient routes; the Shield lay rugged and immense as ever; the wheat and barley rolled in the passing wind even as the tall grasses before La Vérendrye and John Tanner. The *métis*, descendants of *voyageurs* and tripmen, now drove the thundering trucks of the highways. In the great flood of 1950, those of 1852, 1826, and 1776 recurred, and for a few days revealed how Lake Agassiz might come again. Even the Winnipeg River, the sounding fury of its falls choked back and drowned behind the rigid silence of the dams, now brought light and power to the outermost limits of the southern farmlands as in the days of La Vérendrye and his followers it had brought the light of civilization and the Gospel. The barren coast which Button had raised and Fox had probed was barren still, save for the shaft of Churchill's elevator; the southern plains, grasslands once and wheatlands now, were still the source of food for those who raided the northern forest and the Shield. Where so much was unchanged in ceaseless change, the environment and the past, geography and history, were constant and tireless artisans of Manitoban life. All its history, the fur trade and the Red River colony, the pioneers of the farms, the engineers of the railways and the dams, was always and steadily at work on the community of Manitoba.

Geography and history had produced a Canadian province, a proud, self-conscious, yet integrated community. It was Manitoban in virtue of its geography and its history, but geography and history also made it Canadian. It was Canadian because the pulse of its life was the action and reaction of settled south and wilderness north, the plains on the Shield, the Shield on the plains. It was Canadian because while geographically it was North American, culturally it was European in all the strands of its life. Manitoba, like Canada, had severed no ties and foresworn no loyalties. Its life was kept at tension by the pull and counterpull of American geography and European history. And the past would prevail in a community in which the one rebellion had been in defence of the past.

The past would prevail because Manitoban geography and history, like Canadian geography and history, were one and inseparable. The compulsions of geography alone would have taken its people on to easier climes; the past alone would have invoked a sterile loyalty to an unresponsive northern land. Both had combined to set working a precise natural selection by which Manitobans had been made, as Canadians had been made, of those who by endurance in loyalty to older values than prosperity, had learned to wrest a living from the prairie's brief summer and the harsh rocks and wild waters of the north. Manitoba, like Canada, was the response to the challenge of the north, a challenge not quickly or easily met. And those who remained and met that challenge, generation on generation, might hope to see in the life of their country, by work of hand or word of spirit, some stubborn northern flowering.

20

Epilogue: New Growth

MANITOBA IN 1955 WAS A FORMED SOCIETY. THE lands of the province that could be tilled and pastured had been determined. A highly developed agriculture had been established, a truly agricultural population had been sorted out of the very mixed lot of the early settlers, Canadian, American and British farmers, urban immigrants, European peasants, Icelandic fishermen, remittance men and simple romantics. Only three great difficulties of agriculture remained: credit, labour, and crop failure. But much had been learned about the first and third, in Manitoba and elsewhere, and the second was being solved in quantity by the use of power machinery, if not in quality. The farm organizations had created a climate in which agriculture could thrive, and the Faculty of Agriculture and agricultural representatives of the Department of Agriculture made the resources of science available to the farmer.

Towns and cities, railroads and highways furnished abundantly all the services that the agriculture, industry and distributive agencies needed. Schools, hospitals, and to a slight degree even libraries were available throughout the province. Electricity had reached all but the remotest corners of the settled south.

Everything, in short, that had been dreamed of and aspired to had been realized at least to a reasonable degree. The society the pioneer generation and its sons and daughters had sought to build had been established.

Social formations, however, and particularly in the vastly accelerated rate of change in the second half of the twentieth century, are like cloud formations. Seemingly fixed, perhaps massive, in all instances they both change their shapes and are in motion. Form transforms to form.

There were clear and pressing causes of change in Manitoba after 1955. There was first the changed economic climates of Canada and the world. The cycles of boom and depression, underscored as they were on the prairies by drought, crop failure, and debt, had become a fixed part of the thinking of the province. All enterprise, private and public, was governed by the need to be able to reduce costs and carry debt in times of low income. That depression would follow the Second World War was taken for granted. That the dry years would come again was thought certain, if unpredictable. But in fact no major depression, and no serious drought, or crop failure, occurred in the twenty years after 1945. A fundamental premise of Manitoba thinking simply did not hold. The economic climate was buoyant, expansive, beneficient. The hard-taught caution of two generations was confounded.

In the second place the very establishment of a modern society created social needs that had to be met. Of these perhaps the chief was improved opportunities for formal education. The elementary school system that had been created to ensure general literacy had largely succeeded. The secondary school system that had been designed to furnish recruits for the professions and for clerical and administrative work had also largely fulfilled its purpose. But these restricted ends were insufficient for the society which had come into being. For one thing, all forms of work, including farm work, required, or benefited from, more than elementary education. For another, Manitoba society was profoundly committed to the ideal of equality of opportunity. The widest way to the realization of the ideal was through the schools. Social rather than academic agencies, the schools had created out of the mixed immigrant population a new society of equals, for whom education might take the place of capital or family. More and better education was therefore both needed and demanded.

The next social need was better health services. Great as were the changes since the pioneering days, a greater change was in prospect, for the possibility of realizing it was now apparent. That was that hospital and medical services should be available to every one as of right, however the cost should be met. To provide such services meant more hospitals, more doctors, more civil servants. But in Manitoba, as elsewhere in North America, the demand was becoming irresistible. It was in fact revolutionary in character, in that like the abolition of serfdom, it ended an old old order long taken for granted, and also in that even the sceptics could see no way of opposing it and sought to guide rather than to halt. And behind the change lay the possibility that physical and mental health would cease to be a matter of private means and private action and become a public benefit universally available and maintained as a public necessity, like roads and water.

The third factor was the growth of population. While this was relatively slow in Manitoba, it was fast in the sense that the younger age groups increased faster than ever before. This was especially true, because of improved federal health services, among the Indians. There were thus more youngsters to be educated, and more educated. And there would be more young people for whom jobs must be found in a thriving Manitoba or who, like the generation of the thirties in their thousands, would have to find jobs elsewhere in Canada or abroad. The economy had, therefore, to be stabilized and expanded; this proved really only a matter of the rate of expansion.

The fourth factor in change was inherent in the kind of society and government which had been created in Manitoba. That was a society which, because of its experience in rapid pioneering and in the farm organizations, had, without adopting socialism as a creed, made government in all its forms an agency for economic and social development. The politics of creed, class and race were behind; the politics of development had arrived. Government, both the politicians and the civil servants, thought in terms of development. Its function was not to administer routines; it was to create opportunities for enterprise, and even to conduct the basic enterprises, such as the production of power, themselves.

The force of these changes was increased by one fundamental factor, which at once arose from the changes and intensified the need for further change. That was the shift of population from the country to the city. It was a massive and increasing shift. In 1941 the rural population of Manitoba had been 407,871, the urban 321,873. In 1951, the rural was 392,112, the urban 384,429. By 1961 the figures were 332,879 and 588,807.

The effects of the shift were momentous. Most apparent was the decline of the small towns. The little service town of the elevator, the grocery and hardware store, the post office—the tank town of railway days—was doomed. Motor cars on the new highways took shoppers, trucks took grain and livestock, to the bigger towns. Thousands of investments, little businesses, little jobs, homes, were threatened; many ended, others knew the slow erosion of inescapable poverty.

With the small town went, except in a few favoured regions, the small family farm which had been the cornerstone of Manitoban rural society. The uncertainty of agricultural income, the increased overhead costs of an agriculture based on power machinery and the use of artificial fertilizer, ended the marginal farm, unless the owner accepted increasing want outside the main flow of Manitoba life. Many in fact did in the bush country of the Interlake and along the edge of the Shield.

With the decline of the small towns and villages and the small farms went the steady weakening of local institutions, the school districts, the rural municipalities, the towns themselves. In a time when all costs were increasing and more public services were demanded, these bodies found themselves with incomes that decreased, or failed to increase rapidly enough. The rural school system and the rural municipal system of Manitoba were inadequate and failing, as those of Saskatchewan and Alberta had been recognized to be. Change was necessary. Yet these institutions had always been regarded, and rightly so, as the foundations of Manitoban democracy. Men and women familiar with them, and bred to respect them, would not part with them easily. At the same time of course metropolitan Winnipeg grew. In 1951 its population was 354,069; by 1961 it was 475,989, i.e., roughly half the population of the province. The old rivalry of the city and the province therefore continued, as was to be exemplified in the continual bickering over two issues, daylight saving time and the colouring of margarine. The city favoured, the country resisted both. It was a revelation of the course and character of change that both were finally to be accepted.

For the change was not only in the distribution of population, but also in the values people held. What might be called urban values were slowly replacing the old rural ones—a more material and easier way of life, greater social mobility, a freer use of credit, higher educational standards. The change might or might not be for the better; the fact was, it was taking place. It was occurring for two reasons. The first and perhaps most fundamental was that the countryside itself was being urbanized. Black-topped highways, the motor car and the truck, gave the countryman as much freedom and mobility, in winter as well as in summer, as any city dweller. Gone was the old rural social isolation. Electricity in country homes, running water, the use of groceries for the whole family diet, access to the same goods and services, ended all the old distinctions in tastes and manners between city and country folk. Rural values had been replaced by urban ones.

The second reason was that the growing size and power of Winnipeg could now, because of the first, exert their influence without check throughout the countryside. A cleavage that had existed since the "urban revolution" centuries before had closed. The country was now urban in outlook; the city was rural in scope.

Manitoba in 1955, then, was a formed, but also a revolutionized society. In no way is the fact made clearer than by the change which came over the provincial government after that year. It was still essentially the Bracken government of 1922, and was headed by a man elected to the Legislature in that year, Premier Douglas Campbell. No one better personified the first post-pioneering generation. A farmer by occupation on the Portage Plains, he was at home in the rural democracy, plain, direct, practical. Himself of better than usual education, he valued education for its pragmatic uses. Of Ontario Scottish and Presbyterian origin, he was canny, cautious, and realistic. Ideas he valued if useful; imagination he had never cultivated, distrusting its heady quality. Friendly in attitude, fluent in speech, dapper and debonair in manner, this warm and kindly man could at once lead a simple democracy and command the strength to govern. He must be placed among the outstanding Premiers of the province.

His greatest achievement already lay behind him, the assumption by the provincial government in 1954 of the production and distribution of all electrical power in the province, except for the Winnipeg City Hydro, itself a public corporation. His greatest challenge now lay before him, that of leading into the new and sweeping changes that the society desired and that the province realized were now required. No greater challenge could have faced any man than that, having accomplished his work, he should set out to re-make it. It is the measure of Douglas Campbell and of his generation that, with whatever doubt and reluctance, he did so. It is also the measure of the harshness of public life that, having done so, his performance should be judged inadequate.

Yet, in retrospect, the extent, rather than the reluctance, of the changes undertaken impresses the viewer. This readiness to change with caution was shown in four main ways. One was in increased expenditures, particularly on roads; another was in launching an enquiry into the state of public opinion with respect to the sale and distribution of liquor; the third was in an enquiry into the state of education in the province. The fourth was fundamental; it was a decision to alter the distribution of seats in the Legislature, with a specific ratio between urban and rural seats, a ratio more favourable to the urban.

The first of these changes, the increase in expenditure, was significant, if modest enough in retrospect. It was made possible by steady increase in provincial revenues, both from taxation and from federal grants. It was a response to a growing public demand, particularly voiced by the *Winnipeg Tribune*, for the more rapid building of better highways. And it was in road-building that the change was most rapid. A system of highways had been decided, and a standard of construction chosen. The system rested on Highway Number 1 (the Trans-Canada) across the province from east to west through Winnipeg and Brandon, the re-building of the Pembina Highway (now Number 75, the

Lord Selkirk Highway) south from Winnipeg to Emerson, and Number 10, the most exciting of all, from the International Peace Gardens on the border on Turtle Mountain north to Brandon, Riding Mountain, Dauphin, Swan River, and eventually to Flin Flon. The standard was good, not good enough for the clay soils and winter frosts of Manitoba, but it was an improvement over the gravel it was replacing. The extent to which the change to freer spending was accepted and the serious way in which it was undertaken was revealed by the building of the Highway Number 1 through the rock of the Shield to the Ontario Border. Hon. William Morton, himself a farmer and now Minister of Highways, followed this great undertaking with eager interest, the last such project of his service in the government.

The second change was a very different matter, because it was an assessment of how much the personal tastes and social values had changed in the generation since the 1920's. It was undertaken with great caution in 1955. A Royal Commission was headed by Hon. John Bracken, who came out of retirement for this review of legislation passed in his days of power. The Commission found a general desire to allow wine, beer, and spirits to be more easily available, and very little resistance to such a suggestion. The once great power that was the Women's Christian Temperance Union, for example, had dwindled to a mere handful of elderly ladies— the body which had once swept back the sea of drink.

The Commission's report therefore recommended that the sale should be greatly liberalized, that a commission of control be established, that the use of wine and beer be encouraged, and that a foundation be created to educate people in the matter of the evils of intemperance. The moribund puritanism of Manitoba decreed that liquor and wines should never be served on Sundays. The report was thought to be a sane and reasonable document, largely based on recent legislation in Ontario, shrewdly devised to forestall opposition, and it was well received. In 1956 its recommendations were made law, and local plebiscites across the province resulted in a widespread, almost general acceptance of some, or all, of the various ways in which liquor might be sold to the public in hotels, restaurants, or other public resorts. It was a clear statement of the prevalence of urban over rural values, an explicit declaration that the post-pioneering generation had ended.

The investigation into the state of education in the province was provoked by a public revelation of the shockingly bad examination results of most rural high schools in the annual provincial examinations. A Royal Commission with broad terms of reference was appointed in 1957 under the chairmanship of Dr. R. O. MacFarlane of Carleton University, until recently Deputy Minister of Education of Manitoba. It made an exhaustive and searching enquiry into all aspects of the educational system up to the University. Before the Campbell government could consider its findings, there had been a provincial election.

The fourth change was a deliberate grasping of the nettle of the question of the relative proportion of rural and urban representation in the legislature. The last redistribution of seats had been that of 1920. Since that time the representation of the rest of the province had greatly exceeded that of Winnipeg. Moreover, in Winnipeg the system of proportional representation across the city had allowed the representation of small parties, such as the Communist, and even of the election of individuals, such as "Judge" Stubbs. The city had therefore not one, or two, voices, but was a babel of political debate. Now Campbell, of his own initiative instituted an enquiry into distribution and the Legislature passed into law its finding whereby a ratio of seven rural seats to four urban was established. A commission, consisting of the Chief Justice, the President of the University of Manitoba, and the Chief Electoral Officer, were to re-distribute—for the time being—the constituencies at intervals of ten years. It was a major and successful reform, and a classic example of a reform carried in time to avoid a more extreme measure. It gave the Winnipeg voters more representation, twenty out of fifty-seven members. It also recognized generously the rural claim that metropolitan Winnipeg, with its councils and financial resources, had neither the interest in, nor the need of, representation in the provincial legislature that the rural constituencies had.

One other considerable development marked the last years of the government's altering course. That was the agreement entered into with the International Nickel Company to develop the great nickel ore-body discovered in the Moak Lake—Mystery Lake area of the North in the watershed of the Burntwood River. This great enterprise would lead to a town of 8,000 to 10,000 people in a blank part of the provincial map, and would give the province a mining development of major proportions. The province, for its part, undertook to build a dam at the Kelsey Falls of the Nelson River to provide the electrical power. This was done, the new town was built—named Thompson after an official of the company (not the great geographer)—and a gigantic stride taken in the development of the north. This, however, was not in itself a change. It was one more realization of the dream of growth in the north that would give the province wealth and population beyond what its agricultural and urban base in the south allowed.

Change was not, however, confined to Manitoba. It was rapidly taking place across Canada and throughout the world, change in the power and prestige of states, change in the relations of men in society, change in economic production and in social expectations, change in the modes of administration and in government. Suddenly in 1957 the Liberal federal government, in power at Ottawa since 1935, was defeated in the general election in 1957. John Diefenbaker of Saskatchewan, Conservative leader, became Prime Minister of Canada, although his victorious party was still only a minority in the House of Commons. Could a similar political change take place in Manitoba to match the changing circumstances and the altered mood of the province?

An almost identical change did in fact occur in the provincial election of that year. And it did so because, as in federal politics, a political leader was present to catch the tone of a political unrest that called for change at a faster pace and in a more forthright tone than the Campbell government, for all its response to the new times, had been able to give. That man was Duff Roblin.

A grandson of the former Premier, whose tenure of office had ended so badly, a convinced Conservative, a Wing Commander in the last war, and a Winnipeg representative since 1949, he brought much beside a historic name to public life. Brisk, assertive, commanding, he had revived boldness, decisiveness, and trenchant criticism in the Legislature. He restored to public affairs a sense that issues mattered, a sense long dulled by the former government's belief that the whole of government was mere administration, a sense dulled also by the war-time coalition in which the Conservative leader, Errick F. Willis, had served.

Roblin felt strongly about his beliefs, and in spite of his youthful appearance, his seeming coldness of disposition and too ready truculence, he persuaded the members of the Conservative party that they must adopt clear-cut Conservative policies and seek power in terms that the changed mood and needs of the province demanded. Because they agreed, they elected him leader of the party in 1954 in place of Willis, who relinquished the leadership amiably and loyally served the new chief. The government was henceforth challenged by a forceful and persistent critic, the brunt of whose criticism was that the times had changed, and that only a change of government would serve the needs of the times.

The Premier and the leader of the opposition made a piquant contrast, and were well matched. The one in power, easily confident, quick in analysis and in debate, the representative of the farmers' seizure of power from the professional and business men in 1922; the other challenging, high flown, tautly aggressive, a resurrection of the old party politics rejected between 1915 and 1922. Yet the former was now the representative of an old order, the latter the champion of the new in very shining armour indeed. Which would divine the temper of the province: Campbell who said, progress indeed, but with no burden of debt to drive us down in depression, or Roblin who said, progress yes, progress by using every resource we have, including the credit our future warrants?

The election results of 1958 gave no clear answer. The Conservatives elected twenty-six members, the Campbell Government nineteen, the Co-operative Commonwealth Federation eleven. Premier Campbell resigned, and Roblin was called to form a government. Victories in the Conservative southwest of the province, with the new single member constituencies in Winnipeg, had given the Conservatives their narrow chance. In an

autumn session, his programme of legislation received the support
of the C.C.F. and his government, if not capable of carrying fully
Conservative policies, was launched. After a defeat in the Legislature in the spring of 1959, he went to the country, and was
returned with thirty-six out of fifty-seven seats. He had been
given a comfortable working majority. Manitoba had not endorsed
a man, a programme, or an anti-political movement of emotion. It
had returned to party politics, the three parties of the Conservatives, the Liberals (as the followers of Douglas Campbell were
now frankly called), and the C.C.F., an urban labour party, but
one slowly growing in political realism. Manitoba had voted for
Roblin and change, but, ironically, it had done so with a Camp-
bellite caution.

It is therefore necessary to remember that the new government
was not, and could not be, a complete departure from the old.
For one thing, the Liberal opposition remained too strong, both
in the Legislature and in the country, as narrow margins of victory
in the constituencies showed. Any failure of the government, any
recession from prosperity, might bring the Liberals back to office.
For another, the government faced a dual opposition, the rural
Liberal and the urban C.C.F. It had therefore to maintain itself
in the country against the Liberals and in metropolitan Winnipeg
against the C.C.F. While desirous of being a party of progress,
it had to be a party of the centre: yet another factor was its own
internal equipoise between being conservative in principle while
progressive in practice.

The same character of the tight-rope walker was evident in
the personnel of the new ministry. The Premier himself, while a
well-to-do businessman, neither belonged, nor sought to belong,
to the economic and social establishment of Winnipeg. The same
was largely true of his urban colleagues; most were younger professional men, of public spirit but no great civic standing. The
government was not an urban government created in reaction to a
generation of rural government. On the other hand, its rural
members were as rural as any member of the Campbell government. This fact was personified in the second man in the cabinet, Hon. Stewart McLean of Dauphin, Minister in the sensitive

Department of Education. He was as much a representative of cautious, pragmatic rural conservatism as Campbell himself, and would have been more at home in a Campbell than in a Roblin government.

The task of this nicely balanced administration was therefore to tip-toe between the economic reaction of Winnipeg business and the social conservatism of rural Manitoba. It had to advance with deliberation and pursue idealism with hard-headed restraint. In this delicate balance was to be the explanation of both the success and the failures of the Roblin regime.

It was, however, in mood at least a government of action. Its plan of action, adumbrated in the sessions of 1958 and 1959, was taken up with vigour and defined with clarity in 1960. The key to its programme was the resolve to borrow against future development to meet present needs. Here was its real clash with the policy of the administration it had displaced: the core of Campbell's policy was to expand expenditure as revenues allowed, but to abstain rigidly from all borrowing, provincial and municipal. Its purpose was to free the revenues from the servicing of debt, and to be able to contract expenditures should revenues contract. This policy Roblin swept aside as defeatist in spirit and wrong in practice. The proper policy was to borrow wisely and spend wisely in the confidence that such expenditures were in fact investments in development which would yield the revenues to service and retire debt. It was the thinking of the aggressive businessman and of the economist who believed in "social" investment. It brushed aside the hard-won experience of practical farmers and politicians gained in the depression years. This was the central change in the transfer of power, and it was to remain the central issue of politics of the Roblin regime. The Premier had "put it to the touch" on this issue "to win or lose it all."

The policy met with a wide measure of public acceptance at the time, despite the steady criticism of the Liberal opposition and the *Winnipeg Free Press*. It did so the more because one of the chief concrete results was a great increase in road-building. This was widely welcomed for the work it gave and also by a public which, as it shared the general prosperity, bought more and more cars and took to the new highways to seek the new holiday resorts—planned and developed under the Campbell government —in ever-increasing numbers. These numbers were steadily swollen as more and more tourists came into the province in the great summer-scattering of the North American public.

The concept of social investment was carried into education. Provincial grants to the school boards and to the University, particularly to the Faculty of Agriculture, were significantly increased. The recommendation of the MacFarlane Commission that larger districts be created for secondary education was made law, and a commission set up to draw the new boundaries. In this field, however, caution, not "boldness," prevailed. The delicacy of the subject, its impact on custom, religious beliefs and prejudices, the native conservatism of the Minister of Education, all combined to produce an approach that invited obstruction by its timidity. The larger districts were to come into being only after plebiscites had been held within the new boundaries. Elementary education, for the obvious reason that change there would be more difficult, was excepted, a fundamental error. The weight of the government was not placed behind the campaign for acceptance of the larger districts in the plebiscites—as a result, in some districts, notably those in the Mennonite and French districts of the Red River valley, the plebiscites resulted in rejection. This, no doubt, was democracy, but it was not good educational policy on the part of a government which had been elected on the claim that Manitoba could not remain in the first half of the twentieth century. The brave new government had chosen in education to do its leading from the rear.

There was no doubt some need for caution in handling educational matters in Manitoba. The MacFarlane Commission, rather to its own surprise as well as the public's, had proposed, among various recommendations on curriculum, the making of grants to private schools. This was done on the simple pragmatic ground that those schools were educating at private expense pupils who would otherwise be a charge on the public taxes. Neither the government nor the Legislature would touch this simple proposition. But in a prolonged public debate it was made apparent that the Manitoba Schools Question still kept its original heat. And besides the old sectarian feeling was a new one of loyalty to the public schools, most marked in the teaching profession and in the people of other than French or British origin. The schools had established themselves in a social agency of assimilation and equality. Not a shadow of departure from the civic standards it had created would be allowed. Manitoba society had in fact become not mosaic but uniform.

A Social Assistance Act was passed, however, in 1958; it sought to make sure that public assistance would be available to all in need. This was perhaps the one definitely conservative measure of the government, conservative in that it was concerned with the needs of persons, not of classes or of categories, and conservative in that it sought to deal with actual need. The Act of course brought the charge that the means test was being restored, but the actual administration of the Act proved the charge unwarranted. The difference was that the onus to prove need was placed not on the person concerned but on the welfare officer dealing with the case. It proved an example of humane and enlightened conservatism with an enlightened civil service and in a relatively small community.

If Manitoba was indeed to be a better place in which to live, social investment was not all that was required. As the institution of larger school districts implied, there had to be political changes also. Nowhere was such change so much needed as in metropolitan Winnipeg. That area, which embraced half the population of the province, contained the City of Winnipeg (which in turn consisted of only something more than half the population of the area) and sixteen municipalities, ranging from the cities of St. Boniface and St. James to rural municipalities. Each was reasonably well governed, and nearly all provided the essential services of police and fire protection, sanitation, paving, and public assistance. But there was little means of co-operation except through a few agencies like the Greater Winnipeg Water Board. Moreover, the municipalities were, in varying degrees, parasitic on Winnipeg for general services, such as fire protection. One general reason for their existence was indeed to avoid taxation for the full range of urban services. Moreover, the lack of means of co-operation meant that not only could no efficient provision be made for common needs, such as sewage disposal, or a system of streets capable of handling the swollen traffic, but there was also no means for planning such overall development as had to result from the fact that metropolitan Winnipeg was really one community.

After study by a special committee, the government in 1960 brought in a bill before the Legislature to create a metropolitan government for Winnipeg and the sixteen municipalities with jurisdiction over assessment, zoning and building by-laws, arterial roads and bridges, traffic and public transportation, water service, sewage and garbage disposal, parks, flood protection, and civil defence. Police and fire protection were omitted, in what was a bold yet cautious measure. The bill became law, despite much opposition and criticism from the various councils whose functions were diminished and especially from the Mayor of Winnipeg, His Worship Stephen Juba, whose powers, if not his prestige, were restricted. But this pioneer piece of legislation in Canada proved well calculated, in part because of its own merits, in part because in the first Chairman of the Metropolitan Council, R. H. G. Bonnycastle, the government was fortunate to find a man of rare force, business acumen, devotion to public service, and personal integrity. Manitoba-born, Oxford-educated, travelled, he was an example of what the province at its best could produce in public spirit and personal talent when the pervading pragmatism of Manitoba society was not allowed to corrode the mind and heart. Winnipeg now proceeded to deal with the problems of its own growth, and to become what it had set out to be before 1914, a well-planned, well-directed North American city.

In one other way Winnipeg called for the special attention of the provincial government. The near-disaster of the flood of 1950 could not be risked again. The full penalty of the error of putting the political and economic capital of the province at the fork of the Red and Assiniboine had to be paid, either in some future full disaster or by undertaking measures to prevent damage by another flood. The previous government had begun the necessary historical and engineering studies. It was, however, too conscious of the political dangers of spending vast sums from the provincial exchequer to protect Winnipeg alone when other parts of the province also might suffer from flood or from drought. The Roblin government acted boldly. It adopted a general plan of flood prevention and water control, a wise and reasonable procedure even if it could not hide the fact that by far the greater part of the plan must be devoted to preventing the flooding of Winnipeg. To the latter end it endorsed the report of the Red River Flood Commission to dig a floodway east of Winnipeg from above St. Norbert to below Lockport on the Red. Flood waters would be diverted around Winnipeg by the channel. An earth-moving job greater than the digging of Suez or of Panama, it also involved the building of bridges for the railway lines and the highways, and the preservation of the channel in the crumbling Red River clay. Only with federal assistance could the province undertake so great an enterprise. This was forthcoming, to the amount of $31,500,000, and in 1961 digging began.

It was to be supplemented by dams on the upper Assiniboine River, and by the digging of a canal just above Portage la Prairie for diversion of floodwaters from that river to Lake Manitoba. The dam at Shellmouth was begun, but the Portage diversion ran into local opposition and engineering difficulties in finding a suitable route. The opposition was to lead to the defeat of one cabinet minister, Hon. John Christianson, in 1962, and the combined difficulties have delayed the digging of the diversion to this day.

Social investment and social growth, however, assumed and required a corresponding economic response. In this the role of the government was less direct but no less positive. As early as 1957 it had produced a scheme of agricultural credit, designed to meet the perennial need of the western farmer for credit on terms different from those of an ordinary commercial enterprise. In 1959 a Crop Insurance Agency was created to begin the most desired and most doubtful of agricultural needs in certain test areas. Aided by the long run of fair to good crop years, it was to build up and extend over the ensuing years without the disastrous calls on its reserves that a general crop failure would have meant. Those two measures, coupled with federal legislation, really completed all the government could do to create favourable conditions for agriculture. In fact these years saw the perfecting of the economic system the organized farmers had fought for in the pioneering and the post-pioneering generations, and their economic radicalism changed into an economic conservatism to match their social conservatism. This was the fact, coupled with the personal appeal of Prime Minister Diefenbaker, which explained that the Prairies, which went Conservative in federal politics in 1957, remained Conservative for the ensuing decade.

A similar series of measures was enacted for industry. In 1957 a Business Development Fund Act provided financial assistance for individuals and corporations with reasonable enterprises. This was intended particularly to aid small business ventures, and especially those to be situated outside metropolitan Winnipeg. It was, as the Manitoba Development Corporation, to become the central agency of government by 1966. Steady pressure by the Department of Industry and Commerce, and further legislation, had a slowly increasing measure of success in persuading industries to move to smaller communities where water and power were now available, and where most costs were less than in Winnipeg. It was an attempt to bring the dwarfed body of the province to match the giant's head of Winnipeg. Through its own departments and the crown corporations the government could work more directly. The departments concerned continued to protect and explore the forest and mineral resources of the province, but no new development of any size followed the opening of the great nickel mine at Thompson. It was in power that action was possible. With the joint development with Ontario of the White Dog Falls in that province, the power of the Winnipeg River was fully harnessed. Two steam stand-by stations at Selkirk and Brandon gave the hydro-electric network of the south all possible assurance of uninterrupted service. The demand for power continued to grow, and the only remaining hydro-electric power was to be found in the north, with its costs of transmission southward. After prolonged study, it was decided in 1960 to develop the Saskatchewan River, not by diverting the water southward to the

Fairford River, but at the Grand Falls themselves. This great undertaking, the first effort really to tie north and south together, went forward for the next five years. Power from the waters of the Rockies was to flow with that from the waters of the Shield through the expanding grid of the Manitoba Hydro Board. And beyond the Saskatchewan lay the Nelson, draining the much used but unwearied waters to the Bay.

Power was the one great resource the province had, the gift of its position as the basin of the prairie watershed and the western Shield. Abundant power and educated labour—these were the real hopes of the future. Perhaps some recognition was given to these facts by the decision of the federal government in 1960 to locate its second atomic energy plant and nuclear research centre at Pinawa on the Winnipeg River. A second Chalk River, it would not only fulfil its stated purpose, but also aid teaching and research in physics at the University of Manitoba. A cyclotron for nuclear research was made available in the same year to the University which, like its province, had moved far and fast from its origins a mere eighty-odd years before in the missionary colleges of Red River.

Manitoba at the beginning of the sixties was moving rapidly into step with the affluent, the scientific, the electronicized world of the second half of the twentieth century. The good life, with all that the term implies, was available as never before. Certainly it was a better life materially, educationally and socially for most Manitobans. It could have been much better in intellectual and cultural ways, in the provision made for libraries, the arts, and support of the University. The government intended to aid development in these areas as in economic and social life. It increased government grants to art galleries, theatre groups, museums and historical societies. It moved to create an Arts Council. But it moved slowly and cautiously in a realm in which a Manitoba government was a stranger, and in which hostile criticism would be ready and ruthless.

The deliberate undertaking of the Roblin government to promote growth, in itself a declaration that government in Manitoba had consciously and admittedly changed its character and henceforth was responsible for growth, provokes, of course, the question, what growth in fact took place? The answer, in general, down to 1962, was considerable growth, but not all that had been hoped for, or even what might have been expected. In population, for example, the census of 1956 had enumerated a total of 850,040 persons; that of 1961, 909,000. This indicated a good increase, but it was still a long way from the million that had been the goal in 1912. The plain truth was that the province was barely holding its natural increase. Immigration had been slight, and industrial growth no more than offset the decline in the agricultural labour force. In the realm of wealth, the story was better, but essentially the same. Farm income fluctuated from year to year but did substantially advance over the years. Income from minerals and forests was stable; the oilfields had proved limited; the nickel mine at Thompson was not yet in full production. Industrial income advanced at a good rate, but was it enough to make up for the failure of income from the primary industries to increase in a major way? It was not sufficient, and the government's response was to appoint in 1961 a committee of thirty-eight governmental and private people to study the problems and prospects of economic growth in the province.

The fact was that Manitoba was having to run fast to maintain her position in the procession of Canadian provinces. Much of the steady prosperity it enjoyed was indeed owing to the general prosperity of the country as a whole and to the vigorous federal policies of development, notably in the decision to sell wheat to China. But while this was true, what was of immediate importance to Manitobans was that they were using their resources to advantage, that they were prosperous, that life was increasingly rational, humane and pleasant in the province.

One of the results of change from an economy largely primary to one in the main industrial, and from the laissez-faire community to the welfare one—a change long in train, but rapidly coming to the surface by 1955—was the re-appearance of the Indian in Manitoban life. The Indian had been the main labour force of the fur trade; he had helped create the original wealth of Red River, and prepared the way for settlement. Settlement had, however, led to the treaty regime, and by the treaties all those of Indian blood who chose to be classified in law as Indians were set aside from the stream of settlement on reserves. The reserves were the old assembly points of the Indians' nomadic year, and, except those for the Ojibways and refugee Sioux south of the Assiniboine River, were by the rivers and lakes of the Shield, or along the edges of the Shield or in the Interlake. They were chosen, that is, for seasonal hunting and fishing but would not support even the Indian way of life throughout the year. It was of course the hope of the government and of the missionaries that the reserves might prove a transition from the nomadic life of the hunter to the sedentary life of the farmer. But, along with the pull of custom and the lack of capital, the very location of most reserves influenced the Indian not to change and made change difficult or impossible.

For two generations, however, the old way of life, supplemented by government aid, and seasonal work on the harvest fields and in clearing land, continued. The Indian way of life, as it had come to be in the days of the fur trade, continued in the lonely reaches of the Shield and Interlake, sustained by the continuing fur trade, the fisheries, and the still abundant game and fish. In the third generation, however, fur, fish and game began to fail. Land-clearing and harvest gangs were terminated. The inadequacies of the reserves became apparent in increasing poverty and misery in the white-washed log houses of Grand Marais and Sandy Bay. And the public conscience and the federal government, critical of other peoples in other lands, suddenly realized that it too had a "native" problem at least as reproachful and as difficult of solution as any in the world. Increased federal aid, particularly in health, spurred a sudden increase in the Indian population. Manitoba's had always been relatively large, as its reserves were relatively poor. The population of the related *métis* was unknown, but probably as large. What was the Indian to do? What ought Manitoba to do?

The treaty Indian on reserve was the responsibility of the federal government, which had been trying since the end of the war to revise its once highly regarded Indian policy to fit the new circumstances and the widely varying needs of Indians across Canada. But Indians who left the reserves, as they were doing in some numbers, and the great bulk of the *métis*, indistinguishable except in law from their blood relatives, the Indians, were a provincial responsibility, like any other citizens in distress. The collapse of the semi-nomadic way of life left the Indian helpless on the reserves of the north. In the south the Indians, and the *métis* as well, often went to the cities and in most cases ended up on the welfare rolls, in reformatories, or in jail. In short, the Indians and *métis* in the south were simply added to the ranks of the dispossessed, the failures, the incarcerated, of Manitoban society.

At this pass, the matter became not merely a matter of conscience, but also one of welfare costs. Welfare workers of Winnipeg, for some time aware of the special difficulties of the Indian in the city, now began a study which led to the calling in 1954 by the Winnipeg Council of Social agencies of the first Indian-*Métis* conference in that city. It was a well arranged meeting of Indian and *métis* representatives, welfare workers, the churches, interested citizens and representatives of the Indian branch and others engaged in work with the Indians in other provinces. The conference revealed a number of misunderstandings and real needs, and received good and helpful publicity. It became an annual event, which more and more Indians and *métis* attended, and which they came to control. The conferences led to a square facing of the issues. An Indian and *Métis* Friendship Centre was set up in Winnipeg; the provincial government began a programme of study of the *métis* and of assistance in their particular difficulties. More important in the long run was the agreement between the Indian Branch and the Department of Education to have Indian children, wherever possible, attend the public schools. This meant that in fact the treaty regime would survive only as long as Indians demanded it; the decision had been taken to assimilate the Indian into the general society of Canada.

If an affluent Manitoba had faced its most distressing social problem, it was also, at the other end of the spectrum, dealing with its other great area of negligence, the arts. The material slums of Logan and Jarvis Streets were well matched by the intellectual slums elsewhere in the city and the province. The old puritan hatred of the arts was being transmitted into a bland indifference. Small wonder that the decade saw little accomplished in letters, except the continued work of Nan Shipley and the efforts of scholars at the University, such as Professor Richard Hiscocks' fine books on Austria, Poland and Germany. Two of the best writers were expatriates, Margaret Laurence, whose *The Prophet's Bell* and *The Stone Angel* were of high quality, and Jack Ludwig, whose *Confusions* was a witty and wicked piece of academic clowning. Music was, as always, cultivated but undistinguished, the best talent, such as Harry Freedman's, going elsewhere in order to grow and be appreciated. More important perhaps was the widespread interest in the plastic arts, in the serious study of painting, sculpture and pottery, and in the increasing purchase of their material results by a growing public. The Royal Winnipeg Ballet had made, under new leadership, a solid recovery from the disaster of its fire. It carefully built up, under Arnold Spohr and a devoted Board of Directors, a small, highly trained *corps de ballet*. It developed a colourful and varied repertoire, in which "white" ballet was no more than a stiffener of the dance discipline. It was designed to perform not only to the limited, if growing, audience of Winnipeg, but to the public in the small cities and the larger towns of the Canadian West. In these, notably perhaps in Flin Flon, they won their warmest receptions. As its quality became professional, and as grants from the Canada Council gave it a financial assurance it had always lacked, the way opened to tours in the east and abroad. There it enjoyed its undoubted success, success which culminated in the performances at Jacob's Pillow in New England, in those in England as part of the Commonwealth Festival of the Arts, and in 1965 in an American tour sponsored by Sol Hurok, the chief of American theatrical agents. This was not good amateur performance; it was success by general standards of the art.

More novel and perhaps more significant, because of its intellectual quality, was the formation of the Manitoba Theatre Centre in 1963. The Winnipeg Little Theatre had stoically kept the lamp of drama flickering in Winnipeg, but a professional core of actors and solid financial backing were needed to give sustained quality to performances and to create an audience large enough to support a paying run for a play. One man made the difference. John Hirsch, a child refugee from Hungary, educated in the University of Manitoba, developed a flair for dramatic production with a zeal for art and a love for the country which had given him a home into an ability to produce and a mastery of theatre which focussed the efforts of lovers of drama. The old Dominion Theatre on Portage East—about where Dr. Schultz's store had stood—was made available by a local patron of the arts. With almost explosive quickness Winnipeg found itself attending productions which brought the best of classical and contemporary drama and a sophistication and vigour in performance that filled the theatre night after night, and which caught the attention of eastern and American critics. The Theatre Centre became a model for similar developments elsewhere in Canada, and Hirsch a name in the dramatic world.

These extraordinary achievements in the high arts were not matched elsewhere, particularly in the Summer Theatre. That venture, which made so much sense in terms of entertainment for tourists and summer engagements for artists, suffered from bad weather and poor management. It was too much thought of in terms of commercial promotion, too little in terms of the inescapable fact that the arts, in a society which includes the cultural, other than literature, in its education of the young, must be steadily and heavily subsidized if they are to thrive.

The evidences of the easier and more affluent life were to be found in entertainment with a mass appeal. The long record of hair-line successes and obstacles overcome by the Winnipeg Blue Bombers had led to a wide spread interest in football. On the basis of this, the business community, aided by loans from the city, organized a corporation known as Winnipeg Enterprises Limited, and built a stadium and an arena on the western city limits. This at once gave the Bombers a home appropriate to their fame, and furnished a centre for other sports and spectacles, notably track and the Winnipeg Exhibition. The latter still does not rival the long-established Brandon Fair, or in colour the rising Morris Stampede, but it was slowly justifying the obstinate belief that Winnipeg, dour city that it was, should have such a fair. Among other supports, track and field events began to build up as proper coaching became slowly available in the schools and the University. Soccer grew with the post-war immigration of British, German and Italians. The Winnipeg Bonspiel and curling throughout the province maintained its winter supremacy. Of greatest interest was the appearance of non-Anglo-Saxon names on the teams. Hockey, sad to say, declined, injured by the short-sighted commercial greed of the international professional leagues. But the crowning evidence of the acceptance of the easier life was the passing in Winnipeg, after one failure, of a plebiscite to allow Sunday sport. Puritan Manitoba was dead, even if its dead hand still forbade the serving of alcoholic drinks on Sundays, the day they were most likely to be wanted in dining out.

The Roblin government had at least released such a society to fulfil itself; it had even aided it to develop. It could therefore face the provincial electorate with some confidence when it went to the country in 1962. It stood on its record, pledged itself to develop the power of the Nelson, to continue social investment, to aid the Indians and *métis*—for the first time a political matter—and build an arts centre for the approaching centenary of Canada. The results, however, were a warning as to how strong the separate elements of Manitoban society were. The government was returned with thirty-four supporters, two less than in 1958. Cautious as had been the school policy of larger secondary districts and that of building the Floodway, these had cost the government two seats. The Liberals gained three seats to rise to fourteen, the C.C.F., now the New Democratic Party, lost two, which left them with eight. The results revealed that the Liberal party still had deep rural and sectarian roots, and that criticism of the governments financial policy still was influential. Douglas Campbell had retired from the leadership, although not from politics, in 1961, and had been succeeded by Gildas Molgat. The change in leadership made no change in the party. The N.D.P. still was considered an urban and labour party, and had little appeal beyond the boundaries of metropolitan Winnipeg. The one Social Credit member represented nothing but the essentially a-political feeling of his Mennonite constituency. Clearly the change of Manitoban society had largely occurred, and largely benefited Winnipeg. The drag of rural conservatism, expressed through the Liberal party, though only relative, was still strong.

The Roblin government had obviously gone as far as the temper of the province would allow. It had reached the apex of its policy of social development. But at least it had the authority to work within the still generous limits it had publicly stated for itself. And some evidence of the extent of its successes and failures was becoming apparent.

Its successes were extensive. The province, both privately and publicly, was prosperous as never before, except in the last years of the First World War. Every effort had been made to bring intelligence and knowledge to bear on the promotion of enterprises in the province, and the Committee on Manitoba's Economic Future's Report, when it appeared in 1963, won praise both in Canada and abroad. The educational system was improving, and the enrolment in the secondary schools was steadily rising. A General Course was being developed, with some success, despite public distrust, for those who did not wish to write the matriculation examinations for University entrance. Agriculture was relatively prosperous, and other industries were growing considerably. A superior hospitalization scheme had been introduced, and the necessary hospitals, and medical and nursing staffs found. The tourist industry, so called, was steadily increasing its facilities and handling surprising numbers of visitors. A Royal Commission under D. R. Michener was appointed to deal with the problems of an outmoded system of local government and taxation. A major campaign to mark the national centennial of 1967 and that of the province in 1970 was set in operation. The introduction of "shared services" to give a modicum of help to private schools revealed at once the Premier's cold courage, and how inflexibly the non-Catholic public felt about any attempt to help private schools. And a Swiss consortium, Monoca AG, had undertaken, with help from the Manitoba Development Fund, to develop the wood pulp resources of the north.

When so much was done, and so much more promised, it is no

grateful task to list the failures that went with the successes. But the stream of history carries both success and failure. One failure was the result of misjudgment. The attempt to pass labour legislation in 1962 making trade unions and their members legally liable was not only stopped in the Legislature, but earned the government a merited rebuke from the Court of Appeal. Another matter, never a public issue, was the result of negligence. That was the failure to abolish the legislation which removed the onus of proving guilt from the Crown in certain cases and placed on the defendant the burden of proving innocence. The two show how the provincial, like the federal Conservatives, had failed to think out the principles of modern Conservatism. Organized labour is a conservative force; the preservation and renovation of established rights and institutions are the peculiar duty of the Conservative party. These were failures of head and heart.

The remaining failures are both much bigger in scope and less certain in character. The greatest single shortcoming of the Roblin government was not to see that larger school districts had to be carried by the provincial legislature, and that they must include elementary as well as secondary schools. Its own uncertain political position, the Manitoban belief that the more local the democratic process, the more democratic it is, led it to accept the half-way measure of the MacFarlane Report, and the use of plebiscites. The result was the expression of every kind of local and personal obstruction, including that of school trustees who were afraid of losing their petty authority, great financial waste, and the loss of much of the good actually attempted. Only sterner action could now tidy up the shambles created.

Of the same character was the failure to carry out boldly the comprehensive recommendations of the Michener Report. These would have created fewer and larger local government districts, brought education under them, and shifted the weight of local, and especially education taxation from property to the general revenues of the province. Such changes are inevitable, and if carried promptly would have won political support. But again a usually courageous government balked.

That failure brought it face to face with the central issue of the times. Some relief had to be given to the hard pressed municipalities and school boards. While increasing expenditures had been met by borrowing, including the highly successful sale of Manitoba bonds in the province, taxes had not been greatly increased. In particular, no sales tax had been imposed. But increased prosperity had not increased existing taxes enough to meet existing provincial expenditures and the needs of local government. New taxes had therefore to be levied in 1964. The clear and obvious action was to impose a sales tax such as obtained in all other Canadian provinces but one. Fear of what the opposition, always waiting to denounce the government for over-spending and over-borrowing, would do, led to the decision not to impose a sales tax, but to impose instead a number of others, including one on fuel. Public opinion had been resigned to a sales tax—it was irritated by the nuisance of the substitutes.

Finally, although it was in itself a failure of the government, it could only be attributed to a government which had made itself responsible for all development in the province. That was the fact that economic development in the province had not kept pace with social needs and population growth. It was not furnishing the revenues needed to service debt incurred and outlays made. The issue was not closed, but the question marked was underscored in the provincial election of 1966, when the Conservative party again won, but with only thirty-one seats. It was still victory, still power, but not a victory to match the courage shown, the risks taken, and the gains made. Only in Winnipeg was there a clear result: the north half was N.D.P., the south Conservative, with no Liberal. Did this mean that in the affluent society there was at last a real political division, a division of income and aspiration, with no place for a central party? Or did it mean anything general at all?

The historian can say nothing more weighty about the day before yesterday than any other thoughtful man or woman. But some questions he may perhaps properly pose as an observer, questions of today but with some historical ancestry.

One is whether the dispute that raged in the first half of the sixties over the decision of Air Canada to remove its overhaul of work to Montreal when the use of Viscount planes ended, and which ended in failure to have the decision modified, meant that as the Panama had undercut Winnipeg's strategic position in Canada, the advent of the jet transport plane had done the same. Many flights by jet simply overfly Winnipeg. One more of the city's and the province's assets had dwindled further. The long search for alternatives has had to be continued.

A second question is whether the generally critical and even hostile reaction by most of the Manitoban public, and particularly those citizens not of British origin, to the federal Royal Commission on Bilingualism and Biculturalism revealed that in fact Manitobans had never accepted the idea of a dual nationality, and now rejected their own concept of a mosaic Manitoban society? Did the reaction to aid to private schools, even in the form of shared services, also reveal that Manitoban society was a conformist, egalitarian society of the American model?

Had the valiant efforts of the Roblin government, and indeed those of Douglas Campbell, revealed the lack rather than the availability of resources? Much of the development directly undertaken, as that of the Nelson, depended on federal aid. The north it seemed, was beyond the resources of the south to develop, and not attractive, except for rich mineral strikes, to private capital.

Was a government committed to development so committed that it ought to carry out that development itself if private capital would not? Even if this question is to the point, however, more remains to be taken into account. The Roblin government, as thoroughly as it tried to embody the will and aspiration of a new and dynamic society, was in fact a *tour de force*, attempted by one lonely and devoted man. He never succeeded in securing the support of, and indeed he avoided as being of no use, two powerful elements in the province which should either have given the leadership he attempted, or at least have given support worthy of the leadership. One was the wealthy business community of Winnipeg. Partly because so much of it was branch office personnel, partly because so much of its wealth was controlled by widows and others who, not unnaturally, were cautious, but mostly because it was canny, reactionary, untravelled, fearful of ideas and of imagination, not only failed to support the government but became a dead weight on its efforts, neither aiding nor opposing, but deadening. The second element was the University. Despite the increase of support from the Roblin government, despite that government's avoidance of pressing the University to do anything, because it respected the University's freedom to do what it should have done, the administration of the University failed to prepare for the great increase in numbers, and failed still further to prepare for the effects numbers would have on its traditional, involved organization, which nevertheless might have been developed in ways at once conservative and fruitful. The University failed because its administration was dominated by the same Winnipeg establishment that blighted the prospects of the city and the province. This was a failure, an inadequacy, far more serious than any loss of strategic position, or any lack of oil fields. It was that failure of head and heart which damns any man and any society. It was even more serious because, clearly, Manitoba could live up to its past, and to its achievements in business and the public service outside the province and in the arts, letters and sciences within it, only if it were to make the best of what it had of head and heart.

The province of the fur trade, the grain trade, the long freights thundering to the Lakehead, of the city clustered by the Forks like teepees on the plain, of the long, low, brooding mountains of its west, of the lake-set Shield and the coursing Nelson, faced as its first century rolled to its close a clear choice—the mediocrity of survival as it was and had been, or the achievement by intelligence and resolution of what it might be, a prosperous, rational, humane and vivid society.

NOTES

1. Miller Christy (ed.), *The Voyages of Captain Luke Foxe of Hull and of Captain Thomas James of Bristol in Search of a North-West Passage in 1631–1632* (Hakluyt Society; London, 1894), II, p. 353, Foxe, Aug. 23, 1631, off Cape Tatnam, "I cannot see any high land or find any deep water"; p. 484, James, Aug. 18, 1631, on same coast, "We stood in 6 fad., and could not see the land from the Top-masthead."

2. *Ibid.*, I, p. 165. The landfall was at 60° 40′ north latitude.

3. *Ibid.*, pp. xxii-xxix; the *Discovery* was to make four more Arctic voyages, six in all.

4. *Ibid.*, II, Appendix D; Henry, Prince of Wales, was "Supreame Protector" of "The Company of the Merchants Discoverers of the North-West Passage." The names of those incorporated include an unusual number of the nobility and the moneyed men of England.

5. *Ibid.*, 1, p. 165.

6. *Ibid.*, pp. xxx, ci. The date usually given is Aug. 15; the inscribed board which Button left and Foxe in part recovered recorded Aug. 27. As Button's journal was not published and has not been discovered, we are left without the vivid details and exact information it might have furnished.

7. J. B. Tyrrell (ed.), *Documents Relating to the Early History of Hudson Bay* (Champlain Society; Toronto, 1931), p. 5. See also Foxe's account of finding relics, in Christy, *Voyages*, II, pp. 344–9.

8. See Christy, *Voyages*, I, p 770, fn. 2. There may also have been a reference to his princely patron, who, unknown to Button, had died in November, 1612.

9. C. C. A. Gosch, *Danish Arctic Expeditions, 1605 to 1620* (Hakluyt Society; London, 1897), II, p. 23.

10. *Ibid.*, p. xxxix.

11. Christy, *Voyages*, II, pp. 334, 347, 488, 567–8, 572; Gosch, *Danish Arctic Expeditions*, II, pp. 28–9.

12. Christy, *Voyages*, II, p. 347; Gosch, *Danish Arctic Expeditions*, II, p. 24.

13. Christy, *Voyages*, II, p. 571.

14. E. E. Rich (ed.), *Copy-Book of Letters Outward* (Champlain Society; Toronto, 1948), Introduction by E. G. R. Taylor.

15. Christy, *Voyages*, II, p. 322.

16. Gosch, *Danish Arctic Expeditions*, II, p. 23.

17. Christy, *Voyages*, II, p. 337.

18. *Ibid.*, p. 491; see also p. 485, "a very low flat land."

19. *Ibid.*, p. 342; Foxe also wrote (p. 346): "The North side is a clay cliffe, like that of the Nase in *Essex*, but not so high. . . . it was clay clift on both sides and of a reasonable height."

20. *Ibid.*, p. 347; Foxe wrote: "Methought the vallies was good grass." To a seaman merely abundant grass would be good.

21. Munk and Foxe reported the woods to be nearer the coast and farther north of Churchill than they are today. See Christy, *Voyages*, II, p. 346; Gosch, *Danish Arctic Expeditions*, II, p. 23, and Commentary, p. 116, with footnote 2 on the lack of wood at Churchill in 1790.

22. Rich, *Copy-Book*, pp. xxx-xxxi.

23. See J. B. Brebner, *The Explorers of North America, 1492–1793* (New York, 1933), chaps. xii–xiv.

24. Reuben G. Thwaites (ed.), *The Jesuit Relations and Allied Documents* (Cleveland, 1899), XLII, p. 221.

25. G. O. Scull, *Voyages of Pierre Esprit Radisson* (Prince Society, 1885; reprinted New York, 1943), p. 172.

26. Grace Lee Nute, *Caesars of the Wilderness* (New York, 1943), pp. 70–2; Thwaites, *Jesuit Relations*, XLV, pp. 221–2.

27. Nute, *Caesars of the Wilderness*, pp. 73, 187.

28. Nute, *Caesars of the Wilderness*, p. 134. A. S. Morton states that this had been done in 1669; *History of the Canadian West to 1870–71* (Toronto, n.d.), p. 52.

29. Nute, *Caesars of the Wilderness*, pp. 291–2, Appendix 2, "Extract from Mr. Thomas Gorst's Journal."

30. Morton, *Canadian West*, p. 73.

31. Scull, *Voyages*, pp. 262–4.

32. Morton, *Canadian West*, p. 81.

33. The first York Factory was built in 1685, but a French or English party was resident at Port Nelson from 1682 on.

34. Nute, *Caesars of the Wilderness*, p. 224; Scull, *Voyages*, p. 345.

35. Tyrrell, *Documents*, p. 68, from "Journal of Father Silvy."

36. Nute, *Caesars of the Wilderness*, p. 239 and Appendix 8. The lack of canoe bark at York was to be a continuing handicap to the coastal trade; see R. Glover, "The Difficulties of the Hudson's Bay Company's Penetration of the West," *Canadian Historical Review*, XXIX (Sept., 1948), pp. 241–3.

37. Nute, *Caesars of the Wilderness*, Appendix 8, p. 327.

38. A. G. Doughty and Chester Martin (eds.), *The Kelsey Papers* (Ottawa, 1929), p. 111, in which Kelsey declared in 1690 that Chouart and Elie Grimard had failed to go two hundred miles inland; also p. xx.

39. James F. Kenney (ed.), *The Founding of Churchill* (Toronto, 1932), pp. 20–1.

40. The site of Deering's Point is a matter of some conjecture. See

Morton, *Canadian West*, p. 111; Doughty and Martin, *Kelsey Papers*, pp. xxxiii-xxxix; J. W. Whillans, *First in the West* (Edmonton, 1955).

41. Tyrrell, *Documents*, "Letter of Father Marest," and "Letter of la Potherie"; R. Douglas and J. N. Wallace (eds.), *Twenty Years at York Factory, 1694–1714: Jérémie's Account of Hudson Strait and Bay* (Ottawa, 1926).

42. Douglas and Wallace, *Twenty Years*, p. 38.

43. *Ibid.*

44. Tyrrell, *Documents*, "Letter of Father Marest," pp. 123–4.

45. *Ibid.*, p. 128. "Letter of la Potherie," p. 265; Douglas and Wallace, *Twenty Years*, p. 20.

46. Douglas and Wallace, *Twenty Years*, p. 19.

47. *Ibid.*, p. 32.

48. *Ibid.*, p. 35.

49. *Ibid.*, p. 33.

CHAPTER 2

1. James F. Kenney (ed.), *The Founding of Churchill* (Toronto, 1932), pp. 64–5.

2. Pierre Margry, *Découvertes et établissements des français dans l'ouest et dans le sud de l'Amérique septentrionale* (Paris, 1888), VI, pp. 26–34.

3. *Ibid.*, p. 52.

4. *Ibid.*, pp. 77, 514, 522.

5. J. B. Brebner, *The Explorers of North America, 1492–1793* (New York, 1933), pp. 353–4. The Saulteaux were Ojibways.

6. Margry, *Découvertes et établissements*, VI, pp. 50–1.

7. *Ibid.*, pp. 496, 500.

8. *Ibid.*, pp. 504, 512.

9. *Ibid.*, pp. 495–8.

10. *Ibid.*, p. 516.

11. *Ibid.*, p. 510.

12. *Ibid.*, p. 513.

13. L. J. Burpee (ed.), *Journals and Letters of La Vérendrye and His Sons* (Champlain Society; Toronto, 1927), p. 104. See p. 121, where La Vérendrye writes, referring to the Mandans, "their usual diet, like that of our *voyageurs*, is Indian corn [*de bled d'Inde*]."

14. *Ibid.*, pp. 91–2.

15. Margry, *Découvertes et établissements*, VI, pp. 586–7; Burpee, *Journals of La Vérendrye*, p. 95. I have accepted these statements concerning the difficulty of obtaining food as true; Brebner seems to regard them as excuses. The provisioning of the fur trade is a much neglected subject, but a central theme in the history of Manitoba.

16. Burpee, *Journals of La Vérendrye*, pp. 130, 134, 168.

17. *Ibid.*, pp. 96–7; presumably it was also sown at Fort St. Pierre.

18. *Ibid.*, pp. 101–2, 142.

19. *Ibid.*, p. 182. For La Vérendrye's dependence on supplies of wild rice, see p. 260.

20. *Ibid.*, pp. 107, 121, 153, 160, 254.

21. *Ibid.*, p. 141.

22. *Ibid.*, p. 220; see also pp. 267 and 272 on the destitution of Fort St. Charles in 1736.

23. *Ibid.*, pp. 146–7, 182, 240–2. Note that the plans to advance in 1736 were wrecked because the "provisions and necessary effects" were delayed at Kaministiquia (p. 208).

24. *Ibid.*, pp. 197–8.

25. *Ibid*, p. 238.

26. *Ibid.*, p. 242.

27. *Ibid.*, p. 244; La Vérendrye urged the Assiniboins to settle near the proposed fort at the Forks, which they promised to do.

28. *Ibid.*, p. 244.

29. *Ibid.*, p. 254.

30. *Ibid.*, p. 303.

31. *Ibid.*, p. 485.

32. A. S. Morton, *History of the Canadian West to 1870–71* (Toronto, n.d.), p. 190.

33. Burpee, *Journals of La Vérendrye*, p. 486.

34. *Ibid.*, pp. 378–9; C. P. Wilson, "La Vérendrye Reaches the Saskatchewan," *Canadian Historical Review*, XXXIII (March, 1952), p. 46.

35. *Ibid.*, p. 379.

36. *Ibid.*, pp. 126–7; see also L. J. Burpee (ed.), "The Journal of Anthony Hendry [sic]," *Transactions of the Royal Society of Canada*, 3rd series, 1907, p. 321; C. P. Wilson, "Crossing the Prairies Two Centuries Ago," *Report of the Canadian Historical Association*, 1954; H. A. Innis, *The Fur Trade in Canada* (New Haven, 1930), pp. 98–9.

37. *United Kingdom: Report from the Committee Appointed to Enquire into the State and Condition of the Countries Adjoining to Hudson's Bay, and of the Trade Carried on There* (London, 1749).

38. Morton, *Canadian West*, pp. 243–4. For the inland work of the successors of Henday, see pp. 272–90.

CHAPTER 3

1. Alexander Henry, *Travels and Adventures in Canada and the Indian Territories between the Years 1760 and 1776*, ed. by James Bain (Toronto, 1901), chaps. III–V; Alexander Mackenzie, *Voyages from Montreal*, etc. (New York, 1802), p. 46.

2. W. S. Wallace (ed.), *Documents Relating to the North West Company* (Champlain Society; Toronto, 1934), pp. 70–5, Benjamin and Joseph Frobisher to General Haldimand, Oct. 4, 1784.

3. A. S. Morton, *History of the Canadian West to 1870–71* (Toronto, n.d.), p. 267.

4. *Ibid.*, p. 269.

5. *Ibid.*, p. 271.

6. *Ibid.*, p. 290. Morton's narrative, founded on journals of Hudson's Bay Company men, affords the most authoritative record of the penetration of the Northwest by the Montreal traders.

7. H. A. Innis, *Peter Pond, Fur Trader and Adventurer* (Toronto, 1930).

8. C. M. Gates (ed.), "The Diary of Hugh Faries," *Five Fur Traders* (Minneapolis, 1933), p. 223.

9. *Ibid.*; the diary of Archibald N. McLeod gives a vivid account of the busy trade of the upper Assiniboine in 1800. There were twenty-one posts on the upper river in 1794–5; Morton, *Canadian West*, p. 434.

10. Elliot Coues (ed.), *New Light on the Early History of the Greater Northwest: The Manuscript Journals of Alexander Henry and of David Thompson, 1799–1814*, I (New York, 1897), p. 35: ". . . Bas de la Rivière Winipic, the general depot for provisions which are brought from Red and Assiniboine rivers every spring in long boats."

11. *Ibid.*, p. 64.

12. E. E. Rich (ed.), *Copy-Book of Letters Outward* (Champlain Society; Toronto, 1948), pp. xxxiv, 77; *United Kingdom: Report from the Committee Appointed to Enquire into the State and Condition of the Lands and Countries Adjoining to Hudson's Bay*, etc. (London, 1749), evidence of White, Sergeant, Hayter, Thompson, Griffin, and Robson; Joseph Robson, *An Account of Six Years Residence in Hudson's Bay, from 1733 to 1736, and from 1744 to 1747* (London, 1749), pp. 12, 42; Edward Umfreville, *The Present State of Hudson's Bay* (London, 1790), pp. 26, 27, 152; see especially p. 103: "The inland parts produce wild rice and Indian corn; and when our people have sown any of the seed of these, it has come up as promising as in the cultivated gardens of Canada."

13. Coues, *New Light*, I, pp. 188–9, 197, 211, 228: "Oct. 17, 1804. Snow. I took my vegetables up—300 large heads of cabbage, 8 bushels of carrots, 16 bushels of onions, 10 bushels of turnips, some beets, parsnips, etc. October 20th. I took in my potatoes—420 bushels, the produce of 7 bushels, exclusive of the quantity we have roasted since our arrival, and what the Indians have stolen, which must be at least 200 bushels more." Also pp. 242, 252, 267, 280, 291, 430.

14. Mackenzie, *Voyages*, p. 51n.

15. Coues, *New Light*, I, p. 280; John Tanner, *A Narrative of the Captivity and Adventures of John Tanner during Thirty Years Residence*

among the Indians in the Interior of North America (New York, 1830), p. 180.

16. Gabriel Franchère, *Narrative of a Voyage to the Northwest of America in the Years 1811, 1812, 1813 and 1814*, etc. (translated and edited by J. V. Huntington, New York, 1854; reprinted in *Early Western Travels, 1748–1846*, edited by R. G. Thwaites, Cleveland, 1904), p. 379.

17. Andrew Amos, *Report of the Trials in the Courts of Canada Relative to the Destruction of the Earl of Selkirk's Settlement on the Red River, with Observations* (London, 1820), p. 6, evidence of Jean Baptiste Roi: "For twelve years past I have cultivated a piece of ground of my own [on the east bank of the Red opposite the mouth of the Assiniboine]. . . . I used to sell the produce to the gentlemen of the North West Company or of the Hudson's Bay Company." P.A.C., Selkirk Papers, 3, Miles Macdonell to Selkirk, July 17, 1813: "Mr. Henry had bought 100 bushels of potatoes from free Canadians at the Forks."

18. Selkirk Papers, 3, Macdonnell to Selkirk, May 27, 1813.

19. *United Kingdom: Papers Relating to the Red River Settlement* (London, 1819), p. 4.

20. J. B. Tyrrell (ed.), *Journals of Samuel Hearne and Philip Turnor* (Champlain Society; Toronto, 1934).

21. R. Glover, "The Difficulties of the Hudson's Bay Company's Penetration of the West," *Canadian Historical Review*, XXIX (Sept., 1948), pp. 240–54.

22. Morton, *Canadian West*, pp. 434–6.

23. Selkirk Papers, 1, Selkirk's instructions to Miles Macdonell, 1811.

24. *United Kingdom: Papers Relating to the Red River Settlement*, p. 41; Morton, *Canadian West*, p. 533.

25. For these and subsequent statistics of the Selkirk colonists, I am indebted to the researches of Mr. Wm. Douglas.

26. Selkirk Papers, 1, Selkirk's instructions to Miles Macdonell, 1811.

27. *Ibid.*

28. *Ibid.*, Archibald Mason's Description of Hudson's Bay in North America.

29. *Report of the Public Archives of Canada, 1886*, p. cxcv, Macdonell to Selkirk, Oct. 1, 1811.

30. Selkirk Papers, 3, Macdonell to Selkirk, July 17, 1813.

31. *Ibid.*

32. Selkirk Papers, 4, Macdonell to Selkirk, July 25, 1814.

33. *Ibid.*, 2, Selkirk to Macdonell, June 12, 1813.

34. *Ibid.*, 4, Macdonell to Selkirk, July 25, 1814; Colvile to H.R.C., Dec. 5, 1815.

35. *Ibid.*, Macdonell to Selkirk, July 25, 1814.

36. Wallace, *North West Documents*, pp. 290–1.

37. E. E. Rich (ed.), *Colin Robertson's Correspondence Book, Septem-*

ber 1817 to September 1822 (Champlain Society; Toronto, 1939), pp. lxiv–lxvi.

38. Selkirk Papers, 8, Peter Fidler's Narrative of the Re-establishment, Progress and Total Destruction of the Colony in Red River, 1816.

39. *Ibid.*, Semple to Selkirk, Dec. 2, 1815.

40. *Ibid.*, Fidler's Narrative.

41. *Ibid.*, Fidler's Narrative and that of John Pritchard; also evidence of parties on both sides in Amos, *Report of Trials.*

42. Selkirk Papers, 7, Wm. Morrison to Alex Clarke, July 23, 1816.

43. *Ibid.*, 12, Alex. Macdonell to Selkirk, Nov. 10, 1817.

44. J. P. Pritchett, *The Red River Valley* (Toronto, 1942), p. 223.

45. Selkirk Papers, 16, Alex. Macdonell to Selkirk, Aug. 15, 1818; Captain Matthey to Selkirk, Aug. 30, 1818.

46. *Ibid.*, 17, Wm. Laidlaw to Selkirk, July, 1819.

47. Alexander Ross, *The Red River Settlement* (London, 1856), p. 23; John West, *The Substance of a Journal* (London, 1824), p. 81.

48. Selkirk Papers, 20, Robt. Logan to M.G. & A., July 3, 1820.

49. Ross, *Red River Settlement*, pp. 50–1.

50. Grace Lee Nute (ed.), *Documents Relating to Northwest Missions, 1815–1827* (St. Paul, 1942), p. 225.

51. Marcel Giraud, *Le Métis canadien* (Paris, 1945), pp. 644–5.

52. E. E. Rich (ed.), *Simpson's Athabaska Journal* (Hudson's Bay Record Society; Toronto, 1938), pp. xxxviii–xxxix, Introduction by Chester Martin.

CHAPTER 4

1. "Diary of Nicholas Garry," *Transactions of the Royal Society of Canada*, Section II, 1900, p. 135.

2. *Ibid.* From the Manitoba or ash-leafed maple (*acer negundo*), however, not the sugar maple of eastern North America.

3. P.A.C., Selkirk Papers, 15 and 16.

4. "Diary of Nicholas Garry," p. 139.

5. *Ibid.*, p. 193.

6. *Ibid.*

7. P.A.C., Bulger Papers, 2, Halkett to Provencher, Aug. 30, 1822; Halkett to Bulger, Aug. 31, 1822.

8. "Diary of Nicholas Garry," p. 193.

9. E.g., Cuthbert Grant; see Margaret Arnett Macleod, "Cuthbert Grant of Grantown," *Canadian Historical Review*, XXI (March, 1940).

10. A. S. Morton, *History of the Canadian West to 1870–71* (Toronto, n.d.), pp. 575, 805, 808; also A. H. de Trémaudan, *Histoire de la nation métisse* (Montreal, 1935).

11. Selkirk Papers, 15. Twenty-six Canadians, not country dependents, are listed in a return for 1818.

12. *Ibid.* Only 26 de Meurons are listed for 1818; yet Selkirk's party had consisted of 140, and Garry gives the number of 65 "of all ages" ("Diary of Nicholas Garry," p. 193). The 1818 list is men only, while Garry's includes dependents. It is difficult to discover the population of the colony in these disturbed early years.

13. One hundred and thirty are listed in 1818, with 51 "additional," presumably meaning those who had not come as colonists but from the fur trade. Garry gives 221 of all ages.

14. "Diary of Nicholas Garry," p. 163.

15. Bulger Papers, 4, John Pritchard to Bulger, Aug. 21, 1826.

16. Alexander Ross, *The Red River Settlement* (London, 1856), pp. 124–5, a caricature description of Red River farming.

17. M. S. Osborne, "The Architectural Heritage of Manitoba," *Manitoba Essays*, ed. by R. C. Lodge (Toronto, 1937), p. 54. Red River frame was a style of log construction used when a large building was desired, or when the available logs were short; a frame of upright logs was built, and squared logs dropped down slots in the uprights to form the wall. The standard architecture of the Hudson's Bay Company was the Norman French style of Quebec, the chief character being the rectangular form crowned by a roof with four slopes and no gable, with or without dormers. Some of the Red River doorways possess an elegant simplicity. Though the style was French, the stonemasons were sometimes from the Orkneys, but little Orcadian influence is evident in the surviving buildings.

18. H. M. Robinson, *The Great Fur Land, or Sketches of Life in the Hudson's Bay Territory* (New York, 1879), pp. 67–8.

19. See the conflict between Governor Bulger and Chief Factor John Clarke in 1822; Bulger Papers, 2, pp. 329–58.

20. *Ibid.*, Bulger to Colvile, draft despatch.

21. E. H. Oliver (ed.), *The Canadian North-west: Its Early Development and Legislative Records* (Publications of the Canadian Archives, no. 9, Ottawa, 1914), I, pp. 188–9, 201, 202.

22. Bulger Papers, 2, pp. 108–9, resolutions passed by the General Court of Directors of the Hudson's Bay Company, May 29, 1822.

23. Oliver, *Canadian North-west*, I, p. 267.

24. H. Y. Hind, *Narrative of the Canadian Red River Exploring Expedition of 1857, and of the Assiniboine and Saskatchewan Exploring Expedition of 1858* (London, 1860), I, p. 209.

25. Oliver, *Canadian North-west*, I, p. 269.

26. *Ibid.*, p. 54.

27. Bulger Papers, 3, p. 117, March 31, 1823.

28. Oliver, *Canadian North-west*, I, p. 78.

29. *Ibid.*, pp. 87, 286.

30. "Diary of Nicholas Garry," pp. 137–8.

31. John West, *The Substance of a Journal* (London, 1824), pp. 150–1; see also Grace Lee Nute (ed.), *Documents Relating to Northwest Missions 1815–1827* (St. Paul, 1942), p. 156, Rev. S. Dumoulin to Bishop Plessis, Sept. 10, 1818.

32. "Diary of Nicholas Garry," pp. 140–1. Nute, *Northwest Missions*, pp. 353–63.

33. *Ibid.*, p. 179.

34. Archives of Archdiocese of St. Boniface, no. 406, Taché to Bishop Bourget, July 22, 1852.

35. West, *Substance of a Journal*, pp. 150–1.

36. As in the instance of Rev. Henry Budd, one of West's pupils.

37. "Diary of Nicholas Garry," p. 156.

38. See the woodcut in West, *Substance of a Journal*.

39. See, for example, Ross, *Red River Settlement*, pp. 296–7.

40. *Ibid.*, pp. 334–5; Ross, of course, oversimplifies, as was his custom.

41. Bulger Papers, 2, p. 329.

42. Bulger Papers, 3, pp. 215–21, Committee to George Simpson, May 21, 1823.

43. Oliver, *Canadian North-west*, I, pp. 91–2.

44. J. P. Pritchett, *The Red River Valley* (Toronto, 1942), pp. 254–5.

45. P.A.M., Journal of Peter Garrioch, I and III.

46. Garrioch, Journal, IV, pp. 204–33, "Seven Days Experience, or the Pleasures of Smuggling."

47. W. E. Ingersoll (ed.), "A Selection from the Letters of Donald Ross" (unpublished MSS), Alexander Christie to Donald Ross, Jan. 3, 1844.

48. Garrioch, Journal, V, pp. 238–9, 251, 254, 260–3.

49. Garrioch, Journal, V, pp. 295–8, 312; also VI, Appendix D, a letter from free traders to Governor Christie, dated Aug. 29, 1845, asking what rights of trade half-breeds and native whites had in Red River. Christie replied, Sept. 5, 1845, that all had equal rights, but the Company had a monopoly.

50. J. M. Reardon, *George Anthony Belcourt, Pioneer Catholic Missionary of the Northwest* (St. Paul, 1955), p. 81.

51. Ingersoll, "Letters of Donald Ross," Sir George Simpson to Sir Chas. Metcalfe, Nov. 6, 1845; Simpson to Donald Ross, Dec. 29, 1845.

52. W. D. Smith, "The Despatch of Troops to Red River, 1846, in Relation to the Oregon Question" (unpublished thesis of the University of Manitoba, 1951), pp. 123–4; *United Kingdom: Papers Relating to the Hudson's Bay Company, 1849* (London, 1849), p. 112.

53. *United Kingdom: Papers Relating to the Hudson's Bay Company, 1849*, pp. 1–5, memorials of English and French inhabitants of Red River, asking for local self-government.

54. Ingersoll, "Letters of Donald Ross," Major Caldwell to D. Ross, May 7, 1849.

55. *Ibid.*; P.A.C., Diary of Rev. R. Hunt; in entry for Oct. 5, 1849, Hunt reports that Caldwell told him he had deliberately taken no troops to the Court House, because of the rumour that he was seeking a pretext to fire on the people. Two of the rioters were said to have offered to go into the Court to shoot Thom. Caldwell claimed that his decision not to call out troops had prevented bloodshed.

Caldwell, it is to be observed, was severely criticized for his behaviour in this and other instances and in 1850 was set aside temporarily as Governor of Assiniboia by Governor Eden Colvile of Rupert's Land.

56. See the author's Introduction to *The Letters of Eden Colvile* (Hudson's Bay Record Society, 1956).

57. Archives of the Archdiocese of St. Boniface; the papers for 1850–3 contain many references to the activities of the free traders: no. 371, J. Black to H. Fisher, Nov. 14, 1851; no. 465, George Simpson to H. Fisher, June 29, 1853; no. 485, E. McGillivray to H. Fisher, Nov. 17, 1853, from Fort La Corne, "We are troubled with a strong opposition in this neighbourhood [the Saskatchewan; ten free traders are named]"; no. 485, George Simpson to George Deschambault, Dec. 6, 1853, expresses fear that the free traders will enter the English (Churchill) River district. The story of 1766–75 was being re-enacted.

58. See H. G. Graham, *The Social Life of Scotland in the Eighteenth Century* (London, 1899), pp. 166–7.

59. See Major Griffiths' comment of French petition of 1849, on p. 112 of *United Kingdom: Papers Relating to Hudson's Bay Company, 1849*.

60. Hind, *Exploring Expedition*, I, pp. 155–6; Garrioch, Journal, III, pp. 175–7.

61. G. Dugas, *Le Mouvement des Métis* (Montreal, 1945), pp. 220–1.

62. *United Kingdom: Correspondence Relative to the Recent Disturbances in the Red River Settlement* (London, 1870), p. 27.

63. See John Palliser, *Solitary Rambles of a Hunter in the Prairies* (London, 1853), pp. 111–14.

64. Descriptions of the hunt are numerous; see Ross, *Red River Settlement*, chap. VIII, for the most detailed.

65. Archives of the Archdiocese of St. Boniface, no. 437, A. Fisher to H. Fisher, Feb. 20, 1853, reports some *métis* starving, and subscriptions being raised among the English to furnish relief—one instance among many. Prudence, of course, as well as charity, required that *métis* and Indians be helped in distress.

66. P.A.M., Journal of Samuel Taylor, p. 55, June, 1860; the Saskatchewan boats set out on that date.

67. J. J. Gunn, "The Tripmen of Assiniboia," *Echoes of the Red* (Toronto, 1930), pp. 24–58, is the principal source for this section.

68. A Scots word meaning a narrow strip of cultivated land, "a land" in western Canadian speech. See Bulger Papers, II, pp. 385–7, in which Alexander Ross complains of the loss of "a rigg of three full yards in breadth and about two hundred yards in length," by a re-survey in 1822; also Taylor, Journal, I, p. 55, June, 1860: "I were down Grubing on my land on Wednesday 4th, the 5th and 6th, finished two rigs first week 130 yards long, 10 yards wide each rig."

69. Archer Martin, *The Hudson's Bay Company's Land Tenures* (London, 1898).

70. Sugar was regularly made by Indians, *métis*, and whites from the sap of the Manitoba maple. See Taylor, Journal, II, p. 19, date April 1, 1865; also M. A. MacLeod, "Manitoba Maple Sugar," *Beaver*, March, 1955.

71. Garrioch, "Journal," V, p. 254, May 5, 1845: "Gavin threw into the ground four bushels of wheat."

72. The cultivation of this dwarf, acclimated corn, probably of Mandan origin, was, of course, taken over from the Indians; see the author's "Agriculture in the Red River Colony," *Canadian Historical Review*, XXIX (Dec., 1949).

73. Archives of the Archdiocese of St. Boniface, no. 100, Provencher to Dionne, June 20, 1840; no. 207; no. 269, Alexander Christie to H. Fisher, March 2, 1847, reporting the crop of 1846 to be a complete failure.

74. Taylor, Journal, I, p. 75, Aug. 27, 1862, a very dry year; II, p. 1, July 1, 1865: ". . . this is the dryest summer that anyone can remember the wheat looks short and thin"; p. 12, Sept.: ". . . there are some people that have really not one sheaf of wheat." The crop of 1868 was a complete failure, even seed having to be imported: *Nor'Wester*, Feb. 12, 1869.

75. Taylor, Journal, I, p. 46.

76. These names occur in the Garrioch and Taylor journals; presumably they are the present Bird's Hill, Pine Ridge, and the woods of the first slopes of the Precambrian Shield.

77. Wm. H. Keating, *Narrative of an Expedition to the Source of the St. Peter's River, Lake Winnipeg, and Lake of the Woods*, etc. (London, 1825), II, p. 225. Most of the cattle in Red River were descended from stock brought by Colonel Dickson and Joseph Rolette in 1822, 1823, and 1824; see Bulger Papers, II, pp. 296–8, Sept. 1, 1822, when 170 head of cattle had arrived at the Forks. See also Ross, *Red River Settlement*, pp. 380, 389, on the quality of the livestock.

78. Some sheep were brought in with the first parties of colonists, and more from Kentucky in 1833.

79. D. Gunn and C. R. Tuttle, *History of Manitoba from the Earliest Settlement* (Ottawa, 1880), pp. 271–2.

80. Taylor, Journal, I, pp. 45, 67; II, pp. 7, 11, 15, 18, 23, 29.

81. See the author's "Agriculture in the Red River Colony." Taylor's Journal makes it evident how great the variation was.

82. The sickle and scythe were in use to the end of Red River days, but reapers came in from St. Paul in the middle fifties. The sickle was preferred to the scythe down to 1838 at least, when the use of the scythe on the experimental farm of the Company at Upper Fort Garry was scoffed at by the colonists; Ross, *Red River Settlement*, p. 213.

83. Manton Marble, "To the Red River and Beyond," *Harper's New Monthly Magazine*, XXIII (Aug., 1860), p. 307.

84. These are repeated items in Taylor's Journal.

85. Bulger Papers, IV, pp. 71–2. John Pritchard to Bulger, Aug. 1, 1825: "The Windmill is expected to be in operation in the approaching Autumn."

86. Taylor, Journal, II, p. 1, Sept. 19, 1863: "The watermills are all dry and will not be able to grind this fall"; p. 9, May, 1864, water-mills still unable to grind; p. 22, July, 1865, Taylor working on installation of Company's new steam-mill at Lower Fort Garry, the first having been installed in the village of Winnipeg in 1863.

87. Oliver, *Canadian Northwest*, I, p. 316.

88. Garrioch, Journal, V, p. 272.

89. Ross, *Red River Settlement*, pp. 124–5, 201, 296–7, 334–5.

90. A. K. Isbister, "The Hudson's Bay Territories," *Nor'Wester*, Aug. 15, 1861; see also Hind, *Exploring Expedition*, I, pp. 177–83.

91. P.A.M., Ross Papers, Jas. Ross to his sisters and brother, Dec. 24, 1856.

92. *Ibid.*, Hind, *Exploring Expedition*, I, pp. 177–83.

93. Ross Papers, Wm. Ross to Jas. Ross, Feb. 9, 1856.

94. *Nor'Wester*, Sept. 14, 1860; Hind, *Exploring Expedition*, I, p. 203.

95. *Cambridge History of the British Empire*, II, p. 579.

96. Murray Campbell, "The Postal History of Red River," *Papers of the Manitoba Historical Society*, series III, 1949–50, p. 5.

97. The Bishopric of Juriopolis *in partibus* had been made that of "the North-West" in 1847, changed to St. Boniface in 1854.

CHAPTER 5

1. *United Kingdom: Report of the Select Committee on the Hudson's Bay Company* (London, 1857), pp. iii–iv.

2. H. Y. Hind, *Exploring Expedition* (London, 1860), I, p. 297.

3. *Ibid.*, II, 55.

4. John Palliser, *Solitary Rambles of a Hunter in the Prairies* (London, 1853), pp. 269–71.

5. *United Kingdom: Papers Relative to the Exploration by Captain Palliser of That Portion of British North America Which Lies between the Northern Branch of the River Saskatchewan and the Rocky Mountains* (London, 1859), *Journal*, pp. 37–47.

6. *Ibid.*, pp. 6, 16.

7. Lorin Blodget, *Climatology of the United States* (Philadelphia, 1856), p. 530.

8. *Nor'Wester*, I (1), Dec. 28, 1859. Also *Hansard*, 3rd series, V.177, 1865, Lord Wharncliffe on "the disturbances . . . in the balance of the constitution of British North America."

9. P.A.C., C. 364, Correspondence among Hudson's Bay Company, the Colonial office, and the War office, Oct.-Nov., 1856, with respect to the dispatch of troops to Red River in view of the establishment of an American military post at St. Joseph's.

10. P.A.M., Journal of Samuel Taylor, p. 64.

11. See the account of John McLean, who brought his family from Ontario to Portage la Prairie in 1862, in *The Tread of the Pioneers* (Toronto, 1932), pp. 18, 187–8.

12. *Nor'Wester*, I (3), Jan. 28, 1860.

13. *Nor'Wester*, Supplement, 7 and 14, 1860.

14. *Nor'Wester*, III (3), Feb. 19, 1862.

15. *Nor'Wester*, I (1), Dec. 28, 1859.

16. Roderick Campbell, *The Father of St. Kilda* (London, 1901), p. 166.

17. J. J. Hargrave, *Red River* (Montreal, 1871), chaps. xix, xx.

18. E. H. Oliver (ed.), *The Canadian North-West: Its Early Development and Legislative Records* (Ottawa, 1914), I, pp. 523–6.

19. *Nor'Wester*, VI, April 17, 1865.

20. *Nor'Wester*, IV (11), June 11, 1863.

21. *Nor'Wester*, V (5), March 17, 1864.

22. *Globe*, March 27, 1868; July 4, 1868; Feb. 19, 1869; the last is the best account of the episode, free of the facetiousness of Alexander Begg and the use of the erroneous and derisive term "Republic."

23. Oliver, *Canadian North-West*, II, pp. 877–8.

24. Samuel Taylor, Journal, p. 83.

25. *Globe*, Jan. 5, 1869, Mactavish to *Globe*; John Machray, *Life of Robert Machray* (Toronto, 1909), p. 156.

26. *Nor'Wester*, Feb. 12, 1869, and *Globe*, March 20, 1869, quoting *Nor'Wester* of Feb. 26, 1869.

27. *Globe*, June 2, 1869.

28. *Canada: Report of the Select Committee of the House of Commons on the Causes of the Difficulties in the North-West Territories in 1869–70* (Ottawa, 1874) evidence of Archbishop Taché, p. 12; evidence of A. G. B.

Bannatyne, p. 123; evidence of J. S. Lynch, p. 131; evidence of J. S. Dennis, p. 186; P.A.C., Macdonald Papers, 103, Ritchot to Cartier, undated.

29. P.A.C., William Cowan Diaries, 14, July 19 and 23, 1869.

30. *Globe*, Sept. 4, 1869, quoting from *Nor'Wester*.

31. *Report of Select Committee*, 1874, p. 187, evidence of J. S. Dennis.

32. *Ibid.*, evidence of Taché.

33. *Globe*, July 12, 1869.

34. See author's Introduction to *Alexander Begg's Red River Journal* (Champlain Society; Toronto, 1956).

35. *Nor'Wester*, May 15, 1869.

36. Cowan Diaries, 14, July 29, 1869.

37. James Taylor, *The Veterans of the Fur Trade Association* (Prince Albert, 1906), p. 9.

38. Alexander Begg, *The Creation of Manitoba* (Toronto, 1871), p. 78.

39. *Report of Select Committee*, 1874, evidence of Adams G. Archibald, p. 150; M. Giraud, *Le Métis canadien* (Paris, 1945), p. 1106.

40. P.A.C., Macdonald Papers, C. J. Hargrave to Sir Charles M. Lampson, Fort Garry, Feb. 8, 1870: "Our insurgents usually manage the Portage brigade." J. J. Gunn, *Echoes of the Red* (Toronto, 1930), pp. 39 and 58.

CHAPTER 6

1. *Canada: Report of the Select Committee of the House of Commons on the Causes of the Difficulties in the North-West Territories in 1869–70* (Ottawa, 1874), evidence of Rev. J. N. Ritchot of St. Norbert, p. 68.

2. P.A.C., Macdonald Papers, 103, Ritchot to Cartier, undated.

3. P.A.C., William Cowan Diaries, 14, Nov. 2, 1869; *United Kingdom: Correspondence Relative to the Recent Disturbances in Red River* (London, 1870), p. 38, Mactavish to McDougall, Nov. 9, 1869.

4. *Correspondence Relative to the Recent Disturbances in Red River*, p. 53, Memorandum of Canadian cabinet, dated Dec. 16, on the Colonial Secretary's (Lord Granville) despatch of Nov. 30.

5. *Report of Select Committee*, 1874, p. 102, evidence of Sir John A. Macdonald.

6. *Correspondence Relative to the Recent Disturbances in Red River*, pp. 187–8, William Mactavish to W. S. Smith, Nov. 9, 1869.

7. *Ibid.*, p. 41.

8. *Alexander Begg's Red River Journal* (Champlain Society; Toronto, 1956), Nov. 25 and Nov. 26, 1869.

9. *Ibid.*, Nov. 26 and 27.

10. *Ibid.*, Dec. 1.

11. *Ibid.*, Dec. 3.

12. *Correspondence Relative to the Recent Disturbances in Red River,* p. 92.

13. *Ibid.*, pp. 85–91.

14. Macdonald Papers, 101, Macdonald to Sir John Rose, Nov. 22, 1869; Macdonald to Rose, Nov. 26, 1869.

15. *Canada: Sessional Papers,* 1870, III (12), pp. 49–50.

16. *Ibid.*, p. 48; P.A.C., G. 21 (12), John A. MacDonald to Smith, Jan. 3, 1870; Joseph Howe, Secretary of State, to D. A. Smith, Dec. 10, 1869.

17. As Smith reported to Howe. The passages were, however, deleted from the proofs of his report when published: P.A.C., Secretary of State for the Provinces, file 1043.

18. *Alexander Begg's Red River Journal* (Champlain Society; Toronto, 1956), Jan. 26, 1870.

19. The proceedings of the Second Convention are fully reported in the *New Nation.*

20. See the author's Introduction to *Red River Journal of Alexander Begg.*

21. *Canada: Sessional Papers,* III (12), 1870, p. 5, Report of D. A. Smith, April 12, 1870.

22. *Begg's Red River Journal,* Feb. 25, 1870.

23. Cowan Diaries, 14, Nov. 19, 1869.

24. *Begg's Red River Journal,* Nov. 19, 1869.

25. P.A.C., C Series, 363, letter of Frederic Damien Heurter, dated Fort Douglas, April 17, 1817, which describes court martial held under the presidency of Cuthbert Grant.

26. *Report of Select Committee,* 1874, p. 21, evidence of Archbishop Taché.

27. *Canada: Sessional Papers,* III (12), p. 8, Report of D. A. Smith, April 12, 1870.

28. See *Canadian Historical Review,* VII (June, 1926), pp. 137–60, for the letter of Riel and Lépine to Morris, Jan. 3, 1875, in which Riel and Lépine argue that the execution of Scott is not to be separated from the whole course of the insurrection, as it was a necessary part thereof.

29. *Report of Select Committee,* 1874, p. 18, evidence of Archbishop Taché.

30. *Begg's Red River Journal,* March 9 and 10, 1870.

31. Chester Martin, "The First 'New Province' of the Dominion," *Canadian Historical Review,* I (Dec., 1920), pp. 367–70.

32. P.A.M., Sessional Journal of the Legislative Assembly of Assiniboia.

33. *New Nation,* July 1, 1870, a full report of ratification of Manitoba Act by Assembly of Assiniboia.

34. G. T. Denison, *The Struggle for Imperial Unity* (London, 1909), pp. 23–32.

35. *Begg's Red River Journal*, May 10 and May 24, 1870.

36. *Report of Select Committee*, 1874, p. 32, Taché to Howe, June 9, 1870; also Macdonald Papers, 103, Taché to Cartier, June 10, 1870.

37. *Canada: Sessional Papers*, V (20), 1871, p. 91.

38. F. A. Milligan, "The Lieutenant-Governorship in Manitoba, 1870–1882" (unpublished M.A. thesis, University of Manitoba, 1948), pp. 104–26.

39. Macdonald Papers, 252, Morris to Macdonald, Sept. 25, 1872.

40. P.A.C., G. 21 (12), Despatches regarding commutation of Lépine's sentence and North-West amnesty (Ottawa, 1875), Dufferin to Secretary of State, Dec. 10, 1875.

41. P.A.M., Morris Papers, Morris to Prime Minister Alexander Mackenzie, Dec. 8, 1874; also P.A.M., Diary of Kenneth McKenzie, for some details of organization of opposition to Clarke and Girard ministries.

42. *Manitoba Weekly Free Press*, Jan. 29, 1876, p. 5.

CHAPTER 7

1. *Canada: Report of the Select Committee of the House of Commons on the Causes of the Difficulties in the North-West Territories in 1869–70* (Ottawa, 1874), p. 140, "Memorandum connected with Fenian Invasion of 1871," by Archibald.

2. *Manitoba Weekly Free Press*, May 22, 1875, p. 5.

3. *Ibid.*, July 26, 1879, p. 8.

4. *Manitoban*, March 21, 1874; *Manitoba Weekly Free Press*, March 21, 1874.

5. G. M. Dawson, *Report on the Geology and Resources of the Region in the Vicinity of the Forty-Ninth Parallel* (Montreal, 1875).

6. *Manitoba Weekly Free Press*, July 22, 1876, p. 3.

7. A. Begg and W. R. Nursey, *Ten Years in Winnipeg* (Winnipeg, 1879), p. 26; *Manitoba Free Press*, May 18, 1878, p. 3.

8. Dom Benoit, *Vie de Monseigneur Taché* (Montreal, 1904), II, pp. 285–6.

9. *Manitoba Weekly Free Press*, July 29, 1876, p. 3; July 6, 1878, p. 8.

10. *Ibid.*, Feb. 22, 1879, p. 3; Aug. 31, 1878, p. 1.

11. *Manitoban*, Aug. 8, 1874, Sept. 19, 1874; *Manitoba Weekly Free Press*, Aug. 8, 1874, p. 3.

12. P.A.M., E. K. Francis, "The Mennonites of Manitoba," an exhaustive study in typescript; see his *In Search of Utopia* (Altona, Man., 1955).

13. *Canada: Sessional Papers*, IX (7), 1876, pp. 50, 167–74. *Winnipeg Standard*, Oct. 16, 1875.

14. P.A.M., W. Kristjanson, "The Icelanders of Manitoba" (manuscript), a detailed account of Icelandic colonization in Manitoba.

15. Begg and Nursey, *Ten Years in Winnipeg*, pp. 65, 97; D. M. Gordon, *Mountain and Prairie* (Montreal, 1880), p. 283.

16. These figures are taken from Begg and Nursey.

17. Many details of the industrial growth of Winnipeg are to be found in the *Manitoba Weekly Free Press*, April 12, 1873, pp. 5, 8.

18. *Ibid.*, Aug. 12, 1876.

19. Except the census figure for 1871, these are the estimates of Begg and Nursey, *Ten Years in Winnipeg*, and from the *Commercial*, IV (19), Feb. 2, 1886.

20. *Manitoba Weekly Free Press*, April 3, 1875, pp. 5–8.

21. *Canada: Sessional Papers*, IX (7), 1876, p. vii.

CHAPTER 8

1. *Canada: Sessional Papers*, IX (7), 1876, p. xix, and X (6), 1877, p. xiv; the figures are estimates, admittedly not accurate.

2. *Ibid.*, XIII (7), 1880, pp. 71, 75.

3. *Ibid.*, X (6), 1877, p. 41; XII (7), 1879, p. 41.

4. These figures are compiled from the Reports of the Department of Agriculture in the *Sessional Papers*, 1874 to 1881.

5. *Ibid.*, XIII (7), 1880, p. xxviii; XIV (7), 1880–1, p. xxi; XV (7), 1882, p. xx.

6. *Ibid.*, XIII (7), 1880.

7. *Ibid.*, 1881, L, p. 405.

8. *Ibid.*, XIII (7), 1880, pp. 65–70; report of Immigration Agent at Emerson.

9. *Manitoba Weekly Free Press*, April 27, 1878, p. 8; Sept. 28, 1878, p. 8.

10. *Ibid.*, July 18, 1874, p. 8; Aug. 24, 1878, p. 6.

11. *Ibid.*, April 20, 1878, p. 1, May 18, 1878, p. 3.

12. *Canada: Sessional Papers*, XIII (7), p. 65; *Manitoba Weekly Free Press*, May 24, 1879, p. 5.

13. *Manitoba Weekly Free Press*, March 29, 1879, p. 3; April 19, 1879, p. 3.

14. *Ibid.*, May 31, 1879, p. 2.

15. See Nellie McClung, *Clearing in the West* (Toronto, 1935), chap. vii, for an account of this journey by one pioneer family.

16. The advertisements of contemporary Winnipeg newspapers are the chief source of the information in this paragraph.

17. The accepted account of the origin of the Red Fife is given in A. H. R. Buller, *Essays on Wheat* (New York, 1919), pp. 206–18.

18. This familiar story is found in A. Begg and W. R. Nursey, *Ten Years in Winnipeg* (Winnipeg, 1879), pp. 138–9 and the *Manitoba Weekly Free Press*, Oct. 28, 1876, p. 3. Small consignments of seed had been exported in Red River days: *Nor'Wester*, Sept. 28, 1860; J. H. Klippart, *The Story of the Wheat Plant* (Cincinnati, 1860), p. 553.

19. *Manitoba Weekly Free Press*, Sept. 16, 1876, the first apparently of the paper's crop reports. The wheat crop was estimated to be one of 480,000 bushels: *ibid.*, Nov. 4, 1876, p. 1, an exchange from the *Mail* of Toronto, which analyses the reasons for the "Manitoba fever" in Ontario.

20. For example, *Manitoba Weekly Free Press*, March 17, 1877, in which Kew, Stobart and Eden advertised for 5,000 bushels of wheat.

21. *Ibid.*, Oct. 27, 1877, p. 3.

22. *Ibid.*, March 9, 1878, p. 7.

23. *Ibid.*, Oct. 6, 1877, p. 5.

24. *Ibid.*, Dec. 28, 1878, p. 5.

25. *Ibid.*, Feb. 10, 1877; Nov. 16, 1878, p. 5, when meeting for same purposes was cancelled.

26. Wm. Leggo, *The History of the Administration of the . . . Earl of Dufferin* (Montreal, 1878), pp. 601–9.

27. *Manitoba Weekly Free Press*, Dec. 8, 1877, p. 6; July 6, 1878, p. 8, and Aug. 17, 1878, p. 8; July 29, 1876, p. 3.

28. W. T. Phillips (unpublished M.A. thesis of the University of Manitoba, 1948).

29. *Manitoba Weekly Free Press*, Feb. 9, 1878, p. 5.

30. *Ibid.*, Aug. 14, 1875, p. 7.

31. The writer has never seen the words of "Meadow Lea" in print; those of "Remember the Red River Valley" may be seen in J. K. Howard's *Montana Margins* (New Haven, 1946), p. 353; also P.A.M., The Diary of Ellen (McFadden) Rowes, 1882–1900, p. 3.

32. *Manitoba Weekly Free Press*, Feb. 3, 1877, p. 4; Sept. 29, 1877, p. 3; Oct. 13, 1877, p. 3.

33. Begg and Nursey, *Ten Years in Winnipeg*, p. 103; *Manitoba Weekly Free Press*, Feb. 1, 1879, p. 8.

34. *Canada: Statutes*, 42 Vict., c. 66, 1879; *Manitoba Weekly Free Press*, June 21, 1879, p. 6.

35. *Winnipeg Daily Times*, March 16 and Aug. 25, 1881; City By-law No. 148 embodied the contract; *Manitoba Statutes*, 46 Vict., c. 64.

36. *Manitoba Weekly Free Press*, Feb. 1, 1879, p. 4.

37. *Ibid.*, June 7, 1879, pp. 3–4; R. O. MacFarlane "Manitoba Politics

and Parties after Confederation," *Report of Canadian Historical Association*, 1940, p. 51.

38. *Manitoba Weekly Free Press*, Nov. 8, 1879, p. 8, Norquay's Address to the Electors of St. Andrew's South.

CHAPTER 9

1. *Manitoba Weekly Free Press*, May 31, 1879, p. 3.

2. *Commercial*, IV (19), Feb. 2, 1886, pp. 1, 2.

3. *Manitoba Weekly Free Press*, Aug. 19, 1881, p. 7.

4. *Commercial*, I (73), June 12, 1883, p. 766; II (16), Jan. 15, 1884, p. 308.

5. *Ibid.*, IV (19), Feb. 2, 1886, a special issue on Winnipeg.

6. *The Colonist at Home Again*, by "A Retired Officer" (Captain Goodridge), (London, 1889), p. 14.

7. N. E. Wright, *In View of the Turtle Hill* (Deloraine, 1951).

8. *Commercial*, IV (47), Aug. 17, 1886, p. 960.

9. *Ibid.*, I (4), Oct. 24, 1881, p. 72.

10. *Manitoba Weekly Free Press*, Nov. 20, 1880, p. 6; Dec. 11, 1880, pp. 3, 5.

11. *Commercial*, II (9), Nov. 27, 1883, p. 168; V (12), Dec. 14, 1886, p. 223.

12. *Manitoba Daily Free Press*, Dec. 6, 1883, p. 2; Dec. 20, 1883, p. 4; and Dec. 21, 1883, pp. 1, 4.

13. *Ibid.*, March 6, 1884, p. 4; March 7, 1884, pp. 1, 4.

14. See J. A. Jackson "The Disallowance of Manitoba Railway Legislation in the 1880's" (unpublished M.A. thesis of the University of Manitoba, 1945).

15. "Report of the Department of Marine and Fisheries," *Canada: Sessional Papers*, XIX (9), 1886, p. 201, XX (14), pp. 206–7.

16. *United Kingdom: Judicial Committee of the Privy Council: The Province of Ontario vs. the Province of Manitoba, 1889*, Appendix of Documents.

17. *Canada: Sessional Papers*, XVI (10), 1883, p. 171; XXI (4), 1888, p. xxii.

18. W. H. Barneby, *Life and Labour in the Far, Far West* (London, 1884), pp. 364–5.

19. *Report of the Department of Agriculture, Statistics and Health for the Year 1883* (Winnipeg, 1884), p. 115.

20. *Commercial*, IV (40), June 29, 1886, pp. 829, 900.

21. *Ibid.*, VI (12), Dec. 12, 1887, p. 235. The Exchange was organized on Nov. 24, 1887, and incorporated in 1888.

22. The survival of the concept of racial representation is shown by Wm. Lagimodière's letter of May 21, 1888, in which he informed Greenway he proposed to run in La Vérendrye as a supporter of Greenway on certain entirely proper conditions and if Greenway were to give "justice and consideration to our *representation*" (italics in original). P.A.M., Greenway Papers, no. 525.

23. P.A.M., *Manitoba Debates (Free Press)*, April 16, 1888; Letter of Sir John A. Macdonald, dated March 30, 1888, to Greenway.

24. *Ibid.*, April 25, 1888.

CHAPTER 10

1. P.A.M., Greenway Papers, no. 365, Robt. Watson to Thos. Greenway, April 19, 1888; no. 356, R. J. Cartwright to Greenway, April 17, 1888; no. 739, Geo. Stephen to Wm. Whyte, July 4, 1888; no. 747, Geo. Stephens to Wm. Whyte, July 10, 1888.

2. P.A.M., *Manitoba Debates (Free Press)*, April 16, 1888.

3. *Ibid.*, Feb. 4, 1890, a later reference to the Northern Pacific contract which remained a subject of controversy for years.

4. Greenway Papers, no. 1567, Schultz to Greenway, Oct. 26, 1888.

5. Geo. R. Parkin, *The Great Dominion* (London, 1895), p. 57.

6. Dom Benoit, *Vie de Monseigneur Taché* (Montreal, 1904), II, p. 256.

7. *Ibid.*, p. 382.

8. *Brandon Sun*, May 16, May 30, 1889.

9. *Manitoba Daily Free Press*, Nov. 28, 1889, quoting J. W. Dafoe, writing in *The Week*.

10. *Brandon Mail*, July 18, 1889, a Conservative paper, predicting such a manœuvre; R. E. Clague, "The Manitoba School Question, 1889–1896" (unpublished thesis, University of Manitoba, 1938). Both Mr. Clague's version and that in the text challenge, on the documents, the account of the origin of the School Question given by J. W. Dafoe in *Clifford Sifton in Relation to His Times* (Toronto, 1931), chap. II.

11. *Brandon Sun*, Aug. 8, 1889; *Manitoba Daily Free Press*, Aug. 3, 1889.

12. *Ibid.*, Aug. 6, 1889.

13. *Winnipeg Sun*, Aug. 1, 1886, and Nov. 28, 1889.

14. Greenway Papers, Aug. 6, 1889.

15. *Manitoba Daily Free Press*, Aug. 10, 1889, p. 1.

16. *Manitoba Debates* (F.P.), Feb. 6, 1890. Prendergast quoted the saying as the reason given by members for supporting abolition of the dual school system.

17. *Brandon Sun*, June 20, 1889; *Brandon Mail*, July 11, 1889; *Commercial*, July 30, 1888, p. 1139.

18. W. L. Morton "Manitoba Schools and Canadian Nationality," *Report of the Canadian Historical Association*, 1951, p. 53; the story in brief and the references are given here.

19. *Manitoba Debates* (F.P.), Feb. 12, March 6, 1890.

20. *Ibid.*, April 1, 1890.

CHAPTER 11

1. *The Manitoban Colonist*, IX (6), Sept., 1894.

2. The details are culled from the Greenway Papers, P.A.M.

3. *Canada: Journals of House of Commons*, 1895, appendix XXIX, Report of Select Committee on Agriculture and Colonization.

4. *Manitoban Colonist*, VI (12), May, 1892, "The Tide Has Turned"; also Aug., 1893, p. 44.

5. *Ibid.*, X (10), March, 1896, pp. 447, 480.

6. *Manitoba Statutes*, 53 Vict., c. 35; *Manitoban Colonist*, V (50).

7. *Manitoban Colonist*, IX (1), June, 1894.

8. *Manitoba Debates* (F.P.), March 24, 1892.

9. *Manitoba Colonist*, IV (6), Oct., 1889.

10. *The Weekly Review* (Portage la Prairie), May 6, 1891; *The Manitoban* (a monthly magazine, begun Dec., 1891), I (4), March, 1892.

11. L. A. Wood, *The Farmers' Movement in Canada* (Toronto, 1924), pp. 124–130.

12. *Manitoban Colonist*, IX (6), Sept., 1894.

13. Ernest Thompson Seton, *Trail of An Artist-Naturalist* (New York, 1940), chaps. xx–xxvi, xxix.

14. *Manitoba Daily Free Press*, July 1, 1881.

15. *Commercial*, IV (45), Aug. 3, 1886, p. 909.

16. *Manitoba Statutes*, 59 Vict., c. 10, 1896.

17. *Canada: Sessional Papers*, XXXII (10), 1878.

18. See J. E. Ewart, *The Manitoba School Question* (Toronto, 1894), for the text of the judgments and related material to 1894.

19. Greenway Papers, no. 9018, J. S. Hodgins to Greenway, April 4, 1896; Hodgins was Superintendent of Education in Ontario.

20. *Ibid.*, no. 9564, Feb. and March, 1896.

21. *Ibid.*, no. 9487, a typed memorandum on the School Question, noted as having been drawn by Tarte and Bourassa. The religious clauses are much as the later legislation on the subject. The bilingual clause names French only, but there is a notation to the effect "+ foreign language."

22. *Ibid.*, no. 9091, Sifton to Greenway, Aug. 14, 1896; no. 9168, Sifton to Greenway, Aug. 5, 1896. When agreement was reached in November, Sifton entered the federal cabinet as Minister of the Interior.

23. *Manitoba Statutes*, 60 Vict., c. 26.

24. *Manitoba Debates* (F.P.), 1916, p. 8; J. W. Dafoe, *Clifford Sifton in Relation to His Times* (Toronto, 1931), p. 98.

CHAPTER 12

1. *Nor'-West Farmer*, XX (1), Jan. 9, 1901, p. 12; XXII (16), Aug. 20, 1903, p. 907.

2. *Swan River Star*, special no., March, 1900.

3. P.A.M., *Manitoba Debates* (F.P.), April 20, 1898.

4. H. R. Ross, *Thirty-five Years in the Limelight: Sir Rodmond P. Roblin and His Time* (Winnipeg, 1936), pp. 71–2.

5. *Morning Telegram*, Jan. 20, 1899, p. 7, Jan. 24, 1899, p. 3.

6. P.A.M., Pamphlets Record of the Roblin Government, 1900–1909, p. 5.

7. *Morning Telegram*, Dec. 8, 1899, p. 1.

8. *Manitoba Debates* (F.P.), Feb. 28, 1901, p. 9.

9. G. P. de T. Glazebrook, *A History of Transportation in Canada* (Toronto, 1938), p. 337.

10. *Manitoba Debates* (F.P.), March 29, 1901.

11. P.A.M., *Manitoba Debates* (Tribune), March 19, 1901; *Commercial*, Dec. 20, 1902, p. 347.

12. *Nor'-West Farmer*, XXII (2), Jan. 20, 1903, pp. 90, 95.

13. *Ibid.*, XXII (5), March 5, 1903, pp. 250a–b.

14. A. E. Copping, *The Golden Land* (London, 1911), p. 41.

15. *Manitoba: Sessional Papers*, 1911, "Address of the Executive Government of Manitoba to His Excellency the Governor-General on the Subject of the Extension of the Boundaries of the Province of Manitoba and other matters connected therewith."

16. *Canadian Annual Review*, 1905, pp. 90–7.

17. *Ibid.*, 1906, p. 428.

18. I owe these added sentences (1970) to the work of Professor Brian McCutcheon, not yet published. He is not, of course, responsible for my version of the matter.

CHAPTER 13

1. R. McBeth, *Sir Augustus Nanton* (Toronto, 1931).

2. *Morning Telegram*, Sept. 5, 1899, p. 1.

3. *Ibid.*, Oct. 13, 1899.

4. *Ibid.*, Oct. 11, 1899.

5. *Ibid.*, Feb. 24, 1899, p. 5, and March 1, p. 5.

6. This account is based on the unpublished manuscript of E. S. Russenholt, "The Power of a City."

7. The special studies in this field are P. Yuzyk, *The Ukrainians in Manitoba* (Toronto, 1953) and V. Turek "The Poles of Manitoba" (manuscript in P.A.M.).

8. A special study of Manitoban Jewry is in preparation by Rabbi A. A. Chiel, and the writer has benefited by conversations with him.

9. See the statement of Archbishop Langevin in the *Canadian Annual Review*, 1902, p. 465.

10. *Canadian Annual Review*, 1909, p. 511.

11. Catherine Lyle Cleverdon, *The Woman Suffrage Movement in Canada* (Toronto, 1950), chap. III.

12. W. L. Morton, "Direct Legislation and the Origins of the Progressive Movement," *Canadian Historical Review*, XXV (Sept., 1944), pp. 279–82.

13. A. G. Street, *Farmer's Glory* (Toronto, 1934), pp. 165–8.

14. *Canadian Annual Review*, 1909, p. 509; 1910, p. 569.

15. Ruth Harvey, *Curtain Time* (Boston, 1949), a delightful reminiscence of the Walkers and "the Walker."

16. Bernard McEvoy, *From the Great Lakes to the Wide West* (Toronto, 1902), p. 75.

17. Rupert Brooke, *Letters from America* (Toronto, 1916), pp. 103–5.

18. W. L. Morton, "Manitoba Schools and Canadian Nationality, 1890–1923," *Report of the Canadian Historical Association*, 1951, p. 5.

CHAPTER 14

*His duties were to maintain law in the territory, and to promote interest in its resources—in short, to conduct government and development in an area in which there were too few people to organize democratic government and to push the interests of the region.

1. A. H. de Trémaudan, *The Hudson's Bay Railway* (London, 1915), chaps. XX, XXI.

2. *Manitoba Free Press*, Dec. 30, 1916.

3. *Canadian Annual Review*, 1914, p. 589.

4. *Ibid.*, 1913, p. 539.

5. These details are gleaned from the contemporary press, from A. Fortescue Duguid, *Official History of the Canadian Forces in the Great World War, 1914–1919, General Series* (Ottawa, 1938), pp. 11, 33, and Appendix 85, and from Roy St. George Stubbs's excellent *Men in Khaki* (Toronto, 1941), four historical essays on the R.W.R., W.L.I., Camerons, and Grenadiers.

6. *Canadian Annual Review*, 1915, pp. 621–2; this is borne out by the incomplete file of correspondence between the Lieutenant-Governor and the Premier in P.A.M., Roblin Papers, and particularly by Cameron's letter of April 19, 1915.

7. P.A.M., *Report of the Royal Commission Appointed to Investigate the Charges Made in the Statement of C. P. Fullerton, K.C.* (Winnipeg, 1915).

8. P.A.M., *Report of the Royal Commission Appointed to Inquire into Certain Matters Relating to the New Parliament Buildings* (Winnipeg, 1915).

9. P.A.M., *Report of Special Commission to Enquire into Certain Matters Relating to the Law Courts and Central Power House* (April 22, 1916).

10. P.A.M., *First and Second Interim Reports of the Royal Commission Constituted to Inquire into All Matters Pertaining to the Manitoba Agricultural College* (Winnipeg, 1917).

11. *Canada, Sessional Papers*, 1917, no. 230A.

12. P.A.M., *Report of the Royal Commission to Inquire into and Report on All Expenditures for Road Work during the Year 1914* (Winnipeg, 1917).

13. *Canadian Annual Review*, 1917, p. 735; Baribault's name is given as Guilbault.

14. *Canadian Annual Review*, 1915, p. 630.

15. *Manitoba Debates* (T.), Jan. 7, 1916, p. 1.

16. *Ibid.* (F.P.), March 1, 1916, p. 58.

17. *Ibid.* (T.), Jan. 21, 1916, p. 15.

18. *Ibid.* (T.), Feb. 24, 1916, p. 31.

19. *Ibid.* (F.P.), Jan. 13, 1916, p. 7.

CHAPTER 15

1. *Canadian Annual Review*, 1915, p. 650.

2. *Canadian Annual Review*, 1919, p. 463; D. C. Masters, *The Winnipeg General Strike* (Toronto, 1950), is the most recent and extensive treatment of the subject.

3. *Canadian Annual Review*, 1919, p. 484, evidence of H. R. Maybank.

4. See T. M. Longstreth, *The Silent Force* (New York, 1927), pp. 301–6, for a description of the police view of the riot.

5. P.A.M., *Report of the Royal Commission to Enquire into the Causes and Effect of the General Strike* (n.p., n.d.).

6. P.A.M., *Manitoba Debates* (F.P.), Jan. 31, 1922, p. 31.

7. P.A.M., *Killarney Guide*, June 10, 1920.

8. P.A.M., *Dauphin Herald*, June 3, 1920.

9. P.A.M., *Carberry News-Express*, June 17, 1920.

10. See the letter from Aikins to Norris published in the *Manitoba Free Press*, March 21, 1922.

11. *Manitoba Free Press*, April 7, 1922.

CHAPTER 16

1. *Manitoba Free Press*, Jan. 24, 1923.

2. *Ibid.*

3. P.A.M., *Sessional Papers of the Legislative Assembly of Manitoba, 1923* (5).

4. P.A.M., *Report of the Educational (Murray) Commission* (Winnipeg, 1924), pp. 118–22.

5. P.A.M., *Report of the Commission on the Possibility of Re-adjusting the Relations of the Higher Institution of Learning* (1924), p. 34.

6. H. Michell and H. C. Grant, "The Co-operative Movement," *Canadian Journal of Economics and Political Science*, III (Aug., 1937), pp. 406–20.

7. Murchie and Grant, *Unused Lands*, pp. 35–6, give comparative figures.

*Some share in this development may be attributed to the work of one man. That was R. C. Wallace, Head of the Department of Geology in the University of Manitoba since 1910. His interest in the mineral resources of the province had led to his appointment, following J. A. Campbell's entry into federal politics, as Commissioner of Mines for Northern Manitoba in 1918. He greatly increased both the public knowledge of the mineral resources of the north, and worked closely with the Manitoba Chamber of Commerce to attract capital for mining developments. As Commissioner he became deeply interested in the issue of the administration of the north by the Province while its natural resources remained under federal control. In 1921 he completed his report on this subject, the first step towards the transfer of the resources to provincial control in 1930. Perhaps his most important service was his study of the desirability of a railway to the Flin Flon orebody, and his recommendation that it be built, in his report of the same year. In that year he returned to head the Department of Geology once more, but combined that position with the new one of Commissioner of Mines for all Manitoba. In this position he continued to be a strong agent for the development of Northern Manitoba until he became President of the University of Alberta in 1928.

8. F. H. Ellis, *Canada's Flying Heritage* (Toronto, 1954), pp. 198–202, 239.

9. Maurice Ollivier, *Problems of Canadian Sovereignty* (Toronto, 1946), pp. 384–6.

10. *Precis of Discussions, Dominion-Provincial Conference* (Ottawa, 1928), pp. 19, 11–12, 23. *Canadian Annual Review, 1927–1928,* p. 33.

11. *Winnipeg Tribune,* July 23, 1928, p. 1.

12. *Manitoba Free Press,* April 30, 1929, p. 1; May 7, 1929, p. 1.

13. *Report of the Royal Commission on the Transfer of the Natural Resources of Manitoba* (Ottawa, 1929), pp. 41 and 45.

CHAPTER 17

1. W. J. Sisler, *Peaceful Invasion* (Winnipeg, 1944).

2. Ruth Harvey, *Curtain Time* (Toronto, 1949), chap. xxx.

3. "Gee Sharp Minor," *Crescendo* (Winnipeg). This is the story of the Men's Musical Club to 1934, of the Male Voice Choir, and of the efforts to found a symphony.

4. *Canadian Annual Review,* 1930–31, pages 236–7; P.A.M., *Report of the Royal Commission to Enquire into the charges against the Manitoba Pool Elevators* (Winnipeg, 1931).

5. P.A.M., "Report of the Royal Commission on the Impairment of University of Manitoba Trust Funds, 1932–1933."

6. *Canadian Annual Review,* 1933, p. 278.

CHAPTER 18

1. *Winnipeg Free Press,* Dec. 10, 1935, p. 1.

2. Bank of Canada, *Reports on the Financial Positions of the Provinces of Manitoba, Saskatchewan and Alberta, 1937* (n.p., n.d.).

3. *Winnipeg Tribune,* Aug. 16, 1937, p. 1. *Winnipeg Free Press,* Aug. 16, 1937, p. 1. *Report of the Royal Commission on Dominion-Provincial Relations* (Ottawa, 1940), I, pp. 13–14.

4. P.A.M., *Manitoba's Case* (Winnipeg, 1937), pp. 7 and 5.

5. See Mrs. George Cran, *A Woman in Canada* (London, 1911), chaps. v and vi, for a sketch of Larcombe at home and at work.

6. *Report of the Royal Commission on the Municipal Finances and Administration of the City of Winnipeg* (Winnipeg, 1939), pp. 560–1.

7. John Tanner, *A Narrative of the Captivity and Adventures of John Tanner during Thirty Years Residence among the Indians in the Interior of North America* (New York, 1830), pp. 165–6.

8. See W. L. Morton (ed.), *The Voice of Dafoe* (Toronto, 1945).

9. C. P. Stacey, *The Canadian Army, 1939–1945* (Ottawa, 1948).

10. George Ford (ed.), *The Pickersgill Letters, 1934–1943* (Toronto, 1948): Bruce Marshall, *The White Rabbit* (London, 1952).

CHAPTER 19

1. P.A.M., *A Farm Electrification Programme: Report of the Manitoba Electrification Enquiry Commission* (Winnipeg, 1943).

2. *Canada Year Book,* 1951, p. 131.

SELECT BIBLIOGRAPHY

AMOS, ANDREW, *Report of the Trials in the Courts of Canada Relative to the Destruction of the Earl of Selkirk's Settlement on the Red River, with Observations* (London, 1820).

ANDERSON, DAVID, *Notes on the Flood at the Red River, 1852* (London, 1852 and 1873).

BALLANTYNE, R. M., *Hudson's Bay: or Every-Day Life in the Wilds of North America during Six Years Residence in the Territories of the Honourable Hudson's Bay Company* (Edinburgh, 1848).

BEGG, ALEXANDER, *The Creation of Manitoba, or A History of the Red River Troubles* (Toronto, 1871).

——— *History of the North-West*, 3 vols. (Toronto, 1894).

BENOIT, DOM, *Vie de Monseigneur Taché, archevêque de St-Boniface*, 2 vols. (Montreal, 1904).

BINNIE-CLARK, G. *A Summer on the Canadian Prairie* (London, 1910).

BOND, J. WESLEY, *Minnesota and Its Resources: To Which are Appended Camp-Fire Sketches: or, Notes of a Trip from St. Paul to Pembina and Selkirk Settlement on the Red River of the North* (New York, 1853).

BREBNER, J. B., *The Explorers of North America* (New York, 1933).

BRYCE, GEORGE, *Manitoba: Its Infancy, Growth, and Present Condition* (London, 1882).

BULLER, A. H. R., *Essays on Wheat* (New York, 1919).

BURPEE, L. J. (ed.), *Journals and Letter of La Vérendrye and His Sons* (Champlain Society; Toronto, 1927).

Canada, *Report of the Royal Commission on the Transfer of the Natural Resources of Manitoba* (Ottawa, 1929).

——— *Report of the Select Committee of the House of Commons on the Causes of the Difficulties in the North-West Territories in 1869–70* (Ottawa, 1874).

CHRISTY, MILLER (ed.), *The Voyages of Captain Luke Foxe of Hull and of Captain Thomas James of Bristol in Search of a North-West Passage in 1631–1632* (Hakluyt Society; London, 1894).

CONSTANTIN-WEYER, M., *Manitoba* (Paris, 1924).

COPPING, A. E., *The Golden Land* (London, 1911).

COUES, ELLIOTT (ed.), *New Light on the Early History of the Greater Northwest: The Manuscript Journals of Alexander Henry and of David Thompson, 1799–1814*, 2 vols. (New York, 1897).

COWIE, ISAAC, *The Company of Adventurers* (Toronto, 1913).

DAFOE, J. W., *Clifford Sifton in Relation to His Times* (Toronto, 1931).

DOBBS, ARTHUR, *An Account of the Countries Adjoining to Hudson's Bay in the North-West Part of America* (London, 1744).

DOUGHTY, A. G., and MARTIN, CHESTER (eds.), *The Kelsey Papers* (Ottawa, 1929).

DOUGLAS, R., and WALLACE, J. N. (trs. and eds.), *Twenty Years of York Factory, 1694–1714: Jérémie's Account of Hudson Strait and Bay* (Ottawa, 1926).

DUFFERIN AND AVA, HARIOT GEORGINA, Marchioness of, *My Canadian Journal, 1872–8: Extracts from My Letters Home Written while Lord Dufferin was Governor-General* (London, 1891).

ELLICE, EDWARD, *A Narrative of Occurrences in the Indian Countries of North America* (London, 1817).

EWART, J. S., *The Manitoba School Question* (Toronto, 1894).

FITZGIBBON, MARY, *A Trip to Manitoba* (London, 1880).

FRANCIS, E. K. *In Search of Utopia* (Altona, 1955).

GARRY, NICHOLAS, "Diary of Nicholas Garry, Deputy-Governor of the Hudson's Bay Company from 1822–1835: A Detailed Narrative of His Travels in the North-West Territories of British North America in 1821," *Transactions of the Royal Society of Canada*, Section II, 1900, pp. 73–204.

GIRAUD, MARCEL, *Le Métis canadien: son rôle dans l'histoire de provinces de l'Ouest* (Paris, 1945).

GOSCH, C. C. A. (ed.), *Danish Arctic Expeditions, 1605 to 1620* (Hakluyt Society; London, 1897).

GUNN, D., and TUTTLE, C. R., *History of Manitoba from the Earliest Settlement* (Ottawa, 1880).

GUNN, J. J., *Echoes of the Red* (Toronto, 1930).

HALKETT, JOHN, *Statement Respecting the Earl of Selkirk's Settlement of Kildonan upon the Red River in North America: Its Destruction in the Years 1815 and 1816 and the Massacre of Governor Semple and His Party* (London, n.d.).

HARGRAVE, J. J., *Red River* (Montreal, 1871).

HARVEY, RUTH, *Curtain Time* (Boston, 1949).

HEALY, W. J. (ed.), *Women of Red River* (Winnipeg, 1923).

HILL, R. B., *Manitoba: History of Its Early Settlement, Development and Resources* (Toronto, 1890).

HIND, H. Y., *Narrative of the Canadian Red River Exploring Expedition of 1857, and of the Assiniboine and Saskatchewan Exploring Expedition of 1858*, 2 vols. (London, 1860).

KENNEY, JAMES F. (ed.), *The Founding of Churchill* (Toronto, 1932).

MACOUN, J., *Manitoba and the Great North-West* (Guelph, 1882).

McCLUNG, NELLIE, *Clearing in the West: My Own Story* (Toronto, 1935).

MacFARLANE, R. O., "Manitoba Politics and Parties after Confederation," *Annual Report of the Canadian Historical Association*, 1940.

MacKay, Douglas (revised by Alice MacKay to 1949), *The Honourable Company: A History of the Hudson's Bay Company* (Toronto, 1949).

MacLeod, Margaret Arnett, "Cuthbert Grant of Grantown," *Canadian Historical Review*, March, 1940.

—— (ed.), *The Letters of Letitia Hargrave* (Champlain Society, Toronto, 1947).

McWilliams, Margaret, *Manitoba Milestones* (Toronto, 1928).

Marble, Manton, "To the Red River and Beyond," *Harper's New Monthly Magazine*, August, 1860.

Martin, Archer, *The Hudson's Bay Company's Land Tenures and the Occupation of Assiniboia by Lord Selkirk's Settlers, with a List of Grantees under the Earl and the Company* (London, 1898).

Martin, Chester, "The First 'New Province' of the Dominion," *Canadian Historical Review*, December, 1920.

—— *Lord Selkirk's Work in Canada* (Oxford, 1916).

—— "The Red River Settlement" and "The Political History of Manitoba, 1870–1915," *Canada and Its Provinces*, XIX.

Masson, L. F. R., *Les bourgeois de la Compagnie du Nord-Ouest*, 2 vols. Quebec, 1889–90).

Masters, D. C., *The Winnipeg General Strike* (Toronto, 1950).

Morice, A. G., *Histoire de l'Eglise catholique dans l'Ouest canadien du Lac Supérieur au Pacifique, 1659–1915*, 2 vols. (St. Boniface, 1921).

Morton, A. S., *History of Prairie Settlement* (Toronto, 1938).

—— *A History of the Canadian West to 1870–71* (Toronto, 1939).

Morton, W. L., "Agriculture in the Red River Colony," *Canadian Historical Review*, December, 1949.

—— "Introduction," *London Correspondence Inward from Eden Colvile, 1849* (Hudson's Bay Record Society; London, 1956).

—— "Manitoba Schools and Canadian Nationality," *Report of the Canadian Historical Association*, 1951.

Murchie, R. W., and Grant, H. C., *Unused Lands of Manitoba; Report of a Survey Conducted by R. W. Murchie and H. C. Grant* (Winnipeg, 1926).

Nute, Grace Lee, *Caesars of the Wilderness* (New York, 1943).

—— *Documents Relating to Northwest Missions, 1815–1827* (St. Paul, 1942).

Oliver, E. H. (ed.), *The Canadian North-West: Its Early Development and Legislative Records*, 2 vols. (Publications of the Canadian Archives, no. 9; Ottawa, 1914).

Palliser, John, *Solitary Rambles of a Hunter in the Prairies* (London, 1853). (For *Journals*, see United Kingdom, below.)

Pennefather, John P., *Thirteen Years on the Prairies* (London, 1892).

PRITCHETT, J. P., *The Red River Valley* (Toronto, 1942).

RICH, E. E. (ed.), *Colin Robertson's Correspondence Book, September 1817 to September 1822* (Champlain Society; Toronto, 1939).

ROBSON, JOSEPH, *An Account of Six Years Residence in Hudson's Bay, from 1733 to 1736, and 1744 to 1747* (London, 1749).

ROE, F. G., *The North American Buffalo* (Toronto, 1951).

ROSS, ALEXANDER, *Red River Settlement: Its Rise, Progress and Present State with Some Account of the Native Races, and Its General History to the Present Day* (London, 1856).

SCHOFIELD, F. H., *The Story of Manitoba*, 3 vols. (Winnipeg, 1913).

SISLER, W. J., *Peaceful Invasion* (Winnipeg, 1944).

STANLEY, G. F. G., *The Birth of Western Canada* (Toronto, 1936).

STREET, A. G., *Farmer's Glory* (Toronto, 1934).

STUBBS, ROY ST. GEORGE, *Men in Khaki* (Toronto, 1941).

SUTHERLAND, A., *A Summer in Prairie-Land: Notes of a Tour through the North-West Territory* (Toronto, 1881).

TANNER, JOHN, *A Narrative of the Captivity and Adventures of John Tanner during Thirty Years Residence among the Indians in the Interior of North America* (prepared for press by EDWIN JAMES; New York, 1830).

TRÉMAUDAN, A. H. DE, *Histoire de la nation métisse dans l'Ouest canadien* (Montreal, 1935).

TROW, JAMES, *Manitoba and North-West Territories* (Ottawa, 1878).

TYRRELL, J. B. (ed.), *Documents Relating to the Early History of Hudson Bay* (Champlain Society; Toronto, 1931).

United Kingdom, *Correspondence Relative to the Recent Disturbances in the Red River Settlement* (London, 1870).

——*The Journals, Detailed Reports, and Observations Relative to the Exploration, by Captain Palliser, of That Portion of British North America . . . between the Western Shore of Lake Superior and the Pacific Ocean during the Years 1857, 1858, 1859 and 1860* (London, 1863).

——*Papers Relating to the Hudson's Bay Company, 1849* (London, 1849).

——*Papers Relating to the Red River Settlement* (London, 1819).

——*Papers Relative to the Exploration by Captain Palliser of That Portion of British North America Which Lies between the Northern Branch of the River Saskatchewan and the Rocky Mountains* (London, 1859).

——*Report from the Committee Appointed to Enquire into the State and Condition of the Countries Adjoining to Hudson's Bay, and of the Trade Carried on There* (London, 1749).

——— *Report of the Select Committee on the Hudson's Bay Company* (London, 1857).

WALLACE, W. S. (ed.), *Documents Relating to the North West Company* (Champlain Society; Toronto, 1934).

WEST, JOHN, *The Substance of a Journal during a Residence at the Red River Colony, British North America; and Frequent Excursions among the North-West American Indians in the Years 1820, 1821, 1822, 1823* (London, 1824).

WILSON, C. P., "La Vérendrye Reaches the Saskatchewan," *Canadian Historical Review*, March, 1952.

WRIGHT, N. E., *In View of the Turtle Hill* (Deloraine, 1951).

YUZYK, PAUL, *The Ukrainians in Manitoba: A Social History* (Toronto, 1953).

Supplement to the Bibliography

GALBRAITH, JOHN S., *The Hudson's Bay Company as an Imperial Factor, 1821–1869* (Toronto, 1957).

HILL, DOUGLAS, *The Opening of the Canadian West* (London, 1967).

HOWARD, JOSEPH KINSEY, *Strange Empire* (New York, 1952).

LENT, D. GENEVA, *West of the Mountains – James Sinclair and the Hudson's Bay Company* (Seattle, 1963).

MACLEOD, MARGARET ARNETT (ed.), *The Letters of Letitia Hargrave* (Champlain Society; Toronto, 1947).

——— and MORTON, W. L., *Cuthbert Grant of Grantown* (Toronto, 1963).

MORTON, W. L. (ed.), *Alexander Begg's Red River Journal and Other Papers Relative to the Red River Resistance of 1869–1870* (Champlain Society; Toronto, 1956).

——— (ed.), *Manitoba: The Birth of a Province* (Altona, Man., 1965).

MURRAY, STANLEY NORMAN, *The Valley Comes of Age* (Fargo, N.D., 1967).

PETERS, VICTOR, *All Things Common: The Hutterian Way of Life* (Minneapolis, 1965).

RUSSENHOLT, E. S., *The Heart of the Continent* (Winnipeg, 1968).

RICH, E. E. (ed.), *Eden Colvile's Letters*, with Introduction by W. L. MORTON (Hudson's Bay Record Society; London, 1956).

STUART, J. A. D., *The Prairie W.A.S.P.* (Winnipeg, 1969).

STUBBS, ROY ST. GEORGE, *Four Recorders of Rupert's Land* (Winnipeg, 1967).

INDEX